I0817762

TO ABSENT FRIENDS

Harriet Pollack, Series Editor

TO ABSENT FRIENDS

EUDORA WELTY'S CORRESPONDENCE WITH FRANK LYELL

Selected and edited by

JULIA EICHELBERGER

University Press of Mississippi / Jackson

The Critical Perspectives on Eudora Welty series is made possible in part by a generous donation from the family of Floyd M. Sulser Jr.

The University Press of Mississippi is the scholarly publishing agency of the Mississippi Institutions of Higher Learning: Alcorn State University, Delta State University, Jackson State University, Mississippi State University, Mississippi University for Women, Mississippi Valley State University, University of Mississippi, and University of Southern Mississippi.

www.upress.state.ms.us

The University Press of Mississippi is a member of the Association of University Presses.

Designed by Peter D. Halverson

Manufactured in the United States of America
∞

Publisher: University Press of Mississippi, Jackson, USA
Authorised GPSR Safety Representative: Easy Access System Europe - Mustamäe tee 50, 10621 Tallinn, Estonia, gpsr.requests@easproject.com

Library of Congress Cataloging-in-Publication Data

Names: Eichelberger, Julia, 1959– editor
Title: To absent friends : Eudora Welty's correspondence with Frank Lyell / Julia Eichelberger.
Description: Jackson : University Press of Mississippi, 2025. | Includes bibliographical references and index.
Identifiers: LCCN 2025030367 (print) | LCCN 2025030368 (ebook) | ISBN 9781496858993 hardback | ISBN 9781496859006 epub | ISBN 9781496859013 epub | ISBN 9781496859020 pdf | ISBN 9781496859037 pdf
Subjects: LCSH: Welty, Eudora, 1909–2001—Correspondence | Lyell, Frank, 1911–1977—Correspondence | Authors, American—20th Century—Correspondence
Classification: LCC PS3545.E6 Z48 2025 (print) | LCC PS3545.E6 (ebook)
LC record available at https://lccn.loc.gov/2025030367
LC ebook record available at https://lccn.loc.gov/2025030368

British Library Cataloging-in-Publication Data available

To Roy, Ben and Julie, and Sara and Brian

CONTENTS

ACKNOWLEDGMENTS

I THANK THE FOLLOWING COLLEGE OF CHARLESTON STUDENTS FOR HELPING me transcribe and research these letters: Tammy Matthews, Susie Jackson, Brendan Reardon, Blake Taylor, Cara Scott, Mary Scott Gilbert, Stella Rounsefell, Emma Looby, Samantha Sommers, Abby Stahl, and Charlotte Nicely. Research for this project was supported by the College of Charleston's School of Humanities and Social Sciences, the office of Undergraduate Research and Creative Activities, and the Graduate School. I also benefited from Writers' Retreats sponsored by the Center for Effective Teaching and Learning, from logistical support provided by the Department of English, and from the kind encouragement of my C of C colleagues.

In Mississippi, I was often assisted by Forrest Galey, Betty Uzman, Elizabeth Cambonga, and other staff at the Mississippi Department of Archives and History. Many thanks to everyone at MDAH who has given such care and attention to the Eudora Welty Collection and has been so helpful to me. I am grateful to Michael Pickard, Eudora Welty Chair of Southern Literature at Millsaps College, for hosting a long-distance manuscript review session in his office, and for keeping me apprised of his students' research on Welty's correspondence for the Millsaps Digital Welty Lab. I also appreciate the support and guidance provided by the staff at the University Press of Mississippi, including former Director Leila Salisbury, Editor-in-Chief Katie Keene, Associate Editor Mary Heath, Senior Project Editor Valerie Jones, Design and Production Manager Pete Halverson, and Harriet Pollack, editor of the Press's *Critical Perspectives on Welty* series. Insightful manuscript reviews by Hunter McKelva Cole and Suzanne Marrs helped me identify some of the many people Welty and Lyell mention in their letters. Kerri Jordan was an attentive, sensitive, and extremely helpful copyeditor for this project.

Particular thanks are due to those who shared their memories of Welty and Lyell with me: Hunter McKelva Cole, Suzanne Marrs, Mary Alice Welty White, and the late Louis Lyell and his daughter and son-in-law, Louise and Luke Lampton.

I have relied tremendously on the scholarship as well as the friendship of many members of the Eudora Welty Society. I was also helped greatly by the expertise and editorial advice of Scott Peeples, Pearl McHaney, Suzanne Marrs, and especially Harriet Pollack. These scholars' insights have enriched this book, which would never have been finished without their encouragement.

To all of my supportive and patient friends, and to my family, I am more indebted than I can say. I owe special thanks to Roy, for remaining enthusiastic about this project for so many years, and for laughing at the letters he helped me proofread.

EDITORIAL NOTE

THE MATERIAL IN THIS BOOK HAS BEEN CHOSEN FROM OVER SIX HUNDRED LETTERS, postcards, and greeting cards now in the Eudora Welty Collection at the Mississippi Department of Archives and History; Welty's letters to Lyell have now been digitized and are available online.[1] Fewer than fifty of these letters have been transcribed, published, or summarized elsewhere.[2] I provide an inventory of the complete Welty–Lyell correspondence at MDAH in my "Correspondence Calendar" in the 2021 *Eudora Welty Review*, where I list and briefly describe each letter.[3]

This book, containing over 350 complete or excerpted letters, is a scholarly resource, but is also intended to be an epistolary narrative. Whenever possible, I have tried to let the letters themselves tell two unfolding stories. One is Welty's life as she wrote almost all her published works, and the other is her nearly fifty-year friendship with Frank Lyell. The letters cannot speak for themselves entirely, however. Because the correspondents shared so many experiences and interests, they rarely needed to explain themselves to each other. My "Dramatis Personae" list enumerates many individuals mentioned in the correspondence, and within each chapter, my annotations are intended to make the material more intelligible and enjoyable.

For improved readability, I have standardized the format of the letters' paragraphs, greetings, and closings, which were often scribbled in the margins when Welty or Lyell ran out of space. As discussed in my introduction, they often playfully addressed and signed letters using other people's names. I begin each letter with its date and its location and destination, information the correspondents did not always include on the letters themselves. The dates I provide are usually those assigned by the tireless archivists at the MDAH, although in some cases I determined a different date to be correct. MDAH filed letters with the envelopes or other containers in which MDAH received them, but some letters are not in their original envelopes and some postmarks differ from information in the letter indicating its date. Thus I have sometimes relied instead on information found in the letter's contents, other letters, and the growing body of external material documenting Welty's life and times. A bracketed question mark indicates I am uncertain about the date. Welty and Lyell often wrote a date or a day of the week at the beginning of a letter, but I have regularized the format of all letters' dates, unless the correspondent was providing other useful or memorable information in that space.

Within the letters, brackets surround my italicized explanatory comments and also indicate when I have omitted parts of the letter or could not decipher some handwritten word or phrase. Welty often inserted material above the lines or in margins, but I rarely attempt to document this, usually opting to present a fair copy of her letter that includes her added material. Typographical and spelling errors were rare, and I have silently corrected most of these.

In my notes, I cite letters from Eudora Welty to people other than Frank Lyell; some of these have been published, but others are available only through the Eudora Welty Collection. When a note lists only the recipient and the date, I am referring to an unpublished letter archived in the Welty Collection, series 29a. The majority of letters from Welty in this series have been digitized and made available for research through the MDAH website.

DRAMATIS PERSONAE

Lyell, Frank (1911–1977) Jackson native who became friends with Welty when they and other Jackson friends took graduate courses at Columbia University. Lyell studied English literature, earning an MA from Columbia and a PhD from Princeton. He taught at North Carolina State University, served in World War II, then became a professor at the University of Texas. He often visited Jackson, and he and Welty also saw each other often during their visits to New York City. He and Welty exchanged hundreds of letters throughout their forty-seven-year friendship. Lyell maintained friendships and correspondences with numerous other writers and artists, some of whom he met through Welty.

Welty, Eudora (1909–2001) Jackson native who became an internationally acclaimed fiction writer. She is also recognized for her criticism, photography, memoir, and a vast body of correspondence. Throughout her long life, Welty nurtured close friendships and exchanged letters with an ever-growing number of people, but few correspondents knew her as long as Frank Lyell, a friend since 1930. Her correspondence with Lyell sometimes discusses her work in progress as well as their family, friends, and whatever they'd been reading, viewing, or enjoying; the letters attest to their enduring friendship and their shared delight in the cosmopolitan, the beautiful, and the absurd.

Hundreds more people are mentioned in the Welty–Lyell correspondence: family members, personal friends, celebrities, colleagues, and people who were, or would become, important writers, editors, publishers, and scholars. Below, I identify many of these individuals who had an important connection or personal relationship with Welty and/or Lyell. In the following chapters, I also identify most individuals when first mentioned, but they are so numerous that readers may find the notes more troublesome to navigate than the following list, where individuals appear in alphabetical order by last name.

Alexander [Sancton], Seta (1915–2007) Jackson friend of Welty and Lyell who later married Tom Sancton. Her 1987 memoir of growing up in Jackson is entitled *The World from Gillespie Place.*

Ames, Elizabeth (1885–1977) Director of the Saratoga Springs artists' colony, Yaddo.

Aswell, Edward (1900–1958) Editor for Harper & Brothers, and married to Mary Lou Aswell when Welty first met him in the early 1940s. He was then editor for many notable writers including Richard Wright and Thomas Wolfe.

Aswell, Mary Lou (1902–1984) Fiction editor at *Harper's Bazaar* and an early admirer of Welty's longer, more meditative stories such as "The Winds." When she first met Welty, Aswell was married to Edward Aswell. She was then briefly married to Fritz Peters, with whom she spent several months abroad in 1949–1950 when Welty was enjoying her first sojourn overseas. Aswell later became the partner of Agnes (Agi) Simms, living with her in New Mexico. She and Welty maintained a close friendship through regular correspondence and visits, and Lyell also enjoyed spending time with Aswell and Simms.

Auden, W. H. (1907–1973) English poet, dramatist, critic and librettist who became a US citizen and a friend of Lyell's. At the end of World War II, he was a civilian employee of the United States Strategic Bomb Survey. He and Lyell, who served in the US Army Air Forces Intelligence, interviewed Germans to determine the effectiveness of the US military's bombing.

Balakian, Nona (1918–1991) Editor at *The New York Times Book Review* who was beginning her career there when Welty worked for the publication in 1944. She was one of several friends Welty usually visited with whenever she came to New York.

Basic Eight, The Group of friends that began gathering as an informal supper club in the 1950s. They included Jackson residents Charlotte Capers, Bill and Ann Morrison, Eudora Welty, Major White, and Jimmie Wooldridge. Frank Lyell and Hubert Creekmore attended these gatherings when they were in town.[1]

Beachcomber (J. B. Morton, 1893–1979) From 1924 to 1975, Morton was the author of "By the Way," a *Daily Express* (UK edition) humor column Welty and Lyell enjoyed reading, clipping, and sharing. The *Daily Express* later described Morton's column, with its "cast of characters ranging from Mr

Justice Cocklecarrot to the Apostropher Royal Sir D'Anville O'M'Darlin,'" as "a unique daily dose of surreal inconsequentiality."[2]

Beaton, Cecil (1904–1980) British photographer whom Welty and Lyell admired. In the 1920s and '30s, *Vogue* and *Vanity Fair* often published Beaton's images of unconventional, hedonistic, glamorous artists and socialites known as "Bright Young Things," avidly followed by Lyell and Welty. Welty wrote Beaton a playful letter in 1933, asking for a job, and Lyell met Beaton at a party in 1935. A few years later, Beaton photographed Welty for an issue of *Harper's Bazaar.*

Bennett, Willia Wright (1909–1988) Jackson friend and contemporary of Welty and Lyell.

Boros, Eva (1907–1989) Hungarian writer Welty befriended in Paris in 1949–1950. At the time Boros was married to British photographer Bill Brandt. Lyell visited Boros during a trip to London. Both he and Welty were impressed with Boros's 1956 novel, *The Mermaids.*

Bowen, Elizabeth (1899–1973) Anglo-Irish writer whose work Welty admired before meeting her in 1950, when Bowen invited Welty to visit her at her family estate, Bowen's Court. The writers became friends and enjoyed many reunions; Bowen made several visits to Jackson.

Brickell, Herschel (1889–1952) and Norma (1894–1983) Herschel Brickell was editor of the *Jackson Daily News* in 1918 when he married Norma Long, who had grown up in Jackson. The couple moved to New York but often visited their families in Mississippi. Herschel Brickell worked for the *New York Evening Post* and wrote book reviews and essays for other national publications. He became an editor for the publisher Henry Holt in 1927. Lyell and Welty, during their 1930–1931 year at Columbia University, were frequent supper or party guests of the Brickells in their New York apartment. From 1941 to 1951 Herschel edited volumes published each year for the O. Henry Prize. Knowledgeable of Spanish-language writers as well as American literature, he also worked for the State Department in Colombia in the 1940s and 1950s. He died by suicide in their Connecticut home in 1952. Norma then resettled permanently in Jackson.

Burger, Nash (1908–1996) Classmate of Welty's from Jackson who taught high school there before moving to New York, where he became an editor for *The New York Times Book Review.*

Capers, Charlotte (1913–1996) Jackson friend of Welty and Lyell. From 1955 to 1969 she was director of the Mississippi Department of Archives and History; her friendship with Welty led to Welty's donation of all her papers to the Archive. Capers, a member of Welty and Lyell's group of friends who called themselves "The Basic Eight," was a witty raconteur and the author of a local newspaper column, *Miss Quote.*

Carter, Hodding, Jr. (1907–1972) Louisiana-born journalist first known for his strident criticism of Huey P. Long. He then established the *Delta Democrat-Times* in Greenville, Mississippi, and in 1946, won a Pulitzer prize for editorials criticizing the white supremacist senator Theodore Bilbo and the treatment of Japanese Americans by the US government.[3] He had worked as an AP reporter in Jackson in 1931–1932, and Welty, who worked as a journalist in the 1930s, likely knew Hodding and his wife Betty when they lived in Jackson as newlyweds in 1932. In 1947 Carter and Ben Wesson formed Levee Press, which in 1948 published Welty's "Music From Spain." The press also published works by Faulkner, Shelby Foote, and William Alexander Percy. The Carters' eldest son, Hodding Carter III, took over the family paper before becoming Assistant Secretary of State during the Carter administration.

Cheney, Brainard (Lon) (1900–1990) and Frances (Fanny) Cheney (1906–1996) Lon Cheney was a journalist and novelist sympathetic to the ideals of the Southern Agrarians. His wife Fanny was a reference librarian. Welty met the couple at Yaddo in 1941. In 1953 the Cheneys converted to Catholicism, sponsored by their friends Caroline Gordon and Allen Tate, and became friends with another Southern Catholic writer, Flannery O'Connor.

Chodorov, Jerome (1911–2004), and Fields, Joseph (1895–1966) Playwriting team with a proven track record (*My Sister Eileen* and its musical adaptation *Wonderful Town*) who adapted Welty's 1954 novel *The Ponder Heart* for a Broadway production that ran for several months in 1956. Welty felt that their script was disappointingly different from the novel, although she found herself charmed by the production after getting to know the cast.

Clemons, Walter (1930–1994) Editor of *The New York Times Book Review* from 1968 to 1971, then a critic for *Newsweek*. He and Welty became friends in 1970 when he visited Jackson to interview her before the publication of *Losing Battles*. They often saw each other when Welty visited New York. Welty asked Clemons to be her literary executor, but he predeceased her.

Collins, Carvel (1912–1990) Harvard professor who became a leading Faulkner scholar. In 1951, while doing research, he met Welty in Jackson and then again in New Orleans, where they went on a car ride south of the city. This experience inspired her story "No Place for You, My Love."

Comès [Winslow], Marcella (1905–2000) Painter of Welty's 1946 portrait that hangs in the Eudora Welty House. She was the official portrait painter of the United States Poet Laureate and of other writers, including Welty's friends Robert Penn Warren and Katherine Anne Porter. While Lyell was living in Washington and serving in the Army after the war, he made friends with Comès and introduced her to Welty.

Coward, Noel (1899–1973) English playwright, composer, actor, director, and associate of other "Bright Young Things" admired by twentysomethings Lyell and Welty. One of Welty's playful 1930s postcards to Lyell was addressed "Dear Mr. Coward."

Creekmore, Hubert (1907–1966) Friend of Welty and Lyell from Jackson who became a poet, translator, and novelist (*The Fingers of the Night*, 1946, and *The Welcome*, 1948). He and Welty took photographs in Jackson in the 1930s. Creekmore's sister Mittie married Welty's brother Walter.

Daniel, Robert (1915–1984) Friend whom Lyell first knew from Sewanee. Welty, Lyell, and Daniel coauthored a parody literary anthology, *Lilies That Fester*. Daniel became an English professor at Kenyon College.

De Creeft, Jose (1884–1982) Spanish-born sculptor whom Welty met at Yaddo in 1941. His large sculpture of Alice in Wonderland characters was installed in Central Park in 1959.

Dolson, Hildegarde (Hildy) (1908–1981) Writer friend of Welty's who lived in New York and was a client of Diarmuid Russell. In the summer of 1948 Dolson and Welty house-sat in Westchester County while collaborating on a musical revue, *What Year Is This?* Welty met up with Dolson during her 1949–1950 sojourn and spent time with Dolson when visiting New York, sometimes along with Lyell.

Eliot, T. S. (1888–1965) Influential modernist writer who was born in Missouri and moved to London, where he wrote poetry (*The Waste Land*), essays, and dramatic works, eventually becoming a British citizen. Lyell heard him lecture at Princeton and London, and later spent time with him when Eliot came to lecture at the University of Texas.

Engel, Lehman (1910–1982) Jackson-born friend of Welty and Lyell's who left to pursue a musical career but returned regularly to visit family and friends. Engel was studying at Julliard when Welty and Lyell were attending Columbia. He was a composer, arranger, musical director, and conductor for many theater, dance, and opera productions, as well as choral music, studio recordings, and radio and television broadcasts. In 1961 he founded the BMI Lehman Engel Musical Theatre Workshop. In 1968, he composed the score for a ballet based on Welty's children's book *The Shoe Bird*.

Erskine, Albert (1912–1993) Coeditor of *The Southern Review* and an early publisher of Welty's work, during a period when Erskine was married to Katherine Anne Porter. He had a long career at distinguished publishing houses and became Welty's editor at Random House. When the two of them worked together for a week in 1969, editing her *Losing Battles* manuscript, Welty stayed in Albert and Marisa Erskine's home.

Evans, Madge (1909–1981) Actress in theater, film, radio and television, best known for her 1930s MGM films and for a line of hats named for her when she was a child actress and model. She married the playwright Sydney Kingsley in 1939. The couple were dance enthusiasts and hosted a party for Martha Graham's company that Welty attended in 1958.

Faulkner, William (1897–1962) Celebrated modernist author of many fictional works chronicling an invented Mississippi county, Yoknapatawpha, that resembled the author's own home environs in Oxford, Mississippi. He sent Welty a note of encouragement in 1943, while he was in California writing screenplays for Warner Brothers. Many of his novels were out of print when she began rereading them during the 1940s. She met Faulkner in 1948 through Oxford, Mississippi, friends of John Robinson, and in 1949, before he had won the year's Nobel Prize for literature, she spent an afternoon with him and Robinson on Faulkner's sailboat. In 1962 Welty was in Faulkner's company again, presenting him with the National Award of Arts and Letters Gold Medal for Fiction.

Fearing, Kelly (1918–2011) Artist and art professor at the University of Texas, where he became friends with Lyell. Welty admired his art and owned two of his works.

Fischer, Jack (1907–1980) Writer and editor. Welty and Lyell's friend Dolly Wells worked for him when he was at Harper & Brothers. While editor at *Harper's*, Fischer heard Welty give the lecture that became "Place in Fiction" and asked to publish it in the magazine, but ultimately decided not to.

Foff, Art and Antonette Couple with whom Welty and John Robinson became friends during Welty's 1947 sojourns in San Francisco. Arthur Foff (1923–1972), a novelist and a client of Diarmuid Russell's, founded the creative writing program at San Francisco State in 1949. His wife, Antonette (1922–1987), wrote novels as Anton Fereva.

Ford, Charles Henri (1913–2002) Surrealist poet and editor born in Brookhaven, Mississippi. In 1929 he began publishing a magazine, *Blues: A Magazine of New Rhythms*, in Columbus, Mississippi, featuring such modernist poets as William Carlos Williams, Ezra Pound, and Gertrude Stein. He lived with Djuna Barnes in Paris, then coauthored the 1933 novel *The Young and Evil*, about gay artists in Greenwich village. In 1934 he returned to New York with his partner, the Russian painter Pavel Tchelitchew. Both Welty and Lyell saw him occasionally in the city in the 1930s and 1940s.

Ford, Ford Madox (1873–1939) Highly esteemed English novelist, poet, critic, and editor of *English Review* and *Transatlantic Review*. He wrote to Welty in November 1938, telling her that Katherine Anne Porter suggested he ask Welty to show him her stories. He was impressed, but was unable to place her short story collection with publishers, who told Ford and Welty that they were more interested in novels than short fiction.

Ford, Ruth (1911–2009) The sister of Charles Henri Ford; actress and model photographed by Cecil Beaton, Man Ray, and Carl Van Vechten. The siblings shared an apartment in Manhattan in the 1930s. In 1959 she and Faulkner adapted his novel *Requiem for a Nun* for the stage and she performed the role of Temple Drake.

Forster, E. M. (1879–1970) English fiction writer and critic whose works Welty greatly admired. He wrote to her expressing appreciation for her work in 1947 and 1948, and in 1954, spent an afternoon with Welty in his rooms in Cambridge, where she was a lecturer in a summer program. Her 1965 essay "Must the Novelist Crusade?" lauds Forster's critique of racism in *A Passage to India* (1924), stating that it remained relevant "because of the splendor of the novel."

Frederikson, Edna (1904–1998) Writer who was at Bread Loaf with Welty in 1940. She published a novel, *Three Parts Earth*, in 1972.

Gielgud, Sir John (1904–2000) English actor and director. When Lyell met him in London in 1945, Gielgud had become well known for performing and directing Shakespeare as well as more recent plays. Lyell met him backstage after a performance of *The Duchess of Malfi*, where he played Ferdinand.

Giroux, Robert (1914–2008) Harcourt, Brace editor of Welty's *The Golden Apples*, *The Ponder Heart*, and *The Bride of the Innisfallen*. He then moved to Farrar and Strauss and later became partner and chairman of the firm, renamed Farrar, Straus and Giroux.[4]

Gordon, Caroline (1895–1981) Kentucky-born fiction writer and literary critic and friend of Welty's. From 1925 to 1959, she was married to the poet Allen Tate.

Graham, Martha (1894–1991) A pioneer of modern dance in the twentieth century who was living in New York when Welty and Lyell's friend Lehman Engel came there to study music. Engel composed music for Graham and probably encouraged Welty and Lyell to see her perform when they were living in the city during the 1930–1931 academic year. Thereafter, Lyell and Welty delighted in Graham's work whenever they saw her company perform, in New York, Jackson, or Austin.

Green, Henry (1905–1973) English novelist whose work Welty greatly admired. When the two writers met in 1950 at a London cocktail party, they were mutually entranced and spent a second evening together discussing "heaven knows—everything" Welty later recalled.[5] Lyell invited Welty to submit her essay on Green to the *Texas Quarterly*, where it was published in 1961 as "Henry Green: A Novelist of the Imagination."

Greenway, George[6] A Jackson boyfriend of Welty's after college; also a trumpet player, he came to visit Welty in New York during her 1930–1931 sojourn there. He later worked at the Library of Congress.

Hains, Frank (1926–1975) Arts editor for the *Jackson Daily News* and longtime friend of Welty's. Hains directed many plays produced in Jackson, including an adaptation of Welty's *The Ponder Heart* that he rewrote, more to Welty's liking than the Broadway version.[7] Welty was grieved and shocked by his death in 1975; an acquaintance had murdered him in his home, a few blocks from Welty's house. Hain's homosexuality was not entirely an open secret in 1970s Mississippi, and the coverage of his murder sometimes suggested Hains's lifestyle was partly responsible. Welty wrote Hains's last column after his death, lauding her friend as a "refresher of our spirits" through support of artists and the arts.[8]

Hamilton, Bill (1908–1972) Jackson friend of Welty's who was part of the "Night-Blooming Cereus Club" in the 1930s. He became a history professor at Duke University.

Hilton, Ralph (1907–1982) Friend from Central High School who wrote for the *Jackson Daily News* before producing the *Jackson State Tribune*, for which Welty wrote in the early 1930s. Hilton later worked for the Foreign Service before editing and cofounding *The Island Packet* in Hilton Head, South Carolina.

Hollingsworth, William (1910–1944) Artist and friend of Welty's since childhood. After studying at the Chicago Art Institute, he returned to Jackson in 1934, where his work was exhibited at the Jackson Municipal Art Gallery along with photographs by Welty and Hubert Creekmore. He suffered from depression that led to his suicide in 1944. In 1958, Welty wrote the introduction for an exhibition of Hollingsworth's work at the Mississippi Museum of Art, reprinted in *Occasions* and *On William Hollingsworth*.

Hull, Marie (1890–1980) Jackson painter and art teacher from whom the young Welty took lessons. Her body of work, exhibited nationally as well as in Jackson, includes portraits, landscapes, and watercolor sketches.

Jones, Alun R. Welsh scholar who met Welty when he attended a 1954 summer institute at Cambridge where Welty was lecturing. Welty later tried to help him publish his fiction and to find a teaching appointment in the US. He published scholarship on English and Welsh writers, as well as a 1969 essay on Welty.

Lavin, Mary (1912–1996) Irish fiction writer and for many years a client of Diarmuid Russell's. She and Welty met periodically when their travels brought them into the same place.

Lawrence, Elizabeth (1904–1985) North Carolina friend of Frank Lyell, whom Welty met while visiting Lyell in Raleigh in the 1930s. A landscape architect and horticultural writer, she published *A Southern Garden: A Handbook for the Middle South* (1942) and other books, and over seven hundred columns in *The Charlotte Observer*.

Lillie, Beatrice (Bea) (1894–1989) Canadian-born singer and comedienne who appeared in Broadway shows, movies, radio programs, and eventually on television. Welty and Lyell were lifelong fans of Lillie's sophisticated and zany performances. She was married to Sir Robert Peel and worked with Noel Coward and other British aristocrat-artists. Lillie's recordings of "I'm a Campfire Girl," "Paree," and Coward's song "Marvelous Party" were part of Lyell and Welty's shared vocabulary.

Lotterhos, Helen (1905–1981) Jackson artist and friend of Welty's; a cousin of their art teacher Marie Hull. She and Welty enjoyed driving into the country to do plein air sketches and watercolors. Photographs Welty took on these excursions sometimes include Lotterhos.

Lyell, Clarena Hallam (1885–1977) Frank Lyell's mother. Her father, Frank Hallam, had been rector of St. Andrew's Episcopal Church in Jackson. She was an active member of the choir at St. Andrew's as well as a wedding soloist and performer in vocal recitals and plays.

Lyell, Gordon Garland (1874–1961) Frank Lyell's father, a prominent Jackson attorney who served as chancellor of Mississippi's Fifth District from 1906 to 1913 and was thereafter known as "Judge Lyell." G. Garland Lyell and Frank Hallam, who became his father-in-law, were close associates of Governor James K. Vardaman.

Lyell, G. Garland, Jr. (1913–1972) Frank Lyell's brother, who became an attorney in his father's firm and then the state's assistant attorney general. He drowned when his car sank into the Ross Barnet Reservoir in 1972.

Lyell, Louis (1925–2023) Frank Lyell's youngest brother, who grew up in Jackson, served in World War II, and lived in Germany, California, and Washington before returning to Jackson. One of his many acts of philanthropy was to sponsor an observatory, named for Frank Lyell, at St. Andrew's Episcopal School in Jackson.

Lyell, "Tippy" (1940–2024) Wife of Louis Lyell. Allison Jean "Tippy" Reamers Lyell and Louis had two daughters, Lorna Margaret Lyell Chain (Tom), and Louise Hallam Lyell Lampton (Luke), and four grandchildren.

Maxwell, William (1908–2000) Fiction writer and *New Yorker* editor whose association with Welty developed into a close friendship between her, Maxwell, his wife Emmy, and their daughters Katherine and Brooke. Maxwell published numerous novels and short story collections and, during his thirty-nine years at *The New Yorker*, edited many distinguished fiction writers in addition to Welty. Their correspondence is collected in *What There Is to Say, We Have Said.*

McCullers, Carson (1917–1967) Southern writer whom Welty met and disliked when they were both at Yaddo in 1941. Her works included *The Heart Is a Lonely Hunter* (1940) and *A Member of the Wedding* (1946).

McGill, Ralph (1898–1969) Editor of *The Atlanta Constitution*; vilified for his antisegregationist stance by many white readers, a few of whom sent death threats, burned crosses on his lawn, fired shots into his house, and left bombs in his mailbox.

McGrath [Vanderlip], Eileen (1911–1992) New York friend introduced to Welty by Diarmuid and Rose Russell when McGrath and her sister Peggy and brother-in-law David Rockefeller were living near the Russells. Welty nearly always saw McGrath when she came to the city, and through Welty, Lyell also became friends with her. She became a medical doctor and practiced in New York City. In 1959 she married Frank Vanderlip.

Merkel, Una (1903–1986) Film and stage actress who met Welty when Merkel played Edna Earle in the 1956 Broadway production of *The Ponder Heart*.

Mian, Mary (1902–2001) Writer and client of Diarmuid Russell's whom Welty first spent time with during her 1949–1950 sojourn abroad, when Mian and her husband **Aristide Mian (1893–1979),** a French sculptor, were living in Meudon with their three daughters. Mian published short works in *The New Yorker*, some of which were collected as *My Country-in-Law*, as well as young adult historical and fantasy fiction. She and her husband moved to Santa Fe in 1954.

Millar, Kenneth (1915–1983) Author of mysteries written under the name Ross Macdonald. Welty, an avid reader of mystery novels, admired these works and was delighted to receive a fan letter from Millar in 1970. The writers began a correspondence that lasted until 1982, when Miller's Alzheimer's disease made it impossible for him to write back. Theirs was a loving, spiritually intimate relationship. Millar, married to another writer, Margaret Millar, dedicated his 1973 novel *Sleeping Beauty* to Welty and she dedicated her 1976 essay collection, *The Eye of the Story*, to Millar. Their correspondence is collected in *Meanwhile There Are Letters*.

Morris, Willie (1934–1999) Mississippi-born writer who became editor of *Harper's*. He was also great-nephew to two eccentric Jackson ladies, known to Welty and Lyell as "Phantoms," who wore fur coats to the grocery store. Morris attended the University of Texas, where, as editor of the student newspaper, he criticized university and state legislators' resistance to integration. His memoir, *North Toward Home*, fondly recalls taking English classes from Frank Lyell.

Morrison, Ann (1928–2007) and Bill Morrison (1925–1977) Jackson couple who were members of Lyell and Welty's group, "The Basic Eight." Ann Morrison worked for the Mississippi Department of Archives and History as Charlotte Capers's assistant and later as educational program coordinator. Her husband Bill was an architect.

Moss, Howard (1922–1987) Poet, dramatist, and poetry editor for *The New Yorker.*

Nalbandian, Karnig (1916–1989) Armenian American artist who was at Yaddo with Welty in 1941. Welty and William Hollingsworth worked together on an exhibition of Nalbandian's sketches at the Mississippi Art Gallery in 1942. A photo of Nalbandian and Welty on a bicycle appears in Marrs's *Eudora Welty,* and a portrait of him at Yaddo is in *Photographs.*

Night-Blooming Cereus Club Group of Jackson friends who gathered in the playhouse behind the Welty family home in the 1930s. Members included Welty, Frank Lyell, Nash Burger, Bill Hamilton, Lehman Engel, and Hubert Creekmore. Their motto was taken from a Rudy Vallee song lyric, "Don't take it serious; life's too mysterious" and from the night-blooming cereus, a plant grown by Jackson neighbors that opened rarely, at night. Some individuals announced the anticipated opening of their plants in the newspaper.

Parker, Annie (1867–1944) Head of Jackson's public library. She was widowed at a young age, then became a librarian. Newspaper articles often referred to her as Miss Parker.

Peters, Fritz (1913–1979) Writer who was newly married to Mary Lou Aswell when the couple were enjoying a sojourn in Europe and spent time with Welty there. His 1949 novel, *The World Next Door*, was based upon his experience in a mental institution. He and Aswell separated in 1950. In 1951 he published *Finisterre*, a novel about the emerging sexual identity of a young gay man.

Polk, Eddie Mae (1933–2018) Jackson resident who worked for many years as housekeeper for the Welty family at Pinehurst Street. Mrs. Polk was an honorary pallbearer at Welty's funeral in 2001.

Porter, Katherine Anne (1890–1980) Fiction writer who met Welty in the 1930s while married to Albert Erskine (1912–1993), coeditor of *The Southern Review*. She published short fiction (*Flowering Judas*, 1930; *Pale Horse, Pale Rider*, 1939; *The Leaning Tower*, 1944) and a novel, *Ship of Fools*, that she worked on from 1941 until its publication in 1962. Porter encouraged Welty early in her career, showing her work to Ford Madox Ford, recommending her for fellowships, and writing the introduction to her first book of stories, *A Curtain of Green*. Welty became friends with Porter during the summer of 1941 when she was at Yaddo and Porter (separated from Erskine prior to a 1942 divorce) was living nearby in Saratoga Springs. Lyell met Porter while visiting Welty at Yaddo, as documented in Welty's personal photographs.

Prescott, Orville (1906–1996) Book reviewer for *The New York Times* from 1942 to 1966 and something of a nemesis to Welty. He was a hostile coworker in 1944 when she worked as an intern for the publication, and later wrote unfavorable reviews of Welty's books.

Price, Reynolds (1933–2011) North Carolina author of dozens of volumes of fiction, poetry, essays, and drama, who first met Welty when she visited Duke University where he was finishing his undergraduate degree. Welty became his lifelong friend, encouraging his writing and enjoying his company. Price was almost like a son to Welty, and when she could no longer travel, he paid her regular visits in Jackson. Lyell was also a friend and correspondent.

Prince, John (1922–2011) and Katherine (1927–2021) Friends of Welty's who lived in Washington, DC. The three initially met through Marcella Comès, who also introduced them to Katherine Anne Porter. Welty often saw the Princes when she visited Washington, and they traveled in France with her in 1974.

Redmayne, Pamela (1901–1999) English woman who hosted Lyell and other American military officers for weekends in her Cotswolds home while he was stationed in London in 1945.

Reynal, Eugene (1902–1968) Publisher at Harper & Brothers, then at his own firm, Reynal & Hitchcock, which in 1949 was sold to Welty's publisher, Harcourt, Brace. There, Reynal was vice president until 1955 when he left to form Reynal & Company.

Robinson, John (1909–1989) Jackson friend who was Welty's love interest in the late 1930s and 1940s. In the 1930s he lived in New Orleans and worked as an insurance adjuster. During World War II he served in the Army Air Forces Intelligence. Welty began writing *Delta Wedding* partly to cheer Robinson while he was away; she visited Robinson's relatives and read his great-grandmother's diary as research. She and Robinson shared a love of gardening, a topic of many letters to him collected in *Tell About Night Flowers: Eudora Welty's Gardening Letters, 1940–1949*. After his return from military service, Welty encouraged him to pursue writing as a career, and he published a few stories. Welty's hopes for a continuing romantic relationship ended when she realized Robinson was in love with a young Italian man, Enzo Rochiggiani, with whom he spent the rest of his life. She and Robinson sustained a lifelong friendship, writing occasionally and seeing each other when Robinson and Rochiggiani visited Jackson.

Rockefeller, David (1915–2017) and Peggy Rockefeller (1915–1996) A grandson of billionaire John D. Rockefeller. David married Peggy McGrath Rockefeller, whose sister, Eileen McGrath, became a friend of Welty's. The Rockefellers were also friends of Diarmuid Russell and his wife Rose, who lived near the Rockefellers in Westchester County, New York.

Russell, Diarmuid (1902–1973) Welty's literary agent and friend, the son of the Irish poet A. E. (George William Russell). When he and Henry Volkening formed a literary agency in 1940, Welty became one of their first clients. Russell was an important early reader of Welty's work in progress, as well as an effective advocate for it in the literary marketplace, as documented in correspondence published in *Author and Agent*. Welty was close to Russell, his wife Rose Lander Russell (1906–1988), and their two children, Pamela and Will. Welty and Russell's shared interest in gardening was a touchstone in their frequent correspondence, some of which is published in *Tell About Night Flowers: Eudora Welty's Gardening Letters, 1940–1949*.

Sackville-West, Eddy (1901–1965) British music critic and novelist whom Welty met while visiting Elizabeth Bowen. (His cousin, writer Vita Sackville-West, was for ten years Virginia Woolf's lover.)

Sancton, Tom (1915–2012) Writer who married Welty and Lyell's Jackson friend Seta Alexander. He was managing editor of *The New Republic* when it published Welty's essay "The Pageant of Birds."

Segovia, Andres (1893–1987) Spanish guitarist who was the inspiration for a Spanish musician character in Welty's 1948 story "Music from Spain." She heard him in concert in San Francisco in 1947.

Shands [Walsh], Aimee (1909–1996) A classmate of Welty's and a member of the Junior Auxiliary League; one of the Jackson group who did graduate work at Columbia University when Welty and Lyell were there, in 1930–1931. Her father, Dr. Harley Shands, was a prominent Jackson doctor who lived in Welty's neighborhood.

Shotwell [Ricketts], Leone (1910–1990) Friend of Welty's who attended Columbia along with Welty and Lyell in 1930–1931. Her aunt and guardian was hesitant for her to move to New York, so she persuaded Welty to come along, which won her aunt over. She later married Jacksonian Barron Ricketts.

Simmons, Dorothy (1908–1995) Welty's classmate and friend; in 1938 while visiting Simmons in her family's home in Utica, Mississippi, Welty heard a whistle blown to alert tomato growers to cover their plants during freezing weather, inspiring her story "The Whistle."[9] Simmons accompanied Welty when she visited John Robinson in De Lisle, Mississippi, in 1948.

Sims, Agnes C. (1910–1990) Artist based in New Mexico who became the partner of Mary Lou Aswell. Prehistoric rock art inspired some of Sims's most famous paintings and sculptures. She was also a renovator of historic houses in Santa Fe. The home she shared with Aswell was part of a compound, including a gallery and studio, where Sims supported other artists by hosting exhibits and performances.

Sitwell, Edith (1887–1964) English modernist poet who was also known for her angular features and distinctive style. Welty seems to have owned a 1930 recording of Sitwell's *Façade*, a sequence of Sitwell's poems she recited with musical accompaniment, speaking in a manner Welty found incomprehensible. Lyell met Sitwell briefly in 1945 when taken backstage to meet John Gielgud after his performance in *The Duchess of Malfi*, and in 1957, he sent Welty an account of Sitwell's visit to the University of Texas.

Skinner, Mary Frances (1908–1986) and Joe (1908–1995) Married couple from Jackson, friends of Welty and Lyell. The Millsaps graduates attended Columbia University in the 1930s when Welty and Lyell were there, then returned to Jackson. Both became life masters in bridge.

Slocum, John (1914–1997) Junior partner in the Russell & Volkening literary agency; he represented both Ezra Pound and Wyndham Lewis. He left the firm in 1941 to become a press aide to Mayor Fiorello LaGuardia, then enlisted in the Army. After serving in World War II, he worked for the Foreign Service.

Smith, William Jay (1918–2015) and Barbara Howes (1914–1996) Poets who were a married couple when Welty and John Robinson spent time with them in Italy in 1950. William Jay Smith later became the United States Poet Laureate, from 1968 to 1970.

Somerville, Ella (1893–1974) Oxford, Mississippi, resident Welty knew through John Robinson; a friend of William Faulkner.

Spain, Nancy (1917–1964) English journalist, mystery novelist, and broadcaster known for her acerbic and campy wit, whom Welty had met in London.

Spann, Willie (1901–1983) Jackson friend of Welty's who taught mathematics in the Jackson schools, as did her older sister, Pearl Spann. Willie Spann is pictured in *Photographs*.

Spencer, Elizabeth (1921–2019) Mississippi writer who got to know Welty when Spencer was a student at Belhaven College, across the street from the Weltys' home. She published novels, short fiction, a memoir, and a play.

Stafford, Jean (1915–1979) American fiction writer whose *Collected Stories* won a Pulitzer Prize in 1970. She became friends with Welty in the 1940s.

Stern, James (1904–1993) Anglo-Irish author who worked as a civilian employee for the United States Strategic Bomb Survey along with Lyell and W. H. Auden in 1945. His 1947 memoir *The Hidden Damage: A Personal Pilgrimage with W. H. Auden into the Heart of Post-War Germany* reflected his interviews with civilians traumatized by the Nazi regime.

Stevens [Maclahlan Ring], Emily White (1908–1996) and John MacLachlan (1905–1959) Emily White Stevens was Welty's high school classmate and roommate during their first year of college at Mississippi State College for

Women. After she finished college at Millsaps, she went to North Carolina, where future husband John MacLachlan was in graduate school. Both earned degrees from the notably, and to some Southerners, notoriously, progressive sociology department at the University of North Carolina. They were teaching at the University of Florida when John died. In 1975 Emily married Dr. Alfred Ring.[10]

Sumner, Bertha Ricketts (1890–1970) Writer who first knew Welty in the 1930s when a member of the Jackson Little Theatre, along with Eudora and Chestina Welty and many of their friends. She published novels as Cid Ricketts Sumner. In 1970 Sumner died tragically, killed by a teenaged grandson who may have been using drugs.

Sutherland, Donald (1915–1978) Writer and professor friend of Lyell's who corresponded with Welty and visited her in Jackson when serving in World War II and stationed nearby. Among his publications was a 1951 literary biography of Gertrude Stein.

Tennant, Stephen (1906–1987) Wealthy and eccentric British aesthete and socialite, one of the glamorous and transgressive "Bright Young Things" Welty and Lyell first knew through *Vanity Fair* and *Vogue*. He met Welty in New York in 1949 and presented her with a copy of a collection of Willa Cather pieces, *On Writing*, for which he wrote an introduction entitled "The Room Beyond." In Paris in 1950, he took Welty to a performance at the Folies-Bergère. In later years Welty enjoyed recalling this occasion and another experience: dining at an expensive Paris restaurant at the invitation of the wealthy Tennant, who said "Darling, shall we share?" when the check arrived.[11]

Travers, Pamela (1899–1996) Author of the Mary Poppins children's books and a client of Diarmuid Russell, who introduced the two writers. She also became a friend and correspondent of Lyell. Her adopted son, Camillus, was the grandson of Irish writer and publisher Joseph Hone.

Trilling, Diana (1905–1996) and Lionel (1905–1975) Critics whose reviews (hers in *The Nation*, his in *Partisan Review*) often analyzed the political and social implications they found in literature. Diana Trilling reviewed Welty's works unfavorably, interpreting them as accepting or even upholding the social and racial hierarchies that were so deeply embedded in the Southern societies Welty depicted.

Van Gelder, Robert (1904–1952) and Dorothy (1900–1999). New York writer and critic and his wife, also a writer. Robert Van Gelder was a reporter and editor of *The New York Times Book Review*. He published numerous interviews with writers, including one of Welty in 1942. In 1944, at his invitation, she worked for the *Book Review* as an intern for almost five months. Dorothy Van Gelder coedited an anthology, *American Legend:*

A Treasury of Our Country's Yesterdays, with her husband, who authored other children's books.

Volkening, Henry (1902–1970) Cofounder of Russell & Volkening, the literary agency that represented Welty and many other distinguished literary authors.

Waller, Fats (1904–1943) Jazz pianist, composer, and singer whose art inspired Welty's short story "Powerhouse." She began working on the story after seeing Waller perform in Jackson in 1940.

Warren, Robert Penn (1905–1989) Novelist (*All the King's Men*), poet, critic, and coeditor of *The Southern Review*, where some of Welty's stories first appeared in the 1930s.

Wasson, Ben (1899–1982) Friend of William Faulkner and for a time his editor and literary agent. He later wrote a regular arts column for the Greenville, Mississippi, *Delta Democrat Times* and in 1947, cofounded Levee Press with that newspaper's editor, Hodding Carter. In 1948 Levee Press published Welty's "Music from Spain" as a seventy-two-page volume.

Wayne, David (1914–1995) Stage and film actor who played Uncle Daniel in the Broadway production of the play *The Ponder Heart*, based on Welty's novel.

Weeks, Edward (1898–1989) Editor of *The Atlantic* when several of Welty's works appeared there, including a serialized publication of *Delta Wedding* in 1946.

Wells, Dolly (1910–1973) Rosa Farrar "Dolly" Wells, a classmate of Frank Lyell, became Welty's lifelong friend. *The Golden Apples* is dedicated to Lyell and Wells. She lived and worked in New York City for many years before returning to Jackson in the early 1970s.

Welty, Chestina (1883–1966) Welty's mother. Born in West Virginia, she was a schoolteacher before marrying Ohio-born **Christian Welty (1879–1931)** and moving with him to Jackson. An avid reader and gardener and an active clubwoman, she was devoted to her family. Her husband died at age fifty-two, and her younger son, Walter, died at forty-three. In the 1950s, she developed problems with her vision, then suffered strokes that restricted her mobility, independence, and happiness. For much of her life, however, she was an ardent supporter of Welty's writing career, and the two women coexisted happily in the home they shared.

Welty, Edward (1912–1966) Eudora's brother, who shared some of her love of humor, music, and visual art. He became an architect and designed the rental house that the family built on their property. He and Elinor Saul married in 1943. He suffered from clinical depression as an adult, as well as arthritis. After a fall at his home in 1965, he was hospitalized and died in 1966, four days after his mother.

Welty [Thompson], Elizabeth (1944–2012) and Mary Alice Welty [White] (1947–) Welty's nieces, much beloved by their aunt "Dodo," who babysat, drove carpools, took them on trips, and celebrated their own travels, jobs, marriages, and the arrivals of their children.

Welty, Mittie Creekmore (1917–2004) Eudora's sister-in-law, who married Walter Welty in 1939. Her brother, Hubert Creekmore, was a close friend of both Welty and Lyell.

Welty, Walter (1915–1959) The younger of Welty's brothers. Married to Mittie Creekmore, he became an officer in the Standard Life Insurance Company of Jackson. He died of heart problems caused by arthritis.

Wheeler, Monroe (1899–1988) Director of exhibitions and publications at the Museum of Modern Art.

Williams, Tennessee (1911–1983) Mississippi-born playwright. Welty wrote a brief and admiring program note for the Jackson New Stage's 1959 production of *Cat on a Hot Tin Roof.*

Wolfe, Karl (1904–1985) Mississippi-born painter known for his portraiture. He trained at the Chicago Art Institute before moving to Jackson. He created a portrait of Lyell's brother, Louis.

Wolfe, Mildred Nungester (1912–2009) Artist who trained at the Chicago Art Institute and came to Jackson with her husband, Karl Wolfe. Her 1988 portrait of Welty is now in the Smithsonian's National Portrait Gallery.

Woodburn, John (1901–1952) Literary critic and Welty's editor at Doubleday, Doran. He met Welty on a 1939 talent-scouting trip to Jackson. He took her stories back to New York with him and, in 1940, urged Diarmuid Russell to offer to become Welty's literary agent.

Wooldridge, Jimmie (1914–1974) A member of "The Basic Eight," a 1950s group of Welty's Jackson friends that included Lyell when he was in town.

Woolf, Virginia (1882–1941) English modernist writer; an artistic and intellectual heroine to Welty. She and Lyell had admired Woolf's fiction since the 1920s. In 1931 Welty wrote her a fan letter in which she called *To the Lighthouse* "perfect and life-giving" and "light under a door I shall never open," and offered some critiques of *The Waves.*

Young, Stark (1881–1963) Mississippi-born playwright, novelist, painter, essayist, renowned theater critic, and one of the Agrarians who wrote *I'll Take My Stand* (1930). Early in his career he taught at a series of universities, including Texas. Based in New York for most of his career, Young regularly visited Austin to see his sister, Julia Robertson, who was also a friend of Frank Lyell's.

TO ABSENT FRIENDS

INTRODUCTION

> *All* letters, old and new, are the still-existing parts of a life. To read them now is to be present when some discovery of truth—or perhaps untruth, some flash of light—is just occurring. It is clamorous with the moment's happiness or pain. [. . .] What we've been told need not be momentous, but it can be as good as receiving the darting glance from some very bright eye, still mischievous and mischief-making, arriving from fifty or a hundred years ago.
>
> —EUDORA WELTY, *THE NORTON BOOK OF FRIENDSHIP*, 1991

THIS BOOK PRESENTS OVER 350 COMPLETE OR EXCERPTED LETTERS BETWEEN Eudora Welty (1903–2001) and Frank Lyell (1911–1977). In my title I have borrowed from a toast Welty was fond of making: "To our absent friends." Neither correspondent was my own friend, but I have lived with their writing for enough years now to feel as if I were present for part of their friendship, immortalized in letters that would not have been written without absences, all of which I now salute.

Eudora Welty was an exemplar of the short story form and a distinguished novelist, critic, memoirist, and photographer. Her works invite us to reflect upon the lives and societies of the people she portrays, most of whom are residents of her home state of Mississippi. Welty was also a prolific and gifted letter writer. Her correspondence provides an intriguing record of her daily life, adding to our understanding of this remarkable artist as she responded to her time and place.

In previously published Welty correspondence, readers can observe different facets of Welty's personality and different writerly gifts on display. Like another great letter writer, John Keats, who said he believed in inhabiting the personality of his subjects as a "chameleon poet," Welty wrote letters that reflected each friend's interests and passions. Writing to her literary agent and friend Diarmuid Russell, Welty often shared questions about her work in progress along with witty vignettes from her hometown and elegant, lyrical comments on gardening and the natural world. Letters to John Robinson, who for a time was Welty's love interest, covered similar topics while also expressing devotion and concern for Robinson during World War II and afterwards when he seemed unhappy and adrift; she characterized his writing as superior to her own, doubtless hoping that the writing life might bring him a greater sense of purpose and connection to her. To her *New Yorker* editor William Maxwell, a fellow writer who became a close friend, Welty's graceful and lively letters discussed family, mutual writer friends, the roses they cultivated, the literature she and Maxwell were producing, and other works, including one another's, that they admired. To Kenneth Millar, author of the Ross Macdonald mystery novels, who admired Welty's work and treasured her love for him as much as she did his, Welty shared more introspective, poetic letters reflecting on the writing life, memory, mortality, loved ones, and moments of beauty and gratitude.[1] Welty entered into the subjectivity of another person when writing letters to a friend, much as she did in her fiction.

Compared with these letters, Welty's correspondence with Frank Lyell is distinctive in several ways. Spanning forty-six years, it shows us Welty from her early twenties to her late sixties: the first extant letter was written in 1931, just after Welty and Lyell had spent a year at Columbia University, and the last one is from 1977, the year of Lyell's death. The friends never entirely lost their youthful exuberance. In their early incarnations, Welty and Lyell were full of themselves, eagerly seizing upon everything that seemed beautiful, hilarious, profound, or ridiculous. As they grew into more self-contained, slightly calmer versions of themselves, they maintained their cosmopolitan appetites for high and low culture, their veneration of art, and their love of the absurd.

A madcap sense of humor, present throughout the correspondence, is most prominent in the 1930s letters, which are often sprinkled with puns, riddles, gossip, cartoon sketches, and sardonic remarks that must have been as much fun to write as to read. Like Lyell, who sometimes excitedly reported having sighted or even met an artist or star, Welty, too, enjoyed addressing or signing the letters with the names of celebrities and hometown acquaintances. I counted at least 110 fake names across the entire correspondence, some reappearing in multiple letters. Twenty-two names are of famous people or figures in literature and film;[2] the rest are names of Jackson residents, many of whom had attended public school, Sunday school, music or art lessons, or social gatherings with Lyell, Welty, and their families.[3] They were not close friends, and most of them, judging from activities reported in the society pages of *The Clarion-Ledger* (Jackson), seem much more conventional than

Lyell and Welty, so assuming their names in a letter would have been self-evidently absurd, like a false moustache. Both correspondents appear to have found amusement in coming up with an ongoing parade of names from their past, using them as playful flourishes to begin or end a letter.

Welty and Lyell became friends during the Depression, years that, for them, were relatively carefree. Undaunted and bemused, these young intellectuals saw much to ridicule in the grown-up world they were entering, but their letters also convey deep respect and admiration for music, literature, art, dance, and other cultural expressions. After attending a New York concert in 1933, Welty wrote Lyell, "heavens. the effect the sacre d. p. doesn't have on me is not worth talking about," using e. e. cummings–style lowercase letters to express, in an offhanded aside, her intense reaction to Stravinsky's *Sacre Du Printemps* (*Rite of Spring*). Lyell, too, was consistently delighted by almost any artistic accomplishment. As Welty told their mutual friend, John Robinson, Lyell had "a vast appreciation of what is fine, or beautiful, or learned, or luxurious. [. . .] He really knows so much and he really loves, no worships, beautiful things."[4] This reverence and pleasure was a recurring topic throughout the Welty–Lyell correspondence.

Also mentioned regularly in the letters were childhood friends from Jackson who shared Welty and Lyell's cosmopolitan tastes, including a budding history professor (Bill Hamilton), book critic (Nash Burger), poet/novelist (Hubert Creekmore), and composer (Lehman Engel), who had all gone to school with Welty or Lyell. When in their twenties, these friends gathered in the abandoned playhouse in Welty's backyard to smoke, drink, talk about art, and generally crack themselves up. They called themselves the Night-Blooming Cereus Club, after the night-blooming flower and the practice of some of their neighbors of inviting people to come to see their specimens open. The young people's motto was "Don't take it cereus, life's too mysterious."[5] Apart from such diversions, Jackson had little to engage Welty in the early years of her correspondence; in 1932 she reported, "I have 0 to do"; in 1933, she listed her home address as "Loose Ends, Mississippi," and in 1935, she told Lyell she was "sick of Jackson" (after spending part of the summer typing his PhD thesis).

By the 1940s, however, Welty was plenty busy—writing, revising, or reading proofs for her books (*A Curtain of Green*, *The Wide Net*, *The Robber Bridegroom*, *Delta Wedding*), recommending other writers for fellowships that she'd once been turned down for, and spending several extended periods away from Jackson, in New York and San Francisco. In letters from this decade, there was much more to talk about: Welty's work in progress and Lyell's response to it, Lyell's teaching job at NC State, his training and service in the Army Air Forces Intelligence, and his subsequent teaching at the

University of Texas, where he spent the rest of his career. Their letters, often longer than in the 1930s, continued to feature humorous anecdotes, waggish annotations of enclosed news clippings, gossip and sardonic remarks, and discussions of art, literature, and mutual friends. Welty and Lyell continued to celebrate each other's accomplishments and to deride those who failed to appreciate them (e.g., "Many thanks for rising up and writing to the *New Republic*," Welty wrote in 1946 after Lyell had protested what he believed to be a wrong-headed review. "This is noble of you.") By 1949, as Lyell was beginning his third year at Texas, Welty had completed her fourth book, *The Golden Apples*. It was dedicated to Lyell and to another friend from Jackson, Dolly Wells, who like Lyell had read the stories as Welty drafted them. That fall, Welty was finally able to make her first overseas trip.

In the 1950s, letters document Welty's travels abroad and her widening circle of friends, including accomplished writers and artists, many of whom she introduced to Lyell. She continued sharing work in progress with him and reporting on the process of publishing her short fiction (*The Bride of the Innisfallen*), criticism, and a novella, *The Ponder Heart*, that was later turned into a Broadway play.[6] By the mid-1950s, however, her letters included fewer amusements or accomplishments and more reports on increasingly serious health problems in her family. Her brother Walter's poor health ended with his death in 1959, at age forty-three. Welty's mother, Chestina, suffered from declining vision, a loss of mobility, and periods of intense unhappiness, with Welty assuming responsibility for her mother or hiring others to help her. During these years, letters regularly report details of their difficult, confined lives, punctuated by Welty's lecture trips to earn money to pay for her mother's care, and by her guilt over not being able to alleviate her mother's suffering. She and Lyell continued to exchange annotated clippings and report on absurdities they witnessed, as well as books, films, and performances that moved them. Welty sent reports on Lyell's family, who lived in the neighborhood, as well as mutual friends in Jackson with whom Lyell also socialized when he was home. Writing from Texas, Lyell sympathized with Welty's family troubles and urged her to travel whenever she could get away. After the deaths of Welty's mother and surviving brother Edward in 1966, she produced more short fiction and another novella, *The Optimist's Daughter*. In 1970, she finished a long and long-delayed book, *Losing Battles*. When Lyell received his advance copy, he responded with delight, pronouncing it "quite a special novel."

By the 1970s, Welty had developed strong ties with many other people, including Mary Lou Aswell, Elizabeth Bowen, William Maxwell, Reynolds Price, and Kenneth Millar. Lyell was now one of many intimate friends writing to Welty, along with hundreds of strangers who wrote, telephoned, and knocked on her door asking her to sign books. "So glad to be thought of daily on your busy days," Lyell wrote in 1977, proud of her acclaim. Marrs's biography notes that for a time in the 1970s, Lyell had worried that Welty no longer valued his friendship.[7] The relatively small number of Lyell's letters that Welty preserved, particularly in this period, might seem to corroborate this impression, but her 1976–1977 letters to Lyell retain their familiar tone of fondness for an old friend, as in a 1976 card from Santa Barbara concluding, "Let's meet soon and tell our trips."[8]

In the final years of the Welty–Lyell correspondence, the high-spirited young people who wrote the earliest letters were still present, accompanied by some poignant acknowledgement of their own aging. Welty and Lyell were in their sixties, an age that, when their correspondence had begun, must have seemed unthinkable. In 1976, thanking Lyell for sending her a book on the Bloomsbury group, Welty wrote that one photo of Virginia and Leonard Woolf "filled with those years and days in 1939 leaves you just without words. It was good to see them all young and fair."[9] Welty and Lyell had shared experiences and enthusiasms for almost fifty years; few close friends had known her as long as he had. His 1977 death, at age sixty-five, was unexpected; visiting Jackson following a European tour, he was diagnosed with congestive heart failure and died before surgery could be attempted. Welty wrote of her grief to Kenneth Millar, calling Lyell the third of "my three dearest" friends who had passed away recently (following the losses of Dolly Wells and Diarmuid Russell). "I guess I was his closest friend here," Welty wrote Millar. "I know I'm at an age when the loss of friends is not considered surprising," she added. "But I am not going to learn to accept it for being not surprising. I'm going to hate it and protest it straight ahead—I'm indignant for their sakes—up to my last breath. I testify to their absence."[10] In the twenty-first century, the Welty–Lyell letters continue Welty's protest against loss, testifying to the daily lives and the cultural surround of these absent friends.

These letters are rarely momentous; they often contain updates on family, mutual friends, and recent travels or work, but little urgent information. Rarely does either correspondent engage in the philosophical musing or personal reflection characteristic of letters to Millar, Maxwell, Russell, Robinson, or Mary Lou Aswell. In Lyell and Welty's letters, some topics are invoked telegraphically, with little explanation provided. Sometimes the writers only gesture towards things too sad to dwell upon, especially the suffering or loss of loved ones. In addition, there are significant topics these letters do not discuss. For example, clippings and a few glancing references indicate shared disgust over segregationist politics or white supremacist violence in Mississippi, but very little is said on that subject. Lyell, clearly a dedicated churchgoer, almost always refrains from discussing his faith with Welty, whose interest in Christianity seems to have been minimal. Welty's letters rarely hint at her love for, and unhappiness over, Robinson, nor does she discuss, in the 1970s, her love for Kenneth Millar. Neither correspondent mentions Lyell's romantic relationships, if any such existed. Perhaps such personal topics were never broached, though they could have been discussed in person, on Lyell's visits to Jackson or when they both were in New York, or in other letters, many of which apparently have not survived.

Fortunately for us, many letters do survive. Reading them, I have felt like an eavesdropper on a freewheeling conversation that is already well underway and will continue long after I leave the room. Often the conversation recounts a moment that was twice pleasing or hilarious: first when experienced in person, and then again while describing it, or reading about the pleasure it had afforded their friend. "Tell all," Welty concludes a letter to Lyell in Europe on October 29, 1953. On a 1960 trip to New York that Welty had feared she'd have to cancel because of her mother's illness, she wrote Lyell a postcard from Times Square: "I made it! Know you rejoice with me."[11] In 1967, while Lyell was abroad, she wrote, "So glad you're getting this fine summer—Enjoy it every drop."[12] Even when things were not going well, letters often contained a humorous anecdote or a few clippings to amuse the recipient. Some letters contained little *more* than clippings. From the 1930s to the 1970s, any subject—movies, jazz music, radio comics, Jackson bridge parties—was an occasion to clip or quote from an article or an ad and perhaps dash off a comment that the recipient was sure to appreciate.

The letters chosen for this collection, showcasing Lyell's and Welty's gifts in the genre, also demonstrate the value of the seemingly archaic practice of letter writing.[13] Writing a letter brought the recipient to life, like rubbing Aladdin's lamp, throughout almost five decades of friendship. It must have provided a form of company, conjuring up the imagined friend who would be reading the letter. "Now—who was I writing to?" Welty teased Lyell in 1933 after describing the furniture surrounding her.[14] It may seem incredible now to think of the number of messages each correspondent mailed, a habit developed during the early decades of their friendship when letters were virtually the only way to stay in touch. Even after they both could afford long-distance phone calls, Lyell and Welty regularly sent letters, postcards, greeting cards, gifts, and clippings with handwritten annotations. Such letter writing, however rare today, is not altogether removed from our own time. In the twentieth century Welty and Lyell were doing what many do in the twenty-first: bringing ourselves into the presence of friends by reacting to news, food, scenery, and other moments we reexperience by sharing them, in links and photos. The bits and pieces of Welty's and Lyell's lives are captured on paper and in clippings shared by mail, but lovers of text messages and Instagram postings will recognize a similar desire to experience a fleeting moment with a friend. These letters demonstrate that before social media and instant communication were available, friendships were maintained in a similar spirit, through shared flashes of cultural expression, natural scenery, overheard remarks, and quips that the sender enjoyed as much as the recipient.

As a photograph can capture a fleeting instant, these letters now preserve past moments, long after the friends who shared them are gone. The correspondence confirms a belief Welty stated in her 1944 essay "Some Notes on River Country": that "passionate things, in some essence, endure." In that essay, contemplating the ghostly presence of the former residents of southwest Mississippi, Welty suggested that there had been too much life in this place for it to fade away altogether: "A place that ever was lived in is like a fire that never goes out. It flares up, it smolders for a time, it is fanned or smothered by circumstance, but its being is intact, forever fluttering within it, the result of some original ignition. Sometimes it gives out glory, sometimes its little light must be sought out to be seen, small and tender as a candle flame, but as certain."[15] These letters have become the enduring habitation, the place, where Frank Lyell and Eudora Welty's friendship now resides, "intact, forever fluttering within."

As the New York train pulled, close to midnight, out of the station at home, your friends stood waving as though they'd never see you again. Your last view of Jackson from your window was an old dark wooden building by the tracks topped by a hand-painted sign under an arc light: "Where Will YOU Spend Eternity?" This sign was also the first thing you saw in the dawn when the train brought you back home again. [. . .]

I knew that even as I was moving farther away from Jackson, my mother was already writing to me at her desk, telling me she missed me but only wanted what was best for me. [. . .] The torment and guilt—the torment of having the loved one go, the guilt of being the loved one gone—comes into my fiction as it did and does into my life. And most of all the guilt then was because it was true: I had left to arrive at some future and secret joy, at what was unknown, and what was now in New York, waiting to be discovered. My joy was connected with writing; that was as much as I knew.

—*ONE WRITER'S BEGINNINGS*

Chapter I

1931–1939

THE CORRESPONDENCE BETWEEN EUDORA WELTY AND FRANK LYELL BEGAN IN 1931, after each had finished a year of graduate work at Columbia University, along with several other friends from Jackson. That year, Welty and Lyell often explored the city together; Welty found these extracurricular activities much more interesting than her classes. Her father had wanted Welty to learn to support herself, which he suspected she might not be able to do by writing alone. "He sent me to a business graduate school [. . .] and that was wonderful, it gave me a year in New York," she recalled much later. "Almost no work, it was so easy. Anybody could do it."[1] Lyell, who'd completed his undergraduate work in three years before entering Columbia's graduate program in English, also found plenty of time for the city's plays, movies, museums, and nightclubs. He and Welty discovered amusing free activities, such as attending night court to observe cases being argued. Lyell sometimes stood outside of Broadway theaters before a performance, where he could look for celebrities in the crowd, then be ready to blend in and enter without a ticket. Almost anywhere, they might spot glamorous celebrities and avant-garde artists. "I'm getting surprisingly blasé on the subject of famous people we've been seeing lately," Lyell wrote in a letter home, after seeing Greta Garbo and other movie stars in a crowd. The city was a perfect playground, full of highbrow and high-energy experiences that were scarce or nonexistent back in Mississippi. Lyell wrote to his family, "These last have been the grandest nine months of my life."[2]

When the spring term ended, Lyell had earned his MA and set out for a tour of Europe. The degree and the tour, which was probably a reward from his proud parents, were announced in *The Clarion-Ledger* (Jackson).[3] Lyell's trip occasioned the earliest piece of extant Welty–Lyell correspondence, a postcard mailed June 7, 1931, picturing children riding an elephant at a zoo. Lyell wrote in the voice of one of a group of children, whose names he also invented. "It was a gay, gay ride what with the mongoose having died the day before we got there—Anyway Letitia nearly fell off + Hiram (that was what we named the elephant) stepped all over our dollies. And Cadwallader (our little brother) cried all the way," Lyell wrote. At the top of the postcard, Lyell broke character to add, "Do write me breezy words to the SS Homeric, White Star Line, W 18 St, sailing June 12, 1931, N.Y."

This card reached Welty in Jackson, where her father had been diagnosed with leukemia. His condition worsened that summer, and in September, he died after a doctor attempted a direct blood transfusion from Chestina Welty. Their daughter witnessed this heartbreaking event. "My mother never recovered emotionally," Welty wrote in her memoir. "Though she lived for over thirty years more, and suffered other bitter losses, she never stopped blaming herself. She saw this as her failure to save his life."[4]

Welty was now working part-time, writing for the *Lamar Radio News*, a newsletter promoting WJDX. The station broadcast from the city's tallest building, owned by her father's company, Lamar Life Insurance. After her father's death, with her bereaved mother and younger brother still at home, and with no job prospects elsewhere, Welty remained in Jackson, although she longed to leave.

In a fan letter she sent Virginia Woolf in 1932, Welty referred to her hometown as a "ghost-like world" where "nothing may happen."[5] New York was, in many ways, Jackson's opposite. Across the next four decades of the Welty–Lyell correspondence, delight in the city would be a continuing theme.

In 1932, Lyell's studies took him back to the New York area when he began a PhD program at Princeton University. He wrote Welty once while on the road, then wrote the following letter when he arrived the next day. His letter was on stationery he may have gotten from the lobby of a hotel—he wrote that he was hoping to stay with Lehman Engel, a Jackson friend who was studying at Julliard.

September 26, 1932 • New York to Jackson

[*Written on Hotel Astor stationery*]

Eudora:

After being in P (simply marvelous) for only 5 hours, wouldn't I hop the train for N.Y!

Greetings from Manhattan Transfer! My room is swell—dark paneling around fireplace all the way up, good day bed, + 2 swell chairs + upholstered window-seat—the pictures look marvelous—Thank God I brought them—I helped Arthur + John H. move into their room. (My trunk is not in yet—had it been there I'd probably have stayed to settle myself, but need some underwear shorts (yours to me are swell—+ do forgive me) mac, pillows + a grey hat. Will see some show tonight + stay with Lehman if I can find him. Glorious weather + gas, food, hotel + car storage for the whole trip only cost us $15 each! It would have cost me that to express the luggage we brought—A perfect journey + no [*Lyell drew a picture of tire losing air*]

Write soon,

F

Back in Jackson, Welty sent Lyell a food package and questions about a choir he had joined in Princeton.

October 5, 1932 • Jackson to Princeton

Dear Best of All Possible Worlds:

Has the chapel choir any connection with the Westminster, which we are to hear over our radio—Also please advise: will you wear something cute to sing in? Please find time to sing for you love it so.—Does a #2 bass seem to satisfy—[. . .] I wish your chapel choir was across the st. instead of Belhaven choir. Say, the Ch. of Christ is having a wiener roast tonight + didn't ask me. However it is cold, windy, rainy, + foul out, I would almost rather be in bed, + am. I wish you would meet somebody who has seen Virginia Woolf. Maybe we could get our love to her somehow—

I [*"double dog" represented by Welty's sketch of two dogs*] dare you to go see Hanya Holm the only Mary Wigman exponent in U. S. (in the Steinway Bldg) + say "What's the matter? Hanya Holm to go to?" If you won't do it I'll have to get Butler to.[6]

Have not yet heard from Hamburg—American Lines—Their world cruise leaves Jan. 7 + you may see me off, as though you hadn't a million times. Have also applied to the U. S. Lines to London in hopes of taking Va. Woolf something. Probably nutbread—Your mom laughs at me for sending you food (I told her so she wouldn't send you anything for comparison), seems to think it was coals to Newcastle but I think it is more likely like pocket-hdkfs, you can never have too many. The thing is, I have 0 [*zero*] to do. Idleness breeds nutbread like wildfire, or hotcakes rather. Didn't you hate to open the box. Wanted to make it dirty but didn't want to get you in trouble at inspection. Went to "Greeks Had a Word for It" yesterday + I + Ina were as one—Told Mother I wanted to be gold digger (have had further reactions toward radio land) + she says I can't be one I am too fine, but I know it is because I am too sentimental.[7] There is a catch to everything I want to be. In the [*Thomas*] Mann chapter on "Mounting Misgivings" I find the phrase "sublime exertions" + wonder if you could tell me where I could put mine.[8] The attic is full, the cedar chest "doesn't work," + I am slowly giving out of Victrola needles[9]—In fact I am in bed. Hiya, Sleep—

[. . .] Well, don't guess I'll write you any more now, I'll rest on my nut-bread—which I forgot to taste, but I remember flinging in some ginger just for the ride—No Ed Wynn tonight, just the Pres. instead, what a frost. You must learn How Do You Do It[10]—Just swell—

In the following letter Welty encloses several drawings representing the State Fair in Jackson, one captioned "Halfmanhalfwoman offers the remaining fact for ten cents but is not taken up." A sketch of a Women's Christian Temperance Union booth is captioned "Cannibalism in the WCTU Booth." The booth has signs reading "Our Cry: Beers & Wines Never Never Never!!! Boys & Girls Ever Ever Ever!!!" One figure beckons from behind a ledger marked "Sign Here." Another person holds a sign marked "Kiss Me." A prostrate figure in the foreground is labeled "a victim." In another drawing, a fortune teller beneath a sign offering "Your Life History and Name For Fifty Cents Cash," tells her customer, "Of course you understand at the outset dearie, this is only a 10c reading." Welty's cartoons reflect the era's preoccupation with "freaks," eugenics, and temperance. The slur that Welty's letter includes ("Dagoes") is further evidence of attitudes held by some white, American-born people during this era, attitudes Welty may not have shared, but was willing to make use of for this private acrostic.

October 15[?], 1932 • Jackson to Princeton

Hi there! Lady Abdy speaking, in a marked English accent[11]—Thanks for the Hygiea straws. I put them in a cedar box to keep moths and no telling what all out. Was put in glow by letter—How glad I am that Princeton is wonderful—[. . .]—How are the fires in your fireplace—I think if they burn beneath Adam it would be very thrilling[12]—The Woolf call no. is lovely—now it is like knowing she passes a certain corner at a certain time—

I provide you with pictures to entertain you while you are reading the letter—

Escorted Mother to the Fair Flower Show—some things good, some bad—[. . .] Mother is working on a contest, thank God her interests are divided—it's for Frigidaire, making a sentence with the initials of "greater food space"—it gets her—altho it took me but an instant to write under her rueful gaze

God
Requires
Every
American
To
Eat
Rutabagas

Frighten
Off
Odd
Dagoes

Seize
Peakeasies
And
Correct
Eugenics

After the WCTU Booth I had a relapse to Tahitie from which I wrote you a letter in pidgin English—I hope it doesn't throw you back in your studies.

The fortune teller told me I was going to get a great thrill in June 1933 + later said I would be married in June 1933 + I have been worrying ever since—afraid she was referring to only one event both times—I do think she could predict 2 things for 10c—For 50c she offered to tell me my name but I let it go—[. . .]

Saw Louis [*Lyell, Frank's seven-year-old brother*] looking priceless in a light blue shift—

[. . .] Also got Willia a teakettle that whistles when the water boils—splendid entertainment for the money—I shall send her my recipe for boiling water to go with.

Evelyn O'Briant is here with babe (very cute eating strained carrots) + is taking a covey back east [*to NYC*] with her, including Willie Spann but not

The Poor Little Rich Girl

P. S. I just got a Xmas check (life ins)[13] for exactly $42—tempting—isn't it—Will try to get facsimiles. The Rich Little Rich Gal (bong!)

Leone [*Shotwell*] is coming home for a day tomorrow.[14] Fudge cake for her. Am just before reading Faulkner.

By January 1933, Welty had arranged another trip to enjoy New York City and look for a job.[15] *During her train ride, she mailed a postcard to Lyell, written as if intended for Noel Coward.*

January 10, 1933 • Bristol, TN, to Princeton

[*Photo of woman in apron who has won a baking prize using Calumet baking powder is pasted to this card.*]

Dear Mr. Coward—

After seeing your place in Harper's Bazaar[16] we are wondering if you wouldn't like our Mrs. W. E. Farley. We won her in 1902 + up until now just haven't found any place she would go—. Then we saw your studio far from the madding vortex—you have shuttered windows, a pickled pine foyer, space between your two pianos, and plenty of recesses, which we haven't. Mrs. Farley knows many heel + toe positions + has a splendid number of lamé samples, shown here—In our spare time we have successfully trained her to hold anything except beer + a target, + guarantee she can rise to any occasion—What about it?

Calumet Baking Powder Co.

January 17[?], 1933 • New York to Princeton

[*Written on verso of program for performance by Hindu dancer Shan-Kar.*]

you must see Shan-Kar—i don't know of anything you would like more—he is marvelous—very beautiful—he is continuously divine—really his dances are like the humours of the gods—(just as john martin to john martin I tell you this[17])—he has the most enchanting body i have ever seen, he uses it like a voice—i don't know anything about the hindu cosmos but the appeal of all he does is very direct and you are instantly enchanted—the musical instruments you would love to have, one of them is ten jugs filled with water at different heights and you sit on the floor with them all around you conveniently—some of them look like something we might have had in the penthouse—all the music has a time of day—Simkie is luscious too—she has rosy palms and huge eyes—they use all your favorite colors, and all the hindus are the most beautiful color—i can't bear it until I see Shan-Kar again—can't bear it until you see him—& hereafter i can't bear anyone who can't throw his neck out of joint—his last recital is this Sunday night and i'm going back—[. . .] Shan-Kar has a sort of archaic smile, i guess it is the smile of the hindu cosmos tho—he has the most wonderful walk when he comes out to bow to you—they all have a noble and godlike bow, the only paradoxical thing about them—i wanted to bow to Shan-Kar—the audience was not so good—an attitude of happy tolerance prevailed, maybe due to the laugh mary wigman had on the awe-stricken crowd who marveled when she thundered out on the boards last year—i don't see how anyone could fail to surrender unquestioningly to Shan-Kar—how they could fail to know him when they see him—he is unlike anything else but there he is—like infinite wisdom, theirs for the seeing, and so exotic and splendid and divine that no one should be tolerant. The audience didnt give a thing, and i wished for you. There is the funniest dance with Shan-Kar as the Chief of the Demons and little Robindra as the King of the Monkeys—with wonderful false faces—the King of the Monkeys insists on fighting the Chief of the Demons and when he falls unconscious the C. of the D. carries him in his arms to the regions below and he slowly regains his senses; then he immediately starts fighting again—it is so funny—the Gandharva is very celestial—the sword dance is breath-taking—

February 6, 1933 • New York to Princeton

[*Written on horseshoe-shaped greeting cards and on program for "Six Miracle Plays" staged by and starring Martha Graham.*[18]]

Dear Frank—

The Piccoli are amusing—In "The Bull Fight" the curtain falls on the successful matador standing on the bull, with flowers being hurled from all directions, + in response to applause the bull catches a bouquet with his tail + waves it in circles from prone position.[19]

There was a party here until 3:00 Saturday night but got up Sunday + went to see Martha Graham dance in the miracle plays—They were awfully pretty, I would like to have been one of the angels, there were 2. Graham was nobody but the Virgin Mary in all 6 plays, which must have been monotonous for her—I think. But she was lovely + quite holy. I was taken in but the typical dance audience showed the decline of the west.

Couldn't afford the 2nd Depression Gaities but understand B. Lillie was in practically every act.[20]

Saturday night you missed (by the way it was gruesome of you not to call by) Guy [*Lombardo*] in Blues in My Heart + You've Got Me in Between—Also Going Going Gone—[21]

The Radio City art show is rather bad—in fact Russia's exhibit was a disgrace—And there are stupidly + entirely too many pictures. I saved France till last but the Matisse is not even playful + the Picasso is as spiritless as a Peck + Peck window + there isn't anyone else. Vanessa Bell has the largest English canvas—warm + glowing[22] [. . .] But have recovered from flu—

Goodbye—

E

March 10, 1933 • Princeton to New York

Depression's apogee
dE—

What color are you affecting for the bank holiday—I'm wearing all my green so some of the old currency colors will be in circulation. [*The newly elected FDR had just closed the country's banks for four days.*]

[. . .]—much agitation here—all inside tho—I get it from Dean Wicks—[. . .]—Norman Thomas sermon here two weeks ago derailed against such persons + banking programs—so talk, talk, talk—[23]

I listen now to the Phila Symph—Pictures at an Exhibition—+ Le sacre[24] to come—

To our piano duet repertoire we've added overture to Marriage de Figaro, Mozart, very good—Der Freishutz, Weber, very Important, but I loathe it.

How awfully the advertising people duped you—Just a pack of dupes—but try elsewhere to pigeonhole your great talents—There is surely some place that NEEDS you.[25]

Mae West was too grand—who on earth can talk like that?[26]—I've been trying to get some of the inflections but get naught but fiascos—Saw it twice—

Tallulah [*Bankhead*]'s cartwheel absolutely floored me—I haven't recovered yet—Just as if God had spit or something—A merry opening—+ saw Bob Benchley at last—Some of the lines are good—I'm very attached to the "Have you seen my mother?" youth in the speakeasy—Waiter replies: "She was here a few minutes ago; think she's gone up to Harlem."[27]

Guess you heard Gracie [*Allen*] last eve—First time in weeks for me—[. . .] Wish I could come to N.Y. tomorrow—but guess I'll just have to go on hoarding my 36¢.

After Tallulah we did the German beer place + picked up the 3 people at our table (2 men + amazing girl—little more than streetwalker now—but had been in Johnson Hall [*dormitory where women students at Columbia lived*] for a season + as she grew soggier, quoted "Eliza [*Butler*][28] wouldn't let me—no, really, Eliza said, absolutely not—+ we can't wear anything red because it excites men's passion + never any fur because all men like to rub it"—amazing creature) + went to a clam-dump in Hoboken—+ got home at 4.

Incidentally go to this beer place—3rd Ave betw 17 + 18 st—German American Athletic Club—25¢ a glass + food very cheap.

I've been antidoting early + middle English with <u>Rasselas</u> (!) + god knows what—but sometime read Wm Beckford's <u>Vathek</u>; + I've just finished <u>The Monk</u> (M.G. Lewis) corruption + seduction in convents + monasteries with supernatural minglings. Some of it is most gruesome—now I'm at <u>Pointed Roofs</u> (Dorothy Richardson) the first stream of consciousness novel, I'm told (or was at Va.)[29] Could make little of Walter de la Mare's The Return—not good—but it may have been that I failed to get whatever was his main point—Try it + tell me what you think. [. . .]

March 27, 1933 • New York to Princeton

df—[30]

The radio is bringing "drink to me only" into my home + making me misty-eyed—Where is my gauzey handkerchief—

[. . .] Babe Didrickson had 2 pictures in VF [*Vanity Fair*], Guy [*Lombardo*] is off the air for the season, there'll be no beer in Miss., + how can I go home[31]—The ans. is Jesus loves me, + I just won't—Don't know where I'll stay—Wish there was a sweet paper agency. I even applied to Cecil [*Beaton*], see other side—I trust you can imagine me in the Miss Kookoo formal in Vogue; I can, until I am almost ready to take off—I did get a new frock, reduced on Mad. Ave—a Gauguin orange color with black belt + white taffeta collar [*tiny drawing of dress*] which I don't wear—gives a girl new life—all I need is a spray of African daisies to be something very je ne sais quoi—that + a sprightly rejoinder—

Saw "The Song of Life"—lousy—

Angna Enter's drawings are charming—have a dash—

Have had fun with old friends in city—Wish I could have seen Flower Show—

Adios—

E

[. . .] rough d. of the letter I wrote cecil—a little gem of its kind—a diamond in the rough—I think I shall undoubtedly be cabled for—

[*Verso of letter is draft of letter to Cecil Beaton*[32]]

dear mr. beaton—

our dimorphic differences do not prevent me from writing to you in england from a greenwich village apartment; in fact, they are the nostalgic cause for the letter. the intrinsic kinship which I feel, perhaps absurdly, indeed absurdly, with things cosmopolitan, such as your coterie's columns in vogue & spur, a certain assurance in wearing the color yellow, and other forms of gaiety, gives me the courage to write and ask if you need an amanuensis. the reason i thus single you out for application is that your articles are among the slender holds, like maypole ribbons, which i can keep on the world—that is, the best of all possible worlds—(aside: may God forgive me!) and then i can take the most intimate care of water-color brushes, know how to trim a photograph imaginatively, and have a literary education; which i feel might be helpful to you; i see you're being kept busier as the seasons go by. i know I'm fated to help someone get things off to the magazines in time; i believe i arose from a pile of manuscripts as venus rose from the sea.

neither am i untoward like the regular finger-nailed satin-collared secretary; i can maintain a deftly remote attitude and then suddenly at a nod fly to and decorate a Sitwell with decorum, although I realize that won't be required. I am inspired by a glint in the eye to divine puns, am pleasantly double-jointed, and would be generally nice to have available, being inoffensively capable on the side. i could bring a large collection of the best American jazz gramophone records.

i am 23 years old, my home & family are at 1119 Pinehurst Place, Jackson, Mississippi, I used to have enough money, but now I read in the libraries. The closest I have ever come to London was when Walter Hines Page, related on my mother's side, was ambassador, but I have traveled in a confined way other places. i have a degree and graduate work—newspaper and publicity experience—but you're blasé, thank god, so I won't pursue this enumeration. Can also imitate Mary Wigman, a feat which i admit is a little dated, and invent lovely games which so far have been played only in my imagination, i'm an introvert. Which may, among other things, cause you not to reply; but i assure you I am in dead american earnest about applying for a secretarial position with you, think I could fill it, and shall hope to hear from you this spring when you are not too tired. thank you indeed for a figment of your attention,

yours truly,

March 28, 1933 • Princeton to New York

Dear Eudora—

I do hope you like "how would you like a spaghetti dinner" in the N.Y.er last—To me it's the best since—a long time—but I'm the only one around here who likes it—D. [*Dorothy*] Parker's piece is swell, aussi.[33]

We [*Princeton Glee Club and Philadelphia Symphony Orchestra*] do the <u>Parsifal</u> this week-end—Radio carries it Fri afternoon + Sat evening—I don't have any classes now until April 9! Will probably be in N.Y. sometime soon after April 3—keep your eye open for me—

Won't N.Y. be swell when beer gardens dot the park + Riverside Drive—I think culture is on the upswing—[34]

Daddy sent me 25 bucks today—I suppose the Deposit Guaranty is on its feet once more—Mae West has Brunswick discs of her recent songs—+—I meant to tell you this ere now—the original Rhythm Boys have Sweet Sue + Ain't She Sweet + My Sugar in the Rain on both sides of a Victor.

Sigmund Spaeth entertained us tonight—T.S. Eliot was disappointing[35] [. . .]

Had a fling at M. Pound's Draft of XXX Cantos (first on Princeton Library copy) recently—can make o of them[36]—I get no sleep anymore—have that rundown feeling—the holiday will fix me up—I hope—

F

Welty surrounded the date of the following letter with asterisks, it was her 24th birthday, which she had weathered "better than fay wray," the heroine of the just-released film King Kong. *Lyell had apparently sent her a hand-drawn birthday card. Disappointed not to have found a job that could keep her in New York, Welty amused herself with a stream of rapid-fire patter, with many sentences changing directions and commenting upon themselves.*

April 13, 1933 • New York to Princeton

dear frank

is that me in the picture—you didnt make me very pretty, i've got eyes—who is that other one, you? I can't tell whether that is a golfbag with a club and the balls dropping out or just another candle, but it can hardly be another candle when you have got God! too many as it is—you know damn well nobody but february needs 29, whom YOU know, anyhow. i would just as soon have 12 lighted at both ends—however i suppose the extra ones are either to grow on or for my virtues—chastity, chastity, chastity, and chastitee. thanks. i have got thru the day very well so far—better than fay wray could have done i think—was awakened to go see about a job at the waldorf astoria, a birthday gesture from the columbia appointments office, but would have had to take dictation from 5 men, and probably extras, including washing, at vile pay. there was a man on the subway in rags and beard and suffering expr. that everybody gave money to just simply because he happened to look like jesus Christ, this being the season etc. i gave part of malcom's money for tickets to Gay Divorce[37] to him, that's what started the avalanche, but i hadn't thought of easter [*April 16*] or jesus, naturally this is MY birthday. Had lunch with lehman [*Engel*] who refreshed me. tonight there will be a celebration at the home of one of the officers on the ship an eng., who rates all anniversaries,[. . .] the dead, honesty as best policy, etc. high. welsh rarebit is the bait. malcolm is also going to give me a surprise party afterwards, if i can still be surprised after welsh rarebit.

For some reason i no longer dread anything, and will not mind a few months at home. Felicia [*White*][38] gave me some Carolina Pines to bathe in so I have even now begun acclimation and shall be all ready for P'hurst Pl [*Pinehurst Place, Welty's street in Jackson*]—[. . .] when unquestioned on her plans for the summer miss w replied evasively, saying "Pshaw. So far I have only done a little choreography for Section I-A of Lear's Limericks and am now in the middle of "There was an old man in a boat who said 'I'm afloat, I'm afloat'". When they said no you ain't, he was ready to faint, you know, and I haven't got any further."[39] When asked to give her opinion on Easter, Miss W responded "Eggs" and when asked to leave, she left.

I went to Phila. orch. Tues night—heavens. the effect the sacre d. p. doesn't have on me is not worth talking about[40]—i thought it was very very marvelous—on the program margin i was moved to write a short essay on pain, the meaning of its assertion, etc. wh. was gingerly left on the BMT when i got off at 14th st. [. . .] yesterday there was a blizzard and I went to the cherry orchard—how marvelous nazimova[41] is! and how marvelous the play is in the flesh! i do not know why but i sink into chekov as i would into a deep purple bath—i wanted to return last night but had to go to a party—i feel that you do not love the scottsboro case as I do so am enclosing a snap of ruby bates, my favorite, the one who disappeared after the first trial when someone whistled, remember,[42] and months later, when found, said she'd been in NY talking with Dr Fosdick—it's a small world—didn't you love gracie doing tricks for the dog—bud departed last night, i feel bereft, having roomed with him for wks. wilma and i are now just 2 girls together.[43] wilma is very swell, has a good sense of doom. [. . .] i have some swell shoes to mooch around jackson in—athaletic—must gain lbs. and get clear-eyed etc—so i can enjoy my records—i gave out of emma to read at bedtime, so think i'll get the m. l. giant.[44] It is nice to leave your conduct to miss austen's files upon going off to sleep, you know nothing will be done save in the most moderate conversation between 3 people without christian names, at least their christian names are in the front of the book. you would like emma. nettie is now arriving sat. a.m. and i am to help show noel the aquarium, subway, ferryboat, etc. it will be good to see a new face in the city.[45]

goodbye—a light kiss to all—(me in ballet skirt)—

e

Back in Jackson that spring, Welty took photographs, as she had been doing for several years, and sent many contact sheet prints to Lyell. In April, these included close-ups of flowers and of elephant figurines in grass, seemingly feeding in a meadow, or climbing up an inverted pottery basket. More photos followed in May.

May 25, 1933 • Jackson to Princeton

[The envelope bears a decorative stamp that reads "Save the Scottsboro Boys" with Welty's comment, "I got this on an NY letter—" Welty wrote on the backs of six snapshots, including the following:]

[*On back of a flower photo:*] I've been reading The Golden Bough about the external soul + places you can keep it when in danger—my favorite (next to gardenias) is in a white-foot hind named Eillid Chaisfhion—"tho she should be caught, there would spring a hoodie out of her, & tho the hoodie should be caught, there would spring a trout out of her, but there is an egg in the mouth of the trout, + the soul is in the egg—"[46] I think in 3 white doves flying inside a boar on an is. [*island*] is not bad either—Still nobody could call that hind—"Here, Eillid Chaisfhion, here Eillid Chaisfhion. Nice girlie!"

[*On back of photo of mimosas:*] This is the souls of the mimosa going to Paradise.

June 12, 1933 • Jackson to Princeton

[This message is on four postcards labeled I–IV. Postcard I features Welty's drawing of Expressionist dancer Mary Wigman stamping her feet in a saucepan, captioned "Frau wigman making a tapioca pudding—has she gone to pot—and will you have to take pot luck." Welty drew hands pointing "to footnote" and below Wigman's feet, wrote "I consider her at the foot of her class."

In Postcard II, she wrote "Have been hearing the Lallam family (name disguised) touted at every breath—Darena got a medal for yr's unflinching S. S. attendance"—presumably referring to the Sunday School attendance of Lyell's mother's family, the Hallams. After reporting who had won the Little Theatre bridge prize, Welty suggested,]

Do you want to go in with me bootlegging—V-burg once a wk for a case of beer + dual personality ± we ought to be able to think of side-lines or—cars."[47] Barron[48] is going to be in + can represent the law + you can be literature—I'll be Hope—May I borrow your handkerchief . . .
I am pressing split infinitives.
To just see me is to simply love me—
" " " " is to sort of " "
" " " " " " too divine—Of course I am[49]

[*Continued on Postcard III:*]

[. . .] thru assiduous all-day concentration + libation by Leone got "Body + Soul" out of Guy Thurs PM . . . Listen, Semi-Precious, said Diamond Lil, roughly, the other day or night under my eyebrow I got an idear which struck me as a gem + that is for you to see the editor of Harper's about some magazine articles to write this summer—

[*Riddles and puns continue on Postcard IV, made from a family photo of young Welty in a striped dress at a child's party.*]

In summer 1933, Welty wrote several articles for the Jackson State Tribune, *a paper that another Central High classmate, Ralph Hilton, had just started.*[50] *"He got hold of some space up over a store," Welty recalled later, "and under that flat hot tin roof it was like working inside a popcorn popper."*[51] *This short-lived publication showcased an impressive array of Jackson-born talent. In the June 19, 1933, edition, Welty wrote a long essay on Lehman Engel, who had composed works for Martha Graham and had other compositions performed in New York, San Francisco, and Vienna.*[52] *She later reported on sculpture by Paul Manship, whose grandfather had been a famous Jacksonian. She also wrote as the* Tribune's *society editor, placing more emphasis on the arts and less on what attendees were wearing. Lyell, home from Princeton in July, may also have participated in producing the* Tribune *with Hilton. He wrote Welty while she was attending the World's Fair in Chicago.*[53]

July 24, 1933 • Jackson to Chicago

Dear Eudora—

The Tribune is gasping for your return to inject the new vitality thru 3 weeks of features. Don't write yourself out in 4 or 5 emissions; I suggested to Ralph you were good for at least a dozen dontchethinkso? While combining a sunbathe with [*Shakespeare's*] Timon of Athens this A.M. I tried to pull a Beverly Nichols on some very buggy docks—but what I did is no secret: the bugs tormented me + I them + it wasn't very amusing.[54]

[. . .] Saturday I won 30¢ at contract (1 point=1/80 ¢) + quoting the [*Jackson Daily*] News, captured a "coveted prize" at a party for Miss Spinks that night.[55] The award in reality was a badly colored deck of cards depicting "The Gorge" which we already had at home with green instead of purple borders, + despite the Tribune, they weren't "handsome."

Go to lunch at Henrici's in Chi—I've heard it is good. And write breezy words to me.

Yours,

F

August 9, 1933 • Sewanee to Jackson

dE—

Thanks endlessly for the deux cheery notes. Robert Daniel, Bishop Garlan's grandson,[56] read them this morning + is eager to become a pen-pal of yours. He's 18, + I'd rather talk to him than any male hereabouts.

So few people come up that one is instantaneously popular + asked hither + yon all the time. Went to the Wares Sunday—all of the family are riots. And you should see Libo (Eliz.) who looks like M. Graham, affects profanity + Garbo slouch, + talks like a man, low guttural tones. All the older people are museum pieces, + Pete Ware's imitations of several sent us into hysterics one night from which I shall never recover. Mrs. Loaring-Clark fetes us constantly—I'm lunching with her today. A gay soul, drinks like a [*drawing of a fish*], + tells bawdy stories, 3 children. Mrs Shober of New Orleans has 3 too + is just as batty, but I don't like her as well as Mrs. L-C. Played cards last night with Mrs. S. + Mrs. Frank Hoyt Gailor from Memphis, who is a perfect howl. (Will give full descriptions + imitations later) Was made to drink gin which was unfortunate. Then you should see Mrs. Sanburn, also from N.O. I'm looking forward to picnicing with her this afternoon. She uses many [*drawing of a lit cigarette*] + loves to carry on what she knows is good dinner-table repartee. Sample: "So I went to the auction at this <u>ancient</u> place because I knew what prints they had would be old, but when I arrived home I found to my <u>complete</u> amazement that all I'd purchased was a refrigerator + a pair of antlers." Her husband committed suicide. Really, everybody up here is "a character"—Sewanee's always had that reputation; + always will. But I'm wild about it for that reason, as well as for many others.

I rode the bus from Memphis to here because the rain poured in floods all that day. The Binghams with whom I stayed in M. are so perfectly lovely. Mrs. B is one of the sweetest people I've ever seen, + daughter Sarah most attractive—charming house, too. We Peabody Roofed in evening.

Saw "When Ladies Meet" for the third time in Monteagle the other night. Hattibel + Louis [*Hallam, Lyell's aunt and uncle*] are supposed to arrive this week-end, so I shall return with them, I presume.

Yours,
F

In September Welty began filing society columns about Jackson with the Memphis Commercial Appeal, *which had opened a Jackson office and listed Welty as "Society Editor."*[57] *While Lyell continued his studies in Princeton that fall, Welty pursued photography with another of their creative, cosmopolitan friends, Hubert Creekmore, a young writer whose family lived down the street from the Weltys.*

November 22, 1933 • Jackson to Princeton

Loose Ends, Miss.
Dear Frank—

This paper was once the abandoned Tupelo-Corinth road project from the Highway Dept + after being adopted for my new method of bridge scoring (see reverse) was abandoned again + after you read the letter you can make a drinking cup out of it—I am bearing down on "The American Procession"—Am. Life Since 1860 in Photographs—perfectly swell—be sure to look through it[58] [. . .] The Chase + Sanborn announcer is bringing up Helen "who snapped at everyone" till her fiancé (the proper one I think) told her about dated coffee—I am wearing my old blue suit + an old Sak's 5th sweater—You now have the setting in mind I suppose—However the living room has all been changed by me and altho I am by the radio I am in the red chair, + I swapped the love seat and the winged chair, as well as the piano + secy. back again.

Now—who was I writing to? I hope you referred to Vogue's wine table + found our champagne was of the best make + of a good vintage year—of course—

Did you hear Guy play Hinky Dinky Do—best piano work since "3 Little Words"[59]—

[. . .] I'm still hoping to see Shan-Kar at some point during the winter—there's a photograph of Pavlova in the American Procession too—Yesterday I made 2 reflectors for the bright photo—flood lamps—cut coffee cans + painted outsides black—This makes them about 10 times as bright—Hubert [*Creekmore*] + I take pictures for the Jr Aux every day for their Clarion Ledger edition[60]—All look just awful—We flung in Loraine Crockett's police dog for one group + he tossed his head to one side as tho he did not give a damn for the photograph + he turned out to look the best of all—(This makes me feel Aesoppy.) [*Small drawing of dog turning his head to one side*][61]

I am eating divinity—Mother is disappointed at the lack of appreciation it fetches + says that hell she is going to send the next to you—

December 7, 1933 • Princeton to Jackson

[*Written on verso of fourteen numbered snapshots from Lyell's 1931 summer travels.*]

DE—

Many thanks for the New Orleans postal barrage [. . .] Read a paper on [*Percy Bysse Shelley's*] Alastor [. . .] then three of us [. . .] toasted each other

+ F.D.R. + E.R. + god knows who with long[?] ryes + sodahs—It's grand—you can get wonderful results on a dollar—must curb baser impulses more than ever.

Last weekend was a dream. Got rides with 2 Brooklyn school pals up + back + stayed with a friend in Hartley Hall at Columbia so saved some dough that way. Michelina's debut party was la plus chic affaire I've ever attended. I've never seen in my life so many superbly [*illegible*] ladies—the raison d'etre of Conde Nast + his publications viewed for the first time. Some of the ensemble were the most glorious I've ever beheld—I couldn't help contemplating the ecstasy a Jackson lass would be transported into if she possessed even a yard of some of the costumes. There were from 175 to 200 guests—it was a dinner dance in the ballroom of the Colony club. [*Jazz pianist*] Eddy Duchin played + had converse with him—requesting his glorious rendition of Sophisticated Lady—still my favorite. [. . .] Met most attractive people—went afterwards with [*Jackson friend*] Frances McWillie (lured from her bed—via phone) to my first real N.Y. boite de nuit, the very good Place Pigalle. Great fun—swell entertainment in the sophisticated manner, no rough stuff, beautiful dancing [. . .]

Did Harlem twice with Paul Bowles + Ralph Vincent[62]—Gloria's Theatrical Club is the place to go, + nothing is more amusing. I went last Wed night with them, + we didn't get in until 8 A.M!

Saw only 2 plays—"Men in White," fair, + Ham + I went to "Sailor Beware" which was funny if you think things like "Boy, look at them avocadoes" are funny. I managed to sleep thru half of the last act. Did far more parties this time than I ever have before. Norma [*Brickell*] gave one Sat night, nowhere near as brilliant as her Spanish evening, but very nice. Su Chen H, a Chinese versifier, read his verse in his native tongue, + that was charming.[63] [. . .]

Good, good art shows on. The [*Constantin*] Brancusi show is absolutely incredible. You should see Mrs. Eugene Meyer in black marble + priced neatly at $5000. [. . .] You'd love it. The Salvador Dali show is no less amazing—he's a surrealist + loves intestines, fried eggs, excrements, brain fissures exposed, blood, + general depravity + degeneration. Paints very well—in rather a miniature style—but the assimilation of objects into artistic wholes defies all reason—some was amusing, much was revolting. The Renoir room at the Knoedler gallery is the most effective one man display I've ever seen on 52 Street.

Dicey [*Dodds*] + I lunched at the world's best place. The Park Avenue on E + 8 Street. It was Belle Livingston's last stand—Dark blue walls, grey mirrors, 2 stories high, grand egg shaped bar with many sided tall mirror in semicircle behind. A balcony too, + another bar on it. Delicious food—$1.00 lunch—the most epicurean I've ever eaten.

Dined with the Fullers at 325 Park after hearing [*Rev. Harry Emerson*] Fosdick Sunday A.M., then met Conrad Salinger in the Waldorf + we went for cocktails to the apartment of very amusing friends of his.[64]

Saw "Little Women" at Radio City where I seem to stage all my excessively lachrymose outbreaks—'Twas there I kept a stream of hdks [*handkerchiefs*] wet thru Cavalcade.[65] L. W. is splendid + I'm quite willing to toss my hat into the air with all the others for Miss [*Katharine*] Hepburn.

The new RCA building is perfectly stunning at night with flood lights on it. Jack Fletcher tells me it's 78% rented, but I find that difficult to believe—Saks windows have staged a brilliant comeback. Even the monotone petit-point-bag display had disappeared + they are the best on the avenue. [. . .] I go to N.Y. again this Saturday—will go to Sergei Rachmaninoff's concert in the afternoon [*Saturday, December 9*], + to Mary of Scotland at night—Paul Bowles is giving a party afterwards which should be good. [. . .]

[. . .]. The bonfire to celebrate our victory over Yale was kindled Monday night—a marvelous, towering, blaze behind Nassau Hall—much revelry.

Do send me some pictures if you've made any recently. [. . .]

Write soon—

As ever,

[*FL monogram*]

January 20, 1934 • Jackson to Princeton

[*Welty wrote this postcard in the voice of Princess Faucigny-Lucinge*[66] *who'd been cavorting with other high-society people: Cecil Beaton, Daisy Fellowes, Elsa Maxwell. On the postcard photo of a train station, Welty drew an arrow indicating Elsa was on the approaching train.*]

Robt E Lee birthday, '34

Just knew Elsa would be along to carry us all off to some divine place. We are all coming over to your place as Bedouins. Aren't Daisy's suspenders too marvelous. We made Cecil lie across the tracks—awfully amusing.[67]

Yours—(Princess). F. L. (in the white derby)

In Jackson in the 1930s, Welty was, as she described herself to Katherine Anne Porter, "underfoot locally."[68] *In the next letter, Welty encloses a printed postcard sent to members of one local organization she belonged to, the Jackson Little Theatre; the card invited members to reserve tickets for upcoming performances. Welty later wrote of the Little Theatre, "You came to a performance to see your friends, on the stage and off."*[69] *Actors were cast according to their daytime occupations. "I suppose we reasoned that a doctor's part was safest in the hands of a physician. Lawyers of whatever stripe, noble or villainous, were impartially cast from the Jackson bar. Maids were the exception: they were played by debutantes. They tripped out, smiled at the audience across the footlights, opened their mouths and said 'Tea is served, madame,' and brought the house down."*[70]

February 10, 1934 • Jackson to Princeton

[On oversized Valentine cards printed with caricatures and verses]

Dear Frank—

Don't think I'm an opportunist just because I write you on Valentine's now—I'd do the same thing in December that I do in May—All days are alike to one born under Aries (the ram)—any venture undertaken at any time—I have a collection of 102 valentines—[. . .] genuine '04 vintage, says Mother [. . .] They fall into 3 classes—the pleading ("DON'T be a slouch around the house, tidy up, you will find it pays"), the brutal, + the hnyeh-hnyeh—these are a few duplicates I got in feverish selection under no competition—My favorite is "Your Get-Up Is Absurd" + I enclose "Your Enchanting Smile" as the lone instance of ecstatic insult in the lot. Just a transport of BLAH—rather enervating—

How did the papers + exams come out—The Ballet must have been a soothing intermission—Send me the photographs of Shan-Kar—If they can't print them send me the neg, I bet I can get it out—I left one of my overexposed negatives under the light 40 min once before it registered on the paper but I got it out—I now feel fine + do my own housework for 9 + have a 6 mo. old baby boy

—Mrs. T.Q Hawkins, Route 4, Gresham Kan.

"The Bad Man" was the Little Theatre play—of mild int[*erest*]. Dr. Wilde was V.G. + Ruth Hewitt was just terrible. I attended dress rehearsal + in the scene where the villain snatches the hero's gun from his holster while the h. is giving him a drink of water he groped + groped + groped + couldn't find the gun, which was scarcely odd because the hero hadn't any.[71] Also Dr. Wilde, who is the bad man, covered complete cast under his gun + forgot what he wanted with them. However the next night it was better. I had to serve coffee—Rehearsal night I took some photos for the paper which weren't very good in lighting, as there is no spotlight—Young (14) Frank Ellis helped me in great excitement—After the curtain went down he said "Rotten—I'd just as soon see Greta Garbo—[. . .] I like Mae West—'How'm I doin' boys? H'm H'm!'—Hand on hip—[. . .] Hubert was supposed to take me to Billie Vick's dance the night of the play—just his luck, to be away in Washington or NY or somewhere. I craved to make a suit of plum colored linen but there wasn't any altho Richard Harris assured me I'd be stunning in rose-flame instead—So I got some piqué with rows of different colored cherries and hope to look like a slot machine someday. Have a Vogue Cable New Release pattern & cut it out during Die Walkure last Sat. but somehow dropped it after that—We had a freeze— + Brunnhilde sleeps—

I haven't heard Guy [*Lombardo*] in wks.—The last couple Sat. nights Chas. Hurt, the better-looking, more modest, taller, Harvard Law, just visiting from Chicago but still pretty dull brother of sticky Marshall the Ann Pullen escort[72], has been taking me out + about 10 o'clock I begin gnawing the varnish off the chairs in the movie or something + he can't understand, so this Sat. we are playing bridge by the radio, a sacrifice at that—However Eddy Duchin will be thrown in—I am reading Salammbo on which I once bit the dust in "Celebrities," + it is instantaneously hypnotizing, but what outlet would you suggest for a wealth of aroused barbarian impulses? I've been to the movie—[73] Was Alice Brady in "Should Ladies Behave"—Never having got to Mary Boland in "The Vinegar Tree" I don't know how it c.f.'s but laughed all the way through, as did some man on the back row.[74]

Read The Woods Colt the other day—Faithful + touching Ozark material, at least it impresses you as faithful—as deeply [*genre?*] as 20 Yrs A-Growing but not as much inspired as carefully executed—Nice wood engravings, very dark + umbrageous—[75]

Spent yesterday with Willia [*Wright Bennett*]—the baby is getting very expressive—but wasn't at first as cute really as Bitty Creekmore's new one—a lot of black hair + eyes dark + red cheeks[76]—As a matter of fact all babies subdue me, I wasn't easy about Willia's until she marvelously in 2 weeks grew big enough to fit the cap I gave her thank God—I just took Bitty's daffodils—

Guess who I remembered the other day—Mercedes French—you probably don't, she was a lot older—she wore French heels, that's what I remember—+ my grim satisfaction in that. I also encountered her on my first venture into the 1st adult, or F. Marion Crawford, section in the library—cool as a cucumber—

Emily White[77] has an article in the Kappa Delta mag on "A Future Role for the American College-Bred Women" which I am sure all Kappa Deltas are shunning—

Fred Astaire + the views of Rio make their parts of "Flying Down to Rio" breathtaking—See it for them—Oh I wish Fred were at my beck + call—The adagio dancing on top of an airplane, esp. the accident when the dancer falls off one plane + lands on another, is the latest, dearie. Let's don't take it.

Write to me soon—

Yours—

Ozma of Oz[78]

March 7, 1934 • Jackson to Princeton

Frank Lyell—

May I tuck you in this insurance policy and when you are fully covered please let your whiskers hang out—Last wk Guy aimed to please the most exacting—we are his exactors I believe—what with B & S, S & L, Sophisticated Lady—+ tonight, Blues in My [*heart shape*][79]

Tonight is lovely—stars, frogs, & birds—your Aristophanic Medley—Our japonica has not yet made its debut but others have + it's spring now, even Mother admits it—Also Lynn Fontaine comes out in gossamer in Harper's BZ—Daisy, give me your hat—

Grieve with me [*drawing of a glass with drops of water falling into it*] over Edna Best's + Herbert Marshall's parting—Always loved both of them—Today saw news reel of Barbara Hutton + her Mdivani—awful—I certainly don't think he is too too M M divani—nah![80]

Sunday while I was immersed in attic rummaging (I enclose a few old lamé samples) + tossing away curls + theses,[81] someone phoned + asked would I coach a May Day pageant + I said of course. I'd love to, what time, + so here I am, teaching Lee + George School children 7 folk dances every day—wouldn't I get mixed up in a May Day pageant—I certainly do—[82] But it is a lot of fun—yesterday I helped plan the costumes—the dance that really gets me is called Jack be Nimble—there's another one called Ace of Diamonds, no relation to the card, + one called School Day Antics, very athletic, for the 6th Grade boys who agreed all over the city to be in the pageant provided nothing sissy, so I'm teaching them a dance girls can't do, it would kill them—I've found out one thing already (I think one always learns something from whatever one does, don't you, except pressing ferns) + that is that maypoles don't just come. Somehow I'd always had the idea, hadn't you, that there is earth, air, fire, water, + maypoles—But that's begging the question, + false modesty—

A note from Lehman indicates that you + Hubert have located each other at last—Mrs. Creekmore, whom I ran into buying a hat (over 1 [*drawing of an eye*]) says she is afeared H is spending his train $ $—

Have your handwriting analyzed—Mine was awfully favorable—I've got nearly everything, except persistence + discretion, I am fitted, alphabetically, for acting, apartment managing, astrology, aviation, etc. Use an unsigned quotation from Wordsworth as I did—got 10 for originality—

The eraser shield is used, but I thought you could rub out a lot of Anglo Saxon with it + grate interesting cheese—[83]

Can't imagine N Shearer in the Cornell role or Chas Laughton as bad old Mr. Barrett—[84] [. . .] I cut most of Dolly Wells' tea to see Hepburn in "A.M. Glory," here for 1 day—she is fine, so is A Menjou—[85] Did you know that

Patsy Kelly, the only member of the Vanities cast we could hear on our 1st top row night at the theatre, is making comparatively restrained + not v.g. shorts with old Thel Todd—[86] yes, yes—

What with my pageantry I have had to drop Decline + Fall of the R.E.[87] before it even gave a preliminary totter, but anyway I was beginning to be known to myself as "that girl that reads all the time."

Yrs

[*picture of a window with darkness outside and a burning lamp on windowsill*]

April 2, 1934 • Jackson to Princeton

Dear Frank—

Such a blithe evening—a music festival—stringed orchestra, 8 pianos, + 100's of voices—the 8 pianos on the Peer Gynt numbers were very exciting to a packed auditorium + the program went from Amarylis to Verdi quartet with your mother—[88] all presented in bright spirit—on a spring night with low yellow moon + our garden, at least, smelling divine—it's our plum trees—I wish you could go under them down the path—Anyway the concert made us all lovely extraverts + I hope such concerts may be repeated. I am becoming very civic, c.f. the way I used to be. Have I told you about the Milk Fund? The children at Lee School stab the heart, so I thought we could put something on—you know, a revue or something—just the smarties—our own numbers throughout—this summer—You will won't you—Hubert must do the music—I've already summoned Robert [*Daniel*], who is to gladly give up a summer in Heidelberg for us (I've promised it will be like a charade) + am insinuating a Milk Fund into the conscience of the citizens + starting thinking in terms of blackouts.

Help on this too—During a Methodist convention we are likely to have delegates in the house, willy nilly, for 2 wks, + want to mfg [*manufacture?*] an atmosphere of enigma + danger—Edw [*Edward Welty*] is planning to brood an hr on the lawn in early morning + I'm to go "click-click" in the attic (the imprisoned nit-wit)—Wish we lived nearer the Jitney & could utilize experienced Phantom.[89]

The Christ-Is-Risen-Bug-on-Your-Back combination of yesterday (it was also Mr. J. P. Clark's + Miss Pearl Spann's birthday, but few knew to cope with that extra confusion)[90] had me out early to see everything. [. . .] At church Judge Lyell read the lessons with unexcelled magnificence—Splendid music—

Did you look beauteous for Easter? I for one appeared in navy triple sheen with Dobbs hat, a throwback from my first purchase like this—[*drawing of sailor hat*]—the frock being my own invention, consummated by the dressmaker with mutter after mutter—she is an alarmist of the 1st water—like Lachesis, the Fate—It looked all right.

I suppose you went to NY + flung yourself into social ambush for the after-Easter events—Did you miss participating in Parsifal?[91] I didn't even hear it once this season after last year's at least 5 repetitions—I suppose I was exempt.

Hubert sent me some Russian picture books, not of the best subjects but if you see him tell him to come home—Greet Lehman for me also—Tell him Mrs. Istrione McLean, who plays for me when I teach the children, sends congratulation + fondly thinks of him as still going about with her flag of discovery stuck in him—

Rushed by a minute to see Willia this afternoon—her child is Botticellier every day—simply immense! W. just looks like an extra on the scene—sort of hangs around, dressing—

Mother was awarded the Grand Prix for the best naturalistic garden in Miss—I hoped it would be a trip to NY but it turned out to be a shrub—Not a familiar face, either—mother wasn't in favor of planting it as long as she knew only its Latin name—she thinks it may very possibly become a tree—so we don't pet it.

The girlhood chum of mother, her husband (an erl [*oil*] millionaire) and son were here passing through and I started to bring up driving east with them to Va but the son was too stupid. We could have played counting cows on the L & R, and that's all. I'm certain he couldn't have told if anybody was in or out of the arts.

I'm going to be a Cliffordpullen (chaperone) at the Creekmore dance for Mittie.[92] Walter was home last wk, having successfully gone through initiation in John Ricks' pants. I'm taking Vest's picture tomorrow—The last 9 snaps have had the same pose: [*stick figure with hand on one hip, elbow bent*]! I take others but they are so much chaff to Mr. Millstein.[93]

The japonica bush wasn't killed after all + I wish I'd waited to try mailing the flowers—[94] I'm afraid they traveled too slowly though—I got the idea one Sunday, & had to use female wiles to make the boys in the mail car accept the pkg—against all rules, + it probably got held up—damn it—Everyone is beginning to call it camellia japonica, even for everyday—I & Jas. Joyce would like to say Camellia Japonica Penix.[95]

Katherine Cornell is playing The Barretts in N. O. Wednesday but can't go—You will note that even as we foresaw Carolyn McLean is doing Holiday this wk—Need I report? + Mr LeGrand Jewelry Christian Science Radcliffe is doing the drunken brother—Haven't attended any rehearsals, I want it full in the face Thurs night—

On Friday the 13th I shall become ¼ century old—weird, perhaps, but you get used to anything—I might have a party—invite Lee School—Civic again—You should have seen our Easter egg hunt—They like to of never found the eggs, but that was because I came to Oakdale Park with a fresh eye—+ hate eggs, too—

Write soon—

Love—

E

April 7, 1934 • Jackson to Princeton

Dear young blade—

Cheerio, the haw [*hawthorn bloom*] is out! Looks like icing—

I gather from Hubert's posts that you are doing the becoming thing by the visiting Jackson gals in the city—Hurry + write me though + tell me if you sincerely like pink linen trim—I sew relentlessly, having in the 1st blush of spring fever purchased practically a bolt from the pink, and now it's on all my clothes, like icing—

I sit + await Pelleas on the radio—If you heard Gracie on last Wed. rap out a few cracks for me—[96]

I'll be glad when Hubert gets here tomorrow—I know he will be hung with tokens—

Last night Nash [*Burger*] & Bill [*Hamilton*] came over with a new motor + beer + passed the evening—[97] Nash was gayer than I've ever seen him—Coming in he said "Couldn't get pretzels, so I bought a Clarion Ledger"—

Am reading Eva's book, At 33—nicely + simply written, with charming folk all the way through, so far—[98]

I'm going to clean up the penthouse soon—Don't go back on it this summer—The other day I discovered a dead bird on the floor—Too too Russian, I didn't fall for it—[99]

George Greenway is coming down this month[100]—Barron [*Ricketts*] was the only good one in [*the Jackson Little Theatre production of*] Holiday, which in 1934 seems an astonishingly tedious + juvenile play—a "what is it all about anyway" rampage. Carolyn McLean as Ann Harding (she couldn't have been Hope Wms) was simply terrible—in a wrinkled above-ankle-length old evening dress + pseudo Phèdre gestures—Will Wells came through all right, Baldwin Jones was forgettable in her role as Barron's wife, Lorraine Crockett was wooden as money-god sister—The worst play of all, though I saw it in the helpful vicinity of Willia + John, Celeste + BH + Aimee + the Forbes—we discussed N.Y.

I still teach the dances, but sooner or later the fateful last day will come until when I have put off doing a request for the kiddies, the Carioca.[101]

Trial By Jury is to be put on by college glee club here Thurs, I shall attend—

Yours,
Bertha, the Sewing Machine Girl (hmmmmmmmmmmmmmm)

An April 8 postcard is a rare instance of Welty seemingly participating in the casual racism of her era. Printed on the card is a cartoon drawing of an African American girl with two smaller children in wheelbarrow, captioned "How'd you like a box of chocolates?" Under the caption, Welty wrote a racialized pun, "Hershey mouth." She addressed the card to "Massa Frank Lyell" in Princeton. The postcard message seems unrelated. Welty's choice of image and annotation could possibly have been ironic, like Welty's writing on ugly old Valentines printed with sexist caricatures and rhymes, or impersonating a member of the Women's Institute, as she does in the message on this postcard.

April 8, 1934 • Jackson to Princeton

Dear Tom—

Well, Mr Question Box, since you won't let me rest until you know where I got the acquamarine satin that made all gasp at the ball last Saturday, I'll whisper my secret—No, not the Emporium.[102] One night while crying myself to sleep because you had suddenly begun paying marked (X) attention to Agatha Merton, a rich girl, I came across a coupon. In less than a week I was pinned by the Woman's Institute[103]—On initiation night they are going to Picot me—Altho my work on the sewing machine is only in its infancy (sort of a Singer midget) I have already made two camisoles + a couple of slips, + the acquamarine satin was only review work or lesson IV! You won't be able to take your eyes off me graduation week!

Prettily flushed,
Nan

P. S. Mrs Roosevelt is also a member—W. I. '08

April 20, 1934 • Jackson to Princeton

[*Enclosed: 3 small feathers colored white, yellow, and rust, tied together*]

Dear Frank—

First I get a letter from you saying you saw C. [*Cornelius*] Vanderbilt at St. Thomas [*Church*] + then I get a letter from " saying he saw you

—Just the same people over + over—

I enclose a yellow feather which you can win Beatrice Lillie's [*drawing of a hand*] with—[104]

While in the salon of Stella May, my hair artist, I luckily read an article [. . .] on setting up the first home à deux—[. . .] Elsie de Wolfe[105] has charming tables which hang from brass rings + which after luncheon can be thrown overboard + converted into rafts—[. . .]—And on no account must you fall into the expense of a Persian rug when the little woman can, just like one of Daisy's friends, run up a sweet rug on the Singer, using bits of awning—[. . .]

Hubert + I have been doing various things—a few on-the-back snaps of wisteria, a beer party on my birthday with Willia, Nash, Barron etc—a hand-to-mouth afternoon in the strawberry patch—open-letter-to-Time writing etc—the last by H. alone—He writes a story a day—I am going to write a play for the Little Theatre to produce, called "Cain's"—

WC Fields, M Boland, Geo & Gracie will amuse me this afternoon. I hope in VI of a Kind—Did you read in Time that WC Fields wears always a [*handwritten Greek letters Phi Beta Kappa*] key which he found—I saw Death Takes a Holiday, brought here for the teachers on a state convention, + was enchanted by the setting, an immense Roman palace, providing formal + impressive backgrounds—I thought this too good of Hollywood, for I'd expected a layout something like "the Bat"—F. March wears the cinema expression of double entendre, + stares slightly upward, like a lingerie clerk, but everybody else is good + Evelyn Venable is lovely. [. . .][106]

Vanity Fair has all our pals this month, Elsa, Gert, Noel, Mona Wms—Cecil fawns more every day, although in [Elisabeth] Bergner he deserts his usual picnic litter of gauze + gladioli + gets a pretty nice snap—I can't get much idea of the Ballet from the colored photo—

I've been substituting some in the high school, Eng + Spanish, which I taught just like English, since someone had blundered.[107] Took this opportunity of warning youth thus contacted against Gert. Stein, a discussion so impressive that when the Catholic School bells went gong at the end of the hr. they all laughed their heads off. I told the Spanish class about Goya, after which all made puns on him—Let me Goya sweetheart—then everybody asked me to the dance that night.

I'm reading [*Flaubert's*] Salammbo again + shall continue until my crush-a-pomegranate compulsions overpower me once again. Everyone I think of that I like would have made a good barbarian—

[. . .] Write me—tell me what you are doing, not where Mary Taylor[108] might well have been but wasn't—The life here is hypothetical enough—

Love,

Mrs Guy Lombardo

May 11, 1934 • Jackson to Princeton

[Stamp on envelope of letter: "In Memory and In Honor of the Mothers of America Three Cents"]

Dear Frank Thursday

I miss you tonight because I'm Faustian—since you are not here + it is necessary to put something down on paper, it will probably be that I love you always—

I selected essays of Thomas Mann to read, which suited me exactly—papers about Wagner, Durer, time + mythology, love of the past + claims on the future, patience + music + endurance + domesticity—He writes on 19th century German genius, when everything was overabundant, more than life-size, almost mythological in creative effort, + calls Spengler a false + loveless snob—All very cozy after The Nature of the Physical World by Sir Arthur Eddington, which I'm also reading—[109] You must also—it's magnificent—has imagination, wit, + stunning simplicity in presenting utterly unheard of (to me of course) conceptions. No one could help drawing a parallel between his symbolism of physics + the symbolism of human relationships—(Apply the Einstein relativity formula + Eddington's time frame + space-frame conceptions to the problem of communication between 2 people—) I've read only about ½ of it but it's 1000 times more connotative of such despairs + wonders than most of Ulysses—

A few Saturdays ago I remember wishing you could have been in the Astor Hotel; Sir Arthur was broadcasting there at a dinner—He was totally charming—he said "Of course I feel most at home inside a star"—splendid Eng. accent of course—"You must think of the atom as a lady in crinolines"—[110]

The PWA project for putting unemployed artists in the cities to work, you know—went to Mrs. [*Marie*] Hull and Helen McGeehee—Mrs. H. nearly breaking her neck to work her canvases into her schedule—+ what paintings! The governor's mansion, the old capital, [*Welty inserts multiple sets of* " " "] over and over, in various lights at various times of day. Utter hurried bosh— McGeehee's really have something—she chose industrial scenes and different [*drawing of right angle*]'s of approach—[111]

I had Shan Kar's bro.[112] slightly enlarged for exhibit in the coming photo show[113]—For publicity Hubert is going toward to insert a news item in the papers the day it opens. Mrs. Bertha Schmaltz, a tourist, was arrested leaving the University Club with a photograph from the exhibit there under her coat. When asked why she did it, she replied, "It was so beautiful, I had to take it."

We (Hubert) made you something. Watch out for the P.P. soon. We have to find something to mail it in—

Mrs Frank Cannon summoned me to get publicity on the Maternity Center. [*drawing of mother/madonna + child, with caption: By This Sign Shall Ye Know Them*] yelling at me from the porch, as I left, to stress the sacredness of motherhood, after going into the post-natal infection field with me all afternoon (I never did want to go)—I went away whistling—[114]

Have you read "Najnski"—[115] you've probably already seen them but I liked the movie of "Eskimo" (Mala is my idea of a sweet Eskimo!) and "It Happened One Night"[116]—the former has beautiful narrative technique and photography and splendid Mala; + Clark Gable's very amusing in "It Happened 1 Night"—[. . .]

Extra love to allow for the Fitzgerald contraction,[117]

E

In July, Welty's and Creekmore's photographs at the Municipal Art Gallery drew praise from a Clarion-Ledger *(Jackson) society columnist, who noted that "two of Jackson's well known young people" had "beautifully demonstrated the artistic possibilities of photography." Their photographs were exhibited along with paintings by William Hollingsworth,[118] and Marie Hull gave a gallery talk on the three Jacksonians' art on July 13.*

May 13, 1934 • Jackson to Princeton

Dear Frank—

I've been to Utica and the countryside is so lovely—[. . .] I was tempted to marry Knut Hamsun—We'd have acres + I would be very hearty—You, Hubert, Lehman, Willia etc could come down [. . .] We could play making the most words out of GROWTHOFTHESOIL—This would also be a good opportunity for me to find out if the K in his name is pronounced or silent—

(You say something here.)

Another thing I am interested in is old patent medicine labels—I wander up and down drugstores as tho I were in a library. I snatch down a "Mother's Friend," run my finger over the engraving, read the text, sigh, and return it to its shelf—[. . .] We are sending you a record we made, under Mr. Spier,[119] of Gertrude Stein's "Study in Conversation." After you hear it you have to send it on to Gert. As Tambourines. Use only fibre needles, once only[120]—George Greenway says the Congressional Library has her books on the Insanity Shelf, adjacent to the works of an author who prints with a rubber stamp on the title page: "This from the hand of God the Father Almighty"—[. . .]

Yrs,

Garnetta, the Silver King's Daughter.[121]

Didn't you love the Thurber of the day indoors—"This is just like that awful afternoon we telephoned Mencken!"[122]

That summer, Lyell and many Jacksonians made an excursion to the Chicago World's Fair, now in its second year.[123] *Welty, who had attended the year before, composed a letter, illustrated with many drawings, that she probably delivered to Lyell by hand, to read on the train journey to Chicago.*[124]

July 1934 • Jackson to Jackson

Dearest Mr. Lyell—

Here is a limerick for every stop + a stop for every limerick is all you need now.

Pickens
There was a young lady of Pickens
Who read Longfellow, Burns, Scott, + Dickens—
When they said "You're intense,"
She replied, "No offense,
But my interest first lags and then quickens."

Durant
There was a young girl of Durant—
When they said, "What's the news of your aunt?"
She replied, "Poop de doo,
Poop de doo, poop de do,"
That disinterested girl of Durant.

Winona
There was an old girl of Winona
Who lived in a pongee kimona—
When the Lions Club came thru
She politely withdrew,
That delicate gal of Winona.

Chattanooga, Tenn
An oldfashioned girl of Chattanooga
Had an oldfashioned horn that went "ooga"—
+ with little or no pity
Bumped all in the city

Conditioned to "beep" + not "ooga"

Fulton, KY
There was a young lady of Fulton
But this flower of the South was a-wulton'—
She would sleep 24
Hours a day if not more,
On a theory that Fulton's a dull town—

Cairo, Ill.
There was a young lady of Cairo
Who purchased a green autogiro—
When they said, "You'll come down,"
She replied with a frown,
"But not necessarily in Cairo."

Chicago, Ill.
There was a young girl of Chicago
Who liked "Poet + Peasant"—largo.[125]
She said "Ain't it pleasant
To hear 'Poet + Peasant'—
It renders me utterly ga-ga.

I suppose there's next to no possibility, or even a bull's eye of no poss, that you go thru Mottley, Va, a town which I honored several years ago with a limerick on a young lady there, but in case you should pass thru there (it really amounts to the same thing in Eddington if Mottley should pass thru you[126]), here you are all fixed up—

Mottley, Va
There was a young lady of Mottley
Whose cocktails turned out very ottley—
When they said "Are you sure
Your ingredients are pure?"
She replied confidentially, "Hottley."

And now for a few quick games of "Reed Smart" before Terre Haute—Suppose we start at Head of his Class, + try for Grace Coolidge. Just try.

Head of his class, classified ad, add-a-pearl, Pearl White, White Sister, Sister Ann, Ann Sothern, Western Union, Union Square, Square Root, Rooti-toot-toot, Toute Suite, Sweet Sue, S'sue Hayakawa (Didn't work)[127] Now you start with the World's Fair and see what you get—World's Fair, Fair + Warmer, Warmer my Wondering Boy Tonight, Tonight You Belong to Me, Me oh My, My Man, Man Ray, Ray for the Red White + Blue, Blue Heure (transp.) , Heure Night in June, June Bugs, Bugs Baer, Baer Back, Back to My Little Grass Shack in Kalala Kalue Hawaii—Quite a distance—Send me a lot of postcards.

Many people go to Chicago to let their hair grow, why not you? (I don't know why I love it so) Don't go into the House of David, I can't stand for extremes to meet [*drawing that may be an Orthodox Jew with long beard meeting other stick figures with long hair*]

The Travel + Transport Bldg was the best last year—Louis will love it, you too—

So Be It, Be It sic Lillie, Lilly Lucy, Lucy Lillie, Lilly White Hands, Hands Up, Upsy Daisy—Daisy Fellowes! (At least I ended among friends)

July 16, 1934 • Chicago to Jackson

[*Lyell to Welty*]

The journey up here was a touch strenuous, but Elizabeth Holmes got on at Canton + Charlie Swayze in Grenada + we had fun together. Tonight we're convening in the Congress for Eddy Duchin. I think the Fair is really wonderful. We stayed there all day Saturday, + ascended one of the towers at 9 to see all the lights—one of the most dazzling sights I've ever seen, + the half hour we were there Guy was playing on the radio. Spent all yesterday at the Art show + had a grand time.

See you in the Swiss Village—Ohleaydeoo—

That summer, Welty and Lyell continued to participate both in conventional society events and in artistic, intellectual, or bohemian activities. A July "Chatterbox" column noted that Welty, Creekmore, and Lyell attended a dance in the Arlington Room of the Robert E Lee Hotel.[128] *In August 1934 she wrote photographer Berenice Abbott concerning Abbott's photography course at the New School for Social Research and the equipment Welty was currently using, which she feared might be inadequate.*[129] *That fall, Welty was still looking for creative outlets.*

October 1, 1934 • Jackson to Princeton

Dear Frank

You may well wonder how I got this paper [*spattered with flecks of green paint*]—It was with a Flit gun, hope you like it—

Imagine you up there with only Chaucer, Spenser, Shakesp. Milton, Keats, Shelley, and Middle Eng. Lit. betwixt you and the Ritz bar—

Just the opposite of you, no one here has been working very hard—Ho Hum.

[. . .] Will probably be fired off the Commercial unless I quickly begin a 3-piece knitted suit—The new debs will soon be known, they're behind the curtain now—

Margaret [*Harmon*] had a beer gathering but Barron got us all into Henry James + I didn't get well out until an hr. or so after the party had broken up—[. . .] Hubert is going to be head of the Little Theatre workshop this season—Think I'm joining up with the playwriters,[130] I'll do something terribly amusing about a beauty parlor, even though I have been reading Irish plays, + too bad it is you can't fold in the Irish in your program—[. . .]

Jack Benny said he played football for ICS (right, international correspondence School) for yrs., + used to mail them in touchdowns—Once at the last min. of play he sent a touchdown airmail but didn't put enough stamps + it came back—[. . .][131]

By the way let us hear airmail how the exams turn out, that will be something—If you make 100 I will send you something to eat [. . .] Somehow I even gave Marshall Hurt a date, in fact he's downstairs now—probably wondering over the drawings Edw. + I did this morning for "Best Not Mentioned, Any Medium" with which we agreed from the start—in 3 colors of chalk—Edw's is called "All Roses Have 3 Thorns, Except Apples" a still life. Mine is "Sunflower + Velocipede," very sultry—

I'm about to take some more pictures—tomorrow probably—have done everything but file the application with the camera—

Mamie Smith is at the Alamo at midnight[132]—Margaret, Hubert + I are going—

Well goodbye Toots,

[*drawing of a hand raising a champagne glass*]—Success!

A Camp Uh-Fiah Gehl[133]

October 31, 1934 • New York to Princeton

[*Drawing of jack-o'-lantern*]

Dear Frank—

I suppose you boys are out just raising hell tonight—Don't ever spook to me again—

Just been to Dodsworth[134] which I thought splendidly done—Last night attended the Philadelphia Symph—magnificent—the end better than anything since the last time I heard them play Bach, which I do love—

The photo peddling seems to move slowly—I become discouraged, all the publishers profess admiration but corresponding poverty—[. . .] Wish I had my horoscope—no telling what Uranus may be doing in my House—

[. . .] Do come down this wk-end so I can see you even for a bus ride (although Martha Graham may be good). I need a blithe spirit [. . .]

Today I called Random House, found the Stein tea would be 5:00, loaded the camera, + slept through the hour.[135] You might bring the record + we could call dressed as Rutherford B. Hayes or Grant—

Yrs ever,

Etoile de Holland[136]

The following week, Welty went back to Jackson, where the local paper reported her return on its society page.[137]

On Thanksgiving, Lyell wrote Welty about listening to the radio broadcast of the wedding of Prince George, Duke of Kent and youngest son of George V, to Princess Marina of Greece.

November 29, 1934 • Princeton to Jackson

Turkey Day Proclamation: I do hope you were able to hear the wedding broadcast this morning—it was on in these parts from 5:45–7.00, came in perfectly + thrilled me absolutely to the bone. The announcer on top of the Abbey described the 4 royal entries + Marina no sooner descended from her coach than the notes of the organ swelled up inside + you felt as if you were a member of the bridal party entering with her, or at least a duke or peer of the realm. I loved the plighting of the troth with both of them speaking clearly + beautifully—+ I'm dying to know who did all the royal coughing. Perfectly wonderful! by far the most successful transatlantic broadcast I've heard. Shaun Wylie + I have just returned from service at Trinity + will soon repair to the Wicks for the rest of the day. Janet has come home with Mt. Holyokels, so it will be gay. I'll be in N.Y. Friday + Saturday. Have you heard Cole [*Porter*]'s <u>You're the Top</u>—very good—Guy will do it well + you will no doubt produce verses that surpass his. Try to include my 2 loose couplets: You're the band of Sonya, the hands of Dase; also You're Schiaparelli, Voiregnara Jelly—Charles Baker + I are most depressed over Arete Kefner's departure for Europe yesterday—said he had to go + won't be back this year—Distributing his possessions about I inherited a combination radio + Victrola, a bottle of Cointreau + wine glasses, + a wedgewood bowl full of bayberries. We'll miss him.

Goodbye,
FDR

February 2, 1935 • Jackson to Princeton

[*This letter records a game in which participants draw the head of a figure, fold down the paper and pass it to the next person, who draws the body, with a third person finishing the feet. This was a change from another favorite game, Old Magazines, in which people drew cartoon bubbles that supplied absurd statements for the people in magazine photos.*]

Dear Frank—

On reverse see new game, Fold Down the Paper, or Heads + Tails. This head (lady looking into chandelier to see if it needs dusting) is by Seta Alexander,[138] the Boy Scout body by Edw. Not as impressive an example of the game as I would like to show you, but the only paper without somebody or something on both sides. Hubert drew the body of a bird, + after he folded down the paper I drew the head of a man blowing a bird warbler whistle. A laughing horse committing suicide turned up as do many other things Luther Burbank would hesitate to laugh at.[139] Anyone who is tired of playing Old Magazines will love F. down the P. [. . .]

February 16, 1935 • Jackson to Princeton

Dear Frank,

Much w. has flowed under the b. since I last wrote you a letter and I haven't heard from you in a long time either.[140] Migs [*Schermerhorn, a friend from the University of Wisconsin*] came about 2 weeks ago. First we went to N. O. We had much fun. H. was down there going to the dr. and he took us to all the joints and all the places in the Fr. Q. but I am afraid we wore him out.

We decided to pick up two men we saw in Solari's that tried to pick us up and we resisted. [. . .] We had a peculiar experience in the Monteleone after changing to cheaper room with privilege of using ladies room down hall. A team with a coach lived next door and when we would take a bath they would look over the partition and comment. We reported them in huffy manner and house dick was sent up to sit down hall with grey fedora over knee and black cigar, nodding to us every trip. But team got in and wrote on one door Ladies and on other Gents and on bath Both Sex. We fetched house dick who clutched towel and rubbed it off blushing like fire. The day we left team was still taking baths there, calling us "Anderson!" if we opened the door. [. . .]

I never did tell you about Mr. McIntosh. He roomed here for a week, coming the week of the big snow unrecommended but quite old and flossy. Scotch, from Chicago, did nothing, intimating why should he. Sat in door playing solitaire with eye on door all day. Invited me and Dorothy to lunch the first day and was all right but worked up to taking Margaret and me to Browns Wells for the day and breathing on our necks, so we tossed him out. About 80. Threw 20 dollar bills around. Had "girls" everywhere he would buy typewriters and things for. Mother trusted him because he was a good responder to 2 demand bid. I thought he was pathetic, he brought out to show me his collection of silk pajamas, cuff links, studs, medicines, sewing materials, and monogrammed hdkfs. [. . .] He ran around the halls all morning in his pink silk pajamas, squeaking "Am I invited to breakfast?" He walked to town in the snow and while we were out shoveled all the snow off the sidewalk down the whole block. He wore tissue paper inside his cap (Scotch plaid) to keep his bald head warm. Oh well, he's gone now. [. . .]

I am sort of worried about Hubert—he was sick in bed for 3 weeks [. . .]. I haven't heard anything from him since we left N.O. and I think he is building up and tearing down his constitution every day. He isn't going to be able to get out another issue of the Southern Review, which is very sad.[141]

[. . .] I'll probably be up there sooner or later, as I've just about finished my photograph bk. H. [*Hubert*] thinks I ought to wait until I can take a baptizing and a ball game, but I can't wait. I am afraid somebody else will get out something like it or the publishers or the public will become saturated with photography books. I want to get some money for it and then go somewhere else to make another book, like Mexico or Alaska.

Judge Lyell called me the other day to come see a print of Louis' picture, which I did—it is very charming—a sketch, you know—I can't help wishing K. Wolfe had done him in oils.[142] The original is at your house now and I'll see it maybe tomorrow, we're going up that way for tea. I suppose it is much bigger than the print. The sketches are rather photographic and exact—really copies of people. It is good to preserve Louis as he is in any form.

How is your thesis. I'm getting terribly fast on the typewriter—I take notes on it all the time—having nothing else to do all day I read The Golden Bough, the Decline of the West, and all kinds of folk tales and fairy tales and take notes. Not that I'll ever have any practical use for them—but it has always been a pleasant sensation to feel any kind of knowledge mounting up. Have also written some stories and poetry which are much better than I ever thought I'd do. [. . .] That's all the news I know. Write soon. Is your picture of [*singer*] Lotte Lehmann the same as was on TIME today. Great for any boy's room.

E

March 4, 1935 • Jackson to Princeton

Dear Gluck-Sandor—[143]

Semi-tidings of great joy—I leave Jackson Wednesday. Destination N. Y.—IF 100 things, like clothes from the cleaners—

Will be there only short time unless find fantastic job. Hdqtrs: Barbizon Hotel, Lex + 63. Communicate. Hubert is also going to NY soon. We all ought to get a box at B Lillie's or something matey.

Goodbye I'm about to split!

F. Sorel

April 7, 1935 • New York to Jackson

Dear E—

Just a line to tell you of last night's festivity when I emerged for the first time after a week's work in the N.Y.P [*Public Library*]. Got everything done on schedule + it all came out very well.

I went to a cocktail party at Ruth + Bubber Ford's on West 8th Street, + it was wonderful.[144] Guest list in part: Cecil Beaton, Baron George Hoyningen-Huene, Djuna Barnes, George Balanchine, Wm Dollar (great success in American Ballet this year—Balanchine directs it), Peter Neagal (transition person), James Pendelton (wonderful furniture store on 57 street), Augustus John, Nicolai Waldorf (wrote music to Union Pacific), Paul Bowles (whom I hadn't seen in over a year), etc, etc. That lasted until 8:30 when I had to dash to Personal Appearance, after which I went to one of the maddest parties you've ever heard of or conceived at Cecil's apartment in the Waldorf—It would take weeks to describe the place to you—he's done it all over—dozens of artificial flowers, pictures, paintings, scrapbooks (full of Tallulah, Daisy, Tilly, Elsa, the Sitwells, royalty, etc, etc).

The princess Natalie Paley was there among others. But the exciting thing is that Huene is going to photograph me in the Waldorf this afternoon at 2:30! [. . .] He's really a swell guy—hates Dali, mad music, photography, painting, seems a sincere conservative at heart—[. . .] I return to P.ton on the 5:30—will report on result of the sitting—can you believe it? I can't—

F

May 6, 1935 • Jackson to Princeton

[*A clipping enclosed in this letter reports on a new streamliner train named "The Rebel" over the objections of the United Daughters of the Confederacy and Dr. Dunbar Rowland, director of the state's Department of Archives and History.*[145]

An Appreciated Letter

Mrs. Dunbar Rowland acknowledges the receipt of a kind letter from the officials of the Gulf, Mobile, and Northern railroad relative to the name of the new streamlined train and wishes to give this public expression to her appreciation of their warm commendation of her courage and efforts to serve what she believes to be the best interests of her state.

No matter how hard her contest, Mrs. Rowland is always a good loser when she feels assured the ethical standards prompt those who do not agree with her, which she feels sure was the case in the present instance. While she still believes that the new name of the train is not in keeping with what should be the highest cultural aspirations of our people, she leaves that as a matter of taste.]

Dear Frank—

The typing is going more slowly than I thought it would [*Lyell's dissertation on Scottish novelist John Galt*]. If you could write your lines a bit wider spaced and your words not so little nor so close together, it would be much speedier and less tedious. Am picking up with practice, but you must admit your writing gives one pause.

[. . .] When you get the chapter back, I wish you'd look into a few points of punctuation, at least before a final copy is made, and right away, if you can, to prevent errors ahead for me. [. . .] Find out if it is correct to italicize any titles except those of books and magazines? In old days (my school days) poems, chapter headings in books, essays, and short articles, all of which you italicize, went in capitals and little letters, in quotations. [. . .] Also, I believe it is proper to write out all numbers under 100; I left things like "Chapter 23" as you had them on page 49 however. [. . .] Also, be sure you're showing all paragraphs. Some of them are of rare length.

John Galt is a scream—[. . .] The Earthquake sounds like a synopsis of grand opera—would have made a wonderful movie for the Gishes once. You tell it amusingly. As a typ [*sic*] from the typist, to whom only hyphens involved should matter: use less words of Latin derivation. As constant reader I grow tired of unceasing prefixes and multisyllables, esp. since the text and criticisms quoted are so heavy. I'm not a rabid Anglo-Saxon or tabloid person in tastes, but e.g. on pg. 18 when Galt did not feel well enough to go then, you say "but the condition of his health was not conducive to an immediate continuation of his travels." Too much of that sounds pompous and like mockery—pages of it make for pressure.

[. . .] Judge Lyell [. . .] telephoned me to come see your photographs [*presumably taken in April by Hoyningen-Heune*]. I don't think they're overwhelming either. I don't even think they're very good, especially the one you said put in the frame, in the snotty note to your family. The one I like is not the sissy one but the third one. In the shirt. The lighting in it is the only good lighting—informative and revealing and interesting. What did he think of them himself, and what were the others like?

Willie Spann said she and Peter Lindamood[146] had called on me last Sunday while I was out of town, Peter bearing "all kinds of messages from New York and Frank." Peter, from various rumours, sounds most strange, and if still in Jackson, is, I imagine, dead. Is he a Columbus product like Chas Henri [*Ford*]? I can't place him. Tiny with red hair, my mother says. There are no new people in Jackson except a Mr Ticner, who sells books for Houghton Mifflin, who has also been around when I was away; his attraction is the possession of Dwight Fiske records, which I have not heard, but you said they were funny, so will cutivate this Tic.

Am on my way to the Little Theatre; I collect all the food and drink for three teas in The Last of Mrs. Cheney, with Norma Shearer Donaldson in the leading tumble. I am thinking of furnishing trick food, rubber eclairs and squirting sponge cakes from the old reliable Johnson Smith, Racine, Wis.[147] A pretty how-do-you-do? I think so, goodbye.

[*drawing of a flower with stars labeled "Night" in background, flower labeled "Night blooming cereus"*]

Mrs. Zula Cain[148]

May 13, 1935 • Jackson to Princeton

Dear Frank—

Sorry the coming pages are delayed—I am mailing the rest of the MS on hand tomorrow morning (Tuesday), and hope it is in time. The Little Theatre took up much wasted time, had many thankless tasks to do and in attending the rehearsals witnessed much tear slinging and curse fixing among different factions. The organization is in a horrid state, with internal warfare, enraged feelings, flattery from all, and general impasse; the next production is supposed to consist of original plays—I submitted a farce, supposed to take place in the waiting room of a R.R. station, but Mrs. [*Bertha Ricketts*] Sumner[149] says the judges were felled by the presence of MEN and LADIES as exits and entrances, and they can find only one other play good enough. In it, I think, everyone goes offstage. I've enjoyed this portion of the thesis—have devel. quite an affection for old Johnnie. I see you have entered into Scotch rustic life with the customary graceful adjustment! By the way, you could have knocked me into a row of Sitwells when I discovered that PP, whose Memoirs I was after in the NYP, was Mister Pope.

The mimosa, the gardenias, and Livingston Park opened yesterday and I attended each bang, receiving new l. on l. [*lease on life*]

Received letter from Commercial Appeal today saying they had been informed that since my work for them was in the nature of a favor to them and a pleasure to me, and not for the remuneration, and since they wished to expand and could not "impose on my good nature for more than I was already doing," they were releasing me from the weekly assignment, Clifford Pullen [*Jackson woman whose daughter was a few years younger than Welty*] to take my place. This annoyed me, as I knew Clifford wrote the "information," I have been hearing for 2 weeks that she said she was going to take over my job. She appeared yesterday and I didn't. Very coy business. Oh yes, I appeared in Chatterbox simultaneously, or last week, one, I hear.[150] This sounds like an Ayrshire squabble, of about the correct proportion.

Have been [*substitute*] teaching Aimee [*Shands*]'s psychology class lately, Aimee being sick with sinus trouble. It is lots of fun, I take up Expressionism in Art in connection with any synapse that pops up. Doubt if they pass. [. . .]

Did you hear B Lillie Friday—I hear she and the girls were running the fire dept for one day—the telephone rang—"Just one of my old flames"—and after a long chat with someone whose house is burning she rings off with "We'll be right over—we'll stop by the ten cent store and buy some ash trays."

I look for Hubert and Lehman this week—Hubert has been coming home for the last 2 weeks and am exhausted as is everyone else with day-to-day expectancy. Wish he could have gotten a job up there. Did you have him down to see Cointreau. Mrs. Engel was saying the other day that she was looking for Lehman this week but would be a mighty disappointed woman if he didn't show up for Mothers Day. Feel sorry for the boys coming back. Are you?

Much lervely gossip abounds since S Gordon + R Greens alighted from around the world. Why, I don't know, since she and Richard have certainly been able to throw bedrooms together right on President Street without going into Egypt to sin if they wished to. However, Dr Capers stated in church that he was glad to welcome them home—"I don't know what they've done but Mr. Green looks none the worse for wear," goes the tale. She was at the play in a Tahiti print.

The coast ahead looks clear for days of perfect typing, so send ahead the MS and I'll finish it very promptly this time.

Anne Elise Roane ("Horse") Winter.[151]

June 16, 1935 • Jackson to Princeton

Dear Frank—

Have had no thesis + have heard 0—Since you'll be leaving in 2 wks I don't suppose you're hoping to have the completed paper typed + re-typed by the end of school—So I'm going to N. C. tomorrow without misgivings on your account—

Emily White [*Stevens MacLachlan*] + John inhabit a 15 room Colonial mansion in which they sneer mightily at the aristocracy, + I go to chide them. EW also has a project she wants photos for + the publisher at the U of NC Press is int. in my book[152]—Also I am sick of Jackson—Who could ask for anything more—

My trip I am making a charming bus affair + will postcard you when I'm coming round a mt. unless in the arms of Clark Gable, which the Greyhound Lines consider imminent of course[153]—I'm going to Charleston SC on the way + will spend a day there snapping shots + sea food—

Let me go to Calif <u>too</u>—

Hope I'll be back in time to see you; Margaret + I think we should throw something big in one of our gardens at the time—[. . .]

Gloria

In September Lyell took a job teaching English at NC State College in Raleigh. On his long train ride south, he wrote to Welty and Hubert Creekmore.

September 24, 1935 • train from Princeton to Raleigh, NC, to Jackson

In the dumps—N.J.—8 pm

Dear Eudora, Hubert + anybody else that's interested—(that is our group—I'm sure I can count on you to bounce the proper ones)—

I'm just half an hour out of Trenton—+ have been through thirty minutes of tears [. . .]. I don't know why—I'm perfectly satisfied, indeed rather delighted + flattered to go to Raleigh (Telegram: "Application unanimously approved—Expect early arrival, etc, etc—" after 10 days [*deliberation?*] over (I'm sure there must have been) a number of jobseekers—somebody from Yale got the Lubbock [*Texas*] position—I'm telling you sincerely that I was absolutely terrified by the thought of being offered that place. My friend Bob Brittani, who had it before + recommended me for it, but of course couldn't dilate at great length upon it all when I was perhaps in Glacier Park, perhaps in Jackson Hole, perhaps dead, told me in Princeton last week when he was on his way to Ohio State that for 2 months of the year they were unable to see across the street through the dust and sand storms, [. . .] it all sounded ghastly to me [. . .] 450 miles in any direction to a place of similar size. [. . .] this year they revised the stipend to $1500 (which is, shh, to be my salary in Raleigh) but even so I'm much better off being where I am headed now. Princeton instructors get $1800, but with the higher living expenses, they don't get to do any more with their pay than I'll be able to do.

My friend, Lodwick Hartley, is in the department there, so I'm hoping he'll fill me full of dos and don'ts about the place (+ I can count on him to do so) so I can step off with this + that person on the right foot. When I was in N.Y. last week, I tried to find the Frank Fullers at 375 Park Ave, but they had not returned for the autumn—They used to live in Raleigh, and Mr. F (rich + prominent) has a brother (R. + P., I hope) in Raleigh. I don't know where on this globe I'm going to spend tomorrow night, but I hope poor Lodwick or the Fuller family or Prof. Clark, with whom I corresponded this summer, (the letters bothered me—stiff with typographical errors, erasures;—must correct all that in Raleigh first thing) will be able to find me a desirable place. I'm planning to be popular + sympathetic with all the horrible as well as attractive folk and to. . .well, I'll just hold all plans in reserve until I see how they work out—now I should no doubt be outlining the opening lecture, warming up the first ball to toss out, stringing pearls of lovely things to say—but I have to get over all this ground for you little chickadees or you won't write me things to brighten North Carolinian hours as I want you to do. Suddenly today, everything + everybody I like became more precious to me than ever before, and I counted so many blessings that have been heaped upon me that I was completely overcome.

I haven't stopped a minute for the last 2 days—Getting packed was ghastly—A three year accumulation of stuff seemed to have grown to incredible proportions—I gave away things right + left—china, lamps, pillows, bicycle, books I didn't want—all too prodigal—stuffed three huge wooden boxes which I hope God will conduct to Raleigh, besides the trunk, + I got on the train in Trenton with 2 big suitcases, handbag, hatbox, tennis racquet, 2 suit boxes (I went wild in MacDaid's yesterday, + bought lovely garments I hope won't be considered too pretentious in Raleigh) (when people ask where I am, please, Eudora, try to say Raw-ly—I fear you may give it the Sewanny vowel turn which, my dear, makes my blood run cold) + the corrugated box in which I had put all my fine framed European prints. I simply didn't have time to do anything about the latter. Now I'm glad I didn't for they're in an empty berth + I can trust them in my own hands. Porters + conductors still haven't been able to figure out what the hell, but what the hell, say I. (I'm sorry this is all sort of scrawly, but the train lurcheth furiously, + I'm in a state myself)

I analyze it this way: I've been so supremely happy in Princeton, loved + adored every minute of it, that just for a while after I left this evening I couldn't conceive of being able to get along without my friends there. It would have [*been*] much better if I'd seen the group of graduate students I came to loathe in their dull colorlessness + fundamental stupidity + seen none of the undergraduates I'm very fond of, + not many of the faculty people or townfolk, + none of the homes I've had such delightful hours in—but all was just the opposite—Princeton didn't choose even to stage a single rainy, dreary, typical day during the past week, + yesterday + today were radiantly beautiful + I saw practically everybody + they said such endearing words to me that I was all so stirred + moved by them—But at the time I was so busy, I had no time to think about what depths their really sincere feelings reached, + when suddenly it was all snatched away + I had time to think, I absolutely sunk to bathyspheric depths. [. . .] I don't usually melt before anything except artistic triumphs of one sort or another but I came very near it then. And what was so very nice was the encounter with the academic procession of faculty leaving the Chapel this afternoon after opening exercises—naturally, I hated like everything not to sing Veni Creator Spiritus in choir again, but I simply didn't have time to work it in. [. . .] got there just in time to have President Dodds and Prof Wicks coming outside leading the procession, bow nicely to me +, being the only person in front of the chapel at the time, to catch Mr. Gerould's eye—I was to see him before leaving in his office, but here would do just as well—so he stepped out of the colorful lines to say goodbye, only to be followed by all the members of the department present who had heard about my appointment, but hadn't seen me—The unexpected array of brilliantly hooded bigwigs descending upon me was blinding—+ my dear Mr. Osgood made me feel perfectly grand about going + Gerould said don't think about the thesis until I get well under way toward whipping freshmen into shape, + don't hurry, + put it off to next summer if I want to, etc, etc. That, tentatively, is what I plan to do—Of course, I brought all the notes + what I've already done with me, but I couldn't bring all the Galtiana—However, they said they didn't mind how much they had to send me through interlibrary loan service, + call on them for dozens if I chose to do so—[. . .] shouldn't take me over 2 ½ months to complete. [. . .]

Well—anyway—it's all very adventurous + for the best, + all will work out successfully, I feel. I hope I haven't bored you, but at this momentary and sudden turning of the ways I don't [*illegible*] words are superfluous—that reveal my real reactions to it all—

I shall try to end on a cheerful note with an account of Lady Beatrice [*Lillie*]'s duties in At Home Abroad which I viewed the other night in the hoary, merry Winter Garden. The audience was negligible in allure, but [. . .] I noted that Carl Van Vechten devoted the summer to growing a long bob (maybe it was a transformation). It's a swell show [. . .]

Well, I'm weary + must send these leaves winging their way to you—Please keep thinking up things to say to make freshmen courses interesting—[. . .].

Yours,

F

11 P. M. Better now—in Virginia—+ so lovely

November 5, 1935 • Jackson to Raleigh

Dear Frank—

Guy played Blue Skies so magnificently a while ago that I thought I would notify you in case you didn't hear it—also Dancing On The Ceiling, Sophisticated Lady, Between the Devil & the Deep Blue Sea, and even the hit of the week was rather more hit than weak. Poor Guy now has to refer to himself as an Esso marketer or something equally disadvantageous.

It's always in the most unpromising circs. that I want to write a letter—the old eyes hurt like fire and I am liable to throw up any minute (my most embarrassing moment). Hubert won a box of candy yesterday with lucky number and we ate with no reverence for layers. I have got it as dark here as a Loew movie house and feel just as restless as if I were really in it so I must do something. You never write, but I'll write and tell you what we did yesterday.

Hubert, Nash [*Burger*] and I drove over to Yazoo City. H had heard about an old lady named Mrs Mayes who was stinking with confederate literature and Audubon prints. [. . .] Old lady lived beyond impassable barrier of barbed wire, vegetation, and clouds of dust blowing out from her Confederate collections. Had only 1 tooth and it wasn't very cute. [. . .] As for the Audubon prints, I don't know what the scouts could have been thinking of as the only evidence of bird or animal life were a few calendars on the walls and gnawed-away indices of law books.

After we left there we rode home by way of the wild woods to Red Bank, Sartatia, and Bolton. It was wonderful. You could smell the heavy loam in the deep cool woods—the Yazoo and Big Black rivers were running along. The roads were dirt and wound around as if made by somnambulistic cows. We chose at forks by instinct but lost our pride in that when we asked at one crossroads. The roads parted at right angles. The negro said "Dat road goes to Bolton that-a-way, and the other road it goes to Bolton to but take a little longer to git there." We asked one man where the road we were on went and he said "It don't go no-where." There were big live oak trees and lots of sumac and moss and mistletoe. There wasn't anybody else on the road.

I hope you went to class on Hallowe'en in costume. Nash, Margaret, Charles Bonner and I went down Cap. St. in masks and hats, which was very much fun, except that unbearable Charles didn't wear a mask—don't you think he is impossible. Nash went in to mail a letter with a Chinese mask on, which I think will hide forever the source of the letter.

[. . .] We are planning happy parties for the holidays and counting on your presence—although H [*Hubert*] predicted that you will take a flying trip by plane (that worked out all right) to NY before and after your Jackson sojourn. Write us when you'll be home. It's only a month or so off.

Do you have any time for reading. A rumor was afloat that you had 7,000 papers to grade a week, equals 1,000 a day—say not so. I have been reading a lot—just finished [*Thomas Mann's*] Buddenbrooks. Have you read it. It is a tremendous account of a family—within that scope it is as exhaustive as the Magic Mountain—and treats also of gradual disintegration, mental and physical, and the death of the proud untouchable well born family through time alone, which brings to it common blood, madness, errors of conduct, and other taints. In it are several briefly launched ideas which terminate enormously in the Magic Mountain. But in Buddenbrooks he seems to spend his time leading up to things which he then dispenses with heard late, while in the M. M. he dispenses instead with the lead-ups. I have also been reading in Against the Grain until the ganglia start undue palpitations, when I shiver, drop the book, and go out for a Coke. I think it is base, a hoax, unpardonable, and to be admired only in the perceptions of sensuous relationships, in which idle craft I think he works with honesty. I remember reading La-Bas once and finding o to shrink from as I never can get a very big thrill out of someone reciting the Lord's Prayer backwards while spitting at the altar, that's not very bad, if you want to be really bad.[154]

My own witchery becomes more promising each day as the herbs are thriving in their transplanted state and balm smells divine—like liquid candies, you know those little things. Hubert's yard man thinks H is going to be a witch doctor although his herbs aren't doing so well, and says "Mr. Hubert I want to be the first to get your love potions."

Aimee is attempting decorations in the house and Dr. Shands has agreed to let curtains be hung at his windows and an easy chair to be brought into his room—only one of the reasons and signs wherein gossip sees that he is going to marry (a) Mrs. Posey (b) Lois McCormick (c) "somebody up at the hospital." Don't tell A.

Hubert said Louis ate alone in the Belmont the other night—ordered a steak supper, called briskly for "My check, please" when finished, and behaved in all quite for your approval. He questioned Hubert tactfully about work in the highway department and didn't bring up the 6th grade. I also hear that he did some reprehensible Hallowe'en damage.

Ruth Roudebush White made me so mad today that I have been in a bad humor ever since. She regards herself as Inspiration, head muse of Miss. art. Karl Wolfe is immersed even deeper in his hydrangeas. William Hollingsworth shows signs of being somebody but Mrs. White insinuates that he owes all to her especially since he <u>had</u> to get married; and that a wife like that was naturally ungrateful. Such a hideous thing to say in Jackson, where it is considered shameful enough just to be an artist. Don't repeat the slur on wife's name as I don't think it is generally known so far but it's unimportant enough to start the rounds.

I see Willia a good bit. She is fine, so is the baby, who on request says "God is love" and points with a sweet gesture heavenward. She also sings, with static, "We are lit-tle flowers, growing—growing—growing."

Have you a radio. The Sunday night programs are continuous—the ones to be listened to—starting with Jack Benny and ending with [*Jascha*] Heifitz and the like. I thought Heifitz played too well-worn compositions last night except the first one—I was feeling so elated from the Yazoo trip that the only selection that touched my mood was the ride of the Valkyries. Missed Beatrice the other day but I understand she sang "A Baby's Best Friend is His Mother." I thought of a wonderful song for her. The tune is fine but I can only send the words:

The bees and the flies have bright little eyes
But they cannot see like me (very high note)
They crawl on the book and they seem to look
But they don't know ABC.
Cho. A, B, C
D, EEE F G
HIJK, LMN O P
And down to XYZ.

It's an old thing my mother taught me.

Without the slightest sound or warning beforehand, a pack of geese wanders up underneath my window and begins reprehensible noises, all the time, and it is beginning to undermine my daydreams. However I still plan to go to NY.

What with ex-school teachers and girl scout executives making their debuts I think I had better slip quietly out now. I'll only mention that a family named Higginbottom has moved around the corner from you, and Mr H's mother and father run a leper colony in India and always dress for dinner, so the local H's do too because they do. Sort of a colony club. She thinks Jackson is lovely for wearing out old evening dresses and socks, and he is organizing a Hoe and Rake Factory here, after which they will leave and he will organize one in the next place. I'll call on her soon and swipe some of the hoe and rake stationery.

Do write soon, just on the back of an old theme. One of Nash's pupils asked him the other day "Mr. Burger are you an only child?" Ans., yes. Child: I thought so." Exit. Prepare for this.

Yours,
Eudora

Recommend some good movies. However, we get Joan Crawford. Don't you hate the Wake Theatre—reminds me of a coffin.

Lyell sent Welty gifts in early December, apparently thanking her for all the typing she had done.

December 10, 1935 • Jackson to Raleigh

Dear Frank,

What do the general run of typists do when they get cacti in their fingers—have been watering the plants and didn't know they were big enough to bite me. I saw your mother today but didnt dast ask her when you were coming home—no doubt 1 trip to Manhattan will not prove sufficient and you continue to plan the Christmas hop.

I am deliberating whether to thank you now for the Christmas presents, but I think not yet. As far as poss., I have not looked at them very much or played the record with any regularity, as must save them for the proper time—and once I have said thanks would wear them out immediately with abandoned use. They charm me, but you certainly should not have sent so much—heavens! I won't be overwhelmed but you should not have felt indebted—it is ridiculous to feel under obligation to anyone for anything I never do—anyway Miss EW never types in the spirit of a notary public. You will see how spotless is my character when you get back Hottentot Potentate unscratched.[155]

The lights are up on Cap [*Capitol*] St and the Watkins cedar, toy machine guns and G Men pursuit cars fill the windows, the girl scouts put the last stitches in their carol-singing costumes, the phantoms are in their monkey-fur neckpieces,[156] Hubert brings back more sperrits every trip to N. O., and there are parties in the planning. Let us hear for sure when you're coming, when you know.

We had a good time Sunday. Hubert, Nash, Margaret and I drove to Mendenhall and ate chicken dinner off the revolving table.[157] We were very cosmopolitan, veritable gems of hotel guests, as you can imagine. After the usual map-begging and world-discussions we decided to come home by way of Pinola, which we did, taking each other's pictures on the bank of a stream, and drinking. Later in the evening Hubert made some good hot rum drinks and we heard Melchior sing.[158]

Major Bowes' amateur unit (one of the thousands) comes here this week, as does Three Men on a Horse. Jackson is beset with attractions, I have already witnessed Kyrl and his band and Earl Carroll's Fannities, and skipped Ethel Barrymore in an old thing I saw ages ago in Chicago, The Constant Wife. It was on her next stop after this one that she called a newspaper girl a b. Just think suppose it had been Martha Harrison!

TIME is very funny these days, Gracie is funny, Guy is good (played an old no., How Do You Do It, which I used to request in writing every week I believe), the movies are pretty good. Garbo will be here at last next week—if only that ass March weren't in it! I enjoyed Way Down East, which was not what you would think—good color and the melodrama limited to a good Eliza scene.

Glad you had such a good time in NY—don't stay too long before coming here. Is Lehman coming. I hear Emily White and John are—Junior is expected in Feb., unless they come on the bus, I bet. Hope you persuaded Robt Daniel to skip down for a romp.

Jingle bells,
E

In April, a New York gallery exhibited Welty's photographs,[159] *and two of her stories, "Magic" and "Death of a Traveling Salesman," were accepted by* Manuscript.[160]

May 19, 1936 • Jackson to Raleigh

Dear Frank—

I suppose Beauty Fewell, the waterworks' daughter, was before your time. Oh well, I'll go on and write the letter anyway.

Don't despair—the divinity [*homemade candy*] is indeed to come, and is on the way now. Mother was busy last week, what with judging a flower show in Belzoni, Miss., and with termites under the house and a man after them, and with both sons in golf finals. But we never go back on our divinity, as I imagine it would be messy; and you're welcome.

Thanks for criticism on tale [*"Death of a Traveling Salesman"*]. I agree that more facts in the gent's past would have lent clearer perspective and pointed the present more. But I did have all sympathy with him. Perhaps I took him for granted. It's funny how people do, a publisher (at Covici-Friede) wrote me how sympathetically and vividly I made the same character! (Also asked me for a novel, but you know I ain't got one.) Would hate to try to say what I was "trying to do" or what, in the story, because on such a thing I'm not even from the beginning very intellectual! It's just a story. The lack in people's lives etc. Two more sort of sexy items are to appear now and I wish Story would buy my more amiable piece—about a murder—but they won't I guess.[161]

Have you heard from Hubèrt. I guess you have his address, 1723 N St. N. W. Did you know he has a photograph in the 2nd International Leica Exhibit in Washington? Ain't that swell. He seems to have enough to do to occupy 24 hrs each day, and is getting more offers from publishers to submit things. He might get me a show there, don't know.

[. . .] Read "What of It" by Ring Lardner if you can get it. I read "Bury the Dead-"—swell.

Had fun at your mama's last week—fine food, drinks, and fettle. Am now bent for a high school graduation tea for Delia May Horton. Should have had my hair dyed white because they're going to call me "Grandma" anyway, but at least it's not a dance like Mittie's, so I won't be shocked.

Yours,
Verna Calhoun

Welty began working for the Works Progress Administration as "junior publicity agent" covering the work of government agencies all over the state. Although not doing photography for the WPA, she took her camera along when she traveled. Lyell had returned to Princeton, working on his dissertation.[162]

July 15, 1936 • Jackson to Princeton

Dear Frank—

What are you doing with John Galt. You must have been glad to see him, not to be writing former friends. I want to find out when you're coming to Jackson, so I won't be gone. Baker Wynne is coming through tonight he said, and will be back over Saturday. I was planning to go to N. O. but will no doubt see him anyway.[163]

We are in the Tower Bldg where you can smell trainsmoke, and how I've stood not going off on the choochoo this long I don't know, must be getting old. I am just like the Lady of Shallott, my only contact with the world is old drinkingcups which I toss from the windows in the direction of Hunt and Whitaker, the Noble Hotel, etc. There have been several fires out the window,[164] and if the Buckeye Cotton Mill ever catches fire this will be THE place to see it.

Within the office, things are not so promising. There are seven working here doing the job of ½. I write publicity, get it, paste it in books, retype it for files, retype it for mimeographs to the state dailies, retype it for the weeklies, and finally eat it. Last week 200 women came to town for a conference of WPA women and they all contacted me for various things like photographing a trailer from Tupelo, making bus reservations, driving a tour through the city, etc. You know how even one bridge-table of middleaged females can ennervate me. Multiply the exhaustion by 50 and you get a high temperature and bad dreams. Last night I dreamed Jack Benny was put in charge of this office. It ran along about the same.

Have you seen Lehman and Hubert. Wish all youall would come on home.

Spent the ¼ of July in V'burg with Nash, Leone and Barron. We drank large crude planters' punches, but I don't think I'd like them anyway. Would like a nice tall gin rickey every afternoon after work, to remove the spell, which as it is lasts until about midnight. I haven't been able to get any writing done, although am about six stories ahead in plans. So no telling what I will do—unrest, disgust, etc, will probably disfigure me for life. Pardon the demonstration.

Write soon. Come on home.

Thought you probably howled at Maddy Vegtel's takeoff on Cecil in the NYer as well as other Helen E Hokinsons, Arnos, Etc.[165]

Eudora

August 11, 1936 • Jackson to Princeton

[Written on page 19 of a newsletter labeled SR-4426, where articles are concluded that were started on pages 2, 3, 5, 8, 9, and 13. Articles are entitled "Road Beautification," "Writer's Project," "Historical Research," "Meridian Arboretum," "Crime Survey," and "Pontotoc Community House."]

Dear Frank—

When are you coming home. I bet I will miss you. Am making a few trips these days. In a few minutes set out for Newton, Meridian, Columbus, Tupelo, Clarksdale, etc. taking pictures. You should be along to help me collect Mississippiana, my side line. We take all the state papers in the office and I have already filled one scrapbook.

How are tennis, Sylvia Townsend Warner and Katherine Mansfield, none of which appeal to me? Tried Mansfield a few years ago and thought her a bit softy and sickly. Maybe one of my tough moods. [. . .] Probably unjust. [. . .] Have ordered the new Virginia Woolf novel[166] [. . .] Have been enjoying "Stories of Three Decades" by Thomas Mann, re-read "Death in Venice" which remains one of the best ever to my mind, and also like several of the others. Only a few writers remain landmarks for my continued sighting, he's one.

An alleged friend of yours, Blanchard Kennedy, came through here the other day. I drove him as far as Terry, he was hitchhiking somewhere, had just been to Mexico and wanted to go to Paris and hoped to reach New York in a few weeks. Seemed lamentably unstable, I was very unhappy over him, Willie Spann said all his family is screaming mad in Columbus, but although I doubt if he had even change of a dollar in his pocket he spoke for the most part of Mrs Harrison Williams etc and gave imitations of Freddie Bartholomew as Peter Lindamood does them. What is going to happen to all these boys like him. No security or grasp of anything (except Vogue) and not even a desire for any. I could tell it was a cult, of which Peter is probably the priest. Somehow to me the climax was reached when I happened to look down and saw he wore white moccasins. He was very sweet, but he ruined my day—imagine him after ten years. Where did you ever meet him in Columbus? Think I'll go up there and write a novel. [. . .]

Our new house is about half finished.[167] Hope it will be rented by fall, because part of the proceeds will go to me and I can take saved salary from the quote job unquote and go to NY.

Let me know when you expect to come to Jackson so I can plan not to be in Noxapater [*Mississippi*] photographing a cold storage plant. [. . .]

Write soon.

Eudora

September 2, 1936 • Jackson to Princeton

Dear Frank—

You are low-down not to come home this summer, everyone feels the ugly salute keenly. What is so attractive about John Galt, or could it be 3-storied house and 2 cars or 2-storied house and 3 cars. I suspect you.

Have you decided to go back to North Carolina [. . .] Bill Tichner came over Sunday with a fleet of Dwight Fiske records, which surprised me very much—I expected a whisperer, but he (DF) is a bombastic soul and I think very funny. Like Clarissa the Flea and Ida the Wayward Sturgeon with her badge "I Will Share." I played Bill my Lillie records and as much as he would listen to of Edith Sitwell. I have never yet been able to understand a word of Edith. Have you seen her new biography of Vic.[168]

Hubert says they are getting ready to strike in Washington. Think they should. You can't trust the gov't. [. . .] Lehman has been here for the last week though I haven't seen much of him, the family claiming him to the bosom all day and every night out at Maple Grove. He has so much in prospect for next year—contract with NBC, concerts with his madrigal group, records with Columbia, and maybe a trip to Russia.

[. . .] Have enjoyed few movies lately except Mickey Mouses, Silly Symphs, and Popeyes.

Write soon, I have been out on a trip but am back for a couple weeks and may soon be fired, who knows or cares.

Byebye,
Eudora

October 27, 1936 • Jackson to Princeton

Dear Frank—

Just as a Hallowe'en prank, I'm coming to New York for a week. Leaving here Thursday night on the midnight mail. Boo. You'll come down, eh? [*Lyell had remained in Princeton to complete his dissertation.*] I wrote Hubert I'd stay in Washington Saturday, but won't have a chance to hear from him, no telling where he'll be, eh? Why so much eh in here, I feel a draft. Anyway I'll get to NY Sunday and will stop at the Barbizon I suppose. Have a note there for me, friend, and plan to whip down the Avenue with me. Eh? Kachoo!

This is written on a specification prepared for me by Col. Hulen when I said I didn't know how I'd connect a victrola to a light socket at the Fair. An old army man.[169] This confused me so that I blew a fuse.

See you soon,
Eudora

In January 1937, Welty received a rejection that included words of encouragement from Robert Penn Warren of the new Southern Review. *Meanwhile, Welty and Lyell and their friend Robert Daniel amused themselves by creating a parody collection called* Lilies that Fester, *with invented authors' biographies as well as absurd creations.*[170] *The bio of one fictitious contributor, Erdine Praed, identified her as a two-year-old who had already published a prose work in German and a book of English verse,* Ballads in a Bassinet.

February 3, 1937 • Jackson to Princeton

Dear De-Lyellvely:

Erdine Praed is an honey. How did you ever bring her to being! I just typed her off and will send Robert and Hubert copies—have you one? She will do more to fester the lilies than anyone so far, I am happy to say. [. . .] I adore the titles of everything she writes, especially Ha Ha Ha and Ugh. Surrealist Bkfst seemed to spring from the heart, I must say, espec. the last 4 lines. Hymn is really cunning, and Credo is so direct! Of course the sonnet and its debts is I mean are, very veddy English, and that's what we editors are looking for. Thanks lots, and when Erdine writes again, regard L. T. F. as suffering an handicap without you send it in.

The clues to the treasure hunt threw me into a deep lurch from which I only recovered by going to see a return engagement of Horsefeathers.[171] I have been three more times, no matter what anyone wants with me, I am in Horsefeathers, thank God. Isn't it wonderful when Groucho folds his arms behind his head and says Oh the shame of it! Harpo is best of all times in this. A Day at the Races has been completed, I see by Variety, so we may watch for that now and get through another day.

I suppose you've been working hard on that man—YOU know who I mean. I've been doing lots of writing. The exhibit for Robbins, which may or may not have been where I sent you, was printed and mounted over one Saturday night—he was late sending me the necessary supplies. I hope it looked like something, I don't know what.[172] You say something.

I not only didn't make the pun Robert said I was probably making—I don't get it! Isn't that awful, don't tell Robert.

Do you ever read Stage. Ruth Gordon had a story in the Jan. issue about being in a show with Ellen Terry—every time Ellen Terry would speak to her, she would get so fussed she'd go into her dance, regardless of cue. Glad you saw the Bea Lillie show—it must have improved some since it opened in Washington. I heard Reginald Gardiner over the radio, imitating wallpaper, trains, etc. (He was sick when he was in B.'s show the night I went). My grammar is getting so wild I'd better stop.

A Civic Music Association is organized here—I don't know what our first concert will be—the committee phoned me the other day to see if I'd ever seen Angna Enters. I suppose you went to see Shan-Kar's new numbers. I wish we could get him, but he would cost too much.

Will try to get down a day or two of Mardi Gras next week.[173] Will postcard the pals. Write soon, and I love Erdine!

Tee Mitchell

In March 1937 Welty, Hubert Creekmore, and Nash Burger all had stories published in River: A Magazine of the Deep South. *(Another writer included in that issue was Peter Taylor.) Lyell, too, had been writing in Princeton. He sent more chapters of his dissertation for her to type in May. Welty may have shared this letter with another friend; she has written a few wisecracks in the margins.*

April 10, 1937 • Princeton to Jackson

Dear Miss Eudo:

Gangway for Galt! I'm mailing to you this A.M. the first 5 chapters which I have checked and rechecked until I've finally gotten them to the point where they suit me. So you get to work on them as soon as ever you can, but don't hurry through the typing because it must be done most carefully.

I'm afraid you're going to have to play a most annoying game of "footnote, footnote, who's-got-the footnote," because I've put a number of them on the backs of pages without numbering them according to those on the right side. In a few cases I've put two non-consecutive sections to be inserted on the right side on the back + footnotes. But don't let it puzzle you—whenever I've done crazy rearranging or put material somewhere outside the main text I've sprinkled a myriad of **** signs about—look ahead for them, + figure out the puzzle first before you try to type it out—errors will thus be circumvented. I've tried to spell out in brackets all the proper names + weird (Scottishisms) I thought you might be puzzled by. Look for them ahead aussi.

Page 31 is rather a good model for spacing   margins on both sides exactly right. If you wanted to , you could put the footnotes a little nearer the bottom here, + gotten a bit more on the page; but of course you don't want to run the risk of crowding them. Make a mark in pencil or something on the side of each page so you'll note when you get to the footnote danger zone. (A few footnotes are rather longish, so watch out for them. You know, of course, about starting over with 1, 2, 3, 4 on each page for the footnotes, + you handled the <u>Ibid</u> problem so well before I don't suppose I need to repeat that. (However, if an <u>Ibid</u> falls on a no. 1 footnote in any case in your typewritten copy, just look back + copy down the title in its place. Any questions?)

Of course remove all parentheses from the footnotes. I have a few parentheses I want left in the text (pp. 5, 59, 90, 107 and perhaps elsewhere)—Don't hurl them out.

I've corrected this part of the MS so carefully, I don't imagine many things will puzzle you, but I do apologize for all the jaggedness the multitude of carets (is that what they are? Fig. 1: ^) contributes to the general effect. But I repeat: don't type when flustered, stop when you're tired, + proofread with the phlegm of Mrs. Harrison Wms.[174] ([*In margin, in Welty's hand:*] some phlegm eh kid) (Prince L. knows her well, dined with her before recent sailing to villa in Capri where she keeps one Count Bismarck, a p-nsy, grandson of <u>the</u> Bismarck. Match with multimillionaire Harrison (her third, his second) a business arrangement whereby she brought the continental set + social prominence to him, + she obtained means to achieve the title which Prince L. says she richly deserves of the world's best dressed woman. She never has been known to wear, do, or say the wrong thing, + Prince L says underneath it all one feels she's cultivated it all in a rather artificial, deliberate way—"but what the hell—she makes a false gesture, yes, but it's a beautiful gesture + being with her is really an aesthetic experience." Further observations: "Any second rate movie actress is more fun to be with (construe "sl—p with") than a first rate society woman." ([*In margin:*] I could almost have guessed it) When I asked for examples, he began raving about Lily Damita—in such a way that I gathered Errol Flynn knows nothing he doesn't know about her.) ([*In margin:*] In other words, this guy with Harrison his chest wants Damita)

Well, back to business: let me know by penny postcard that you've received this precious document, + are guarding it with your life.

And I repeat this golden rule: When you have to go afield from the text for inserts, <u>don't forget to go back to the point from which you made the detour.</u> ([*In margin:*] All that jitters is not gold.)

Of course, I want the original MS back. You needn't make a carbon copy. Get enough paper so it will all be alike, + try not to change typewriter ribbon in mid-thesis. Put <u>Chapter 1</u> in capitals; the subtitles of chapters in little letters, but put a black line under them also (I'm waiting to do the preface last.)

There's more to come, of course, + I'll send it as soon as I get it ready—if you strike snags let me know, but don't telephone. ([*In margin:*] Or if I just strike.)

Your proposal of "Galt with the wind" was hailed by everyone at dinner tonight as the best pun heard on that much punned upon work.[175]

Endless gratitude,

F

In summer 1937 The Southern Review *published Welty's story, "A Piece of News." They would eventually publish six more. Welty continued her photography; a news article reported she'd be exhibiting photographs and giving a talk on "art photography" in November, and* Life *magazine published six of her photos.*[176] *The following month, Welty seems to have visited Lyell en route from New York; her letter enclosed a program from Benny Goodman's January 16 New York concert.*

January 26, 1938 • Jackson to Raleigh

Dear Bessie Culbertson the communist's daughter:

What a lovely time I had in Raleigh! So rare. You were all lambs—tell each one. I shall look through the postcard file for the best to send to the boys. Your mother I've talked to on the phone but haven't been over there yet—I shall soon. I gave her whatsoever was of good report, as Miss Boyd would have done. I don't know why highschool is so with me this morning, last night I dreamed about hunting my seat in the balcony (Miss Stokes wouldn't let me sit there until I was a senior, for talking) and finding it! o boy! there it was! it was thrilling. it was where i could look down at miss hampton, my crush. Please send me some themes to read, by the way, all of you. [. . .]

It has been terrific weather, including cloudbursts, dust storms, and freezes. John [*Robinson*] came in during a cloudburst and went the next day up around Tupelo, where I saw in the paper there was a small cyclone, and the next day was our dust storm, so I turned on the porch light, but he didn't take advantage of the dust for some reason. [. . .] John and I woke up Joe and MF [*Joe Skinner and Mary Frances Skinner*] around one o'clock the other night and went over the new house, which is very spacious and nice. They have moved in, of course, and there is a cabinet for bridge trophies. [. . .]

Tell everyone, Anna, Mrs. Riddick, Wallace, Katherine, Baker, Lodwick, and the niece of the woman who drowned in the lake and made pg 23 of the New York Times, my best hello. It was all lovely in Raleigh.

Yours,
Troy Funchess

That spring, Lyell completed his PhD. The society column of The Clarion-Ledger *(Jackson) congratulated him on his degree on May 14, 1938. The following week, the columnist congratulated Welty for a less definite accomplishment: "And to Miss Eudora Welty we present an orchid for the splendid short story she wrote and its accepted publication."*[177] *Lyell traveled abroad that summer and sent Welty a postcard from John Galt's birthplace in Scotland, followed by this one from London.*

July 26, 1938 • London to Jackson

Dear Fay Cook:

Thanks so much for your letters + the Wodehouse + the Cutting cuttings. Will leave tomorrow for Paris via Bruges + Ghent, + read the W. on the way. Do send the rest if it's good. I went to the ballet for the 4th time in a row last night—twice to Covent Garden, twice to Drury Lane—Only had to take myself once! You have no idea how wonderful everyone has been to me here. I can't bear the thought of leaving.

Spent hours in the BM [*British Museum*] yesterday [. . .]. Saw E [*Edith*] Sitwell[178] at the Noblissima Visions—7th Symphony of Beethoven, ballet evening—she looked like the other side of this—incredible! [*The postcard reproduced a Persian painting from the British Museum's collection entitled* The Ascent of the Prophet Muhammed to Heaven.]

Xxx

George R—

The next letter refers to the "Crisis" that occurred after Hitler announced plans to invade Czechoslovakia on October 1, 1938. The following undated letter is likely October 6, given its references to the weather, Neville Chamberlain's speech, Welty's Junior Auxiliary League activities, and the State Fair.

October 6[?], 1938 • Jackson to Raleigh

dear frank—

am i supposed to address you the way you wrote it—"224 woodburn road, anna being 225"? might cause talk among the postmen between here & raleigh, beginning here—glad you're settled, and now i have somewhere to send the clippings i clipped for you [. . .] yes, hubert left for columbia—when i found he was really going, i tried to switch around and be encouraging, but still doubt the wisdom—but who knows, he may like something about teaching—nobody's heard from him—we had 2 or 3 parties before he left and he took off on the midnite mail in good spirits with everybody waving at him—i don't guess he had time to stop off there—[. . .] be sure to send me some interesting themes this year—The Crisis was terrible here, was it there? everybody was so miserable, even belhaven girls on the bus would say "gee that old bad hitler, i'd jist like to break his neck!" did you hear chamberlain's address—so touching and wonderful! i love him.[179] mrs annie parker was sitting on her front porch and said Well, this time next year, Hitler'll be sitting on this porch."[180]

[. . .] If you see Bill Ticknor tell him Ginger Ray is back with the Chez Paree show on the midway next week[181]—or just tell his sister to tell him, just want to get the message to him. It is awful—nobody that likes the fair is in town this year. Nash, who always went twice every day—nobody. willia and i didnt paint a screen this year for "best other than named" and somehow the spirit seems to be lacking all around—

i agree with you that the records you gave me are not very hot—go hear fats waller doing "i'm the shiek from araby" with good piano in "in the gloaming" on the back—victor—at spiers the blonde (sends you love, mentions you every time i go) has a grand no. of "Sleepy Time Gal" arranged for tapdancing—over ½ of it is made up of silent stretches that you have to fill in with tapdancing—big exit finale—a decca, hear it at mccrory's—i have toscanini's new mozart symphony—a negro man was playing on the black keys in spiers and joe asked him if he could read music—he said "i can read it—but it hurts my eyes." isnt that grand. i know a new game that clarence moore, a g-man, taught us at a party—instead of shooting at us—the raleigh group could work it up i think—you make these fast and furious—the answer has to be two words rhyming with each other—like "heavy child actress?—burly Shirley"—what a girl puts on to go to church?—sunday undy"—etc—just the rhyme is all that counts—the sense can and should be mad—[. . .]

spent the last two days collecting dough for ywca, because the jr auxiliary [*Junior League*][182] just pledged me—the first thing i had to do, go to a luncheon at the ywca,[183] dolly [*Wells*] and i fell out of a swing and did back summersaults—didnt look very good—i had to make a speech, too, didnt like that—i didnt know whether to join or not, but they say no one has ever refused—i'm just not a joiner—[184]do you remember shady rest? hit the jackpot there not long ago, when john was here—people clapped me on the shoulder and led me to the roulette room[185] [. . .]. this month i'm in the Parararari̇e Schooner and Sou Rev, two sad stories[186]. [. . .] i've worn the scarf from London and people all but applaud. if only i had something to go with it! dolly gave me a record of the lambeth walk and taught me the walk,[187] so now i have that, and the scarf. tell anna, lodwick, baker and everybody hello [. . .]—be sure to read "out of africa"—

write soon—what do your pupils think of Europe? it is still just as hot here as when you were here, and everybody is nearly dead.[188] with this thought i will close.

always remember harriet fletcher. the most expensive middy blouses in JHS and i don't mean perhaps.

Harriet Fletcher[189]

March 29, 1939 • Jackson to Raleigh

Dear Alfrieda Misterfeldt—

the records are so fine—and so cheering, being signed Ford Ford[190]—thanks—my favorite is the Maxine [*Sullivan*]—night and day—i love the way she says "why is it so that this longing for you follow wherever i go, in the roaring traffic-boom—" the whole record is grand—of course, bea [*Lillie*] is good too, and everyone around is trying to get all the words, which always takes a little time—played it for willie spann the other day during intermission at pingpong, when her resistance wasn't good—it nearly kilt her—next i like best "i cry for you" and "time on"—and they came just as i was having my swing reaction—what all did you do in n. y.—write and tell us—i am sending a card which i bought in tougaloo[191]—just at random, supposing it will fit in somehow—the woman said the "Hello Sweetheart" cards went just like hot cakes and i had to choose between "Happy Easter" which was good, and "(something) Mother Dear!" (Mothers Day) and "Top o' th' marnin'" (5c discount, acct St Patrick's day being over now)—but Tougaloo is a mine of greeting cards, it's a pity—i just bought robt penn warren's novel [*Night Rider*] to read, have you seen it—jeanette macdonald is singing here tonight!!! but i'm reading—armand coullet[192] phoned me to come take her photo for the paper but I didn't have any lights—somebody else did, and what a smirk! I would have gotten one showing her teeth I think—

write soon,
congratulations! from,
charles galloway.[193]

April 15, 1939 • Jackson to Raleigh

Dear De Los Garret—

I loved the Bea Lillie show, feel like I been—Seta, Willie + everybody too—How could I have not mentioned Never Again first? I love it—Thanks for Never Again—"Time On" is "My Hands," silly—Lehman was here 2 days—would have been here 4 days if it wasn't for plane sickness—(Is that clear?) [. . .] Unwin of London sent back the MS—a nice note—said the sales of short stories etc—FMF never sent anything but the records—never wrote—I wrote him + said if he couldn't make the stories salable then I guessed nothing ever will, I started to say, like Gosky patties![194]

[. . .] Charlie McC is grand when they saw him in ½ + Fields is grand in the chariot in "You Can't Cheat an Honest Man"[195]—Did you hear the Marxes last Sun? They tore it up grand—when R U coming home?

Yrs,
Robbie Dunford

Ford Madox Ford's efforts to help Welty find a publisher were welcome, but he was ultimately unsuccessful. In May 1939 he wrote that Knopf was considering the collection of short stories, but Ford died in June, and Knopf passed on the collection. Even so, Welty's star continued rising. One story was chosen for the Best Short Stories of 1939 anthology, another for the O. Henry Prize Stories of 1939. *New York Times* critic Robert Van Gelder mentioned her story in the November *New York Times Book Review*, and John Woodburn, an editor for Doubleday, Doran, paid a visit to Welty in Jackson that November. Despite this recognition, multiple publishers who reviewed Welty's work in 1939 told her they could not accept a collection of short stories by a writer who had not first published a novel.[196]

Jackson society, meanwhile, was only vaguely aware of Welty's career. A 1939 news article, "Provisional Members Use Talents Widely," said of Welty's ongoing participation in the Junior Auxiliary League: "Eudora Welty was trained in Journalism and Publicity Work at school and although she enjoys all types of service, she especially enjoys publicizing the various projects that the Junior Auxiliary sponsors."[197] In December, the Jackson newspaper reported that the Fine Arts Club would be discussing *The Best Short Stories of 1939*, which included a story by Welty, which it misidentified as "The Green Curtain."[198]

So then Uncle Rondo says, "I'll thank you from now on to stop reading all the orders I get on postcards and telling everybody in China Grove what you think is the matter with them," but I says, "I draw my own conclusions and will continue in the future to draw them." I says, "If people want to write their inmost secrets on penny postcards, there's nothing in the wide world you can do about it, Uncle Rondo."

[. . .] But oh, I like it here. It's ideal, as I've been saying. You see, I've got everything cater-cornered, the way I like it. Hear the radio? All the war news. Radio, sewing machine, book ends, ironing board and that great big piano lamp—peace, that's what I like. Butter-bean vines planted all along the front where the strings are.

Of course, there's not much mail. My family are naturally the main people in China Grove, and if they prefer to vanish from the face of the earth, for all the mail they get or the mail they write, why, I'm not going to open my mouth. Some of the folks here in town are taking up for me and some turned against me. I know which is which. There are always people who will quit buying stamps to get on the right side of Papa-Daddy.

But here I am, and here I'll stay. I want the world to know I'm happy.

—"WHY I LIVE AT THE P. O.," *A CURTAIN OF GREEN AND OTHER STORIES*, 1941

Chapter 2

1940–1949

DURING THE 1940S, BOTH WELTY AND LYELL EXPERIENCED INCREASING PROfessional agency, just as the war took control of their lives and almost everyone else's. As Welty was breaking into the New York publishing world, her brothers and many close friends were being drafted. She was in love with another friend from Jackson, John Robinson, who was drafted in 1941 and, from 1943 to 1945, stationed abroad in the Army Air Forces Intelligence, witnessing the invasion of Sicily and sometimes accompanying pilots on night missions in Italy. Lyell was able to avoid the draft and continue his teaching for almost two years before he joined the Army Air Forces in 1942, eventually securing a military intelligence assignment. Although he never saw combat firsthand, he went to Germany after V-E day to gather Germans' accounts of the impact of Allied bombing, for the United States Strategic Bombing Survey. After returning stateside in 1945, Lyell served for several more months. In the fall of 1946 he began teaching at the University of Texas, where he would spend the rest of his career.

During these years, in addition to writing hundreds of letters to friends in the military, Welty wrote fiction—*A Curtain of Green* (1941), *The Robber Bridegroom* (1942), *The Wide Net and Other Stories* (1943), and *Delta Wedding* (1946)—as well as book reviews, occasional essays, and invited lectures. She won several awards, including Guggenheim fellowships in 1942 and in 1949. For several months in 1944, she worked for *The New York Times Book Review*, hoping she might somehow get an overseas journalism assignment, but was unsuccessful, and she did not see Robinson until late 1945 when he returned, showing signs of depression. After the war, with travel restrictions eased and her brothers safely home, Welty spent more time away from Jackson, in New York, New Orleans, and San Francisco. After publishing *The Golden Apples* and receiving a second Guggenheim award, Welty embarked on her first transatlantic trip in October 1949.

Welty's writing career gathered momentum while the United States was undergoing the largest military mobilization in history. In 1940 she secured a literary agent, Diarmuid Russell, who would become a close friend as well as an effective advocate for her work in the literary marketplace. She met him in person on a trip to New York that summer, then enjoyed a fellowship at the Bread Loaf Writers' Conference in Vermont.

August 17, 1940 • Middlebury, VT, to Jackson

Dear Frank,

Too bad if you don't come up—it's so grand up here—good places to swim, one with 3 waterfalls—The atmosphere is a little odd—rare, literary, talky when you wish it were quiet—all sorts of people—The fellows go over to a secret place + drink with the staff—before every meal + after the night lecture—

A lot of notes are taken at the lectures—I have made a collection of spied-on notes:

"Character alters events
Event " characters
Greatest burden that we can carry:
Superiority"
(Like a song?)

"Read—then wait 2 hours + let it settle"
"Swinburne made use of vowels + consonants for effect."
"Feel bones of story."

A lot of old ladies are here, they change hats for every meal—I'm in the cottage with the Nashville novelist Brainard Cheney + his wife, lots of fun, + the wife of the Charlotte, N.C. judge who got Vincent [*Rousseau*] out of the shooting scrape[1]—also Carson (Lonely Hunter) McCullers, who is an odd bitter 22-year old with long hair, bangs, cigarette cough, boy's clothes, + a new pal of Louis Untermeyer the wit. Went swimming with the group yesterday—Herschel + Norma [*Brickell*] arrived 2 days late + I've just caught a glimpse—he doesn't come to the hideout, so far—Katherine Anne Porter is to be a guest lecturer next Wed. night, 21st—wish you could come[2]—Auden next Saturday—

In N.Y. I had a wonderful time with my agents—weekend in the mts. + Cafe Society, Calypso, good things—Will tell all. Diarmuid Russell is a wonderful Irishman indeed—Hubert I saw in Norfolk + we had a good time—He + James may come up next week-end.

Must go to hear Miss Mirrielees, who wiggles her nose[3]—

The new Fats sounds superb—thanks—I have found 2 Fats devotees here—

Yours,

Eudora

Welty had attended a Fats Waller concert in 1939 that inspired a story she workshopped at Bread Loaf, where she was told it was not publishable.[4] *Four months later, however, Russell managed to place "Powerhouse" in* The Atlantic, *a few weeks before landing a contract at Doubleday for her first book,* A Curtain of Green and Other Stories. *Welty continued writing new works and getting encouragement from Russell, who assured her that she need not try to write a novel if she preferred shorter forms.*[5]

In summer 1941, while in residence at Yaddo, an artists' colony, Welty often spent time with Katherine Anne Porter. Welty's photographs from that summer show Lyell with Porter and John Woodburn, Welty's editor at Doubleday. Porter had agreed to write a preface for the collection, introducing the new writer to a national audience. Porter did not complete it on time, but her endorsement was so important that Doubleday was willing to postpone the book's publication until she was finished. The following letter reports Porter had finally completed the preface, some of which Lyell read while visiting at Yaddo.

September 15, 1941 • Jackson to Raleigh

Dear B.Y. Glover,

[. . .] It has been terribly hot here except for many fine nights. Nothing much has been happening. Tom Sancton, Seta's friend (they're to be married Christmas) has been here and we have sat around on various porches drinking beer, etc. John Robinson was up last weekend and we did the same with Old Taylor's [*bourbon*] which has gone up to the sky out to the Pocahontas road—Mister Beasle's has been closed, didn't you-all know?[6] I had been tired of swallowing things from Yaddo and hadn't done a bit of it since. Katherine Anne wrote me that her eyes had given her hell but were better now. She finished the introduction, the date is definitely November 7, and John Woodburn tells me you are coming to the party and that I had better. Don't know yet, but glad you're coming. The introduction is long, xxiii pages, just about what you read when you were up there, all sort of joined together, and a nice job, modesty forbids me to say more. She says she is whizzing away on the novel too so I guess all has been resumed and is well with her.

I think I know what you mean about the "plot" business which is lacking in her work, but it is not so much a lack of a thread of action as a lack of action itself which would be visible to the eye. Instead she depends on a thread of emotion, which is like the working of a miracle if it works [. . .] For myself I must have at all times something visible or apparent to the other senses, either in a dual play with my story or completely identified with it—it is a form of projection and I could not get the story out at all without it. [. . .] and if I develop my way of doing it would never get to be like hers. Diarmuid writes me Harper's Bazaar took First Love and The Purple Hat both—wonderful news, especially in the case of First Love, which I didn't think anybody would take at all. I've finished a story since I got home, called The Wide Net, with the Natchez Trace in it for a line or two. I want to have a second book ready by the time this one is out, or almost, and the stories are all in my head so it is just a matter of getting them written.

I had the most wonderful letter from Jose de Creeft[7] which I will send you to look at but send it right back. I had despaired of writing him anything in words, so I just said a little, but enclosed a clipping from the paper advertising a "no slip, no slide, no spill" watermelon tray, which was made with the drawing from the patent, every part numbered up to about 50, very complicated looking, and told him this would be for his bicycle—he already had his racer's bicycle covered with gadgets and carry-alls.

Saw you mother the other afternoon, and one afternoon saw Louis ride by in a wrecker (he had given out of gas on the N. Trace) looking proudly out and smiling. There were some gardenias in your house, don't you wish you could have whiffed them.

Write soon—you must be busy getting the year started. It's still too hot to write a letter and say anything here.

Yours,
Maude Williams
& her long long plait

Beyond Lyell's classrooms in Raleigh and Welty's typewriter in Jackson, world events were exerting a greater influence. In anticipation of entering the war in Europe, the United States was reinstating the draft, training soldiers, and producing munitions, tanks, ships, and planes. "Jackson is filled with air bases, air schools, air fields, and barracks and tents," Welty wrote Russell in September.[8] Lyell received his draft notice in November 1940, but obtained a deferral to continue teaching at NC State College. In Welty's next letter, written the day after the Japanese attacked Pearl Harbor, she wondered how much longer he could be spared.

December 9, 1941 • Jackson to Raleigh

Dear Frank—

How is it with you—deferment, does it still hold?[9] I hope nothing calamatous [*sic*] applies to it. None of these words look spelled right and perhaps they aren't. To think Sax Rohmer and all those boys were right when they kept hissing about the Yellow Peril.[10] Jackson seems very calm, [. . .] but Mother of course has her ear at the radio all day & night. I have been going out to work in the yard in absolute & final preference to any of that, so far.

My books finally came from Doubleday and I wanted to send you one but by this time you may have gone to NY or something and it might miss you so I will keep it till I hear from you when you are coming for Christmas or whatever. I do think it is pretty and want you to see it before it is such old hat. The reviews seem to have been pretty good all over, except for one written by Rose Feld for the Herald Tribune which was a strange strained effort and I didn't agree with any of it even if it was unflattering. (Hard to believe.) If you go to NY go by to see John Woodburn. Mrs. Herbert is doing OK by sales here I think, and Kennington's has now put 4 books in the window along with 50 other objects with a sign "VOGUE'S GIFTS UNDER $10.00"—you know, highball glasses, shoulders-length pink gloves, etc.[11] It takes a set of 4 books to make this gift and if the competition with non-books is not too terrible there is one chance in 50 that the set will be bought, by a few. I know some people that are just as likely as not to buy books as double-size coffee cups and saucers, of which you get only 2 for the money.

The New York trip was swell, and the party was a nice one, at the Murray Hill Hotel, I was surrounded by a little cordon of friends so the rest did not scare me. Lehman came, de creeft, Nalbandian, Dolly, and of course John [*Woodburn*], Diarmuid and Henry [*Volkening*]. The only glamorous (I protect myself with a sic) personage there was Viki Baum, who looked like Grand Hotel with a lot of velvet makeup, tasseled eyelashes, and plush bosom.[12] Everybody just sat around or stood around and talked and there was a bar in another room and two soldiers came, thinking it was one of those hospitality stations, and went with us all evening, if I remember even to the Village to eat. We went to Café Society afterwards, a few of us, so the party lasted into the morning. The next day I went to Henry's for dinner and then home with Diarmuid for the weekend. The Aswells (she of H. Bazaar, he of Harper's) were at Henry's, also Joseph Kesselring and Peter Monro Jack (that I always thought was 3 people trying desperately hard to make a living by reviewing every book published, but he is a little tiny argumentative Scotsman) and their wives. Mrs. Aswell wore a leopard jacket (real) and a leopard top to her evening gown (unreal) and was gay and invited me to lunch and couldn't remember whether she had and asked Diarmuid on the phone and he said she certainly had.[13] So I went to lunch, after numerous phone calls from her secretary to the Bristol (getting Dolly, and asking: "Is this Miss Welty's maid?" I told Dolly she should have replied, "No, Miss Welty is my maid") and changing times, and finally we went to the Passy where you have probably been and Kay Boyle came also wearing unreal leopard. They were nice to me at the office and showed me all over and I got to see George Grosz's original drawings for my story last month, which I hope you loved in reproduction. Let me see. All this time I have been waiting till I had free time to write all, and now it has left me. I got interviewed by Robert van Gelder but it was not scarey, just like a date—he took me to a place to eat down on the waterfront, some ancient & noted place which I have forgotten the name of, and then out driving up the Hudson, and was very nice. I don't know whether it has ever been written up or not, but I did not mind it as feared.[14] Lehman gave me such a nice cocktail party, with all the good foods & drinks well known. We missed you there as everywhere.

The day I left, John [*Woodburn*], who had been on jury duty the entire time of my stay, and whom I did not see, but only flowers coming instead, took me (correct this sentence) to the Algonquin, at which, he declared, I should have been staying instead of the Bristol and to which, he averred, I should stay on my next trip although I laughed. There he pointed out imaginary celebrities and when a horrible looking dark bellboy walked through he muttered "Saroyan."[15] We came nigh missing the train, taking flight down the Pa. stairway and just leaping onto the train with baggage sailing after me onto the platform as it pulled out. All the way there in the taxi the driver was saying "Maybe <u>you</u> think you are going to make this train." "If we miss it," John told me, "I'll come with you." I rode all the way home with a lady from Boston who would say, "Do they celebrate Christmas in Mississippi?" She was going to Wesson.

I went to New Orleans Thursday to see John Robinson and drove back with him Friday night for Anna Belle [*Robinson*]'s wedding Saturday. It was a nice wedding, and we had a good time. N.O. was being very tropical with azaleas in bloom and everything green. I was eating lunch under a palm tree in some court by myself, (while John was still coming from Florida in an airplane) and some middlewestern people went through looking and stood right over my plate and stared at the food (trout marguery) and one said, "They eat this kind of hot food all the time here." I looked up and said, "We can talk, too." Touristas all over the place. I bought Seta a wedding present and myself a little map, and Katherine Anne some vetivert roots she asked for, but nothing else. We went around, and had dinner with John [*Robinson*]'s friends the Beins that he lives with, and out to nightclubs, but I hadn't been to

N.O. in a year or more and it got me down, I stayed in bed yesterday coughing and sneezing. But the radio was too much, so am up today. Write soon and give the news. Tell me if you want the book there or when you come home.

Yours,
Eudora

Welty enclosed poetry Lyell's father had written in celebration of her book's publication.[16]

There is a pen pusher Eudora,
As a writer she is a top-scorer.
Her "Curtain of Green"
Is a beauty, I ween,
And surpasses a Northern Aurora.
- - - X - - -
This girlie is surnamed Miss Welty,
So tall and so lissome and svelt-e.
For her stories so good,
Such a la carte food,
All critics have praise and no pelty.
- - - * - - -
There is a girl in our town
And she is wondrous wise.
She wrote some dandy stories
And won O. Henry Prize.

We are fond of our Eudora
And so's the whole darn town.
She is a home-brew product
Of very high renown.

Her name and fame have gone around
This fine old land of ours,
And placed her high, both far and near,
With literary powers.

And so may our home-brew girl
Intoxicate the nation,
And sell a million books, or more,
Around the whole creation.
—"ROYALTIES"
11-25-41 G. Garland Lyell

January 27, 1942 • Jackson to Raleigh

Dear William MacMurtry,

[. . .] Hubert has been in N.O. seeing about getting a commission in the navy (lieutenant, which comes from being an M.A., somehow, outside reason I think) because he has been called up for final examination in the army. He will know soon, I suppose. You must lie low. Edward's number came up again too and though his doctors say he should not be in the army he is now automatically 1-A; he is trying to get something in line with drafting or map-making, but will probably end up in the heavy artillery, they don't seem to be making much effort to consider the individual at all any more. Walter has a nice little dependent, which will be good for one year, I guess, then become null & void as far as deferment goes.[17] Mother made a good crazy remark the other day—"I think less of this war every day." [. . .]

I have been reading Biographia Literaria and how piercing and true and often inspired it is.[18] Also I love the footnotes—like this one: "April, 1825. If I did not see it with my own eyes, I should not believe that I had been guilty of so many hydrostatic Bulls as bellow in this unhappy allegory or string of metaphors! How a river was to travel up hill from a vale far inward, over the intervening mountains, Morpheus, the Dream weaver, can alone unriddle. I am ashamed and humbled. S.T. Coleridge."

I love the wonderful tempo of those times (especially "at a time like this," favorite phrase of the radio commercial).

Had a govt. postcard from Vincent [*Rousseau*] saying he is now transferred to Moultrie, Ga., a place where he feels he is going mad. He said a native standing on a scaffolding watching an army plane do stunt flying fell off and sued the pilot of the plane.

I'm enjoying the Mozart and especially since the radio has been fixed—it is beautiful. What a disappointment that I did not win a Magic Brain Victrola and $200 worth of records as I expected to when I wrote 25 words on "I like the Victor Record catalogue because." My entry was so good and so condensed that I wish I had it back now, I would get Diarmuid to try to sell it to the Reader's Digest.

Had a postcard from Seta with a picture of the Boston Massacre. She wrote, "This sort of thing must stop!" Her address is (Mrs. Thomas Sancton), 13-A Ware Street, Apartment 3, Cambridge, Mass. [. . .]

Eileen McGrath, the girl I was staying with in Mt. Kisco when you phoned me last summer, says she is coming through here at the end of February. She is the one that works on syphilis.[19] I told her if she came here and did anything conspicuous I would pretend I never saw her before, I hope she doesn't hire a hall and threaten our Bailey Avenue set with extinction if they don't wake up, or something. She is now with the miners in Ky. And is going to N.O., a rich field.

The MSCW Alumnae honored me at a meeting at Miss Etta Mitchell's.[20] They asked me to speak to the girls on the famous people I had got to meet, and I declined, so they said they were going to review my book and read a story while I was present. Miss Etta met me at the door murmuring that I would be allowed to sit in a chair that was brought over from England by her ancestors in 1675, one of a set of 18, to give me some idea of the size of the room, and ordinarily she allowed only brides to sit in it. It was placed in the center of the room with the MSCW Alumnae around in a circle, very trapping. They had sent me a pink corsage. I moved back by Miss Gayden. Then somebody got up and said she just couldn't write anything about the book so she was just going to ask Janie Melton to read that thing in the front (the blurb on the jacket). So that was the criticism, and then Janie Melton read Worn Path. I sweated and afterwards they passed around a "plate"—they were being nice to me but I suffered. Mrs. J.T. Calhoun was not present, she is the only one I had absolutely known would be there, and I didn't know any of the others, except Miss Mabel Bridges and Miss Gayden and Flo Scott.

An old lady in the Research Club told me that her sister had once written a book that she would like for me to see—she couldn't afford to have it printed in New York, like me, but had it printed in Natchez, and a picture of their mother was the frontispiece, and the name of it (this is what really made me jealous) was "Wreaths Around Natchez." She said it had a world of things in it, and I will bet it did.

Sent John Woodburn a wire on Jan. 19 saying "Happy Robert E. Lee's Birthday, and was this delivered on appropriate blank?" and he wired back "Same to you and many of them and it wasn't." But otherwise have had no communication from Doubleday since I left—don't know how the book is going but I guess as expected, or not as expected, bound to be one way or the other. I come out in H Bz next month with First Love. I had a wire from them too asking me if I had any good source for saying Burr was tried at quote Washington, Territorial Capitol of Mississippi unquote. I wired back I did, and it was a good thing, as I would have hated to send back their money. I think they are going to use another story, The Winds, soon, but they have not quite all decided to, they and I both thought it was not very clear so I did some more work on it and it is now better from my point of view. I think the Wide Net at the Atlantic and it is the first of the old friends D.R. has tried it with, having tried to get me thousands of $$ for it at the slicks and they would not offer it. I'm glad you liked Hazel, but I wanted the story to be the river-drag—[21] I had at the beginning some idea of writing it as another story, Hazel's, and she is so complete in my head that I may have unconsciously led the reader to expect more divulged about her. What would be some good names for little negro boy twins? I am beginning a new story but am as usual stumped because I can't name the characters to suit me. Do you like Pearl Lee and W.D.? A.C. and D.C. would be good. The worst I thought of was George and Norge, those are out.

The new Dr. Fell is out, "Death Turns the Tables" and I am midway through it. It is not a sealed-room mystery, and this baffles me at the outset. Don't tell me that Mr. Carr has run out of sealed rooms.[22] Not one decent movie has been here except "Suspicion" and I missed that. [. . .] I had a letter from Elizabeth Ames, the lady that runs Yaddo, and she said she didn't think K.A. would get into her farm until spring, and hoped she would not, and she didn't think she could cope with it all alone out there in the ice and snow (neither do I). She said KA has seemed very tired lately. I have no doubt she is. I wonder if she has scratched at "The Itching Parrot" yet.

Dolly has a job in N.Y. with a man on 42 st. and Bway, isn't that wild—he goes between the govt. and the movies seeing about our morale—ugh. For instance, she says in a new Donald Duck, Donald fusses about paying his taxes, but then Uncle Sam comes along when he needs protection, and he is so grateful and happy he rushes fluttering down to pay gladly. Isn't it too much, that we must infect ourselves even through D. Duck? However the job itself that Dolly has is probably pretty interesting.

Spring is nearly here, and we have one camellia in a flower to the extent of one blossom, and some crocuses and snowdrops, and at Mrs. Anderson's old house on State St. those two early flowering quinces are in full flower. In a few more weeks it will be wonderful. Where are you going for Easter vacation? Why not come to New Orleans with Eileen and me (is that the end of Feb.?) She says her pal Wystan Auden may come down, if it coincides with his Easter vacation, from Michigan. I will just wait and let that take care of itself, I guess.

Yours,
Beauty Fewell

In March 1942, Welty was awarded a $1200 Guggenheim prize.

April 7, 1942 • Jackson to Raleigh

Dear Frank (Groboski)

Many thanks for the letter with the news about the possibilities about you and the war. It does sound hopeful and I keep fingers crossed that the right thing happens [. . .]

The N.Y. trip sounds as crammed as usual. [. . .] It was wonderful about your going by Doubleday and giving them hell about the Robber Bridegroom. They will probably think you are the first of a posse from my home town coming up there to get them, if they don't publish it. I had a letter from Henry Volkening (of Russell and) whom I wrote about it, and he said he wished he could buy you a drink for doing that, and then maybe you would go back and do it all over again, as a different man.[23] [. . .]

This is a wonderful spring and you should see it here again, the magnolia fiscatas are opening and roses beginning to bloom. The camellias were never as wonderful as this year—I hope you didn't really miss seeing them altogether in Charleston. I work in the yard all day every day, and hope to have some good things in time, besides muscles.

Miss Fannie Thompson called me tonight and said, "I want to tell you that you are an Outstanding Person, you have Gone to Town and it hasn't Gone to your Head, you are Not Snooty." (Capital letters hers of course.) She said, "I like to see the ones I have watched grow up Amount to Something. Success is important but it is the real Dough that Counts and you have got the Dough. What I see in you, is Balance." Isn't that wonderful! She was screaming these fine things out almost too fast for me to remember them to report to you but I wanted to give you a few good reactions. Aunt Mary's: (I said, "O Aunt Mary, I've got a Guggenheim!") "A Guggenheim what?"[24]

Hubert is still here—I take it the navy has to run up a few uniforms before any more yeomen can begin work. Edward has a job in Memphis with the U.S. Engineers, Military Division, in his line of work which defers him for 6 months and I wish for longer, but of course they may simply draft him out of the office before the 6 months are up. Little Vincent [*Rousseau*] is now a Sergeant! Still in Moultrie, Ga. Lehman seems to have a good chance of getting into the Navy.

Many hopes and wishes for the good place [*military assignment*], and go down and make them do what they said, don't let there be any catch in it. The task of keeping up school work and trying to manipulate all these strings, threads even, must be enormous and hard, and I hope soon something definite and good will happen and settle it, as well as possible. [. . .]

Write the news when it comes, and good luck. If I go to N.Y. before your school is out I'll drop by, but that's only a vague thought—haven't yet decided on any trip, or on anything. In fact you could have knocked me down with a f. I wish I could take the $$ and buy all my friends out of the army & navy, ransom money. But at least, good luck.

Yours,
Juanita Seale

Late April 1942 • Jackson to Raleigh

Dear Ernest Gosling,

Thanks so much for letters and clippings. [. . .] Have you been back to Charleston yet? I hope the promises they made you there will hold and you will find out soon just exactly what you will be doing. If the suspense and uncertainty can be ended, that will be something. Walter has gone to New Orleans today to be examined for the Navy and hopes for something in statistics or mathematics, but is eating bananas and water to weigh enough and I don't trust that. Edward has a job with U.S. Engineers at Memphis (you know, U. S. E. D. signs) and is either to be given a uniform and continue, or be sent to the army, he doesn't know which, but says one or the other will be soon. Hubert is still here and says it may be 5 months before he is called. I don't see him much as he seldom comes by. Flo Lehman said Lehman expects to be in the navy immediately—Juliet went to N.Y., then accompanied him to Chicago, and expects to pack his clothes for him for the navy at once! But I think the thing he is hoping for hasn't been definitely settled at all.

As to my trip to N.Y., I don't know when I'll go, the family affairs being more or less in a state of uncertainty, and so much having to be done each day and every day in the garden. I'm sure it will be before June though, probably in May. I would love to go somewhere in Vermont or the mountains [. . .] I will let you know as soon as I can make any plan, and it will be fine to stop off a day or two in Raleigh. [. . .] If you are still reading murders, try Nicholas Blake (Day Lewis) on "The Smiler with the Knife" and "Shell of Death," and I like Simenon, though many don't. He comes out in those 25c magazines editions now, "The death of M. Gallett" etc. Other than such, I have been reading "Mont-Saint-Michel and Chartres," [*by Henry Adams*] and writing a story (I am still tired from it, if this letter sounds languid) which I enclose my copy of, so don't lose it in case I have to send for it. I might think of ways to improve it. See how you like it. Write the news when you hear any. Good luck.

Marguerite Beckermann [. . .]

May 6, 1942 • Jackson to Raleigh

Dear F,

Glad you like the story—which you did more than I thought.[25] Isn't it a bad title—I can't think of a thing, but am still trying—Do you have a suggestion—I too wanted to build up the scene between Livvie + Baby Marie + did in fact, originally but toned it down again for it got too much emphasis—The comments were helpful + I am going to do a little revising before it is printed—Atlantic took it + it's coming out in July issue—so the title will have to come quick—I hit my forehead every day but nothing comes out—

[. . .] I hope you're getting along with the application + it will come through, soon—Walter has applied for something [. . .] having to do with spotting planes or something—his statistics + math being the basis—I talked to John R. tonight + he has heard nothing from his application in the N. made months ago + the draft is coming up. Jimmie Wooldridge is in Peekskill, N.Y. Vincent R. is a sergeant—about maps + charts—Mims [*Wright*] may go overseas in 2 months—Willia [*Wright Bennett*] is going to Pensacola where John [*Bennett*] is stationed, in 3 or 4 weeks—All unsettling + I have my fingers crossed so much I couldn't uncross them, for everybody. Good luck, let me hear—Thanks again for reading; + criticizing story + I am glad you liked it—will write when I'll pass through—

yours,

Eddalee Bodker [. . .]

August 21, 1942 • Jackson to Princeton

Dear Frank,

[. . .] Your trip sounds just grand and I enjoyed all the cards so much. Hubert had brought the brochure of the same voyage over to my house while he was here [. . .]

John Robinson has been here on furlough and is now with the Air Force. I hope to God something good will turn up for him soon though. Jimmy Wooldridge will be home on leave the first of next month. Hubert as you no doubt know has been sent to Corpus Christi and Judge C. says he has gained weight and feels much better now. He looked like a wraith when he was here, especially about the ankles. Edward is suspended in the air, between his job with the War Dept. and the draft, with wires going back & forth about him all day between one office and the other, and nobody knows what will happen.

Edna Frederikson[26] was with me 6 weeks and I was glad to see her and yet glad when she left—I guess the strain of the past weeks, the army and all, kept me from being quite the perfect hostess I really am, but it was just the wrong time for me to think of anybody's novels in any minute degree, especially when I'm not given them to read, only told about them before they're done. I think writing should be seen and not heard. Edna is very nice and I wish you could have seen her. She's gone down to N. O. for the time being. She has written an excellent book, though not sustained or containing any plot, which all publishers like but want her to revise. She is on No. 2 now and nobody's seen it.

I hope soon to clap eyes on the photographed thesis. If you don't get copies to give away, you could send one around the country where you've got friends, like the real live mermaid with the wrist watch, on a freight car. I hope it looks nice and satisfies you.

I couldn't read the card just when you got to the part about the records. But what I thought I read sounds fabulous. Glad you're stocking up. Afterwards, let's all just gather and play them and play them. John sent me a beautiful Bach aria one day that I keep playing, and I play records all the time now and work in the yard and read poetry and make rugs—have to. When will you hear any news about yourself in the army, please let me hear as soon as you can.

I wrote a story about Rodney—that is, "modern" Rodney—but can't tell yet if it's OK or not.[27] Have been reading proofs on the Robber, so I guess they won't take back the contract this late. My book C. of G. sold to John Lane in England, to be published sometime next year, isn't that nice—I didn't even know Diarmuid was working on that, until one day he sent me the contract with a little 'x' where I was to sign my name. 'Livvie' was supposed to be out in July Atlantic but hasn't come out till yet.

It's hot and rains every day and yet there's just a smidgen of fall in the air. Do you think you might come home for just a bit before long? [. . .]

Write soon and give the news. If you see John W [*Woodburn*] again talk longer and cheer him up if you can. When he is high he is high, and low, low.

Do you remember the pent house.[28] The little boys in the neighborhood told mother they were the Junior Commandos and were taking it over for collecting scrap metal. She was helpless—but one day asked them not to trample the flowers. The leader replied, "The Jr. Commandoes don't walk on the flowers, however I think the Black Legion was in here this morning."

K. Nalbandian wrote me K. A. P. was back in Yaddo and would not be in N.Y.C. this winter after all—three cheers—but that's all I know. Write soon.

Yrs—

E—

September 4, 1942 • Jackson to Princeton

Dear Frank,

What a wonderful two volume surprise—they are beautiful and terribly welcome and I'm so pleased—thanks ever so much.[29] So far I have just gazed at them out and in and opened them at random (Dorothy is always on a walk of course, whatever sentence the eye lights on) and looked at the beautiful drawings and maps scattered all through. But that was the first day and today I start reading them, the first volume first—have always wanted to see them but didn't much imagine I would. I got the cards from New York and am glad you're still having a vacation but it will be nice to see you here. [. . .] Seta is having some kind of operation in New York today [. . .] I hope she is getting along all right. Jimmy Wooldridge is here on leave from guarding N. Y. harbor and last night he and Charlotte [*Capers*][30] and I talked till one or two o'clock, Charlotte in fine form. Willie Spann and I went to New Orleans for two days this week—that's why I was late opening the books, they were here when I returned—but though we ate fine and drank fine I felt the worst depression on account of John being gone. But it was nice, really, we ate at G. and A. and had drinks at Pat O'B's and stayed at the M.[31] I sent Diarmuid's little girl and Katherine Anne each a little tiny painted chair out of a shop on Royal St. Had a nice letter from Elizabeth Lawrence, several in fact.[32] Are you going back through Raleigh? Jimmy couldn't get a reservation down on the Southerner so he took the Tennessean, which is a streamliner down through Chat. and Memphis, but it takes longer than the Southerner by a long shot. But easy reservations. Haven't heard anything from Hubert but Judge C. said he was gaining weight and liking it in Corpus Christi. Have a good time and come home soon. Thanks again for the beautiful Journals.

Yours
Eudora

In September, Lyell enlisted at Camp Shelby, Mississippi, and began waiting for a slot in an officer's training program, hoping to receive a noncombat assignment overseas.[33] *He spent a few weeks in Camp Shelby before being sent to Florida. Welty wrote him at his new address, beginning and ending the letter with more Jackson names.*

November 1942 • Jackson to Miami

Dear Elizabeth Parsons,

Needless to say I was pleased greatly to hear you were in Miami Beach for the season, which I know started with the first Planters Punch you had. Judge phoned me when they got your letter, then yours to me came next day. Mother has got it in her purse now to read in the beauty parlor! so I will have to answer it out of sections committed to memory. The set-up does sound as good as it ever could. All I hope is that you stay a while. The swimming etc. ought to make up for everything endured at Shelby for those bad weeks. [. . .] Let me know what the training is like when it starts and you have a moment to write. Have you any idea about what you might be going into, or do the tests etc. that will begin to come upon you daily decide things for you?

My brothers are both in Virginia, within 65 miles of each other, but I don't know when they will meet. Poor Edward, the day he got out of the hospital, went out for training which meanwhile the others had got a two-weeks' start on, and in swinging over a lagoon on a rope he fell wrong and broke his right arm. It is enough to make you cry—he's right back in the same ward again, and will be for 3 or 4 weeks. He feels that he is missing out on all training and any opportunities. But he is a lucky person in general and this may be some form of good luck in disguise—can't tell about that. Walter is at Fortress Monroe, as suspected, and we haven't heard much except that he got there and the training was about to start. [. . .]

My copies of the Robber came yesterday so I will get one off to you today. I'm glad you have given the other to the Army, for it will have such a good influence over Camp Shelby and teach people to mind their manners. [. . .]

I'm glad you think the book looks OK (except for the jacket, with which I agree).[34] [. . .]

The Victrola came and is wonderful. It plays everything like new. I think it is pretty too. Mozart sounds like nothing ever heard before in this house.[35] [. . .]

Must go now. Oh yes, I had a letter from Chas. Henri Ford—as follows—I haven't the nerve to send that to be returned, and I want Diarmuid to see it too—"Dear Miss Welty: I have been meaning to write you for a long time, ever since I read the story in Accent about the second-hand clothes.[36] The next number of VIEW will be on and of Americana Fantastica and I wonder if you do not have an incredible story which you would send us? We go to press Nov 10 and the issue will be our most elaborate to date. Incidentally have you seen View? Please let me know where to send you copies . . . Did you ever see my other magazine Blues which I edited from our homestate (Mississippi) a long time ago? As most of our articles etc are illustrated, if you have a fantastic MS to send, perhaps you could suggest some illustrations? Looking forward to hearing from you, Yours with great admiration (signed in purple ink). PS Another Mississippian, whom you perhaps know, Kennedy Blanchard, will also be represented in the Fantastica: with a statue of an Homonculus . . . Your Robber Bridegroom sounds marvelous and I am looking forward to reading it—have you an unpublished 'fairy story' which you would send View?"

Didn't we know Kennedy Blanchard under the name of Blanchard Kennedy? Or am I fantastica? Must really go now. All luck and take care of yourself and let me hear all.

Yours

Maggie Stewart

PS Livvie is out in Atlantic [. . .]

November 25, 1942 • Jackson to Miami

Dear Frank—

I saw the beautiful Galt [*book publication of Lyell's PhD thesis*] and it overwhelms me to be in the dedication—thanks, thanks—but it's undeserved—far too generous on your part—but of course I am proud. The book looks elegant, beautifully made up and the binding and title page most tasteful. [. . .] You should be proud of the book, and you should see how proud your family is—and as I said, I too. [. . .]

I just got your letter too, and I'm glad you've moved back to civilized quarters again. What kind of work are you doing—or is it anything specialized yet? I hope you get to stay there for the winter. [. . .]

Thanks for the clippings. Li'l Abner[37] I will send immediately to Edward—it was grand. [. . .] The Robber is selling all right, they tell me, and they said at R&V that John [*Woodburn*] phones in play by play descriptions of each sale, practically—up to Nov. 11th, Armistice Day, sales were 2,329. I must send you the Hearst review, but I haven't got a copy of it. I copied it and sent it to Hubert the day it came, and it said among other things "Snuggle down into the Robber Bridegroom and kiss old Sourpuss Reality goodbye for a couple of hours. This has got the Crazy Beauty. And what is the Crazy Beauty? you ask. Etc." by Benjamin de Casseres.[38] A hooper dooper. [. . .]

Must go now, but thanks again for all. Good luck down there—write more soon.

Yours,
Eudora

[. . .]

Welty had written in August about playing Lyell's record collection "afterwards," but the end of the war was a long way off. The Japanese were capturing British soldiers and conquering more territory, General Macarthur had been evacuated from the Philippines, and the US government was placing Japanese Americans in internment camps. Robinson and Welty's brothers were unable to come home for Christmas. Rationing had begun in the US. In early 1943, Welty was lending her support, somewhat reluctantly, to the war effort, writing promotional materials for the War Savings Committee in Jackson.[39]

March 3, 1943 • Jackson to Charleston

Dear Frank,

How are things going—send a report on the special duties—I was glad to get the cards and to hear life in Charleston will have some existence for you—even camellias, maybe—How have they endured the cold waves? Write me about them.

[. . .] . Edward was home on a 5-day furlough and it was grand. He had been given 3 furloughs before this, but this was the first he has got. Always just as he gets one foot on the train they jerk him back, and this time, as he was getting in a plane he heard that 50% of his camouflage outfit (not he though) had just been taken to go across to fill out a marching unit. Since getting back he has been issued mosquito helmet and arctic overshoes, but thinks nothing, just cancels them out. He was crazy about his work and seems to have been doing ideas, specifications, and renderings, as well as booklets needed for the truck drivers—elementary stuff, such as drawing of a truck casting a shadow beside a box casting a shadow with message, "Your Truck casts a shadow just as this Box does, and can be seen from the air," etc. He is in barracks with a bunch of Italians who sing opera in the shower and all are like Chas. Atlas above the belt and dwindle down below with short legs and he says one, the most like Atlas, flexes his biceps and makes a full turn every night, after taking off his clothes and before getting into bed, flexing, flexing, for everybody. John is leaving OCS, this is Graduation Day. Then he goes to combat intelligence school in Pa. Without a leave yet.

We've had the limit in weather now—seven cold waves, and all of them after I thought it was spring and had done much work in the garden. Much was hurt—bulbs in full bud, sap in everything, all camellias blooming or far advanced so nothing much in the way of cover could help. Last night it was 16 again. We have had wonderful camellias though. I hope those in Charleston did well. We got a new spray and pump outfit for Xmas, and the other day Mother and I had a Mack Sennett 2-reel comedy in the backyard with it[40]—squirting the wrong way, getting us drenched to skin and in eye, etc. and I wish there had been somebody to see it, it must have been grand. [. . .]

I saw "The Glass Key" and thought it was good. I think Veronica Lake is O.K. myself, and Alan Ladd fine. See her in "I Married a Witch" which has good things in it, Benchley, and wonderful near-wedding scene, Rene Clair. It was the first time I'd seen Veronica and I thought her a wonderful witch, but Charlotte [*Capers*], who was along and loathes her, said she's always like that, witch or not, and I guess she is, but she just suits Glass Key and the like. You can miss "For Me and My Gal" though some old Ruth Etting songs are in it, also Gene Kelly, also Ben Blue, but a mess—ends with World War One, than which o can more profoundly depress me at this point.

Write the news soon and I hope all of it is good, or better.

Yours,

E

PS—Tacky news—I have to copy over all my stories [*The Wide Net and Other Stories*]—as the MS was lost in mail—out of magazines and such, law me.

March 26, 1943 • Jackson to Charleston

Dear Frank—

This is from J. Woodburn and I'm sending yours to him—simple, isn't it! he says "Enclosed tracts—I come from across them" and says I can hand them out in front of the cinema—"let him who is without cinema cast the first tract." How is the work—the set-up sounds swell. I hope you get it going the way you want it. Write developments.

Hubert got his commission, Mrs. C told me, and he is very pleased. Don't know what next.

MF is going to meet Joe [*Skinner*] tomorrow—she was going to drive up and I was going up with her—picking up John's car on the way—but the scheme fell through when Joe wired her to come ahead on train—probably changes up there. Will write later if anything happens.

Did you know Willia is near you—address care Gen. Delivery, Beaufort, S.C. She sometimes comes down to Charleston or is planning to, I think—J. B. [*husband John Bennett*] is going to be away about 3 months, I know no more. Worth [*nine-year-old daughter*] wrote me today and said P.S. "Please write me some letters because I feel as if nobody had ever heard about me." She enclosed riddles. Sample: "Q. Why is the letter F like a banana skin? A. Because they both make all fall."

Was asked to write a piece about [*Jose*] de Creeft—could <u>anyone</u>?

I haven't a copy of the Times review I did but they cut out all the critical (sic) parts—for instance I was mainly concerned with the question, Was the hero feeble-minded? (Literally) I said this should be told clearly yes or no to the reader, but they cut that out. The book had good things, I thought.

This is just a note—must run to express office before it closes to send my ms. up for the second time—if it is lost too I will expect a note from the black hand in the mail saying "Final Warning, quit writing this book, hear?" [. . .]

Yours,

Eudora

Welty visited New York in April and was able to see Robinson, who was in Pennsylvania for military intelligence training and made a visit to the Russells in Katonah. Lyell, too, saw Welty during her New York visit. In the following letter, he wrote Welty about rereading Robber Bridegroom *shortly after* The Philadelphia Inquirer *had published an abridged version in its Sunday supplement.*

May 1943 • Charleston to Jackson

[. . .] The other night—Saturday—I did what I've been wanting to do a long time—read the Robber straight through again. Again thanks and renewed praise. I enjoyed it even more the second time. Sunday I took the Smiths a copy of A Curtain in honor of their kindness to me on so many occasions. The Sunday I came back from NY was the Sunday the Philadelphia Inquirer published the supplement by you, and it was fun to see peoples' heads in it on the coach to Washington and beyond. I captured a copy to bring on with me. Where are you now? Write soon and tell me about Walter, Edward, and Hubert. Where is Hubert? It's been a month since I had a line from him. Any summer plans, or will you stay at home? Write soon and tell more about the NY sojourn. [. . .]

Yrs,
F

May 19, 1943 • Jackson to Charleston

Dear Frank,

The pictures came safely and I was proud to get them—they really are grand, and thanks very much. I still can't decide which would have been my choice for one, so it's nice to have the two. Mother, Walter and Mittie think they're wonderful pictures.

Life has been hectic around here—Edward was home on a short furlough, and Walter, along with almost every man in his V.O.C. [*Volunteer Officer Candidate*] contingent at O.C.S. [*Officer Candidate School*], was returned home, to wait on the next step—I guess he'll be drafted in as a Corporal with basic training completed, and no way to tell what they'll do with him. It hurt him pretty badly, I think, but he doesn't show it and is back working until he gets called.[41] [. . .] I had fun in N.Y. after seeing you. Went to the country for two weeks and worked in the garden, painted porch furniture, etc. etc.[42] The children are wonderful now—you should have seen them on the Easter

Egg Hunt. William, 2 1/2, would find an egg and cry "Look! Look!" without moving, and Pammy would come loping up, seat low like Groucho Marx's, and snatch it from under his eyes. John R. came out the first weekend and we all had a picnic—J. Woodburn, Henry, and a British writer named Christine Weston, whom I didn't like, were out too, and Henry's wife and little girl. The weather was perfect both weekends, though it blew and blasted in between. D. came home early at night and we had a nice time—mostly sat and talked.

It's been so hot since I came back—I've been doing much needed work in the garden, when I could—and had publicity for bonds etc. waiting for me. Did I tell you Harper's Bazaar commissioned me to do a piece on Rodney? I don't know how Diarmuid got that! But I think it will be fun to write, even if they don't print it.[43]

I was glad to hear reactions of train crowd to Robber B. and glad you still think it stands up. I had a funny letter from Wm Faulkner, signed simply "Faulkner" and beginning "Dear Welty." He said, "You're doing alright. You're doing fine. Bought your book called Green something, read Robber Bridegroom and thought of Djuna Barnes, just as you were thinking of Djuna Barnes when you wrote it. Can I help you? I will be at Warner Bros. until July." Strange stuff.[44]

[. . .] Edward said at Richmond they are teaching their illiterates to read, and he saw a text book. Under appropriate, colored pictures the text ran:

> This is my RIFLE.
> My pack is HEAVY.
> The food is GOOD
> I like my LIEUTENANT.

He also said on the train with him was a firey-haired lady who talked forever about her son in the army and finally Edw. asked what her son was in, and she replied, "He's in the audience." We decided it was ordnance, but she was very complacent. Mittie said at the U.S.O. a lot of Japanese soldiers going to Shelby stopped by and gave her dozens of postcards each to mail. She took a gaze at a few and all were messages like, "Hello, Fat Stuff," etc., and were addressed to Japanese girls who must be in internment camp, because all had numbers. Worked in camp laundries.[45] [. . .]

Yours,
Eudora

[. . .]

May 25, 1943 • Charleston to Jackson

Dear E,

[. . .] I don't understand about Walter at all. Does that happen to many V.O.C.'s? Was he in OCS? You didn't tell me he was. I should hate to have to get out of all this unless I could stay out, but I don't see that it's anything to be embarrassed about and any getting home to a job that can be picked up where it was left and the wife and family is a real blessing. Does he have to wear Khaki? And GI shoes, etc.? Please explain.

[. . .] Amazing Faulkner letter. "Can he do you a favor?" I'd write back and say stop having the nerve to mention or think of you and D. Barnes in the same second. He's really crazy.

Savannah is grand. I know you'd love it. Sunday we spent at the beach, going out via Bonaventure Cemetery, tremendous, drenched in moss with everything so overgrown that it's more like a park. It—and the whole city—must be beautiful at azalea and camellia time. Bushes of both everywhere. We thumbed our way out and back (18 miles), having good luck in getting direct, immediate connections both ways. I got on the Champion at 6 and was in Charleston an hour and 45 minutes later. Fine weekend.

Must run to calisthenics (triweekly) now.

Yours,

F

July 3, 1943 • Charleston to Jackson

Dear Aline Hewitt,

[. . .] The OCS papers have left the Base, and several days ago I received a postcard from the Adjutant General's Dept. in Washington telling me that my papers had been received and were being considered. I put down AAF Administration first (Miami Beach again), the AG's Classification School second choice, and the AG's Administration school third. [. . .][46]

Charleston is still a miracle of loveliness to me. Church Street or Legare in the late afternoon or the Battery are out of this world, and I love them dearly. The Villa Margherita, now a Merchant Seamen's Home though many of the old tenants keep on living there, has reopened its dining room to anybody in uniform. Low prices and better than average food; so you'll find me there when I eat in town. Last Sunday I met lots of nice people at Mona Martin's mint julep session after church. She and her mother have one of the most charming houses on East Bay and the Robber is covering that waterfront now.

[. . .] I believe I'll ask for an early August furlough; but I can't even ask until the end of July. It's better to ask suddenly a day or so before you want to go; then they don't hem and haw and decide not to let you go.

Must go to lunch. Let me know when the Rodney piece is to appear.

Yours,

F

P.S. Before sealing this my AG application was returned—"no openings in classes at present, but this will not hinder you from applying for other officers' schools." Now you see why I hate to mention things like this until they're settled. The AG gets separate application and never like to be 2nd choice, I'm told. [. . .] They keep them till they rot, holding fast to them to fill vacancies they hear about. [. . .] Please say nothing of all this. I haven't even told the family I've applied for anything.

July 29, 1943 • Air Forces Officer Candidate School, Miami, to Jackson

Dear Ernestine—

It's amazing—got here Sat morning + I'm glad we did because we had the afternoon + evening free for shopping—had to buy $60 worth of shirts + pants (6 each of those) + matching accessories—

On the train coming down I ran into Norman Creech of Guthrie, Ga who worked at the Bell Telephone Co. in Jackson for 5 months + lived at Seta's—awfully nice!—+ we're doing everything together. Grand to have somebody congenial to laugh and groan with [. . .]

Powerfully hot + we drip + sweat all the time. The confinement isn't at all bad, because there's so much to do—+ outside we at least look at + pass by all the hotspots—

I really like it, though as John said, staying awake in classes (?)—all under palm trees outside so far—is the great problem. 4 old students of mine are in the new class!

Much, much to tell, but have to put the lights out—Write soon, please, and tell me the news. I haven't had a line from anybody yet—

Yrs,

O/C [*Officer Candidate*]

Allied forces were attempting to weaken the Axis by taking control of Italy, a campaign that was expected to take months. Welty wrote Lyell a birthday greeting after receiving a letter Robinson wrote as he was moving through the Italian countryside with the infantry, eight days after the invasion of Sicily.[47]

August 7, 1943 • Jackson to Miami

Happy Birthday—I should have remembered it before the day. How is everything? Write when you get a chance. This is not a real letter (or could you tell?). Will write soon—have to get in the car, Helen [*Lotterhos*] is blowing horn to take me to town. Nothing funny has happened. Except here's a clipping.

John's on the front in Sicily. I got a letter yesterday—written July 18th. Feel very upset. Edward got married last Friday—and Walter and Mittie are going to have a baby. Big items for a little note.

I hope all is well. [. . .] Wish I could send you a singing telegram with "Officer Candidate Lyell Frank H." worked into the last line. Try to imagine this to yourself.

Yours,
Eudora

Well out of harm's way, Lyell missed his friends (asking Welty, August 5, "Please write a lot") but weathered his OCS experience fairly well. He described it in more detail after seeing a film about OCS that Welty had seen earlier that summer.[48] *The film was probably* Wings Up, *a short documentary created by the Office of War Information and narrated by OCS graduate and film star Clark Gable. The opening scene shows a man in a fighter plane who's exhausted, unable to read a map, and sure to lose his crew and expensive aircraft—a nightmare that could be avoided by weeding out all men who are unfit for this demanding role. The rest of the film—a remarkably tedious sequence of scenes—demonstrates the rigors of the new OCS at Miami.*

September 7, 1943 • Miami to Jackson

Dear Eula McClesky,

Many thanks for letting me read KAP's letter—How I wish she could pull herself together, make an end or two meet—It seems pretty hopeless at the moment. The Wide Net will now be the best book of the fall season, not The WN and The Safe Harbor.[49]

As you see from the enclosed they did show us OCS Miami style if we wanted to look at it. I did + ran across the street to the Governor to look. There are basic similarities of the present life, but I'd say that in general what looks impossibly exaggerated in the film isn't nearly so much so in reality now. We move quickly on the stairs (to get to our rooms + collapse), but never run up + down them. The white collar on the bed does not have to be within a gnat's head of certain dimensions. (I now live in the Adams Hotel instead of the Tyler—had to give up my perfect bed for a sort of damask upholstered divan daybed which never has to be made up at all. I just cover it with one sheet at night + throw the pillow on + there's my bed—Sheet + pillow go into a small chest in the room in the mornings)—

The parades are as exhausting as they look, but they must have been even worse when the school was 3 times as large as it is now + you had to wait for other squadrons to form, pass the reviewing stand, etc. [. . .] bracing (as shown in the film) is now out—[. . .]—There will be posturizations, but on the QT + no foolish questions asked + all v. corrective + informative. Contrary to expectation I found that the bracing doesn't, or didn't, even faintly resemble hazing. I call hazing mild torture, beating with paddles or worse, + deliberate intent to make the victim look foolish. Posturization for me was done in dead seriousness here the first 2 weeks + after that the middleclassmen who did it before asking the "when is the noon balloon from Rangoon" type of question (Ans: "Delayed by typhoon") At that point they get awfully disappointed if you don't laugh + it's no strain at all—just a bore like so much of the routine here. I found early in the game that the more horrible I made myself look (i.e., like the people in the film) the fewer questions I was asked—Another good trick I found was just to begin reciting answers I knew, then passing bracers felt I was properly wound up [. . .]

Sorry to bore you with all this again, but thought you would like to know my reactions to the picture.

Classes never look that way to me: immaculate OC's enthralled by an expert intelligent whiz of an officer [*illegible*]. We're soaked to the skin in the heat, sleepier than ever, 3 or 4 people are always doddering in their chairs, + though I now have 3 or 4 capable instructors I have encountered no officer yet that I would call an inspiration. [. . .] Everything John told you about the place I ditto. Leaving, getting out, never thinking of the place again, is our goal. [. . .] There are some sad, stupid souls here + I wouldn't call the average squadron an impressive body of men by any means. The business of the navigator losing his way in the plane, etc. hasn't even a faint connection with our business. Navigation isn't taught here, but any OCS candidate faced with reading any map after our so-called "course" in map-reading would be just as baffled as the man in the film when faced with a decision to be based on knowledge gleaned at OCS. [. . .]

Must go to lunch—

Yrs

F

[. . .]

October 11, 1943 • Miami to Jackson

Dear Doris Comby—[50]

Open post on the bivouac has taken us to a [*joint?*] down the road for the evening—simple but they have got Myers rum—I like the bivouac—it's grand to be in the open + informal + away from all that fife + drum corps stuff + the things we murder with endless repetition—If only the mosquitoes would leave us alone all would be well. [. . .] Speaking of advts, one on the road out here says "Miami Shores Memorial Park—Exclusive—Futuristic—Eternal"—!

Yrs eternally,

F

October 13, 1943 • Jackson to Miami

Dear Marion Tobias,

The Schubert Trio came safely and is just magical—I have just played it again and will probably play it another time as soon as I finish this. Thanks very much—I don't see how you find time to dash a record album into the mails like this but it is grand to receive such. Hope you get a furlough when this is done and can hear it.

Out there where they have rum and futuristic eternal cemeteries must be at least nice for being out in the open. When is OCS over—I lost count. [. . .]

Walter got off for Tucson yesterday. He & Mittie have been staying with us for ten days or so, also Smoky the spaniel, and it was a big vacancy when all departed (Mittie of course just back to 1607 Pinehurst). Walter looked so nice—Mother was showing him around and when she got to the cook, the cook said, "Yes indeed!"

Hubert wrote me from New Cal [*Caledonia*]. and seems to like it all right. He wrote the family a long long letter (illegible), telling of the voyage and the islands, which I am sure were Fiji as he said natives with big spheres of hair were beating the hammers with old oil tanks when they landed—a form of welcome he presumed. [. . .] . He told me about the initiation when they crossed the equator, how they cut their hair and ducked them in water and threw eggs in their faces. The stars and constellations are all so different which must be strange.

Pamela Travers[51] phoned me from Santa Fe the other night and said she would come by here in a fortnight. I'm sure she assumed Santa Fe was just around the corner from here, being just so far from N.Y. She's bringing Camillus—that will be fun, he is an enchanting child. I can't think of anybody for him to play with since the Lotterhos children have gone—he's 4—but think I will give him Cornelia Long and Ellen Holmes and Mary Ricketts and they will average up for him maybe. [. . .] Went to Leone's party for Mary on her birthday and took another set of pictures with somebody's camera—can't buy films except by luck. It was a nice party, like the one you were at the year before, Mary was excited and very cute. It was attended by the same circles as last year. Ellen Holmes was there etc. Much sliding on slides, swinging, pulling curls, slapping, eating.

The Fair is here! Nash came over the other night—he is teaching radio code at JHS—the only trouble is, they learn it quicker than he can. He and Marjory want to go to the fair and I suppose we will ere it is over. Willie and I were supposed to go tonight but it is raining this morning and we might not slush it. Have to sell hamburgers Thurs. and Sat. nights, ugh. The World's Only Hawaiian Midget is here—and I dread to see whether or not "Remember Pearl Harbor" is in sequins on her behind, as they say she does the Hula.

[. . .] Must tell you that Mrs. Parker [*Jackson librarian*] thinks that Martha Hamilton's Baha'i is "the Antichrist!" She is not going to put their magazine on the front of the rack, regardless of what they want. She could spit on it.[52] (This from Nash.) Did I tell you Martha has come back to Jackson and is going to have twins? Even she is staggered.[53]

Must go now—many thanks again for the music. Oh I forgot to tell you Katherine Anne is closing South Hill for the winter and is moving to a little inn near N.Y.C. where she hopes to do a stretch of work and then "look about for a job"—sounds bad. She sent me her new vintage of hot pepper, sherry, and rum sauce—hotter than the other—very good. She says nothing about the novel. I worry about her.

Yours in the golden circle 4th degree,

Miriam Ezelle[54]

October 25, 1943 • Miami to Jackson

Dear Lucy Van—

The New Republic has just arrived with the bird pageant [*"A Pageant of Birds"*]—delightful.[55] Still don't understand why T. Sancton puts your stories into such ungrateful [*reviewers'*] hands.[56] The review of the Net in the last issue but one was no reflection on you, but on them + the author (who is he, by the way?). John Woodburn sent me a copy, which will be the Army Net until I send it to the Smiths in Charleston, for whom I have earmarked it when ballast (pardon, please) must be dropped. You can't keep anything but the OCS essentials in these closets (restrictions + the fact that there's little room for everybody's belongings) + I know that it will fall into kind hands on Church Street. Don't tell J, however.

Please send me Hubert's address again + letters from him to the family if they'll lend them to me to read. Hope Walter is getting along all right.

Had a room at the Roney Plaza + a hot bath (3 of them!) this weekend. Nothing but cold showers here for the Army until Dec. 1. Good food + drink + an amusing floor show with the boys during rounds on Sat. night. Today we paraded in a downpour—wet clothes spread everywhere tonight—An upperclassman now, but still tired. Intelligence is the stiff course here, but I do like it a lot. Praying to go to H'burg [*intelligence school in Harrisonburg, PA*], but counting on nothing. Must to bed.

Yrs,
F

Lyell's next letter updated Welty on his next assignment and on his sighting of the Duke and Duchess of Windsor, who had been testifying in a local murder trial involving one of their friends.

November 24, 1943 • Miami to Jackson

Many thanks for the letters + the book. Today things became definite. We can leave here Nov 29 + are free until Dec 11 when we must report in H-burg by noon. Am thinking about what to do in the Roney Plaza bar now—home first anyway. Saw the Windsors here yesterday afternoon—The trial over, they can go home. Her right stocking was crooked, otherwise she was completely up to expectations. Flash: W. [*Walter*] Winchell [*syndicated gossip columnist*] is at the next table.

Yrs,
Robert Rush

Lyell spent a week of his leave in Jackson, as Welty reported to Robinson: "Frank came by and blew the horn—he had some furlough gas and we rode out the Canton road to the turnaround place—the fall colors a little misty and dim in the late light."[57] *From Pennsylvania, he reported on his quest for living quarters in a town overrun with military trainees and their families.*

December 15, 1943 • Harrisburg, PA, to Jackson

[*Written on Harrisburger Hotel stationery*]

Dear Emma Maud,

This is the world's coldest hotel. Stayed the first two nights in a room overlooking the river, with no way to close the slats on the door + clung to the blankets for dear life with no results. Good preparation for the huts, where I have caught the cold I have now anyway. 10 minutes after I started looking I found a house with much extra room rented (mainly to teachers in the school) by Miss Mary Sachs who has a large ladies' store next to this hotel. A gray stone exterior as on Jefferson St or such with a completely done over interior à la House + Garden modernity—black floors, potted greenery, blond furniture, thick woven rugs, mirrored [*lamps?*]—everything new throughout—10 bucks a week. The only catch being that I should have had to share a room with somebody + maybe 2. Haven't met any of the occupants, but I'm sure they'd be OK to live with, + one of them is a Lt. Will Robinson's friend in Miami told me to look up! The Adjutant of the school thumbs-downed me when I asked to be allowed to escape the huts—said all single men had to fill them up. Maybe I can work something later. I shared the secret find with 2 OCS friends (married + thereby vaccinated against hut life) + they couldn't believe such a place existed when they saw it, + now occupy quarters for 2 which Burgess Meredith + Gilbert Roland lived in when they were here. I shiver now + am sick when I think about what I see about me now—maybe I can wiggle out later, will try.

We were processed Sunday AM, finished by noon, + told we didn't have to reappear until Tues at 9 Am. I looked at the [*Pennsylvania*] Capitol after dinner (did you see it? Incredible in spots. The all-out chandeliers of bronze + cut glass in the House of Reps (20 tons 20, in wt) are so godawful that they're a must for the H'burg visitor), listened to the symphony + took the 6:30 for NY to spend Monday shopping. You're supposed to receive a Xmas book from Brentano's (where I bought Louis (!) The Great Image.[58] Had to give it to a family member—so much did I like it). After giving Jackson addresses to the clerk, I looked across the way + there were Joe + M. F. down on a 3 or 4 day pass. A long chat followed of course. [. . .]

The school is overcrowded, but really wonderful—in spite of the huts. Am delighted to be here. The address you know [*Robinson studied here in 1942*]—So let's hear from you.

We get out at noon on Friday for Xmas + ditto for New Year's—the latter a very handsome surprise to me.

Yours,
Lee Gainey[59]

Lyell spent Christmas in New York with his eighteen-year-old brother Louis.

December 27, 1943 • Jackson to Harrisburg

Dear Frank,

The beautiful Leonardo came three days before Christmas but stayed sacred under the tree till the appointed morning—and then opened at our tree, during the eggnog and everything. It is wonderful—I've been looking at it slowly and mostly at stolen times, because Mother has been in bed with flu and Walter & Mittie staying here, and am not through it yet for the first time, but it is wonderful to have it. Many thanks. I hope your Christmas was a good one in the city—write about it when you get a chance. Of course we missed you badly and the day was a little on the thin side. I went over to your house in the afternoon but everybody was gone—the Christmas array was on the piano, all looked festive, and a big envelope shining on top with what i feel was a poem for the day inside, from Judge—will have to learn more. [. . .] Seta and Tom came over Christmas night late and we had a drink out of my bottle of Bourbon I got from the feathery lady at Hickory Grove Tourist Cabins. [. . .] Did I write you about the horrible night of The Living Christmas Tree [*"Singing Christmas Tree" was an outdoor choral concert presented by Belhaven College, across the street from the Welty home. Singers stood on a multitiered platform shaped like a giant Christmas tree.*]—the carols were beautiful, and I heard yours and Jimmie's and all's favorites wishing you were listening—but Aimee phoned me that 8 members of the Shands family were coming. Aunt Mabel, Harley's bride, etc. All. Dr. S. But all didn't come in—the house wasn't close enough to the Tree, Aunt M. said. Aimee left with them all after she had insulted all my invited guests all around, to Seta she said "Is that your husband? I never did see him—forgot to come to your wedding." So as soon as she left we lit into all the Shands—the genus—and in the thick of it Harley poked his head in the door silently and said "We thought we'd come back." (he + bride—very nice) Willie brightly told a long tale of Pete Slater's Egyptian marriage and how they went gazelle hunting on their honeymoon, and we played 2 games of Peter Coddle—but we didn't sleep of course, wondering. Christmas was cold, dark, rainy, and still freezing at night, etc. [. . .] I'm glad the school satisfies you. Write soon.

E

January 18, 1944 • Harrisburg to Jackson

Dear Robbie Dunford,

Many thanks for sending the DeCreeft piece—I like it very much—You did just the right thing: gave a picture of him which explains the great variety +

abundance of his work much better than indexing, cross references, analysis of styles, etc. I should think they'd welcome such an approach as a most welcome departure from the usual. Please let me know when they print it so I won't miss it.[60]

Awfully tired tonight. The work has been tough—or "rugged" as we say—of late, so much so that last weekend I had a hard time getting downtown for one drink on Saturday night. We had a problem to do outside of class that took me 14 hours to complete! [. . .] nothing will keep me from N.Y. this Saturday—The Magic Flute on Sat night + Lehmann's recital Sunday afternoon (an all Schumann program).

Will be graduating here Feb 4. For prisoner of war interrogation absolutely fluent German is necessary + I need much more practice in speaking before anybody can make me an interrogator—in 4 weeks, during which there's no time for working with language except to make it military. [. . .] I believe I like Combat Intelligence better anyway—so that's what I "graduate" in. Also—putting everything together—I don't believe anybody except people who have been in service a long time stand a chance of going abroad so soon as I expected—as soon as John did, for instance, after leaving H'burg. Can't tell of course, but it sounds as if recent Miami Lts will be kept over here for a few months anyway. [. . .]

Have moved out of the huts! To [. . .] the only dormitory available to single men (+ reserved + unmentioned when you arrive so that they can fill up the shacks first). I'm in a bed vacated by a Photo Interpreter, who had to stay only 4 weeks. Still not worth the outrageous sum of $45 they take out of our pay for "adequate gov't housing," but better than hut 90, + I'm feeling better, but still not entirely rid of the cold.

Must go to bed. Thanks for the snapshot—good.

Yrs,

Cecil Dyer

After his Harrisburg course, Lyell completed further training, writing Welty from many locations. On a postcard mailed from Lexington, Kentucky, he wrote, "Theme song of all such joints I've been in since the Black Hills 'Cow Cow Boogie.' On to Asheville. Ky is nice. Yrs, F."[61] The postcard below depicted the Empire Room in Chicago's Palmer House hotel, where Lyell had seen a vaudeville performer, A. Robins, whom Welty had first seen in New York in 1942.[62]

March 10, 1944 • Chicago to Jackson

You can never tell where you'll see what funny face. In this vomitously ornate room, Hildegarde, still getting away with murder, of the customers, has A. (for Albert) Robins as part of the show. We arrived at 11, but I stayed up to see him after your recommendation. The head waiter, who let me in the crowded room + sat me at his desk, tells me Robins is Viennese. It's an incredible act. The watermelons, + the melting violins!

Yrs,
F

Lyell maintained a keen interest in Welty's career. A March 4 postcard sent from Nebraska told Welty, "Look on page 309 of the March 6 New Republic for a misleading statement about you. Except for the Life photographs, have any of the magazines mentioned up to that point ever published anything from your workshop?"[63] He offered some critiques of another new publication, "Some Notes on River Country," then assured her he enjoyed it and would love to read whatever she wrote next. In the following letter, Lyell assessed a review essay that Robert Penn Warren had written on her work.

April 19, 1944 • Camp Mackall to Jackson

Dear Velma Simpson,

[. . .] The Woolf review[64] looked elegant in the Times. Sent it to Hubert. I haven't quite finished the book. Will return when I do. From Lodwick I learned of the R P Warren article in the Kenyon Review + sent for it. [. . .] I don't like his trailing after D. Trilling in comments on style. I've told you myself that I've occasionally found your wealth of simile + metaphor distracting—touching something outside the story so vividly that for a moment the mind shifts away from the theme—but how this opulence is taken for "insincerity," "false poetry," "narcissism," or "Look-at-me exhibitionism" is beyond me. I agree with him that the variety in A C of G makes it a more entertaining volume than The WN + that The Purple Hat + Asphodel aren't entirely satisfying, though "hocus pocus" + "straining" for atmospheric effect are unnecessarily strong epithets to use against them. I should say that you survived the typical LSU Catherine-wheel analysis remarkably well + can therefore rest assured that you are among the blessed. Don't fail to tell me your plans about going to N. Y.—arrival, length of stay, etc. May be able to come up while you're there. Enjoyed The Burning Court,[65] not one of the best, however—B or B+—Write soon.

F—

In Jackson, Welty tended the garden, painted, and wrote: book reviews, the story "A Sketching Trip," and many letters. Welty spent May through June of 1944 in New York City, where she worked for The New York Times Book Review *and shared an apartment with Jackson friend Dolly Wells.*[66] *Lyell saw her during the summer; when off duty, he was allowed to fly to New York with pilots who were completing their flight training. As he explained to Welty, it was "easier to get to N. Y., Cincinnati, Cleveland, etc. of a weekend than to anyplace nearby, when one hasn't a car."*[67] *Lyell was in the city in May when Welty received an award from the American Academy of Arts and Letters. She wrote Robinson that Lyell "took me up to the St. Regis's roof which he says is the only place, gave me a Planter's Punch & a fine hearty lunch, and stayed by me at the doings and clapped when I got the award, which I thought was very handsome of him. [. . .] After the doings there was 'Tea on the Terrace' for about 5000 people [. . .] and Frank said 'Don't mind them' (they were just mowing me down in their path) 'They are the ones who donate the money.'" Welty reported that on this visit, Lyell had trouble finding a place to stay in the city. He shared a room "with a Navy friend who worked nights so they could use the same bed, until Frank got to staying out so late, at El Morocco, I think, that he got on the same shift, so he would use my bed in the hotel while I was gone all day—bawled out everybody that phoned—'I haven't the vaguest idea where Miss Welty is.'" Later in June, she wrote Robinson, "Frank caught a ride up in one of his C-47s this weekend and he went straight to the Waldorf. We went only to the 'best' places. He tells me they are all what he is dreaming of all week. We had to stand up in '21' at the rail, it was so mobbed, never the whole time got a seat. 'Frank, I can't hear a word you're saying.' 'I said that's Lucius Beebe*[68] *right behind you.'"*[69]

Welty had hoped that she might find a way to visit Robinson, whom she'd last seen in May 1943, by landing a journalism assignment that would authorize overseas travel. Very few women received such authorization, however; even while stateside, Welty had limited opportunities to write about the war. The New York Times Book Review, *where she was working as a reviewer and copy editor, published several reviews of her books about the war, but under a male pen name, "Michael Ravenna." Welty wrote Robinson that one colleague on the* Review, *Orville Prescott, disliked her fiction and her presence as a staff member, and had partitions installed in the office so he could be separated from her.*[70] *To Lyell, Welty said little about the war, but included other news and vignettes she knew would amuse him.*

August 4, 1944 • New York to Camp Ritchie, MD

Dear Robert Dyer,

How are things shaping? Let me know. I hope nothing grim is shaping up but it's that kind of business either way, I think. How much longer is Ritchie? Lehman told me last Sunday he saw you but didn't give news and I couldn't think how he would know much of your work to ask about. [. . .] Lehman looked well, I thought—he was at the Ritz—you and he! Drinking rum with friends. I enjoyed seeing him. [. . .]

I feel bad today after a good party last night—I gave it myself, but the van Gelders insisted it be at their house—which was very nice. It was from 6 to 4 (instead of vice versa). Planters Punches. The Van G.s are both swell to me and about 8 people came—Dolly and the Farleys, Diarmuid and Henry, Margaret Cousins, and John W., who got very very drunk and insulted all, mostly Dotty van Gelder whom he told how beautiful she was but dumb. (not true) O me.[71]

I've been working pretty hard, and you don't know how hot it's been—still is. I must tell you about a little rainbow we had though, it was down near the ground—a little, tiny rainbow—and it was right over the sign [*for*] Mae West in Catherine Was Great. (Do you want to come up and go to that? It's probably awful but it would be fun to go to see Mae.)[72]

[. . .] Write the news when you get a breather, if you do, and let me know what happens. Mind out—

Yours,

Cary Johnson

Welty remained in New York until October. Lyell was being posted from one American military base to another; on October 5, 1944, she wrote Robinson, "Frank got sent on maneuvers and guess where he was sent—Camp Shelby [Mississippi]. Just in time for the Fair." Robinson, by contrast, was now assigned to a "Night Fighter Squadron." Home from New York in the sanctuary of her Jackson garden, Welty wrote Robinson, "you <u>have</u> to be all right—That's all I know but I wish you were here, on this day, so hard—"[73] *Distressed to learn that Robinson had been volunteering to accompany pilots on night missions, Welty soothed her anxiety in the mild fall weather, working in the garden or driving through picturesque Delta landscapes.*

In early November, Lyell wrote Welty that new orders preempted his scheduled leave to Jackson. "Don't know what this calling back is about—It may be an alert for overseas, a change of post, a maneuver, another "course," or a mistake—Anything is possible, so don't speculate + <u>don't</u> <u>mention it</u> until you hear from me again," he wrote on November 7.

November 9, 1944 • Camp Ritchie to Jackson

[*Written on stationery of Washington, DC, hotel*]

Dear E—

It was an overseas assignment! From Washington, dated Nov. 3, the day my leave started. Haven't any idea what to expect, but I go to Greensboro, N. C. on the 1 PM train Sunday—arriving that night at 9. I'm praying for leave from there in order to come home—the War Dept really wants everybody to have at least 10 or 11 days—but I have done little to get ready because I don't know what to get ready for. [. . .] I'm rather excited, but baffled—Say nothing of the above—

Came down here today to shop for winter things I needed anyway.

Yrs,

F

Lyell managed to get to Jackson the following week. Welty described his arrival to Robinson: "I thought now I can just cry, in peace by myself, for you. I haven't heard since a letter you wrote 4 weeks ago—and just as I ran upstairs the phone rang and it was Frank—leave, had just flown in—so I had to rejoice with him."[74] *A few days later, Lyell was packing, "taking so many things with him—is so prepared. Do you think he should take* sheets, *and pillowcases?" She described to Robinson how Lyell's friends and family pampered him in his last days before he was to report to North Carolina. "Everybody bore in cakes and candy, all kinds of goodies, and of course his mother baked steadily and brought up hams saved six months—never did I see so much food, it was sort of Roman at the table—hundreds of grapes sprawled in the center, even. Anna Belle [Robinson's sister] brought along her Scottish bottle one night too which was the height of the leave and Frank's last glad gulp as he left Jackson."*[75]

December 11, 1944 • Greensboro to Jackson

Dear Elna Berry Evans,

[. . .] Saw Wilson in Raleigh—it's really a series of tableaux, with love, politics, war + peace, etc. common-denominatored to almost unrecognizable simplicity. Now I see why at election time the Republicans carried on for suppression as far as they could. The whole party is made the villain of the piece in no uncertain terms as indeed they should have been + now—Senator Lodge seems merely the spearhead of unanimous isolationism. Ruth Elizabeth Ford wears pince-nez throughout + does very well in a part that calls upon her for no really distinctive pressure in any direction—except as a sort of spinsterish mainstay for father. I do wish she could get a role that demanded something of her, for she handles herself most intelligently. The film lasts forever + I don't recommend it to you, but see it if you haven't anything else to do.

Saw Meet Me in St Louis tonight. This one has a great deal of family, childhood, turn-of-the-century charm + gracefully managed musical numbers (orchestrated by Conrad Salinger whom I knew during Columbia + early P'ton years in N.Y. + had lost track of lately). J. Garland + little Margaret O'Brien are ruinously self-conscious, which is too bad, especially in the case of the latter. For naturalness Father is best of all. There is a delightful Hallowe'en sequence you will love, in which Miss O'Brien after the evening's coup de grace does one of the finest bits of child acting I've ever seen + her announcement of success is so hilarious that for this moment alone you must see the picture. There are several grand touches by the children all too rarely thought up in Hollywood. When the oldest sister forgets that for the safety of the public it's not such a good idea to put dummies under steel cars, the other one—not M. O'Brien—says, "Oh, Rose, you're so stuck-up." (And she is.) There is also a wonderful scene at the Xmas dance, with J. Garland + all the worst dancers—I'm sorry to be driving you to so many movies of late—but this + Laura + None But the Lonely Heart have so much of merit in them that you must see them.

[. . .] As you know, much about Ritchie pleased me greatly; but I still rejoice daily that I'm out of its clutches.

And that reminds me of another movie, 30 Seconds Over Tokyo, the most effective presentation of Air Corps life + personalities that I've seen during the war—except for the run-in-the-ground Southern hamming of the pilot from Texas. Otherwise the Wunderkinder who dare the eagles' flight emerge here just as they so miraculously are + this will show you better than anything else I can think of why I like the Air Corps + would never feel chez moi [*at home*] elsewhere. The shots of the mission from the Hornet are thrilling + beautiful. It's really a swell show, with excellent Chinese scenes + players toward the end.

I've started A Passage to India + it's wonderful. The way Chapter 3 opens, for instance—superb writing. The point about Forster + us is, I think, that we tried him too early. For me it was my freshman year in college. That was like my reading Pride + Prejudice on the train going to California at the age of 13 + wondering afterwards what all the shouting was about. He's like Miss Austen—worldly-sophisticated to the nth degree + one must involve oneself in the human comedy before he can have any idea what either is driving at. Then one sees immediately that theirs is the master touch.

Good night—

F—

By Christmas, Lyell was still stateside. Welty sent a Christmas box to North Carolina that missed him because he managed to come home once more. To Robinson, Welty described Lyell's appearance during the Weltys' Christmas morning ritual of eggnog. "In a minute, in burst Frank—you aren't surprised, are you? Flew home from ORD since his boat not quite ready and the CO turned out to be a brother of one of Judge's old school debating society team or something. He went over Jackson on a foggy night and they put him down in Texas—the Adolphus Hotel—but he was here for Christmas morn—it was fine to see him." A week later, Welty wrote to Robinson about Lyell's departure for New York. "I hated to see him go, he was sick with a cold, and eating fast, still while the family was blowing the horn, standing up in the kitchen over something chocolate."[76] *Lyell spent all January in the "hurry up and wait" posture known to many in the military. Waiting in New York was no hardship. In the next letter, he reports on going with Peter Lindamood, a friend from Columbus, Mississippi, that Lyell and Welty knew in the 1930s, to an exhibition featuring the art of Pavel Tchelitchew, partner of another former Mississippian-turned-bohemian, Charles Henri Ford.*

January 18, 1945 • New York to Jackson

Dear Eula:

Many thanks for the Abners [Li'l Abner *comic strips*]. Keep it up if your fingers can hold out. Enclose re[*mark?*] by Mr Jewell on Tchelitchew is when the Times equilibrium is[77] [*illegible*] balled-up. P Lindamood I learned was in town at the Chelsea + we had a meal together + he invited me to this opening. P owns one called "The Pearl," too much of a death's head for me, but the painting in all is extraordinary. Loveliest—the one I wanted—is "Melisande"—perfectly beautiful. The heads + eyes with nerves exposed were amazing, just gruesome. C. H. Ford at the show showed me the "banned" issue of <u>View</u> (absurd censorship, but it pleased him to death) + he said "Who on earth could object to <u>that</u> (the [*harmless?*] female nudes)—it's just meant to be pinup girls for intelligent G. I.'s" He got off some other good ones I haven't space to set down.

Wish you'd read a long letter I wrote the family yesterday about the 5 day leave. Private to you: No one seems to think we'll leave before Feb 1 anyway. There's certainly not tension at the moment. [. . .] Hope to be at Don Giovanni Sat and Lehman's all Brahms [*program*] Sun. afternoon. [. . .] Write soon.

Yrs,

F—

Lyell shipped to England at the end of January. En route, Lyell wrote Welty, describing the concerts and parties he had attended and Bea Lillie's performance in the revue At Home Abroad. *He enclosed an annotated program rating each skit or song and citing favorite lines or stage business. He also described some of the men traveling on his ship.*

February 4, 1945 • Military boat to London, to Jackson

Dear Menna Harris,

[. . .] There's nothing to write about from here except people. There's one grand character in our group named Roland Haas, a Hungarian Jew who has lived 14 years in NY. [. . .] He's short, plump, 37, and has a thick accent which sounds funniest when he uses GI expressions—he revives all the corniest ones for me, especially the "Hubba Hubba" rallying cry, still of baffling origin and significance to me. He complains rightly and frequently about absurd regulations (I always love to have people around who say what I'm thinking in no uncertain terms). He has excellent taste and has been everywhere and seen everything and is a real gentleman. Quite the reverse is [. . .] Barney who I drew in the BOQ lottery as a temporary roommate to move in with the mad Texas gambler, nearly drives me wild. He has oyster brains, can't remember anything, chatters all the time, eats the apple you brought from the mess hall, wants you to open a new package of cigarettes when he has just as many packages on the shelf, loves to be nursed (+—to their shame—finds plenty of nurses), voted for Dewey (+ asked me perfectly seriously why I thought it would have been calamitous had he been elected), etc, etc. His current amour is little Patrice Munsel, the Met's new Lucia,[78] though his wallet is mainly full of [*film star and pin-up girl*] Ella Raines, who he says, pretends she's true to a flyer-husband overseas but really isn't.[79] [. . .]

Must go to bed. Another move tomorrow to what I hope to heaven will be our final resting place—

Yrs,

F

Either spoofing or complying with military restrictions on disclosing military assignments, Lyell announced his safe arrival in a telegram.

February 5, 1945 • London to Jackson

OPERATION OVER. CONDITION SATISFACTORY. MAY THE PASSOVER BRING NEW HOPE AND COURAGE. REGARDS TO THE GANG—FRANK LYELL.

February 10, 1945 • Jackson to London

Dear Geo. Bourgeois—

How are you? The passover cable came, and is being shown the gang, and I guess besides Seta, Willie, Nash, Frances McWillie and all, you mean of course show it to Lois Fisher, B.Y. Glover, Hanson Murphy, and Seabelle Gates[80] which has me carrying it around in my purse ready. Was so glad to get it—the U-boats have been right busy as I hope you didn't necessarily notice. By now you should perhaps be at your point of work and might have started business—of course even that comprehensive cable you got together couldn't tell everything. No telling when this letter will reach you at this obsolete APO but will send it while waiting for a better address just to ask how you're doing. The Second Immolation[81] has come from Meyer's and is perfect, and perfection, and many thanks again for it—it is beautiful to listen to. Your long letter to the family, which Louis kept and kept, was brought to me by your mama the other day (I had been in with a sprained foot and couldn't go get it) and I was glad to get a clear account of all the NY visit—it couldn't have been more complete, could it? Or more just what you wanted. So pleased about it all. [. . .]

Have had overseas letters from John (today) and Jimmie (4 or 5 days ago) and Walter (yesterday) all of whom are well and getting along OK. I feel very hopeful about the Russians now. [. . .]

Tomorrow I'm going to drive up to the Delta to see John's cousin Nancy Fitz-Gerald and read old diaries of Miss. in the 1830s and '40s and so on—and look at the Delta—am looking forward to it.[82] The gas board gave me 20 gallons to go on—very swell. Plan to stay 2 or 3 days—don't know Cousin Nancy at all but John arranged it from Italy and she wrote me a special del. note yesterday to be sure and come in time for Sunday dinner.

"Laura" came to town and I went as directed and liked it very much—wasn't Judith Anderson wonderful in the one scene she had? Clifton very good too, but I don't think there could be much doubt as to his being the murderer from the start. It was well done though, I thought.[83]

It's nearly spring—the jonquils are beginning to open and are being sold by the tub full on the corner, and the little white hyacinths all in flower in the yard. The big camellia by the steps has millions of buds and the first ones opening. Birds singing, the air soft, and the flowering shrubs coming out—it's lovely. Willie and I went for a walk this afternoon.

Write as much about the job as you can, now that you're in it—and if you can write nothing, that will be a kind of clue in itself (the kind I'm not very good at). Just so it is a thing you like and that interests you. Be careful and let us know how you really are. I'll write more when I get a good address.

Yours,
[*signed*] Eudora
[*typed*] Claribel Hunt

Lyell delighted in the arts and entertainment of London, as Welty reported to Robinson: "Frank has already joined a club in London. He is sightseeing. It seems unreal to me. It seems mad to hope he can stay so elated through the war." The war meant that Londoners had less to eat, especially chocolate. "It's never seen anywhere outside and people beg you for it. Do send my box, now," he wrote on February 19. Rationing affected food supplies in the US, but some items were available for purchase to send to US military personnel who had requested them in letters. Welty was quite willing to comply, reporting bemusedly to Robinson, "Frank is a model overseas friend, he has sent back a tin box that was in his Christmas present and the first letter I got from him, today, starts out with a request. (Cakes, candy, Vicks Nose Drops, something to read,—choices.)" To Lyell, she expressed only pleasure at reading about his London experiences.[84]

March 5, 1945 • Jackson to London

Dear Harmon Alley—

Fine letters are coming from you with clippings, programs, and all the things that would go in "galore", and I'm enjoying them so much. The life there sounds very full—and it's grand you are managing to work all in. Keep things as they are! I've enjoyed the accounts of the theatre particularly and hope the rest of the productions are as good as "Vanya" and the rest—the Vanya sounds like a beautiful job. The Churchill Club fascinates me—be sure to report on the talk by Miss Rebecca West as I am curious about her. I remember all the stuff she used to contribute to the old Bookman and her break with it—very high spirited—I thought she was high-handed some of the time too. [. . .]

Everybody we know is OK. Tom has been here and e & Seta were over. Saw Nash & Marj. Katherine Anne is in Hollywood. Guess what she's making, $2,000 a week. [. . .]

I went to the Delta a few weeks ago to visit John's cousins the Fitz-Geralds near Webb and read some wonderful diaries that his great-grandmother kept beginning in 1833 when she went as a bride from Port Gibson to the wilderness near Sidon. They are really beautiful things. Very moving—unfortunately many of the years have been lost, most of the Civil War for instance. But I had a fine visit and learned much of the old times, though I don't feel I am able to use the material for writing since in itself it is already so fine it shouldn't be tampered with. I'm working on a long piece now incorporating the nightlight story[85] and it should end by being as long as the Robber—if it works out. I don't get too much time to work at it but hope to finish it this spring.

The art piece by Maurice Collis was good—wish you could see him. Pamela [*Travers*] should arrive one of these days—you will no doubt run into her on the street ere you get this or I know her address. Hope so.

Yours acreeably,
Jane Acree

April 18, 1945 • London to Jackson

Dear Elna Berry Evans,

Forgive my long, even postcardless, silence. [. . .] I wrote the family a long letter on the 14th + 15th + want you to borrow that for full details. For me there is just so much to do + see around here that I just can't produce more than a few such extended accounts. Every inch of London fascinates me—if you don't look hard, you miss all the characteristic details, + practically every overheard conversation is a vignette.

Back to an old question: Rebecca West. I liked her all right but was by no means enraptured. She's plain, short, neither fat nor thin—comfortably in between—pleasant, etc—but by no means the subtle sophisticate I thought she might be. [. . .]

Much more to my taste were Rose Macauley + Stephen Spender answering questions at a Brains Trust [*BBC quiz show*] I went to at the Royal Empire Society several weeks ago. They were both brittle + sharp as steel + I couldn't have liked them more. R West looks like the average housewife; these 2 proclaim themselves aesthetes a mile off, Spender tall, drooping, handsome after that Hollywood version of a poet—but never for a minute offensively so—+ Miss M. ghostly pale, toothpick thin, severely tailored though v. feminine, + ever so witty—

[. . .] [*After seeing Raleigh acquaintance George Dix:*] He invited me over the phone next morning for a drink at his flat + I learned the woman with him was Sybil Colefax![86] He also had a note from her asking him to dinner with T S Eliot; so I've seen the handwriting + it is awful. After addressing the envelope (badly enough) she goes completely to pieces [*Lyell provides a scrawl*] Sort of like that. In one sentence on the back page the only word you could be absolutely sure of was "Veronese."—Maybe he was coming to the dinner too. George says she lives at the Dorchester, gives a regular dinner party every Tuesday night + several days later sends each of the guests a small bill. But they all go because of rations demanding that people entertain [*illegible*] + the fact that Sibyl is the best bringer-together of the last war generations. George also brought me up to date on the Internat'l Set of yore. Daisy Fellowes also lives at the Dorchester where her husband lies v. ill. Ditto for Lady "Emerald" (real name Maud) Cunard, who "backed" Mrs. Simpson into Duchess of Windsordom, + still gathers together the remains of the Duke's "set." She + her daughter Nancy ("negrophile") never speak. G says Daisy is really chic, but the hats, etc. generally a little too much so. When I asked G to come along to M. Teyte, he said, "Who's that?" + then confessed he has absolutely no ear for music.[87] I told him he'd better not confess these gaps to Sibyl. G. is the original burner of incense before the social register, but is ever so much more entertaining + balanced in talking about it here than I ever found him to be at home where he usually bored me to tears. I envy his going with the Duchess of Kent on his second trip to The Circle[88]—he says she's charming, but that the Balkan-Greek accent is v. hard to get used to. Sibyl is partner in a wartime decorating shop—Colefax + Fowler—neat prices—e.g. they asked £800 for doing 3 rooms for Hermione Gringold. The people who go to her Dorchester dinners, incidentally, refer to the place they're given in as "The Ordinary." Mrs Dodge, at the Eng [*English*] Speaking Union, also lives at the Dorchester. One day I'll take her to tea there + make her point out these fellow boarders. Otherwise it's v. dull—We go to the Ritz, the Berkeley or Claridges when we're moving in this hotel world—The Berkeley's cocktail bar + lounge is the most British of all, jam-packed from about 7:30 to 8:30 + the only place you're sure to see a few long dresses + whiff some Chanel. Sample remark: "What are you doing back here?" Second Army Capt: "Oh, I'm posted in town now in an administrative job. You know, something to do in the middle of the week." [. . .]

The news of the President's death [*April 12*] profoundly shocked everyone over here + people everywhere still offer Americans their really sincere condolences. They know they have lost their greatest friend + I love them for it. James Agate, whom I see often at one of the spirits-until-11PM-clubs I belong to, came over the other night to express his sympathies to me + bought me a drink as he continued his eulogy of FDR, though he added that he considers Lincoln our greatest leader + I think I agree. I regret that I couldn't attend yesterday's memorial service in St Paul's, but I heard the broadcast near my office. We had a service here on Monday + the chaplain put first things first, to my mind, when he said the greatest things about FDR were his making the desires of the underprivileged articulate + his carrying a vision of the world at peace which no one else seems to have. The British want peace, all right, but outside their Empire they never seem to be properly interested [*or?*] concerned. And not shaking them up more vigorously was ever to me a great weakness in FDR. I'm sure he could have retained their respect at the same time he might have used his influence to change many of their national + international ideas, which are still dangerously isolationist. Tributes fill the papers this week [. . .] I won't hear a word of pessimism about Mr. Truman—A tremendous responsibility but I see no reason for qualms on any side.

[. . .] Tonight I'm going to the opening of The Duchess of Malfi at the Haymarket (Gielgud, P. Ashcroft, Yvonne Amand, Leslie Banks, etc.)

Upon my return to town I achieved first lieutenancy + a flat in town on the same day, the latter in particular changing my outlook on life for the better. [. . .] There is a jewel of a Hungarian housekeeper who brings me breakfast every morning before I go just around the corner to Grosvenor Square to get the bus. Couldn't be more convenient to work or places I'm always in of an evening. [. . .] V. quiet + comfortable + I'm delighted with it.

Must run. More later—

Yrs,

Frank [*"Frank" spelled in Greek letters*]

April 19, 1945 • Jackson to London

Dear Frank—

Li'l Abner is starting on a wonderful adventure now and I enclose the opening scenes—will try to save all, which will probably go on into your move to Germany and the end of the war and everything (please God). I don't see how it can last much longer. Any day now—I hope daily it will be the last. The death of Roosevelt so terrible—and for the men overseas fighting I hated it most—they must feel such a personal blow—and the prospects now, with Churchill—I just don't know. You no doubt were at the memorial service—it must have been impressive, and very moving that they held it. I still feel that the people everywhere want the peace to be the right one—and have hope in their force. It's a beautiful day in Jackson—cool and bright, roses blooming, the last irises, and peonies opening. Do you ever visit gardens there? Write me about them. (Have you written me lately? Haven't got any letters.) What about Kew—or did they uproot everything for safekeeping and put plants in pots inside some sandbagged building—after all the English regard flowers.

We are anxiously awaiting news from Walter—he was almost certainly at Okinawa and it has been 19 days since the landing. Mary Frances and Joe are in town with their baby [. . .] ! Our baby and their baby met yesterday—long looks on Elizabeth's part, delight on Mary Martha's. Not too friendly. Our baby is wonderful now too—so funny—she loves music and goes to the piano and waits for somebody to play something on it, then she claps her hands in time, and when she touches a key gently and it sounds, she tries to pry it loose from the keyboard and take it off to examine. She holds out her arms to Mittie when hot boogie woogie comes over their radio and Mittie catches her up and dances with her in her arms, but when she sets her down again she screams. [. . .] Am still working when I can on the long story but look at it with a little discouragement—so many words for a simple story, I fear. Mother sends her best. Take care. [. . .]

Yours,
Eudora

April 19, 1945 • London to Jackson

Dear Louise Patterson,

Enclose program for "my first Duchess."[89] Haven't read it [*The Duchess of Malfi*] since the U. of Va. days, but must do so again to see whether the motivation for Ferdinand's + the Cardinal's torturing of their dear sister is so weak. Both could have put more blood + guts + deliberate love of horror + persecution into their acting. Gielgud was fine in many scenes, but seemed to have too much real affection for the Duchess + stopped too far short of incestuous overtones if that's the side of the contradictory character that he wanted to play up. P. Ashcroft was sweet + lovely + looked perfectly beautiful, though she was very grand. This gory tragedy should be overplayed, I think, + the inhuman, not the human, qualities emphasized. It's long, but no one was bored + there are wonderful lines from time to time + nobody laughed in the wrong places—compliment enough to the performers.

Bob Whitfield, with whom I went, is a friend of J. Gielgud + we went to see him afterwards. Was terribly glad because while the 3 of us were in the dressing room—Mr. G. at dressing table removing makeup—a bearded man in Navy uniform came in. He proved to be Mr. Furse who designed the sets—v. good too. I was talking to them by the doors when a woman in black + white poked her feathered head in the door + said, "Jon, dear, may I bring in Miss Edith Sitwell?" [*illegible*] I was glad when Mr. G. put on the velvet robe over the final mad-scene tights + bade her come in. A terrific sight—chalk face, over yards of black satin—dress + cape to the floor—with gold + pearl hung at the neck—+ the head tightly bound in light green silk with sort of Medusa snake-rolls in front. I thought she'd be skinny, but she isn't—lots of bosom + midriff—she's of rather monumental height—with a wonderful rich voice, booming first, "I know this play well, John, but I had no idea it could be so terrifying." She introduced all round a youth named Russell—v. blond + pale + tall—British—nice looking withal—who came up to me (the unlikeliest choice in the room) + [. . .] asked, "Ah ah ah ah ah ah ah ah you Mr. Furse?" I said sorry no + turned him over to the Naval blackbeard. The Sitwell nose is remarkable—v. long + pointed with a big broad bump in the middle. I was spellbound + felt after awhile that long association with this poetess might make me talk that way too. How I wish I had a picture of her + Gielgud talking on the large star's-dressing-room sofa. Quite a sight. This dressing room at the Haymarket is the most proper one I've ever seen—old playbills + engravings on the walls, big furniture, everything comfortable, mixed Spring bouquets of flowers everywhere, full length mirrors, fancy big dressing table—not the barren prison cell we see usually in NY—A good evening!

Yrs.,
J. L. Roberts[90]

Lyell was about to begin the field work for which he had trained so long. Germany had surrendered on May 8 and a team was preparing to enter the country to assess the effects of Allied bombs upon industry, infrastructure, and morale. This was intended to guide the Allies in their campaign against Japan. Civilians who worked for the US Strategic Bombing Survey, or USSBS, included the poet W. H. Auden and another writer, James Stern, who was a friend of Pamela Travers.

May 15, 1945 • London to Jackson

Dear Allie Blanche,

In bed after a good evening with Pamela. She looks grand, ever so much thinner—I had to look twice when she came in the Berkeley (where we had dinner) to be sure it was she. The Berkeley is just at the end of Berkeley Street, corner of Piccadilly, v. near me, + afterwards we came back to the flat + Luise produced a large bowl of ice cream—with a jumbo Hershey bar from Jackson melted over it. She was ravenous—as indeed we all are over here—+ I had already given her my 3rd course (mushrooms on toast) which she ate after her ice cream at the hotel. It was grand to see her again. I do like her so much. [. . .] She told me much of James Stern who she says is on his way to join the USSBS. W. H. Auden dedicated his last book to them (Stern + wife)—He may already be here. We've got so many new civilians lately. After WHA appeared nothing will surprise me. If you really want to come over, why not investigate the OWI [*Office of War Information*]? Lots of writers have come under their wing + I think you might like it.

P. sat on the enclosed review—her creases [. . .] This is the first long one I've seen + I think it's excellent—in fact I think it's the most discerning piece I've seen about any of your volumes.[91] Will send others if they come out while I'm here. I will be in Darmstadt June 1 somewhere "in the field." My address won't change, at least that's the story so far—I'd presume it means we'll come back here. Sometime in August I should think. Could you mail me a book? I wrote a sort of V-E day letter to the family, which you must read. [. . .] Must go to sleep. Write soon + often—Yrs, + thanks for book soon—

Earl Beyard[92]

Back in Jackson, Welty's relief at the German surrender was tempered by casualties among Jacksonians and ongoing worry over those in the Pacific theater. For more lighthearted topics, she wrote about another Jackson resident, Benjamin Franklin, a Jackson high school student and neighbor of the Weltys, whose art had been featured in a solo show.

May 17, 1945 • Jackson to London

Dear Frank—

Have so enjoyed your letters—and the Sitwell vignette—it seemed ordered for you—she must have turned her little friend to stone and he lost speech first. The theatre season sounds lovely-and the countryside with those jolly energetic hostesses too. [. . .] I am sorry for you to leave London. Thank God this is ended though—the Germans ended it badly too, didn't they. I'm sure by now you know C.D. Jones is liberated and the story about his standing up for the prisoner's rights in front of the guns. Little Francis Stevens is at Camp Shelby—he had 3 bullets in his neck all night in a foxhole, the Germans did nothing for him, but a Russian doctor (lady) operated on him—saved his life. We are so depressed over Effie Lee Scott's child, Walter—on the last day of the fighting in Italy to be killed.

Have heard from John and he is OK, on the day it was over there. Anna Belle also heard from her husband, who was up in the Alps with the Inf., on the 2nd—so he is surely all right. We are anxious about Walter, as he seems still to be around Okinawa and being "interrupted"—and when I think about that place anyway it is more than I can bear. How I hope none of ours get sent to the Pacific now. What about Garland [*Lyell, Frank's brother*]? The late V-mail I sent that got that blurred photograph was probably just shot down a couple of times and got to you on the 2nd or 3rd trip. You've probably missed airmails along then too, don't you suppose? [. . .]

I hope you got a letter from me with Benjamin Franklin's art show in it. Mrs. Franklin called on me the other afternoon, as I had certainly not gone to the opening, and she wanted to re-urge me to go—"But you've missed so much in not hearing Benjy's gallery talk!" I went around to look lurkingly at the show and it would kill you I hope. He seems to have a dash of talent, normal in a young beginner and showing up in his first things, but later—"abstractions" with those names I sent you—and his abstract portrait of Edgar Allan Poe was where I shut my eyes. He had some dreadful botanical studies, mainly I think to entitle them, because (I wrote it down for you) one is called "Phalaephaenopslpus Specie." He is a ruined child. Mrs. Franklin says Benjy is so glad the war is over in Europe because he wants to go to school in Turkey. "Turkey??" "Oh, it's India, I believe." He composes on Saturdays (music). Poor Mrs. F., I could give you an imitation but hesitate to write it! Speaking of art. John writes me that in Florence they are bringing out the bronzes—and hauling up the Judith and Holofernes with ropes around Judith's neck[93]—and that it is a wonderful sight to see, little groups everywhere busy repairing and putting back up.

[. . .] . I thought of you listening to Churchill's speech—all so stirring, and all so empire. It was really magnificent to hear him tell of the evil-doers now prostrate at our feet—and the end—Advance, Britannia![94] [. . .]

Carpe diem. Write soon.
Love from all,
Eudora

May 25, 1945 • Bad Nauheim, Germany, to Jackson

Dear Hulda,

First let me thank you for the recent Abners + the marvelous Poetry Society piece + the utterly incredible Vary Thrower account of B. Franklin + his brushwork. My God, My God, My God!."[95]

Pamela [*Travers*] had a long Whitsun [*holiday for Pentecost Sunday*] in the country, so I didn't see her after our evening in the Berkeley + in my flat, but we had a long goodbye conversation on the phone. Isn't it a howl to have her friend James Stern turn up in my section of the USSBS along with Auden, who got him in. They're old friends + I'm delighted to have them around. All the way from London to Frankfurt in the plane on the 23rd J + I talked together + among other things he explained, was Camillus. He's Joseph Hone's (friend of Yeats) grandson, a twin, + why P doesn't say so mystifies him as much as it does me. Won't C. have to know some day? J. says she's never been married to anybody. Why the "Mrs"? That's how she wants to be addressed [. . .]

He's extremely nice + knows so many people we know—Woodburn, KAP (saw much of her in the Paris-Pressley days + says No Safe Harbor was written then—that when he saw her at that pre or post-divorce writers conference in Colorado, + showed him the MS with "40 days to go" whispers, it was the same thing he'd read near the Seine!) [. . .]

I spent my first night in Germany in Darmstadt to which we drove though shattered Frankfurt. Auden had been there over 2 weeks + graciously let me go to sleep after dinner in his bed (a real one—most of them in the house were cots) while he went Jeeping to Bad Nauheim, whither Jimmy had been sent, to see him + bring back 6 cots for the people who arrived with me. I was dead tired when I arrived after 2 nights of late packing + going out in London. Yesterday it was thought best to move the 6 of us to Bad Nauheim—OK by me—See all the country you can, I say; so now I'm sitting on a chaise longue in the Park Hotel, with Jimmy as roommate (instead of Auden + a Columbia philosophy professor—They're still in Darmstadt.) + he's asleep in the bed as I was yesterday afternoon. I went out this morning only to take a mineral bath at the section of the spa commandeered by US Troops. Endless big bathrooms with wooden tubs which they fill up with hot bubbling sulphur water + then leave you on your own. You soak + then let the mineral water give way to fresh for soaping + final rinse. Delightful! Will return tomorrow. By this weekend all our people should be here for final instructions before we set out in teams for the area we work in. I still don't know which one I'm going to, but by the time you get this I'll be Jeeping around no telling where. But we can say where we are, so you will know.

Don't know where Auden + Stern will go, but hope we'll be running into each other. Both express great admiration of you + sorrow over never having seen you. I think you'd like them both. A. rather gives me the creeps at times, but S. never—He's v. quiet, v. intelligent + most charming—Have you ever read any of his stories? I haven't—Pamela says they're v. good. Please tell all you know of him.

The next few days here should be v. pleasant now that I've rested + caught up on sleep. I hope to see Heidelberg + Wiesbaden before we move away. Don't know whether we'll have our meetings in Darmstadt or here. These places are in completely different directions from Frankfurt, miles apart, but nobody seems to mind, least of all me, + USSBS transportation flies out to all points of the compass daily. I could be sightseeing now, but I don't feel like it.

[. . .] I left footlocker + bedroll behind, but brought endless stuff with me: suitcase, duffel bag, musette bag, gripper handbag, briefcase. No trouble to carry them about, however, because the Jeeps have trailers. It's all been such a grand experience so far—I've loved every minute of it + am praying my good fortune holds out in getting into interesting spots, with heaven-knows-what-next people. [. . .] The last package of food she [*Lyell's mother*] sent me took 6 weeks instead of the usual four—dunno why. Think of eating fudge cake from 935 while flying over Brussels—Well I did it day before yesterday + loved it because it makes distances seem v. short indeed—Like writing on Swing Dan stationery in Bad Nauheim![96]

Toodleooo,
George Neely Raines

June 4, 1945 • Bad Nauheim to Jackson

Dear Annie Payne Lott,

This will be a request letter among other things so I'd better start over: Dear Eudora Alice Welty:

Enjoyed KAP's letter v. much. Will try to drop her a line soon. Did you know about her long long illness? Jimmy Stern said a Dr in Mexico told her she had only 5 years to live unless she laid absolutely still for 8 months + then did hardly anything for 7 years. She complied, stayed in bed in Mexico + calmed herself during all the Presley years in Paris. That was when Jimmy knew her best. Hence those innocent, girlish, light-through-the-hair photographs she had along with Presley in Yaddo. Delighted she's so rich, but her health sounds poor. Too bad. How can we work Garbo into the Robber Bridegroom cast?

This is being scribbled while I'm moving up in a friseur [*barber*] queue. I'm next in the chair if a Colonel pacing the floor will just leave—good, he's gone. I'm leaving tomorrow, headed for Hamburg—Will probably fly to Essen + Jeep from there [. . .]. We're going via Hannover + besides Hamburg will work in Lübeck (which I hear is lovely), Neumunster + Eckenforde—(Look around Kiel on your map to find these places.) Don't know how long I'll be in that area—a month anyway, + maybe most of July. All new to me—Am looking forward to it with joy—I'm really having a marvelous time—Couldn't like the USSBS more. Read yesterday the most interesting military document I've seen in the Army—recorded interviews with Albert Speer made in Flensburg (way up on your map) by people in another section—He was head of [. . .] the entire armament industry in the Reich. Fascinating + revealing on every count.

Please send me sugar + spice + everything nice [. . .] So nice of you. Books, anything is appreciated. The last nut cake arrived in time's nick today—Will be eaten in Essen, Hannover, etc after tasting in Bad Nauheim tonight. Also ink from 935, v. precious. [*Beside this paragraph is stamped "Jackson Miss Parcel Post Jul 18 1945"*][97]

Cheer Nash en route to N. Y. So glad he's going. Hope good news from Walter comes through. My best to your mother.

How many pictures from B Franklin's show had the red "Sold" star on them? Is Mrs. R. R. [*Ruth Roudebush*] White taking full charge of him too? Won't he have to go in the Army? I'd love to see his version of the Pacific conflict.

Yrs, Frank H. Lyell, 1st Lt AC (Official enough?)

June 4, 1945 • Jackson to Bad Nauheim

Dear Frank—

Fine to get your letter from Bad Nauheim—it didn't take long, from May 25 to June 4—and I had wondered in spite of no change in address if mail would come or go very quickly there. I am in such wonder over what you are doing, is it to observe what Strategic Bombing has done? Does this take poets? and am hoping to have a little enlightenment. It's good you can at least tell where you are freely. Let me hear all. I think you've made a very good start in your hope that all will work out with fortunate and interesting places and people, with Mr. Stern, Auden, baths, and all. I'm so glad you saw Pamela and it was good to have first-hand news of her. She hasn't written herself yet and I have been wondering how she was. I am trying to get her off a box with some sweets, since she had such yearning over the Jumbo Hershey—fine of you to bring that out for her! All your days are as thick as plum pudding cake which I relish but can just say now "Good!"—and mean to write better—I'm trying to do the housework, which I can assure you is literally never done and besides, to water the yard and type up my story—Mr. Weeks of Atlantic suddenly wanted to see it by the 14th of June but I don't think I can make it—about 200 pp. So I must write a stupid letter. All the literary gossip from the ruined towns of Germany is interesting—I haven't heard any in I don't know when. K.A. was working on No Safe Harbor when I was at Yaddo with her and she said much had been written on it a long time ago. I know it far pre-dated any war, and that the war when it came rather beat her to what she had been saying—what has happened now to the novel she hasn't mentioned. Yes I did send you the letter—hope it does turn up—haven't heard from her since. Pamela calls herself Mrs. for Camillus, I imagine. I miss them so—C. is so darling and I owe him a letter. I have the New Yorker of letters from all the world capitols on V-E day for you, if you didn't see. Will put in next box. Thanks so much for the review—what an overboard one—it pleased me of course, rather scared me in places. I sent it and let Diarmuid read it. It's wonderful to be getting copies of the English books—this is sweet of you and I will be glad to have them. Will mark some for you and keep. Yes I did read something James Stern wrote, a little informal account of a day he had with Camillus on the lake in the park—which I enjoyed—had hoped to meet him at Pamela's but it never worked out that way. It's nice you came over with him of all people—the old habit of yours, which no longer keeps it a coincidence. Let's see, what all little items was I going to mention. [. . .] B. Lillie was on Information Please last Monday [. . .] [*Artur*] Rubinstein was on the week before—wonderful. He got off on Queen Victoria's children. "Seven." "No, Mr. R, nine." "Maybe with the dead ones nine—I only count living. Seven." He knew all. "I think I was a king in my other incarnation, I so well know these families."

My new story is about 80 pages typed up today—it's the 1923 Delta family story—I can't tell much about it yet, but hope when I finish typing it I can then rest and look at it with a fresh eye. I fear for John Woodburn's reaction—for I don't hate anybody in it, no matter what they do. No indignation. He can't conceive of this, I feel sure. My little story [*"A Sketching Trip"*] about the Wells, Hubbard's or what, is out in Atlantic this month—you read that last summer I think. I wrote you about all the news I heard from the boys but in case that letter might be among the lost ones (I know and count on some lost, do you), John is OK in Italy and doesn't know what now, Walter is, or we think surely he is, in the fleet off Okinawa but all right as of the 19th, Donald Sutherland is all right, you might see him in Germany. [. . .]

Had such a nice time at your house the other night [. . .] I will indeed go by and get the letters there to read—hope to soon—it has been hard to meet with your mother out doing Red Cross and all kinds of things or just out, and me so tied here—which must sound amazing from Germany—when as you say you can take a bite of 935 Bellevue fudge cake while flying over Brussels. That part is just wonderful. Write soon and take care. Thanks for all clippings and enclosures. All well here. It's a little cool today—rained yesterday—and the Cape Jessamines are in full bloom—the mimosa tree—

Yours,

E.

[. . .]

June 17, 1945 • Neumünster to Jackson

Dear Ruth Gainey,

You are the richer for my having seen The Uninvited. We arrived here from Lubeck today, settled down in my abode for this week + after supper went to see what was on at the cinema. The Uninvited. I declined + took myself a step or 2 down the street to the local officer's club [. . .]

There were 3 copies of the Summer Punch, so I took a whole one. Restrained myself to the old Jackson Public Library technique with the Tatlers. I don't think anybody saw me.

[. . .] There looks to be nothing to do in Neumunster, but we are busy all day interrogating + writing reports; so it doesn't matter very much.

Many thanks again for the box—I'm nibbling malted milk pellets as I write.

I've hit one or two genuine anti-Nazis, but the kind who could speak up only after the surrender. Most of the Germans I've talked to make me boil with rage with their air of informed innocence + they're all repulsive looking, especially the soldier-prisoners you see being herded around all over the place.

In Lübeck we lived for 3 nights in a hotel opposite the Bahnhof from which I could see the streams of French + Belgian slave laborers + war prisoners being taken to a camp for the night in British Army trucks after the journey from Schwerin + Russian territory. In a pathetic group of 200 I inspected closely, as a French Lt told me, there wasn't a single one who hadn't been away from home at least 4½ years. He said they didn't begin to feel happy about anything until they entered the British zone, when all cried, "Maintenant, nous sommes libre [*Now, we are free*]," + sang the Marseillaise. The Russians saved them from the Germans, but didn't hesitate to take their wedding rings, knives, watches, or anything else the Germans didn't steal. Also, said the Lt, he saw very few Russian-operated vehicles that weren't American made + endless American guns + small arms. Why do we let the Russians do us like they do do do? That to me is the great mystery of World War II. Inscrutable Russians indeed. Inscrutable American State Department!

I've been so eager to fraternize with the Russians + have so far seen only one: an officer in Wiesbaden. It looks as if it's going to be a long time between Rhine wine drinks before the next one comes along. We must be friends somewhere besides on paper.

Think of me when the lovely Mississippi fig season is in full fig.

As ever,

Harmon Alley

[. . .]

June 25, 1945 • Eckenforde to Jackson

Dear E—

I'm sending a lot of pictures in this same post "free" to the family. Be sure to see them sometime.

Have just arrived at this fishing village on the Baltic—It doesn't seem nearly so far up as it sounds. Got your letter in Hamburg at our HQ there when Nick Nabokov[98] + I went down to see Richard III again—Yes, people like N + WHA [*W. H. Auden*] can well do the job at hand—in fact they are perfectly suited to it—interviewing German civilians of all ages, sizes, classes + prejudices.[99] [. . .]

Must run—Just wanted to send the enclosed—

Yrs,

F

Lyell continued send annotated news photos of London to Welty that summer, including one picturing "Edith Sitwell's stuttering friend," whom Lyell had met backstage in John Gielgud's dressing room, and another of a Lady Stanley, on which he had written, "Ex Mrs. Douglas Fairbanks socially on view at [. . .] the English Speaking Union."[100]

July 20, 1945 • Jackson to Bad Nauheim

[*Written on back of a religious tract, a drawing of an anchor with caption "Faith, the Anchor of the Soul"*]

Dear Lynelle Wright—

This was handed to me at a bus stop by the longest waisted person I ever saw, girl with bushy hair. Nothing can compare to the British Criminals clippings you sent—I loved every word—[. . .] So glad to get your letters + it does sound interesting though hard. Will send you a better letter but now Walter is home on leave + Edward + his wife came from Va. + we are <u>seven</u>—The baby runs with Walter's cap + won't let him go, but he goes today—has a mo. in Portland while his ship is overhauled, Mittie is going out with him. Karl Wolfe is getting discharged soon—J. Bennett is on Bougainville—Marjorie + children are joining Nash in N.Y. next week—had letter from J. Wooldridge, he's in occupation + was in Munich—Hq. 551st AAA Aw Bm APO 403, he's W. O. (j.g.) [*Warrant officer, junior grade*]—If you get a chance look him up—know he's homesick. Miss Sue Brame called me on the phone + had long talk. She has over 700 (?) dressed dolls, she says, representing her ancestors back to 1790, + the kind of thing that gets in print these days. She thought they would make a book—what publisher? Hope to see your family + their letters soon—

Yours,
May Hitch

July 18, 1945 • Bad Nauheim to Jackson

Wonderful evening—We've just had "Information Please"[101] with everybody including Beatrice Lille in the garden bandshell behind the Park Hotel! Her accompanist played solos first, then Reginald Gardiner imitated wallpaper + trains, then she came on in the silver dress of the opening British-canteen-for-the-troops scene in the 7 Lively Arts. Program: "Rhythm," "Wind," "Paree," "There Are Fairies,"—a howling "Three Little Fishes" encore + an encore medley of songs which she said she was singing at the end of the last war. "Wind" is marvelous—a grim lament of the lovelorn with "wind around my heart" in nearly every line + something about knowing how "we shouldn't have eaten that dinner à la carte." This one was in a London review called The Big Top of 2 years ago. The question + answer section had the typical spontaneity [. . .] The whole thing lasted about an hour + a half + everybody loved it. My pictures won't come out I know, but I had to try one of Bea + joined the autograph seekers on the stage afterwards for a closeup of her signing marks, dollars, etc. There was grand business between songs when she retired to a multicolored handkerchief on the piano—dainty dabs behind the ears first, then brisk wipes holding ends with both hands behind shoulders—like a prizefighter.

Took a truckload of boys in another Rhine journey last Sunday—all the way to Cologne! Upon the Autobahn via Limburg (charming old town in spots) Siegburg + back along the river to Koblenz—through Bonn, Bad Godesberg (along here Siegfried slew the dragon + Hitler slew Chamberlain at the pre-Munich meeting) [. . .] Perfectly beautiful ride all the way—long + tiring toward the end, mainly on account of the roads, but extremely interesting. Cologne is a wreck in the center of the city, the cathedral pocked all over with shell fire, but essentially the same. [. . .] Have you a copy of your reply to J [*Joseph*] Cornell?[102] My God!

Yours,
F—

August 4, 1945 • Bad Nauheim to Jackson

Dear Bessie Smith + Jane Power,[103]

Here's a recent Bad Nauheim shot of me, sitting under the Sprudelhof fountain. [. . .]

Jimmy Stern + Wystan Auden howled over the B Franklin–Vary Thrower critiques the other evening—simply couldn't believe them. I have a grand picture of Wystan standing in a Jeep on the Naziparteitag Gelände Hitler speechplatz in Nüremberg[104]—Had a perfectly wonderful trip to practically every place I saw in 1938 in my own Jeep recently—Read recent letter to family telling all.

I'm flying back to London tomorrow. I enclose a distraught letter from PLT [*Pamela Travers*] [. . .] Jimmy has written her, he tells me; mail has gone wrong somewhere—I feel v. sorry for her. Do write + cheer her up. I'll call her + go to Mayfield if I can. Please return this letter to me. Give Willia my love. So glad Walter came home. What next for him?

Yrs,
Dabney Purvis

August 1945 • Bad Nauheim to Jackson

[*Postcard is picture of Lyell in uniform in front of the Führer Building.*]

Telling a German passerby not to do something, but too late![105] Another title might be "How I Felt About the Munich Pact," signed in the Führerhaus behind me. What looks like smoke on it + beer-hall-putsch victim temple (whence US authorities have removed the bronze coffins to squelch forever, I trust, that attempt at typology) is really tattered camouflage netting. Too bad these things didn't get the bombs the other Konigsplatz buildings got. F

August 13, 1945 • Bad Nauheim to Jackson

Dear Robbie Dunford,

The birthday box is really wunderschön—such variety + usefulness! A culinary, literary triumph [. . .]

Terribly sweet of you to be so lavish + discriminating with infinite riches in a little room[106]—

Returned to London last Friday, August 5. [. . .]

Wystan [*Auden*] + Jimmy Stern are flying back to the USA today. W. has to get final citizenship papers before he can return to Germany, to join the

Information Control Division in Bad Homburg (between Bad Nauheim + Frankfurt) through which the magazine he's interested in must be engineered. He hasn't definitely committed himself to return, but they want him to + I rather think he will.

I'm now working as an editor in the Publications Section of the Survey—going over final reports from all divisions thoroughly—If I stay at this post, I'll certainly be in the London sector until at least the end of September.

We eagerly await end-of-it-all news. Piccadilly crowds celebrate every night regardless of Hirohito's failure to bow to the atom—The little shrimp, they ought to [*drop?*] one on him. [. . .]

Yrs,

Roy DePriest

In August, Japan surrendered after the US dropped atomic bombs on Hiroshima and Nagasaki. Lyell returned to London, where he edited reports on the impact of conventional bombing on Germany. Lyell's desk job meant he could regularly enjoy the cultural pleasures of London and spend time with English friends, including Pamela and Camillus Travers. In Jackson, Welty worked on the novel she was calling Shellmound, *later to be titled* Delta Wedding.

August 19, 1945 • Jackson to London

Dear Frank,

I got the 2 pictures—The Good Little Boy and the Bad Little Boy if I ever saw them—and many thanks. The Good is really good (and the bad really bad) and so satisfying to have. You are back in London now and I don't doubt you got there just right for V-J Day—hope you were in the thick of it and will be anxious for that report. I'm so glad you had that <u>full</u> trip to Germany—[. . .]. Was sorry to know that Pamela is feeling unsettled and <u>hungry</u>. I'm ashamed not to have written her better, but did send her a box of groceries—don't know if they've had time to come. [. . .] I do love her, and Camillus—I haven't had a letter from her but maybe she hasn't had one from me—the mails do seem unreliable.

I love the story of your mother going over to Jessie's house and calling through the dark from the porch, "Jessie you don't need to come to work tomorrow!" and Jessie meekly, "Is it peace?" We went downtown and stayed a minute, I saw a lady walking down Capitol St. holding a flag with 5 stars on it right over her stomach—where the sons all came from in the first place. People sitting all over the mansion and church grounds, like the Fair. Nash sent me some Confetti from Times Square—I enclose a confettus. I talked to your mother—know she is relieved and glad beyond words. Us too—Walter is still in Portland, Mittie with him, and she supposes he will go out on his ship as scheduled but at least sweeping mines won't be combat now (I hope). Such a dragged out thing though—We can't feel much here—no relaxing in the body at all—I guess when people come home it will be realer. [. . .] John is still in Italy—hope not for much longer. Got a victrola record from him yesterday—unbroken.

I knew you would love the Vary Thrower pieces—the name alone is a guarantee. [. . .] I was crazy about the postcard which I sent to Seta with a clipping pasted on out of the Beachcomber.[107] She is your most ardent second-hand clipping enjoyer. [. . .]

I'm finishing up my novel (sic) and hope to be all done by next week.[108] It's called Shellmound—do you like the name? It's really a town but in my story it's a plantation. Wish you could read it and give your reaction to it—when will this be?

Did you ever get some packages from me? I have one to send—all of them just fill up with nothing and there's 5 pounds. A little boy has moved in next door and plays the piano all day with heavy hand. I don't mind though because I've so cleverly discovered he has a Familiar Airs book in alphabetical order—Anitra's Dance, Anvil Chorus, Ave Maria, ending with Valse Triste I can't wait to see.

[. . .] I guess I wrote you that Dolly was OK after the bomber blasted into the Empire State—she wrote that although it was 14 floors above her it was on her corner and that there were terrifying moments of seeing flaming stuff and hunks go by their cracking windows, hearing explosions, and not knowing what had happened, how much of the bldg. was on fire, or what to do—Dolly you know worked for one of the invention depts. of Columbia Research and has the keys to the safe where inventions for the next (ugh) war are kept and probably the atomic bomb—and it must have been terrifying in a special way for her.[109] Nash likes NY fine, the children and Marjorie there now. Had a postcard from Hubert from Cape Cod: didn't like it. Mother sends her best.

Love,
Eudora

Welty continued to write Lyell between August and November, when he returned to the States, although no Welty letters are extant between August and November. She seems to have sent Lyell a local news account of a night-blooming cereus opening in Jackson, because this letter is addressed to the Jackson woman who sometimes invited neighbors to witness the blooming on her porch.

October 1, 1945 • London to Jackson

Dear Mrs. Zula Cain,

The N-B Cereus has just arrived. Lovely. Wish we could be around the wash tub smelling it together. [. . .]

You would have loved yesterday afternoon's reopening of the London Philharmonic. Sir Thomas [*Beecham*] was in fine form, acting out every note, shifting baton from hand to hand, + taking court bows at the end of each piece—good program: Overture to Prince Igor, Mozart's "Paris" Symphony, a delightful Handel—Beecham suite called "The Great Elopement," Dvorak's Golden Spinning Wheel, + Delius' "Walk to the Paradise Garden," and Berlioz "Roman Carnival" overture.

To the Churchill Club for dinner. J. Gielgud was there and asked me over to his new house for a drink. Charming place in a little Street behind the CC, which he went to school in as a Westminster School boy. He's taking Hamlet and The Importance of BE to CBII in 2 weeks.

Went to the old Vic's reopening Wednesday with J Dobbin—Henry IV Part I. Ralph Richardson was a fine Falstaff, but I thought Wesley Addy of M. Webster's NY production an infinitely better Hotspur than L [*Laurence*] Olivier (haven't heard of W Addy since and he was new to me then, but it was a stunning performance I shall never forget.) Mrs. Churchill and Sarah C sat in front of us and N. Coward, Mr. A. Duff-Cooper, etc were much in evidence, but the person I was most glad to see was GB [*Gertrude*] Stein—I expected an iron gray Amazon but she's really quite short—has completely white hair (in the same bob), and was wearing what looks like a blue green satin housecoat—just a braided wraparound—very peculiar. I'm returning this Wednesday to the opening of Part II.

Hope you got in some autumn glory in New England or the country somewhere during your trip. Tell me all about Nash, where they live + how M and the boys like it, Hubert + where he works, etc.[110] What is Willia's address at home? Tell her that even Sir Thomas B [*Beecham*] couldn't get "Yes Sir, That's My Baby" out of my head yesterday and whenever I think of that tune I think of her. Then I was plagued by minstrel tunes ("It takes a long tall brownskin gal to make a preacher lay his Bible down," etc) we used to listen to from seats K-C 1 2 & 3 at the Century (W, Mamma Mims + I) + the spectres of Myra Brown and her gigolo-looking brother Ace Brown.

[. . .] Write soon.

Yours,

F

PS Who gets Shellmound? The Atlantic, H-B, or both?

October 8, 1945 • London to Jackson

Dear Allie Blanche Ruff,

Pamela gave me the enclosed to send to you. I went to see her Friday night to see how she was progressing in the new home—my God what a job she has on her hands! No lights, no telephone, no water, nothing arranged yet, all confusion; but she was perfectly calm + cheerful about it and in time of course it will be an attractive place. [. . .] Write her a cheery line, but don't refer to my impression of the state of things chez elle above.

Had cocktails with J. Gielgud at the Ritz yesterday afternoon. So sorry he's leaving for India on Wednesday just as I've come to know him. He's thoroughly delightful and I like everything about him except his remarking that Bim, the DT Ward attendant, in The Lost Weekend reminded him of me! As in the case of G Sanders in Rebecca, I said there was some consolation in my feeling that both are good performances.[111] Have you seen it? Excellent on the whole. It just came to London last week, but I suppose it's been available to you for a long time. Anyway don't miss it.

Must run

Yrs,

Philip Kolb

October 15, 1945 • London to Jackson

Dear Mae Hitch,

A good Beachcomber today. Will get to hear [*Pablo*] Casals play with the BBC Wed. night + the opening of Oedipus and The Critic Thurs night.

Pamela took me to a 'poetic drama' at the Mercury Theater which has a whole season of this sort of thing. [. . .] Mighty long + not very elegant. But there was good music by Benjamin Britten, white young hope of English composition, + I was glad to see him. [. . .]

P. + Camillus were dining out recently and when she was surprised at the freshness of the blackberries in the pie after October 1, Camillus, making conversation with straight face between bites, said "In the country we say the devil weewees on the blackberries after the 1st of October." Two of his menagerie go to school with him every day + when P. asked why he didn't want to take Piglet + Pooh one morning, C. said, "No, they've had their treat already. They had milk from my breasts." (This derives from P's attempt to persuade Gladys the maid to nurse the newest of her illegits properly—which she isn't v. much interested in doing.)

Yrs,

J. L. Roberts

October 25, 1945 • London to Jackson

Dear Louise Patton,

I enclose recent newspaper comments of the same day on the weather.[112] [. . .]

Heard Sir Thomas again Saturday afternoon. Haydn #99 was wonderful. [. . .] Pamela is supposed to meet me at the Churchill Club at 6:30 for dinner + TS Eliot at 8. I'm wondering whether either will show up. P still has no phone + no telling what's happened since Sunday. [. . .]

Must swim out to the bus.

Yrs ,

Felix Grant

PS (Later at home) Pamela came + 10 minutes early! TS Eliot came with Sybil Colefax (a quiet short oldish mouse, like a DAR convention-woman except quietly dressed). He is terribly stoopshouldered and looks far too old for his years, but he spoke extremely well (about Poe) + P. + I talked briefly with him afterwards. P is giving Camillus a Guy Fawkes Day party which I hope to go to. She sends her love to you. F

In September 1945, Welty's novel, still titled Shellmound, *was sold to* The Atlantic *for serialization and to Harcourt, Brace as a novel. Both would be published under the title* Delta Wedding.

October 30, 1945 • London to New York

Dear Miriam Ezelle,

The news about the novel is wonderful. Many congratulations. So glad H-B won't wait until the Atlantic finished running it to bring the whole thing out. I'm all impatience to read it, but still don't want you to risk a MS in the mail. [. . .]

Grand for you to be staying on in NY. Nicer weather here now—will hear Myra Hess + Casals play an all-Bach session Sunday afternoon—That should be good—

I give up trying to write more—Am in office + have had a dozen interruptions. There's a <u>slight</u> chance for me to be home for Xmas, but this is v. private to you. Don't mention it at all. Don't worry—I've never sent a single letter from you elsewhere—I agree with you, I understand and you understand—<u>it saves time</u> and it's all entre-nous—

Yrs,

F

November 11, 1945 • Jackson to London

Dear Frank,

Some letters here from you when I got home from NY, including the one with Sayings of Camillus. Keep this Goat from Camillus! [*Stationery features a goat design.*] Also the one with weather notes and T.S. Eliot mentions. Poe such a dreary subject, why does he fascinate the English? You are probably doing something somewhere to celebrate Armistice Day fittingly. I saw your mother the other night and she doesn't have much idea whether you'll be coming home for Christmas or not. I say you will be, for you've never missed Jackson yet at such moments. But drop a little line when and if the news gets hot. Surely the editing job must be nigh over as I see quotes from it etc. Hope you don't get shipped over to help on the Japanese version.

John [*Robinson*] is down at Shelby, I'm going down to bring him home tomorrow, Anna Belle going with me. That will be wonderful. He got in last Wednesday and called me from NY and is getting discharged at Shelby. It has been a long time. Walter hopes to get out by Christmas but expects it will be more like Jan. or Feb. Joe is out and home and back practicing law. I hear Jimmie is on his way. So all will be well and just leaves you if you don't make it back by Xmas. But I count you in, and hope for it. [. . .]

Dolly is coming home from NY for her vacation in the morning. I stayed with her the last 17 nights on a cot in her room at the Albert ($17), the only available sleeping inch in NYC, and it was swell for we are old room mates and love talking all night and giggling over our quart of ale.

[. . .] Did I tell you I am a godmother, just as you are a godfather? I'm sure I did—being so proud and delighted, as William Russell chose me himself. I think even though he is 4 years old I ought to get him a silver cup, maybe mug, though I am sure what he would like me to bestow on him is an electric train with 2 semaphores and a tunnel. He is an adorable child—just now he is more wonderful than he's ever been—a radiant, outgoing child. Tell Pamela how wonderful the children are—her godchild Pammy is lovely—very meditative and leading her own life absolutely. She reads the Oz books to herself—is 6 ½. Diarmuid says sometimes she takes down a book of A.E.'s and he sees her open it and quietly read and quietly put it back—what she thinks she doesn't say.

It's lovely in Miss. now—soft days—not a bit cold. I've been working in the yard—separating and resetting daffodils. [. . .]

Yours,

E

Lyell wrote Welty from New York on December 5, 1945, reporting on having seen John Woodburn (apparently "well off the wagon") at a production of The Glass Menagerie. *Lyell expected to be home within a week, he wrote. "Please start assembling Δ Wedding MS. First thing I want to do at home: read it." By the time Lyell arrived, Welty's happiness over Robinson's return had begun to dim. "John seems not so rested or well," she wrote Russell in mid-December. She was also depressed when Gerald L. K. Smith, founder of the Christian Nationalist Crusade, promoted his antisemitic, racist, fascistic ideas at an appearance in Jackson. Disturbed that* The Clarion-Ledger *(Jackson) treated the event so casually, she protested their lack of concern in a letter that they published on December 23. Welty sent Russell a copy of the letter. "I've gotten less and less able to bear idiotic doings in Mississippi," Welty wrote, adding that she "got some phone calls of approval and one anonymous letter saying I was known as a dirty Communist and to keep my mouth shut." A few days later, she told Russell she felt "nervous and bad, really not like any way I ever felt before." Later that January, she referred to Robinson as having "been a little low in his mind." In February, she told Russell, "I feel a little better in my mind most of the time now."*[113] *She did not share such observations with Lyell, but in the following letter, she referred to her brother's low spirits after returning from military service, as "the same familiar symptoms." Lyell, not yet released from his duties, was now stationed in Washington.*

February 16, 1946 • Jackson to Washington

Dear Frank,

This is a Sat. and you are probably in New York—is there any more [*Lotte*] Lehmann? She sounds beautiful—so glad you are able to go hear her.

[. . .] John and Will cooked a wonderful meal the other night and we ate desert that made us all think of you, dish of chocolate and cream over a sunken cake that had been soaking up rum and brandy for days. Jimmie arrived in Jackson this week and already has a room—your mother got it for him, at Marian Brister's—so that is nice. He was moving in today. Walter is back, I think I wrote you that, and he and Mittie and Liz will move into their house in a few weeks. He looks well, just somewhat tired and doesn't want to do anything, the old familiar symptoms.

[. . .] Tell all the contingent hello for me—I miss them all. The camellias are blooming and the flowering quince and Jap. magnolia, and a few early jonquils. Pearl River is UP. Did you hear any further news of Woodburn, since J.S.'s note? Did you hear B. Lillie on Fred Allen's Sun. eve. program recently and Info Please? Just wonderful of course. I hoped you were listening.

Write soon—
Yours,
Eudora [*drawing of a large head*] Eddie Stiles!!

February 28, 1946 • Washington to Jackson

Dear E,

Had a good W'ton's B'day visit in NY. Went to the Symphony—Brailowsky playing Rachmaninoff's 2nd Concerto + Shostakovitch's 5th were the main dishes. Otello was a real thrill at the opera. I'd heard nothing previously except broadcasts—I think it's the greatest Italian opera of all—so v. human + well constructed + with all the set pieces set in so naturally + not causing breaks for applause—Marvelously subtle orchestration + deeply moving at the end with the love-duet surge coming in again during the death-kiss. Some of the singing missed fire, but everybody aimed in the right directions.

Enjoyed State of the Union very much. A good play, much funnier than Born Yesterday to me + Ruth Hussey's performance is absolutely first-rate. A charming actress, who never struck me as extraordinary before, but she is. There's a grand New Orleans woman who gets drunk on Sazeracs at the dinner party in the last act—that rare thing on B'way, a woman who looks + sounds Southern. The girl in Born Yesterday is perfect for the part + has an incredible voice—just right—but the play is the sort you can hear all too much about in advance so that when you see it there's little surprise left in the lines. It really isn't worth seeing, but State of the Union is. [. . .]

Yrs,
F

This letter includes an annotated clipping describing how Mississippi representative John Rankin had gotten into a prolonged argument, almost coming to blows, on the House floor. The argument erupted after another representative, Helen Gahagan Douglas of California, had criticized the House Un-American Activities committee. On the clipping, Lyell wrote, "Isn't it awful? Our 2 bushwackers were out of the Senate when I visited the FEPC filibuster one afternoon, but Sen. Ellender from La was just as bad. Sample come-on from supporters: Sen Johnston from SC 'You've heard how the colored folks have "hot suppers" on Saturday nights. Did you ever hear of a white man dropping in on one of these hot suppers and not getting into trouble?' Sen Ellender: 'Never, Senator, never. Thank you.' Etc etc. That day Cong. Douglas looked quite unglamorous. Very unmade up and dug in for business." His next postcard to Welty was playfully signed as President Truman and his wife.

February 28, 1945 • Washington to Jackson

[*Postcard of the White House*]

Write me in your next whether you've ever read The Labyrinthine Ways by G. [*Graham*] Greene now reissued as The Power + the Glory. Come up soon + stay a long time. We'll always keep your name in the chili con carne pot.
Harry + Bess

April 11, 1946 • Washington to Jackson

Dear Mary Flower Jackson,

Mamma has set a pace up monuments + down sewers that's so fast I can't keep up with it. Joined them for a White House Tour yesterday, however, + last night [. . .] to the Philadelphia Orchestra where Harry + Bess appeared with the Independence, Mo. Tuesday Bridge Club, 3 tables straight out of Grant Wood.[114] Mamma was thrilled because McKinley was the last president she has seen in the flesh. They're going to NY tomorrow. ASCAP[115] crashed through with 3 tickets for the Lunts and 5 for Oklahoma. [. . .]

Must run to lunch with them at the Shoreham.

Did you get the matches?

Happy Birthday!

Yrs,

George Bourgeois

April 16, 1946 • Washington to Jackson

Dear E—

Have just put Mamma on 8:45 plane for Atlanta. She had a grand visit + you must hear about it. I decided not to attempt New York. Washington is all abloom + Dunbarton Oaks on Saturday afternoon and Mount Vernon on Sunday were lovely sights.

Under separate cover I send publication day pages from the Times and Tribune. O. [*Orville*] Prescott will produce a piece from his daily worker shop later on I presume. Will try to catch other hosannas for you.

Happy Easter + write soon.

F

As Lyell predicted, Prescott, a book editor for The New York Times Book Review *and a very unfriendly coworker during Welty's time at that office, wrote a very negative review of Delta Wedding.*[116]

April 17, 1946 • Washington to Jackson

Dear E

Your timid, insensitive ex-colleague-on-the-other-side-of-the-wall Mr. Prescott has no business reviewing ordinary fiction, much less Δ *Wedding*. I gave up reading him long ago, but this really finishes me with him. "Only" result, indeed. What else did you set out to do but present the Fairchilds intimately in the plantation setting? Ain't that enough? I don't see how anyone who reads the book can continue to think of Mr. P, if he ever did before, as a "receptive and willing reader." What cheek to call himself one. "Sit up, take notice, pay alert attention, concentrate"—ridiculous, but he certainly needs to. Hate to pass this on, but knew you'd be interested. Read it, but don't weep.

Yrs,

F

April 18, 1946 • Jackson to Washington

Dear Frank,

[. . .] Thanks for the pretty + mighty cute birthday present [*fancy matches*]—I've lighted + lighted with them—+ they all do fine—+ you were sweet to remember it was my birthday—They ought to last me through the Easter season + St. Swithins' Day. I could chain-smoke, maybe. My book came out in due order on the 15th + I sent you one which ought to trail in soon—It was right much from here, Office Supply gave me an autograph party which I had dreaded but which was nice + cheering—will tell you all the funny things if I see you soon—I think I'm coming up to N.Y. about May 1 so hope to greet you at some moment there—will write when I'm real sure—J. Woodburn is in hospital now but O.K. + getting out soon, Diarmuid reports. Gall bladder + appendix removed. Seta is here + they are coming up to N.Y. last of April I understand. Will tell all news if any when I see you, so trifling a letter writer lately for no reason. Thank you again for my present.

Yrs,

E

April 22, 1946 • Washington to Jackson

Dear E—

Herewith another copy of the Times review if you want one and last Sunday's book gossip column.

Sat in the chancel surrounded by hydrangeas, on Easter at 88 Bartholomew's. Marvelous music with organ augmented by trumpets, trombone

+ drums. Beautiful day and Fifth Avenue was so jammed it wasn't pleasant to stroll. The hats were beyond belief—you should have seen them in the Plaza. On Saturday there were three black straws in a corner of Bonwit Teller's window, one a roped haystack, another a plaited arrangement, another a huge round brim with a white bantam rooster (I think) for a crown—black neck + tail feathers + red beak + trimmings—+ a sign: "Who but Adrian could have designed these."[117] Who, indeed? On Easter Sunday the sign was gone + the rooster hat had moved from the pedestal to the model's head, so everybody could see it I suppose. We saw nothing on the streets to beat this number. Passing St Patrick en route to St B's a policeman guarding the portals yelled "Hey Lt, come here"—an ex-USSBS—Sgt from Bushy Park days in London!

Stayed with Hubert who is okay. More later. Busy day—

Yrs,

F

April 23, 1946 • Washington to Jackson

So glad you are planning trip up here. Keep me posted on arrival time, Bristol or whatever bookings, etc. Try to include a Wton [*Washington*] stopover. Forgot to tell you that in [*Brentano's?*] where I went to see <u>Δ W</u> in the flesh, the "Recent Fiction" table looked thus

[*Drawing of stacks of books, including* Brideshead Revisited, The White Tower, *and* Member of the Wedding. *Stack for* Delta Wedding *has only one copy left.*]

April 29, 1946 • Jackson to Washington

Dear Frank—

Came down sick and can't start on my trip as I'd planned—have been on the weak side all spring and though I feel better [. . .] I just can't face a trip and the hardy life of the city after a bout with cold, sinus, and some kind of infection around my ear—still have fever. It is a disappointment—I had hoped to see you on the weekend of next week maybe. Have you seen Lehman's show?[118] [*Walter*] Winchell [*theater critic*] gave it a nicecrack this morning—just made up that word for him. Thanks for the copies of reviews and the ad you sent—glad to have them. Herschel was through here and I was pleased to have him say he likes the book very much and wished he could have reviewed it, or Stark Young—he said no northern reviewer could do anything better than say the writing itself was satisfactory, only a southern one could say what the book was getting at—true, I think. [. . .] Jimmie gave me a very elegant party at the R.E. Lee Sat. night and I tested my powers for going to NY at it, and fell down low—it was a very freeflowing party, John made oldfashions, and we missed you—Seta and Tom, Charlotte, Willie, Barron (Leone was sick), Helen Bataille, Helen and Ary (probably the only ones not prostrated the next morning) [. . .] I'm pleased the book got there—I thought I'd never get any from H.B. and when I did, Mrs. Herbert didn't have a one to sell and pleaded with me for my small stock, so I let her have them against her own shipment. Hubert sent me his and I too think they did him dirty with the jacket and bookcover—but the paper and print are nice, aren't they—I like the book [*Fingers of the Night*] very much, do you? Write soon and I will do better when my health gets sturdier—don't know how I got so rundown.

Love,

E

P.S. I was depressed by my co-worker's review in Mon. Times, certainly. [. . .] He just didn't know what was being attempted in mine and at the same time thought he did. I dread Edmund Wilson's in NYer like poison. It will probably dispose of me with one whack, like the heading to Carson's review—"A novel that leaves you blank."

May 15, 1946 • Jackson to Washington

Dear Frank,

Many thanks for rising up and writing to the New Republic—why didn't you send me a copy of your letter.[119] This is noble of you—and I must say after reading the review I felt I needed some kind of championing. It was a gem of reasoning, I thought, that review. But it makes me sad to think how simply unintelligible a Southern book is to such readers—and simply per se. It's a kind of symptom—How do you like the reverse side? [*Verso was letter that began "Dear Lady," inviting Welty to come stay on her goat farm in Florida. "We will be more than glad to have you, and you can drink as much good goat milk as you like."*] I wrote Mr. and Mrs. C. to be careful, as authors are a lazy race and they could be doomed to spending the rest of their lives listening to the slow tap of one on their typewriter, and spooning goats milk down his throat.

Later—Thanks again for the reply from Mr. Cowley—and you evidently put the fear of G. into them. It gives me a self-righteous feeling to be stood up for. Was interested to see the Trilling review—but do you think swinging under the chinaberry in Rosedale will make her take back that for instance ever since I stopped writing about poor white trash I've been guilty of xenophobia and narcissism? She would hate to take back such grand things. Was thrilled over the New Yorker being so fine to H. and me—and in the same issue and with a Bemelmans cover. Yes I knew you would adore about Benjamin [*Franklin, of Jackson*] in the Delta. Mrs. F. phoned me and told me all of it over again—she said "Just the kind of audience Benjy loves—he lapped it up with a spoon!" He sent a copy of my book as a thank-you gift. Saw him last night at the Jackson Symph. Orch.—in the aisles, up and down, gazing into the balcony, strolling across the front of the stage, a dazzling smile on his face—you couldn't believe. What will happen—he escapes the draft, being only 18 or 19. [. . .] When are you coming to Jackson? Do you have any idea? Your mother says you might go on a trip. You had better get here to vote against Bilbo. [. . .] Am reading the Berlin Stories.[120] Here is a little review Auden hand-wrote for the Times while I was there that I saved for you and just ran across—you might or might not want.

Yours in the magnolia-xenophilia,
Eudora

Honorably discharged from the military as a Captain, Lyell began teaching at the University of Texas. During that fall, no letters from Welty to Lyell are extant, although she may have written him regularly. She wrote many letters to Robinson, who had moved out West. Welty responded to Robinson's writing and encouraged him to try to make writing a career. She even retyped and, without his knowledge, submitted one of his stories to The New Yorker, *a nonfiction account of a difficult landlady he rented from while in the military, "Room in Algiers."* New Yorker *editor William Maxwell, who had become friends with Welty but had not yet been able to persuade the magazine to accept Welty's work, accepted Robinson's. Maxwell had hoped his magazine would publish "The Whole World Knows," a story Welty had begun contemplating on her way home from New York in August, about a young married couple in a small town where everyone knew that husband and wife were carrying on affairs.*[121] *Welty told Russell "in the train I felt I could hear voices like that all sad and intense, coming out from all those little places in the night. . . . and I felt open to them or something."*[122] *She was also working on another story, about a piano teacher and her small-town pupils, which would eventually become "June Recital," the central story in a story cycle Welty would publish in 1949,* The Golden Apples.

Over the next two years, as these stories began to unfold, Welty shared more drafts in progress with Lyell. She was weary of life in Jackson, writing Robinson that she spent time in the garden "avoiding people to whom I can't talk. When I get a letter or story from you things seem different and real."[123] *That fall Welty suggested that she and Robinson could use her recent royalty earnings to found a magazine, an undertaking Welty had no experience with. She made a trip to New York in November to discuss the idea with people she knew who worked in the magazine industry, but this venture never materialized.*

While she was in New York, Robinson invited her to come to San Francisco, and she went there directly instead of returning to Jackson for the holiday. En route, she wrote this letter to Lyell.

December 17, 1946 • Train to San Francisco, to Jackson

Dear Frank,

You were leaving Texas today, Hubert told me, for Xmas at home—+ he'll be leaving NY at the same time. It's might jolly on here—Crossing Great Salt Lake just at sunset, looks Wagnerian in distance—John is in San Francisco + asked me to come out for Xmas there too—it sounds wonderful + I know I'll like it out there—at the same time missing our usual day at home—the eggnog after breakfast + on—Will be thinking of you + hoping the Jackson Xmas is fine—[. . .] + do write me—Use John's Box, 706, San Francisco.

Love + Merry Christmas—
Eudora

January 4, 1947 • San Francisco to Austin

Dear Frank,

Thanks for the Christmas Eve note—and for Diana [*Trilling*] + the boys for 1947—sweet of you to send me The Nation, which I always mean to read—Thanks for the tree present too—will see it when I get home + I did miss you all Christmas. Write me of it—Loved it about Mrs. Bell's gems. Couldn't have liked it maw.[124]

I'm staying on a few weeks as I got a chance to rent an apt. on a weekly basis—imagine a chance to rent one at all!—for a few weeks. So why not see more of the town? I'm going to try writing a story here—It's a small apt. with bed that lets down in the living room—big kitchen—nice + quiet—great luck. Write me ℅ J.R. Box 706 still—+ let me know what Xmas was like at home—I like San Francisco—a beautiful view from every street + hill—+ wonderful ocean.

As for stopping over, it doesn't look very hopeful, as I now travel by <u>Tourist Pullman</u>, dear—a fine invention, can get home for $72.00 in all, but no route through Austin—goes through Galveston—I wish I could—Are you coming home for Easter? Or going to NY?

Write soon—Thanks again for the nice Santa Claus—
Yours,
Eudora

January 20, 1947 • San Francisco to Austin

Dear Frank—

Grand about your trip to NY! I hope weather + all behave, so nothing will be in your way for a fine holiday. It's wonderful + clear out this way—maybe it's a sign it is fine there. It looks like my trip home will about coincide with your NY trip, so nice as it sounded I expect it's out, this time. I'm really in no fit shape to "visit" with Chicks [*Austin hosts*] & people at any rate—my 3 or 4 dresses I set out from Jackson with in November are about done for—Another day I'll see you in Texas. [. . .] Thanks for all the Jackson news. [. . .] I've put down words in a couple of composition books but not too well yet—Did you read my story "The Whole World Knows"—I think you did—anyway it had been at the NYer since I wrote it, Aug. or Sept., + finally Ross returned it the other day after, Diarmuid told me, a big fight with Maxwell etc. Harper's Bazaar bought it + paid fabulous like—$750! The other story of the summer + fall is still at the Atlantic + probably Mr. Weeks still hasn't opened the envelope—a procrastinating gent.

Wish you could be out here in this fine weather—+ S.F. is a lovely place, I think. I do have the apt., don't know what Hubert was referring to, + think the woman wants it back last week in Jan. It has a nice kitchen—very modest place—on Larkin St., near Sutter—close in. Going to hear Segovia Sunday night—Yes [*Pierre*] Monteux is with the Symph and Piatigorsky[125] Sat. night—Have a wonderful time—Write all—

Love,

E

If you should see John Woodburn, give him my regards—I tried to get in touch with him in NY and never could. Tell him I'm now in San Francisco—the scene of all his wild stories. Hope you locate him.

January 31, 1947 • San Francisco to Austin

Dear Frank,

Got to stay on a little in the apt. so not evicted this week—So won't be going home while you're in NY anyway—Tell me all—I hope the trip came off OK on both planes—the tornadoes in middle west not nearly enough to rock you I hope—

You may have seen much in NY but Mae West is here—I ain't been but the name of it is "Come on Up"—[126] I too have Elizabethan Reader + going through Dr. Faustus—Would love to see Colin McPhee's book—so handsome sounding—My story is laid in S.F.—+ has Segovia[127] in it—will have to disguise him—Write soon + give me tidings of NY—[. . .].

Must buy some ink (wasting it saying so!)
Yours,
Eudora

February 14, 1957 • San Francisco to Austin

Dear Frank,

Good to get a report on the NY trip—but sorry you always get a cold when you travel How is it? Thanks for the grisly Chatterboxes—makes me want never to go home. Enclosed a clipping also from a home paper, sent here—did you see? It's lovely + springlike here—wish you could sample this nice clear air for your cold, would help. I have the apt. till March 1. Have investigated about the San Antonio stayover (yes it's the Argonaut) + I just don't believe this time I can—I'd have to time it for a weekend so you could be free enough, + March 1 is on Sat. The train connections to Austin from San A. are hopeless + it would mean a long drive for you or bus ride for me—+ I'm tired—really don't feel like seeing or meeting people in a new place—Have worked very hard on my story + it is still not right—All afternoon + evening tonight, it's midnight—too late to clatter the typewriter. I'd of course be so glad to see you but don't believe I can do a stopover. When will you get home, Easter is not far from March 1. Write me about that. Please don't be disgusted if I just can't make it to Austin this time. The other night I phoned Katherine Anne, she sounded well. Here are some letters from her, please send back eventually—I hope you are taken aback by her idea of my novel—+ don't know what I could have said about it myself to be so interpreted. [. . .]

John has written some but is not very settled or happy at all it seems to me—he is still more or less nervous—on edge—I hope he'll get to feeling better—He comes out to eat dinner a lot, + I try to cook, which I enjoy. He wrote a fine story in the summer which Diarmuid is handling but the Atlantic after over 3 months of holding it sent it back—They still have my long 60 page one[128] after a couple months too—Saw the NYer review of Hubert's poems what do you think of them? I've not yet seen. [. . .]

I'm hoping to hear [*Mischa*] Elman + the SF Symphony play tomorrow night—It's a fine outfit here—really exciting—+ a nice, small opera house with good acoustics, do you remember it? Also, Danny Kaye is coming (in person, to a movie house) Wednesday, + I'll be at the opening performance, along with the screaming bobby soxers, I guess.

Write me more of your trip when you have time—
Love,
Eudora

February 19, 1947 • San Francisco to Austin

Danny Kaye is here—+ I met him! Bennett Cerf who's in town took me back-stage with him[129]—How nice Danny is too—as you might expect—adorable. His act is a riot—my favorite song being a sulphurous "Love me or Leave me" + a "Tiptoe Through the Tulips" obsession with stampings + forthright rendition that would kill you. Did you see Hubert's poems reviewed in New Yorker?[130] Ash Wed. greetings. How is your cold? I hope well.

Yours,
E.

March 6, 1947 • San Francisco to Austin

Dear Frank,

Thanks for the clips—glad the Lavin got such a good review—and did I ever thank you for the superb Abner? I tried in vain for the next Sunday installment—it just doesn't seem to be in any papers at all out here. What in the world happened?

I'm still here, and just now have a little cold and don't feel much like leaving. It's wonderful springtime weather—I had to move out of the apt. (wait till I tell you the history of the landlady and another Italian lady by the name of Mrs. Hagerty) but am in a little hotel around the corner from it, nice and quiet, sunny, and have my story to work on. Will try to send you a copy if and when I ever get it all typed up, it's laid in S.F. Today I dragged myself out on an excursion I know you would approve of, so I felt I should report, went to Florine Stettheimer's show at the de Young Museum. [. . .] Just as I was going down the hall to leave I caught a glimpse of a statch [*statue*] in the distance and said "De Creeft"—and it was—a little figure called "Sullen Woman", in some traveling show of painting & sculpture. Marble, very buxom and buttocky, very sullen. John has had the flu and is better, almost well now, but had a hard time as he lives away out on the edge of the ocean which is so damp and foggy now. He feels better though. Have you read about the lady called Gypsy Buys and the house that Peace Peace It's Wonderful Brown wants to buy, out here in California?[131] A fine story but I can't find the funny beginning of it, only this little P.S. today. Hope you saw it when it started.

Must go eat something—this is the worst part about not having my little apt.

Yours,
Eudora

March 20, 1947 • San Francisco to Austin

Thanks for the Abner—it's glorious. Saw the French 19th century drawings on loan show here—all. The finest I've ever seen. Will Monteux come to Austin? He's playing at "4 cities in Texas" on tour. Hear him if you possibly can. My story ["*The Whole World Knows*"] in H. Bazaar this issue. Can you find?

Love,

E.

After returning to Jackson, Welty worked on editing her story for Harper's Bazaar, *then titled "The Golden Apples," but later renamed "June Recital."*

April 23, 1947 • Jackson to Austin

Dear Frank,

Many thanks for the Bali book—it looks fine, doesn't it—very attractive—and I'm anxious to read it. The photographs as splendid as ever.[132] [. . .]

I was on the Coast lately—the Lotterhoses took me down to Margaret's cottage—and the game was a rainy night—you were wrong as to Who Was It. Helen, Ary, and Mrs. Lotterhos. Did I save the one about somebody running through Miss Martha Enochs? The only way. We had a nice time down there, though it was cloudy and rainy a good part of our days, but so beautiful—dogwood, azaleas, wistaria, and Cherokee roses. Of course they were cutting down live oaks for a 4-lane highway, enough to turn you sick. The great big bulldozer or something bigger was ploughing through right in front of their house while we were there. [. . .]

I did quite a lot of work on the SF story, and typed the whole over again. Hope it's better—renamed it "Music from Spain." Have been going over the long 60 page one Mary Lou Aswell has suggested conglomeration of cuts in, to decide whether to cut at all or not—and if so, these or others—a hard dull task.[133] Write soon—hope all goes well there. It's fine weather here, and roses are just beginning to open and the fine irises. Magnolia fuscatas now.

Thanks again for the House in Bali. And for the Beatrice Lillie birthday card! A cheering note on the day.

Love,

Eudora

Abner is gorgeous now, don't you think?

May 18, 1947 • Jackson to Austin

Dear Frank,

So glad you'll be in Jackson after school—Hope all goes off OK at finals—

Do you believe I got a letter from E.M. Forster? I enclose it—guard it with your life + return to me—Felt so proud + delighted.[134]

Have been laid up more or less with a sprained back 4 or 5 weeks—couldn't type or drive—Still not too good but can get around some now. Too much garden work or something. Excuse not writing, this is why. [. . .]

Isn't Abner wonderful! I can't wait for denouement. [. . .] Write soon—

Love,

Eudora

I have a little "piece"—not a story, in June Atlantic. [*"Hello and Goodbye"*]

In August, Welty gave a talk on the short story at the Northwest Pacific Writer's Conference in Seattle, then traveled to San Francisco, eager to enjoy the city and John Robinson's company. This visit seems to have been as uneven as the first, with Robinson setting out on a solo vacation in September and Welty worrying about his state of mind and his career. Welty also continued writing stories and sharing drafts with Lyell, who was back in Texas for the fall semester.

September 21, 1947 • Austin to San Francisco

D. E.—

Just a line to tell you I've arrived safely at the old address—2406 main building. Put an ad in Jackson papers + it produced a Baylor (Waco) passenger + two or three possibilities to share driving back + forth from here. Brows are still wet + I hate to think of restewing in classes, which begin on Monday—but off we go. Lucky you. Hubert says New York has been awful. Also that his MS though finished needs much revision—hope it gets it before publication. The "golden apples" were as delicious the second time as the first.[135] Don't miss [*illegible*] of NYer cartoonists in Sept 15 *Vogue*.[136]

Love,

F

September 26, 1947 • Austin to San Francisco

D. E.—

Many thanks for the Beebeish view of the Opera opening —v. amusing. Yes, please send the new story when you can spare a copy + the lecture too—would love to see them. Moved back into the place I lived in last year after a vain search for improvement on it which could be occupied at once. Things are still unsettled there + in the classroom, but all will simmer down by this time next week, I hope. Weather agreeably cool now. Please, please, please try not to be tired and in a rush when you go home from SF this time so you can stop over briefly in Texas. Getting back and forth between here and San Antonio in a car is ever so simple. You must do it.

Love,

F

September 29, 1947 • San Francisco to Austin

Dear F—

Here's my new story, (separate cover after all)—If you're not too swamped with other themes, would you read & report? I'd be glad—My main problem now is: have I a bunch of short stories intact, or an incipient novel? You recognize Jinny from Whole World, as a little girl, + Loch from Apples, a bit older—Do you have any strong feelings on the subject? I put an envelope inside so when you finish with it (no hurry) you can please mail it to Dolly to whom I spoke of it—But if you mark anything on the MS etc + want to return to me, do that, but at the moment I don't know where I'll be after this coming Sat. when I must leave the apt. Will send word—

How is school? Let me know your news—You must be terribly busy right at the start, at least—What became of the poor girl who fell down on her fanny at the church social?

The other night I dreamed a casement opened out on faery seas forlorn[137] & guess who looked out? Caroline Gordon—I wrote her at once—

No hurry on this MS but drop me a line when you get to it—Good luck —Hope weather is good—

Love,

Eudora

[. . .]

October 10, 1947 • Austin to San Francisco

D. E.—

Have just finished reading Moon Lake again —so wonderful and very touching—the nasty remarks of the nice (?) girls, and the moving, living quality of the woods + the night. I always have that feeling about the woods when I go through them—that they're going somewhere too—like boats even when they're tied up—excellent touches about the boats too. The darkies, the cat, Loch, and the dull older people—most appropriate for the setting—I have only a few suggestions:

Page one: are they "councilors" or "counselors"? Not sure. I can't imagine P. Hatch and + Mrs. G considering themselves a "council."

Page 32: I think Easter's fall should be pepped up a bit after the tickle. The suggestion—later on—of her being disembodied in the blue are okay, but the opening sentences of the paragraph—"Easter went into a body that has been but in the hit in the hand by a stone. Her body seemed to languish upright for a moment, and quite seriously it fell" seem to me to be a bit slow in pace—All is quiet, then the big event of the story happens and I think she needs a little more resounding send-off—just a bit as to how her fall looked to Exxum would do it.

Page 43: Miss Willie's bosom . . "like a cloven white hide. Like legs." I think I see the hide, but not the legs. Show me, please, the next pair you see when I'm around.

Page 45 (near top): "they looked back at her through the yellow and violet streams of dust—just now reaching them from Miss Willie's Journey—the air coarse as sacking let down from the tree branches." Miss W. has been on the scene for a long time—too long, I think, for the dust to be just arriving. If you want dust at that point, couldn't you stir it up some other way?

Back to page 1: " . . . he stood against the tree with his arms folded, jacked up one-legged, sitting on his heel, like an old fellow waiting for Kress to open." The simile seems too extraneous to the setting and not common enough with reference to Kress to be referred to so casually. Anyone, young or old, might stand that way waiting for anything to open or for a conversation or a play or an opera to end. One of my favorite poses!

Otherwise I see nothing I should change. An incipient novel? There are certainly endless possibilities in Jinny and her [*illegible*] poisonous attitude. Nina is a fine foil for her here + Miss Willie is grand + I love Loch. The stories are complete enough in themselves, but in a novel about Jenny the "Whole World" [*short story, "The Whole World Knows"*] situation would be there I should think more or less as is. She could take music from Miss E. of "Apples" + so could some orphans, because when I "took" from Miss Mary Williams, Emania Pyron (can't you possibly work that name in somewhere?) did + she lived in the institution at the end of West St. For the most part you would have to start all over with Jenny + her group, so I don't see why you can't have two cakes—a new collection + a novel on the fire too—

And you have <u>another</u> story? Of course I'd love to see it if you have a spare copy. I'll send "Moon Lake" on to Dolly, who I presume will return it to you.

I've been meaning to ask you whether you ever read War and Peace. I spent most of the end of the summer on it + finished it shortly after I returned to Austin, finding it what Mr. Forster + others of his caliber say it is, the supremely great novel. It overwhelmed everything else I can think of on account of the scope of the thing + the perfectly astonishing variety of character + feeling he displays. I hadn't read a Russian novel in a long time + expected to experience remembered difficulty with names + places + so on. But none appeared because everybody in W + P is presented with such triumphant reality of speech + gesture + attitude to life that it's impossible to confuse the characters. Nobody surpassed Tolstoy in turning types into individuals + all the historical element is completely clear because the characters you know take leading parts in all the action. And there's nothing special about them—no one is a genius or exceptional in any way—everyone an ordinary human being. One wearies only of Tolstoy's effort to prove historians and historical methods wrong in introductions to later chapters, + too much repetition of his deflation of the "great-men-are-the-makers-of-history" theory. But he was interesting even while arguing these points, + I've never read anything with more absorption.

After so much of the oblique approach in fiction of our day, it's so refreshing to see a writer approach all the deep recesses of the heart + mind head-on, but still with the greatest subtlety [*illegible*] about "scenes"—he can do any kind, about any sort of people—anywhere—all leaving you with the most satisfying sense of completeness though the separate episodes are really quite short—The intensity + the focus of the detail do it—It's easy to see how he mixes his elements to get the effects he wants, but still the technique is breathtaking. There is always vigor in his presentation, but an emotional sensibility as delicate as what Lotte Lehman and Maggie Teyte put into their singing. It's after midnight + if I start enumerating impressions of the characters I'll never get to bed—Suffice it to say they're all wonderful + the major ones "developed" with extraordinary skill. It's 1146 pages long, but I was sorry when I finished it because every page contains some brilliant flash + there's nothing like enjoying them the first time—You must read it again if you haven't looked at it since you started writing your own stories—Nothing could be more stimulating. Be sure to tell me [*illegible*] whether you ever get all the way through it. Everyone started it some time or other I suppose. I did, but too early, I think. Having been through a war makes all the difference. The military types and war episodes really demand it for full appreciation of them. [. . .]

My schedule: MWF 11–12 The Novel Before Scott

2–3: Second semester of freshman English

3–4: Second semester of Survey (Wordsworth, etc.)

TTS 11–12 Second semester freshmen again

Would much rather have two on TTS—I'm speechless by four on MWF. The Novel keeps me frightfully busy, but I'm very glad to be teaching it. Have had little time to play. Have been to only one movie here, but like that one much more than most recent ones: Crossfire—many refreshing touches in it—

Write soon, + again [*illegible*] thanks for "Moon Lake"—

Love,

Frank

October 14, 1947 • San Francisco to Austin

Dear Frank,

Thanks for the fine mail—your nice long letter yesterday [. . .].

Thanks ever so much for reading my story and so carefully—it's good to think you like it. Perhaps Easter's fall should be pepped up—yet I wanted to keep it sort of pure in space—which probably sounds mumbo jumbo—but I could still make it quicker, if it seems slow—for as you say, it took a long time to get up to the point. Councilors—counselors—oh I wish I knew which was which—I knew I'd get the wrong one—which is it? I looked them up in the dictionary in a bookstore and still couldn't tell.[138] Will show you a Miss Willie bosom. Like opera singers have, lots. Maybe the legs are a little too—no they're not!—One of my favorite poses too, to see, I had a feeling it is "of the place," I never saw it anywhere but in the S. Did you? But thanks for all these things—I intend to ponder further on the story—No, not an incipient novel, but my new plan is to go ahead with the stories and have a book of inter-related stories. What do you think of it? Not to bother with plot-threads and all that, but just to take up these people whenever and wherever in their lives that might interest me. For instance, I see Virgie in New York living with a gangster! I'd like to deal with Loch later, Easter later, Virgie, and have done so with Jinny of course, and I don't know what all. The new story, one I wrote off in a day, imagine, after my usual agonizing for months on one, is the earliest one of the set—Mother has it and I told her to forward it to you, I think, I know I told her to forward the lecture, which she now has. If she doesn't put "Shower of Gold" in the envelope, let me know.

War and Peace I did just as you did, began a long time ago and abandoned—and during the war, often I thought of it, but just couldn't, while the war was happening. Now I must certainly begin it all over again—it's foolishness pure & simple not to have read this book. Your letter about it makes me anxious to get into it. John spoke the same way of it, he read it before the war, and of course Forster in "Aspects" [*Aspects of the Novel*] just sort of says "Well . . . !" Lately I've been reading Euripides—I heard by the way that Medea was going to be performed this year, and when I said, who, Judith Anderson? they said yes. But not as by Euripides, I understand but as by R. [*Robinson*] Jeffers. Hm, as Dick Tracy always says. I took some notes on the Eurip. Medea and had them in my purse, and took a bus ride yesterday over to Sausalito, and thought if anything happened to us on the bus what a wonderful suicide note the Medea made! My notes say Let our whole house go to ruin. This unlooked for thing that hath befallen hath broke my heart; I am foredone; the joy of life is gone, and I am fain to die, my friends. Amid all things that live and are possessed of wit, we women are the wretchedest of creatures. Aye, and they say we live at home secure, while they are warring with the spear; but they deem falsely. I had liefer far thrice take my stand in battle than once bear a child. I shall go the road of daring to the awful end.

But came back without incident.

Your schedule sounds interesting in content, but rather heavy on MWF I should certainly say. You must have to take cough drops by the 3 o'clock one. But the TT day must be nice. I don't know what I will do, or where do it. (Medea again.) This hotel doesn't drive me out after 5 days, but that's all they do. Charge daily rates. They wouldn't promise the room ahead, either, and I didn't know till the day I had to leave Olson's that I could get in. But I'd like to stay on if I had a place, and work on these stories I'm thinking of. The weather in Oct. is supposed to be nice here—it has been so far—

Last night went to Tristan [*Tristan und Isolde*] by the SF opera, with guest Helen Traubel. She was of course gorgeous, but for the rest, I'm not good enough judge, but was very weary—it began at 7:30 and we got out at 10 minutes to 12. Also, for some reason, I just expected Melchior to walk down the steps in Act I and here came a little man about the size and bearing of Dr. Sullivan, Set Svanholm, only he had Melchior's hat on, I think—and he pranced and did stiff piteous gestures, and the galvanic and matronly corseted and overpowering Traubel advancing toward him made you feel like yelling "Careful!" The duet was beautiful, so was at long last the Love-death, but poor Tristan dying on the rock was on a rock too big for him, so that he had to keep getting fixed and watching how he fell back (with little jumps to get himself back up in place) and he just had such a hard time, though his voice was good. Very elaborately staged—in the last act instead of just that big rock, as I recollect at the Met, there was a smaller rock, but still too big for our man, and lots of black and white hides decking it, and a white pillow, and red silk cover, and he had on a kind of royal blue nightgown, ankle length, and over all this was a big tree with autumn foliage which shed during the singing—leaf falls to the right, next leaf falls to the left. Opera is of course the big social event in SF and hour is come, I saw a beautiful Indian or Egyptian maid all wrapped in white gauze to the floor and eyes—

[. . .] Thanks for the clippings—they just this minute came—to know there are Abners is fine, look forward—no I don't see him here—he comes out in a very obscure and not-often-seen paper called the News. Must go out now, I generally buy groceries and eat a sandwich in the room—Thanks again for the letters—when you've read lecture and new story, would it be too much trouble to send them back to Jackson for me—my only copies—just at your leisure. And let me know what you think of them, when you get a chance, for I'd like so much to know.

Haven't seen movies you mentioned—C. Chaplain is here in M. [*Monsieur*] Verdoux[139] and will see—we're late getting things—Danny hasn't ever come in Secret Life [*of Walter Mitty*].

Yours,

Eudora

[. . .]

October 27, 1947 • San Francisco to Austin

Dear Frank,—Let's see how near I can get as much as you do on a postcard. Thanks for the letter. I was scared what you might think of the lecture—it's <u>your field</u>! + it was a relief + pleasure to learn you thought it did all right [*Welty's lecture on the short story delivered at the U of Washington in August*]. Don't know what its fate will be in print, if any. L. [*Lambert*] Davis + Atlantic are giving it the eye. Thanks for the Abners! Fine. Sent you a copy of a new story last week—no hurry about returning that, since I have one at home—Think I'm leaving about Saturday for Chicago—Sorry won't see you—You'll be home Xmas, I suppose? Will Hubert, do you know? Saw <u>M. Verdoux</u>, good as ever in first ½—where he counts the money is marvelous. You'll <u>love</u> Martha Raye! The last ½ is a bit tiresomely significant.

You win on the postcards. Hope all is well there.

Yours,

E.

Back in Jackson, Welty was still hoping her relationship with Robinson could improve, although she does not refer to this in her letters to Lyell, expressing only occasional concern for Robinson's health.

November 17, 1947 • Jackson to Austin

Dear Frank,

Thanks for the notes, clippings, Abners & all—was glad to get. Isn't Abner wonderful—and even Lower Slobbovia is getting into this now, he is as complex as Wodehouse, who could say more?

Wasn't Available grand with Stupefyin?[140]

I finally got home, the last three days were mighty slow and I ended up on the day coach from Amarillo on—had to change trains every day! Usually at dawn. It reminded me of my old trips to New York on the day coach where I once got off at Meridian, B'ham, Chattanooga, Bristol, Washington, and by mistake Pittsburg, New Jersey, and NY. But the stopover at Grand Canyon was superb—I stayed on several days, for it seemed silly not to—it was off season, perfectly beautiful with the yellow aspens and the snow on the mountains and the clarity of air and the cold—all welcome after California to me. I'd been reading books on geology lately, so attended a little lecture on the Canyon with much pleasure while there—It was all very fine.

How does school go? I wish I could hear some of your lectures on the novel. Maybe you will do a book of them some day? Thanks for returning the MSS—will have to send you a lot of stamps to pay you back.

Had a letter from Mr. Weeks to Diarmuid this morning, saying the speech "makes fresh and perceptive reading. But the lecture as it stands would fill 18 Atlantic pages. I should love to use the piece in the magazine but if we are to do so well shall have to have Eudora's permission to carve it down by more than a half." I am so weary of the old thing that I told Diarmuid I wouldn't do any more work on it, I didn't care what they did. [. . .]

Glad you like the new little story. I hadn't thought of the meet me in the woods business as being solely Columbus—do you reckon so—I was thinking of more a Greek god idea—visitation etc—his name is King and the title Shower of Gold. Surely I wouldn't want anybody to think I was making comments on his family or origins—if you think that seems possible I may withdraw the story—certainly Peter L. [*Lindamood, from Columbus, Mississippi*] would both see it and call it to little B's attention, with pleasure—

Have read Elizabeth Bowen's "Friends & Relations," an English Penguin [*edition*], that was sent me—I like her writing very much and this was something I'd never seen of hers, even mentioned—a novel—some fascinating parts. The children are highly superior. It's one of those "Brief Encounter" plots, which is a bit stuffy, but that doesn't count so much against it. Have also just read [*Edmund Wilson's*] "The Wound and the Bow" with a good deal of interest—it's just reprinted.

When do you arrive for the holidays? I heard that Hubert might come—that is, his family wanted to give him the trip home. Seta wrote she would be here. Maybe Dolly.

The weather is nice now—the trees are colored and the woods beautiful—I love our fall. Haven't done a thing since I got home, only a little garden work—but must get to work on my stories sooner or later. Must call people & say hello—your mother among them—I feel inclined just to stay outdoors in the nice air not lifting a hand. [. . .]

Love
Eudora

November 28, 1947 • Jackson to Austin

Dear Frank—

So glad you did get a little audition of sorts on the wedding [*of Princess Elizabeth and Philip Mountbatten*]—I thought of you, for it's the first really big Occasion you've missed for a while now. The broadcast sounds a little lacking though. How was T'giving. It was so beautiful here, you would have loved the day—perhaps we'd have had the old tea with cake. The leaves have been so wonderful—more color than I ever saw here in my life, that I can remember. Have been out on the N. Trace and down to the River nearly every day—bright warm sun, frosty nights, cloudless—the trees really look "clothed", like trees in poetry—wish you could see. The crape myrtles & tallow trees are just torchlights up and down the streets. [. . .]

Glad to know you're planning your ride home—it's just a month before Christmas. Some were looking for you Thanksgiving—Willie Spann was. Would you like John to ride from Austin to Jackson with you? If you have room, could you write him (better airmail him where to be) ℅ Rollo Wheeler, Box 222, Cedar Glen, Calif. [. . .] Will indeed find & send Caroline's letter[141]—shames me, I haven't answered—and haven't written to find KA's news, but Caroline said she was ill last spring [. . .] I still fail to see how she lives & breathes in Los Angeles. Will be writing her soon, so maybe will have a letter during the holidays—my manners are so bad—I'm just not a Letter Writer you know. And she is—

Hodding Carter and Ben Wasson are starting a little private press in Greenville and are bringing out the San Francisco story I wrote about the guitar player, as a little book, limited edition[142]—they plan to make stories of Faulkner and Gertrude Stein among others—sounds nice—

Must dash—will write again before long. Hope you and John can get together—When we all get in one place for Christmas we will Dance And Sing.

Love,
Eudora

December 2, 1947 • Jackson to Austin

Dear Frank—

Enjoyed the clippings, which I've just had time to read—[. . .] I think Rebecca West felt deeply as we all do the utter vulnerability of that little princess [*Elizabeth*] and that good "decent" royal family in the world now. That's really where the feeling leaps up—

I loved the trumpets—and the darling little boys, they were in a newsreel of the wedding, did you notice them? [. . .]

I'm a little under the weather this AM and writing notes in bed, getting up later to plant some pansies. So looking forward to the holidays. Trust you & John get together all right—guess I'll hear—I'll go to N. O. and get some Scotch and we'll have a nightcap when you get here.

The woods are just glorious—The crape myrtle leaves blew down last night but most are still thick and bright—remarkable—

Am getting lots of English reviews of Delta [*Wedding*], seem favorable, and D. wrote today he would send me an entire one by Eliz. Bowen—anxious to see, as I admire her. Mr. Weeks may take the speech, he wants somebody to cut it, but I said "Not me."

Love,
Eudora

Christmas in Jackson included a visit from Art and Antonette Foff, whom Welty and Robinson had befriended in San Francisco. Welty reported on the visit to Diarmuid Russell, who was Art Foff's agent: "The Foffs got here Monday night before Christmas and left the day after Christmas, and it was fine to have them—but I've been a little anxious as to whether they really had a good time or not—the house was full all the time of people, family & old friends back for Christmas, and I think Art and Toni thought it would be instead a nice quiet meeting of them and John and me all talking about books and writing—I would be on my knees sweeping out the crumbs from under the table and Mother hurrying in and out, and Art would be asking me what I thought about a story by Katherine Anne Porter, and I think Christmas may be a bad time for visits—."[143]

February 10, 1948 • Jackson to Austin

Dear Frank—

Thanks for the letter and the fine clippings—enjoyed the Trilling review and the Crosby radio piece both. I don't think Trilling is so far wrong, just ever so extreme—that is, I can go along with her in believing the reader is entitled to receive an attitude and an explanation, only I don't think they should necessarily be "the right" one or "constructive" or solving a thing on earth. The novel is not to me a bit "the medium for bringing both sympathy and moral-social discrimination to bear upon the individual human plight." But I think with her that plots ought to get more thought and attention (plot in the Forster sense) and be positive affairs, relating motive to action and "assessment", and dealing with values more—but in the name of "truth" and "art"—not morals. Do you think so yourself? (Yes I was glad I came off without a whack this time, but only because she was so very hell bent, with Capote by the scruff of that delicate little neck.) How is your weather? Ours is bad again—after I thought spring had come—and froze ice on everything, with some camellias open on the bush. But the sun's out just now, and birds have been singing for ever so long, so maybe now it will be spring—I hope the cold lets up out there soon. Poor NY, it must drive them nearly crazy.

Did you see, by the way, KAP's piece on Stein in the Dec. Harper's? I thought it was delightful—one of her very best things—and agreed with every word of it.[144] [. . .] Must have pleased her to write that piece.

Had a letter from her not long ago—will enclose, and please return sometime. I wrote and warned her good about the SF climate, which would do her harm I fear. Do you think she's going to finish that n- - - - ?

Just judged some awful stories from Mississippi College. Don't know why I said I would. I should have known all the characters would pray. Speaking of motivations and plots, God did everything in these stories, and everybody in them is either a good Baptist or a bad Baptist. You'd love the one about Dragonwick. That's the name of the house where lightning strikes a man that killed Mr. Judson over some cotton debts, while the heroine speaks to God.

Mr. Weeks still has all my stuff, the speech and the last two stories, and Diarmuid can't get a word out of him. He said he would like to apply a blowtorch to him, and in the Atlantic I just read where Mr. Weeks got a roof load of snow down his neck as he was bowing to his wife and daughter who stood in the window—thought Diarmuid might have fixed him. Have been writing, tried two stories, but neither one came off. Maybe the spring will help, if we have one.

Joan of Lorraine[145] came and Charlotte and Jimmy and friend and I went. Thought it really muddled in its aspirings, but it was interesting to see Diana Barrymore. She seemed to have the bones, Barrymore bones, in the final scene with head thrown back in a single spot, but otherwise she was pretty cuddly. She had the Barrymore curtain call act down good. [. . .]

Have been judging (I'm a judge) drawings and letters children send in for a Jr. League radio series about lives of the composers—they would kill you. There's one little boy I wish I knew more about, he uses crayons exactly like a Roualt of 6—name on back, Donnie Fairbairn, Lee School, Royal Hotel. Ellen Holmes hasn't yet contributed—but have seen some more of her work lately—a watercolor undersea imaginary scene—including within a beautiful blue-green, blue-purple change-about color for the sea, numbers of fishes, sea shells, seaweed, and a golden treasure chest with a mysterious word on it. Really a beauty. She goes to Helen [*Lotterhos*], who had given her just one little real seashell to look at, and she made up all that from it.

Must we live in Mississippi, how do you like all this stuff in the paper?[146]—I guess you read about Versie Lee Brown being Cleopatra in the Mardi Gras do—crowned with an "enormous sequin vulture".[147] You know he's the man (her papa) who bought the Creekmore manse and always advertises his store with a picture of himself in the middle of "Brown", in the O.

Love,

Eudora

Yes, I too enjoyed Lions & Shadows—for the most part—Auden was the best.[148] But so much trivial stuff—surely the British public schoolboy leads the most sheltered (or how would you describe something more fantastic than "sheltered") life on God's earth. I got bored reading all those old things he had written. I'm ignorant, was Chalmers Spender? Or who? Hear Ruth Ford has a blonde picture in new Vogue. For laff read Mrs. Knickerbocker Makes Her Own Clothes in Harpers BZ—there's a Va. Woolf essay reprinted, but didn't get to read all

March 22, 1948 • Jackson to Austin

Dear Frank,

Many thanks for reading the story, and for your opinion—I felt there was something in the first reaction—even though you changed your mind on another reading. But just now I think not to change it, this being one story I dashed off mostly, a thing I enjoy and don't do except rarely—and will leave any revision till later, not feeling rushed about it—I felt cheered to know you liked it—seemed to me it would either be good or else utterly bad—and I felt all was staked on a fine point. The other version of Sir Rabbit verse is much better—changed that—D. wrote me he was going to try it on Atlantic, so let's see what Sir Edward will say. He took "Shower of Gold", the other one about Sir Rabbit, and will run it in May. No other news—

How's spring in Austin? I trust it came—it seems to be honestly in Mississippi. Today big winds—equinox and stuff—But all in bloom, camellias, daffodils, the flowering trees—looks very fine. John [*Robinson*], who is down on the [*Mississippi Gulf*] coast writing stories, asked me and Dorothy[149] to drive down a day or two, which we did, and it was lovely down there, dogwood, azaleas, etc. Enjoyed our excursion.[150] Dolly was home for Alice's wedding, just before that, and it was fine to see her—she looks well, and as usual dashed about like a debutante. We went to N.O. for a day on the Rebel, and did you get our card? We sat all alone in Pat O'Brien's courtyard on a black cold day and drank some old-fashioneds—[. . .]

Did you see Virginia Woolf's new book?[151] I've not, but wish maybe Harcourt would oblige me with—will send on, if so. Did you read Diana [*Trilling*] on Virginia in the new Times Book Review? Had some interest, but how Diana does drive her same old point into the ground, to the loss of a lot, and faintly ridiculous in this case I think—spends two columns or more telling us she is getting ready to say something unorthodox, as if we need preparing, and says her same old spiel about social responsibility, etc. Can't really enjoy Mrs. Woolf because she was a born lady and didn't protest or apologize for the fact in her whole life. The last sentence I thought the payoff.

[. . .] Hasn't Abner been good lately, with Fosdick and the Chippendale Chair, which got the chair this morning, with admonition that Crime Does Not Pay addressed to all Chippendale chairs.

Write soon—hope all goes well there.

Love,

Eudora

[. . .]

May 10, 1948 • Jackson to Austin

Dear F—

Excuse me for not typing—taking it easy with a bit of malaria, usual May stunt[152]—Thanks for recent letter & clippings—enjoyed all—did you see the Time comparison photos of Capote & [*Max*] Shulman—the full length sofa-full of each? [. . .]

Since my last, I've acquired a lovely second-hand red Ford '46 convertible—I feel fine and free in same—You must see—Have had one or two trips, like Vicksburg for gin and Piney Woods School to take books—and this last week went to Oxford for 2 days, with John, to visit the Culleys, + had a fine time—met Mr. Faulkner at last—+ and he is besides being the greatest writer to me, an attractive, darling person—quiet, listening to all kinds of stuff, amusing when he speaks—The Culleys' house, do you know it? a beauty—we had a dinner partly in the garden, mint juleps + turkey—the Faulkners, the Bob Farleys, + Ella Summerville (Nina Culley's sister you know) who had many enthusiastic things to say about you—next day Nina, John + I went out to the Faulkners' for coffee, & they showed us over the place—the house is same age as Nina's, built by same architect in fact, but is less "restored"—has old wall paper, soft old wood, a lovely patina—+ I felt that cool you always said was in such houses in the country—Faulkner has three oil paintings stuck over his mantel, of himself + a lady + man, ancestors—all of whom look like Robert E. Lee—his mother painted them, I understood—and there is a bronze owl on his book case—He (F., not owl) had on shorts + a blue shirt, had come in from seeing about his race horse—which daughter Jill rides. We had lunch with Ella + then left—a real nice time up there—They seem to think in Oxford that Hubert is coming there this summer—

Will write letter better with typewriter soon—I'd planned to go to N.Y. this month, Dolly + Diarmuid asked me up—Will let you know when I get plans in shape—Hope all is fine there + not this hot.

Love,
E

Mr. Weeks turned down the new little story, said he could make neither head nor tails of it.

June 20, 1948 • Jackson to New York

Dear E—

Will spare you the Len McCarty trial horrors, but you mustn't miss the latest chapter in the Daily News' delectable sizzle-by-sizzle saga of Mississippi's portable electric chair.[153] (The McCarty tragedy was news to me. It happened the day I drove back to Austin, Jan 4, + I didn't get the paper until shortly thereafter + nobody wrote me. After a week of fighting a murder charge, the defense entered a plea of guilty to manslaughter + the court accepted it. Sentence hasn't been finally handed down, but it can be 15 years. Seems a settlement that will hardly cure homicidal mania. So sad. Paul Dains was the 12th man called to the jury.)

Lehman's piece sounded first-rate this afternoon.[154] I thought it had more dimensions + richness+ suggestiveness than any of his compositions I've ever heard. M. Redgrave read extremely well, didn't you think? When I called Juliet [*Engel*] she said she'd just hung up on Miss Boyd, who said "I knew when I had that boy (in Civics, I suppose) that he'd do all these wonderful things."

[. . .] Have a good time. Will write more later when plans are formulated. Hello to Dolly, etc.

Love,
Frank

Welty spent the summer away from Jackson, staying with Dolly Wells and the Russells, vacationing in Martha's Vineyard, then house-sitting in Westchester County, New York. Welty and Hildegarde (Hildy) Dolson were working on a musical revue, What Year Is This? *with Hildy. One skit Welty wrote,* Bye-Bye Brevoort, *was set in a New York apartment building that is being demolished while "obliviously occupied" by eccentric, quasi-aristocratic, elderly residents.*[155] *Lyell visited the city as well; in Welty's photographs from this summer, Lyell appears with Wells and Dolson.*

Both Lyell and Welty were back in Jackson in September. Welty described their late summer activities to Robinson, who had moved back to California, taking graduate English classes at the University of California, Berkeley: "Frank did get his fig ice cream. Clarena had put some figs in the deep freeze—made the cream when Frank came home—I too had my dish. It was all just right. He leaves in about 2 weeks for Texas."[156]

September 22, 1948 • Austin to Jackson

D. E.—

Here is the H.T.'s [*Herald Tribune's*] review of Hildy's book—another of those cursory glances that say absolutely nothing.[157] Surrounding material enclosed so that you can see how the comments will probably get no more attention than they deserve. Hope Hildy fares better in the Times + the others.

Still getting settled in the new room—not entirely agreeable, but mostly so—It's big + has a private bath + is in walking distance of the university + only $25-Best all-round in my search, so I moved in Sunday. Will probably seem okay when I get everything arranged.

Enjoyed An Ideal Husband the other night.[158] Beautiful colors in the super deluxe Mayfair. See it if it comes to Jaxon.

More later,

Yrs,

F

November 8, 1948 • Jackson to Austin

Dear Frank,

Base ingratitude not to have written before now to thank you for the careful reading you gave my story, and the helpful words on it.[159] I appreciated it—and will keep the advice in mind against whatever day I revise it for the book. It had gone off to Diarmuid and he sold it to Harper's Bazaar. I don't feel the uncertainty you do about some parts—had worked them out with care best I could—but want all of course as clear as I can get it. I agree the title is bad, but hadn't thought of any others at all—just my usual failure to get a title. The jerky quality of some of it, lack of transitions, were intentional—part of Virgie's state of shock—but again I don't want the stories not clear. When I have to read all the stories in a batch, in getting them together for book, will go over carefully, it will be fresh to me again then.

Hasn't it been a beautiful fall? Hope it has been there—here the finest in my memory. I stay outside a lot—go here and there—had a good time in Greenville with the Carters. By the way, Hodding is going to speak on the radio along with [*Ray*] Sprigle in Town Meeting of the Air tomorrow (Tuesday) night—hope you hear him.[160] They are terribly nice—she in particular. [. . .]

Have read Hubert's book [*The Welcome*], and felt depressed, though didn't think it a failure, as you did. I thought the characters were one or two dimensional, not developed enough, and all of it dreary beyond saying, but the facts he deals with are dreary, the towns are like that beyond doubt, and in many parts of the book there is the sensitivity and fineness of Fingers, but the book never reached Fingers [*Creekmore's* The Fingers of Night], to me, did it to you? As ever, I think Hubert underestimates and deprecates his female characters—and I simply couldn't believe a word about the wife that wanted the Lincoln.[161] Had a long letter from Hubert from Iowa, guess you had also, and glad he seems to be liking it all right.

Thought Intruder [*in the Dust, Faulkner*] was wonderful—and wrote an answer to Edmund Wilson's review in the New Yorker, but didn't send it—what's the use? Did you see how in 2 weeks 3 Mississippians were slightingly referred to, Faulkner, Creekmore, and Spencer, as to their place of origin? There was one paragraph in Wilson's review—about the Industrial era, and the precision of novel writing and Faulkner's inhabiting an antiquated community preventing him from taking his place with the truly great, etc., that simply set me wild.

We've been going to see the Museum of Modern Art Historical Films—have you seen that series?—at Millsaps these days. Theda Bara in A Fool There Was last time—Thanks for tip on Marlene—will watch for—had heard it was dreary or something and yet always look for hers vaguely. Wonder if some day she will be as screaming as Theda. "Kiss me, my fool," says Theda, dropping rose petals on the prone form—the Fool is so overcome by love of her that he staggers, walks on his knees then, and at last comes down the stairs on his belly, like a snake. Theda wears window curtains on her seat, and powders her chin with a chamois. A beggar at the dock stops the Fool saying, "Must you follow her? I in rags, and our predecessor, Van Dam, rots in jail." Endlessly long. The drunk scenes look real—may have been.

Bill Hamilton was here, to make a speech to the Historical Association—enjoyed seeing him one evening. He said a special bus met the Southerner to bring the historians to Jackson, and whom they passed through Pelahatchie—one of your favorite names I always remember—somebody asked about the name. The bus driver turned in his seat and informed the car, "There's lots of towns in Mississippi named after Indian chiefs—Pelahatchie, Kosciusko, Philadelphia—" Bill said all the historians took it without a murmur, too timid to smile or seem dubious.

Hope all goes well there. Thanks for the clippings and enclosures, have enjoyed. Write soon. Have had sinus—going now—and mostly stayed outside, not read or written much.

Yours,

Eudora

November 12, 1948 • Austin to Jackson

D. E.—

So glad the story was sold so quickly.

Just a line or two about Mr. Sumner, whose lecture I attended [*J.B. Sumner, winner of 1946 Nobel Prize in Chemistry*]—Glad I went because it was good + gave me ideas about sciences, the humanities, etc. He looks a bit like those Chon Day men in the New Yorker—sort of neat + tight + quick, with knife-thin lips + round, bald head + not much chin. A new man in the Psychology Dept introduced him—said he was living across the street from the Sumners for 20 years before coming to Austin + worked + played with them, tennis especially until Mr S. outclassed him. Mr S arose + I'm sure the first thing everyone noticed was his lack of a whole left arm. Half of it was there, but what to throw up tennis ball with???? Opening sentence: "I like to think of life as an orderly functioning of enzymes." [. . .] one of his daughters had convulsions in Belgium after eating roundworms from a hog's intestines on a lettuce leaf. The cure for this? Milky sap from fig trees. I'll spare you of other repellent biochemical details, of which the pursuit of enzymes seems pretty full. [. . .]

The fall season here? I must remind you that there is no such thing in Texas. Nov 4, I remember remarking, was as hot as July 4. Nov 5, however, was a cold day + I've worn a topcoat ever since, but have yet to see a red leaf. Can't tell you how I miss them.

Love,

F

November 23, 1948 • Austin to Jackson

Tuesday—
D.E.—

Thanks so much for letting me see this.[162] So glad you sent it in after sounding at first as if you wouldn't.

Never see Saturday Review regularly; so I'm glad you told me about John's review.[163] For H's sake I'm delighted he wrote it because as I told Nash last summer, skimming misogynists will look with most favor upon this novel + I hope he sent it to such a one for the Times. Which reminds me that John contributed something vital to the plot—the car-baby business, I think.

May be seeing you this weekend. Brother wants me to be a Godfather for Garland III, + of course I want to be present at the christening. Can ride back + forth to Dallas with Tom Cranfill + have a seat on the 1:55 a.m. plane to Jackson Thursday [*illegible*]. The christening is set for Thursday morning after the Th'giving service at St Andrews.

Hope all goes well so that I can make it. Will be dead tired when I arrive, I fear, but will call you as soon as I can.

In haste,
F

In winter 1948–1949 Welty worked on a variety of projects, including a hoped-for screenplay version of The Robber Bridegroom *that she was attempting to write with Robinson. In early 1949,* The New Yorker *published her letter complaining about Edmund Wilson's remarks on Faulkner, and in February, her essay on the short story was published in installments in* The Atlantic.

February 26, 1949 • Austin to Jackson

Dear E—

Thank you for letting me see the Wilson apology [*apparently lost*]. How lame it is! Of course F. could hardly be considered a genius by anyone who got hadn't got around to reading him. The explanation presents an absurd picture, doesn't it, of him correcting and revising as the article goes to press but still refusing to retreat from his critical position. "Yours with much admiration . . ." ! How much? It's like a preacher cursing a sinner from the pulpit + forgiving him in the vestibule on his way home from church.

Heard 45 minutes of Louis Armstrong [*at University of Texas*][164]—Love the way he talks + sings, but it really wasn't much fun. At least as many whites as blacks present + never over a dozen couples dancing. There was no band, no really grand surge of jazz—just a virtuoso sextet: trumpet, clarinet, piano (a tiny upright), double bass, trombone + drums. Velma Middleton is a huge, jolly woman, sings + dances, or rather wobbles + swirls + waves fat arms in the air. She was the most amusing one.

[. . .].

Yrs,

F

March 15, 1949 • Jackson to Austin

Dear Frank—

How was Martha Graham last night, I wonder? Did she dance Cave in the Heart? (or of the?). The dancing, the wonderful sorceress she did with its inner horror, self-horror—that red string!—and when she put on the Noguchi tree for a hat—all that one was thrilling, I thought. Hope you met the young people I did—so full of life, intelligence, curiosity about places, etc. I remember telling them to look out for you there.[165]

[. . .] Did a good bit of work on the story Juba is in before finishing with it. The collection [*The Golden Apples*] is in now, thank goodness—just under the line. Diarmuid called me up yesterday to say he thought it was good—so pleased to hear that word! It's not just a collection this time as all the stories are connected, so I was really working on all 7 simultaneously a good part of the time! Interesting but tiring. Anxious for you to see. It's dedicated to you & Dolly (but I had meant to surprise you!), hope you like.

Is Bidu Sayo singing there? How lovely she is! She sang last week here, two arias from Marriage of Figaro, one from La Traviata, and some lovely songs of French, German, Italian, Portuguese, English, all countries represented. Bach, Debussy, Brazilian Weed Pickers, all perfectly beautiful. She is such a beautiful person, isn't she—Erica Morini played recently also—marvelous—I imagine all these are on their way west and you hear the same ones.

Your azaleas are in fine fettle over on Bellevue Place—I hope to find your mama at home one afternoon and to see them close. Today it's beautiful and sunny and rather cold (killing frost tonight they say) after days of spring rains and winds. How is it there, the same? I had a letter from Caroline Gordon yesterday saying she and A. were driving down to Memphis [. . .] It would be most fun of all to meet in Oxford—[. . .] Intruder [*in the Dust*] has started the filming up there—I must put my sunbonnet on and go hitch up at the Square—I want to be cast as some Snopes or Gowrie "on sight." [. . .]

Had a letter from Hubert the other day, and he seems well. Said he'd saved the money to go to Europe but had forgotten about making reservations—has

3 people working on them. Hope he finds them. He repeated an invitation to come by Iowa if I ever go to NY by the streamliner again, but I hesitate to do that though it would be fun to see Hubert of course. This season I got 7 or 8 invitations to come to writers' conferences and of course turned all down—never again! saying I never would. If I show up at Iowa they will think my faith is bad, though it's no conference I understand, just a continuous workshop. I shrink wholly. The thing at Ole Miss is just to be on hand. I said no to that too but would like to go in the audience to meet Stark Young, though probably will wait till things bring it about naturally if they ever do.[166] All this business of the writer appearing as a personality before young writers appalls me. So many think that is the end in view anyway, and to encourage it—! [. . .]

Seta, who first expected her child on Washington's birthday, is reaching St. Patrick's without it being born yet and is getting weary of pregnancy, need I say. She was talking to me on the phone the other day and we kept hearing little high-pitched words thrown in. "Who was that?" cried Seta. "Me on upstairs phone," said Wendy's voice. "Oh I thought it might have been the baby." Seta lost her skirt at the Little Theatre the other night—she'd unhooked it and forgotten. "There I was in my shimmie and gold lame blouse." Had to sit down and wait for the auditorium to empty. When she bent over laughing, Clay thought it was Happening.

Bessie [*Cook*], Willie [*Spann*], and I have a reservation at the Edgewater Gulf for this weekend, and are planning to drive down and put the top down—hope all works out so we can go. I yearn to send them back with my car and stay on—but guess I'll have to make that later. Am really very weary with nothing but writing at this typewriter since, really, last October.

Write soon—send us postcard to the Edgewater Gulf, Edgewater Park, Miss., if you think about it—and we'll send you one of the Historic Biloxi Lighthouse—

Love,
Eudora

With The Golden Apples *completed, Welty's thoughts turned to a trip abroad. She was awarded another Guggenheim, which would partly finance her long sojourn. She spent several months in New York, visiting friends and sometimes writing Lyell about parties and meetings with new literary friends. At a party given for Eileen McGrath by her sister and brother-in-law, Peggy and David Rockefeller, Welty told Lyell she "stayed 45 minutes and never did get a single drink." The heat in New York drove her home "to cool Mississippi," she wrote when wishing Lyell a happy birthday.*[167] *In October she returned to the city to embark on her first trip to Europe.*

November 2, 1949 • Genoa to Austin

Dear Frank—

So glad to find your letter in Genoa when I arrived. Hope all goes well with you + the schedule running smoothly + to suit you. Sorry too about Benchley—What will happen to him?[168]

Italy is so lovely that already I'm planning on my return here after Paris. There was just time enough to get the feel of Naples—half-a-day—+ then the beautiful sail of the coast. Genoa Italy is mostly bustle + feels Northern, but is of course interesting to me since I'm getting a chance to inspect a European city. You would have loved a guided tour I took on Hallowe'en through that cemetery you spoke of. The guide so eloquent, his whole soul + gestures in "Don' you think that soul seems to be coming out through that tomb, h'mmm?"—+ indeed the soul has got her hem in the tomb door which is represented as slightly ajar, + is all through but an inch of her. "Ladies + gentlemen" (only I) "I beg you, the next tomb please—this artist was a special for angels." But on All Saint's Day itself I went in the country + down as far as San Remo, + saw besides that wonderful shore + sea + hills, all the celebrations for the festivo, parades with flowers to the cemetery etc., + coming home we passed a procession with lanterns + the priest dressed up + under a canopy, the bus driver removing his cap as we barged through.

The first sleeper I could get to Paris was Nov 11, so after that I'll be c/o Am. Express, Paris (11 Rue Scribe, as I recall Hubert's.) Meantime I'm seeing some spots nearly, but saving the big things—Florence, etc.—till I return + will have lots of time.

Thanks for Betty's address—

Meantime this is "first hotel" (the Colombia, natch, in Genoa) + I'm enjoying the good food + linen sheets—Cheap too.

The boat was so wonderful, the passengers—+ the ports—that I'll have to tell you all that sometime—Did you get my cards?

Take care, and come over to Europe too, soon—better make reservations now, as remember, Anno Santo![169]

Love,
Eudora

November 18, 1949 • Paris to Austin

Hotel des Saints Peres
65, 5ue des Sts. Peres
Paris VI, France

Dear Frank—

This is the address—it has heat & breakfast, and is near Louvre, Luxembourg, Cluny—and is cheap. I believe. Betty [*Lyell's friend from Austin]* and her friend Houston and I have had a meeting and lunch [. . .] . We ate so fine—of course I don't know where. Further up (or down) along the Left Bank.

It would be so fine, as we kept saying, if you were here too! We would be buzzing around much more madly. I mostly wander about on foot, go to Am. Ex. by Metro—and am thinking on my trip to Chartres, etc. (Must go there before it gets any colder—freezing in all public buildings.) The Sunday I arrived (just passed) I went to Notre Dame and saw a notice that the Strasbourg Choir was singing that very afternoon—wasn't that luck? Bach, Mozart, Couperin—Les Beatitudes, Liszt—what a way to see the church for the first time—and all the candles lighted, and those red hats hanging down.

Only opera ticket I could get this week was to Samson & Delilah, may not go—Have mostly just not planned all, just wandered about. Went to see Italian paintings in the Louvre—the French yet to see, aha. It gets dark very early, so there are only about two good hours during the day when the museum is both open and bright enough—which suits me, for I see too much as it is. Also it's icy cold in there—But the leaves are still on the trees along the Seine, falling now—and when the sun first breaks out of the mist, about noon, and the bridges appear through it one by one, you can imagine how beautiful.

It didn't appeal to my pocketbook to spend 2 weeks in Genoa, but the little side trips on the bus made it worthwhile, to Rapallo, Santa Margherita, San Remo, etc., and I could always come back at night & sleep in a warm bed. The journey through the Alps was wonderful—by night, but all was a-glitter. Where I'll go or whether I'll go from here is the next question, though I won't try to decide at this point. Paris, or back to Italy—Florence, or Naples? Or Spain? Somewhere where I can settle in a bit, learn the language, save as much money as possible—will have to think.

Mary Lou [*Aswell*] & Fritz [*Peters*] arrive Sat. Am to see "Genet" [*Janet Flanner*] tomorrow at lunch, should be nice[170]—Have taken out a library card. By now your paper should be coming along somewhat—is it? The best of luck with it. Write me your news. I hope all is good and the <u>health</u> good. When you write the family and Louis, give my love—what is Louis' address? I have a postcard of some cats singing "La Vie de Boheme" I want to send him.

Write me at hotel, not AMEX—too big & careless looking. Hope to hear from you soon—Wish you had the trip too!

Love,

E

December 11, 1949 • Paris to Austin

[*Welty notes in the following letter being conscious of the cost of mailing letters to the States. This seems to have motivated her to eschew paragraph breaks in the following typed letter, which she managed to fit on a single sheet.*]

Dear F—

Such a fine letter from you, and the priceless Li'l Abners within—no, of course I never see them over here, the H-Trib doesn't carry—too much to ask that you send the end of the story (they weigh so much, and the postage!) but TELL me—that is the most fraught of S. Hawkins Day races yet and I am on the qui vive. [. . .] Yes, I've read Benito [*Herman Melville's Benito Cereno*]—isn't it marvelous? Read it last summer for the first time, also the Pacific Island pieces (Enchanted Isles), though had read B. Budd before—yes, also wonderful. I bought a little paperback book by him, "The Confidence Man"—strange, and about a boat on the Miss. River of all things—have you seen that? [. . .] Have been having fun, and am sorry to be so tardy with a letter—the truth is we had a very cold spell and of all our little group here I was the only one who had heat—so we had a more or less permanent sitting room in my room, and drank hot tea, Pernod, and covered up with the comfort. You can just imagine how cold the Louvre is! And dark as pitch in there—I think I told you the only lightbulb in the whole place is the one over the desk where you buy your ticket. But right lately the sun came out two days, a good part of each day, and was so wonderful that we have darted forth like birds in spring—up the E. Tower, into Notre Dame and Sainte Chapelle to see glass, and to see some paintings in decent light. Cold and dark again today. Out to the Mian family, about which I wrote you, is so much the nicest place I go.[171] Meudon is about 12 minutes from Paris by streamline commuter train—a beautiful old walled village, with garden behind house—and big dining room with Aristide's sculptured heads, & paintings, books, music books lying around—a white cat, old and fat, "but she thinks she is beautiful"—and the three little girls, who are just amazing. They asked me and Fritz & Mary Lou out to dinner Wednesday night (I told you I ate Thanksgiving dinner with them, a goose!) and two of the little girls sang for us, one a medieval love song, and the littlest, Pauline, about 8, wearing her new boots and a pinafore, did a song taking dramatic parts and exiting and entering in a complete absorption in it, about a man returning to the chateau and finding his wife had been unfaithful and poisoning her, then dying himself. Genet was there too, forgot to say just now—she is without doubt the brightest lady for miles around—will tell you some funny tales she told sometime—she and Aristide had long argument, he will allow nothing to be said against the United States, where he spent some time—suddenly he cried, "A moment!" and rushed out—the little girls all cried, "Oh papa! Not your papers! Oh no!" "I get my papers!" And he rushed upstairs and came back with an article he had contributed to American Scholar and another he had broadcast to the French Underground—He is an adorable man, and I wish I could see his studio and what he is sculpting now. He lost part of one foot in World War I, and limps a little. Went to dinner with Genet and some of her friends, ladies with the Embassy, have you ever heard of Helen Kirkpatrick and Monica Sterling, both of whom seem to be contributors to Atlantic probably on politics. I knew so little of what they were talking about. I hear that Eliz. Bowen is coming to Paris, and that E. Hemingway is here now—would enjoy seeing Miss Bowen if occasion rises. Another person I like is Lady [*Maudie*] Hervey, the British Ambassadress—met her through strange Mr. [*Stephen*] Tennant, but we liked each other and am seeing her again soon. She says she likes to bolt. Did I tell you we heard a concert by J. Thibaut, three Mozart concertos? Such a wonderful evening—We are going to a Moliere play Monday night and I'm trying to read it beforehand—have done one act—Les Fourberies de Scapin—with delight, even though I go ploddingly. John sold a story to Harper's—will be out soon—so glad.[172] He has done another, which Diarmuid likes, and hope that sells soon. He doesn't like being in Mexico City—and that's cold too. He will go to Acapulco Xmas. When are you going to decide about NY? I bet you do go. But if it means the air—stay out of it, as you said yourself. I think the Peters and I will likely go to Nice after Jan. 1 and will write you for sure, with address, as soon as I know. It's sunny there—if we can just find a room with heat. The Saint Pere is so toasty warm—Have a good trip home—Write soon—

Love,
Eudora

You must never betray pure joy—the kind you were born with and began with—either by hiding it or by parading it in front of people's eyes; they didn't want to be shown it. And still you must tell it. Is there no way? she thought, for here I am, this far. I see Cork's streets take off from the waterside and rise lifting their houses and towers like note above note on a page of music, with arpeggios running over it of green and galleries and belvederes, and the bright sun raining at the top. Out of the joy I hide for fear it is promiscuous, I may walk forever at the fall of evening by the river, and find this river street by the red rock, this first, last house, that's perhaps a boarding house now, standing full-face to the tide, and look up to that window—that upper window, from which the mystery will never go.

—"THE BRIDE OF THE INNISFALLEN," 1951

Chapter 3

1950–1959

DURING WELTY'S FORTIES, HER REPUTATION AS A WRITER WAS FIRMLY ESTABlished. Stories from her first two collections were reprinted in a Modern Library edition and in college textbooks. She wrote criticism, book reviews, and a novella, *The Ponder Heart*, that became a Broadway play. She received invitations to lecture, serve on boards, and even record herself reading some of her fiction in 1952. She traveled often during this decade, translating some of her experiences into fiction that appeared in her 1955 collection *The Bride of the Innisfallen*. Her letters also document the intense joy she took in her overseas journeys. Welty seems to have enjoyed writing to Lyell, who had enjoyed similar experiences, or could be impressed by something that he hadn't yet seen or done. Welty was enjoying Europe with new friends, such as the Irish writer Elizabeth Bowen, as well as old friends, including Mary Lou Aswell, Dolly Wells, and John Robinson, with whom Welty wished to sustain a romantic relationship. Welty's hopes for this connection seemed bright during her first European trip, but faded within another year when she realized Robinson was in love with a young Italian man. She did not discuss her disappointment in letters to Lyell, but continued sharing with him her delight in travel and other experiences they both loved.

Lyell, too, traveled whenever he could, often sending reports to his increasingly famous friend. He continued teaching four classes each semester and writing reviews for *The New York Times* and local arts organizations. The Welty–Lyell correspondence in this era, though less playful than in the earliest years, still reflects their appetites for humor, absurdity, and occasional celebrity gossip, as well as their abiding devotion to literature and other forms of art. One of Lyell's students during this period, Willie Morris, recalled him "reading a passage from a novel and asking, 'Isn't that marvelous?' The sorority girls sat there taking down everything he said, while in the back of the room I could see three or four ranch boys, who always sat there in a self-contained group, nudging each other and snickering over the teacher's unusual recommendations."[1] Morris recalled Lyell as "a literary person in the best sense: he *lived* for literature."[2] Welty later reflected on teachers who loved their subject as Lyell did. In *One Writer's Beginnings*, she wrote, "The word is *passion*."

The 1950s letters contain many updates on family and friends, with special affection reserved for Jackson pals. In Jackson, Welty was part of a group known as "The Basic Eight" who ate supper together weekly. Six lived in Jackson; Lyell and Hubert Creekmore, when in town, brought the number to eight. In 1956, when *The Ponder Heart* was playing on Broadway, two of "The Basic Eight" and other Jackson friends were there for opening night; even Welty's mother, who had been having vision problems, was well enough to attend a later performance. These joyful moments contrasted with increasing periods of worry over the health of Chestina and of Welty's brother Walter, who lived in Jackson with his wife and two young daughters. His health problems continued until his death in 1959. In a letter of condolence, Lyell expressed his profound sense of connection to Welty and her family. "Words sound so futile, and I shall not try to summon any to tell you how deeply I sympathize with you all because I know you know."

Welty made numerous friends during her sojourn in France. Her social life was less constrained than it would have been at home, where many Jacksonians disapproved of unchaperoned women, left-leaning intellectuals, nude statuary, or interracial socializing. In the following letter, Welty reminded Lyell that even her supportive family might not wish to hear all the details she was recounting.

January 16, 1950 • Beaulieu, France, to Austin

Dear Frank—

Your wonderful 75c letter and the one written Friday the 12th both came today—I got one at the Colbert and one at Am. Ex. So that's heartening! And thanks so much. As for the $10 letter, no not yet, and I fear for it—and as for my letters, sure I wrote you (to Jackson) during the holidays, and am mad but not quite surprised—the record is disgusting! So many letters <u>can't</u> be checked on, but ones giving addresses or with enclosures that don't arrive are proof enough. Also there are 2 parcels I've never received, presents from Bessie and Dolly. And no little books from Harcourt, which I was looking for.[3] But what I'll do about the Xmas $$ is just buy myself a bottle of champagne and we'll drink it to Fessor Lyell here in Beaulieu-sur-Mer, and consider it a Saint Agnes' Eve Gift. Which brings me to your reviews, which

Welty in a velvet pantsuit, posing in an angular attitude befitting a modern dancer. Parts of the cut-out figure were rearranged, then mounted on red paper, in the early 1930s. *Image by Eudora Welty and Frank Lyell, courtesy of Louis Lyell family.*

his June 1933 postcard from Welty, the first in a series labeled I to IV, reflects Lyell and Welty's love of nodern dance. "Frau Wigman" is Welty's rendition of Expressionist dancer Mary Wigman. *Courtesy udora Welty LLC and Mississippi Department of Archives and History.*

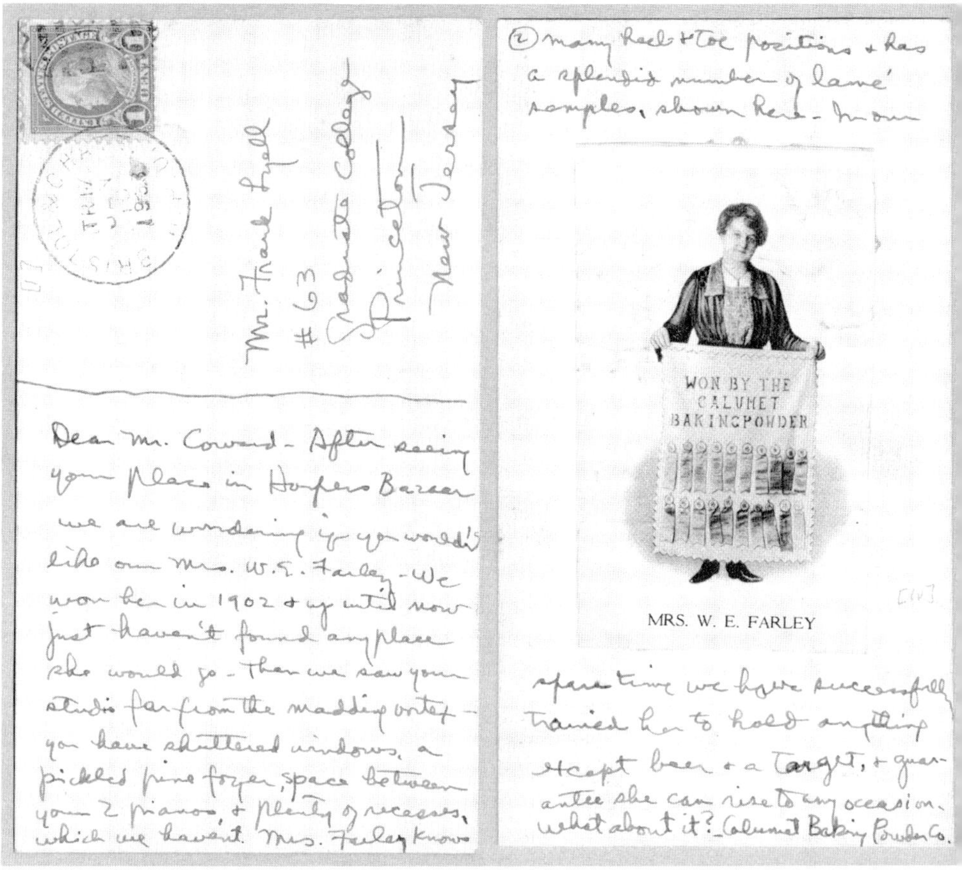

Mr. Frank Lyell
#63 Graduate College
Princeton
New Jersey

Dear Mr. Coward - After seeing your place in Harpers Bazaar we are wondering if you wouldn't like our Mrs. W. E. Farley - We won her in 1902 & up until now just haven't found any place she would go - Then we saw your studio far from the madding vortex - you have shuttered windows, a pickled pine foyer, space between your 2 pianos, & plenty of recesses, which we haven't. Mrs. Farley knows

(2) many heel & toe positions & has a splendid number of lamé samples, shown here - In our

WON BY THE CALUMET BAKINGPOWDER

MRS. W. E. FARLEY

spare time we have successfully trained her to hold anything except beer & a target, & guarantee she can rise to any occasion. What about it? - Calumet Baking Powder Co.

January 10, 1933, postcard on which Welty pasted a clipping of an image of a woman who won a baking contest. The message to "Mr. Coward" offers the playwright this woman, a prize the writer won in 1902, to use to decorate his apartment. *Courtesy Eudora Welty LLC and Mississippi Department of Archives and History.*

Welty pasted this sticker, resembling a one-cent stamp, onto the back of a 1933 letter to Lyell. The stamps were sold to support the Scottsboro Boys, nine Black teenagers accused of raping two white women in 1931. "ILD" in the image stands for the International Labor Defense Fund, sponsored by the American Communist Party, who were defending these young men. Welty sent this letter May 25, 1933, shortly after the Supreme Court ruled that they deserved a new trial. *Courtesy Eudora Welty LLC and Mississippi Department of Archives and History.*

elty enclosed this drawing in an October 1932 letter, after attending the State Fair in Jackson. The draw-g depicts the presence of the WCTU (Women's Christian Temperance Union). Fairgoers are invited to gn a pledge, presumably to abstain from alcohol. Welty seems to have titled the picture "Cannibalism the WCTU Booth," the phrase she wrote in the lower right corner of the drawing. To the left is a prone gure, labeled "a victim." *Courtesy Eudora Welty LLC and Mississippi Department of Archives and History.*

FRANK HALLAM LYELL

935 BELLEVUE PLACE
JACKSON, MISS.

July 24, 1933

Dear Eudora —

The Tribune is gasping for your return to infect the new vitality then 3 weeks of features — Don't write yourself out in 4 of 5 emissions; I suggested to Ralph you were good for at least a dozen — don't he think so? While combining a sunbath with Timon of Athens this A.M. I tried to pull a Beverly Nichols on some very buggy docks — but what I did is no secret. The bugs tormented me & I them & it wasn't very amusing. V. (efficiency) Irgne informs me you exhausted all the black moulding with your Mi'angelos, so the Princeton chapel & my Lorenzo have yet to be framed. Oh did anybody ever frame a Medici? Saturday I won 30¢ at contract (1 point = 1/80 ¢) & getting the news, captured a "coveted prize" at a party for Miss Sprinks that night. The award in reality was a badly colored deck of cards depicting "The Gorge" which we already had at

July 24, 1933, letter from Lyell while Welty was visiting Chicago. That summer she was writing articles for the *Jackson State Tribune*, a fledgling newspaper. All but three of Lyell's letters to Welty were handwritten. *Courtesy Louis Lyell family and Mississippi Department of Archives and History.*

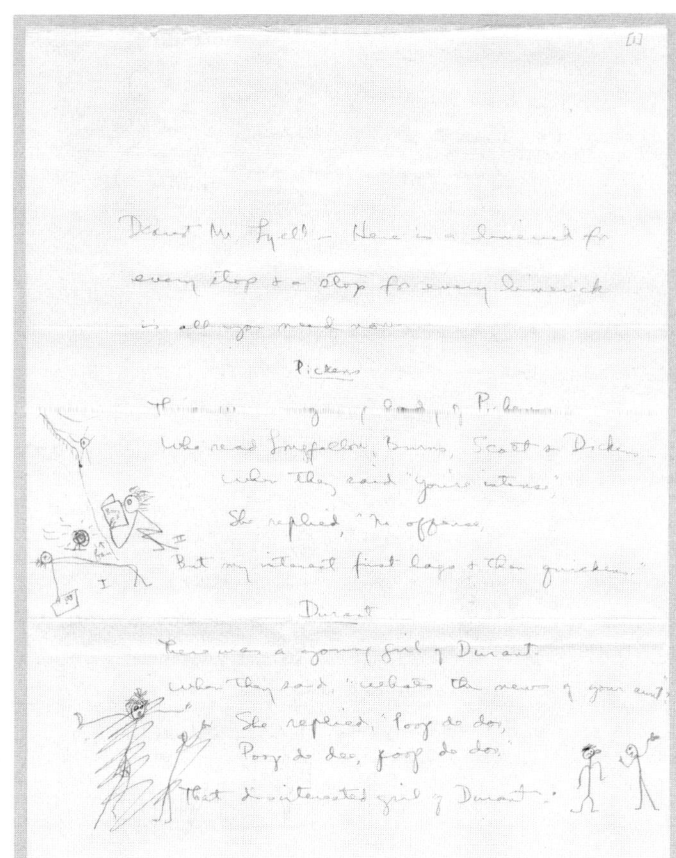

[1]

Dear Mr. Lyell — Here is a limerick for every stop & a stop for every limerick is all you need now.

Pickens

[illegible] lady of Pickens
Who read Longfellow, Burns, Scott & Dickens
When they said "you're intense,"
She replied, "No offense,
But my interest first lags & then quickens."

Durant

There was a young girl of Durant.
When they said, "What's the news of your aunt?"
She replied, "Poog do doo,
Poog do doo, poog do doo."
That disinterested girl of Durant.

irst page of a July 1934 mes-
ıge Welty gave to Lyell to
ntertain him while riding the
ain from Jackson to Chicago.
he pages contain "a limerick
or every stop," each illustrated
y Welty. *Courtesy Eudora*
Velty LLC and Mississippi
epartment of Archives and
listory.

Frank Lyell poses on a riverbank with Welty's friend Helen Lotterhos and another unidentified woman. Welty took this photograph in the 1930s. *Courtesy Eudora Welty LLC and Mississippi Department of Archives and History.*

In this 1930s photo, Welty poses in a tree, draped in a shawl and extending her left hand expressively. Lyell, wearing gardening gloves and hat, earnestly serenades her on a bugle-like instrument. *Courtesy Eudora Welty LLC.*

Welty and friends on a mid-1930s excursion to Brown's Wells, Mississippi. Hubert Creekmore sits in the front row; in the back are Welty, Margaret Harmon, and Nash Burger. *Courtesy Eudora Welty LLC.*

Monday night

Dear Frank--

Guy played Blue Skies so magnificently a while ago that I thought I would notify you in case you didn't hear it--also Dancing on the Ceiling, Sophisticated Lady, Between the Devil & the Deep Blue Sea, and even the hi... of the week w... was rather more hit than weak. Poor Guy now has to refer to himself as an Esso Marketer or something equally disadvantageous. It's always in the most unpromising circs. that I want to write a letter--the old eyes hurt like fire and I am liable to throw up any minute (my most embarrassing moment). Hubert won a box of candy yesterday with lucky number and we ate with no reverence for layers. I have got it as dark here as a Loew movie house and feel just as restless as if I were really in it so I must do something. You never write, but I'll write and tell you what we did yesterday.

Hubert, Nash and I drove over to Yazoo City. H had heard about an old lady named Mrs Mayes who was stinking with confederate literature and Audubon prints. She lived on the Peak of Tinneriff (sic.) which all the negroes of whom we asked directions designated as Peetinnery. It turned out to be just an erosion sample, whichwas only to be expected after the gal in the drugstore warned us that it wasn't what it used to be that it was acl worn down now and wasn't much. Old lady lived beyond impassable barrier of barbed wire, vegetation, and clouds of dust blowing out from her Confederate collections. Had only 1 tooth and it wasn't very cute. She was scared as Mrs Price and Mrs Scott from Jackson had been there only the day before looking for antique furniture, and she hasn't any furniture, even a chair. She had to sell out and the furniture went first and I suppose the religious book collection will go last. We didn't find much we could use (how? I don't know). H was interested in a set of Swift which was supposed to fill 17 vol. but 8 were missing. Mrs M said the negroes who hauled the books there when they saw that there were several of the same book always took out some

First page of a November 5, 1935, letter from Welty, telling Lyell what songs Guy Lombardo had just played on a radio broadcast, then describing an excursion she made with Hubert Creekmore and Nash Burger. Welty typed many of her letters. Early in this letter, she reported she was suffering from eyestrain, but she managed to continue typing for four pages. *Courtesy Eudora Welty LLC and Mississippi Department of Archives and History.*

Edward Welty, Eudora's brother, 1930s. *Courtesy Eudora Welty LLC.*

August 17, 1940, letter sent while Welty was a fellow at Bread Loaf, Vermont. *Courtesy Eudora Welty LLC and Mississippi Department of Archives and History.*

Bread Loaf Inn

Bread Loaf, Vermont

Dear Frank — Too bad if you don't come up — it's so grand up here — good places to swim, one with 3 waterfalls — The atmosphere is a little odd — rare, lit-erary, talky when you wish it were quiet — all sorts of people — The fellows go over to a secret place & drink

Frank Lyell, Katherine Anne Porter, John Woodburn; taken when Welty was at Yaddo in 1941. *Courtesy Eudora Welty LLC.*

Velty took this photograph of the Lyell family in 1937. Standing are Garland Lyell and Frank Lyell. Seated re Louis Lyell, Clarena Hallam Lyell, and Garland Lyell Jr. *Courtesy Eudora Welty LLC and the Louis yell family.*

Welty in New York City, 1940s. *Courtesy Eudora Welty LLC.*

Snapshot of Frank Lyell in uniform, sent to Welty in January 1945. *Courtesy Eudora Welty LLC and Mississippi Department of Archives and History.*

Frank Lyell, Hubert Creekmore, Dolly Wells, Hildegarde Dolson, 1948, Westchester County, New York. *Courtesy Eudora Welty LLC.*

Eudora Welty's mother, Chestina Welty, 1940s. *Courtesy Eudora Welty LLC.*

Walter Welty, the younger of Welty's brothers, with his daughter, Elizabeth, 1940s. *Courtesy Eudora Welty LLC.*

Left to right, Elizabeth Welty, Mittie Creekmore Welty, Mary Alice Welty, Chestina Welty, 1940s. *Courtesy Eudora Welty LLC.*

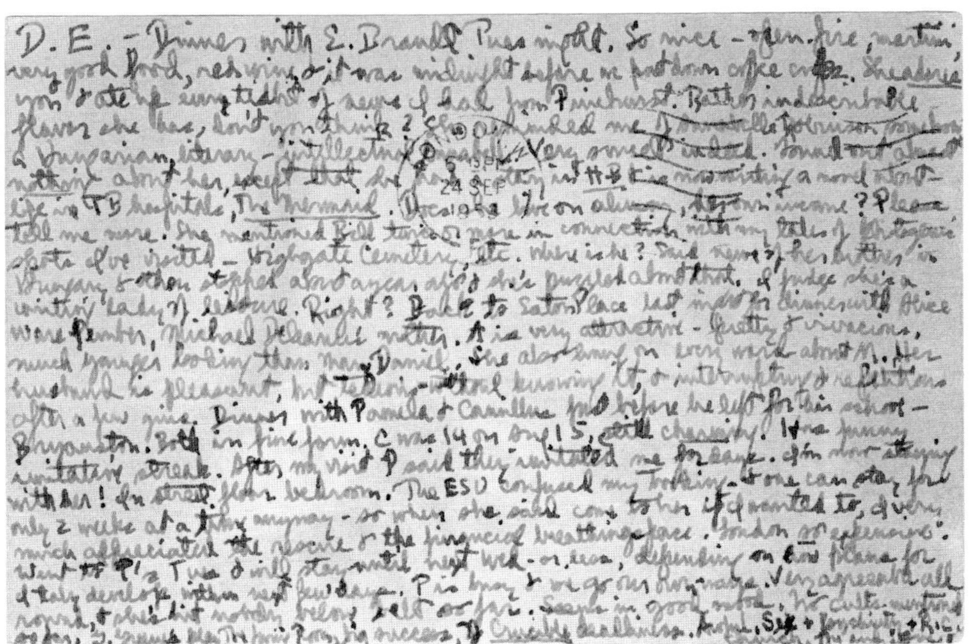

Postcard from Lyell to Welty, September 24, 1953, while he was in London. In her response, she notes the compactness of his handwriting, calling the postcard "your smallest cuneiform to date." *Courtesy Louis Lyell family and Mississippi Department of Archives and History.*

Welty, Mary Lou Aswell, and Frank Lyell in New York, June 26, 1954, before Welty's boat departed for England. *Photo by Louis Lyell, courtesy of Lyell family.*

Postcard from Welty to Lyell wishing him a happy birthday on August 7, 1961. The picture is a 1924 photo titled "May Day by the Scholars of Bryn Mawr College." Welty added a banner for Lyell. *Courtesy Eudora Welty LLC and Mississippi Department of Archives and History.*

Welty and Lyell during her visit to Austin. She lectured at the University of Texas on May 13, 1963. Welty is holding a book called *The Murder of Stanford White* (1962), written by Gerald Langford, Lyell's English Department colleague at North Carolina State University and then at Texas. *Courtesy Louis Lyell family.*

Darling! Is this for me?

It's a Valentine.

IF THE MASTER CAN'T COME TO MOUNTBATTEN . . .

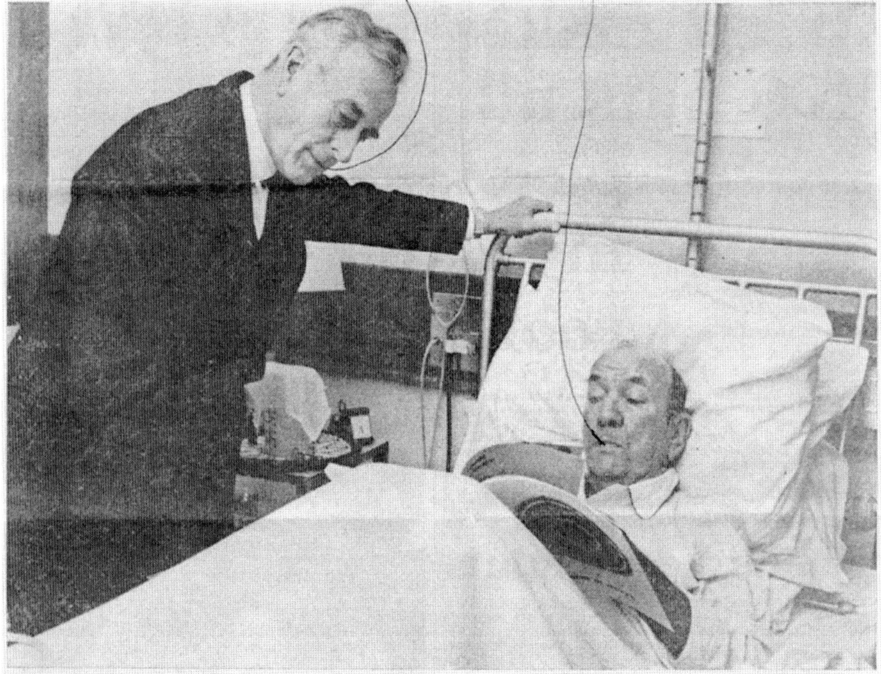

. . . Earl Mountbatten must turn up at the hospital bedside of his old friend Sir Noël Coward

SUNDAY AFTERNOON—the traditional time for the British to visit the sick. And among those who went to London's St. Thomas's Hospital yesterday was Earl Mountbatten, carrying a box of chocolates. They were for Sir Noël Coward, who is progressing well after his attack of pleurisy.

Naturally enough the conversation among the two old friends, both 70, turned to tonight's Royal Festival Hall charity concert, which the Master was to have compered and the earl largely organised.

Lord Mountbatten drily reminded Sir Noël of his reply when invited to take part in the concert —"I'll be there even if I have to come on a stretcher."

Even so, there are few people in the world who are able to bring Mountbatten to them when they are unable to go to Mountbatten.

★ ★ ★

Sir Noël's illness has brought Princess Grace of Monaco back into show business after an absence of 16 years. The former film actress Grace Kelly flew into London last night to compere the "Night of Nights" concert in his place. Today she will have a secret rehearsal with Frank Sinatra—sporting a rejuvenating £3,000 hair transplant—and Bob Hope before the first performance.

HICKEY ASIDES

SIR OSWALD MOSLEY is 74 today—and feeling "better and more energetic than ever," he tells me from his home outside Paris. "My ideal birthday," he said, "would be to spend the morning in the great Paris galleries, lunch in a favourite restaurant, pass the afternoon reading, and go to a concert in the evening." In the event, he admits, he will probably spend the day in his study. "My mind is so full of everything happening in England I cannot stop writing about it."

THE THAMES CONSERVANCY, which as the title suggests is concerned with preserving the beauty of the river, is being accused of doing exactly the opposite. The broadside from Rear-Admiral Roy Foster-Brown, 66, is aimed at the holiday encampment of brown tents which the Conservancy erects every summer on Upper Island, Hurley, Berkshire. Says the admiral, a local councillor: "It is one of the ugliest sights I have ever seen on a river bank."

FOR 41 YEARS Gilbert Dyer has supervised the cooking for the principal, fellows, and undergraduates of Oxford's Hertford College. But now 64-year-old Mr. Dyer has removed the "Head Chef" notice from his door. He has changed his title to "Head Cook" because of his opposition to the Common Market. "I've always been against it," he tells me. "It seems to me nowadays that other people abroad tell us what to do." English cooking, he insists, can be as good as French. And he has already anglicised some names on the dons' menu. Ironically he is founder-master of the Oxford City Guild of Chefs.

News clipping annotated by Welty and enclosed in a letter sent February 10, 1971. In the photo, Lord Mountbatten is visiting Noel Coward, who is reading something while lying in a hospital bed. *Courtesy Eudora Welty LLC and Mississippi Department of Archives and History.*

I judge from the quotes you favored me with as TEMPERATE. Lord! How far do these birds go? I feel annoyed that the first Times review you did had to be on such a book, though—and hope they do better by you next time.[4] I thoroughly enjoyed the review, except I could wish you'd said more on your own + not let the quotes speak for themselves for all—while giving gasps and cries all through it whenever I saw a single word out of that man. And how wonderful you were to clip all the Lil Abners! It was truly wonderful, the wedding with Fabulous Jones—and Mary and Aristide Mian are a-waitin for the outcome, so will send the entire set straight to them. I did write you about the gay Reveillon at Meudon, did you maybe get it after all? [. . .] I could never remember now all the funny little things, like little Pauline Mian, the youngest child, 9, standing in a chair in her sock feet leading a song and a cigarette (chocolate) hanging out of her mouth—or Ami, the middle girl, running to Mary and reporting, "Mama, Pauline has just broken a bottle of champagne over the piano!"—which just seemed a nice christening-idea. [. . .] Aristide is one of my favorite people—at one point he and some friends rose and carried a long ribbon of confetti around the table singing the Volga Boat Song to a communist present. We all had paper hats and noisemakers, my hat had a face on it with tongue sticking out—wonderful time. After the Meudon party (I am telling all again after all) I dashed in on last train and went to party at the apt. of the Peters Sisters, colored singers with the A.B.O Music Hall. (This I didn't tell before, thinking wouldn't be so good for Jackson Xmas reports!—you would like this part though.) They are vast black ladies who do a wonderful show—there are 3 in the act and 2 others and Mama, a California Unity Church member. She had made eggnog and potato salad and chicken salad—and they expected to throw a huge party, the trees all decorated, mistletoe hung, then had to go fill an engagement at a club at 2 AM, which is just when I arrived—and all put on baby blue velvet gowns and rushed out. I imagine the party began with most of the same guests when they returned at 6. The way the Peters and I know them is complicated, and funny, but will have to tell you when I see you—well, they're a name given to Fritz as people who want American dollars for French francs, as they pay their rent in American dollars—so there's a money exchange between them—and they (Peters black) invited them (Peters white) and me to come up for Xmas after we went to their show and saw them backstage. Fritz had already met them—they sounded so funny—that interview is the part I'll have to tell—have an apt. overlooking the Arch of Triumph, 3 bathrooms, etc. An old Lincoln, with French chauffeur. Having a wonderful time in Paris. [. . .] Anyway, after the potato salad and eggnog (made with thin French milk and Scotch!) I went with Ira Morris to have a last drink of champagne—he was the Peters' (white) host that night. He was feeling like another champagne.

[. . .] The only place open was a brasserie on St. Germaine called Royal-St. Germaine (which Hubert told me he used to frequent—he should have seen it for the Xmas Reveillon!) All tables had been reserved—by what looked like lots of people who had come on motorcycles—boys with fur collars on leather jackets, girls in striped suits and hornrims, etc etc., all in paper hats too, and throwing darts with burrs in them at Ira and me, Ira made such smiles at one lady in horn rims! That was a third kind of Reveillon, and fun too. Looked like the setting for a Simenon murder to me, that last place. Anyway—all Christmas I was having a good time but so conscious of Jackson, Miss. and my friends. You were very sweet to come round the Welty tree—I was really hoping you would, and Mother was just delighted. I'm sorry she hadn't got the little books—but glad you're getting one. I would have sent from here, but had not received either. (You know Harcourt.) [. . .]

The place we're staying in now is nice—much nicer than Nice. Do you know it? It's 10 kilometers away from Nice toward the Italian border, and I saw it on a bus ride to Menton last Sunday and fell in love with it, so small and set right between tall rock mountains and the sea, and it's called "Little Africa" and supposed to be the hottest place on the Riviera—and the Riviera just now ain't too hot. We came down and looked around and found a fine pension, small, with wonderful food really, plentiful without end, and comfortable beds, sun, balconies, but just a little cold up until 5 PM when the heat comes on for a few hours—but we stay outdoors in the sun in the mornings. Just now I'm wrapped in dressing gowns and sweaters and bedsocks on top of clothes to write at typewrite before night. But so beautiful—and I feel it will warm up before long. The rocks are opalescent colored and remind me in shape and a kind of translucent air of Goya's "City on a Rock," all pink and blue and sky. [. . .] John is coming over, did you hear? He got his Fulbright at last, and will be at Florence. He's on the Saturnia now. He wrote he was writing me where he'd land, but of course that letter too is among the missing—so I don't know quite when he'll come, but he said he would come to Nice for a little while before studies began, so we look forward to a houseparty at Beaulieu—would you were joining us! What about that summer trip? Do you think you really might come? You will have to finish the work you started in California first, I suppose, but what then? Dolly too thinks she may come to Italy in May—did she tell you about the possibility? How amazing about the Rattler leaving <u>and</u> arriving at reasonable hours! Jackson is just getting too big.

[. . .] I'll be in Beaulieu, the way I think now, for the rest of January and into Feb. probably—because it's lovely and cheap ($3 a day for room and 3 meals!) and I like the sun. Have done most of work on a story, and will try to send carbon to you when I type it up[5]—god knows what will become of it, but will start it out.

Good luck, and write soon. Love, and thanks again for all the news about everybody at home, and the clippings—much joy to have here.

Yours,

Eudora

No, haven't read "Ceremony of Innocence"—Have you read "Loving" and "Back" by Henry Green? Strongly recommend. My little Circe story in new Accent—[6] [. . .]

During February, traveling on a Fulbright fellowship, John Robinson caught up with Welty and her friends in the South of France. He was along on the excursion Welty describes in the following letter. At Nice's Carnival, festivities featured roaming puppets with enormous heads and the practice of stuffing confetti in the mouths of strangers. A few of these puppets appear in Welty's Photographs.

February 14, 1950 • Beaulieu to Austin

Dear Frank—

Indeed I did get the lettre grasse, though late—all mail seems delayed these days both ways, stormy. So pleased to have all the good clips, and think the Fearless Fosdick case intriguing. We all read every line, and I sent on to Aristide Mian in Paris. [. . .]

The Pension here continues good. The rains came and I think went, tho today it's clouded up a bit—but it has been just perfect—sapphire sea, flawless sky, and the olive trees blowing in the breezes all the way up the beautiful mountain. John arrived for a week, and when he left, Mary Lou and Fritz accompanied him to see Florence under his care—they know no Italian at all—and are going on to Rome from there. Then they may return to Sous Les Palmiers, as both are working, and although they have a house given to them outside Paris for March, hints are everywhere that it will be simply freezing there at that time. John hopes to return this week, after he gets all in order, and stay another week or so. Hildy Dolson is here—sends you her best—and Mary Mian. It's all like a Russell & Volkening houseparty, in fact I warned Diarmuid we would have a panorama group photo taken with banner, "The Riviera for Russell & Volkening!" sent him, suitable for hanging in the office. Mary and Hildy are both working, but I feel so lazy—have never gotten that one story typed up in the last stages. What are you doing about that paper for Austin? Do you think you are going to have it finished by vacation time, and then what? Had a letter from Hubert saying he is thinking seriously about Europe but doesn't know. I do wish everybody were here, right in Beaulieu—it's so nice, and so cheap. The room, board, wine, coffee, and bath bill for a whole week amounts to about $20 American money. [. . .]

We went in to see Carnival open, and it was fun—all strangely orderly, though, compared to our second visit—Sunday afternoon—when we were caught up in great T.s of H. (Hope you know that's tides of humanity.) I got separated and lost—later found—and the method of throwing confetti here is specific, thus:—You grab somebody from behind, bend their backs down, and with your fistful of confetti keep pushing it in their mouths—sort of apache style. Ladies to men, men to ladies, children to all. The first time a man grabbed me and fed me confetti I was so mad I turned around to do I don't know what, hit him, only to find he had a little child of two riding his shoulders throughout, quite detached child. Little children are the worst, they throw from below, and you can't hit <u>little</u> children, esp. with glasses on! Wonderful floats and best of all the Gros Tetes—I esp. liked the Cave Men, and hope they will be in some newsreel—a whole company of them, with long yellow hair, big clubs, and big pink muscles and fierce expressions—we had to run right under some of them to get through the parade opening night, and saw one of them smoking inside, blowing out his little peephole, which was in the Cave Man's tummy. It was so cute seeing the little children throwing confetti down those holes, and peeping in. There were some beautiful costumes that looked as if they stemmed from the medieval days—and one company rode black horses and were dressed in feathers, big wide blue wings spread out, bird heads, and each carried a staff made to look like a miniature telegraph pole, in which were sitting tiny golden birds. I tried to take some pictures yesterday, but you can imagine my chances. Came home with confetti all over and inside—Mary said it was all inside her girdle. We intend, nevertheless, to go to the Battle of the Flowers and the Battle of <u>Plaster</u> (?!)

Had a Christmas card from E.M. Forster. When John came over he brought a little bundle of cards that had arrived in Jackson, this was one. It was another photo of his studio, but this time he was in it—a little note inside said "Have been intending to write, but have not been well. I enjoyed your book, especially Moon Lake."—Did I ask you if you'd seen a little story of mine in the Autumn Accent, which I just received? About Circe.

No, never did get out to Chartres—[. . .] Have been to Vence—think I wrote you about that, the visit to Matisse's church. I still like his paintings better on canvas, and there was something about the Vierge's looking like any and all of his jeunes filles that seemed wrong—all right when part of design, but as the religious center of a window or a painting—don't know. But you have to be delighted that a man in his 80s is still attempting something he's never tried before, and the idea of using glass as the coloring agent, light instead of pigment, is fascinating—would love to see the actual, finished church.

Friday, went down to Monte Carlo to see my friend Lady Harvey from Paris—I told you about meeting and liking her, the British Ambassadress—she wrote she'd been banished there to recover from bouts of flu. We had a nice lunch—and talked a long time, she too loves Forster, though doesn't know him—she has read <u>much</u>. Heard a story you'd love—she said they'd noticed old Rothschild there at their hotel, (Hotel de Paris) constantly with a girl that didn't seem his type at all—youngish but dowdy—not a lover, not a typist since he doesn't need one—what was the relationship? Then a mutual friend remarked, "I say, have you seen old Maurice Rothschild and his <u>blood</u> <u>donor</u>?"

Which somehow reminds me of those psychological criticisms you're reading and I'd like to see the second review, if not too ghastly to cut out of paper and send, or somehow. But like you, I think enough is enough, and I hope you get something really worth your time and effort to read and review next time. [. . .]

Love, and do write me soon here—I don't know plans beyond, and expect to stay here while it's so cold everywhere else.

Happy Mardi Gras!

Eudora

February 25, 1950 • Beaulieu to Austin

Dear Frank—

Mother mentioned you <u>did</u> get a letter from me, so maybe the mails are getting innocent again. Your letter, with all the good clips, happily received. The Abners choice indeed—+ I was amused too at the Wilson Atonement for the Easter season—yet in <u>perfect</u> character—Yes, flatterer! [. . .] Amazed about Jean [*Stafford*], somehow—I've owed her a letter since Jan., when she went to Yaddo—not sure whether I met that man at her apt. or not, did meet one Luce man, who came with Jean to a party I had—Hubert will remember, that heat-wave party. Anyway, Jean needs badly to be happy, + I hope this is what will do it for her.[7] Glad to have the news.—Good about applying for Fulbright—to England, I assume? John applied in June, & heard Feb. 1 he was to sail Feb. 9—the message finding him in Acapulco. This was the first year of the Italian awards, which probably accounts for the delay & all—the Eng. would be all in order + prompter, I'm sure. The Fulbright people were very nice about all, to John, + assured him he <u>would</u> get it, but explained about new set-ups, etc. + advised him to enter another school first semester—hence

Mexico. He is having a funny time at the U. in Florence—all in order now, I think—

Mary & Hildy are still here—On Tuesday, Mary is going back to Paris (a wonderful letter from Pauline, 9, this a.m. "Come + defend me, mama, against papa, against Ami, against Mickey, against Simone" the whole household—"Every one is mistreating me. Come bringing many presents".)—Hildy to Capri, + I'm going on to Italy at last—to Florence by bus. John says weather much better now, but he has had flu—The Peters are back in Paris, they have Edita Morris's cottage for Feb. & March, + both hope to write—though it's certain to be cold,—they will have to build their own fires to keep warm—

[. . .] Address next will be ℅ Am. Ex., Florence—do write soon. I think letters come safely now that the Xmas season is over—Hope so—

Good luck and send the news—

Love,

Eudora

Will send report on Carnival when have typewriter—writing this out of house—

April 7, 1950 • London to Austin

Euston Sta., London, Good Friday

Dear Frank—

You, I know, would be in St. Paul's at this time, & I'm in a 3rd class coach starting off to Ireland. Maybe as it is you're in Monterey? I hope so, for it sounds like a lovely Easter idea—Happy Easter! I guess I'll be in Dublin—

Forgive the recent lack of letters—Florence was busy—+ so beautiful, as you know, that I was always dashing out to look at something new or something again. The Spring was perfect there—all the fruit trees, almond, cherry, apple, peach, came in flower, then leaf while I was there. I stayed at Hotel Berchielli, on Lungarno + for 10 days had a Room with a View—right over the river—[. . .]. John was then in Florence too, has by now gone up in the hills to a house he has rented—on the remote side, so he hopes to write there. The life in Florence, so pleasant + a good many people always to be seeing, that privacy is next to impossible. Bill + Barbara Smith, a young couple living at San Domenico, are the nicest people I know in Florence—he came over to Eng, as a Rhodes scholar, she joined him + they moved later to Italy, have a 6-month-old baby—both write, + he, I think, is very good indeed. Recently he's sold a book of poems in U. S. + here too, + is working on a novel.[8] They have a car + took John + me on little trips—Siena—They also took us to lunch at Berenson's, amusing time—the old man is scheduled as everything, operates for lunch tea, + dinner each day, with selected guests,

+ exercises his wits and humors on them, cross-examines them on their own subjects, you know, about which he knows more than they're likely to, & knows the latest.[9] He asked me all about Faulkner—says Pylon is his favorite, + I suppose that's because he sees a parallel between it + Dante—! Do you know a British critic named Raymond Mortimer? He was a house guest at the time—sat on his neck, hugging his knees—said "Everyone writing these days is named Green—Graham, Henry, etc.—you ought to be named Green, B.B." Mr. Berenson didn't seem to take to that so well.—You might have visited the place too, did you—and the library? The gardens were wonderful—18th century, though the house is in part old. The wonderful Sasetta on the drawing room wall! One of the St. Francis ones. The Sienese school is the one I prefer to all, so far—those Duccias in the Cathedral Museum in Siena! Also I love Lucca. John + I went down on a bus tour for a day—he knew it during war while at Pisa—and the earlier churches are more exciting than those at Siena to me, in a way—Of course I haven't seen Pisa yet—[. . .]

Enclose your clippings you wanted back—so many treasures you sent!—+ will send you a few but our airmail must be so featherweight. An item in the morning Times "from our Special Correspondent" on "Spring Scenes at Kew" ends, "At Kew there are ample signs that Spring, though not unduly hurrying, is with us now in earnest—and not least is the chiff-chaff calling industriously from the boughs." Could send you lots of that! + I love it.

Pamela [*Travers*] & Camillus send you their love. [. . .] By the way, have you read "Christ Stopped at Eboli" by Carlo Levi? It's a fine book. It's about that part of Italy near where I was invited for Easter, + would love to have gone—by Jimmie Festa, the young dancer I met on the boat, whose relatives live on a big place near Benevento. He came by Florence while I was there, + renewed his invitation so attractively—a wonderful houseparty!—making me so sad to miss it—The family give a big feast to the village on Easter Monday—+ there are all kinds of doings to be seen, + it's away from everywhere—old, old, pre-Roman—Jimmie by the way is to be in a musical show over here co-starring with Anna Magnani—+ is eager to start!

[. . .] I miss the beautiful hills + springtime + food of Italy—but hope the green of Ireland is as lovely as I've imagined it. Will be writing soon—Thanks again for your fine letters, + keep me posted on all.

On May 8 I'll be in Naples, + on 25th of May in Florence—probably the safest Am. Ex. P.O.'s—For about a week each—I don't enjoy this jumping about as much as the lolling about I've done up to now—but all is great joy—

Love,
Eudora

Welty continued to meet and befriend literary people, including the novelist Henry Green, whose novel Nothing *had just been published. At the party she mentions to Lyell in the following letter, another attendee, John Lehmann, said the two writers "flung themselves at one another." Welty later said she was "captivated" by Green.*[10]

April 29, 1950 • London to Austin

Dear Frank—

Delightful to have the good news of the grant-in-aid from the Huntington! Of course you should have had it, but that's not always a guarantee—such a nice thing—now you can finish up the work you began last summer & maybe have time still left over for other things—So pleased to hear about it—

This just a line, owing to pressure of getting errands done, etc. before Sat. closing time everywhere—+ to see some plays! Seeing the 2 Hermiones tonight, + Venus Obs. this aft.[11]

I leave Genoa June 2 + I reckon that puts me in NY around the 13th—No, I don't plan to hang around NY—no money will be left, for one thing—Maybe you'll be there then—Is school out that early?

Met Henry Green—talks a blue streak——very funny—"Nothing" is out just now—Shall we be going into bookstores + asking them to wrap up Nothing, if they have it?

To Paris tomorrow, then Naples as of May 8 to meet Dolly, who has sailed now from NY—Thanks for birthday greetings!

Love,
Eudora

May 16, 1950 • Assisi to Austin

[*Postcard of fresco painting of St. Clare of Assisi*]

Dear Frank—

Dolly went to Lake Como and I stopped off in Assisi—so lovely here now—do you know this place? You must have come to see the Giottos and Martinis! Went up to see the monastery in the mt. where St. F lived—his bed (cold and short) cut in the bare rock—+ some caves where some of them lived—expected to see lions. The view of all Umbria from there! So many pelegrini even here, had to find a bed in a private home—very modest + the finest *** view in the world.

Love,
E

Sending English clippings by regular mail.

May 24, 1950 • Venice to Jackson

Got your letter + clippings safely in Florence + thanks—In Venice for 3 days—what a lovely and fantastic city—Dolly + the Smiths + I are together—Today took steamer to Torcello + saw those wonderful mosaics—Have been visiting the Tintorettos here—we hope to stop in Padua to see Giottos on way back tomorrow. Spent 4 days in John's fine villa + he had a dance for us + Italian neighbors last week. Hope school ends successfully + you have good trip home.

Love,
E

June 5, 1950 • Transatlantic crossing to Jackson

[*Postcard of a ship*]

Dear Frank—

Here we come—a lovely ship, grand food, + so far, cielo sereno, mare calma—+ so blue. We pass through Gibraltar sometime in the night. Are you in Jackson? I'll be there soon as I don't plan to tarry long in NY. Are you visiting NY? I so hated to leave—you know how it is! Love from Dolly + me—

Eudora

July 20, 1950 • Jackson to Pasadena

Dear Frank—

An astounding bit of news, which I'm loath to tell you—Willia [*Wright Bennett*] got married—I know so little to tell, too—the family so far as I know haven't reported it, but Willia phoned Worth [*Willia's daughter*], who was at a little camp near Allison's Wells, + Worth told Catherine Lotterhos, who told her mother—A man of 45, a salesman, from the Delta, named Sessums (?)—a divorcé, who bought Willia a car + they are gone off to the coast + New Orleans—I feel completely apprehensive about it all.

"Where does Willia meet the man?" Mother asked. I wonder if it could be in hotels on her occasional little trips with Bertha. W has been asking me how much money it would take for two to live in Europe—

Helen Lotterhos, who phoned me about it, says that before this, Willia was deeply interested in another man who would come see her, but the family made so much objection + fuss that Willia has therefore kept this new friend a secret. She told Helen, à propos the other friend, in her most emotional way, that it meant so much to her to have a new interest + affection—Of course, what she's done is understandable, but have you ever dreamed of her doing anything more foolhardy and dangerous? It really frightens me not to be told anything by anybody. Worth told Catherine that the man's first wife was "a millionairess"—he may think Willia one too, I fear. He plans later on to take her to Mexico City—Well, if I hear any more news, I'll let you know, + I hope it may be something to alter the present complexion, but I don't see how it can—

How do things go at the Huntington?

Love,

Eudora

August 17, 1950 • Jackson to Pasadena

Dear Frank—

Here's a grim one ["*The Burning*"]—not, somehow, about France or Italy, but about the Civil War in Ole Miss, yes indeed—Read when you have time, + see what you think—Have just finished—so hot + West Va. company was here—children staying now with us while Walter + Mittie on trip—Eliz. only wants to play 20 Questions—we got Janey's left eye (nurse)—but missed Baby Jesus's Star—Will write more soon—Hope all goes fine, have enjoyed your cards. How is that paper? I saluted you of course on your birthday, but was a sitter—

Love,

Eudora

P.S. Would you please return MS. Thanks!

September 15, 1950 • Jackson to Pasadena

Dear Frank,

Wonder if you could send me that story back by return airmail? I need it—thanks—Appreciate your reading it. I think now it may be the better of the two versions after all, at least I want to do a bit with the two together. Hope you hadn't already sent it and it got lost somewhere. Mary Lou likes it and I want to get it just so before she gets a decision on it.

Thanks for the Labor Day Midnight note from SF—isn't it a lovely town? You sounded as if you were having a gay time—of course you loved the cablecars—I used to live out on Washington St. at the end of one of the lines—Powell or something I think—there where it goes high along the bay all the way up to Golden Gate. Did you ever take the train across the Bay Bridge—wonderful. [. . .] The hills and all the interest of SF must have looked specially fine after Southern California. There are some fine Italian and Chinese restaurants I used to go to but did not memorize their names or where they were—usually with other people. I liked going to Top of the Mark too—every sunset different of course. Wonderful at night too. Did you go in the old Palace bar? With all the red plush and gilt and so on—fun. [. . .] I loved the De Y. museum too—the site of the other one's more impressive and they had some nice things too, but of course De Young has more treasures. I used to love to go to the beach—Cliff House and all—envy your being there. Too bad if Monteux wasn't playing—such a nice concert hall too. There was usually wonderful music on Sundays at the War Memorial—did you hear any there?

Willia hopes to go to Mobile soon to join her new husband—she has had a hard time, suffering from family pressure of the most ruthless sort I think. It's her life, and if she's done this she has a right to go ahead and try to make it work, I am on her side absolutely—just so she isn't harmed—even so, I think she should do what she wants. Maybe she'll get to leave soon—is waiting to get word about an apartment, Mr. Sessions [*Willia's new husband*] being there now looking for one I understand. Worth has gone back to All Saints. She looks well and talks with great control and so much hope. Jackson has never had so good a time as talking about her—you'd be astounded at what even so-called friends don't hesitate to say—and such curiosity. Of course Aimee distinguished herself as usual with the worst and nastiest, but others did their part.

It's beautiful weather now—that fall feeling—muscadines were ripe, I made jelly, the woods are beautiful. Went to Oxford last weekend to visit Ella [*Somerville*]—Hubert, Jimmy and I drove up picking up Eliz. Spencer at Carrollton—had fun. Rained the whole time—missed seeing Faulkner, who was out at the lake—but we sat, ate, drank, and laughed till the cows came home. Ella is fine and we spoke of you. I'm anxious to hear how the Richardson work looks now.

We sure do miss your return trip—wish you could have grabbed a passenger and made this flying visit, but can see it would have been an ordeal. Hope all goes well with the return to Austin, and you get settled and all to suit you. Let us hear from you. Thanks again for sending the story. I think I went too far with it the second time and underlined and explained all too much—it stayed more meaningful with less of that. I did name it "The Ghosts" but may not leave that—don't know yet. Am now working on a new one—not very far along though. [. . .]

Write soon—Hope all goes well, and the summer profitable.
Love,
Eudora
Hope you haven't missed Abner lately. Suprisin smith—

Welty continued to revise "The Burning," set in 1860s Jackson, about three women entrapped by a slave society. Modern-day Jackson, as she reported to Lyell, was attempting to rein in their friend Willia, whose sudden marriage was deemed unsuitable.

September 20, 1950 • Jackson to Austin

Dear Frank—

Much obliged for sending the story + so promptly—Sorry I put you to the bother when you'd just got back—had thought I'd mentioned it was my copy—Is the weather any cooler? It's hot here too—a small shower falling just now.

Anne Wright planned to ask your address, + wondered if I'd told you of Willia's marriage, as she "couldn't bring herself to mention it"—said I could add to what I'd told you that she'd just had a letter (dictated) from W.—She left for Mobile—saying she was fine, but not rereading much—"like getting word from behind the Iron Curtain"—but then W is bitter toward them. I hope all is safe with her. I don't feel any less anxious about <u>that</u> part of it—I only meant that the step is taken, + that W., granting her the premise that the sudden step was OK, should be allowed to try to work it out from there, + to feel hopeful, now + at least as long as she can, + to think of her life as her own. Of course it's easy to see all the Wrights' side too—the shock + anxiety + fright—+ I feel especially for Worth, who must not know <u>what</u> values to trust now—Will let you know if I hear anything. Willia doesn't want her address given out but I asked Anne if I could write her a note + leave it with her to send—I'm <u>sure</u> she needs cheer—if you feel like a note (I <u>don't</u> know what I'll write exactly!)

Isn't Surprisin Smith surprising? Hope you haven't missed any on your travels.

The fantastic hotel sounded like a scene from a play—grand—Loved the conversation—Kauffmanish.

A right good movie is "Mystery Street" with Else Lanchester as a gin-drinking landlady, & Richard Montalban, who I think is good too.

Yes the Palace has its old bar (restored after the Fire) intact—do wish you'd found it—amazing—

Love,
E
Did you read Mrs Keyes in Atlantic?

November 3, 1950 • Jackson to Austin

Dear Frank,

Here a few items—

How is all with you? Do you have time to do work on the study—Richardson? We're having a change in the weather—rain, cool—has been 88. Got caught with bulbs unplanted—and going up to N.Y. for a few weeks tomorrow night. (Sat.)—Have been working hard but tired out with various interruptions, etc. Staying at the old Bristol Hotel, not visiting—for about 2 weeks, hope to work on a story I'm writing, in the mornings—play in the evenings. May go up to Vermont to visit two friends from Florence, Bill & Barbara Smith, later—Need a trip, I feel—don't we all.

Hubert's been down with bad cold, Willie Spann is now + Charlotte is too.—Hubert better I hear—Helen had a letter from Willia yesterday, all seeming well—she said the parents of her husband had been over for a visit—He seems to be still there (traveling used to be his business, don't know whether he's working, not working, or what) + W. says he does all the grocery shopping + likes to fool around in the kitchen—She seemed content + well.

Was grieved to hear from Mary Lou that she + Fritz have separated—shocks me, as well—they seemed so happy & well—One reason I want to go up is see M.L., it's gotten her down—

[. . .] Did you know the old Henry house on Fortification is now the Arthur Murray School? All day + night you see all lighted up + couples ball-rooming by the windows—chesty ladies in flowing gowns—neon sign + jukebox—!—

Please return these letters of Thurber—what do you think of that? I finally decided he meant it + wanted me to write Faulkner, so I did—rather deadpan and of necessity—

[. . .] Love,
Eudora

Saw your mother and father a little while the other night—seemed well + fine—
P.S. Ruth Ford told William Archibald—know who he is? I don't—to read Robber Bridegroom + do a musical, + he wrote me about it—asked could he a year from now. Nice of her—is he a composer or—mercy!—a producer? Will try to see him in NY—[12]

Welty saw Elizabeth Bowen in New York, and Bowen visited Mississippi a few weeks later. In the company of her glamorous, magnetic guest, Welty appeared to take much more pleasure in being in Mississippi.

November 30, 1950 • Jackson to Austin

Dear Frank—

What a grand time Elizabeth Bowen and I had, and what a joy it was to have her—she must be one of the nicest people in the world—just to come down so far, in between lectures in Massachusetts, shows you how sweet she is. We took off Thanksgiving morning (she'd had her turkey the night before, on flying in) for the river country, and went all over the place, Natchez going and coming, and dipping down below Baton Rouge to see that old Belle Grove plantation ruin—crossing the river twice, on ferries, and the St. Francisville one is amazing as you may know, no towns visible on either bank, just the wild river and trees, and it was just sunset and a brilliant one, with wild geese flying over. She saw and took in the whole shebang of course with the most rapidity, and I think it delighted her, which gave me pleasure. We went to Rodney, Windsor—Longwood, Melrose, Rosalie—Parlange on False River on the La. side—I had her eating fried catfish and enchiladas, and drinking chickory coffee, all of which she liked and we played slot machines and took walks, talked, took along some good gin, rode and rode, had really a tremendously lovely time. How good it was to see her. She fascinated them all, from the waitresses and bellhops, up, and got in long talks with all kinds of people. As to people here, she didn't see a single soul, and although I was selfishly relishing that, I felt badly about not getting back in time for her to see Hubert. We just made it back in time for her to go. I was never sorrier to see anybody leave. She is supposed to fly to India when she gets back, which I hope she won't do—things look so awful in that direction, don't they.

How is everything?

I was glad of the clippings—and have more Beachcombers for you, are you tired of them?[13] When home for Christmas?

Love,
Eudora

Welty's extant letters to Lyell from early 1951 do not record her family's health emergency. Walter Welty developed respiratory troubles that led to an operation and prolonged stay in a New Orleans clinic, where Welty spent several days with his wife, Mittie. In late February she wrote Lyell that Walter was "getting along all right" and that she was preparing for another trip to New York and then abroad. Their friend Willia [Bennett, now Sessums] was now at Mineral Wells, a Texas clinic. "Wish you could see her, is it far? For an indefinite length of time—"[14]

While abroad again that spring, Welty took a train and ferry ride from London to Ireland to visit Bowen. This journey inspired "The Bride of the Innisfallen." The protagonist had been experiencing difficulties in her marriage and found anonymous travel to be liberating and magical. This story would become her first to appear in The New Yorker. *William Maxwell, who like Bowen was becoming one of Welty's close writer friends, became her* New Yorker *editor. "I love your train story beyond all possibility of telling you," he wrote her in June.*[15] *On the same date, Welty wrote Lyell from London.*

June 6, 1951 • London to Jackson

Dear Frank,

Are you home? When do you go up East? I hope school ended satisfactorily, you got a rest (and no cold) and have heard some news by now of the Fulbright. ???

[. . .] Thanks for the reassuring words on The Burning—Hubert had written me something like that himself. It's not such a difficult story—is it? Did you know Herschel [*Brickell*] gave it 2nd in the O. Henry, so that's $200—hooray for cash. The one I wrote in Ireland is at present at the New Yorker which is wanting it with some buts attached—I will have to make up my mind when I see what the buts are. It is by the way in Jackson, and I would like you to read it when you have time. I sent it by boat a few weeks back—[. . .]

I just got my typewriter in the honey. The little flat is mine now, and I fix breakfast and write on this card table. We are having divine weather—at long last—oh, I wish you could be here for it! I went to the Festival last night with three friends—for the first time—to the South Bank, then down the river by boat to the Battersea place for the fireworks—it's all very light, gay, airy, and entertaining I think—shows imagination all around—I feel everybody who hates the idea has a lot of right to, yet since they've done it anyway, I think they should have credit for some delightful foolishness—[. . .]

Elizabeth and I went to The Three Sisters with Ralph Richardson the other night—I'd seen it previously a few weeks ago—The first act is so awful [. . .] But the second and third are just wonderful—the play got them, I think that's what happened. R.R. is very stylized—but I think good. He has such vitality—and in Act 2 when he says "I feel in such a strange mood tonight—I want to speak about the future!" while all is burning outside and the others are stretched exhausted on floor and couch—wonderful!

I'm going to Ireland tomorrow for a few weeks, then back to London—write me to 21 Wellington Square, London S.W. 3—do you know where that is? Right next to Smith St. P. Travers is okay but spends at least 6 nights a week at some Gurdjieff class—rhythmic dancing, etc.[16] and is in a remote mood from the everyday world—she sent love to you—Lots of luck + love, + write soon—

E

Welty remained abroad through July, spending more time with Bowen in London and in Ireland, at Bowen's Court, then returning to resume her life in Jackson. On October 10, in one of the only extant letters from fall 1951, Welty encouraged Lyell to come home for Thanksgiving, since Elizabeth Bowen would be coming for another visit. On January 27 she wrote Lyell, "I'm a professor too! No, was elected to the National Institute of Arts + Letters." Another informative clipping she enclosed in February was entitled "Catholic Information: God Has No Beard." It began, "God is not an old man. He does not sit, enthroned in Heaven beneath a halo, looking severely at the world He made one week, long, long ago."

Welty continued to encourage Lyell to apply for a Guggenheim fellowship for the coming year, when he had applied for a research leave. As she notes in the next letter, she was also lecturing. In April, Katherine Anne Porter canceled the reading she had agreed to do at MSCW, introduced by Welty, so Welty had to give a lecture in her place.

May 14, 1952 • Jackson to Austin

Dear Frank,

Thanks for letter + clippings. I hope the Dallas operas were beautiful. Mother got the grandest Dallas card from you. It was so sweet of you, she was proud to death to be so thought of. [. . .] I'm dashing up to N.Y. this Thursday 15th, for about 3 weeks, I think now. [. . .] Wish you were going to be there! Are you still thinking of it at all, or have you dropped the idea? Costs are so formidable—the ticket (R.T. + berth one way) from Jackson is $119.70! (My royalties check just came & was $120.40, so that was a sign—whether to go or stay home I won't say, but I am going. [. . .]

Finished my story—45 pages—which I like, but suppose it's not saleable at that length—+ just mailed in. When Mother has ploughed through the carbon I'll save or send it to you—but it's rough reading—My new typewriter doesn't produce a clean one—Name—"Kin"—I do like it! But my long one still not finished. So much interruption—not the least of which was going to Columbus to make a speech. I was put out with Katherine Anne! [. . .]

Let me hear from you in NY if you aren't too busy finishing up—c/o Rosa F, 31 East 120 Apt. 4—F. So I can present your messages & greetings to all our friends. (Mary Alice's message to Hubert: Tum home.)

Thanks for Gugg lists—Next year, it must include you. How much more work now lies ahead?

I hope all goes fine—

Love,

Eudora

The New Yorker accepted "Kin," and William Maxwell spent a day editing it with her while she was in New York.[17] *She sent Russell "No Place for You, My Love" on July 20. In it, two strangers meet in New Orleans, then take a long car ride together "south of south" through an exotic landscape teeming with untameable life, each seeking temporary escape from troubled relationships back home. By this time, Welty no longer thought of herself as being in a partnership with Robinson, whose relationship with Enzo Rochiggiani had become evident to Welty in summer 1951.*[18] *"No Place for You, My Love" may reflect a drive Welty had taken in 1951, shortly after realizing Robinson loved Rochiggiani; Welty's long drive was with Carvel Collins, a Harvard scholar who was visiting Mississippi and New Orleans for his research on Faulkner.*[19]

July 29, 1952 • Jackson to Sewanee

[*Typed on verso of letter from Jackson College for Negro Teachers, inviting Welty to speak at "75 Years of Literature by Negroes in America."*[20]]

Dear Frank,

Thanks for all communiques—I've been so glad to get them. The set-up there sounds fine, except for traffic & heat & maybe the heat will abate (or what are mountains for?) and the traffic, being gotten used to, will settle down to a drone—hope so. I'm glad it's worked out, though we miss you here. When Robert Daniel comes, tell him hello. (Thanks for info on Inn but I'd best stay in one place.)

Thank you so much for letting me see the Faulkner piece. Strange combination of the honesty, unsparing as always and youthful at the same time, and moonings—and some of his key things in it—highly interesting. Here it is back. I have one issue of the Double Dealer, somewhere, with things by Faulkner, poems—I'll look for it again when you're back. [. . .]

I heard one [*expression*] I'd never heard, "looks like the last of pea-time," meaning of course tacky, specially tacky. Saw Willia twice and she seems full of life. Willie S. asked Louise L. and me to drink a mint julep at 6, which sounds cheering. Look over this Gugg. list and be inspired to apply. It's all right to study the universe I approve, but when it comes to poultry artificial selection and earthworm inheritance—! The usual large number of earthquake and tidal boys, plus a few of the enzyme boys. You apply. John suddenly sailed for Italy, "job-hunting."[21]

Love,

E

[. . .]

August 19, 1952 • Jackson to Sewanee

Dear Frank,

So sorry you've got that wretched cold—[. . .]. The trip I planned to N.O. to an air-conditioned hotel to finish up a story in is also off, but can do it later. Had the New Yorker taken the 3rd story when I wrote? [*"No Place for You, My Love"*] The short (25 pp.) one I finished lately—Bill Maxwell called me up on the phone for the questions this time, which was sweet of him—though I can't say I was very bright at my end—it's supposed to come out in Sept. This is how I'm having the rooms painted & getting colic. The next 2 stories will be too long for any magazine at all but I'm rather enjoying them. One is called "Never Mind, Uncle Daniel," which I guarantee has nothing to do with our friend Robert—to whom HELLO—but I think I named him during the Billy Graham revival. There've been such good Voice-of-the-people letters, on + on, about B.G., liquor election, + presidential election, usually all 3 subjects fit naturally into one letter, but having misplaced the prize one I haven't felt the rest were fit to send you.

I go to Whitfield [*state mental hospital*] 2 or 3 times a week to see Alice,[22] who has finally been moved to convalescent this last time—She must therefore be better in the doctor's eyes, but with me she concentrates on pleading to get out so they are painful visits + I'm uncertain how much good it does her to let go like that. Listen: if I ever end up out there in White Female Receiving, I don't want anybody to come to see me there. Just send me detective stories (English country house) and then English Literature if I'm moved to Convalescent, there's a bench by the lake. Send me War + Peace then.

Did you see Katherine Anne's piece on Willa Cather in Mademoiselle for August—think I memo-ed you[23]—Like most of her recent pieces it's a good bit to do with how the other writer differs from Katherine Anne but is interesting—+ I guess part of her collection that's coming out—Do you know how her health is now? [. . .] I still hope to go to N.Y. this fall—when are you?

Love—
Eudora

Letters from New York shortly before the presidential election record Welty's support for Adlai Stevenson, running against Dwight Eisenhower.

October 27, 1952 • New York to Austin

[*To Lyell. Postcard with no greeting*]

Glad to get yours. Nice but full time here. Katonah this weekend + leaving right away for New Haven with R.P. Warren, spending night with the [*Cleanth*] Brookses. Lehman's Mikado opening very exciting—hope it keeps on. Working on my Kin proofs at NYer Wed.—think of me. Hope all goes well. Nash said your F. Brawne review in + fine.[24]

Love,
E

Terribly excited for Stevenson and hoping.

November 3, 1952 • New York to Jackson

Dear Frank,

Best of luck on that committee—hope it meets soon and does you right and all goes beautifully now [*presumably Lyell requested a research leave*]. Let me know.

I heard the news about John Woodburn too late to go to the funeral or anything, but it seems he simply dropped dead while shaving, at home in the country. Very much distressed about it—I have never met his present wife, but everyone says she is extremely nice, a lovely person—and she must be so terribly shocked by the way it happened.

Yes, I've seen Katherine Anne, we had a warming reunion. After 3 or 4 false starts at getting together—she kept cancelling—she asked me to dinner the other night—lives right around the corner, 117 S. 17, and cooked a fine steak, had bourbon, wine, salad, etc. and we had a nice evening of talk in which she said nothing but nice things about all our mutual friends, and me, and was full of good feeling toward the world it seemed, instead of bad. I hope this has really happened to her. At any rate, relations between her and me are now easy again, thank God. I hate that feeling that there is animosity somewhere at work between me and an old friend. Also went to hear her read at YMHA

[*92nd Street Y, Poetry Center*] the other night. Flowering Judas, That Tree, and The Grace, and answered questions from audience. I must say she still said, with perfect aplomb in answer to a question "Do you revise much?" "No, I never change a single word in writing my fiction. My novel is a single draft." I suppose it is kind of a defense against this terrible delay or block she has—don't know. She looked lovely, and read of course beautifully.

All I can really think of today is election, and I feel if Stevenson is not elected we had all just better get out of the country. I feel so strongly moved by that man, think him so great. I've been mailing his speeches home, as of course none of them get printed down there. I hear Louis went to N.O. and heard him in person—good boy.

Went to Lehman's Mikado opening night, much fun—Lehman had sweetly sent me a ticket, and afterwards Harry C. Joe, Mildred, and Wyatt Cooper and I were for a while at his apartment—he had a huge, enormous basket of flowers sent to him by the restaurant where he used to eat during rehearsals—lovely! I enjoyed the performance and hope to go the Iolanthe before coming home. Hubert, who's here now, says he wants to go too.[25]

Have seen our Bea [*Lillie*] twice and would I could see her again!

Made a record for Caedmon, reading Why I Live at the P.O., A Memory, and The Worn Path—do you approve selections? Haven't heard it played back or corrected it yet, so don't know what it sounds like. Worked on proofs for Kin the other day, but Bill Maxwell and I mostly talked about Stevenson and just rubbed the questions out as they showed up with a big eraser—it comes out in Nov. 15 issue. Another wall has crumbled, Bill says—the NYer printing a spring story in fall.

Enclosed a little paragraph on Nalbandian's show—I wish you could have seen it. I longed to have one of the paintings—beautiful.

We are going to lots of election parties tomorrow night, as the only way to get through the evening will undoubtedly be to circulate. I supposed it will be next dawning before anything's known. Let's pray.[26]

Nash told me about your good review—will be looking for it. They whacked my lead off my little review of the E.B. White book, which annoyed me so—since there I said how I adored the book—that I sent it to Mr. White, by Bill Maxwell.

Must get to typing—am diddling through the day by typing up an 80 page story, for some reason.

Good luck, and love,

Eudora

November 24, 1952 • Austin to Jackson

Dear Eudora,

Treasure-trove discovered recently right under me nose! The anti-Peron deposed editor of La Prenza Alberto Gainza Paz, here for dedication of new Journalism Bldg. After lecture, there was a reception all over the new structure. In library on bottom shelf were loose copies of London Times + Express. Student attendant at desk when I dropped in to cheer up a bit the other day says they throw them away, desiring to keep only issues of latest two weeks on tap. So I just left with an armful! Best clipped + enclosed herewith. Please return as soon as you've read them so I can pass them on to Louis [*Lyell*]. [. . .]

Letter from L. yesterday saying he'd seen you + enjoyed it so much. Glad to be set at ease about the heavy coat. Said he found one for $54 at a place behind Abercrombie & Fitch. Was he in good spirits and excited about going? I should think so. His address in Berlin: ℅ Am Exp, 2 Onkell Tom Strasse!!!!!! Better than Goebbelsplatz or Hitlerstrasse but not much!

Hope you ended New York visit happily. Tell other things about it when you have time. Did you see any of the J-L Barrault plays?[27]

Love,

Frank

December 2, 1952 • Jackson to Austin

[*To Lyell; message has no greeting.*]

So cheered by the Beachcomber! Thanks a million for sharing the treasure—I'll pass on to Louis on Onkel Tom Strasse, with Mary's address. Louis looked well, full of ideas and hope, + I felt confident for him too—was very pleased to have my glimpse of him—we met + ate at the Blue Ribbon, then went up to the Times to see Nash [*Burger*] + Nona [*Balakian*]. Enjoyed your Fanny B. review—fine. [. . .] Still so downhearted by the election. Did you have a nice T'giving in Dallas? What are your Xmas holidays? Seta is coming. Have talked to your family on phone + hope to see soon.

Love,

E.

[*On verso*]

Which name (character in story) do you prefer?

middle aged hotel keeper doing the talking

Edna Earl Ponder

Edna Earl Palmertree

Etta Ponder
Etta Palmertree
[. . .]

December 6, 1952 • New Orleans to Austin

Dear Frank,

Bet you never had a letter writ to you at 5:10 AM—waiting for the taxi to the Rebel [*train to New Orleans*]. It can't make sense! But I am so captivated by (A) the candy which came yesterday, + is as heavenly as hash never was, + is being feasted on by me + Mother very steadily—and (B) the question about my evening dresses!

Well! I have a choice, if you want to know it—(first time in 25, 30, donkey's yrs.) Grey silk short one + long wine colored crape with sleeves + some beadwork (doesn't that sound awful, esp. at the hour at which I contemplate it). I have to wear one or the other at the YMHA reading of stories in NY on Jan. 22—did I tell you? So take your pick, + I'll follow! I am highly interested + pleased in advance with anything you can do!

What news? I'll write soon—

Taxi!—

Love,

E

January 28, 1953 • New York to Austin

Dear Frank,

The scarf was a great success, admired by all. It really is the loveliest piece of "material" (!) I ever saw. In the end I bought a beautiful new dress to go with it—short black lownecked long sleeved silk, with lace top + full heavy silk skirt—shot the wad on it. So the combination helped me live through the evening. The audience was nice—warm, + all my pals. I read, in the end, Why I Live at the P.O., Powerhouse, + Worn Path. Immediately afterwards I lost my voice + have been in with laryngitis + cold or flu ever since, so it was a miracle I got through Jan. 23. I did a foolish but highly enjoyable thing, went out the night after, fever + all, to take the Smiths + Mary Lou (on those tickets I'd had 2 months) to Bea Lillie—She was in top form, + had added on many little touches + lines since I saw her last. In the opening skit, where she's the star's friend, in the dressing room, she throws a scarf around her head, over her head, etc. + murmurs "Yasmin, that's my baby." Delicious evening! Well worth 101°.

Elizabeth Bowen is in New York (since Monday) + I've seen her each day at some point—she too has a cold, but nothing can quell her energies—we're meeting at the Plaza for tea this afternoon, if both able. (Eileen has inspected me—and said, "Now, Eudora: <u>when</u> do you want your voice <u>back</u>?" Like it was out at the cleaners.) Mary Jones, a country friend living in town for winter, is having a dinner party Friday night where I'm taking Elizabeth, + Red Warren + Eleanor + Anne Lindbergh will be there, I hear—so I hope that will be nice. Shall wear the scarf (+ clothes).

Our friends here seem to be all right—<u>all</u> have colds—Have you? Take care. I hope the post-Xmas work has slackened some at least. Soon Europe for you! I enclose Louis's nice letter. Give him my love & I hope to answer soon—I hope he's found that lady.[28]

Love from

Eudora

I move to that apt. if all goes well, for Feb. 1–March 1. Best address me c/o Dolly. Finished a 97-page story—will arrange somehow for you to read when you have time—

March 31, 1953 • Jackson to Austin

Dear Frank—

[. . .] Here's everything returned that you asked for back, I trust. Sorry to be such a laggard at letters these days. I've had an Italian exchange man, Eugenio Vaquer, from Florence, whom I knew slightly when there, and now feel I know well—he stayed five days—really charming, and I hope you will feel inclined to look him up when you're over there. [. . .]

Dolly has taken a new job (her boss went to be on the magazine, leaving her with nobody very interesting to work for at the house) with the new New Republic—just bought by a millionaire to be brought out along the lines of Stevensonian politics, and with the idea of supporting Stevenson. She will assist this new editor, and there'll be one other person in the office to help—so it sounds interesting, starting at the bottom of a good project. They hope to bring the magazine back to its old repute before the Henry Wallace troubles etc.[29] I had to go see the Wellses to console them about it, since they don't want Dolly to work in NY anyway and especially for anything that announces itself to be liberal and moderate—they of course being neither—and they are upset about it, poor people.

[. . .] Send me news—forgive such a dull letter. I've been working hard, indoors and out, with old pages and weeds. Everything does look beautiful—such a spring as we've never seen. Today had the first call from [*neighbor*]

Mrs. Macgowan to come and see an iris—so the fine late spring is here. Magnolia fuscatas in bloom, making me swoon this minute at the window.

Thank you again for all this good reading matter. I meant to enclose a "Mississippi Singing" poem about the termites of pain, but lost, maybe mercifully.[30]

Love & Happy Easter.

Eudora

During his upcoming leave of absence, Lyell had planned to serve as leader for a group tour of Europe, but this job fell through due to an unexpected change of plans by the tour company. Welty wrote on May 11, "What in the world is this, about the tour? Your mother called me + told me what you'd told over the phone—How infuriating + just a little less than that, how mystifying! Do you think there could be some mistake so that you got a letter meant for somebody else?" She concluded "So glad about the Leave of Absence + all." Lyell went ahead with his plans to be abroad for the rest of 1953.

August 30, 1953 • London to Jackson

D. E.

Vastly enjoyed seeing this place [*Hatfield House, Hertfordshire, England*] [. . .] Have seen no familiar faces yet except Bobby Heilman[31] and Spencer Tracy at the Covent Garden bar. Margot Fonteyn entrancing in Cinderella. Off to Edinburgh on Monday [. . .] Hope you had a good time in New York.

Love to you and Elizabeth [*Welty*],[32]

F.

Re [*Carson*] McCullers: husband swindled c. $2 000 monthly via checks, so she left him.

September 24, 1953 • London to Jackson

D. E.—

Dinner with E. Brandt [*Eva Boros*] Tuesday night[33] So nice—open fire, Martinis, very good food, red wine—it was midnight before we put down our coffee cups. She adores you and ate up every tidbit of news I had from Pinehurst. Rather indescribable flavor she has, don't you think? She reminded me of Annabelle Robinson, something of a Hungarian literary—intellectual Annabelle. Very sweet indeed. Found out almost nothing about her, except that she had a story in H-B and is now writing a novel about life in TB hospitals, The Mermaids. Does she live on alimony, her own income? Please tell me more. She mentioned Bill twice or more in connection with my tales of photogenic spots I've visited—Highgate Cemetery, Etc. Who is he? Said news of her brother in Hungary and others stopped about a year ago and she's puzzled about that. I judge she's a country lady of leisure. Right? Back to Eton Place last night for dinner with Alice [. . .] Her husband is pleasant, but tedious—without knowing it, and interrupting and repetitious after a few gins. Dinner with Pamela and Camillus just before he left for his school—Bryanton. Both in fine form. C was 14 on August 15th—still charming. Has found imitative streak. After my visit P said they imitated me for days. I'm now staying with her! In street floor bedroom. The ESU [*English-Speaking Union*] confused my booking—+ one can stay for only 2 weeks at a time anyway—so when she said come to her if I wanted to, I very much appreciated the rescue + the financial breathing space. London so expensive. Went to P's Tues + will stay until next Wed—or less, depending on how plans for Italy develop within next few days. P. is busy + we go our own ways. Very agreeable all round, + she's hit nobody below belt so far. Seems in good mood. No cults mentioned so far. G. Greene's play The Living Room big success, [*illegible*] Crucible deadliness. Awful. Sex + psychiatry + R. C. Church. The end!

Love

F

October 5[*?*], 1953 • Paris to Jackson

[*Postcard picture of a street in Paris from Pont Neuf*]

D. E.—

Love the Saints-Peres [*hotel where Welty had stayed*]. Quiet room on top floor overlooking court—twinkling male desk clerk remembers you—fondly—[*Kirsten*] Flagstad in concert at the Theatre des Champs-Elysées the night after I arrived! Boris [*Mussogorsky's* Boris Godunov] at Opera, with the superb Boris Christoff. J-L Barrault in Claudel's Christophe Colomb followed by amusing visit with A. B. Toklas! The show of stained glass at eye-level still on in Louvre—stunning. This food! What a change from England—All divine.

Love,

F.

Alice B—2 blocks from this street. Picasso lives nearby. Old Paris—new to me—fascinating streets all round.

October 13, 1953 • Florence to Jackson

Dear Eudora,

This marvelous place! Was there ever such a feast for the eyes + the mind laid out anywhere in the world in such small compass? Sublime weather for 3 days, that heavenly light flooding everything. Have reviewed most of the familiar sights + seen much that's new to me. [. . .]

These palaces here—aren't they marvelous? Just the grandeur of the walls as you pass on the sidewalks—And the courtyards of the Strozzi or Medici Palaces, especially the Strozzi—nothing but columns + arches, but what a breathtaking grace + elegance in their proportions + line—Also the market at night—full of claptrap by day but empty, in the dark as noble as a classic temple—

Brief chat with Sir O. [*Osbert*] Sitwell in Pitti Palace! He was leaving as bells clanged + I had a couple more rooms to go. Said call him in London.

Must get some sleep. Motor scooters still buzzing along the Arno—No room with a view for me either. Am back on alleyway but can still hear them.

Love, F

Extravagance in Genoa but did you see this place [*enclosed bill from restaurant*]? The restaurant atop the "skyscraper" ? was there at sunset—Red glow in clear sky behind black mountains, lights all over town + harbor—superb view. Had to stay + eat there. The funghi dish was marvelous—those big mushrooms done up in olive oil + garlic—could eat that every day! [. . .]

Spent the night at pensione near station. Saw a good deal of the town—Cemetery closed, alas, when I arrived.

October 28, 1953 • Florence to Jackson

D. E.—

This beautiful thing [*painting of the Basilica of San Francis, in Assisi*]—Do you remember it?—wish a good color print were available, but can't find one. The main sights this morning and drove out to the Hermitage Saint Francis illegible in the hills after lunch—Seems to me you wrote about seeing this—The rock bed and wooden pillow he slept on. Amazing, isn't it? A good many of the pillows I've been sleeping on have been made of rocks and wood too. Had a non—Franciscan one here at my Assisi hotel last night, however. Pouring rain now. Not a trace of cold so far, but rain has fallen off and on ever since my last day in Florence. Talked to E. Spencer in Rome station last night (on phone) between bus from Naples and train here. Like her so much. Brief visit with Wystan [*Auden*] on Ischia. Perugia tomorrow.

Love,

Frank

October 29, 1953 • Jackson to London

Dear Frank—

I've relished every communication and passed every one along—to Hubert, Charlotte, and exchanged with your family, and you've been so sweet about writing. Is your cold gone? The only bad thing that's happened. What a marvelous trip this one is. Edinburgh sounded full of joys—I was especially enchanted to hear the notes to Roughead, along the way[34]—and I'm glad all's as full and rewarding as should have been. The card about Eva (your smallest cuneiform to date! But accomplished) pleased me much. She is a dear person—warm, with a lovely mind, imagination—a real romantic. She is not too well off, and with that Hungarian freeness may have thrown her all into that fine dinner she asked you to, I've seen her do that so often—but I believed her father-in-law makes her nice presents now and then. [. . .] Didn't you love her apartment—all little things picked up with infinite searching and care, and all just perfect. Bill [*Brandt*] took the beautiful photograph on the wall. I love that room—I stayed there, where the fireplace is, before Eva had gotten all her furniture, and when I arrived—cold—she made a beautiful tea on a suitcase for a table, elegant. Maybe you'll be calling her again—[. . .] and when you do, much love to her. I hope all went well in the Travers menage. P. is an inveterate inviter of people to stay with her, then they are a little sorry, is the old story—I was warned not to. But I hope this time all went gaily. Glad she's out of her bitter streak, for her real gaiety is there, to like so well (couldn't bear for her not to be cheerful to you). Perhaps she resents me because I'm another female writer—not unheard of little quirk—and it's no more than that. I was also afraid at one time she was going to eat Camillus. How is he? A darling boy.—Don't you (still + forever!) love London? There is a wonderful map and old print shop on Oxford St. near my old Montague Hotel, that you might have fun looking at—like the history of London in print form, and there might be some glimpses of Richardson even, who knows? So propitious the way you kept running into the very persons who could best tell you the facts you were waiting to learn. When will you return? I heard you were touring in France and Italy now. I hope you took the bus from Nice to Italy along the Corniche, with the old sites looking down at you, Eze and La Turbie—did you visit them?—and the whole panorama—the train spends its whole time in tunnels. Will you go to Siena? the Duccios [*paintings*]! And you see "Monteriano" and Poggibonsi, where [*Forster's*] "Where Angels Fear to Tread" happened, on the bus ride. And Assisi. You have to visit those Giottos. Did you come down through Provence from Paris? That drenched gold light—& did you see Cezanne paintings come to life without mistake, and Van Goghs—and see le Pont d'Avignon (lunch stop)? I long to hear about all this. Can't you make this last a year????? Memo: you deserve it.

The reason I've not written is just work. I had to read proof on Uncle Daniel [*The Ponder Heart*] for New Yorker and Harcourt both, still have a last set each to come. Then have completed a new story [*"Going to Naples"*], which in turn finished off the collection, due in now so the book can come out next year. This in the course of being typed. I'm doing a carbon on this thin paper with the idea of shipping it to you, if you had time for it, since it's laid on a boat going to Europe (Italian—the Pomona.). But it turns out to be 50+ pages long so it will have to come in sections. Hope to finish the drudgery this weekend. It gets harder and harder to find the good times to really work, just domestic life etc., to be expected—but frustrating at moments. Anyway, after this, I can begin on new work, which I long to do.

Everybody here seems all right. Hubert and Jimmy and Major are all out of town, or I guess some of them may be back by now, so we haven't had any gatherings. By the way did you get our combination, all-purpose wire on the boat the day you sailed? A party at Allison's Wells was held in celebration of your trip, and the wire we sent from Jackson about midnight. [. . .] Tell Louis if you think of it that I mailed him Stevenson's speech in Chicago to the wrong (Berlin-Schoneberg) address—where if anybody finds it, I hope they read it. Also give him love & wishes. Life there sounds very strange, strict, and interesting.

[. . .] We've had not a drop of rain in Sept. or Oct., and everything's parched and tinderlike—we water all day long. I forgot I didn't tell you a thing about E [*Elizabeth Welty*]'s and my trip to NY—it was the heat wave then too. Very successful—she is a darling travelling companion—and all we did, from the Whale at the Museum of Nat. Hist., to down-front seats to Guys and Dolls, turned out to be a happy choice for her. About Guys and Dolls, she said, "If Miss Adelaide hadn't told her mother that story, all this needn't have happened." I loved that myself, had never seen it. We saw Wonderful Town (thought it sprawled, and I wasn't captured by Ros. Rus.), The King and I, Fan-fan la Tulipe, Planetarium show "A Visit to Saturn by Rocket Ship", "The Band Wagon" and Rockettes, 6 Charlie Chaplin comedies, the Emp. State, Boat Trip around the Island, etc. Went to Katonah for the weekend and she got to cool off in the swimming pool twice a day, and see trees again. The Algonquin is nice to stay in, convenient and cheerful and friendly, and we had a window air-conditioner in our room, without which we should have died—the temp was 100, probably 112 in the streets. She went to see The New Yorker and Harcourt and Russell & Volkening, by necessity, but quite matter-of-factly, and turned out to like all my friends—who were sweet to her.

Keep well, have fun, see all, hear all, know all. Tell all.

Love from E—

P.S. [. . .] Can't decide whether to send this to Rome or to E. S. U. Lots of love & wishes—we all think daily of what a good time we hope it is. Let me hear soon again. I'll try to do better with the work off. Buona Fortuna!

Eudora Oct. 29

I know I don't get a thing for neatness on this letter, 'Fessor

November 21, 1953 • Jackson to London

Dear Frank,

I love hearing so. You couldn't have sent a more welcome card from Assisi—isn't that Lorenzetti straight out of Heaven? And the card from Paris, my old neighborhood. (Did you walk in the Luxembourg some afternoon with the leaves falling into that Medici fountain, and past those sad queens?) I just feasted my eyes. Also I was so glad, as you knew I'd be, to have word straight from the Berchielli, Nandina's, those streets—and from Eugenio Vaquer, who I think is such a nice man. [. . .] I hated it so, about 935 [*Bellevue Place, the Lyell family home*]. But it's all being fixed right along and all, of course, borne gallantly by Clarena and Judge, as you would know. Glad your room and your things are all safe—I must say, my first wild thought on hearing of the fire was all those <u>things</u> of yours. Clarena wanted to 'spare' you and Louis, but I'm one of those who voted to have you told—wouldn't you rather have been? (I was in Europe when the tornado hit our house and yard, and owing to a hitch in the mail I at first got only little hints and snatches from other letters, which drove me crazy. I thought exact news would be the best.) Last Saturday night, after a wedding, Judge came bringing a Vogue your mother sent, —and Mother said she felt like telling Judge not to tarry after a wedding but to rush on home and see if it was all right. (The Vogue has a piece on Elizabeth Bowen by David Cecil, which you will enjoy too.) Your whole Continental trip sounds full and good, and I hope the rains didn't last forever after Naples, though they had held off so fine. I hated for Assisi not to have a certain look for you that it had when I was there, the sun going down across that great plain under the hill, with the river shining, and the whole thing like a big bowl of light. Did you see the little wild cyclamens near St. Francis's bed? (Were all those people dreadfully <u>short</u>? Or did they sleep with their knees up?) Glad you liked the Sts. Peres in Paris too (remembering that short quilt). Did you get room 25, the one with the pipes through the wall to make it warm? If you go there again, ask for it. Oh, I remember now, you had a room on the Court.—It was grand the way you and Elizabeth Spencer[35] ran smack into each other and immediately recognized each other—of course—and I was delighted at the joint p-c. Isn't she fine? I think she'd be a perfect person to sightsee with—so fresh and quick and full of good questions—and laughs so well. Did you go to Capri and see the Bat Woman? (Not worth the trip, but Capri is.) Maybe Ischia is the same beauty without the Bat Woman. Is it so that Auden has a running hot water spring running through his living room? I forget who told me, but I used to think of it when I was cold.—Your mother let me see the packets you mailed home from England and Scotland—beautiful—Hatfield House and Glamis Castle little booklets are gems. I hate for you to leave off all this for work, but suppose that too will have excitement about it when it's being done in London. Let me know how things go. [. . .]

There's not too much news that I know. [. . .] Charlotte just this minute phoned that the little Morrison baby has come—little Dan. Which reminds me I had a Halloween party and Charlotte, Ann and Bill arrived in identical costumes—covering sheets, padded inside, witch masks, and tall witch hats, and as they stood on the doorstep each carried a placard and they read across, "Witch Is Witch?" [. . .] I've at last got through with the various proofreading and so on, and guess my story [*The Ponder Heart*] will come out in NYer the first week in Dec. and the book first week in Jan. Am now typing up the stories for a collection due in at Harcourt, but am getting some help from a college girl across the street (she calls me "Ma'am.") Have really felt snowed under by various pieces of drudgery this fall, but soon all will be in at the printer's and I can start writing again. I want to do a play—!

[. . .] We all miss you. It's lovely to think where you are, though. Keep well, don't get a cold in England, cling to that hot water bottle, and have a marvelous time. If you see Eva again, give her my love. I had a letter from Mary Lou saying she wasn't coming over after all—I don't know her reasons, but maybe you could persuade her.

Lots of love,
Eudora

November 28, 1953 • London to Jackson

Dear Eudora,

Many thanks for the letter. Oh yes, I'm glad you voted for telling about fire—like you and tornado, I wished for all details at first, but didn't get picture of event in full until Mama's second letter. In her first she had Miriam emerging from shower into flames but no more of her until she appeared on doorstep half clad at 12:30. [. . .] Not enough about results of fire either, so I imagined awful things and thought Clarena was minimizing. [. . .] Please try to go by there and cheer up C. and take a look around and tell me what repairs look like.

Delighted to have comments on Italy, which bring back heavenly pictures to my mind. In Assisi I never saw what you did at sundown—Arrived in dark the first night, and it was overcast after rain the next. Marvelous when I left, however—all clear, blue sky and great drifts of low white rising clouds stretched all over that huge valley! and every view of the same landscapes from all sides in Pienza, where I spent the day, was superb. Of course, the view from the heights in Assisi is better—on account of the enchantingly homogenous antiquity of the town, its smallness, [. . .] that serenity over-all—just divine. [. . .] [*Ravenna's*] mosaics are magnificent—They are also up to their reputation in San Vitale—[. . .] Spring in Wystan [*W. H. Auden*]'s living room? Not shown to me. There are many hot springs [*illegible*] in the island, of which I'd heard him speak previously. He never drinks anything but coffee, wine and tea. I asked for water and trembled when I drank what he gave me because it comes from wells which he said could be polluted lower [. . .] To flush the toilet you scoop rain water out of a barrel standing in small open court [. . .]. Street floor full of junk. His study and bedroom are the second floor overlooking street. No running water there. I shaved in bowl on iron stand in my room—in rainwater. He said I should have asked for hot. It's all so primitive I didn't think there was any. One telephone in the whole town! We bathe at a public bath house—200 Lire for tub. Queue always there. That's where he reads the newspaper, which comes over after lunch from Naples on bus. Did I tell you he showed me some new poems? A series of eclogues. Grand. [. . .] Lovely morning, summer-warm, when we walked all over the town.

At the Saints Peres I did look at room 25—not so nice as mine, I didn't think—I had 8 the first time, 9 the second. Only drawback: walking up all the front stairs. Both rooms bigger than 25, High ceilings, cozily furnished, and off that noisy street. Up in 8 & 9 over the court you can't hear a sound. Love the way these girls at desk sing bonjour monsieur when you come down in the morning. Couldn't be cheerier. [. . .] oh yes, those statues of Queens in Luxembourg Gardens walked by them after matinee of Phedre at the Comedie Francaise—chilly day, but the garden was full of people—Armistice Day, on which all shops and offices were closed—so so much that was new—I'd never been in the Palais Royale gardens—How lovely that is—Or to the Place des Vosges—Now that's the best of all—Run down in appearance, but another one of those splendid harmonious layouts [. . .]

[. . .] Could keep this up forever, but must stop! Suppose the country is rocking with joy over Uncle Daniel now—Oh, must tell this, the other evening at 7 I waited on (influence of Richardson) Baroness Moura[?]) [. . .]

It was one of those drop-in groups (I think, though I was invited for that particular day) with everybody drawn up about a bottle of gin and a bottle of orange water which she poured into thimble glasses—simple, comfortable flat, lot of books about—being read, too—I talked mainly to a lively American woman, Mrs. Constance Huntington, [. . .] she lived long in Italy in early days. Something was said about McCullers, and Mrs. H said, "yes, I think she's talented, but I always feel that everything she writes has a sink behind it." Sums her up neatly, what? [. . .] [*Asked*] if she read Miss Welty. Oh yes, and love everything but "I don't understand Delta wedding," (!) I said that's what she gets for living in New York London Italy most of her life. [. . .]
[*Written on enclosed advertisement for a Maggie Teyte and Gerald Moore concert*]

[. . .] Maggie Teyte sounded most of the time like a girl of 56 instead of 66 [. . .] in the second of the "Chansone de Belita" she stopped at the most rapturous moment—"La Chevelure", beat head with hands, and said she'd forgotten the next verse. This was pretty bad and the Times called it "most regrettable" and the Express rapped her quite hard—but most of it was absolutely lovely + she sang "Psyche" just as beautifully as she does on any record, dedicated another encore to "two policemen" (!) + was so enchanting that I'd go to her again tonight if she were performing anywhere else. [. . .] Cedric Wattis [. . .] took me back to meet her afterwards, + I couldn't have been happier if I'd been you going back to see Danny Kaye. [. . .]—after tea with Peggy and Cedric at his house I went down to the Royal Festival Hall for the first time [. . .] Enormous audience, + Sir Thomas [*Beecham*] was superb—walking in and out like Mr. Marcellus Green at 92, but conducting like a stripling genius. All the music was the kind he does to perfection: Boccherini Overture, Haydn's "Surprise" Symphony, one Mozart viola concerto, Beethoven's Haydnesque Symphony Number 2 perfectly ravishing—never heard Toscanini get what he got out of it—It was one of the best symphony concerts I've <u>ever</u> heard. After the Haydn he just sat down on a stool behind him on the podium + mopped his head—When he finished mopping, he signalled to the orchestra to rise + bow a while. Then as if he was noticing the cheers for the first time, rose slowly + took forever to turn around + bowed from the waist as if the Queen + nobody else were there. Really killing, but majestic at the same time. Same deportment again after the marvelous Beethoven—the last item was a rousing Chabrier piece "Marche Joyeuse" + you would have thought he was leading the cheering section at a football game. I was in the balcony, far from the stage, but could still hear him singing the melody when a new theme entered—or rather growling it—<u>So</u> amusing—An ovation at the end + an encore—a dance, 18th century affair in style, for the horns mainly. Then a speech. He said when he came to the hall he saw "to his consternation" that this leaflet had been inserted into the program. If anyone wanted to "flaunt it in someone's laggard face" it was no affair of his. "It's very late and you wouldn't want another encore after that lovely piece for the horns?" (Shouts of "yes" + more applause) "I thought not"—+ began to take his leave! Memorable evening.

Please circulate this to Hubert, Charlotte, Jimmy, anyone interested. So good to be settled at last. Spend every day at the V. + A. where working with the MSS is, yes, just as fascinating as all the above. Living very near. Can walk from car to library table in 10 minutes. This glorious city! So satisfying. Heaven to be here.

Love to all,
Frank

December 16, 1953 • Jackson to London

Dear Frank—

Yes! Oui! It did come—such a delicious Parisian present. It will be on the Christmas tree Christmas morning, and then how lovely that everyone will know, by my handkerchief, that I am prevoyante, modeste, et capricieuse! As of course any daughter of April is, or ought to be. It came in the safety of your warning on the envelope quite on time. Thank you, and I do love it.

Your house looks elegant in its new paint and all the work that's been done. You'll like the color of the walls in those front rooms so much, my feeling is—a gray that has softness and warmth, and with the white woodwork is truly elegant. [. . .]

We'll miss you so much! What will you be doing on Christmas Day?

It was grand to get your letter—all the bright memories of Italy being still with you, and I was excited to know you had gone to Ravenna—and Venice—did you go out to the island of Torcello—wonderful mosaics? But I guess nothing after Ravenna could smite you that much again. [. . .] So glad you did go out to I Tatti. Isn't he [*Bernard Berenson*] an astonishing and concentrated, consecrated, intense little hard and gemlike flame?[56] He can't see a person or object without questioning it to see what he could learn, or verify, there. And the schedule and operation of the house, so highly organized, is amazing and amusing too—[. . .]

The Beecham concert sounded superb. Isn't it grand how he carries on at his own singing (sic)—I remember hearing him do it even through the vastness of the NY Stadium concerts—and remember the record of Damnation of Faust where he does keep silent through that almost silent dance of the sylphs (is that it?) but then gruffly his voice comes at the end, "Thank you veddy much" to the orchestra, and then a great sound like everybody tumbling down. To hear Haydn and Mozart under him* (*This sounded like under him as he tumbled down from preceding sentence!)—! You have run into the great music on this trip, haven't you—marvelous luck in the halls.

Yes, Uncle Daniel [*The Ponder Heart*] is out in the magazine, and I felt glad when that crisis (I sometimes have authoritis, or something—this time a 5-weeks sore throat, like I was choking—maybe with all those words; throat-doctors couldn't find anything) was over.[37] You should have been here to get me through it with your cheer! But people have been nice—I saved up some comments to report to you. Louise Love: "Haven't enjoyed reading anything so much since 'The Little Colonel.'" But I'll save the letters to show you. Oh, must tell you—the cashier in the Jitney [*grocery store*], Mrs. Coker, said, as she cashed a chk, "Sure do want to read your life story. I hear it took up the whole New Yorker magazine." Me: "But it's not the story of my life, it's a story I wrote." Mrs. Coker: "AWWWWWWWWW." Utter deflation and disgust. "Now who could have told me it was the story of your life? I've been telling everybody to go read it." Had a letter from a lady in Columbus, Miss: "The courtroom scene was not exaggerated at all." Mrs. Herbert has arranged to get some copies ahead to sell for Xmas; as she realistically said, "I don't think I could sell any copies after Christmas." But they'll get in just under the line—if indeed they do—and she seems downcast when she sees me in there. [. . .]

Hubert speaks not on Uncle Daniel—don't know whether he's not read, or not liked, which. He is having a Christmas party tomorrow night—buffet supper and the evening. We will all talk about you, as we always do ensemble, and miss you. With a good start for the holidays.

Some long letters I've sent to Europe have been lost lately, I find, and it makes me curious if you ever got a real long one I sent to ESU while you were in Rome—it may have been forwarded and now be languishing at Am. Exp. or somewhere—or maybe the plane mail got lost [. . .] I enclose a little snapshot of the Place des Vosges just as a souvenir, for you can see it's a poor one, but you can use your imagination on it. When you said it was cold in Venice I couldn't help but remember Stephen Tennant's rebuke when I said it was too cold to go to Venice in Jan.: "But it will be quite warm from the chestnut vendors on every corner!"—Merry merry Christmas love, and think of us at eggnog time. Hope work goes with all success & expedition to insure a Happy New Year. We'll all hope for a sight of you in Jan!

Mother sends love too—

With love & wishes—

E.

(Re-reading Northanger Abbey, came upon Miss Thorpe's pronouncement: "Sir Charles Grandison! That is an amazingly horrid book, is it not? I remember Miss Andrews could not get through the first volume." + Catherine replies: "It is not like Udolpho at all; but yet I think it is very entertaining . . ." Remember?)

The Ponder Heart *appeared in the December 3 issue of* The New Yorker, *then in book form in January 1954, dedicated to William and Emily Maxwell and to Mary Lou Aswell. The book was an alternate selection for the May 1954 Book-of-the-Month Club, and to Welty and Russell's surprise, there was also interest in turning* Ponder *into a Broadway play. Amidst positive reviews were some that William Maxwell called "excruciatingly stupid."*[38]

Welty continued to receive recognition that year. The Modern Library published a one-volume edition of A Curtain of Green *and* The Wide Net. *Welty prepared more stories for publication in a new collection. That summer, she traveled to Cambridge to lecture at the American Studies Conference.*

July 1, 1954 • United Lines to Jackson

Dear F—

It was lovely to be seen off + you + Louis were gallant to come out in the steam of that morning + brave all the Germans for it.[39] The heat stayed with us + hung over the ship for 3 days, then it got fresh + beautiful. Last night a wonderful sky-wide sunset—you know the kind—a gently rolling sea—+ against the horizon, I give you my word, a four-masted schooner. I thought it was a hant + came out of the Ancient Mariner—it finally faded away—It turned out to be a Coast Guard navigation class on it, that crosses the ocean on it once a year.

The company on this boat is real uninspiring + seems mostly like a 2nd rate Yorkville beer hall, but I was lucky as it turned out, for I eat with the Irish + only have to sleep with the Germans. [. . .]

I hope you had a fine time the rest of your visit in N.Y. Did you + Louis see Eileen, + perhaps Peggy + David? Write me the news when you have time. Address is ℅ Fulbright Conference, Peterhouse, Cambridge. (I didn't get much work done, because when I either read or write, my cabin mates watch me. Have not seen a single book opened by anybody else, once.) [. . .] love to you & I wish you were in England!

Yours,
Eudora

A postcard to Lyell the following week lists friends seen in London. By contrast, Lyell was home in sleepy, sultry Jackson, eager for reports.

July 16, 1954 • Jackson to London

Dear Eudora,

Murderous heat all this week. Hubert + Jimmy took to Pensacola Beach for 10 days. They report a good time, but a hot time. Lehman just left for two weeks in Jamaica, Haiti, + Puerto Rico. Was here 5 days, fat + frisky, + I saw him several times. Circulated your letter from boat to him + all mentioned there in. Thanks for that + London card. Tell about H Hamilton's party.[40] Was Wystan really present? Nancy Mitford? Nancy Spain? Nancy Astor? No telling who. Hope you found nothing Girouxish in H. H. What of E. Spencer? Glad you saw her. [. . .]

Aimée [*Shands Walsh*] just called—typical, regional. "Do you ever write poetry for friends, dear?" She wanted an announcement—party jingle to print under baby picture of Harvey Garrison's daughter Jackie, who is marrying someone named Jack. Was not satisfied with 2 or 3 of her own. Could I improve them? "This sort of thing is just like finding an inscription for Daddy's tombstone." "What did you choose?" " Well, I chose 'Well done, thou good and faithful servant,' but I had a dream one night, + Daddy said he heard that's what we were going to put on it, but he said please not to, because he didn't like to think of himself as <u>anybody's</u> servant." [!!!!] "So you gave up?" "Yes, we caught them before they started carving + told them just to make it 'H.R. Shands, M.D.' and the dates." Gales of laughter from her through all this. When Mama + Eliz Craig went to Miss Linn Hemingway's funeral last week, they took Aimee to the cemetery from the church. When the service was over, A. said, "come over here to our lot + let me show you what I did to Grandaddy. He's been moved over to make room for Alma + Miss Chris." Isn't she quelque chose?

[. . .] Can't remember whether you saw <u>H's Bazaar</u> before you sailed. It's played up well, on cover, with "A Long Story by E.W." [*"Going to Naples"*[41]] printed first to catch the eye, + also inside. I read it again + thought it much improved for being shorter, + now it's certainly 'Italian' enough. It still seems a little jerky as you go from topic to topic in the early course of events, but not much, + there are many good things in it. Not one of my favorites, however (as almost <u>all</u> the others are!) because I just don't like the people very much. Your mother + I agreed on this point the other day over the phone after I discovered she hadn't seen a copy + took her one.

Got C. [*Christopher*] Isherwood's new novel [*The World in the Evening*] at the Holliday in N.Y. + read it on the way home. A big disappointment, as about half the critics have said, + I don't know why all of them didn't. Just plain dull. Nothing for the films, but as I read along + wondered what <u>is</u> this like, I decided it was like sitting through a dreary movie with people like Kay Francis + Melvin Douglas in their most tedious roles. You couldn't care less about them.

Katherine Harris brought us some figs last night—what few there are are ripe now. Blissfully delicious today, on top of the vanilla bean ice cream. Hope you aren't confined entirely to gooseberries at Peterhouse.

Has Shaun Wylie come to see you? Wrote him you were there.[42]

Best love,

Frank

P. S. Correspondence card from Louis today. "No news yet." [. . .]

P. P. P. S. Did you get a letter I sent to the America addressed to Cobb??

July 19, 1954 • London to Jackson

[*Among the clippings Welty sent home on this date were a photo of an heiress in an attitude of hauteur, wearing a headscarf and sunglasses, who had admitted to stealing jewelry; a tally of votes for and against "That Hat"; and a column by British journalist and broadcaster Nancy Spain, whom Lyell and Welty both knew.*]

July 31, 1954 • Jackson to Cambridge

Dear Eudora,

I'm longing for a letter from Cambridge, with comments on the conference (exactly how much performing you've had to do, how many Englishmen attend classes + whence they come, the point + purpose of the gathering, etc—whether any of these turned out as you anticipated—no need to say that what you've given them has been a smashing success!) Do tell about the people, from Forster to Mizener (sublime to ridiculous—by now you must have formed some opinion of Arthur [*Mizener*]—what is it?) [. . .]

In the morning mail I did get the second batch of Express clippings. Many thanks. Loved them. The Sitwells will never speak to Nancy Spain after that blast at Sir O [*Osbert Sitwell*]! Your mother has passed on a lot of welcome news, but it makes me long for more [. . .] Sick over your not getting my boat letter to Cobb, which was returned. In that rush from the America, I forgot the skirt! Pinned hope on your checking when you saw me waving emptyhanded. That 1st class deck steward near me must have picked it up. It could still be in the boat's Lost + Found. So stupid. Please get a new one + charge to me. [. . .] Please remember me to both Pamelas![43] Have you called P. Travers? They'll be sorry if you don't, I'm sure.

Best love,

Frank

August 3, 1954 • Cambridge to Jackson

Dear Frank,

First of all, it's been so fine to have your letters—the first big thick one came just before I had to stand up to give my opening lecture, and set me steady, and that I needed. All the news I gobbled up, and I felt bad about not writing back, but you probably knew exactly what kept me from it—never a minute to myself. This is the day the second session opens, but I have 2 hours free, and intend to write this letter even if two painters are standing on a ladder painting the windows at my back. So much accumulating to tell, where can I start? I had lunch with Forster. He wrote me a note saying he had learned from David Daiches (They asked me to lunch—great fun. What a nice man. His father I'm told is the leading rabbi of Edinburgh.) I was in Cambridge, was just about to set off for the Continent, and could I have lunch with him, in his rooms at King's the last day, which was also the next day I think. I of course had overwhelming feelings of joy—had meant to write and ask if I might "wait on him", but had not yet done it. He had all his own things in his rooms, bookcases 2 rows deep, the electric heater was on—for my benefit, I'm sure, because later on I heard him agreeing with the gyp [*college servant*] that it was quite hot today—sherry waiting, and the lunch brought in and served on his own little table—hors d'oeuvres and chops and vegetables and fresh raspberries and cream, white wine, and then coffee by the fire. He talked about his family portraits hanging round the room, and some letters and papers he'd just come into possession of—and when I asked if he might be going to write something about them, he said a sketch was rather in his mind. He asked if the college people attending the Conference knew anything about books—"They generally don't"—and was very kind about what I was up to. He said he hardly saw how he would ever get back to America, because of the need, if he came, to lecture, and to be put on show, and said the same thing was true of India—that he would very much like to go, but just didn't feel he wanted to undergo any more of that. Isn't it sad? He was going to Beireuit (you spell it) and later on to Switzerland, to be back in the Fall. After lunch he put on a jaunty fat tweed cap with a button on top and took me for a walk. We cut across the grass (!), and went down into the Backs and along the river, then back and into the Chapel. He showed me over it, and then at the last took me up the winding stair into the organ loft, where a man was playing Handel (I think, but I was having such a lovely time I can't remember exactly), and we looked down into that lovely place from above. He was absolutely darling. As we parted in front of King's he said, "I shouldn't worry for a moment about what to tell them about writing—just tell them to stop it!"

And then, that night, at something called "General Discussion—Literature," Arthur Mizener oratorically said, "Now you can't go saying Passage to India is a great novel, come come! It's simply a novel of manners that's gone wrong. When you finish it, you're left with nothing but a vacuum!" I was put in the ridiculous position of having to defend A Passage to India. You know what I think of him. He regards the conference as a show, that's obvious, and doesn't really care what he's saying, so long as people gasp, laugh, defend themselves, get mad, and the rest—all of which I do, to my fury. I was so upset after General Discussion: Literature that as I was coming home I literally kicked myself and got in with my foot all covered with blood. The last thing he said as I was leaving had been, "Well! Thanks for working so hard." He says Faulkner is finished. The writers he covers in his lecture on the American novel are Sinclair Lewis, T. Dreiser, J. dos Passos, Hemingway, Fitzgerald of course, Faulkner, and then John O'Hara, James G. Cozzens, and J.P. Marquand! He has lent all these people Sanctuary, which is the only Faulkner they read, and then they all demand of me why I think it's good. I brought the Portable [*The Portable Faulkner*], and talk about The Bear, Spotted Horses, etc. etc.—Well. I can't say I've been happy with the combination of Mizener and me, but we don't have many joint sessions, and he doesn't attend my lectures, so doesn't raise any arguments after those. (A discussion period, pretty good, comes after each.) I've gotten along all right with the lectures, I guess—read the one on Place in Fiction in two parts and cut down the one on Short Stories to ¼ and used that for the last. The new set will get only 2 lectures, and I'll see what (I mean which!) they want. The first set of people were all terribly nice—their interests were in the main in the other lecturers' subjects—economics, education, history, politics, race (Dr [*John Hope*] Franklin is a Negro lecturer from Howard.), etc.—but there were 10 or 12 very bright ones indeed who were interested in books. [. . .] the ones I really got to like best were some much shyer ones, who came from Wales & Scotland—they reacted to the Place in Fiction thing like anything, and have brought me some wonderful samples of Welsh writing. Besides the lectures, I had 3 classes a week, at any hours from early afternoon till after dinner at night—and they never went home, of course. I would end up giving them sherry, or whisky, or we would all go out to tea—at which point they would begin having convulsions about the funny things the other lecturers had said. [. . .] (And Mizener [. . .] prowls up and down the platform, never stops swinging his Phi Beta Kappa key, and baits them—After a question—"Now, I'm afraid, we've come to a question of <u>taste</u>.") Oh I meant to tell you, the first thing he did was announce he was giving a concert of New Orleans Jazz in his room, for whoever was interested—[. . .] He'd bought the records all in Cambridge, which brought a big laugh. Well. I should have been telling you all the other things that have been nice, instead of airing myself on Mizener. All sorts of things are going on in Cambridge besides the Fulbright Conference! The Cambridge Arts Theatre Trust is having its Summer Festival, and I've gone to poetry readings—George Rylands, David Jones, and Donald Beves, reading from the poets who attended Cambridge—I never even thought Spencer had ever been alive, much less been a student at Pembroke—with music for Shakespearean plays written by Cambridge musicians, Vaughan Williams etc.

[. . .]. I met Mr. Rylands, by the way—a friend of Jamie Hamilton's and Roger Machell's in London (the partners, of the publishing house, who wrote him). He invited me to meet him in King's. He is the Dadie in Virginia Woolf's diary.[44] Quite a boy. While we were having a gin and french in his rooms, someone came to the door and Mr. Rylands went and measured out (he has a magnificent voice) "No, no, no. Take it away. I won't buy a copy. I wouldn't be seen with a copy. I wouldn't be found dead with a copy. If I bought a copy I'd be pleased to give it to you. Only take it away!" I thought it must be the Salvation Army people, but it was a student trying to sell him a copy of "The Confidential Clerk"! (Does it go on from door to door?)[45] He told lots of stories all through lunch, which was a welcome breath of the Other World—I forgot to say we ate in the Arts Theatre Restaurant, very nice, and it was nice to eat in a chair and have a napkin, much less wine. I am the first female ever to have sat down at table in Peterhouse Hall—in 600 years!—and can well understand that, as there are simply long trestle-like benches that go the whole length of the hall, and ladies have to sling a leg over both coming and going. I'm told the university isn't really all that bothered by ladies appearing in Peterhouse, as when we have gone all will be wiped away as on a slate, no memories remain of us. Where I actually live is down the street from Peterhouse, with guess what in between—the Fitzwilliam Museum! (I've been in several times when I had a few minutes.) It's called St. Peter's Terrace, and is a block of houses set back behind a hedge, on Trumpington St., with very nice big rooms, comfortable enough. I'm on the first floor front, have 3 enormous big windows, a mahogany dining room table, a big press, a dresser, a desk, a sideboard, a sink behind a curtain [. . .], 4 dining room chairs, big leather settee, big leather chair, liquor or shoe cabinet (I use it for both), studio couch in which is a big trench where the party who stays here in term has been sleeping—he must be very long, narrow, and heavy, and never turn over. (I guess he "sleeps like a log," because it looks just as if a log has slept there.) There is a marble mantlepiece and a little electric-wire heater, like a toaster. Secretly, I burn it. It seems un-English of me—but the weather has been terrible. Not more than 2½ days of sun since I got off the boat, and they were not whole days. Rain and cold. I know it must sound glorious to you. Is it any better? I don't see how you've been doing your work—but it sounds as if you have been right along. I hope that's going well.

I meant to tell you about Singing on the River, the plays, about the bus ride to Thaxted—but later, for I must take a bath for I hear the new set of people all stamping up the stairs (either to bathe or come in here). I do love the town of Cambridge itself! How lovely in the evening—often the rain stops, or if it is still raining there is a rainbow in it, about 9:30 at night—and this heavenly blue strange Northern sky color, with those spires up against it—I wish you could see it again!

[. . .] Excuse this badly organized rush of a letter, I'll write again from the wilds. The academic life is too big a whirl for me! But it has been fun, + wonderful + new. Love to all + lots to you,

E—

August 9, 1954 • Jackson to Cambridge

Dear Eudora,

What a fine letter! Did you plan for it to arrive on my birthday? Well, it did + made the day very joyful. Know you've really been busy every minute with the Conferees, but it sounds interesting + rewarding—An Experience, even if you never care to repeat it. Glad you liked a lot of the people who attended. Mizener sounds as if he's been outdoing himself on the objectionable side. Did you find any <u>other</u> side? Guess not, or you would have said so. How funny for him to have played them jazz records. As I told you, precisely what he did to me the first time I went to his room at the Graduate College in P'ton! With him it must be some sort of test. But of all people to give that sort of test! So sorry you've had to cope with him in arguments; but I'm sure you set others straight even if he kept on his own crooked way. Love the account of Mr. Forster—Grand that he was there. [. . .]

No particular news since I wrote last, except that Louis sounds as if the W'ton job [. . .] is coming through. [. . .]

Still boiling hot. Terrible that you've had so much rain + cold. My Xmas Eve + Xmas Day there were so beautiful + sunny + blue. Hope you haven't caught cold. As for those benches in the dining halls, I remember sitting at the high table on the dais during a weekend at Trinity during the war + being amazed to see the students down below at the end of the meal rise from the benches back against the wall, stand on them, walk across the table + down on the other side! By that time of course a number of people + most of the dishes had been removed. Glad you're going to Wales. Donald Sutherland wrote me to London that he "discovered" it last summer +

thought it marvelous. Said he didn't know he could react to landscapes that way anymore. Will you go to London first, then Wales en route to Ireland?

Love,

Frank

If you go to Paris, please see if you can find me a copy of this small booklet of color photos of the city. Charlotte brought one back. Lovely shot there in of one corner of the place des Vosges which is the reason I want it. you'll probably want one too. Will reimburse you. Couldn't cost very much—even in a London bookstore. Title page:

Paris Par Jacques Donvez [. . .] Don't bother about this if it's too much trouble [. . .]

September 10, 1954 • Bowen's Court, Ireland, to Jackson

Dear Frank,

Thanks so much for the letters and the clippings, and the nice picture Louis took that day on the boat—it's so good of Mary Lou especially, isn't it? Good news about Louis' job—please give him my best wishes for Washington. Did you leave all well at home? I hope the car did nobly on its new tires and on its new battery, and you got the heat and the desert safely behind you. The summer sounds absolutely awful there, and of course it's been absolutely awful in the other extreme here. I feel I never had a day of summer at all. Still going to bed with a hot water bottle here, and drawing close to the fire [. . .] Wales was simply lovely, and real peace, and Scotland was grand—Edinburgh, that is. I didn't get to the Highlands or anything, what with Festival things to see, and the wretched weather that shrouded the mountains and sea. Yes I did love the look of Edinburgh—to those closes, and hills, and haunts! I went down the Royal Mile on foot, and went in a bus on a tour of the city twice—so as to see things more carefully and again—and of course walked miles everywhere all day! The feeling of savagery and wildness you get permeating the grand things is marvelous, isn't it? Helped I must say by the presentation of Macbeth in the Assembly Hall—so much space and so much darkness to act it in, on that big apron stage that held the banquet with ease, and where the fights could range all over the place [. . .]

Elizabeth is well, and has just got the proofs on her new novel—which I hope to read before I go. Very happy busy times here—we go out a lot, either riding or visiting, and have company in for dinner, etc. It's rained madly at times—and the little girl who brings in my breakfast said, "'Twas a wild night in Ireland last night!" Eddie Sackville-West is visiting here too, and he is such a sweet man. Very Edwardian—travels with a little barometer in a case, and changes of stones for his ring. I wish for you when he gets to talking about his family. He said his grandmother, who was Irish, was a fearful old party, and when her breakfast toast was not done absolutely uniformly, she sent it back to the kitchen with pins stuck in to show where it was wrong. [. . .] He is supposed to inherit Knowle when his father dies, but does not want it [. . .]. He does want to buy a John Nash castle near here, a Gothic one standing empty in a perfectly beautiful situation—it really is marvelous, we've been to see it twice and are going back. In a ring of mountains, settled in the fold of a little valley, with the most romantic views from the arched windows in the octagonal rooms, and from the balustrades of the terrace—where, by the way, magnolia are now in bloom. [. . .]

Did the Beachcomber books come before you left? I meant them for your birthday but only sent them on your birthday, from Foye's and wished they'd come while Louis was there too. They may not be his best—I don't know, but were all I ever saw anywhere.

Jack Fischer [*editor*] came to Cambridge to lecture and heard me do mine, and wants to print it in Harper's Magazine—so I was very pleased. I want you to read it, but will have to type up a copy when I get back home. It's called Place in Fiction—though as Howard Moss said, probably the English would assume I meant Plaice in Fiction & may have done. I long to know if you got through with your work??

[. . .] Will write again—sorry to have been so late this time—I've been thinking of you of course and wishing you were here—Elizabeth sends her best to you too. So glad you encouraged Mother to fly up [*to West Virginia*]—she did and loved it. She enjoyed your visit so, and the conversation on the phone—thanks for being so sweet to her. Love, & good luck settling back in.

Love,
Eudora

October 4, 1954 • New York to Austin

[*Postcard of Manhattan skyline*]

Here I am! Hubert & Jimmy are here too. Got home safely after a nice calm, if slightly dull, crossing—all old ladies! Hope all goes well there + you're liking your new rooms. Letter soon. Home Oct. 13.

Love,
E.

November 24, 1954 • Jackson to Austin

Dear F—

Out on an errand to Old Men's Home, bringing Helen, + she decided to sketch so I'll write a note. Just took time out, all at once—so swallowed up it seems in stuff—errands [. . .]

I've been reading proofs on the collection of stories, getting that article in order—+ thanks so much for reading it! I am glad you thought well of it. You can see I re-hashed it rather, in brief, for the Times Lit Sup.—+ trying to catch up with nagging dull business correspondence accumulated from all Summer.[46] [. . .]

Ponder has got the most terrible reviews in England! You should see what they said, + turn your head away. My new publisher is feeling pretty glum. Think I'm signing a contract now with Lehman's friends Fields + Chodorov, who want to write a play on Ponder—Hope this too won't fall through [. . .]

Glad you thought the Rain Lady story [*"Ladies in Spring"*] OK on new reading. It was just as it was, only I added one sentence. (Years later it occurred to him that the lady in the woods might have been Opal too.) I hope the collection as a whole is a good enough one—I can't really tell—only 7 stories. Had hoped to have 1 new one to add but didn't make it.

Write if and when you can—Hope you have a fine Thanksgiving tomorrow—See you pretty soon—

Love from

E

December 7, 1954 • Jackson to Austin

Dear Frank—

MMMMMMMmmmmmmm!!! Before this last gorgeous bite is gone I have to say thank you and thank you again—how I love that Dallas surprise. It's really the best candy there is, as is agreed by all who come in reach of those good black and brown pieces—Mother well to the front. It was grand to have the Thanksgiving treat—I guess you must have been having one of your traditional good times in Dallas. It was so sweet of you to send it. Hope you brought a box full home to grade papers to the crunch of. How soon are you coming? Hubert of course predicts you will be here just a night, then whizz away to the city—is he a good prophet? I hope you have enough time here to draw the breath—so much to hear & tell of the summer.

I'm still buried in work not caught up with—you can see I've worn through the typewriter ribbon, and all on back stuff and drudgery. But I shall finish up and be ready for Xmas Cheer. You know of course B. Lillie is on the air (I mean TV) tonight with Bob Hope—I was told in time and mean to hear her. Did you see Lehman's Macbeth with J.A. and M.E. last Sunday?[47] I did—TV is a terrible medium, isn't it? But Evans was moving and impressive, I thought, and Anderson what you'd imagine, but in black-and-white TV, filmed for color, her make-up too often looked like a plate of asparagus (au gratin). Charlotte's young Morrisons say their baby who witnessed the show has been washing his hands in pantomime constantly, just like Lady Macbeth. Dolly is home, looks fine, will likely be here for several months. [. . .] Be so good to see you come in! Are you going to get yourself an LP record player? So many records you'd like! Lots of love, & drop one of your P.C.'s saying when you're coming. Thank you again for Anna Clairs of blessed memory—

E—

[. . .]

January 4, 1955 • Austin to Jackson

D. E.—

The card announcing the weekly arrival of Punch awaited me here. I thank you again because I shall love seeing it regularly.

Our chauffeur did not arrive at the Robert E Lee until 8 Sunday morning. Thick fog over all the roads, and for us it lasted pretty far—beyond Monroe. But we had lots of food in the car + got here at 7 p.m. Warm as June in Austin.

Saw my review in the Times today. All the juice removed, + whoever edited it didn't bother to insert transitional words and phrases to make it sound coherent. The author [*Mordecai Richler*] is really an anti-Jewish, resentful Jew. My suggestion of that has been eliminated for the Sulzbergers' comfort I guess.[48] Mr. Richler's debut isn't an important one, but he's better than average, + as a warning to him and others of his ilk, I wish they'd hinted a few more of the references + critical phrases I put in. [. . .]

Such a good Christmas. Hated for it to end.

Best love,

Frank

February 3, 1955 • Jackson to Austin

Dear Frank,

So happy to have your letters and please excuse my own delay—just the old pressure. Your own may have lightened a little by now—are exams over and end of term done with? I hope all's well—no colds, no snows or wind storms. [. . .] Thanks for the reviews of Elizabeth [*Bowen*]'s book—[. . .] I myself think the book's a short story in feeling, scope, temperament, and treatment, and Elizabeth agreed she thought of it rather that way herself. It's all weather and hallucination—heat & wraiths and oppression and moonlight, wonderful atmosphere and brooding quality. The Irish scene of course is marvelous—the dinner party that John Lehmann printed is hardly typical of the book though it's the liveliest chapter—but that's the only time any of those characters, except for Antonia and Jane, make any appearance.

[. . .] It was disgusting the way the Times cut your other review. It's to their own detriment, but that doesn't help any, and is so infuriating. I remember how mad I was with them [*in 1952*] when they cut my entire lead to a little review of "Charlotte's Web"[49]—all the best praise!—I went up and told them about it, as I was there, but that didn't change anything of course. I've now subscribed to the Times Bk Rev, but unfortunately missed your Acrobats piece, too early for me, and have never caught up with it. I've been sent some really dreadful new books (not to review, just for "quotes" ugh!)—haven't read much of them, but what I've read depressed me.—Went back and read "Howard's End" again the other night. Restoreth the soul.—About Harcourt, had a letter from Eugene Reynal saying he was clearing out—could not work well where surroundings were not congenial and harmonious. Giroux has systematically made things hopeless for everybody around him, it does look like—I'm not sure who's left there now, besides him—I can't think of anybody! No word from him about it, but I hear my book of stories is due out in early April now. Read proof on it before Christmas, I think. Wrote a little piece I promised R.P. Warren for a new edition of "Understanding Fiction", on the writing of a story ("No Place for You" in NYer), and when Va. Quarterly asked me for something for anniversary issue I tried that there, not thinking they'd take such a specific thing, but they did—it's prefaced with general remarks, but I don't know how good—I hate trying to write criticism and agonize and rewrite a thousand times, then feel unhappy about it. Have done a draft of a 60-page story, which I hope to cut down considerably when revising. Kind of Smith County. Names: June (Junior—hero), Miss Dovie (his mother), Willowdean (his wife), Essie Dee, Empress, & Elvie (his sisters), Lady May (his baby), Aycook Odom (his friend), Mr. Seeb Matthews (a neighbor), Judge Moody (his enemy, sent him to the pen) and Mrs. Moody. Scene is combination family reunion and welcome home from the pen. He didn't do anything much, just tried to teach Old Man Mix, at the store in Toonigh, a lesson.[50]

Stayed two nights in N. O. [. . .] Pamela [*Redmayne, Lyell's British friend*] had just come from Atlanta, where she visited Warm Springs and told them how to run the March of Dimes campaign, showed them where to take the pictures they used in publicity, etc. Had been to Bellingrath ("Shocking weather!")—had been in Virginia ("I used the word 'apprehensive' and a young girl said to me, 'Oh, Miss Redmayne, please don't use any more of those 3-syllabled words, we don't understand what you mean.'") Had a wonderful lunch at Galatoire's—drink, truit amandine, green salad, creme caramel, coffee, and I asked her to order the wine which she did—a lovely imported Chablis and she even approved the temperature of it. I don't know if she approved the lunch, but she couldn't have helped eating it, it was just divine. Seta and Mrs. Alexander and Fidelia were sitting across the room, but Seta said in a note today she didn't come across and speak to us for fear Pamela would have thought that was typical American bad manners! Met Seta the day before, also at Galatoire's—why eat elsewhere?—and she was grand. Is wearing size 13. Tom [*Sancton*] has 3 books finished but has never let her or anybody else read a line. She thinks he has some sort of block that might be fear of criticism—anyway she is fairly sad over it though not unsympathetic—wonderful Seta! She and the ladies had been to a ball the evening before (not the one in clipping!)—she looked lovely & gay as ever & sent you love. I go to Duke and Raleigh Feb. 20 or 21. Will be writing. Keep well.

Lots of love,

E.

Guess you know Charlotte's going with new paper and Lilian Bell is to write the column for Daily News—"These Delightful People"!![51]

While visiting North Carolina, Welty met Reynolds Price, a student and aspiring writer who would become an important part of her life. Welty wrote Lyell while staying with a friend from his Raleigh years, Anna Riddick. Knowing Lyell's appreciation for beautiful interiors, Welty began by describing the living room.

February 28, 1955 • Raleigh to Austin

Dear Frank,

Anna is fine + her house is beautiful. While she takes her bath—her family is coming to dinner—I'll write you from the living room—It's a cloudy soft day outside the 4 glass doors that open out to trees + brick paving + green—fire burning in the fireplace, in a lovely Pompeiian color (I asked) papered room—with soft gray greens + dark green + barky colored + brass—over her table against the wall across are 2 magnificent Chinese horses—charcoal rubbings on nice paper—big—in silver frames—On the dark marble mantle are Chinese + Indian things—a peacock + 2 heads—green plants in jars—books up the wall on either side. I'm on a long, soft sofa (hence the writing). I forgot to say over the mantel is a large darkish 18th cent. looking painting of ripe fruit with column, vines, + sky (I'll ask*. [*Handwritten note on the side:*] *It is revealed as an American primitive of harvest produce inside a barn! Very elegant + dark though—+ framed in gold.) Soft gray green rug to match her cat. Cat is asleep now on chair to match him. On the secretary op. the mantel are 2 pewter vases with flowering plum branches in white bloom—We've been having such a good time + your name is spoken every whipstitch.

[. . .]—I got through the Duke thing all right—The paper was over with the 1st night. I asked for a loudspeaker, being afraid they couldn't hear, + when they plugged it in it began picking up ghostly jazz—from outer space?—+ so I went on without it—but read as loud as I could. They claimed they could hear. Bill Hamilton + the Lewis Pattons (Frances Gray Patton) were wonderful to me throughout [. . .]. Harley + Janet Shands came to lecture—looked well—I thought that very comradely of them. Had a "seminar" with the 2 writing classes next day, + enjoyed it—Had read a dozen stories + discussed—good stories, too. A next year Rhodes scholar from Raleigh, Reynolds Price, is especially good—he edits the Duke magazine. [. . .]

I was much honored + pleased by the question about coming to Austin—+ do appreciate it very much indeed. Just now I can't make any plan that would take me away from home, because in March Mother is at last going to have one of her eyes operated on—as you know she has cataracts on both, + by now her "good" eye is hardly good enough to see to read—or garden—Dr. Hughes is going to operate on the "bad" eye—on the chance + hope that removal of a cataract of 35 years standing will give her some vision in it—She will still have the vision she has now, should the operation fail, + sooner or later I supposed the 2nd operation may come up. Anyway, the operation though a comparatively simple one means a rather long convalescence—no glasses for a minimum of 6 weeks, etc.—so—I don't know how things will be. I hope so much the first operation is a success—Anyway, I'll be needed at home for awhile, so can't commit myself about any job. I find I do like working with young people—though if I did try something like that, I'd grow less likely to write myself, because I take it all (students) hard. I guess the answer is "Count me out" then—at least for now. But I thank you. [. . .]

Love,
Eudora

[. . .]

March 26[?], 1955 • Austin to Jackson

[*Stationery—Department of English Memorandum*]

To: Eudora
From: Frank

So very honored to have a copy of the book [*The Bride of the Innisfallen*], another star in your crown. Pretty binding, don't you think? + I know E Bowen will find the Irish green appealing, in addition to swelling with pride over the dedication. Started reading The Bride again + couldn't stop—it made me long to hear such talk again. Such a wonderful story. Many, many thanks.

Hope the worst is over for Mrs. Welty. Was reassured to have your report on diagnosis + her progress after the operation in addition to what Clarena has written. Please give her my love + best wishes for a successful issue to what she has gone through. Don't forget to let me know how she's getting along.

Forgive brevity. Very busy with mid-semester quizzes + other papers.

Love,
Frank

[*Program for March 20 Houston Symphony Orchestra concert in the university gymnasium conducted by Sir Thomas Beecham, with this message on verso:*] Grand to see him here—in the Gym! Went early + sat on the front row. The Houston Symphony played well, but even under Sir T, they aren't virtuosi enough to cast the spell of the royal Philharmonic, + this program—light, pleasant, tuneful—wouldn't be thrilling under any circumstances. Appropriate enough, however, for the place and time—a hot Sunday afternoon—+ I loved watching him. He looks old—sort of shuffles across the stage—but as in Toscanini, the flame burns as bright as ever. Sir T is finishing the season in H. for Ferenc Fricsay (of Berlin Philharmonic), who went home for Christmas and had such a bad case of rheumatism that he couldn't return. They're getting Stokowski next year.

April 11, 1955 • Jackson to Austin

Dear Frank,

Thanks ever so much for the kind cheers about the medal [*William Dean Howells medal from the American Academy of Arts and Letters*]—so glad you think well of that. I was of course pleased & overwhelmed—to tell you the truth I'd never heard of such a medal—had you? [. . .] This is just a little note for the present, as things are still cramming the days, though Mother's so much better and gets around fine, with bandage only at night. Dr. Hughes now thinks she'll have pretty good (instead of the previous verdict, pretty good) vision in the eye—it's a miracle really, with her not having seen out of it for about 30 years, and nobody knowing what might lie back of a cataract that old. She's been very well behaved, too—has been patient and not downcast through all the dark weeks, and done what the doctor told her, exactly. Your mother's been our grandest ally and standby! Moral support, too, as well as the famous and inimitable physical support she is. I've enjoyed seeing her so much and she's helped me so much. [. . .] Don't know yet what I can manage about NY. Can't leave very early or stay very long, with Mother still needing to be careful and with new glasses not due to come till later on [. . .]. More later.

Thanks—much love, and write soon—I'm sorry for such a meagre letter—

Eudora

May 12, 1955 • Jackson to Austin

Dear Frank,

Such a late little note to say Thank you and for "Paris"![52] Of course I was carried away the same as you by that heavenly photograph of the Place des Vosges. And the Louvre and the Pont du Carrousel, which is the very way I went there every day—a lovely picture—I cherish the whole book, and sitting here in Jackson you want every one of those views exactly, conventional or not that isn't the point—I hope, though, you have a little book for yourself. You should have it to hand too. And after all your trouble to get it. I love having it, keep it by my bed to look at before I go to sleep—who knows, I might be transported there in the next dream. Thank you so much!

What are your plans for getting home, and getting to NY? Where and when will we coincide? [. . .]

Mother had a slight setback with her eyes, not serious, only a sty and then an allergy, but a nuisance to her. The progress is still slow and she hasn't had glasses yet; but is still seeing as she always did out of the other eye. It may be a month or more before she has glasses. I have an uneasy feeling about going off, which is morbid—I hope I can shake it off with the dust of Jackson, as, for one thing, I'm sure Mother is tired of having me hover over that eye like a chicken with its one egg (her words). But she's kept cheerful and fine, and the prospects are so encouraging that it's worth the wait and patience. Your mother's been so grand to us. She really saw us through.

[. . .] We miss you a lot these days—there seems to have been a slight surge of gathering again, after the longest lapse—since you were here, I guess. I had them to supper one night, and Seta came to town unexpectedly and joined us—a gay evening, nothing but laughing, and we missed your laugh. [. . .]

Dolly writes she still hasn't a job [. . .]. I hope things are looking up a little—for whatever your patience, it's hard on the morale to be job hunting. Especially with your mother writing "Come home."

This is an interrupted and confused little letter, and I may have left out some of the news—but I'm hoping soon to see you, and we can catch up properly. Let me know your plans when you have them made. Your horoscope said to lie low for a while, but I believe now it's OK to stick your neck out! Mine told me I could too. Mother's told her to be careful of attachments, and I think it meant electrical, because the hall light almost fell on her head yesterday. (So I thought, oh, I can't go!—really I suppose I'm only a little tired or something.) Write soon—I hope the dust has abated. This must be a terrifically busy time. Hope things clear up without too much trouble this term. Will you have to read many papers on Shakespeare?

Thanks again for beautiful Paris.

Much love,

Eudora

September 29, 1955 • Jackson to Austin

Dear Frank,

Does Punch follow you? If not I'll send on "The Stars Look Down", diary of a horoscope addict. Mailed my last envelope to you understamped by half—sorry—it registered on the brain long after I'd carefully weighed it and poked it through—the letter, not the brain. Don't know why I just don't send on the whole paper, except it's so much fun to cut it out. Are you getting settled all right? Glad the lodgings look all right so far.[53] I hope the new schedule is a merciful one. You must have heard Stevenson and I hope for a report that he looks ready to run. The paper said he'd speak at U. of Va. some time soon and maybe the radio station will carry it hereabouts.

Your mother came to see us and we enjoyed her visit so much. Will drop by to see her soon—know she feels the house empty. Louis popped in one afternoon just before leaving—said the visit home had restored him in energy and spirit to a good degree, and he seemed all ready to tackle the East. I hope he finds things congenial and people ready with ideas useful to him. [. . .]

[. . .] Yes, that is a trifle odd about Elizabeth and the little piece—since she's such a stickler for doing what she says for editors. I haven't heard from her since before she set off for Italy last spring—I'd love to know her news, whether she's coming back this fall or not. We seldom write, just take up where we left off talking usually. [. . .] Mother is taking a stronger medication in her eye and Dr. Hughes says maybe this will do it. Meantime she was well enough one day to get glasses fitted, so when they come maybe that will help too. Hot and humid are here too. [. . .] Hope all goes well.

Love,

Eudora

Ps. Did your mother tell you she had a piece of glass taken out of her right thumb by Dr. Johnson yesterday morning that had been in it ever since the fire? [. . .] She says she can drive all right. You know the way she never wants anybody told about anything, but she forgot to warn me not to tell you, so I'm being literal and disobeying her in spirit—anyway she seems to be fine. I'll catch her in soon. She was proud because she's told the doctor that was glass in it and he said it couldn't be, it was a wart, and she was right. [. . .]

E—

October 4, 1955 • Austin to Jackson

Dear Eudora,

What a feast of enclosures along with all the news. Many thanks. (No extra postage demanded so far!) They came just at the right time to cheer me during the first cold I've had since last October. The ghastly humid weather continues—just awful—Wet with perspiration day + night + going in + out of frigid air-conditioned interiors, classrooms, restaurants, houses, etc, I feared I would catch one [. . .] + I did early last week. Felt worst the day Adlai [*Stevenson*] was here (last Wed.)—all I could do to meet morning classes that day—so I missed him, alas. He arrived late in the afternoon, spoke in the gym + was off to someone's ranch for the night. So there was just one public appearance. I feel better now, but still cough + blow the nose + will keep on doing so, I fear, until something resembling October weather arrives.

Yes, Mamma told me about the pane of glass [. . .] but not about pain in her side which stopped once it was out—+ was probably the thing that finally sent her to Dr. Johnston. So foolish to put off doing something about anything that hurts. I can put things off too but not if they hurt. Please help me chastise her for this. Hope Mrs. Welty's glasses are okay + a comfort to her. Let me know how they work. Terrible for her to go on + on + on without any really encouraging Improvement.

Looks as if the Ponder Plane won't take off this year, what? Hate for it to be delayed. Let me know if Joe Fields indicates there's any chance it will fly this season. Don't suppose you've heard from him, but when you do, tell me what he says. He seems the most reliable informant about what's cooking. [. . .]

Thanks very much for the Colette volume—So glad to have it. Here, too, in Walgreens I saw six copies of Hubert's Chain [*Chain in the Heart*] on the 59¢ counter. But no Colette! [. . .]

My enclosures aren't too good—only a few feeble flickers of fun in the Beachcombers. But I love the interview with R Mitchum. No, I hadn't seen the Spain-Waugh bit in the Times. Will look out for her tirade in the next batch of Expresses I pick up.

Love,
Frank

October 10, 1955 • Jackson to Austin

Dear Frank,

Grand to get your letter, and all the clippings. [. . .]

Have to go. Mother got her glasses, and practices using them an hour or so a day. She still has the flare-ups, but when the glasses are on she can see through the floating particles—which is grand, but for the flare-ups to happen at all makes us uneasy of course. But I believe now things will be coming along. [. . .]

Love, and hope you're all right again now.
E

Ps. Must report that Mr. Jovanovich, the new pres. of Harcourt, telephoned me from his desk to ask if some textbook editors who wanted to use "The Worn Path" in a textbook could delete the word "Negro" from it or else would I change the story and not call the character "Aunt Phoenix" but "'Mrs. Jackson". I said I wouldn't. Told him the story was written in its own terms of time and place and vernacular, and it wasn't up to me to change those—that I had never meant disrespect in the first place, and didn't think it was up to me to prove it by making changes—that the feeling was what mattered, and if the textbook editors couldn't see the feeling plain, they didn't know what the story was saying anyway.—No, over the telephone I couldn't think at all,—as I never can, and especially at such a request—I just said no, I wouldn't change it at all, and I wrote this all to him afterwards. I know it was a small matter, and these are cautious times, but I think it's still an important point, a matter of the truth. Don't you? It really made me mad, to imply that I meant disrespect and that if I did they could easily correct it for me by changing a few words. Ugh! How far could such "editing" lead? Trespassing into what realms of gold? On the way to Othello they could hop on poor Robinson Crusoe for not saying "Mr. Friday" on the island and -----------

Hallowe'en, 1955 • Austin to Jackson

D. E.,

Oh yes, you were so right in your reply to Mr Jovanovich—Agreed with every syllable + hope you expressed your views even more finally + firmly to him than you did to me. Shocking, as P. R. would say, especially from a supposedly first-rate publisher.

Do tell about the director of the (*heart drawing*) + his visit to Jackson, + whether he thinks he'll really have a cast rehearsing in December. Exciting if true. Hope you liked him + educated him about the necessary Southern touches.

So busy—Big classes—Two freshman sections, but "specials," the better prepared ones this time. Schedule OK—

MWF 10—Freshmen—	29 [*students*]
MWF 11—The Novel—	28
TTS 10—Freshmen	22
TT 1–2:30—Sophomores	50
	129 Too many

Have pretty good reader—a girl, but can't use her long enough.[54]

Lovely weather lately—mainly cool, but not a drop of rain.

Big meeting of English teachers last weekend—South Central Modern Language Asscn—much reading of papers—some quite good—talking + cocktail parties given by publishers' representatives—on the whole rather fun.

The Sheep Has 5 Legs here now—Didn't laugh as much as I expected to—I think because I knew all about it in advance, from friends who had seen it. Close your ears to such summaries, + you'll enjoy it more. Comedy of situation, rather bordering on farce, shouldn't be bereft of surprises. Fernandel excellent, of course, I liked the Miss Lonelyhearts (Tante Nicole, he's called) episode best.[55]

Doctor in the House also amusing—lots of good touches—Dick Bogarde + others as London medical students. Very funny, even if it isn't meant to be, is Female on the Beach—Joan Crawford doing the things we didn't find in Johnny Guitar—see this if it returns to Jackson.[56] [. . .]

So sorry about Mrs. Welty's moving downstairs. Hope this doesn't mean the glasses aren't working at all. Hope Bride reviews are cheering. This one is what the Book Review Digest would designate +-, I suppose—but I'm glad it's mainly +. You must just try to ignore them.

Best love,

Frank

December 6, 1955 • Jackson to Austin

Dear Frank,

Dallas must be Heaven, where Annaclairs grow—just at Thanksgiving time—(I notice this sounds like the beginning of a ballad—the verse.) You know how we love them—truly the richest + most delicious ever tasted in our house. You were so sweet to send them and we gobbled them up with instant pleasure + gratitude—I hope your Thanksgiving was fun and you had a good holiday after the big push of work you were in—When do Christmas holidays begin? It will be good to start in on them fine to see you. Let me know by p.c. if you have time when we can look for you.

I meant to write you a decent long letter on the typewriter, having various little items to recount + report on. The days fly by full of nothing but chores + errands and lists (unfulfilled) for me this fall, I seem to be a poorer + poorer manager of time the less I have of it! [. . .] I must tell you of the director's visit—not really very rewarding (for the play), at any point, I felt, but he let me read a new script of the play and it was news (dreadful) to me—its direction is all toward gags and gadgets.—the new title is perfect for it.[57] [. . .]

Elizabeth Bowen wired from Lynchburg Va. to ask if I could possibly meet her in N.Y.—I couldn't possibly—So sad to miss seeing her.

Worth [*daughter of Willia*] was here with baby last weekend + I took pictures—Willia wanted one exactly like the ones I took of infant Worth at his age. He's a fine cute baby. Kicks like a demon when lain on his back (the pose). Worth kept poking a little flower for him to take + crooning, "Now Mimsy! Do like Wawa did!" By a fluke on his part + mine we may have got it! He weighs 23 pounds. "He's reducing," says Worth.

Must go—Hope this finds you well + no cold anywhere near—+ feeling ready to come home for Christmas real early this year—Many many thanks again for that delicious box—

Much love from

E—

As the holiday approached, Welty was in good spirits. "I love Christmas this year! Things seem better here, and we get along fine," Welty wrote William Maxwell. "Friends are beginning to get home—In Jackson I belong to a bunch of old friends, half of us are old maids and old bachelors off teaching school or something, that have been spending Christmas together since early childhood, and all still get back for it—We have eggnog Christmas morning here—It's always warm, usually raining by nightfall, and we're still talking."[58]

The Chodorov and Fields play based on The Ponder Heart *was now in previews in other cities before premiering in New York in February. Welty, having discussed many details of the project with theater aficionado Lyell, shared reviews with him.*

January 10, 1956 • Austin to Jackson

D. E.—

So glad to see these [*reviews*]. Please send whatever else you receive from Phila. + Boston + I'll return promptly. Cheering news all around, however remote it all is from your original. At least you got your title back. Teahouse comparisons probably arise from D. Wayne's presence, I should think.[59] What a low aim to think that pleasing to that extent is sufficient! I thought that piece obvious from first to last + recall nothing about it with real pleasure. No denying that it pleases the millions, + that's what they're most interested in. Here's hoping this is a hit too, regardless of the beating the book has to take.

Got back OK—left Jackson at 9:30 and arrived in Austin at 9:30 p.m., stopping only for coffee in Alexandria and Navasota.

Classes are scheduled for next semester in our new English building + office furniture arriving, which means we'll be moving offices during exams. Don't know how fast that will go, but rather imagine I'll have to transfer my belongings about the time I finish grading papers. This, alas, will pin me down when I wanted to be free, and narrows chance of getting to New York—still a tempting but costly prospect. Will just have to wait + see. Don't mention this. [. . .]

Love,

Frank

Please return Miss Murdoch. Want to send her to Mildred Hancock who recommended the book to me. Go to see Summertime—beautiful to look at from start to finish. Stupid plot + K Hepburn ridiculous, but Venice is superb.

Lehman Engel had been hired to write incidental music for the Broadway production of The Ponder Heart. *After the preview, Engel wrote her his assessment, which she passed on to Lyell.*

January 18, 1956 • Jackson to Austin

Dear F—

Copy of a letter from Lehman, of Jan. 13—

"This is the very first second when I have had any time to sit down and write you a letter about Ponder Heart, which I saw in Philadelphia on

Wednesday. You probably already know that the reviewers at New Haven and in Phila. have been on the whole extremely favorable and hopeful. [. . .] My opinion is that it's going to be a great big hit and that you will probably earn something better than a thousand a week out of it which I would say is a good function of the Ponder Heart as a theatre place.

"However, I did not like it at all and I hope you will be prepared in advance so that you have great control of your most personal feelings when you go to see it. It lacks the essential quality of your book and is about as far away from genuine Southernness as anything could possibly be. [. . .] I believe that most of the folk music which I have put in—if not all of It—will be out very soon [. . .]—I think all Southerners like Cat on a Hot Tin Roof for the very reality that non-Southerners find unacceptable ([*Welty's comment in the margin*:] I do too) and I think the reverse will be true of Ponder Heart.

"Anyhow, this is my opinion, based on what I saw and what I feel is going to be added to it and I think that you are going to end up quite rich, which is a very good thing (Paramount is already asking for the rights for a movie to be made starring Bing Crosby!!!!). So there."

All of which confirms my only too succinct impressions from seeing the script. The money I feel sure is an exaggeration of kind thinking on L's part, hoping to compensate me. Anyway, you can be glad if you, as is probable, won't be able to go; or, if you might be able to go, you can be glad you'll be on hand to help me sit through the show. I mean, please do be!

[. . .] I am <u>really</u> mad with the boys for not using his music. It is certainly a sample of the way they're tossing any good things out as they go. [. . .]

I saw Helene Canizaro in the Jitney, who said she telephoned the Music Box theatre on hearing the show would open there and asked for 2 tickets to the opening and they said OK, send about $10 apiece! Whoever answered the phone (??? probably the janitor) didn't know the name of the show that was coming next, but thought it was opening the 14th. Surely the boys couldn't pass up a chance to open Heart on St. Valentine's Day and probably they are going to do it, instead of on the 16th?

Hope all goes well and write me the news soon.

Love,

E—

January 22, 1956 • Austin to Jackson

Dear Eudora,

Swamped by exams. Please forgive me for keeping enclosures so long. Like you, I feel that Lehman sounds ever so right about it all, but maybe N.Y. like Dolly will be "enchanted" most of the time. Is L's music <u>entirely</u> out? If so maybe some of his impatience is due to that—that is, his failure to respond at all. He's bound to be affected by total excision of his suggestions, which could well have struck notes that didn't harmonize with the production. Oh yes, the Music Box couldn't be a better spot—[. . .] it's long been occupied by hits. Would give anything to be there, but of course duty will necessarily pin me down here on Feb 16th. With all this work surrounding me at the moment, I wonder I ever thought I could get as far away as San Antonio. I'll write again when the clouds of blue books begin to lift toward the end of the week.

Send any other reviews, please, that may have come since you copied out L's remarks. Promise to return more immediately!

Did you read the I. Murdoch book? If you did and liked it, I'd like to see it.

Now that I finished it, I must exult some more over [*Colette's novel*] The Vagabond—really marvelous. What that woman can do in a sentence, a phrase! And is there a better literary illustration anywhere of the French virtues of economy + fastidiousness? You know just what it meant to Renee to be told her arms were "the color of a spoiled banana." The ride to Meudon in the new car—when "the happiness of Fossette, who sat on my knees craning towards the door, provided us with occasional conversation, as did also the charm of that still wintry wood, with its great twigs against a chinchilla sky"—On every page, almost, there is a similar marvel of distillation. Also fine is the way she tells how she feels about him at the end of Chap 5 of part II—the last page and a half of exposition. When I praised her to Stark, he said she was "slick," which I said wasn't nearly flattering enough + implied shallowness; that I liked suggestive, poetic, overtonal writing too—but ever rejoiced in such clarity + completeness as one finds here, the deft, firm stroke that may not leave much to the imagination but reveals all with lightning brilliance. The way she weds her feelings with something everyday + palpable + concrete so that you move about + see + feel with her is really superb.

Went to see The Tender Trap to look at D. Wayne [*David Wayne, playing Uncle Daniel in* The Ponder Heart]. Yes he'll look old enough under makeup regardless of what he sounds like. Thought it, incidentally, a rather charming film. F. Sinatra and Debbie Reynolds very good, didn't you think?

If you have absolutely nothing to do, see The Big Knife.[60] Hollywood searching its sordid conscience(?) As Spenser is the poet's poet, this is the movie industry's movie. There are a couple of killing scenes with the producer [. . .] to warm the hearts of every underling in Los Angeles County. I believe C. Odets wanted us to sympathize with no one. Bids for sympathy are made, however, for Jack Palance, who doesn't want to, but does, sign the 7-year enslaving contract + Ida Lupino, who loves him regardless of temperament + philandering. JP hasn't enough (1) talent (as an actor—very strange vocal equipment) or (2) frailty (he's monstrous) to make you feel he isn't being honored beyond his deserts by the contract, + I.L. (who can act and is very appealing) can't help looking much too intelligent to keep on lusting for him (they're separated throughout or supposed to be). It would be a good film if everyone was made out to be totally worthless both as artists + as human beings. It's interesting anyway in a depressing sort of way.

Best love,
Frank

PS (Monday morning) Came to Tower before posting this and found little memorandum book for 1956. So nice! Many thanks.

With her mother's condition improving, Welty traveled to New York for the February 16 opening of the play.

February 8, 1956 • Jackson to Austin

DF—So glad to get your messages. Just getting on the Midnight Mail in a few minutes. Would you were going too! Shall be at Dolly's Friday night, probably at the Russells Sat. & Sun., Dolly's Monday—then move to Algonquin, until I leave on Feb. 21. A full 2 weeks away. Mother's eye is better and she feels, I think, all secure about it now—though of course I can't help feeling anxious. Let me hear from you if you have time before curtain goes up. I am too confused to know what I expect—Latest word is, Burton Lane song is out, title is back to P.H., and it is now 3 acts instead of 2. There is no business like show business, Virginia! Will miss you sorely, + report on all, + write a better letter after restful train trip.

Best love from E.

February 27, 1956 • Jackson to Austin

Dear Frank,

Of course I've been saving up all till I had time free and a typewriter to write you, which has taken till now, Monday morning. It was grand to hear from you at the crucial moments and as of the crucial moments. It was indeed a witching a hour. It will never cease to make me sad that you weren't there. As it turned out, I lived through it—And after it was over I decided it was OK. The thing I hadn't counted on—though I don't know why not, really—was the spell that actors can work out of just any material. The play was really not very well written—I'm prejudiced I know, but still I think so—and it had, as a script, little connection with my story as I see it. But performed, it was another matter. David Wayne is really a lovely actor! He has what the boys never dreamed of having, real warmth and sweetness—and whereas the story is about innocence, of which there isn't a single line in the play, he has such gentleness and tenderness that he conveys it—he puts in what the boys took out. His Uncle Daniel is a quite valid creation of his own, and I think he's good. Also I like him as a person. [. . .] We were supposed to pose for a picture (Clarena sent it to you out of the State Times I guess) and there were in that bound book of scripts at least 5 or 6 of the more recent versions! Una Merkel said "O Lord, don't let me see a word, I'll forget everything I know!" She too is a terribly nice person, I think—warm and real—David told me that he didn't think they used the same script 2 nights running a single time on the road. Imagine how tired and troubled they must have been. Anyway, on the night they did well. I went back afterwards and much hugging and kissing, but never did I see the boys together with Douglas or with the cast. There was no party, I hear, just each going their separate way.

Mary Lou had a buffet supper before the play—starting at 5:30. The Jackson group, Hubert, Dolly, Charlotte, and the Russells and Maxwells and Lehman. Lehman couldn't make the play—he had really been done dirty by the boys, as before reported—but came in fine fettle, bringing me two lovely white orchids that he said were the nearest he could come to the Night Blooming Cereus. We all dashed to the theatre after that, and that was when all sorts of Mississippians began showing and cropping up—Helene Canizaro, Velma MacLaurin, Cary Johnson Richardson and husband,—and the Harcourt Brace bunch came (Denver and Frances Lindley and Bill and Martha Jovanovich), Henry and Nat Volkening, Gene and Kay Reynal, David and Peggy Rockefeller, Eileen and her date (she asked me the night before how she could get in!), Hildy Dolson, Nona Balakian—we had all worked like beavers to get tickets for each other, Dolly, Diarmuid, and Bill Maxwell and I—Hubert and a friend (we tried to reach Elizabeth Spencer and couldn't). I didn't know who any of the critics were—Louis Kronenburger is the only one I know, and I didn't happen to see him—and didn't actually realize I was sitting in their thick. (Lehman told me to sit in the Row G seat—our tickets were only in pairs, no pairs together). When the final curtain came down, everybody I could see rose up in one body without waiting for a curtain call, and pounded out—of course they were the critics heading for their deadlines, but I thought Lord, nobody likes it. There was lots of applause though. After we'd been backstage and milled around gaping and losing each other, Dolly, Charlotte, Hubert, Hildy, Diarmuid,* Rosie and I went back to the Algonquin and sat downstairs having some drinks to wait for the papers. [*beside asterisk at bottom of page:*] (Diarmuid Russell has been infected by the theatre. He says "There's nothing like sitting around the Algonquin Hotel at one in the morning in a dinner jacket and the reviews coming in, and I'm going to start calling everybody 'dear.'") About one o'clock I was paged to the phone: Mark Baron, an AP reviewer, who didn't know me at all, called me to say he'd read me his lead if I wanted to hear it—which was a good one, and extremely kind of him, wasn't it—and then he called back in a few minutes and read me Brooks Atkinson's. (What a crack that was from Stark Young.[61]) (I can hardly believe for a minute that the one man on whom the fate of plays seems to hang would be so frivolous as to write something he didn't mean.) By this time, I was so on the side of the actors, and so full of suspense, that I don't think I could have stood it for the reviews to be bad, regardless of what I had thought of the play. When we heard from the Times, Dolly and Charlotte and Hubert and I went upstairs and had a drink from Charlotte's pint bottle of Old Crow, Hubert went out to buy us all copies of the first papers, and I called up Mother and reported to her. If I'd known how to call you I would have! Everybody was so fine to me—it was wonderful—One of the gestures was so funny really, in its McGrath way—Peggy and David sent me about a million red roses in a big trunklike box to the Music Box with the instructions on the front "Please Present Over the Footlights." ! Anyway we lugged them home and put them in the bathtub. I went back to the theatre on Monday night after the show, when they told me if I wanted to I could watch the play being photographed for Life. Dolly and Ruth had had a fine party that evening—fried chicken and cheese souffle for all, and an open fire burning on the hearth of Dolly's new apartment, new rug, white lamps, white tulips—all very extra fine! when we wished aloud for you, Nash (well + fine) among them. Hubert, Dolly, Ruth, and I went up to the Music Box about 11:30 and they were photographing the play backwards—the sets being up for Act III. This was fun, because David Wayne kept coming down into the orchestra and sitting with us and talking. I'll have to tell you about the photograph of the ball of fire. "A dry run of the ball of fire!" they'd call. They took it about a dozen times, the actors going through that climax over and over. Once David called, "Eudora, what did you mean, sitting down there in Mississippi and writing this in? You're a stinker!" Finally the photographer thought of having one of their men walk through the scene with a flashlight, instead of taking the real thing. "Walk, Henry!" Then "Rise, Laura!" and Laura stood up from behind the sofa with a flashbulb which she let off. "That will probably do it," said Life. The ball of fire, by the way, looks like two skillets put together, works on a trolly, and takes 3 men to run it—one to start it, one to guide it, and one to catch it, and cost $2,000.00! Watch Life for the pictures sometime soon—I don't know if it's certain they'll publish them or not, but if so, it will very likely be soon.[62] Wednesday I saw David again at lunch, before the matinee, and had a nice talk with him. He is, as you pointed out, a real person, and seems really so nice. He has a wife and 3 little children, lives in Westport. He asked me why I didn't try to write a play myself, and of course I have always wanted to. I might be able to put my mind to it now.

It was fun to see the matinee, because it was a "real" audience—the G.W. birthday holiday crowd—and much laughing and warm applause. All seemed neater and easier, and more relaxed. The courtroom scene really is funny. Well—when are you going to see it? I hope to the lord it stays open till you do. [. . .] Diarmuid says I should have started to earn some money on it already, though, so that will be nice. I have no idea how much or for how long, but it will all be manna from heaven.

I saw your mother and daddy yesterday, and they seem fine—your mother says her bursitis is much better since X-Ray. She was wonderful to Mother while I was gone, and had no business to be, for her knee hurt—yet she made us a wonderful coconut cake, some spiced pear salads, wonderful mayonnaise and there was that feast waiting for me when I got home. [. . .]

I'll send you all the clippings I have when I've cut them out and you can look over the ones you haven't seen and send them back. "Eudora, you'll have to go up to Mark Cross [*stationer's*] and get a scrapbook," said Eileen. Think I will get a local version, though—nothing like this will ever happen to me again! Thanks, thanks, for all powerful wishes sent up from Texas that night—I was relying.

Much love,
Eudora

That spring, Welty, who valued Lyell's knowledge of show business, asked him about a possible production of Robber Bridegroom, *what she had the right to agree or object to as an author, and which actor might play Clement Musgrove; Zachary Scott was being proposed. This production did not materialize. In the same letter, she reported news that would be more consequential: the health of her brother Walter.*

April 6, 1956 • Jackson to Austin

Dear Frank,

[. . .] Walter has had a bad time with arthritis, has been confined to bed for several weeks, and been to Oschner Clinic in New Orleans—they switched him away from cortisone too much aspirin and ACTH which was tapered off, then he had a "remission" and has had to go back to ACTH—is better and today went to work for a few hours. We worry about him—he never says it hurts, just that he's had a little fever, but I know it does hurt, and Mittie says even with loads of aspirin he's had 102. But things are better now.

Much love,

Eudora

P. S. I sent you Iris Murdoch and an odd one yesterday.

Chestina Welty's condition improved enough that she was able to attend a performance of the play in May.

May 14, 1956 • New York to Austin

Dear F,

When are you coming? Let me know when you know—so if I possibly can I can stay to say hello anyway. I am at present still here [*Algonquin Hotel*]—will let you know if I move—but it's convenient and in the saving on time and taxis, not as expensive as moving I imagine. Mother had a whirl—she found she could see and enjoy the theater—so much brighter than real life—+ so we went to 5 shows—Ponder included, which she enjoyed, differences from the book didn't upset her—Everybody was so sweet to her—We had 2 country visits, Russells' and Maxwells' and several lunch parties etc—she was so pleased when Jimmy offered to escort her home so I could stay the interval until Smith (June 3rd). But Walter has had another bout with arthritis—I feel I ought not be playing up here with my family all invalids—yet I am tired—+ need a bit of holiday for health reasons I feel somehow—. Have had laryngitis + bad cold since arrival, but after weekend mostly in bed am up today. Lots to tell you. [. . .] You must see the Matchmaker—R [*Ruth*] Gordon a circus[63]—The Lunts are as ever in a frail little opus but it serves—I want to see the Iceman Cometh + Uncle Vanya but have put off Waiting for Godot—am dubious of Beckett though I love Bert Lahr—

Vassar was nice—I got along all right and like the teacher, William Rose, so much.[64]

Will write more when I get some paper! My only sheet—

Love, and write news—

E

May 22, 1956 • New York to Austin

Dear F—

See this typewriter! The New Yorker sent it over to my room as a surprise—luxurious. Glad to hear from you about coming up, but feel sure I can't possibly still be here. I ought not to be gone so long as it is—need to be home, costs a lot to stay on and also I'm tired of the city already—you know—happy to see friends, but the days exhausting. I guess the sinus trouble I've been having the last three weeks has contributed to tiredness. Eileen insists on having me into her office this aft., but I immediately got better! The worst is over anyway.

I sent the picnic installment of Lady Diana to SJ Perelman and hope he will like it.[65] [. . .]

Hope all goes well with you. I'll probably see you in Jackson. I go to Smith for June 3, then straight home I hope.

Love

E

June 18, 1956 • New York to Jackson

D.E.—.

Went to Sat. matinee. Enjoyed it so much in spite of compromises with your originals. D Wayne very warm + radiant, always keeping everything in focus. Of course, so much more could have been done, even on the Boys' terms. Sarah Marshall [*who played Bonnie Dee Ponder*] should have come South—to look + listen, being quick enough, I should think, to pick up inflections, gestures, + a general tackiness she would have had to see to achieve, in a short time. [. . .] House mgr walked me in at theatre. Miss Lyons said do that when I called. House about half full. Spirited throughout. Many thanks.

Love,

F

Back in Jackson, things were very quiet. Welty wrote Maxwell that the main news was the purchase of a small air-conditioning unit for one room, now being called "The Cool Room" by her nieces. Her mother's eyes were "about the same," not free of difficulty, and the Weltys hoped air-conditioned air might help. Welty told Maxwell that, other than a good crop of figs, she had little more to report: "now and then a few of us go up to a little country hotel and sit on the upstairs porch and rock awhile quietly, having drinks in the shade and country stillness, or we sit in the dark in somebody's Jackson porch to talk and play records. There's something hypnotic about the steady heat."[66]

September 25, 1956 • Austin to Jackson

[*Stationery—Department of English Memorandum*]

To: Eudora
From: Frank

Thanks so much for letters and enclosures. [. . .]

No mishaps on trip back, but it was a hot ride + the heat is still on in Texas—up to 100° every afternoon—awful. Classes getting organized. Pygmalion is the first play in a new sophomore drama text, + I'm playing them you know what [*probably* My Fair Lady *album*][67] first thing tomorrow.

Thanks for the Guggenheim letter and suggestion that I be a part of the "prime vintage."[68] Will think more about it, but my first reaction is against the idea—mainly because I know how the committee favors scholarly vintners with higher vineyards + well-stocked cellars that they normally know about already. Leo Hughes, a deserving colleague, is now in England with his family, + he told me he was recommended by 3 former Guggs + how much that meant to him in getting chosen—though I'm sure his project is as good as anyone else's. I just don't think I have a chance. Am dining with [*artist*] Kelly Fearing tomorrow night + will talk to him about applying, as I've done often before. He's far more gifted than most artists on their lists + so much needs to go abroad to see the galleries + landscapes beyond this unpaintable world about us here—but he never seems to feel the urge as strongly as I feel it for him. If he's at all interested, I'll write + ask that you mention him if you have no one else to mention. He's painted stunning things in recent years, better all the time. At his show last spring when I was admiring the new ones alongside Mr. Wayman Adams, I was so pleased to hear him say, "Kelly has a sense of beauty that surpasses anybody else's in these parts" + he meant to include himself. [. . .]

So glad your aches are subsiding + that Mrs. W feels better. Get good + strong before the Little Theatre premiere!

Love,
Frank

September 27, 1956 • Jackson to Austin

Dear Frank,

So glad to get your letter and will reply more fully later, and send back Alun Jones' letter,[69] which I haven't yet read—just came to typewriter to say don't dismiss the Gugg. thing without thought, because it means a trip and an absence of what's dismal. This is the first time I've ever been asked to suggest anybody—don't know what it signifies as to attention paid the application as one not instigated by the one applying—you probably know more about the Guggenheim practices and expectations, from colleagues etc., than I do. Yes it would be grand for Kelly but it would be grand for you and that comes ahead.

I had some bad news, that Diarmuid is in the hospital after a heart attack. He is out of pain and cheerful, but recovery will be slow. He had taken his little boy to school at St. Paul's and was spending the night with friends in Boston on his way home, and is now in Emerson Hospital in Concord. Isn't that bad.

More later—
Love
Eudora

Lyell wrote to Welty just before the presidential election, in which Adlai Stevenson was again running against Eisenhower.

November 4, 1956 • Austin to Jackson

[*Stationery—Department of English Memorandum*]

To: Eudora
From: Frank

A nauseating Republican program in progress—[*Thomas*] Dewey answering questions fed by Helen Hayes + others. D says Stevenson never gets any of his facts straight, especially about Foreign Affairs, so ignorant + poorly informed. Dulles' operation comes at a convenient time, doesn't it—when he ought to be on radio + TV constantly, telling us about the US position toward unrest in Europe + Egypt. For the next 3 weeks Herbert Hoover, Jr will be in charge! How can people vote for government by Dulles + such substitutes + Tricky Dicky. Did you read Time's current piece about Nixon—A pitiful attempt to make something out of nothing? I should think even Republicans would be upset by that.[70]

You won't be rushing to read War + Peace if you see the film—a pale shadow of the book. Lunacy to cast H. Fonda as a person in whom deep stirrings of mind + soul—or anything very far below the surface—are going on. Still the bumbling undergraduate, playing for laughs. Only for a moment for me was the spirit of the novel caught. When Nicholas Rostov comes home + all the family rejoices around him. A. Hepburn okay on the whole, Mel F. fair to middling. Napoleon looks like Oscar Levant. All varieties of accents—from

British English + American through several versions of broken English. Not boring, actually, but not exciting—mainly pleasing to the eye—pretty dresses + uniforms, lovely interiors, + a beautiful ballroom scene.

I hope you're all well now.

Love,

Frank

November 21, 1956 • Jackson to Austin

Dear Frank,

Happy Thanksgiving! So glad to hear from you. How I've let time go by, not thanking you for letter and clips, not sending mine to you. I'm glad you're well (at last) of The Long Cold, and hope you have fun in store for the holiday this weekend. Will you eat your usual Thanksgiving dinner with Tom and family? Maybe there'll be something sparkling in Dallas or San Antonio or somewhere. I hope your car is well. [. . .]

We are all right, with the ups and downs of Mother's eye and Walter's arthritis, all doing very well at the moment. We have the girl to come an extra day in the week, which helps unbelievably. Yes I've been trying to do some work, and every day for the last 2 weeks I've been at it—some of it seems satisfying at the time, though I don't know how it'll mount up or come out in the end. I'm almost afraid to say it's a play, but that's what I'm trying. Don't tell! It's wonderfully interesting & instructive to me no matter if nothing at all comes of it.

[. . .] KAP send me the Autumn Yale review in which she has an article on writing Noon Wine.[71] It's the same request from RP Warren I had, when I tried my say on writing the Below N. O. story. Read it!

Reynolds sent me a story, but I haven't had time to read it—it looks long, and I want to give it a good study. I'll enclose a letter from him if I can find it (my desk looks like one belonging to Melancholia by Durer these days) and I've already hunted for and failed to find—have I sent it to you already??—a picture of Reynolds Dr. Blackburn took in England, complete with black beard and suitable expression. By the way have you seen the photographs in David Garnet's latest reminiscences—Bloomsbury snaps, in which you can't tell any of the men from the women, some lovely. I thought the book could have been much better—amiable and chatty, but not really telling anything. Harcourt sent it to me.[72]

Hasn't the news been black beyond belief. I think of Eva so much—what she must be feeling—<u>for</u> Hungary and <u>about</u> England![73] [. . .]

Guess Lehman's show [*musical* Li'l Abner, *conducted by Engel*] opened all auspiciously, and he wrote that he was to record it the Sunday after the opening (last Sunday) and have his Carnegie Concert this coming Sunday. Mrs. Engel and Flo were supposed to go up to the Abner opening, and Lehman was praying Flo wouldn't back out, though it all depended on the outcome of the usual bickering among the Three Sisters.

Ponder was done in normal [*Jackson*] Little Theatre style, with I think everybody trying like everything to make it extra-special.[74] The direction seemed to me to be nothing at all—no focusing or rise and fall to a scene or good grouping or fall of emphasis—nothing like that, and often the characters would be talking in some crucial scene barricaded behind two or three pieces of furniture, and the doors were so placed that nobody's entrance or exit was ever noticeable—but of course all of it was an attempted without an acting version of the script, so I suppose it couldn't be helped. Cliff Bingham played the part in a sort of head-on-one-side pouting way (can't describe it), not often smiling, and no fluidity or grace or radiance or any of the things David Wayne had—natch. But he was a flaming success and everybody says "I know they couldn't have been ANY BETTER than Cliff Bingham, or near as good (some add) because he's just not Suthn." I was more or less anesthetized to the whole thing by just going enough to know what to expect. Charlotte [*Capers, as Edna Earle*] did fine, and the little Fort child looked the part much more than Sarah Marshall, [. . .] every fault of the play script was <u>cultivated</u>! But on the other hand there was something nice and all of a piece and genial about it (the whole performance) that was attractive—I guess just Suthn. Anyway I was delighted that people liked it. Your mother did, and saw it twice! I knew of course that it was beside the point and also ridiculous to compare any amateur with any professional performance, but I simply couldn't erase from the mind what the play amounted to with David W. in it—in fact I appreciated overwhelmingly what he had made out of a sow's ear, by sheer talent and personal giving-forth.

Camellias are starting to bloom—roses still are.

Happy T'giving, and write soon when you can. Have noted the movie advice. Didn't go to War and Peace on purpose when it was here, so glad you agreed with my instinct.

Much love,

E

November 24, 1956 • Austin to Jackson

[*Stationery—Department of English Memorandum*]

To: Eudora
From: Frank

Thanks so much for sharing Reynolds' letter. [. . .]

Our Th'giving comes <u>next</u> week. Yes, I'm going to Dallas with Tom on Wednesday. We're having pretty weather too, at long last—but no autumn color, alas. Just doesn't exist in these parts.

[. . .] Did you see this week's <u>Time</u>? <u>The Mermaids</u> [*by Eva Boros*] is reviewed first (glowingly) and there's a picture of her—with <u>fluffy</u> hair—not worn that way when I saw here, + it didn't much resemble my recollection of her. How she must be suffering for Hungary now—No, the news couldn't be worse. So glad Eva's picture topped Mary McCarthy's. $15 for <u>her</u> book, from Reynal![. . .]

[*Jose*] DeCreeft's sculpture looks more enchanting than ever. How wonderful it would be to own one! That charming little cat in black granite—+ I love the upside down figure on the cover.

That <u>Variety</u> piece about Cecil "Paramount" DeMille "faith in faith" dinner was marvelous. <u>Time</u> printed a grand review of the film, + this week they did the needful to Elvis Presley. [. . .]

Love,
Frank

P. S. [. . .] The other day in class I made an irreverent remark about Joan Crawford + afterwards a youth, pretty dumb + naive, asked why I didn't like her. I tried to explain how I really loved her for her faults, which baffled him all the more, then asked him if he liked her. "Oh yes, she's my favorite actress because she always <u>lives</u> her parts." End of conversation.

April 7, 1957 • Austin to Jackson

[*Written on memo that begins "The Graduate Newman Club has asked for and received the privilege of having Dame Edith Sitwell for Saturday evening."*]

She [*Sitwell*] has a sprained taped up ankle—came from station wagon to her house in a little wheelchair. Opening remark: " I fell and blacked my eye on skid row! Hate to be such a nuisance, but it's better now." <u>Where,</u> on what skid row, we asked? Chicago? She had fallen over an open drawer in the St. Regis!!!!!!

Just in from this—so wonderful to see her again, looking not a minute older than when she was here in 1950. (Four huge rings, sable coat, gold + black turban.) She stayed an hour + a half, talking all the time + of course everything was quotable. A living room full of people, with various ones asking questions, mainly Beverly Boyd, a convert—instructor in English Department—the talk by no means centered on religion always, but B has the young convert's eagerness + what she asked elicited answers I was glad to hear. Why did she join up, etc—Said she was "unhappy," had never had a church, never belonged to one or attended any + felt the need. Well, are you "happy" now, B asked—well, no, but she felt disciplined, secure + brave. I asked which church she went to for mass. Answer: the Farm Street one (the tiny one in Mayfair, near Berkeley Square). "I creep in at odd hours"—which means that she doesn't go at Renishaw, where she is most of the time of course; + she announced to all that she "wasn't a good Catholic"—I was so pleased that for this group she was full of contradictions + that she said she didn't like T. Merton's poetry, didn't think he was a poet. "You have to be born to it, like me. If you're a hen, you can lay eggs—+ he isn't one + can't." !!! [. . .]

Couldn't help asking if she read My Dog Tulip[75] + wish you could have seen her expression—of course she had—"I love Joe Ackerly, one of my oldest and dearest friends—but I avoided him for months after that book came out because I didn't know what to say to him about it. [. . .]" I said maybe you don't like dogs or any sort of pets. Oh no, I have marvelous cat, who adores me + protects me + at lunch I feel her velvet arms about my legs. She won't let me out of her sight." "But, Dame Edith, that's just the way Tulip felt about Mr. A." "No, my cat's quite different—she's a real lady—" (Silly contradiction here, of course—she just doesn't like that kind of book, or wants to have Mr. A write a better one.) She said she didn't think much of Hindoo Holiday either, but repeated that she was devoted to "Joe." [. . .] Who are your favorite contemporary poets? The early Eliot + Ezra Pound. Who are the best novelists? No great ones but Elizabeth Bowen is very fine. She told all about becoming a Dame, honorary—says it's an insult to the queen if people don't call her M'lady + she's very proud of the honor. Etc, etc.

Chestina Welty continued to be troubled by her eyes and by the thought that her daughter might cancel any trips because her mother needed live-in assistance. Welty continued to work on fiction and wrote an essay about reading, "A Sweet Devouring."[76]

In the following letter, Welty refers to events in Little Rock, Arkansas. When nine Black students attempted to desegregate Central High School, mobs of hostile whites gathered, and President Eisenhower ordered federal troops to restore order. News reports noted that some troops were carrying bayonets.[77]

September 27, 1957 • Jackson to Austin

Dear Frank,

So glad to hear from you that the trip went off all well and you got there not too weary and in decent weather. Is the heat still on? We are having cool, windy, rainy weather—rather gloomy to look at, and the events in the Situation don't help any. Bayonets! Seems everybody is pulling the greatest possible blunders on all sides, and the wounds might never heal. And how many more will they make?

It was so heartening to read your account of the Roman interview with Isak Dinesen in the Paris review. Doesn't she sound a marvelous person? I was so glad to get the word about her health, too—it also helps explain the title Last Stories, no doubt chosen at the time she was going to make the farewell broadcast! And to be reprieved at the last minute is like something that might happen in some story of hers. I suppose you've read Out of Africa—I'm now certain you have. Anyway the spirit of herself that shows in that is full of wonderful humor too, do you remember—the concern of the servant over how she was ever going to expect all those MS pages in loose array over the desk and the floor to become a book—as she so fondly expected—"But I am sure" (anyway) "that it never can be <u>blue</u>," he says. That Eugene Walter is a Mobile man [. . .] He wrote me to contribute, one time, saying we've never met but he once hollered at me from a wall as he saw me walking up the steps at the Cloisters! [. . .]

Helen [*Lotterhos*] brought out an issue of the Chicago Sunday Tribune dated July 2, 1911, to show me that the sack dress was in its full glory then, you should see. You could buy one from the Boston Store (bargain for the 4th) for $2.29. There's a column run by Lillian Russell, answers to correspondence—most of them (signature: DISCOURAGED) want to know how develop the bust, and she advises them to breathe deeply. She also peddles her own ointment, that will help. But maybe you think the tone's not high. This is to A READER: I shall mail you the English dietary for gaining flesh and the recipe for a harmless bust developer." (Harmless bust? query mine) "Your trouble is not primarily one of digestion or lack of assimilation, but of nerves. Cultivate Repose. This 'letting go' is indeed the one thing needful for the excessively thin woman. You must acquire indolence, not matter how great a cross it is to your eager spirit. Sleep without weaving the morrow's plans, rise leisurely, and throughout the day's work hold yourself calmly to the moment's task without attempting to carry the burdens of the entire day." There is a feature on "Little Helps for Lone Woman When She's Traveling Abroad" which tells you not to get on board in your feathers. [. . .]

We all miss you so much. Ate over at Charlotte's last Saturday (Anne's birthday) and all seemed well and Jimmy was back in town again. Saw your mother and she seems well. We are all okay, Walter still gets better. Here are a few little items for you to read. More soon. I didn't read Towers of T, but did read Ordeal of Gilbert P, and the ordeal was all mine.[78] Like hearing someone tell a boring dream that you know all the time is just a dream and he's still with you, undamaged after all. Sentences of Catholic piety like "Holidays were over and the children returned into the care of monks and nuns" made me hear a groan deep in the heart of Texas. Hope all is going well there. Write.

Much love,

E

Speaking of 12 Angry Men with two girls, MSCW is going to put on Ponder [*drawing of heart shape*] with all girls. I'm asked up—some of the characters will have to be in pants + blackface—

September 29, 1957 • Austin to Jackson

D. E.—

To The Sun Also Rises last night—a plodding pointless film—Interesting in a way because it shows how little there is under the crackle of Hemingway's prose. The feeblest possible acting—but what is there to act? Every character assigned only a string or two to play. Mel Ferrer just ambles through as Mel Ferrer. Only Errol Flynn seemed a real individual, different from the essential E Flynn. All mighty bogus, though the Parisian and Spanish backgrounds are the real thing + some of them beautiful.

But I strongly recommend A Face in the Crowd—full of imaginative lines, sets, types, situations, everything. Some killing Deep South touches (Arkansas), especially the drum majorette contest + events ensuing from it. Devastating satire on Madison Avenue + the TV world. Improbabilities creep in towards the end, but on the whole has a ghastly reality + much of it is very funny. Didn't you say you met Patricia Neal chez Lehman or somewhere? She's the leading lady and that should add interest for you.

Had a letter from Nash saying Harvey [*Breit*] is leaving the Times. Did you know this? N. says he has an offer of a "plush job with CBS + is also dickering with Saturday Review and other organizations. He wants, like all of us, something with lots of pay, long lunch hours, + a minimum of labor. I expect he will find it." Who will take us so urbanely in front of books + drape them in Prufrocks???

Hope you and Mrs. W are OK.

Love,

F

October 29, 1957 • Jackson to Austin

[Stationery—Green Park Hotel, Half Moon Street, Piccadilly]

Dear F,

Are you all right?[79]

This doesn't come from the Green Park on Half-Moon St, it comes from the Fashion Beauty Salon at Norwood (alias Tripps Crossing)—("Helen, will you saturate Miss Welty?")—chance at a letter. Hope all goes well with you.

Walter had a little setback + is at the hospital—not dangerous, but he must rest his heart—This don't, please, pass on to anybody. It's been weakened by fluid from arthritis. I gather that eventually it will be all right—but I'm sure they feel discouraged—who would not—but don't show it. I hate this on top of all the rest for him. Mary Alice is as busy as ever + said it might be necessary for her to trick or treat Wednesday night, since she has to go to 2 Hallowe'en parties on Hallowe'en. (Told her to expect short shrift.)

Did you see the Danny Kaye UNICEF film, televised again on Sunday programing for children to ask for funds for UNICEF instead of treats? First time I'd seen it. Moving and good—he is a wonder and the children know it. [. . .]

Did you also see Jose de Creeft in Oct. 15 Vogue with wife and daughter + cat, + shadowy figures in background? Good picture of him—he looks as ever—darling face.

Have done not a lick more work—Did the [*Texas Quarterly*] magazine understand about my not contributing right now? I'm sure you made it all right + expressed my interest in submitting something in the future. I hope it's going great guns with good things staked out. They ought to get hold of a chapter from you on Sir C Grandison [*novel by Samuel Richardson*].

Saw the Sun Also Rises about the same time you did and felt the same great hollowness. I thought one bad trouble was that all the actors were people who are about the age of the characters at the time the characters were, back in the twenties and now they are so old and solid—Tyrone's jacket was mighty tight across him—and when the pals got tight at the bullfight you just thought, two old fools. I'm sorry but Tyrone's ailment was boring to me finally—you'd think that was why the Lost Generation was lost, literally—and they were scared to call Cohn a Jew and cast the most untypical face there for the role. Tyrone looked like more like Robert Cohn then Mel F, and more than he looked like Jake. But lovely of Paris and Spain—Brett was never Ava Gardner, an American! Write soon—keep well—

Love,

E

November 6, 1957 • Jackson to Austin

[*Stationery—Green Park Hotel, Piccadilly*]

Dear F,

Back in the beauty parlor, as you see. Wrote you last while getting a perm. Worried a bit because no word lately and with the Asian [*flu*] all around and hope you aren't laid low. We are better here in the health department, Walter home from hospital + looking + feeling much better at home. He will have a month in bed.

Leaves so beautiful now! Wish Texas had this—

I'm about to finish one story [*perhaps part of what would become* Losing Battles], thank the Lord. Not ready to send off though—[. . .]

Charlotte and I off to Columbus Nov. 14th (Friday, that is, whatever date it is)—I dread it as I have to sing for my supper by "a few minutes talk of your experience as a writer"(!) in chapel. Hope to just settle by reading a story—Charlotte could easily be the one to make the speech, and I can't see what she'll be doing there otherwise![80] [. . .]

Just a note to ask if you're okay—Write when you can—

Love,

E

January 12, 1958 • Austin to Jackson

[*Stationery—Department of English Memorandum*]

To: Eudora

From: Frank

Wystan [*W.H. Auden*] flew in from Indianapolis yesterday afternoon. Met him at airport + had a drink in his room at hotel before others took him out to dinner. Gave cocktail party for him this afternoon which everyone pronounced big success. Mrs. Friedell [*Lyell's landlady*] really plunges into a party + is a big help, making dips + getting in touch with a cheese straw woman. Robbie (Mrs.) Chick made masses of chicken salad sandwiches, + I did the punch: 2 bottles of sauterne + 2 bottles of champagne and one bottle of brandy + 1 bottle of soda—Pour all over ice in punch bowl, stir + serve. The sauterne was French, the rest domestic but OK, + the result awfully good. ($35 worth of liquor!) They drank every drop—42 guests—started coming at 4:30, left at 7. Had invited 45, but three wives couldn't come. Just as glad since at 7 there was only a bit of the dips, three little sandwiches + a few salted nuts left. Wystan seemed to enjoy it + I did too—so I feel good about it. He wanted me to dine with him at the Driskill afterwards, so I did of course, my slight weariness vanishing because he told so many entertaining stories about all + sundry in the international literary world. He speaks tomorrow afternoon at 4 on "The Quest Hero" after which there's another cocktail party, + I'm to have dinner with him + a couple of others after that. Very refreshing to see him—He's in good form, feeling + looking well.

Hope you + Mrs W are well, + being cooked for by a regular daily maid.

More later. In haste with love,

Frank

January 23, 1958 • Jackson to Austin

Dear Frank,

We surely miss you. I hope the pressure of exams and end of term will be over with soon. Such a pleasure to read of your fun with Auden. Sounds to me as if he must have had a rousing good time himself. An item enclosed here's about him, rather interesting.

We've had to have Walter in the hospital again where he had a bad time but he's back home now, still in bed, and I hope this trouble won't return—a spooky business of fluid around the heart, caused by the arthritis. He feels fairly comfortable now (fluid drawn off). You and your mother helped us more than you knew, for the servant problem at our house is solved now and just when we needed it solved most. Clarena put us in touch with Katie—[. . .]. She comes every day but Sunday and cooks dinner and cleans up—real, real luxury. While we were keeping the children, getting them to school at cetera and being away all day at the hospital, it was really heaven-sent, Katie's being here. So thank you too. When things get eased up a little, as I hope so much they will, I can start in at the typewriter and maybe, for a change, get the things done that I ought to have done long ago. [. . .]

Much love,

E

March 10, 1958 • Jackson to Austin

Dear F—

[. . .] How are you? Spring is here, and lovely and blossoming. Shall write later, meantime some clips. Walter and Mittie went to New Orleans on Panama this morning to Foundation Hospital to see if they can't help him. Nothing constructive at all was happening here, and things looked most gloomy. [. . .] No, I didn't go to NY. Next time set for Library meeting is April something—15 or so—and if things go all right so I can leave, I hope to make that one. Hope all is well with you.

Love,

E

March 22, 1958 • Jackson to Austin

D. F.,

Did you see Bea Lillie on TV? I nearly sent you a telegram. Last Sunday on the Dinah Shore Show. [. . .] She flexed her muscles—sang "Nanette" and danced Honeybun in the South Pacific sailor suit inside which she was able to turn around. Material not anything wonderful—but just her very being on TV living and breathing! She looked so well and healthy, darling as ever. Saw in some paper that she and Cyril Ritchard are going to do a show together in the fall—in New York.

Mittie is home and Walter is getting help from therapy at the New Orleans hospital—feeling easier and stronger. The specialist didn't find any damage to his heart—the nightmare, of course. So all is easier with all our minds. [. . .]

I hope, if all goes reasonably well, to go to N.Y. soon—perhaps Saturday week. I was asked to Martha Graham's opening night—+ a party afterwards given by—Madge Evans—!—which I think would be nice to be able to accept, don't you—The Library [*of Congress*] meeting in Wash isn't till April 18th. I'll just see from day today how long I could be gone. I do need a brief change. When is Easter by the way? Don't tell me that if I go I'll miss you, coming to me again? Might you come, and if so when? Write me when you can. [. . .]

Much love—

E

March 28, 1958 • Jackson to Austin

Dear F—

Hope you are in good health, and all goes well. Are you, and does it?

We do better, Walter feels better and stronger, is still in Foundation Hospital in N.O., and Mittie is down for a few days to see him. Children with us. I hope if news keeps on being favorable to get my trip to N.Y. starting this Saturday night on the Rattler. Can gauge my stay by the way things go.

[. . .] Fannie Cheney, [*novelist*] Brainard (Lon) Cheney's wife—you know—was in Jackson to make a talk, and Bethany Swearingen had her + me to dinner + to an evening at Millsaps, where Prof. Sanders and the new English professor, Mr. Stevenson, made talks—both good, and Prof S's really warmed the spirit, because it was about how he spent his time since retiring 2 (?!) years ago. Reading: (a) the classics again—Horace, Homer, Euclid, the song of Roland, Don Quixote, and comparing them; (b) literature of a country unfamiliar to him—Turgenev (rereading), Tolstoi and Dostoevsky; (c) skips + omissions of his earlier years—George Eliot + Dickens ("I think I waited too long for Dickens—I could not go through with that"); detective stories "too numerous to mention—I may mention Simenon . . ." I thought this a wonderful account 80, is he? + starting over.

As Fannie and I were upstairs waiting on Bethany, she sauntered into the stacks and murmured, "Ah, the life of Saint Whosis"—I forget who—"Lon's favorite saint." This cosy remark about a hearty, hard-bitten newspaper man made me disbelieve my ears. She went on to say that while working on his novel, Lon had persuaded the local priest to let him say the mass at noon each day—such a restful break—"We are quite ardent Catholics now, as you see."—all in such <u>cosy</u> tones. She went on to say cosily that Flannery O'Connor is on her way to Lourdes this summer. She is suffering from lupus, she says—sounds dreadful, and I don't know whether she's taking any other, profane treatment or not—She said the Tates had spent Xmas with them—and they'd been with the Tates in Rome—all so cosy. And, I felt, just a shade smug. The Cheneys were fun 15 years ago when they were rather poor, brash, gay and full of beans—Now Fannie made me sad a little, giving out incense like that [. . .]

Hope you're well. I'll not miss you here, Easter, will I? Wish you were coming to New York!

Love,

E

[. . .]

April 1958 • New York to Austin

Dear Frank,

Thank you for the birthday message! And for good letters and clips. So much here you'd like to be seeing—I'll write a real letter real soon—just a line to tell you Random house is taking Reynolds' book of stories![81] Hiram Hayden the editor, Diarmuid just told me—

[. . .] I'm having the finest, + luckiest sort of trip—Elizabeth Bowen, even, turned up in town! and we had two good lunches—she's been teaching (or what) the writers at U of Wisconsin, and is now off to Virginia—so what luck! She looks grand, and we just took up where we left off talking—

Martha Graham was stupendous and you would have been excited so to see the present season—Clytemnestra is so frightening—powerful and archaic and wild—I didn't take to the end, because Clytemnestra seeks redemption, + the two speakers (one on either side of the proscenium arch) chant "Rebirth! Rebirth! Rebirth! "—Unbelievable, don't you think? as a concept. But I gather she has changed it somewhat now—as she seems to do as the season goes on. So complicated and so amazing that I'm not equipped to describe it, but I felt terribly moved by its power and beauty—MG is in wonderful form, has boundless energy + is in gay spirits. She closed the season Sunday night, they said 29 curtain calls, standing room sold out, everything—I was asked to the party afterwards for the cast, at the de Rothschild house, which was very sweet of them, as I was the only non-dancer there! except for Mr + Mrs Sydney Kingsley (Madge Evans, a darling, + exactly the same profile + clear eyes + wavy hair as when she wore those beaver hats.)[82] Such a nice group of young people, so interested in other things (as painters so seldom seem in the dance, for instance, you feel!) + "clean-cut," nice—A champagne supper at about 1:00—that was the night of my birthday [. . .] I also went back at various performances—saw the other new work, "Embattled Garden" (Eden)—and the new form of her Joan of Arc, "Celestial Dialogues "—did you ever see that? Like Chartres—color, costumes, attitudes, spirit, all—my favorite—"Night Journey" (Jocasta—where she cuts (whack!) the umbilical cord!—) "Deaths + Entrances"—others—A party afterwards at the Kingsleys—KAP was in (incessant) high good form + having a lovely time at the <u>other</u> end of the sofa from Martha Graham! Stayed till the very last, + so did I, as I was seeing KA home—lasted till 2:30—after which I think Martha G went home + changed + sewed a few more costumes! before starting rehearsing next am. I asked her, and the 2 men who manage her, Leroy Leatherman + Craig Barton, + the Rothschild lady (Bethesda? I can't yet get her name—she's the one everybody kissed on opening night, put up the $$) whose party I was at, to come to lunch tomorrow with me, and everybody's coming but Martha! ([*In margin:*] They did join me for drinks here one night after the performance) who had promised K. Cornell to run up to Boston + design + sew <u>her</u> costumes <u>she's</u> in trouble with for <u>her</u> new play. Last night at the Russian dances at the Met she sat in the Russian ambassador's box as our finest ambassador to the East etc., + went to the party for them afterwards, along with—but you read the Times story I know. I'm going to the Russian dancers tonight—taking Eileen [*McGrath*]—wonder if she'll like them? I haven't seen her yet, as she's been busy moving to a new apartment—East 69th Street, I'm seeing it tonight for drinks—

I still love "Look Back in Anger"—[. . .].

Nash, Dolly, Nona, Ruth, all are fine + asked about you [. . .]

Well, I did write the letter anyway—Lehman is fine, about to go to Europe for 4 weeks—Hubert seems still the same—not very much in tune with all this! We went together to see "Look Homeward, Angel"—about which I felt a mild disappointment—haven't seen his apartment—he says not able to have company yet—but he seems happier over it and over anything else—

I'll write when I get back (Mon AM) + thank you again for the unknown birthday present. Very cheering, but I wish you'd been here for all this!

Love,

E

April 23, 1958 • Jackson to Austin

Home yesterday, & all the summer green. Azaleas all over the place. My trip did me a lot of good, + the news from Walter is good + he is coming home from Foundation hospital this week. Girls with us while Mittie is down to fetch him. Letter soon. Love, Eudora

June 2, 1958 • Jackson to New York

Dear Frank,

Hooray! So cheered that you are in New York! I thought of you on Memorial Day as being right where you were—at the matinee of Look Back in Anger. [. . .]

I've meant to write for such a long time. [. . .]

Your mother came by the other day and let me read the letter about Eliot. So glad you were with him so much and got to hear so many good things. [. . .]

[. . .] If you see Eileen, she is in a new apartment, so call her at her office—give her my greetings and apologize for my manners in not writing, tell her how awful I have been. I took her to see the Russian dancers at the Met. In the wonderful "Partisans" dance—will you by chance see this, at the return engagement at Madison Square Garden—but I hear tickets are going for $80 a pair—in the "Partisans" dance, where they move in long floor-length cloaks in a ruddy light in a silent company, like soldiers by night on horseback, giving a marvelous illusion of horsemen, she said "Oh, they're on little bicycles under there!"

Give my best to Nash, Nona, Dolly, Ruth, Hubert—to all friends you see—Have a wonderful time. I'm so glad you're there. Will be nice to see you here too.

Love,

E

Thank you for kind words about Bryn Mawr [*Welty had been awarded the Lucy Donnelly Fellowship*]. A real blessing—the award is cash, and all they ask is a visit at your convenience simply to be there for students to talk to—I hope to go up about Oct. if possible.

September 1958 • Jackson to Austin

Dear Frank,

So glad to have your letters, which I've meant every day to answer. Miss you a lot here, and the nice movie evenings etc. Your return must have been a bit tiring—but hope even with the work setting in that the routine's established and smoothing the days out by this time. [. . .]

I'm thrilled that Kelly [*Fearing, artist friend of Lyell's*] let me have that drawing, if I can afford it, and I am determined to—but it's horrifying to think of his making a second one, or even framing of it. Creases or whatever (and that was a crime—and after he wouldn't let them pay him, either!) I think that ought to be the one. I hope he can iron out what they did. Tell him to let me know the price of it, and if he needs being told that, you tell him it's straight business. I would so love having it—have always wanted a drawing of his since that evening in the Chelsea Hotel. Thank you a million for speaking to him and making it possible.

(Note: I'm supposed to be getting the Bryn Mawr check any day now, so I shall be feeling plushy.)

[. . .] Haven't heard from H. [*Hubert Creekmore*] myself, have you? I sent him a manuscript—by his niece, M. A. Welty, a story called "In New York" about a little girl named Elizabeth, who "was a bad type." From the top of the Emp. State Building she jumped onto the window washer's thing (sic) and "her aunt fainted, her uncle was stunned." And on from there. Just something she wrote for English.

As you see, I didn't get to Yaddo, since it looked to me as if I couldn't leave with nobody in the house, and Mother only at the last minute would tolerate the idea—too late to get anybody but it might pave the way to my getting somebody—just to sleep here and be present in the house at night—when I could go up in November. She understands now that it would be for me and my peace of mind. All working out, I'll go up for Washington Nov. 3, Bryn Mawr for Nov. 4–18, and then hope for a fling in NY. Making a month away. It would be wonderful. But we must get the right person, that Mother wouldn't mind. [. . .] I'm glad you thought V. Woolf review was done well—but I didn't do well on S. J. Perelman—don't read it! How is Benet biog.? Such a chore right now for you unless it is good. Sent you Mary Mian's book for some moment of leisure.[83] [*The word "leisure" has tiny line marks all around it, suggesting rays of light, plus three question marks.*]

Love,

E

October 14, 1958 • Austin to Jackson

D. E.—

So glad you're arranging the New York coda to your trip. Wish the Bible major [*Belhaven student Welty had hired*] could stay on after your return to do all the chores you shouldn't be troubled with. [. . .]

Love, F

(You didn't enclose F Hains' piece!)

October 18, 1958[84] • Austin to Jackson

[*Written in margins of a flyer announcing Katherine Anne Porter's lecture at the University of Texas*]

D. E.—

Look who's coming! Or will she???? This is the first lecture in this year's series. There will be fewer people this year than last + reduced funds to operate on + it sounds to me as if there's not enough left to ask you to come. I told [*English Department chair*] Harry Ransom what you said about the spring being an agreeable time—A number of bids went out during late summer apparently, in addition to those in the spring, and when they arranged the calendar it was full. Now they say you must come next year + stay at least 2 weeks, etc, but I'm very much disappointed because I wanted it to be this year. Not that it matters to you, but it would be so much better to have you than 4 or 5 of the "critics" who are coming: Yvor Winters + such. Spender and Allen Tate are the only definitely booked ones that interest me especially, besides KAP. I'm going to meet her at the plane at 7 Tuesday night. She'll be here just Wednesday + leave for Oklahoma for another appearance on Thursday morning, U of Okla, I guess. The other greeter will be Bill Handy, a newish colleague who teaches courses in New + old criticism + corresponds with the visitors + helps steer them around—I say "other" but he's the main one; I'm just going along. Bill is among Harry R's inexplicable choices for doings of this sort—he's like Hal March on The $64,000 ?[85] only without the surface slickness—all grins + chatter + heartiness [. . .] I'm curious to see what he does vis à vis KAP. She wrote him a killing letter: requested "an amber or rose-colored spotlight full into the face," no overhead lights or spotlights + a microphone no matter how small the hall. Said she'd wear an evening dress + hoped everyone "kind enough to come and hear her" would be pleased + hoped these "important little details" would be attended to because they were important in setting the "tone of the evening." Of course she's right, because she'll do better if she feels properly lit up. Said she hadn't been to Texas since 1934 + must talk about "Noon Wine" because she thought of it as happening near Austin.

This will be posted from San Antonio, where I've come just for the evening to hear Elisabeth Schwarzkopf sing with the San Antonio Symphony—their opening concert. More later—

Love,

F

October 22, 1958 • Jackson to Austin

Dear F,

[. . .] Thanks for both letters, and I really feel relieved that the U of Texas says No Room! this year, much as I'd like, always like, to come out, for I feel I'd do better another year. It's given me a feeling of relief every time I've turned down a similar invitation this year, and it's petrifying me if I think about it that I have to go on at the Library of Congress in only about 10 days. KAP may be able to put all her trust in those rows of amber lights full in the face, but I could give a better performance on a postcard if given my choices. Tell me all about KA. Was she in good form? Did she stay out there longer than 25 minutes (her Jackson program)? Did she read Noon Wine—that must have been gorgeous if she did, she reads wonderfully I think, and that happens to be my favorite of all her stories. Tell me all. I'm sure something happened I couldn't possibly visualize.

I'm leaving Nov. 1 and going up from Meridian on the Southerner [. . .] before the ordeal at the Library. Then on to Bryn Mawr[86] [. . .] Then to New York on 18th. Touch wood, touch wood. [. . .]

Love and let me hear.

E.

October 23, 1958 • Austin to Jackson

D. E.—

1:30 AM Thursday, but must write. K.A.'s visit huge success. She looked grand—at her best in every way. Met plane + had drinks in her room after arrival Tues night while she was briefed for Wed by me + Bill Handy. Picked her up at 11:30 with Bebe Steves, an adorable senior student friend from San Antonio (has been in 2 of my classes) + is related to all of KA's special SA friends ("Cousin" Lily Cabill, the actress, etc—who died 3 years ago). This gave her a good "family" start. Lunch in faculty dining-room with interested colleagues. Photographs + autographing of her books in Rare Book room afterwards. Then she went to hotel + I to classes. Lecture was reading of Yale Review article of 1956 about "Noon Wine" sources. Preliminary remarks about Texas childhood—charming—Full hall + many standees at back. She read extremely well—Everything worked—lights, microphone, etc. Pretty dress—dull mulberry chiffon with sequins + long black gloves. Gave party for her afterwards. 35 guests, all enchanted. KA never stopped talking. Seemed delighted throughout. Almost nobody left till midnight. All said it was fine party. I certainly enjoyed it to hilt. Beautiful weather today.

Love,

F

October 28, 1958 • Austin to Jackson

D. E.—

[. . .] To Dallas Friday afternoon for the old Vic's 12th Night—delightful, with v. good actors playing Viola (Barbara Jefford), Sir Toby, + Maria. Stayed with Tom's sister Isabel, lunch with Miss Mabel C. on Saturday, + dined with Betty that night. On Sunday Bob + Mary Ann Clark gave a large cocktail party + seated dinner (in tent on lawn) for gathering opera forces + patrons. Maria Callas + all stars there. Loved meeting + talking to her, natch. Surprised to find her so responsive (she sees + hears all, + gives full, direct reply to every question) + so chic. She really looked stunning: black inverted mixing bowl hat with black ostrich coming straight down from flat crown, rich electric-blue moire dress—square neck + 3/4 sleeves + short flared skirt, + black sable cape—all very high fashion, but flattering. Blue eye-shadow matching dress on lower half of lids!—a little startling up close, but somehow it seemed OK too. Somebody brought John Neville (the old Vic's Hamlet on this tour—a poor Aguecheek in 12th Night, so I didn't go to Hamlet on Sat.) + Judi Dench, the Maria of the night before; a darling Yorkshire lass, + I concentrated on her rather than him—so glad she came so I could say how I especially enjoyed her. Back to Dallas Saturday afternoon for Callas' Sunday performance of La Traviata + back the following weekend for her Saturday night Medea (Cherubim). She seemed in good health + spirits. I hope she remains so through the 2-week season. [*Gossip columnist*] Elsa Maxwell (!) is staying with the Clarks this weekend + I think on through Medea, too. The paper said Leo L was coming down. No telling who else.

Hope you get off all right. Stop being "petrified"! All will be well. Grand for you to have this trip. Your Perelman review, I forgot to say, was fine, properly including so many funny quotes.

Love to all,
Frank

October 31, 1958 • Jackson to Austin[87]

Dear Frank,

So pleased to get your communiqué on the KAP evening—she sounded in superb form and must have been a joy to everybody—I remember now reading the Noon Wine–sources piece—your party put the fine gay touch on the evening of course—KA must have loved it—of course she talked every minute! You are right back in stride with your welcomes to the visitors—what a godsend they must find you—who's next?

This is written 8:30 a.m. under the dryer—my last day before leaving (Jimmy is driving me over to catch the Southerner). Have 1000 things to do—one is to catch your mother at home. The other day I was suddenly smitten with the realization that besides seeing my old cronies in N.Y. I was going to have to face a lot of young college girls, strangers, and that I ought to get my clothes in fitten shape—So got a new beautiful wool dress, and a new beautiful dinner dress—can wear the latter (black chiffon is back!) to read in Washington—so I'm fortified—indeed as the time nears I feel I'm setting out for a lovely time—Write me c/o Eng. Dept, Bryn Mawr till 18th—

In Washington I'll stay 2 nights with John + Catherine Prince—like them so much—Marcella [*Comès*] I guess is still in Europe—In NY hope to stay at the old Algonquin—Have seats to Visit, Touch, Pleasure of, Susie (that was Wong), Goldilocks—that one I'm seeing, I note on the tickets they sent me, the evening of Lehman's opera premiere in Jackson![88] I feel bad about not being on hand for that—hope they don't murder it.

So glad you shook paws with Callas—She sounded quite attractive personally—+ good costume. Elsa! That old bat, following along + clinging to every rafter. If you see her, don't give her a party. Dallas season sounds lavish—

Jimmy had fun in NY, he says—found Hubert in spirits 100% improved—As you know, H will be here for Christmas.

Thanks for letters. Glad Mary A. is doing all right. What a handwriting M. Jarrell has![89] My idea of Madame Bovary's—

Write me—Happy Hallowe'en!

Love—

E

November 18, 1958 • Bryn Mawr to Austin

Dear Frank,

So glad to have your letter—I haven't yet read Hubert's under it, but thanks for it. There's been so much to tell I haven't written anything—14 pages or nothing, you know. Anyway a few items after Elizabeth Bowen + I get home from dinner with two of the English faculty—I must have said on a postcard E. was coming—she came down to Philadelphia to lecture the day after she flew into this country, + was invited by the college to come + visit me at Bryn Mawr—a sample of their kindness + imagination toward my visit. [. . .]

I'm going to be in town for Thanksgiving but going to the Russells' for the rest of the weekend. So you can see how fortunate + gay this all is. I feel well (better—had been so tired + a bit unable to relax lately). So if all still goes all right at home, I'll be having this holiday 2 more weeks.

When do you get home?

[. . .] I forgot to go on with M. L's [*Mary Lou Aswell's*] family. The children were both in Chappaqua, and after Ed [*Aswell*]'s funeral had come on down to Penllyn.[90] Nobody really knows when he died—it could have been 6 days before a policeman was asked by his office to look in the house + he found him—Horrible. [. . .] I'll see Mary in New York Thanksgiving.

Such a late hour. By day the little girls trail in, + by night I've been too tired to write, but so set off tonight by seeing Elizabeth. She is in fine form + looks ever so well, as she always is + does. [. . .]

It will be better fun to talk, before long—write me c/o Algonquin if you can. What about the drawing of Kelly's, by the way?

With love,

E

December 8, 1958 • Jackson to Austin

Dear Frank,

Here I am home, after some delay due to jammed trains after the plane strikes. You'll be home soon I hope? Send me the date, just to have it to look forward to. [. . .]

The trip was so fine. In N.Y. the best of luck held—with Elizabeth B. in town, Mary Mian (who sends best), the Smiths, among those I never expected to really see there. Of course enjoyed all the ones I did expect to see—will give my report in person. Did see My Fair Lady at last! (Mulhare + Howes)[91]

Walter about the same—All the others well. Shall see your mother soon—Much love—Come home early + safely + merry Feast of the Immaculate Conception Day, which this is—

Eudora

On January 9, 1959, Walter Welty died at the age of forty-three.

January 16, 1959 • Austin to Jackson

Dear Eudora,

What an eternity this past week must have been for you all! I feel so sorry for Mittie and the children, for their anxiety during Walter's long months of suffering, all of which you + your mother have shared every minute. Words sound so futile, + I shall not try to summon any to tell you how deeply I sympathize with you all because I know you know. Have been able to think of little else no matter what I've been doing since Mamma sent me the sad news. Please be sure that my loving thoughts are with you, and don't try to write anything now, that is to me. Kelly asked to be remembered to you and gave me these enclosures to pass on to you last night. He is overjoyed that you have the drawing + like it so much.

I had a charming letter from Katherine Anne, which I'll share later on. She's definitely coming here for the first semester next year.

Blessings on you all + much love,

Frank

Great fiction [. . .] abounds in what makes for confusion; it generates it, being on a scale which copies life, which it confronts. It is very seldom neat, is given to sprawling and escaping from bounds, is capable of contradicting itself, and is not impervious to humor. There is absolutely everything in fiction but a clear answer. [. . .] Writing fiction is an interior affair. Novels and stories always will be put down little by little out of personal feeling and personal beliefs arrived at alone and at firsthand over a period of time as time is needed. To go outside and beat the drum is only to interrupt, interrupt, and so finally to forget and to lose. Fiction has, and must keep, a private address.

—"MUST THE NOVELIST CRUSADE?" 1965

Chapter 4

1959–1977

AFTER WALTER WELTY'S DEATH IN JANUARY 1959, CHESTINA WELTY EXPERIENCED increasing challenges to her vision and her mobility. For the rest of her mother's life, family concerns affected almost every decision Welty made. Often caring for her mother and always worrying about her, Welty updated Lyell often on Chestina's health and her own struggle to find time to write. Traveling to deliver lectures at universities provided some income and respite. In 1963 when she and her brother concluded that their mother should be moved to a convalescent home fifty miles from Jackson, Welty was terribly distressed. In the remaining years of her mother's life, she regularly drove to visit her, sometimes writing notes for her fiction during the trip.

Beyond Pinehurst Street, astonishing changes were underway. The South's seemingly immutable color line was being challenged by Blacks and by some white allies, especially young people. Technology advanced the speed of communication and travel, as well as humans' potential for mass destruction and environmental degradation. Social categories of gender and sexuality no longer seemed natural and permanent. Welty remained an avid student of world events as well as a voracious reader, but rarely saw herself as a participant in the era's transformations. She rarely responded to requests to speak publicly on race or the women's movement. She followed the news closely, however, and worried for her mother's safety as civil rights demonstrations and violent reprisals against their supporters intensified. In 1963, she told Lyell, "If I had a way at all I'd pick up Mother and move away from this place for good."[1] Considering Welty's sense of vulnerability and near-imprisonment during this period, it is remarkable that she managed to create works that interrogated systemic racism in contemporary Mississippi, some now widely known and admired ("Where Is the Voice Coming From?", "Must the Novelist Crusade?", "The Demonstrators"), and others that remain unpublished (*The Last of the Figs/Nicotiana*). Ironically, some of her insights into contemporary Black experience came out of her mother's confinement, when Black women were working alongside Welty to help care for her.[2]

Letters became harder for Welty to find time to write, but they helped her weather these difficult years. They kept her in close touch with Mary Lou Aswell, now living in New Mexico with her partner, Agnes Simms. Lyell, too, sympathized with the troubles Welty shared with him, though he never had caretaking responsibilities in his own family. Most of his letters from this period do not survive, but Welty's letters indicate he consistently inquired about her family and offered continuing support in the form of letters, cards, gifts, and in-person conversations when in Jackson.

Welty's caretaking ended in 1966 after the deaths of her mother and then, four days later, her brother Edward, leaving her with only nieces and sisters-in-law in her immediate family. Over the next few years, she translated her grief into a novella, *The Optimist's Daughter* (1972), finished another project long in the making, *Losing Battles* (1970), and published *One Time, One Place: Mississippi in the Depression* (1971), a book of photographs from the era when she and Lyell first exchanged letters.

The correspondence from this period is mostly from Welty; only six letters from Lyell are extant. She seems not to have kept most of his letters, though hers make clear that he often wrote. This may be partly due to the enormous volume of Welty's other correspondence and her ever-increasing fame. Her letters to Lyell report on awards, requests for interviews, speaking engagements, television appearances, and close friendships with people she had once admired from afar. Her *New Yorker* editor William Maxwell and his wife Emmy continued to be part of her life, as did Reynolds Price, whose writing career Welty encouraged and whom she grew to love almost as much as her own nieces. Price, the Maxwells, and Mary Lou Aswell were among her regular correspondents. Letters helped her develop a deep friendship with another writer, Kenneth Millar, who wrote mystery novels under the name of Ross Macdonald. He and Welty exchanged loving, eloquent letters from 1971 until 1982; she continued to write Millar after Alzheimer's disease made it impossible for him to reply.

Relationships with these friends clearly occupied some of the time and energy that Welty had once used to correspond with Lyell; she told him often she was behind on her correspondence. In the early seventies, some of Welty's friends believed Welty "was distancing herself" from Lyell,[3] but her letters to him show that she still thought of Lyell as part of her extended Jackson family. "Let's meet soon and tell our trips," she wrote him in 1976. Shortly after another trip he took in 1977, their correspondence ended when Lyell died of congestive heart failure. The few extant letters from Lyell in the 1970s suggest that their relationship maintained much of its essential character until the end, with Lyell happily recounting his travels, reflecting on art and culture, or enclosing items in which, as Welty once put it, "the old spontaneous true nonsense bursts through."[4]

January 25, 1959 • Jackson to Austin

Dear Frank,

Thank you for your sweet message and your letter—you know how good it was to hear from you. Mother, Mittie, and the girls too—

This is just a short note for now, but just wanted to let you know we're all all right + getting along pretty well—Mother is really being fine. Mittie is, as all the way through, calm + wonderful. The little girls, so shocked + crushed at first, have after the first day been little towers of strength themselves. Elizabeth by her nature holds all in—+ comforts Mary Alice—who of course also has all that born ebullience and is apparently fine—they've helped me a lot—by just being there of course, but also practically.

Everybody has been wonderful to us—your mother! She comes, brings food—you know well how she does, + does.

Two cousins from West Va. flew down for the funeral, + this comforted Mother a good deal—Eudora Andrews and Ed Andrews (another brother's son). As for Walter, + how well he did—it was plain heroic. Every day that goes by, with letters that come to Mittie + us, + what people say + do, I realize more what a well-loved boy he was.[5] The doctors—everybody—wrote to say such things—It's still incredible, all of it, + incredible that a disease like arthritis, that you hear of everywhere, that goes clear back to Greeks, that so many people put up with in mild forms, could reach such devastating proportions, + in a young, healthy man—+ could remain so mysterious—One of the research doctors said he hoped they'd learned something about it from this—which I guess is something.

I'm so glad you expressed to Kelly my joy in his drawing—it was thoughtful of you—and I'm going to write him myself, and the Vogels too—

Glad Allen came, + tell me more about KAP's coming sojourn—sounds fine—for her + you.

Had to cancel the Chicago visit of course + they were so generous + nice in their reply about it—they got two in my place, they said (!)—Flannery O'Connor + Dorothy Parker—

Had a nice letter from your Mr. Handy inviting me for next fall, + I'd love to come. Hollins has asked me but I will have to find the letter to see when—for a long visit as I recall—should I go?

Two copies of the Observer are coming to me so I forward one to you. And Punch has started punching! So good to get it again—and many thanks to you again—You're probably so busy with exams you'll have little time for a while to read—I'm writing this in the car, so as to have uninterrupted moment, because company is still coming steadily—I am OK. I did have to go to Gayden [*the Welty family doctor*] last week, had some small ulcers he said, but he thinks he can cure them right up—medication + rest, he says—back to work, say I. (Don't tell your ma.)

Heavens, Elizabeth Bowen passed through! Seems so unreal I was about to forget to tell you. She stayed at a hotel (she planned it all over long distance from N. Y., didn't know till she called, about our trouble) + Charlotte fed us—She + a friend were on a trip, + E. is going to do a piece about Natchez + the river country for Holiday—She was in her usual good form—

Am giving out of ink, so must close. Much love to you and thank you again for all the thinking about us you did, which helped—

Eudora

February 9, 1959 • Jackson to Austin

Dear Frank,

Bloomsday was wonderful! no candy was ever as good as theirs, and it was much appreciated + enjoyed. Eliz. + Mary Alice said you'd sent them some candy too—This was sweet of you—Many thanks.

We're doing all right here. I'm working some, + hope to get somewhere this spring—You must still be tired after exams—Hope the new semester will give you some changes for refreshment. [. . .]

Saw a rehearsal of "Cat," thought they [*Jackson's Little Theatre*] did well. Enclosures show its fate. Frank Hains asked me to do something to help take off the curse of the shocked folks + I turned out something—not v. good you see—+ he wrote some sensible program notes but no [*illegible*].[6]

Saw Kenneth's review of Requiem—Tynan strikes again![7]

Love,

E—

March 12, 1959 • Jackson to Austin

Dear Frank,

I'm so sorry about your uncle [*Louis Hallam, Clarena Lyell's brother*]. Clarena was at our house when Judge called and told her about it, but she's only just told us—you know how she holds things in [. . .]

Hope your work has settled into its routine for the semester. Wonder if you'll get home Easter—ever since you did, I always think there's a chance—

I'm supposed to go back to Bryn Mawr + they write that sometime between April 7–May 1 is best. Do hope to complete a little work in the meantime—I'm feeling better + am off the wonder drugs, which were only of brief duration. All the family's doing pretty well. Elizabeth will be 15 tomorrow—+ is celebrating by taking a written test at the Highway Dept, first step towards a driver's license. My.

I saw Separate Tables, did you? (movie, I mean) [. . .]. Think you'd like it for the main performances + small bits. D. [*David*] Niven terribly good.

It's been warm + bright here—lots of camellias—Redbud time—How is your Spring?

Hope you're well.

Love,

Eudora

P.S. This letter in car got out of sight in glove compartment—So comes late.

The Christian Science Church is putting up a church building on Riverside (right shoulder to shoulder with that Memorial Bldg.) on the hilltop—at present you see long low building + skeleton tower with the cone of the steeple a-top. I told Mary Alice what the building was and she said 'Oh, I thought they were getting ready to launch a rocket.'

Clarena says you are reviewing another book—what?

Much love,

E

April 30, 1959 • Jackson to Austin

Dear Frank,

Thanks for all the cards. I've meant to write before now but busy. Mother has gotten along fine considering she had such a terrible fall—with deep cuts all around her eye (her good eye) it didn't get hurt—no broken bones—mind clear—just has to rest + heal until sure she won't black out again—which we all hope will be never. [. . .] Of course I was devastated because it happened while I was gone, but [*Dr.*] Gayden Ward says I could not have prevented it coming out of the blue. The maid was right beside her + she fell too quick for her. Good quick help she got—Well, I am hoping that she'll gain her strength back now + can go home. She is very weak, sits up a little when helped into a chair. She must be watched carefully against dizziness or anything—she'll hate that! I'll have a practical nurse for a while. And somebody to sleep in her room, me or another, to be safe.

I'll have to cancel my Texas visit, I feel—for I'll be anxious about Mother from now on, + wouldn't want anybody counting on me. [. . .] I wrote the

Denver thing + they didn't like it a bit—rather hinted that for them to ask anyone from Mississippi at all, where they won't even hold a meeting on account of "certain restrictions," should be enough to make me come, sick mother or not!

[. . .] I never got to report to you that when the Bolshoi opened at the Met I was there! What happened was Sidney and Madge Evans Kingsley invited me (by phone to Jackson) to come sit in their box [. . .] and I was the only one in the party who had a good time! [. . .] I myself thought that [*Galina*] Ulanova was magical and quite apart from anything, either on stage or on earth. [. . .] She gave a marvelous dramatic performance all apart from her dancing—as she did in the movie of Giselle—conveying the most poignant youth and innocence. Motions like water or flames, really—Before the performance I went to the Kingsley's (at 1 W. 72, you know, the Dakota) for a light meal—then after the perf. to the Plaza. Guess who came + I didn't get to meet, because he was at other end of long table, until he came to say goodnight to his host—Kenneth Tynan. I was dying to hear all he was saying [. . .] Very attractive (His wife—blondined and in red chiffon was either very Empire or very pregnant. Or a combination.)

Guess I feel better today than I have yet about Mother—+ hope she'll be up soon. Thanks for your messages—she was glad to get them too—

I'm sad to have missed Mary Lou—she's in N.Y. now—and I don't see now how I'll get out to Santa Fe in near future but maybe things will turn out easier than I think now. I feel I must never go off for suppose it happened again?

I forgot to say during my 1 afternoon in N.Y. I showed my 141 pp. of MS. to Diarmuid + he thinks it's good. Not to be modest—"just marvelous." I hope to continue with the typing.

I hope all goes well—Write soon as you can—Know you're busy of course. [. . .]—This written in snatches and will go mail.

Love,

E

I hate being disappointed about Texas—But no use thinking about disappointment. Maybe it will work out some day yet—

Love,

E

In July, while Lyell was in Boston and New York, Welty wrote to him, "We're getting along all right, mother is getting stronger—I still have little time of my own but it'll work out—Have done something." On September 19, Welty wrote Lyell that Chestina was hospitalized with an episode "like a mild stroke." The following day she wrote, "If I said anything to you about a stroke, forget + never mention it, as if it was one, Mother doesn't know it. It was a pretty terrifying blackout, whatever its nature. She seems bright + well today + has eaten 2 good meals already."[8] *Welty sought to make her mother feel less disabled than she actually was—an impossible task. In the following letters to Lyell, Welty tried to strike a positive tone, gamely recounting the latest challenge in hiring caregivers to assist her.*

October 22, 1959 • Jackson to Austin

Dear F,

I've got these things to mail so will just enclose a short note this time instead of waiting for time to write a letter. Your mother looks so well [*Clarena Lyell had recently had cataract surgery.*] [. . .]. She paid us a visit the other day—drove herself over [. . .] It was so grand of her to come, and especially—when I never would get to see her otherwise—I appreciated her visit. Her spirits of course she never lets show as anything but up—admire this above all, and don't really see how she does it.

[. . .] This note written in such spurts I'm sure it's making no sense. We're getting along all right—Slow but I feel less terrified each day at the possibility of a recurrence right away—+ she's gaining strength. Depressed about Walter all the time, of course. If only Dr. Hughes thinks she can stand the eye operation I think she'll risk the all-or-nothing deal, for she sees so little as to be almost blind as it is. To see again would change everything [. . .]. Carrie still comes all but one or two nights a week, but I let her off whenever she's tired, as she has a sick mother she also nurses. We have a real stupid lazy white baby sitter part of the daytime most days so I can work—Am sure they're all like her! But at least she's unobtrusive and I reckon that's lucky. Have reached pg. 193 (in a year's time) on present draft of story typing—so that looks hopeful. [. . .]—Lehman's and Una Merkel's play opens tonight[9] [. . .]—Write when you can [. . .]

Much love,

E—

January 21, 1960 • Jackson to Austin

Dear F,

So sorry about the wretched cold—Are you better? Hope you can stay in this weekend, + get it licked—

KAP is to be on Camera 3 this Sunday (10:30 AM here, but check). Frank Hains just called + told me.

We've been upset again, another blackout 2 weeks ago, but a mild one this time. We stayed home and have been getting along all right on the whole.

Sorry your mother hasn't felt good either but saw her in the Jitney day before yesterday and she was feeling "lots better." Wish I had time free to get to do something for her, + hope to before long—at least pick up her stuff at the grocery sometimes—It's cold, 22, this morning, but brilliant sun—I really like it. [. . .]

Lehman was here, as you know, + was looking grand—minus those 46 pounds. I went by to see him + Miss Eva Sussmann burst in at the same time without being asked, so we passed not one word! Lehman came by here the next afternoon + stayed about an hour, so we did get a visit. Good to see him—George Stephenson came out one evening + we had a good conversation—in result of meeting that night at your good party—So glad you got to do it again—Nothing more worth repeating!

Do hope all's better with you. Oh, those Express items—I thought they were good, maybe you were just feeling bad with the cold. Nancy Spain at L'Etoile! in her trousers, can't you see her?[10] I remember that cape-like coat lined with red—she wore it at Bowen's Court, where she also dined in trousers—[. . .]

Love and take care—

E

February 12, 1960 • Jackson to Austin

Thanks for your delicious Valentine! Crazy about it. This is second-hand (Edward sent it to me) but had to pass it along—After all, he's your valentine too. [*Valentine is "signed" by a pasted newsclipping of a photo of a man who's not identified, whom Welty and Lyell would recognize as Gov. Ross Barnett, who had been inaugurated in January.*]

So good to hear from you + will write soon. Hope health is good now + keeps good.

We are doing fairly well. Your review looks fine, good position + handsome layout, richly deserved.[11] Couldn't help but wish you'd taken on F. O'Connor! Did you see the good Osbert Lancaster[12] profile in the Observer? Have been working a little last 2 days. Will be writing soon + mailing the review.

Much love,

E

February 15, 1960 • Jackson to Austin

Dear F—

Let me send your review while I can still lay hands on it. [. . .] And I meant to tell you—*please* look in House Beautiful for February (I *think* Feb.—or Jan?) for the ultimate in gracious living raptures—the house called—oh lord, what? the way of living, or something—anyway, the whole issue practically's devoted to it, and you couldn't believe that prose, *or* the house, unless you just sat down under a dryer in the beauty parlor + *saw* it. Edward was fascinated too. Read about the whole thing those master switches, + on + on. [. . .]

We get along about as usual, good days + bad. Carrie, bless her heart, came right on in our snow storm of last week. Our night nurse quit + at present I'm still looking, but suppose we'll find one as we always have before. Bea Lillie is supposed to be on TV on Feb. 24—with Cyril Ritchard—check this—+ do try to see. Hope it comes here. [. . .]

Much love,

E

[. . .]

February 28, 1960 • Jackson to Austin

Dear Frank,

Wonderful news, which I must share. The Ford Foundation has awarded me a grant, to write a play—Two years of cash, and arrangements to study at Actors Studio with their playwriting group—Nothing I could have desired more, but the question is when the time comes (fall of 1960) will I be able to leave + go up there? [. . .]

We're getting along all right, got a night nurse this week which is a relief. Carrie is still, + I hope always will be, our mainstay. [. . .]

I've done some work on my long story [. . .] Do you feel attracted to any of these titles?

The Wings of an Angel

A Shining Mark (quote in context of story, "Death Leaves a Shining Mark")

Willowdean

[. . .] Must go now—Hope you're feeling better—write when you can.

Love,

Eudora

March 29, 1960 • Jackson to Austin

Dear F—

Have started you several notes and letters only to be interrupted—so glad to hear from you + know you're about well now—You know how much I'd like to have Peter T [*Taylor*]—no, nobody's sent me a copy and it would be a great treat to have it for a birthday present from you—Your review whetted my appetite and of course I had one already. Many thanks! [. . .] I forgot to remark before that I enjoyed report on Flannery O'C. Do you remember, I reported what Fanny Chaney of Nashville told me, that she has lupus, a hideous kind of skin disease akin to cancer, incurable, + that she + her mamma were (last year I think) going to Lourdes as a last ditch try to help her. What a misery her life must be. Glad you didn't have to take on that book, though.[13] Did you see Stark Young's piece in recent Harper's? I wonder if he wrote it since stricken. Not that it is poorly done, but a bit unfocused, don't you feel? Is he better, have you heard?[14] [. . .]

Love,

E.

[. . .]

In April, Chestina Welty "had another spell and has been in bed since last week, not able to eat much + not feeling too much better yet. It's so hard on her, to do this over + over—This time she never actually blacked out, but it has been the same story otherwise. We didn't take her to hospital + know she is more comfortable here."[15] Chestina's condition deteriorated further in August; Welty wrote Mary Lou Aswell that her mother "no longer trusts me or believes me." Thanking Aswell for a comforting letter, Welty wrote that she needed this message "as much as if my mother had died or something." Chestina's distress was eased when doctors discontinued one of her medications.[16]

October 6, 1960 • Jackson to Austin

Dear Frank,

So glad to get first your card that you were there all right (but not reporting on bad back) and then the letter. I've missed you and meant to write. [. . .]

Things are perhaps better here than they were for a while. Mrs. Andrews, v sweet old lady, was just too old + couldn't be asked to cope as I needed someone to, + she resigned (so as to spare me explaining anything) after a week. Now I've turned up a new one, Mrs. Renfroe [. . .] Carrie has been filling in but that's been hard on us all because Mother's so down on her—so unfairly!

But of course that's nothing Mother can help or be blamed for, and I only hope Mrs. Renfroe can hold her own and also be a buffer for a while. [. . .]

This is an ungodly hour to write a note, 6 AM, just made my coffee and now to try a little work on Henry Green. I'm afraid I've messed it up, just as I may have messed up my story, by my present way of trying to work. I'll send you a copy.

Hope all goes smoothly now and classes not too demanding. Wish you could get time off, a really good long time, + tear into the Richardson[17] for good + all.—Work on this.

Love,
Eudora

October 8, 1960 • Jackson to Austin

Dear Frank,

I was so honored and tantalized together by that invitation—and how generous a one it is, both in the willingness to consider me again and in the arrangements and the cash. You know how much I'd love the chance to come, held out to me another time. But how can I say anything but no when it would be impossible to rely on my being able to get there when the time came? [. . .]

I believe Mother is better—The hostility has melted away, and she's stronger in every way—takes vitamins + food in capsules etc. now. Carrie quit, but Mrs. Renfroe, God willing, starts tomorrow. Hope it works—

Thank you again for everything and I must go mail this [. . .]

Beautiful days here—bright sun, cool air—

Love,
Eudora

October 14, 1960 • Jackson to Austin

Dear Frank,

Thank you for your letter—and the note and the clippings just before—and the announcement about the Texas Quarterly. [. . .] Of course I am pleased to be asked to contribute, and I'd specially like to since you are the one to ask me. But what? is the question. As you know, I've had so little output lately, and nothing new finished.

The long story about the family reunion is out, at least for now—I feel that the New Yorker, wonderful as it's been to me, should have the first refusal

[. . .] of course nobody does, or can, pay the rates the New Yorker does and so that's an item. [. . .]

I've been working on a second story, off and on this summer, and what its length will be I don't know yet—it too looks over-long.[18] [. . .] should I by some fluke turn out a nice short good one I will let you know first thing. [. . .]

About the visit to Texas—how I've always wanted to come. Yes, the question of getting away makes me a bad risk. I'd have to get somebody to come and stay with Mother, if I leave any more; and this is a delicate matter, for she thinks she would be "perfectly all right" by herself, yet can't cook or get out in the allergic air, or really, now, see well enough to be left alone. She gets furious if she thinks I give something up. But that would be my problem, not somebody else's. I've turned down 5 or 6 such invitations this year already, which didn't bother me one bit, for I didn't want to go, but of course I'd <u>like</u> to come to Texas. [. . .] What date would be a good one? Maybe after Christmas? I haven't had any plans for going away (except for Columbus, Miss., Nov. 15—Charlotte is going with me), reasons above. [. . .]

I wish I could sound more positive about both these things. The fact is I'm willing, but feel without what it takes, just now—material and freedom. But I've already made up my mind to apply myself to getting more work done, first of all—and with that much underway, perhaps action will follow.

[. . .] Beautiful weather here—wish you could come Thanksgiving.

Love,

Eudora

Oct. 14. (Your letter came today—took 4 days!)

October 30, 1960 • New York to Austin

[*Postcard with photograph of Times Square*]

I made it! Know you rejoice with me. Came up on Southerner—a little tired still but about to revive. I'm pleased with things at home + am crossing fingers. Will hope to be here through next weekend, will write—am at Algonquin.

Love,

E

November 14, 1960 • Jackson to Austin

Dear Frank,

So glad to hear from you in New York—and thanks for all messages. [. . .] All went fine while I was away, as far as I can tell, and Mother was glad to see me when I got back—some of her old humor even has come back—so, even if it's not to stay, it's making things easier now.

I'll write about my trip real soon—am so rushed today, the maid is home sick etc. Must say the whole thing did me a world of good—everybody was wonderful to me and couldn't seem to do enough, it was such happiness to be back. Just rested in hotel and went out to see friends for a meal or show, so good. [. . .]

This will amuse you—one day on way to Eileen's I stopped by Holliday Bookshop and on way out heard my name called—Nancy Spain! "My dear, I'm only passing through, I'm on my way to Las Vegas!" [. . .] She had on a skirt. Her hair was done up in some sort of pompadour, the same mad smile.

I also typed up my little piece on Henry Green in the hotel, rented a typewriter from across the street. I was hesitant about it, for many reasons—left it with Diarmuid, who said he'd try the Atlantic but was there a magazine I'd like him to send it to, since it's more quarterly type—I wondered if the Texas Quarterly would like to read it over if I submit it? [. . .] I know how busy you must be—but if you have time to read and report—it would help me. [. . .] I would so hate for Henry Green himself to be made to feel uncomfortable by anything in it in the unlikely event he'd ever see it. [. . .]

Much love, and I will see your ma soon—

E.

November 26, 1960 • Jackson to Austin

D.F

Your mother proved how well she could see by pouring us two glasses of wine exactly to the brim. And she plays bridge and has driven the car. Her eye <u>looks</u> well too. How wonderfully relieved she must be feeling, + you for her. [. . .]

We are OK though nurse won't nurse on weekends (understandable)—Mother is doing well though not still glad to see me but may be a change again for the better—I can do better for my trip. Have sinking feeling you disapprove of Henry Green piece, do you? Tell when all the term work is past.

Much love,

E

P. S. I did get Merrill award! Remember you told me Mary Lou's plot under my window? A blessing from her. So glad, will write.

December 8, 1960 • Jackson to Austin

Dear Frank,

it was so sweet of you to give such care + thought to reading my piece and you can imagine how much better I felt about it. I'm trying to do something about those mixed metaphors etc., + also putting in a paragraph that somehow slipped its pins + got left out when I typed it in NY. What great luck for me if I get to submit it in time for the Texas Q![19] [. . .]

So sad your holiday so short—But look forward to the time so much. John Robinson is here for 3 weeks, from Verona, now his base. Last night [. . .] went out + ate at Rotisserie, a welcome relief from the house which has been strenuous lately but I hope relaxing now. Mother is gaining strength, just mad at me.

I'm writing this at the hairdresser's out of my purse. [. . .]

Much love,

E

Drive Carefully

January 18, 1961 • Jackson to Austin

Dear Frank,

Went by the hospital last night and was glad to find Judge was resting well[20] [. . .] and was relieved to find Clarena planning on a night's sleep at home. It has worried me a lot, her spending those nights sitting in a chair, + then the day time too—Do insist that she arrange to get more rest—I'm sure you do anyway, but knowing how she wouldn't complain I keep feeling you might not know, in Texas, how much she's trying to do: Too much. [. . .] maybe Judge says he won't have anybody else, as Mother does about me—but you just have to accept this in the long run and take on what you need for the endurance + welfare of all. I don't mean to meddle, you know that, am just concerned, + you are the one of all she does listen to. Just because she's so dauntless she needs to be protected from letting herself go past her endurance as I'm afraid she might let herself go. I'm sure she'd despise my very words! or feel I was disloyal to her to write you like this. So don't report me but underline an extra time what you write her yourself.

This is a scrap of notepaper found in my purse—am at hairdresser's—Such a heavenly day, like spring on the Riviera—Blue sky, fresh, light air, birds singing, temp 55°—I am having a ramp built onto porch soon to get Mother outside. Things go about the same here. Mother is anti-everything but getting stronger and I hope with this her spirits maybe will lighten. It is her defense against things she doesn't abide or understand to lambast all, so—. She sends you her love, she just told me. She looks better. [. . .]

I was invited to the Inauguration! Long telegram signed by Pres Elect + Mrs. Kennedy "In recognition of our writers, artists, scientists, philosophers + cultural leaders." etc. "Reservations are being held for you"—Aren't you impressed? I am!

Love,

E

[. . .]

Welty shared her Henry Green essay with Green himself and reported to Lyell her delight that the writer approved of it, "and so proud the Texas Quarterly will run it. At last I have a small tie!"[21] *She read the essay at Vassar on her next journey out of Jackson, which also included a residency at Bryn Mawr.*

March 30, 1961 • Jackson to Austin

Dear Frank,

I'm so glad you're having your trip, + hope it's just the change you need—Love to you in Monterey at Easter. Excuse me for not writing before now. My trip was wonderful. Listen who I got to see—Elizabeth Bowen, Mary Lou, Elizabeth Spencer, and almost got to see Pamela Travers! all from such far places, plus of course the dear New York ones I always count on seeing. [. . .] Pamela Travers was supposed to spend last weekend with the Russells as I was doing (they collected me at Vassar), the 2 godmothers of the children, but she got a virus + postponed her trip—which is out to the Disney studios which are (ugh) about to negotiate on Mary Poppins. (Diarmuid thinks she won't like this too but he isn't her agent.) Camillus, Rosie says, has been involved in all sorts of heartbreaking things, stealing, forging, smashing up cars, even drugs, and Pamela has paid out ever so much money + suffered one or more nervous breakdowns. Isn't that terrible. I wonder if this explains Disney deal—hope cash comes, at least. [. . .] So glad you liked Caught—It's all waiting, then when the fires begin it's some kind of dreadful release, didn't you think? [. . .] I saw Little Mary, and had fun [. . .] Saw Virgin Spring and was depressed and horrified beyond words—Have you seen Breathless? Go.[22]

[. . .] Mother seemed genuinely glad to see me, + stronger. They didn't have too easy a time at home but I knew I had to be away for that relief, to go on. Feel better now.

Since 1955 Welty had been working on a "long story" that she began to think of as a novel, about a family reunion in northern Mississippi. She would eventually publish this novel, Losing Battles, *to great acclaim, but not until 1970.*

April 24, 1961 • Jackson to Austin

[*For Welty's fifty-second birthday, Lyell sent a bird statue and a pop-up card featuring an orchid.*]

Dear Frank,

[. . .] Thank you so very much for thinking of me on the ancient birthday. [. . .] I was much cheered to be remembered, in both animal and vegetable kingdoms. [. . .]

Did I tell you Virgie quit one Monday morning cold? But Carrie is back and she + Mother both seem happy with that. (Mother is now working on the night attendant to make her quit! But we get along anyway + it will work out.) It's confined me on weekends and after Carrie leaves each day, though I've managed to get pages sent to up to The New Yorker + they whizz them back in beautiful shape—Have sent all Part II + part of Part III—Then after III I'll put together part IV, then see if I is needed! So my news is OK. [. . .] Many thanks again for the bird.

And much love,

E

May 16, 1961 • Jackson to Austin

Dear Frank,

Your mother looks pretty well, I think, though of course she worries with her two greatest cares.[23] [. . .]

This is coming from, of all places, the Meridian R.R. Station. I'm going to Birmingham Southern to read a paper—at some cost of peace of mind because Carrie quit the day before without a word and owing me $40 (for bailing her husband out of jail and costs for driving accident). I don't understand for all had been going well so far as I knew. Anyway having promised this in Virgie's day, I felt I had to go on, so have a substitute I have used before till I get back. This is why I hate to plan ahead. Yet it's really so lovely to be away, I'm really enjoying it—bus ride over, beautiful day, and though I have to be with groups 4 times—eek!—I don't care. [. . .] Needed the money so it's all OK. Have done some more work and Mother is feeling pretty well.

Wish things could be better at your house. Much love + see you soon I hope

E

May 19, 1961 • Jackson to Austin

Dear Frank,

Glad to have your letter waiting for me when I got in from B'ham at 10:45 last night. [. . .] I had the busiest time you can imagine [. . .]

Carrie never got in touch with me but this morning I went to see her, and she says she's been in bed with aches and "nerves" all week. She has washed her uniforms this morning, she said—and I believe she means to come back Monday. I have no pride, and besides she is so good, and so essentially sweet, and it would be foolish of me not to beg her, I think—but I did find her assuming that of course I wanted her to come on back to work when she got well. It's all too deep for me, but I need her, as the substitute gets nowhere with Mother. But they got along all right. Edward has been in terrible pain with bursitis and tendonitis and other things—not arthritis—but is some relieved now. [. . .]

Love

August 6, 1961 • Jackson to Washington

[Postcard of 1924 photo of "Day of the Scholars" at Bryn Mawr. In honor of Lyell's August 11 birthday, Welty has drawn a banner held by the head of procession, reading "FRANK."]

Dear Frank,

Many Happy Returns—of the day and the good holiday away! Eat the best they've got (whoever "they" happen to be on Aug. 7) Also drink ditto. Many thanks for the cards—So glad you got to Stratford as hoped. Hot as the devil here too, so glad you can be there to be hot [. . .]

Much love + hope you stay as long as you can—

Eudora

September 18, 1961 • Jackson to Austin

Dear Frank,

So deliciously cool and bright here, hope you're having the same [. . .]

I'll be at Algonquin Mon. and Tues. nights, maybe Wed. We have lost 2 helpers since you left, but Virgie is still in good standing and still working well. So I am going, touch wood. Talked to your mother several times on phone and she seems to be very well.

Am taking up what story I have by Wednesday, hope it's more than half. Can work on train. Isn't it awful about Mr. Hammarskjold.[24]

Love,
Eudora

During the 1950s, civil rights activities in the South had become more organized. The 1955–1956 Montgomery, Alabama, bus boycott had successfully challenged the practice of requiring Black bus riders to give up their seats to white riders. In 1957 Martin Luther King Jr., one of the organizers of the boycott, became the head of the new Southern Christian Leadership Conference (SCLC). The first student sit-ins at segregated lunch counters occurred in Greensboro, North Carolina, and Rock Hill, South Carolina, in early 1960.

Activism in Mississippi became more visible in the early 1960s. In March 1961, Tougaloo students had entered Jackson's "white" public library and were arrested for a breach of peace. In May 1961, a larger coalition of activists brought a new form of civil disobedience to the state. Groups of Black and white volunteers, many of them students, began traveling on interstate buses as "Freedom Riders," crossing the color line when they entered station waiting rooms. They sometimes faced deadly groups of angry white citizens. While some newspapers in these Southern cities, including Jackson, portrayed the Freedom Riders scornfully, national press coverage brought all eyes upon the white supremacist violence erupting along the route as the bus approached Jackson. The Freedom Riders were not attacked in Welty's hometown, but were arrested after they attempted to use whites-only facilities.

When Welty attended her first Yaddo board meeting that fall, she met one of the Freedom Riders, the wife of another board member.

October 3, 1961 • Jackson to Austin

Dear Frank,

Was so glad to hear from you while away—yes, I went! [. . .]

I came home with the cold you always get on the train—so hot still in NY, then icy cold on the sleeper. But had such a nice time! [. . .] KAP didn't come (in fact this was her 6th [*Yaddo*] meeting to miss, as it would have been mine, and they were supposed to throw her out, but you know they didn't.) [. . .] At dinner the first evening [. . .] up came a smiling Negro woman, the wife of [*composer*] Ulysses Kay, a board member—one black one, you know!—saying "Miss Welty, are you from Jackson? I was a guest of your city for 39 days—I was a Freedom Rider." Now what would you have said? I told her she was the first one I had ever seen, and how did she find the time? She said [. . .] she was so well treated, they were simply sweet down there, it was one of the most moving experiences of her life. Well, but every time we sat down to another meal (carrying the tray to some table), next I knew they'd be one on each side of me, and whoever was new at the table would hear the same account. [. . .] The board meeting lasted 4 hours and was my first board meeting, like Mrs. Kay's first freedom ride.[25] Now and then I thought of [*James Joyce's story*] Ivy Day in the Committee Room, for some reason.—There are still more little signs everywhere, Do Not Put Anything on this Fragile Cabinet. Please Direct your Morning Walk in Another Direction. Please Be Careful in this Bathroom, Yaddo's Plumbing System Is Old. [. . .] All had gotten along tolerably well here. I have no help at all all weekend now, so am just now gathering my strength. Let Diarmuid read part 2 of the story and he likes it. And left that and all of part 3, finished and unfinished, with Bill [*Maxwell*], hope he will have time to read & comment soon. D. read all one day in the office on my stuff (he also saw part of 3) and altogether I felt their warm kindness on it. Hope to get done soon. Am supposed to go to Richmann's Institute [. . .], and Morton Zebel is trying to arrange a lecture at Chicago to tie in, which will give me more cash. Smith College asked me to come for the second semester to read 3 papers and consult with the girls at "office hours", at a handsome salary, and although 6 months ago I wouldn't have dared even think of it, now I feel I might try. Don't speak of it to anyone though. I explained my situation to the president and he said they did not now want to invite anyone else (they asked me so late because of a last minute cancellation) and for me to come if I could. A salary of $7,000 plus an apartment, and I do need the money, the time away, all. But of course I don't really know what to do—with Edward not well and harassed, and all the other things, as you know.[26] Mother is getting along pretty well. Of course she does not want me to go. Virgie is still reformed and very good and kind.

Well, I must go do some errands. Talked to your mother on the telephone and will see her as soon as I can. [. . .]

Lovely and cool and sunny here, hope it is there, and that you are feeling well now and all goes as it should.

Love,

Eudora

[. . .]

November 28, 1961 • Jackson to Austin

Dear Frank,

So glad to hear from you, thanks for the Thanksgiving p.c. this morning. Of course I keep meaning to write. Usual distractions but believe Mother's getting better, a little at a time but straight along. It will be so good to see you Christmas, I'm already looking forward so hope you get a nice long holiday this year, Hubert said he was coming, Dolly is.

[. . .] Have managed some work since I got back in spite of some things including a review I had to do of a poor book on Isak Dinesen—tried to get out of it (because it was so poor) + they wouldn't let me. I hate to whack an author, isn't it hard + upsetting.[27] I am writing this in the beauty parlor, Frances Bloomfield just walked in! And last week Hilda Howie + Celeste Colbert were getting permanents together!

Much love,

E.

January 25, 1962 • Jackson to Austin

Dear Frank,

Glad to get your notes [. . .] Your mother and other ladies came back the other day and played bridge with Mother again, so sweet of them, and she enjoyed it so much. Told me to look up "therapy" in the dictionary for its exact meaning & derivation, then said yes, that was what playing bridge was to her.

It rather kills me to be going off [*to a semester-long residency at Smith College*]. Especially when she feels hard toward me most of the time for doing it. For a while I felt I wouldn't make it because we couldn't or didn't keep a nurse at all, lost 4 since Christmas. But now we have at last one who's congenial to Mother, a retired practical nurse, ladylike, never says she has "a gnawing and a craving for fresh meat" or that the Lord spoke to her last night in bed about missing church. And just 5 minutes ago—at last!—I hired a weekend one, who has highest references too, and who will come this weekend—my last—to get into the job. Oh lord, but really I am tired, but it will be different sort of days up there, and perhaps I'll get into the job without too much agony, they all sound so helpful. Do when you can write me—my address I see is to be 142 Green St., Northampton, Mass. I'm going to leave Wed. on the Southerner and spent that weekend HOLED UP in the Algonquin, with this story, which is at the stage when I want to be with it for a good stretch—I do hope this works. Then Mon. to Mass. First lecture Feb.

8. It was so good seeing you Christmas. My glasses, my vase, so beautiful! I wish I could take them with me.

Much love,
Eudora

April 10, 1962 • Jackson to Austin

Dear Frank,

Forgive again such lack of letters. Have had a lot at home to catch up with, but have been (still am) minus help on the weekends, which means finding a good one for sure before I go back [*Welty was home during Smith's spring break.*] All seems to have gone well here, Mother is getting along so well, + is so sweet to me. Have been able to take her for rides a lot owing to absolutely beautiful weather at first + again now, after a rainy spell. Also had to get MSS of lectures in shape to turn in at Smith as they want to print them at the college—still have some of this to do. Have meant for so long to write a long letter + don't know how to say it short. (My greatest fault anyway.)

[. . .] [*Remainder of letter is written in margins.*] When will you be home? Are you going to get to go to England? I wish you could! I'll be home about 1st of June. Must say I look forward. Will try to write after Spartanburg next week + give a report on Mary Flannery.

Paper has given out, so love + Happy EASTER from E.

This is at the hairdresser's, my best privacy. Your mother's coming with 2 other ladies to play bridge with my mother at 2 o'clock. Blessings on her.

April 12, 1962 • Jackson to Austin

Dear Frank,

O those Chewies! I love them. It was a thought both generous and apt, because I not only love them but need the energy—from all that good rich butter & chocolate & Texas Pecans, I ought to be able to gallop through all the days left of my vacation—which of course I need to do. Thank you so very much—and, as you see, ahead of time [*Welty's April 13 birthday*], because when I heard the shake of the box I knew candy and jumped the gun. I have just now had 2.

Your mother looked very well, I thought, but her knee must be giving her trouble and she of course scorns the doctor. I know knees do bother you a long time when anything hurts you there, so I hope time is beginning to bring relief & recovery. She and two other ladies and Mother had a bridge game

Tuesday and that did our household a lot of good. It gives Mother some real pep to think she's accepted back as her old self, well enough to hold her own at the bridge table—and it is darling of your mother and the other ladies to help this along.

After days of interviewing and hunting I think I've replaced my lost nurse so that I can get away as I must next Wednesday A.M. She's to come this weekend for the first time. Gayden came by this morning for his periodic checkup and found Mother doing fine in every way, as I knew he would. Really we have been lucky and blessed. You can't imagine what deep breaths of relief I draw all the time about her—knocking wood at the same time. She is so sweet to me and when I'm away sends long nice letters in her good handwriting that looks the same as ever, with allowances made for poor eyesight.

[. . .] Your poor eyes—no doubt you're about to do a lot more awful reading of awful papers, which is the time I choose, or rather find to send you a Verifax copy of the one essay of mine you haven't seen—I made it on the Verifax myself and from a carbon, and it's my first attempt, so it's rather fuzzy. But if you ever have time or eyesight to take a look, I'd like to know what you think of it. [*This was probably "Words into Fiction."*] The Verifax is something I indulged in and have a little Bantam type of my own—it is no end of help, as I must have copies of the lectures, and it helps me on the story too. And if this summer you would like to use it, you could doubtless produce better copies than this.

Thank you once more for the Chewies—I've not had another, while writing—so good—and now I must go but shall try hard to do better about writing.

Much love,

Eudora

April 23, 1962 • En route from Spartanburg, SC, to Smith College; to Austin

[*Enclosed is program for the conference where Welty spoke, the Southern Literary Festival at Converse College. Welty annotated the program with the phrase "Spartanburg is dry." Also enclosed is a clipping with a picture of three women in Easter hats: Ethel Merman, Hope Hampton, and Hedda Hopper.*]

D.F.—

Happy Easter! I wonder if you had a good refreshing trip somewhere. I hope so. [. . .]

My weeks at home had the complications I've come to accept as normal, a shuffle of nurses, hunting for good new one (found her, I think, hope) and at the last minute a new turn, Eddie the maid in the hospital—pregnant + threat of miscarriage—She's in there now a second time (I left because she was expected to be all right last Monday) and I almost returned home from Spartanburg without coming on, but Mother is being grand about it, in fact stimulated, I think, + of course the nurses are there, to cook—I often do this but now it does get tiring.[28] [. . .] from now on just crossing my fingers.

Conference was OK.—town looking radiantly beautiful, pink and white dogwood, tulips, wistaria—warm days + cool nights. They managed things smoothly. Was glad to see Cleanth Brooks again—and it was nice to meet Flannery O'Connor. She is frail + blonde, sort of the size + coloring Mary Frances Horne used to be in high school—on crutches—with a real sharp tongue, all rightie! I was glad to be enlightened (but felt a bit suffocated) about all this religious background they are all trying to bolster up "Southern literature" with—Flannery with Roman, Cleanth with unspecified but "high church", "ritual," etc. He said in our dreadful "panel" (a real flop I thought, completely unorganized) that all the Agrarians if they had it to do over would "fall back on" not the agrarian philosophy but religion. Oh dear. Meaning nothing against anybody's church, but can't we all just try to work out things (fiction and poetry) with what's in front of us, + so on. And not be in this or anything else a Southern clique. I felt depressed after the self-laudatory, self-infatuated, almost, session. Mr. A. [*Andrew*] Lytle, though a nice man, was hottest on the subject, as you'd expect. Flannery was understandably tired or perhaps disgusted + said v. little at all on the "panel." But her lecture was funny besides holy. "People ask me why it is that Southerners write about freaks. I tell them it's because we can still recognize one." "They call Southern novels 'grotesque' except when they are grotesque and then they call them 'realistic.'" (She said it better than that.) "Faulkner has conditioned all of us by his mere existence. Nobody wants his wagon standing on the track where the Dixie Limited is coming roaring down."

This is on the train to Northampton and so rough I must stop, you can't read this. Let me hear. Hope the worst of your work's over.

Much love

Eudora

P. S. I found that Henry Green had been invited to this festival + had accepted! But couldn't come. [. . .]

After completing her residency at Smith, Welty presented an award to William Faulkner—the National Institute of Arts and Letters Gold Medal for Fiction. Welty spent the rest of the summer of 1962 in Jackson, where she was able to work on her novel until her mother broke her hip in August. Mississippi was again in the national spotlight after the US Supreme Court ruled that the

University of Mississippi must admit Black applicant James Meredith. Governor Ross Barnett ordered state troopers to prevent him from coming on campus, and the federal government sent US Marshals to enforce the Supreme Court's ruling. On September 30, students and other segregationists supporting the governor threw missiles and fired rifles at the marshals. The next day, national news broadcast images of burning cars and reports of two people killed. Hundreds were injured. William Maxwell was anxiously watching reports televised from Oxford, thinking of Welty 160 miles south in Jackson. He wrote Welty that he knew "how you must feel, the frustration of being misrepresented, helplessly."[29] *Two weeks later, Welty wrote to Lyell, enclosing the telegram* The New Republic *had sent on October 1, along with an October 13 article torn from* The Clarion-Ledger *(Jackson) with the headline "Barnett May Defy Some of U.S. Court Orders; Big Fines, Imprisonment Braved by Our Governor." Underlining the word "Braved," Welty wrote, "Typical of our local press."*

October 17, 1962 • Jackson to Austin

Dear Frank,

Thank you lots for the cards + cheering words thereon—[. . .] Have meant to write but all has been awful—The news + goings-on in Oxford, + Mother has been <u>so</u> unhappy + torn. I hope she will eventually recover her good feelings toward the world. Her bone is knitting beautifully (had 6-wks X-Ray, results: perfect) So that's that much. She's OK towards Edward + me, which is all that makes it bearable for her, evidently—or us. They (the household) all say she's better toward them when I'm clear away, so I'm going to try it on the 25th, when I plan to go to Phila. Pa to speak at some do at La Salle College, whatever that is, and Moore Institute of Art. This will finance a week's vacation for me which—if all goes well enough for me to leave—will give me some peaceful train rides + a night in NYC which I'll be v. happy to have—We'll always have 2 in the house—to operate the lift, etc—+ get outdoors in the rolling chair—+ therapy. So I believe it will be OK. Will postcard you. Letters + work have been out up to now. It breaks my heart to see Mother so miserable. I may not be <u>able</u> to leave, yet need to for several reasons. I'm ashamed not to have done more than phone your mother (and when she has the TV on, she says, she can't hear the phone, explaining why I often get no answer) + have not seen Mrs. Burger, which must do. (A stupid letter with no news!) [. . .]

I can't even <u>start</u> to go into the Oxford mess. The really depressing thing is that Miss. thinks Barnett is a 100% glorious <u>hero</u>. Wish I was in Timbuctu—or Xanadu—

Writing at the hairdresser's—Can you read it?

Love,

E.

[*Telegram enclosed*]

EUDORA WELTY

1119 PINEHURST ST JACKSON MISS

WOULD LIKE YOUR REACTIONS TO MISSISSIPPI CRISIS PUBLICATION IN TWO WEEKS PLEASE ADVISE TELEGRAM COLLECT ROBERT EVETT NEW REPUBLIC.

[*Welty's handwriting on telegram:*]

They also phoned and said "Speak for the unheard voices in Miss."

I said no because

(a) I'm a coward—look what they've done to R. McGill[30]

(b) It wouldn't help

(c) I don't madly admire the New Rep. though haven't seen it lately

October 27, 1962 • Bryn Mawr to Austin

Dear Frank,

Thanks for letter. I got away Thursday on the Southerner and guess who was waiting to meet me at 30th St. Station in Phila, Alden Wickes [*Moore Institute of Art*] from your old Princeton days! [. . .] Fun to see him. Straight on to La Salle College which is holding a Writer's Conference. Kay Boyle is there too + K.A.P. arrives (??) today to speak tonight—sent word to the Brothers to "hold Eudora till I get there." My do was last night. Came over here afterwards with Bryn Mawr friend to spend night + have peaceful morning here. Hope to go to NYC Sun + spend a few nights at least. Shall see how things go at home + how long the lecture money holds out. Isn't the Cuba thing awful? So headlong + full of danger of God only knows what.[31]

The Brothers at La Salle seem to live high on the hog. They have Muzak + intercom going on all the time—as I entered to be greeted by priests, I heard the strains of "Tenderly"—They put me up (or do I pay, I wonder?) at a motel decorated in pure Evelyn Waugh Polynesian, with flambeaux, + ice machines on every corridor.

Feel refreshed though, just coming + now work is over with—

Love,

E—

November 2, 1962 • Meridian, MS, to Austin

Dear Frank,

I'm not sure I can write in this bus station in Meridian—pinball machines, juke boxes (2—white & col.) and weak light, but shall try.[32]

New York was good—was there from Sun. PM till Thurs. after lunch. Just what I needed—saw Diarmuid, Dolly, Bill + Emmy Maxwell + the children, Hubert [. . .]

Ate twice with Diarmuid, and with Hildy, then I took her to Beyond the Fringe—Just had to go after hearing the record that night. Extremely diverting—they're grand to look at. I saved the program for you, somewhere in my suitcase—Peter Cook and Jonathan Miller outshine the other 2, I think, for their different reasons—P.C. is wonderful deadpan—as [*Prime Minister Harold*] Macmillan with belly forward + wooden gestures—and as the soldier in Aftermath of War—and J. Miller is zany in the Danny Kaye spirit—Wished for you—House packed + jammed, a great hit—opened Sat. night.

Had a very fine warming evening at the Maxwells—Emmy had cooked a wonderful supper, the children jumped upon me (as I came in) from 2 directions, above and below, in Halloween costume as I entered, and cut out the pumpkin in the living room as we drank old fashioneds—So good to see them—

Diarmuid is fine and has a new grandson as of last Friday.

K.A.P. didn't come. She sent one of those telegrams about the doctor thinking she'd better not, the day of her lecture. However, I feel more concerned than I would at another reason for it—she said "another stupid accident"—I hope it didn't mean another fall—and that that doesn't mean a blackout of some kind. She'd told Bill (Maxwell) about the other fall that she was unconscious + knew nothing at all about it till she woke up in the hospital—"Let us all pray for a violent death."—Just like her, as Bill said!

[. . .] How do things go? When do the holidays begin? (A secret, Hubert says, so don't tell your mother, but he's not coming home for Xmas. Can't face all the jumping on him from Big Mamma, Wade, Rufus, etc. about being a brainwashed intellectual who doesn't love Ross Barnett.)

I hope all's well at both our houses. Felt low about leaving + low about getting back at the moment, but maybe I'll find everything did a lot better without me. Hope so. Will surely see your mother soon—

Much love,

E—

The situation at the Welty home remained a struggle. In early 1963, she wrote Aswell of being "tired in body of course but what is beginning to worry me is I'm tired in mind. But if the [physical] therapist keeps coming, & mother tries (she adores him, 'my only friend') [. . .] maybe the atmosphere will lighten."[33] *Reporting to Lyell in January, Welty was less expressive emotionally, but her exhaustion is evident, her continuing despair leaking out alongside stoic cheerfulness.*

January 11, 1963 • Jackson to Austin

Dear Frank,

I thought of you when poor Stark Young died. [. . .] Good to think of such a civilized person coming out of Mississippi. I sometimes doubt if one ever does again.

[. . .] I didn't get off because when finally Miss Ricketts returned it was with a sprained ankle, + she had to "favor it." Now Emma has had the axe, (so have I!) isn't it really remarkable how it keeps on like this—dear, patient, kind Emma. Mother is very much better in her leg, and can actually stand alone at her walker. Otherwise, I just don't know what I can do beyond what's being done. Oh, well, when I get the breather all will work out. I wrote Mary Lou that I'd be west of the Mississippi on March 21 (Univ. of Ark) + maybe I could get a chance (time, + some $$) to go farther west—Wish I could spend a day with you + one with her. [. . .] This is being written in a laundromat (raining + bad weather here for days) so I don't know at all how Austin + Santa Fe + Fayetteville lie in relation to one another etc! Must go now.

I worked on story yesterday + can finish with a few free days.

Love,

Eudora

It was so good to see you. Felt refreshed by your visit before leaving.

Welty reluctantly began investigating a different living situation for her mother, after Chestina's favored therapist told Welty about a new facility in Yazoo City. The idea of moving her mother away from home "nearly kills me," she wrote Aswell in March. "It seems so wrong. I won't think of it except as temporary, to let me earn some money to keep us going some better way."[34]

March 23, 1963 • Fayetteville, AR, to Austin

Late Friday night

DF,

I will write—As you know I've made a great, if temporary, change—A hard decision—I just got here by the skin of my teeth and have been working at the lecturing etc. every minute [*at University of Arkansas*]. Very pleasant but am tired and the bus trip—the best way to come, after all—got me into Fayetteville at 1:30 AM Thurs. and I leave at 5:30 AM tomorrow, Sat. I'll write after I get back. All seems pretty well at Yazoo and Louise Love + friends have helped. Your mother seems cheerful + feeling better.

Love,

E.

P.S. Much too hard and expensive to go further West. But I passed a corner of Texas at Texarkana and Atlanta, Tex!)

March 30, 1963 • Jackson to Austin

Dear Frank

It's been so good to hear from you—and to get the elegant Valentine, complete with corrective verse! Wonderful—in the bad times. Things seem much better now and I hope I have done the right thing. I had to do something. We'd had no help at all at night since before Christmas, and the day help I could get never lasted more than a day or two. Mother would not consent to be nursed by me either, and I had tried till I didn't know what to do next for we were getting nowhere. At last I went down to Yazoo City to see the Martha Coker Convalescent Home. It is not a nursing home, a depository, but a facility across the street from the Kings Daughters Hospital [. . .] brand new, with first-class equipment—such as elevated bathtubs that the hydraulic lift can go under and let you down so you can have a real tub bath again. It is attractive, non-hospital-looking, more like a hotel, with a sunny patio planted in pretty shrubs and just now blooming with tulips. Good food. And since it's so new it isn't full yet, so everybody gets a lot of attention. And Virgie—who has been on again, off again more than any other soul, but who Mother really does think helps her and she has done it—now lives in Yazoo and comes on a 7–3 schedule to be Mother's personal attendant. So she has familiar faces there.

We went down by ambulance nearly 3 weeks ago now and I believe I can say it's working. Mother is responding well, has taken 15 steps at a time in the walker (never went over 5 here, I think, at best), is gaining weight, has good color in her face, eats well, has been on the whole co-operative—they are really all such nice people there—and has only been glad to see me, not pleading with me to take her home—which I don't know whether I could have stood. You know how I feel about her being anywhere except here. Mr. Gilbert called me after seeing her Thursday and said she is really doing very well indeed. She now is willing to go out on the patio and be talked to by other guests, patients, and contributes some—so much better than the ingrown situation that had [*been*] helplessly developing here. She stays dressed most of the day—I took her clothes, and bought her a little white sunhat with a pink ribbon. Well, it was hard and I couldn't write about it at first. I had so much work to do, that I plunged in and completed some—my children's book (84 pp.) and wrote a lecture mostly over. Went to Arkansas, when I wrote you that line, and got home late Sat. night. Went to Yazoo Sunday—again Wednesday—going back tomorrow. [. . .] If you have a moment, could you write Mother a postcard? C/o Martha Coker Convalescent Home, Grand Avenue, Yazoo. It would make her day, I think. Do you think it sounds all right for a little while? I have to do the lectures, being so much in the hole financially. And I'm coming to Texas! Isn't that unbelievable? [. . .] I'll write again—but had to tell you what's been going on. You know how it's all made me feel. I hope everything's all right with you. I am after your mother to see something about her knee. She should.

Much love,

E—

April 16, 1963 • Jackson to Austin

Dear Frank,

Thanks so much for your letter and clips. [. . .]

Am getting ready to do Millsaps Literary Festival this weekend, then go to Vanderbilt April 24 and 25, to Yale April 29 and 30, and then come to Austin. [. . .]

I'll write you. Had a good time at Duke and also at Davidson. Will tell you. But Mother is so depressed I can hardly bear it. It kills me to start off again. I don't know what to do. But I do have to do these lectures, for every reason—financial, and obligation to the schools, all. She is well looked after, but feels abandoned. All so terrible to me.

Love and I'll write,

Eudora

April 21, 1963 • Yazoo City to Austin

Dear Frank,

You ought to've had a better letter from me long ago. I'm sorry. Always, as you well know yourself, something presses so you put off the thing you'd like to do. It's grand to think I'll be seeing you May 13. I'm so glad I don't actually conflict with the Opera, and as it is we (you and I) ought to be getting in to Austin at about the same time! I still don't feel certain in my mind whether I'd come there direct from NY, or by way of home. I'm hagridden about being away from Mother and to not come by here means I'll be away from April 22 to May 13. On the other hand, I'd have only a day or so here if I did come by home—and I'd so like a breather in N.Y. if I can possibly afford that 5-day interlude. I'm earning well on my lectures —Texas is doing me best of of all!—but most of it's spoken for, and to come + go takes a large bite out of the fees. [. . .] Anyway—you asked about what I'd speak on and I think I'd like to give my new lecture plus a story reading, just because it is new, and the other 2 I have are in print in some shape or form.[35] It's usual with me to also meet with the students who want to ask questions etc. for an informal hour or hour + a half—if that would be liked. [. . .] I'd love for you to make me a reservation at the Driskill—with all due thanks to your good friends. I'm really quite tired—and do want to enjoy Texas, which I can do best by having a hotel retreat. I'm sure they, and of course you, understand. About a party—oh, what do you think? I don't want you worrying, you can't anyway at that busy time, [. . .] But for heaven's sake, just so I get to see you, and exactly the friends you like, that would be wonderful. [. . .]

Writing this while Mother's asleep. She is looking + feeling better today than she has during the last several weeks. It nearly kills me to have her gone from home. She isn't happy, of course, as she wasn't at home, but Mr. Gilbert—the therapist, who sees + treats her 3 times a week, says at her poorest here she's still better than the worst she was at home [. . .]. But the poor little thing—If she could see to read—or to write to us. Well—I write to her with a brush + India ink, so she can read that. She was delighted, as I told you, to have your sweet card.

Love and good luck,

Eudora

P.S. Safest address after May 1 is probably c/o Russell and Volkening, 551 Fifth. I'll be with the Russells the May 4 weekend. And he would get a letter to me if I'd left.

May 20, 1963 • Jackson to Austin

Dear Frank,

To all appearances your mother is getting along fine. She's cheerful, as you might guess, [. . .] I was so surprised to find she'd already had the operation done and was home on my first day here. [. . .] . Of course Miriam is there at night, and Louis, but don't you think she might use a bell just in case she wants somebody—I'll take her one, [. . .] and I will take her some whiskey. It's good you will soon be home. She said the reason she pressed to go straight ahead with the surgery was so she'd be up and about in time for your return home.

I gave an account of my fine visit there to Clarena, of course. And how fine it all was and how happy I was to come at long last. I had a grand time. Thank you for all. You did far too much to give me a good time, and see that I had every possible comfort and pleasure, and run interference for me with the TV etc etc. Thank you for that beautiful party—it was like Old Jackson in ways, didn't you think—so gay, in such spacious and beautiful surroundings, so plenteous as to food and daiquiri—(the Greek accusative of specification)—and I did like the Chicks, and the people you'd asked, and did really get to talk to them and see a little bit of them. The Sunday was just perfect—the good lunch with the Langfords, and the fine evening with Verna and Kelly [*Fearing*]. And seeing the paintings. We got in the luncheon at the Driskill, so good—we got in everything, I'm sure, that was fine & outstanding. I hope it didn't play too much havoc with your end-of-the-year schedule. [. . .]

Mother seems stronger and plumper, and had walked well the day before, but was at swords' points with Virgie, and I've let Virgie go and replaced her with someone I hope will work out all right. It tears me to pieces all the time to have her away, and I don't know how long I can hold out. I know it's good for her in some ways, for she's improving, and I want her to get the full benefit before she comes home, but it seems so terrible for her to be kept away from her home, and I don't know if it's really the right thing or not.

I hope to get work on my long piece starting tomorrow anyway—I want to read it all, in a consecutive piece, and then see.

[. . .] Thank you again for everything—

Love,

Eudora

With her mother now being cared for in the Yazoo City convalescent home, Welty was comparatively free to write. A compelling occasion arose June 12, when NAACP field organizer Medgar Evers was murdered in his driveway in Jackson. Almost immediately afterward, Welty wrote "Where Is the Voice Coming From?" Her story dramatized the racist attitudes that Welty imagined to have motivated the murder, attitudes that many white Mississippians in power had been promoting all Welty's life. (Accurate as much of the story proved to be, Welty was mistaken in depicting the murderer as working class; the actual killer, Byron de la Beckwith, from Greenwood, Mississippi, was as upper middle class as the Welty family. Welty's story was published July 6, the same day Bob Dylan sang a song about Evers's murderer, "Only a Pawn in Their Game," at a voter registration rally in Greenwood. Dylan, too, mistakenly assumed the killer must have been working class.[36]) Welty must have been gratified by the praise, as well as the top-of-the-line royalties, that she received for the story, but none of her anxieties seemed to have eased as the summer continued. In late July, she cancelled plans to be interviewed by Ralph Ellison on CBS, fearing that a TV interview with a Black intellectual might have repercussions for her mother, who was being cared for in a town even more conservative than Jackson.[37]

In August, Welty brought her mother back home. She wrote Aswell that guilt "drove me down there every other day anyway [. . .] and I've got things set up that I'm hoping will work better."[38]

With her mother's care a day-to-day uncertainty, civil rights activism and white supremacist rhetoric were less immediate concerns to Welty, disgusted though she was by Governor Ross Barnett and other white leaders who continued to portray white supremacy as received wisdom and an expression of courage and self-respect. The narrator of Welty's "Where Is the Voice Coming From?" had invoked the governor when he stated defensively that he murdered the civil rights leader, not at the behest of Barnett, but only "for my own pure-D satisfaction."[39] *Lt. Governor Paul Johnson had underlined his white supremacist stance before national news photographers in 1962, physically blocking federal marshals who were escorting James Meredith at the University of Mississippi. On August 27, Johnson won the Democratic party runoff election. Since the Democratic party was the overwhelming majority in Mississippi, his election in November was a given.*

Three days later Welty wrote to Lyell, who was spending the summer in Europe. Her mother's well-being (and that of Clarena Lyell) were top of mind, but Mississippi politics made her wish that she and her mother could leave the state.

August 30, 1963 • Jackson to Paris

Dear Frank,

It's been so lovely and cheerful hearing from you from all points—and wonderful to get the card about the Prado. So glad you are everywhere you are this summer [. . .]

Your mother seems pretty well, though her leg pains her still somewhat—naturally, I guess. She got a ride and came to see Mother last week, which was terribly sweet of her. We keep in touch, though I've been up to the ears. Mother is very well, though not as happy about things as I'd hoped—I'm always hoping for what would mean a <u>difference</u>, and there won't be much difference. She <u>is</u> glad to be home, but the nurse problem is as much with me as ever, 3 in 9 days. But she was so homesick, and I was so homesick to have her here. Have not got to work any, but am beginning the early AM secret working, in hopes.—[. . .] Paul B. Johnson won the election for gov. and if I had a way at all I'd pick up Mother and move away from this place for good. No hopes for us I can see with somebody even worse (because without even the cunning he's got) than [*Governor Ross*] Barnett. Ugh! [. . .] Longing to see you and hear everything. Safe trip home.

Lots of love, bon appetit and the complete B. Lillie recording of <u>Paris</u> is what I sign off with[40]—

Eudora

The civil rights movement remained in the national spotlight. Writing to Lyell in Paris on August 28, Welty did not comment on another national news story, the March on Washington, where thousands showed support of the civil rights movement, celebrities performed, and Martin Luther King Jr. delivered his "I Have a Dream" speech on August 28, 1963. Three weeks later, the Sixteenth Street Baptist Church in Birmingham, Alabama, was bombed, killing four children. Violence, against Blacks and their white allies, was an ongoing possibility.[41]

September 30, 1963 • Jackson to Austin

Dear Frank,

Thanks for card, and also for others trickling in from Spain, sent early August [. . .]

We have a new lady coming this morning (it's 6AM now) and I am hoping and praying, but the pattern is so set! She's said by the Agency to be tops, + made a very nice impression on <u>me.</u> After a weekend with no one I am waiting with open arms. ([*In margin:*] Mother is <u>so</u> sweet when she has nobody but me—of course that's just how she wants us to keep it, poor little thing—) [. . .] I suddenly recalled my standing invitation to come to Yaddo + work, rest, etc. So I impulsively asked Elizabeth [*Ames*] if she could have me anytime this fall or winter, + she replied [. . .] I could stay as long as I wanted. Isn't that a wonderful solution for <u>me</u>—if only I can get things sewed up at this end. Shall see. Of course I can't possibly leave right away—+ the new lady may not be willing to remain without me being in the house—this has come up before. But I cross my fingers—Knew you'd be glad to hear of even the chance I'd be getting the breather. [. . .]

Nancy Spain's book not here yet but I'm delightedly awaiting it. I'll send you some of her fudge, perhaps.[42] [. . .]

Love,

Eudora.

Wasn't Elizabeth Ames sweet? She said she had had my experience + this rest should not be put off till too late. I feel so, too, by now.

November 12, 1963 • Jackson to Austin

Dear Frank,

So good to hear from you at Yaddo. Every golden minute there I used for work, so though I meant to write you, I never got to that even. It was so surprising to me that it took me a while to unwind, or whatever was needed to get down to real concentration on the novel, but I did get about 70 pages typewritten + more than 40 ready to type—Maybe that sounds like a tiny amount, and it is in comparison with the whole, but though I haven't read it over I believe it went well enough. Two nights in NYC. Elizabeth Bowen got in touch with me [. . .]—Mary Lou landed from Europe [. . .] saw Bill Smith, who was down for the first time in 4 months + was at the Algonquin. Isn't all of this lucky?

Hubert seems well, his new apt. is full of space + he seems very happy in it. He's still planning, though reluctantly, to be home Xmas. [. . .]

Wish I'd had more time, both at Yaddo and in NYC for a stopover more than overnight, but things fell to pieces here + they sent for me. Still have no nurse (I left 4, on shifts!) but have a sleeper-in for the moment. She leaves at 6 am, and so I'm writing you by the dawn's early light. We'll work it out again but I'm not too sure I'll make it, just forever, like this. Mother was glad to see me and really doesn't mean at all to engender these crises—

So glad you've had some respite + some music—Will be so good to see you. Forgot to say I bought myself a bottle of Powers [*whiskey*] to have in my room at Yaddo—aside from the usual contributions to the West House bar—It is truly the worst—

Best love + will be looking forward to seeing you before too long,

Eudora

December 10, 1963 • Roanoke, VA, to Austin

Dear Frank,

This is the first chance I've had to drop a line—thanks for your notes + thoughts meanwhile. Mother is back at Yazoo City as of Friday. Things got so bad we couldn't do anything for her at all at home, and the doctor—Dr. Fyke, a very good + sympathetic man—said there was not another choice to it. It is heartbreaking to me + to Edward. At least the Convalescent Home is a nice place [. . .] I managed to get her the only private room left, and 2 nurses—one is Virgie! again welcomed with a smile by Mother. She protested terribly + was terribly bitter toward me, poor little thing. But the actual going was painless, I think she enjoyed the 40-mile ride in the ambulance—If only she now gets to where I can take her out for rides, etc., the difference that will make!

I didn't have time to call everyone, so your mother doesn't know this news—Had to get ready to come to Hollins + get the house in order in the one day before departure. Am weary, but perhaps all this rapidfire activity will distract me.

[. . .] When do you get home for the holidays? It will be good to see you. I'd dread Christmas so much if it weren't for the friends returning.

Have had my public lecture—last night, soon after arrival—and now have 2 days of full activities—you know! [. . .] Flannery O'C. was my predecessor here so I have a lot to keep up with—

Much love from Eudora

I can't even start on the assassination [*President John F. Kennedy, killed in Dallas November 22 while campaigning in Texas.*]—Like you I was glued to the TV—the whole week—and thought of you of course, in Austin where they were due just 3 hours from the time—sickened and really awestruck at what is now possible to happen—

If only Lady Bird [*Johnson, now First Lady*] would get rid of that name—<u>and</u> the Muzak piped into every room in her house—do you think she'll install it in the White House now?

Welty visited her mother several times a week in Yazoo City, fifty miles from Jackson. She kept a notepad in the car so she could jot down material for her novel, sometimes while driving solo. Welty recognized the situation was unsustainable. She also feared that civil rights activism would lead to more upheaval that might place her mother at risk. Civil rights organizers had announced their plans for Freedom Summer, a voter registration campaign aided by hundreds of young volunteers who would spend the summer in Mississippi. The state's governor and other lawmakers responded with new measures against picketing or leafleting, and police were given broader authority to intervene against these efforts.[43] *Welty wrote Mary Lou Aswell that Yazoo City "is reputed to be now the headquarters of the Ku Klux Klan. Our state is authorized to get 200 more patrol cars on the roads and arm the highway patrol."*[44] *Amidst these developments, Welty continued lecturing at universities to offset the costs of her mother's care, wondering if she could move her mother "clear away."*

April 1964 • Jackson to Austin

Dear Frank,

Such a long time without writing but when things are over for the day I feel too stupid to start the letter I've meant to write. Thanks for yours + I hope all goes well with you—Knowing how hard you're at it too. Keep well.

Your mother drove over to pay me a visit the other afternoon and I was delighted at how much better she looked [. . .]

My mother—about the same, I can't think of much else but her being away from her home and unhappy. The doctor says she seems about the same, though she has an ailment now (a hernia in the diaphragm) [. . .]

Have been working on days not in Yazoo trying hard to get novel ready for typist by "early summer" as Harcourt asked. (When's that? It's 78° here today!) Finished final reading + revision of my children's book + turned it in. ("The Shoe Bird"—illustrations to be by Beth Krush, wife of man who illustrated Ponder Heart—they're a team).

Must tell you about NY, Wellesley, Ole Miss, + now coming up, Denison U in Ohio—[. . .] The main thing to tell you is I'm not going to lecture <u>one time</u> next year, if I can help it. All so pleasant everywhere, + I honestly enjoy it, but it mounts up to exhaustion when what I <u>need</u> is more energy than ever. But it's cash. [. . .]

What of your summer? It's bound to be hell in Jackson, Miss,[45] + I wish I could take my ma + get clear away—I thought (in a frantic mood I suppose) of Santa Fe, + wrote Mary Lou, who instantly urged it + wants to help—but the hernia, the trips, the cost, the novel, the lecturing all seem to prevent it—Mary Lou is so whole-souled in her wish to help her friends I'm sorry I alerted her—She even got me a date to lecture at the university to pay for a trip to come out + look things over, but I can't go.

[. . .] Also thought in case you didn't come across it in Forum you might be amused by the piece on <u>The Ancient Mariner</u>—

Which poem, by the way, I read aloud to Mother recently—along with some Robert Frost, some Milton (because she can recite from <u>Paradise Lost</u> + James Stephens—

I'm writing this at hairdresser's—full day today + tomorrow getting things ready to go. if you have time drop me a line after Apr. 14 c/o Prof L.N Downs, Dept of English, Denison Univ, Granville, Ohio. Would cheer me. How is KAP? How is Flannery O'C?

Best love,
Eudora

During the months of Freedom Summer in 1964, white supremacist violence, often sanctioned or carried out by law enforcement, continued. James Cheney, Andrew Schwerner, and Michael Goodman, three young organizers, disappeared in Neshoba County on June 21. Their bodies were discovered August 4; during the FBI's search, bodies of eight other murdered Black men were also found. Numerous churches, businesses, and residences of Black citizens and civil rights workers were bombed and burned. In August 1964, Fannie Lou

Hamer spoke on national television during the Democratic National Convention, when the all-white delegation to the Mississippi Democratic Party refused to recognize Hamer and other members of the Mississippi Freedom Democratic Party. Hamer, a civil rights organizer from Sunflower County, Mississippi, had been brutally beaten in June 1963 in the Winona, Mississippi, jail with other civil rights workers. President Lyndon Johnson delivered a live address that preempted some of the live broadcast, but network television news later played Hamer's entire presentation, in which she described numerous attacks she had endured after trying to register to vote. Welty did not comment on these events in extant letters to Maxwell, Aswell, or Lyell.

Sometime during 1964, Welty apparently revised the first section of "The Last of the Figs," which she had begun in 1957 (later titled "Nicotiana" when Welty was contemplating including this story in a book of civil rights stories). Its characters experience some of the same helplessness and bewilderment that Welty must have felt as she struggled to provide care for her mother while being asked to explain Mississippi to outsiders. The main character, a white artist named Sarah, makes a sketch of a Black woman who works in her home. The protagonist, while sketching her housekeeper, ceases to see her fully. Welty's story, however, registers a strong awareness of Sarah's interior perspective, distinct from her role as "the help."

That fall, Welty found a job that did not require travel: teaching a creative writing class at Millsaps College.

October 3, 1964 • Jackson to Austin

Dear Frank,

Glad to get your letter. I hope everything's cooling off and straightening out and settling down [. . .]

Millsaps goes all right, I think and hope. A nice class. 18 [*students*] now, about half boys half girls, have had three stories turned in, and we talk back and forth. [. . .] I like the class because it's well rounded—a biology major, some French majors, etc. [. . .]

Was up to see Mother yesterday and told her I'd heard from you. "What did he allow?" She was in pretty good spirits. Have felt worse about her lately though—her homesickness, and then I guess the change of the seasons, which makes me think of all she used to do outdoors. I dug up the iris bed and am getting some new irises for it—it had been so jungly. [. . .]

Love and take care,

E

[. . .]

President Lyndon Johnson was reelected on November 3, 1964. That night, news cameras recorded him emerging from the Driskill Hotel in Austin before making his acceptance speech. Welty mentioned this to Lyell in a November letter that also discussed a lecture she would soon be delivering at Millsaps. It would later be published as "Must the Novelist Crusade?"

November 18, 1964 • Jackson to Austin

Dear Frank,

Thanks so much for writing and I was glad of all the news. [. . .]

But I was looking at Lyndon in the Driskill on TV—and never dreamed you'd be there, knowing you were down on him, and don't tell me you were right on my little screen! I was watching on purpose to see him go to that very hotel where I knew he'd go [. . .]

I turned in my grades yesterday too—only one class, but baffles me how to grade it. It's a good class, awfully nice boys and girls, and some do good work, many talk intelligently, and altogether I find it stimulating and pleasant—just a bit frequent. My first public speech is Dec. 2 and I have just finished it and sent it to Diarmuid with a note to submit it to Wm Morris if he thinks well of it.[46] It's far too long for Harper's, but a portion could be used if he likes it, and if the doors aren't closed on the issue. He may (Morris) not like it at all, of course. It expressed a low opinion of the crusade novel.[47] [. . .]

Have just come in from Yazoo, where Mother is doing pretty well—is most alert and so quick when I'm reading to her, and I've taken her riding a half dozen times or so this beautiful long fall. Have been slow with my novel writing but the days sort of fall into an organization with the teaching that they didn't have before, and now that I can draw a breath from the first onrush of school and lecturing, maybe I can settle to it. I've got one of the little children's books [*The Shoe Bird*] for you. [. . .] Nash sent a review from the Times, which was favorable, then somebody sent Miss V. Kirkus' which was agin it. Well, I can't help anything about it now. The roof it was to pay for leaked during [*Hurricane*] Hilda, but not so badly as it would have done if I had NOT written "The Shoe Bird."

Did you by chance see Danny Kaye do "From Turkey with Dressing" in which he again played James Blond? Not as good as the first take-off, "Dr. Yes." but amusing. [. . .]

Love,

E—

In December Welty gave her Millsaps lecture, initially titled "The Southern Writer Today: An Interior Affair." This was her first public response to white supremacist violence since "Where Is the Voice Coming From?" in 1963. Her lecture proposed a distinction between activism and the "interior affair" of writing and reading literature, which may enable readers and writers to contemplate complex and disturbing realities. Referring to the white supremacist violence of that summer, Welty said, "To deplore a thing as hideous as the murder of the three civil rights workers demands the quiet in which to absorb it." Reflecting upon a literary writer's role in society, she noted, "There is absolutely everything in fiction but a clear answer." Accordingly, she offered no direct answer to the questions she posed, which seem to have been directed at herself as much as anyone else.

> *What must the Southern writer of fiction do today? Shall he do anything different from what he has always done?*
>
> *There have already been giant events, some of them wrenchingly painful and humiliating. [. . .] This hate seems in part shame for self, in part self-justification, in part panic that life is really changing [. . .] in the rest of the country people seem suddenly aware now of what Southern fiction writers have been writing about in various ways for a great long time. [. . .]*
>
> *Every writer, like everybody else, thinks he's living through the crisis of the ages. To write honestly and with all our powers is the least we can do, and the most. [. . .]*
>
> *History will change in Mississippi, and the hope is that it will change in a beneficial direction and with a merciful speed.*[48]

After delivering her lecture, Welty read her story "Keela, the Outcast Indian Maiden," about a man's shame and defensiveness over having participated, without full understanding, in the imprisonment of a disabled Black man in a 1930s Mississippi carnival.

In 1965, Welty continued to struggle to find time to work on her "reunion story" novel while teaching at Millsaps and regularly driving to Yazoo City. Race relations in the South were still a national topic that winter. Welty may have tuned in when the US Commission on Civil Rights hearings in Jackson were broadcast. For five days in 1965, Mississippians and Freedom Summer volunteers testified in chilling detail about the refusal of law enforcement to protect Black citizens and their allies from violence. More brutality was broadcast on "Bloody Sunday," March 7, 1965, when unarmed citizens trying to march peacefully across the Edmund Pettus Bridge were bludgeoned by Alabama state troopers. In April Welty completed a portion of her novel that Russell could show publishers in hopes of getting her a favorable advance contract. She had told Russell she was worried that the novel might be deemed "inconsequential" because it did not deal directly with racism, a worry he told her to put out of her mind.[49]

Welty was a guest of the Southern Literary Festival at the University of Mississippi that spring. The theme was "A Tribute to William Faulkner." Welty appeared along with Malcolm Cowley and Robert Penn Warren. Segregationist protestors, still unhappy over the University's token desegregation, picketed against a group of attendees from Tougaloo College, a Black college in Jackson.

April 24, 1965 • Oxford, MS, to Austin

Dear Frank,

All kinds of souls from out of your life are in Oxford right now—Ruth Ford + Zachary Scott, Mrs. Douglass Wayne (?), Peter Lindamood, John Robinson,—no connections anywhere that I know of unless Peter L. came to see Ruth. The Sou. Lit Festival has had a very meaty program—Malcolm Cowley—whom I love!—did a marvelous lecture about the history of The Portable Faulkner + the story of its editing, etc., with the letters he + F. wrote throughout—R.P. Warren lectured last night—I did the opening speech, tribute to Faulkner, that being the central idea of the Festival. In addition we had a photo exhibition, a movie, (both on Faulkner country) a luncheon at the Chancellor's (where Mrs. Wayne was), a cocktail party at Ella Somerville's, a demonstration against the Tougaloo delegation (of which we weren't aware till next day, but so bad of them), a banquet with showing of movie, party after Red Warren's lecture at Country Club—you know how these things go. But the company's been exceptionally nice. This morning Ruth Ford does the program on Requiem for a Nun. Zachary was to assist, but I hear he got sick last night so I don't know. We start at 9 am + at noon it's over. I'm staying on tonight to see the Farleys, Ella, etc. + tomorrow going back with John + Jack Wiseman, who are staying at Ella's house. Perfectly beautiful early summer weather—green + radiant. I saw Elizabeth Welty my first night here when I ditched 2 rival cocktail parties + took her out to dinner.[50]

[. . .] Charlotte + Mary Brian Barksdale are here too, + Frank Hains—but I've had no chance to mingle.

Love,

Eudora

P.S. [. . .] And Carvel Collins is here—don't you know him too? Such a nice man.[51]

July 12, 1965 • Jackson to Florence, Italy

Dear Frank,

Your mother just called, had just had a card saying tell me to write you and today only would reach you—this in haste. The Hermes pkg came safely but the card came too late—I'd opened it and had been wearing it! So after this warn me by airmail card else put on outside pkg Not Pour Vous! Glad London was so good. And esp. glad you went by to see the Mians. Long to hear more of them. Must write to them. If you should see John [*Robinson*] give him my love and tell him letter follows. I went to NY en route Suffield and return, just a few days—hot, water shortage, taxi strike, but good company. Reynolds was in the Algonq. when I checked in and we had a good weekend playing around NY (saw the Beatles in A Hard Day's Night, it was funny) and at the Russells where we went for Mon. eve. party & spent night. The Cowleys, Hildy [*Hildegarde Dolson*] & her new husband of 3 weeks, etc. to dinner. I liked the husband. Hildy a country girl now—seems the odd part, not being married. [. . .] Saw Hubert who is well. The Vietnam battle in people's houses goes on endlessly.[52] Have been working hard but not as far along as hoped. [. . .] Have a grand time and store up all to tell me.

Love,

Eudora

P.S. Was offered $5000 to travel for 9 mo. in Asia, Latin Am., or Africa by some new Cultural Office. Sounds nice & strange! But had I been able to take it I'd have been sorry in the Congo I wasn't on the Corso.

Read your good letter from London to mother who was tearful—I think because "it sounded just like you". Saw Martha Graham, with Kingsleys, at dinner in NY—she is splendid, they are splendid [. . .]

That fall, Welty worked on a short story set in present-day Mississippi, with the civil rights movement hovering in the background. "The Demonstrators," which she completed in November, is a disturbing and mysterious story—in many respects, a mystery, but without a detective to show the reader who is responsible for the deaths and suffering depicted in the fictional town of Holden, Mississippi. A white sheriff, near the story's end, tells a reporter, "Please take note our conscience is clear," a signal to Welty's readers that this assertion is patently false. No guilty party is explicitly identified within the story. This ambiguity was in keeping with the thoughts on fiction writing that Welty expressed in "Must the Novelist Crusade?" Fiction, she wrote, "abounds in what makes for confusion; it generates it, being on a scale which copies life, which it confronts. [. . .] There is absolutely everything in great fiction but a a clear answer."[53] *Welty's "The Demonstrators" was published in* The New Yorker *a year later.*

November 24, 1965 • Jackson to Austin

Dear Frank,

Wish you were coming home for Thanksgiving, but barring that hope you have a good refreshing trip to San Antonio or somewhere. I know I've been a long time writing and can only tell you Edward's been in the hospital with a broken neck—isn't that awful?—Getting along all right, I guess, in traction etc., and I've been trying to see him + Mother as much as possible + not let her know about him. He fell down in the bathroom, 5 weeks ago. Heaven knows how long it will eventually take. He was advised to go to Veteran's Hosp. where a lot of fine + strange equipment is. They seem to be doing very well by him. (I'm there now waiting for him to get back from therapy.)

[. . .] Have talked to your mother on phone and do expect to see her soon—Trying to see Edward daily. Have done work but scattered work—articles, one story, etc, + teaching a big class, prolific. [. . .] [*Clarena*] does seem to be somewhat low in her mind—She doesn't know I might understand why, of course. [. . .] My mother seems frailer + sadder—which I guess just has to be—Took her some camellias—The weather's been just beautiful—

Soon after this letter was written, Chestina Welty suffered a stroke. Welty was now facing "a crisis with two heads," as she wrote William Maxwell. For some time, she hoped Chestina would make a recovery; she told Maxwell that when her mother was able to speak again, she told Welty "in a little tiny voice" that the doctor "was a moron."[54] *December letters between her and Maxwell primarily discuss edits to "The Demonstrators," which* The New Yorker *had accepted. Welty continued visiting her brother and her mother, not telling either of the other's condition.*

January 21, 1966 • Jackson to Austin

[*Telegram*]

MOTHER DIED PEACEFULLY LAST NIGHT. FUNERAL TOMORROW SATURDAY AFTERNOON. LOVE
EUDORA.

Welty's mother was eighty-two. Four days later, fifty-three-year-old Edward Welty, Eudora's only surviving sibling, died of a brain infection.

During the spring of 1966, Welty kept all her previously booked speaking engagements, perhaps as a respite from grieving these two tremendous losses.

She described some of her travels to Lyell in the next letter, which begins by thanking him for a birthday gift of a subscription to the London Observer, *the Sunday weekly published by* The Guardian.

April 18, 1966 • New York to Austin

Dear Frank,

So glad to get your messages and you well know how happy <u>The Observer</u> makes me—Many, weekly thanks for it—[. . .]

I've been plagued by this bug, whatever it is—after the laryngitis in Washington I got OK in Bryn Mawr, then came down with a flu-like thing here + had to also cancel Centenary College—total loss of income $650, which is worse when you consider how much it costs to get here + be sick! I'm well enough tonight so I can start out tomorrow for Agnes Scott [*in Decatur, Georgia*] + Ala., + hope the voice holds out. Then back to NY for a week, I guess. Haven't felt like doing much but have seen <u>wonderful</u> exhibitions—I must have written you about the Mellon Collection in Washington—truly one of the most beautiful I ever saw in my life—the Boudins! 15 or 20 of them, and never had I even thought much about him one way or the other, until this dazzling array of them. The whole exhibition was full of new aspects of old painters for me—Then here, I went to the big Turner show + it was so jam-packed—it seems to be that tiresome word IN, here, + beatniks + their babes + dirty beards + chattering suburban Schrafft-eaters + schoolchildren and mixed couples and the rest were crowded right up to the canvas—with Turner of all people. After 2 visits, both jammed, then I had the great treat of getting to <u>really</u> see the paintings when the Maxwells were invited by Monroe Wheeler[55] to come in on Sat. morning an hour before the museum opened, + they took me along—all those Turners to ourselves! I felt as if I were seeing them for the first time—I <u>was</u>. Peace + quiet and all the distance they require + the space they need around them.

Also saw Lauren [*Loren*] MacIver's show—good[56]—+ some new drawings at the Met. + misc. [. . .]—Called Hubert Fri + we had dinner Hope to call others—Nash, Ruth, etc. when I get back + feel better company.

Love,

Eudora

April 25, 1966 • New York to Austin

Dear F—

Have survived the Agnes Scott–Tuscaloosa trip—a killing 5 days.[57] As I rushed from a late train to platform for a panel at the Sou. Lit Festival in Tuscaloosa, R. [*Robert*] Drake jumped up from the audience + embracing me on the steps to stage asked "Have you read the galleys of my book on Flannery? Your quote hasn't come in." When I said no, he cut my lecture! (Told me so, or how'd I know?) Caroline [*Gordon*] was there + rode back on the Southerner with me as far as Princeton—Fine!

Brandeis ceremony last night—very nice. Letter one day soon.

Love,

E—

Extant letters to Lyell do not discuss her grief over her mother and brother, nor a third bereavement later that spring, her friend Hubert Creekmore, who died unexpectedly May 23, 1966. A member of Welty's extended family (Walter was married to Creekmore's sister Mittie, so Creekmore and Welty had two nieces in common), he had also been part of the 1930s "Night-Blooming Cereus Club" that included Engel, Lyell, and Nash Burger.[58]

During the rest of 1966, Welty began to resume the life of a full-time writer, no longer a heroically devoted daughter. That summer she sent another portion of the long novel to Russell and to Aswell; both responded with encouragement.[59] *The next surviving letter to Lyell is from December, after she had sent him a copy of "The Demonstrators," which was about to appear in* The New Yorker *and which Welty had read at a meeting of the National Council of Teachers of English.*

December 9, 1966 • Jackson to Austin

Dear Frank,

Many thanks for your card. Glad you found my story well done but sorry it seemed "nauseating"—hope it wasn't truly so, especially since I read it at the banquet in Houston to 2000 teachers who had just et![60] I did want it to show (demonstrate, I guess) the break-down of so many ties and of lines of understanding and communication, wanted it to be sad, but not nauseating. It's just a picture of the way I feel things have got to. [. . .]

Hope all goes well with you. Try to get home without a cold—and without a pile of work to do on the backseat—but easier advised than done, I know. I read about the bad weather there—it was black rain while I was in Houston. I hope Macbeth was worth your trip—wish I could have been there, for more reasons than one. Enclosed a few items you might've missed. Take care, and hope to see you soon. Major is back on this side and heard he'd taken an apartment on Lauren St. in Jackson. Saw him one night after he'd returned, looks well and had a fine time.

Forgot to say I'm glad you thought the news story in my story was well done—I thought well of that part myself.

Dolly is dismantling the house and plans to go up to NY in Jan. At this moment Dolly phoned, sends you her best.

Best love

E

In early 1967, Welty reflected indirectly on her bereavement in a new work of fiction that would eventually become The Optimist's Daughter. *"Writing on a story—feeling less depressed," she told Lyell in a note sent on Valentine's Day. In her next letter, Welty enclosed a poem about Creekmore that Barbara Howes [formerly married to William Jay Smith] had sent her, saying she thought it was "quite beautiful, don't you?" Then in a final afterthought, she added, "I am writing on a long story—It may be grim but can't help it." She also shared a less "grim" letter from their mutual friend, Seta Sancton, telling Welty that she had gotten Welty's unlisted phone number from another, but had since misplaced it. (Welty had decided in 1966 to get an unlisted phone number, since her fame had led to so many calls from strangers.) Seta explained how she had jotted down the number on a postcard, then accidentally mailed that postcard to someone else, along with a recipe for charlotte russe. Seta concluded that since Welty's name was not written on the card, her phone number would remain secret.*[61]

In May of that year Welty finished a version of the "grim" story, initially called "Poor Eyes." The New Yorker *immediately accepted it, although it was almost two years before they published it. Russell made plans to maximize Welty's earnings by securing a book contract to follow the magazine publication.*[62]

Lyell was traveling in the summer of 1967. "So glad you're getting this fine summer. Enjoy it every drop," she wrote him June 15. After Lyell's return to Texas for the fall semester, Welty wrote on September 28 that she and Jackson friend Charlotte Capers would take a nonworking vacation to Santa Fe, visiting Mary Lou Aswell and her partner Agnes Sims. Her spirits were better that fall, although the novel she'd worked on for so long was not yet ready for publication.[63] *By February 1968, Welty told Lyell she was still enjoying the creative process, over a dozen years after it had begun.*

February 7, 1968 • Jackson to Austin

Dear Frank,

Glad to hear from you, and thanks for the news and clippings. I'm sorry I haven't written—to you or anybody—it's just work and being too tired by the end of the day.

Your mother seems to be much better now, and I saw her last night when Tippy [*Louis Lyell's wife*] very sweetly invited me to the birthday party she and Louis gave in their new house. [. . .]

I want to thank you very much again for my egg coddler. By now I've used it dozens of times and with lots of different combinations. Of egg, herbs, cheese [. . .]

Have worked with long daily concentration trying to get the boxes of novel pages down to the best number—I xerox them as I go, without bothering about carbons, so the typing goes faster + freer—I still enjoy it—Maybe I'm a nut.

Bright and cold—It's been the most delicious balmy weather here—has it there?—but now while still pretty there's an icy wind blowing. The war news is so shocking + mind-stunning, life seems hard to believe outside the daily thing[64]—

Hope you're keeping well. With exams over, you can at last catch your breath, I hope. Write soon—

Love,
Eudora

Lehman Engel composed the score for a ballet version of Welty's children's book The Shoe Bird *that was to premiere in Jackson in April. He had intended to conduct it, but decided against it when he learned the number of orchestra members and rehearsal time had been reduced.*

March 21, 1968 • Jackson to Austin

Dear Frank,

So sorry to hear you'd got a wretched cold and couldn't make the trip to San Antonio. Hope it's on the mend now.

[. . .] Blow-up with the ballet here—I'll have to tell you about it, but the upshot is Lehman is quite rightly refusing to conduct it, and the whole thing is pretty sure to be a mess. Very sad. I had 2 weeks of much anxiety + strain about it. Everybody mad and shouting on the phone. [. . .]

My New Yorker story is to come out next October, due to a tight they got in—doesn't make any difference to me.[65] Am working hard on novel + hope for it. [. . .]

Had a wonderful inspiration + gave Elizabeth a car, a new Mustang, + at the same time traded in my '54 model on a new Fairlane. So both of us are dashing about in Brittany blue Fords! Elizabeth is doing well at Archives,[66] Charlotte brags on her highly, + she just got a raise and a parking space with "Miss Welty" on it—So I felt she should have her own car. You can imagine how much pleasure it gave me. [. . .]

Much love,
Eudora

January 17, 1969 • Jackson to Austin

Dear Frank,

It was good to get your letter this morning, and I'm glad you got back safe and fine [. . .]

The Buchwalds I love. He [*columnist Art Buchwald*] appears in the Daily News in Jackson, but I just buy a paper when occasion offers, and of course they don't run him with any regularity. [. . .] He was a life-saver during the campaign and election,[67] when I did work hard at finding his pieces as they came. I enjoyed your Beachcombers too—when he writes about hats (remember, wearing 2 hats?) he is like the Beachcomber of old—I remember the old one, "Should Mice Wear Hats?" It's sad to see some of the forced and strained ones, yet worth it when the old spontaneous true nonsense bursts through. [. . .]

Must stop. Wish you could see the camellias—they'd refresh you from the horrors of exams.

Much love,
Eudora

April 20, 1969 • Jackson to Austin

Dear Frank,

The paralysis of my letter writing is terrible, it's been 100% except for answers to those getting up lectures etc. so all I do is write No No No. I've just worked from early morning till I stop in exhaustion, and still have a few days to go till I deliver last pp. to typist. I must tell you that all of a sudden here came [*arts magazine*] APOLLO—three at once! (a few days apart only) and this lavish dreamworld stays by me and I escape into it. Pages i-cxviii are all ads from fabulous auctioneers and gallery people, with full page photographs of dazzling objects. Then the text is full of further dazzling objects, plus some endearing Royal Academy treasures—I look and look, but you were too lavish to send it. You must see! [. . .] Your mother says you are planning on London, which is wonderful—hope it works out, in every good way. [. . .]

I must also thank you for the Observer—meat & drink, as you know, but I had intended to write ahead and warn you you were not to send it this time—too much, and it's gone up so, and everything—I was going to subscribe, or renew, myself. Remember this now for next April 13 (if I'm here and still breathing, after all this work). [. . .] Some grand things in it lately, don't you think—and it was fun reading the results of the Christmas competitions (which I always love and admire) around Easter time.

So much I had to tell you—I'll write again right after I finish up. [. . .] Hope all is well with you.

Best love and so many thanks,

E

Welty completed Losing Battles *that spring. Although* The Optimist's Daughter *had just appeared in* The New Yorker *and most of Welty's works remained in print, her publisher, Harcourt Brace Jovanovich, was lukewarm on the long-awaited manuscript, saying it must be shortened. Welty wrote Aswell that they told her to "cut out many of the images" and to "combine several characters into one."*[68] *Welty and Russell decided to end her association with that publisher, placing the novel with Random House.*

July 29, 1969 • Jackson to London

Dear Frank,

Happy Birthday! Where will you be, down in Cornwall or Kent, driving on the left? We'll have to celebrate it again when you're home. It was lovely to have your letter yesterday, thank you for telling me about seeing Elizabeth Bowen. [. . .] Yes, I've been here all the time, working and settling things—Random House is bringing out my new novel in the spring, all very happily settled, with some excitement. I'm feeling much better, now that I know how much everybody likes it, and how shocked they are at Jovanovich. [. . .] Marvelous to think of your being in Glyndebourne—give the delphiniums a deep bow for me. Yes, I saw both TV shows, the Investiture [*of Prince Charles*] (he's most appealing) and the Moon—couldn't take my eyes away from that, it was like being in an hallucination. Heard here that the BBC was going to wake up people there by letting them go to bed with the TV on and ringing an alarm clock when the Moon Walk was to happen.[69] Mary Alice would have been seeing the Parthenon by the Moon that night—just as magical, in its way, wouldn't it be? She's having a grand time. She just sent me a large Edam cheese. From the Greek Isles she's on to Istanbul and still has Rome and Florence and Venice yet to see. O joy! In the swim is where Mary Alice is.

Have a wonderful time all the rest of the holiday—Keep well, take it easy occasionally. Give my best to Pamela when you see her. I'll be calling your mother one day soon again.

Lots of love,
Eudora

October 30, 1969 • Jackson to Austin

Dear Frank,

Such a long time since I wrote last, and you know I've wanted to—It was good to get your letter % Dolly, which I got just before leaving N.Y. I'm glad the Buick behaved well (the Buick in my novel doesn't) and you got back + into the semester smoothly—Still all fine?

Thanks for the good wishes about the Random House association—it all couldn't be any nicer. I stayed with the Erskines a week in Westport, Albert having hired a Hertz car to drive me out from the city rather than make me go on his commuter train, and we had the finest time—he stayed home from the office + we went over the book, getting all the copies alike + the best way (there were 3, each a little different here + there), all 750 pages. (It'll not be over 500 in print, if that's any relief.) Albert's lovely young Florentine wife Marisa is a superb cook (she was trained as a concert pianist) and we ate homemade breads + pastas and wonderful dishes every meal [. . .] So—I had a lovely time, and Random House too gave me a welcome in the city—now let's hope they are not sorry when the book comes out—you know it may well be jumped on for not being <u>with it</u>. April is the present date. I have to go back to N.Y. next week, for Institute, + proofs are scheduled to be ready. So I'm being asked to read them on the scene to save time. [. . .]
[*In the margin, Welty added, with a drawing of a ladybug*]: Have had house painters, pest controllers (squirrels in the wall), sewer root eradicators, rug cleaners, and no help—aside from <u>their</u> help. Have been making a map for the novel, giving papers to Archives, etc. etc. Reasons for not getting a letter to you (or anyone else).

[. . .] Elizabeth, my niece, is going to get married in January! To a young man named Fred Thompson. She seems so happy—more about it when I know more—It isn't announced yet but she's told family + friends. He went to Murrah [*High School, in Jackson*] + Ole Miss but ahead of her + she only met him this year—has a printing business—Mittie likes him, + his mother—his father is dead. So that's all happy, I hope—She's 25, independent, smart, + has gone with plenty of boys + I think knows her own mind—Of course I feel so tenderly toward her—[. . .]

Write if you get a moment—I will do better—I enclose a horoscope for you for last week in which I thought it recommended you try a little spot of blackmail! Now that the danger's over, you can have this.

Lots of love,
Eudora

Welty's comment on the horoscope, in the last paragraph of her letter, shows her back to madcap form. The clipping, enclosed in the October 30 letter, reads. "LEO (July 24–Aug 23) You have clever way of using old information gleaned from others. Put convictions in action. Work or health problems solved. Send unconventional messages."

December 17, 1969 • Jackson to Austin

Dear Frank,

Just called your mother to find out when you'd be coming—and how long you'd be here. She says Saturday, until—when? You must stay through New Year's Eve. I think Elizabeth Bowen will be here—and I'm sure Reynolds will be. Won't that be fun? I'll have a small gathering on New Year's Eve and of course you have to be on board. It ought to be a fine time, don't you think?

Call me when you're home, and we'll exchange news. I've meant to write—Have been correcting proofs + getting house in order after the painters finally got the cracks mended + the walls covered, etc. Tired, but looking forward—Come safely—will you be in a new car? Your mother says you need it now—

Lots of love,
Eudora

March 7–8, 1970 • Jackson to Austin

DF,

Happy Total Eclipse Day—we can't see a thing for clouds and fog[70]—And the TV just has hillbilly music, I found—I hate to miss wonders! Are you well? And is the new Impala performing properly? I hope so. It would be a lovely surprise to see you drive it home for Easter. [. . .]

R.P. Warren came to lecture at Belhaven + was here Wed. + Thurs.—So fine to see him—He read "Audubon" + commented—Beautiful evening—Saw him for drinks (here) + dinner (with group) both nights. Wed. he was given the Belhaven Award. Elizabeth Spencer was in Jackson 2 days the week before that, in good health and spirits—asked about you—[. . .]—And before she came, Reynolds was back here to lecture at Belhaven—He stayed here at the house, but I learned from that not to try to put up more Belhaven lecturers—it's not really any easier for them, and Belhaven and me were always being Alphonse + Gaston—[. . .]

My book exists—I've been sent the first copy—(436 printed pages) which looks nice to me, and after I get my 9 author's copies I'll have one on the way to you—I do long to know what you think—after all the long time I've been at it. [. . .] Keep well.

Much love,
Eudora

March 15, 1970 • Austin to Jackson

[*Postcard is photo of beach at Outer Banks, North Carolina.*]

D. E.

Was ecstatic to receive the book so soon after your saying it was on the way. [. . .] Boundless, eternal thanks. I've loved what I've read so far—all in your finest vein. Relish every line—+ the texture is so rich I'm not going to rush through it. Wonderful handling of the gathering of the clan, the fracas at the store, the retrying of the trial. The Banner Top scene is superb—so amusing + full of tendresse. Aycock is grand ("Always glad I ain't you!") As refreshing as the waves of the sea + I hated not being able to swim on today (Sunday) but will do so this week. Have a drab, scrawny Stovall girl in class now who could have been born in the store![71] More later.

Love,
Frank

March 28, 1970 • Austin to Jackson

Dear Eudora,

I went to Dallas early Tuesday morning + returned Thursday morning with Ronnie [*during the University of Texas's Spring Break*]. For some reason I began to feel bad when I arrived + spent more time inside than I anticipated—nothing special going on that I missed—but as I took preventive doses + rested I finished the book; so thanks to you I didn't mind the confinement—on the contrary! Was doing what I most wanted to do [. . .]

The novel is full of <u>wonderful</u> things throughout. I especially liked the episode of Lexie's altering the dress. All the revelations about Gloria's past + the revelations of Miss Julia's connections with everybody far + near are beautifully meshed + sustained with mounting interest. Miss Julia is an outstanding addition to your already rich portrait gallery—Everything about her rings true in a deeply touching way. You've also made Jack + Gloria very strong, positive, appealing characters + focused attention on them with customary skill, without diminishing one's interest in their elders. Miss Beulah and Granny are also strong linking characters—Hell, they're <u>all</u> distinctive, young + old, + making so many come alive is a real triumph. I loved the moonlight scenes in the closely-woven episodes after dark—the excellent pictorial effects all through that part. So glad you included a night-blooming cereus! There is superb momentum in all the final scenes—from the Monday morning rescue of the Buick to the end. There + everywhere there are so many amusing touches. I questioned next-to-nothing: e.g., could Miss Beulah's nightgown really be 11 years old—if she's been wearing it all that time?! Would so many Beechams so automatically assault poor Gloria with watermelon? It seems such a violent way to make her "say Beecham." Ten lines up from the bottom of page 221 I thought "eaves" should be "leaves." Suspicion confirmed ten lines down from the top of page 336. Four lines down from the top of page 56, "aded" is the only other proofreading slip that I noted. I wondered about the total absence of Negro characters—not that you needed any. The self-sufficient do-it-yourself Banner world is convincing + complete without them + you shouldn't get any beside-the-point criticism for leaving them out.

I think as a whole it's a wonderful performance, but it's a quite special novel, + it's too much to hope that it will fall into completely appreciative critical hands. It shouldn't be reviewed by anybody who doesn't know all your other work very well. The piece by Miss Oates in the <u>Atlantic</u> doesn't tell enough about the book. <u>Time</u>'s criticism—of books + everything else—has gone down so badly I don't know what to expect from that quarter. Hope you liked the <u>NY Times</u> man who came to see you [*Walter Clemons*]. Tell about him + about Lehman's visit when you can.

By now you should have received an Indian scarf from Dallas. Thought I'd go ahead and let Nieman's send it—an advanced print for April 13![72]

Lots of love,

Frank

April 8, 1970 • Jackson to Austin

Dear Frank,

Many thanks to you for your card and letter about the book—which it was so good of you + understanding to read right away—Of course I'm so glad you found it good and I'm happy + grateful for all that generous praise. I do think it's a handsome job of bookmaking, don't you? The woodcut, the typeface, the paper + the binding? The limited edition was not so pretty, to me—or to Albert—So far the reviews I've seen advance copies of (Sunday Times, Life, Newsweek, Sat. Review + Atlantic) were in the first 3 cases extremely kind, while Mr. Aldridge in the Sat. Rev. and Mrs. Oates at Atlantic were I think intending to be moderately kind but feel they must be professorial or pontifical—anyway they succeeded in being pretty pretentious (Sounds like an alphabet book, what P is for)—Oates didn't really catch on to what the book was about of course. I only hope + pray the Sunday Times will come out this Sunday. If the strike does happen, Albert says, the review can still be used in quotes for advertising, since it is in print, but I would like it as a review, which it was written for (by James Boatwright), not as an ad.

The heavenly silk square from India + from Nieman's + from you arrived and oh, I think it is truly the most beautiful one in color + design I've ever looked at! I love it. What a special birthday present. Thank you, thank you and I'll wear it on the day itself when Charlotte, Jimmy, Anne and Bill + a few are gathering. Seta will be here for it. Only wish for you. Also, Major is coming—though Charlotte and I feel Jimmy is stirred up by it, but after all he is one of the Basic,[73] as he used to say—

[. . .] Guess you saw the Times Sunday review of her [*Katherine Anne Porter's*] book of essays[74]—I wish she could have been talked out of including those unworthy of her—It's a shame—[. . .] I do hope she's getting along better than this clipping sounds, I must say (though I love her calling the psychiatrist "kid".)

So beautiful here now! I'll write soon again but had to say Thank You for the communiqués I value so, and for the beautiful scarf.

Lots of love,

Eudora

P. S. Jose de Creeft is opening a new show today, Kennedy Galleries—Hooray!

And speaking of a third venerable and venerated, I wish you had been looking at Huntley Brinkley for once the other day—interview with Segovia—who's just completed a new U. S. tour and was going back to Spain to await the Event—his 28-year-old wife is expecting!

October 8, 1970 • Jackson to Austin

Dear Frank,

Good to get your messages—to Maine and then here [. . .]

So pleased you like the Auden—I do too—exactly the book I need + want late at night + early in the morning with my waking-up coffee. (The poem to Forster (his) not being in it disappoints me, but of course he didn't make this book around work of his own.)[75]

[. . .] Maine was wonderful from start to finish. I'll have to tell you, Xmas. Cadillac Mountain, the Rockefeller Gardens, the lobster picnic in front of the house by the water—there was Diarmuid, Rosie, Pammy, Willy, his wife Maudie, his 2 little children Daisy and Liam, + me in the house. [. . .] The party the Rockefellers [*David and Peggy*] had was a celebration of their 30th wedding anniversary—It was on an island called—oh, <u>what</u>?—about 4 1/2 hours out by sailboat, a small piece of pure wilderness they hacked a clearing in and built a sort of lodge. [. . .] Freezing cold by midnight, but worth it. And riding on the boat away out of sight of the fires and lights, when it was nothing but wild, Maine <u>night</u>—the stars! Just <u>blazing</u>, + thousands of them, in that pure clear air. Well, you can tell, it was a real holiday for me—complete change, and all just beautiful. Pammy, who lives in Amherst, drove me back to Boston where I caught the train home.

Since I got back, I've been involved in Educational TV—they've been rehearsing, then taping the New Stage version of my stories called "Season of Dreams"—Frank Hains directing and I've been sitting in on the arduous work.[76] [. . .]

Must get busy, + I'll call your mother real soon. I saw Garland III yesterday when I went to the courthouse to register, and he gave me the news that his father was much better and would be at home now—I know your mother has felt tormented by it all—So sorry for her to go through such a thing.

Take care, + drop me a card or a letter when you get a chance.

Lots of love,

Eudora

Reynolds' book—Have you had time for it? So good, + another new way of working tried—[77] Did you see the long essay in Sat. Review?

P.S. So sorry I couldn't accept the much appreciated invitation to speak by your Speech Department—but you know I have stopped this for good.

Clippings include photographs of hippies, one topless, on Isle of Wight; Gina Warwick walking through London airport in bikini; dolphin holding up an umbrella in its mouth; a socialite in a fringed miniskirt; wedding of Elizabeth Taylor's son; people skinny dipping. Several of these are annotated by Lyell as well as Welty. This continued the game "Old Magazines" from the 1930s; friends take turns writing cartoon speech bubbles drawn onto photographs of people in magazines or newspapers.

October 31, 1970 • Jackson to Austin

D.F.,

[. . .] Have you found a better reception for [*Kenneth Clarke's television series*] Civilization? It's such a treat—he's marvelous, and the combinations of time + place + object + his living persona there with them are just what TV was invented for—The set here at my house has so far got them most clearly + perfectly. [. . .]

Beautiful, beautiful weather here! I hope it's like this there, + that maybe you have a good project on for the weekend. If you go to San Antonio at Thanksgiving, Mary Lou + Agi are going to be there. The big museum there has just opened a new wing and the director has offered Agi a one-man show—His wife's asked ML + A down for Thanksgiving so Agi can see the new wing + plan her show for next year. In case they're friends of yours, the museum people, get in touch. Lots of if's but you nearly always connect on if's.

From what Maeve Brennan[78] told me over long distance (she called as a friend of B + all the family, had visited them) the day after Bertha's terrible death, the grandson had been at prep school where he'd got started on pot—+ was sent home. [*Bertha was the writer Cyd Ricketts Sumner, whom Welty had first known in the Jackson Little Theatre.*] He was probably on a search for some loose change for pot in his grandmother's house—certainly didn't come there to kill her, he loved her. Bertha never locked her house, but kept a hammer on her bedside table. The best guess seems to be she woke and went to see, with her hammer, and the boy panicked.—I told you, didn't I, that Bertha drove over from Duxbury to see me at the MacDowell? So like her to surprise me with the glad sight of her, and we had a joyous, if brief, reunion—which I cherish. She asked me to Duxbury and spoke with particular pride of young John. More than you can stand—.

December 9, 1970 • New York to Austin

Dear Frank,

It was worth coming for that I went to see Home first thing, and I can't tell you how beautiful the [*Ralph*] Richardson performance is[79]—(I'll try when I see you Xmas.)—(If I get home—Trains may or may not be running on the 16th!) Temp was 17° yesterday but in the 30's today—I get to hear Auden read something at Institute [*National Institute for Arts and Letters*] Friday.

Love,

E

February 10, 1971 • Jackson to Austin

Dear Frank,

I so much enjoyed the Buchwalds and had missed three of the best—thanks so much for sharing. Here they are back with some stuff saved for you, plus the old-magazines.

[. . .] I read Buchwald's "bad news" piece on the morning after the terrible Los Angeles earthquake news—it really was a horror. Dolly and I had been watching the splashdown, where everything went perfectly and the whole thing was so miraculous and exhilarating, and then the news came on to the picture of "earthly" devastation and horror.[80] (Did you hear the astronauts say they were hungry for some "earthly food"?) Ross Macdonald lives in Santa Barbara and I hope they're all right. My review of his new one comes out Feb. 14—if you'd like to see it. [. . .]

Happy Valentine's Day!

From [*drawing of a heart*]?

Guess Who

In one of the enclosed clippings, a photo of Lord Mountbatten visiting Noel Coward in the hospital, Coward is reading something. Welty added a speech bubble over Mountbatten, "Darling! Is this for me?" and a bubble for Coward saying "It's a valentine."

February 27, 1971 • Jackson to Austin

Dear Frank,

Just a line from the Library, where I xeroxed you Walter Clemon's review of Ross Macdonald in the Daily Times in case you didn't see—so you could read in addition to my own, if you like seeing them—

Confidential: Sewanee is giving me an hon. degree this year—on June 6. Thought you'd like to know. [. . .]

I'm going to Norfolk, VA [. . .] + shall be with some beloved elderly cousins of my mother—just a few days. I doubt very strongly that I'll have to go to NY first for the Nat'l Book Award, but Albert tells me to hold myself in readiness (I've washed a second pair of white gloves.)

I'm told that Bertha [*Sumner*]'s granddaughter, Gayle Cutler, has enrolled in Millsaps for the rest of the year and that she'd just arrived back in this country from studying in Italy. And not surprising that she's deeply troubled about her brother, who, I'm told, is in a juvenile detention home but "they hope" to transfer him to a hospital. The source of all this is Alice Moore, who is not too fortified with sensitivity, between us, and was just blabbing this out in the Jitney over the snapbeans. If I learn more I'll let you know. Would like to see the girl, but she must be having a hard time with first adjustments. I don't want to make her think I'm prying or being a ghoul. Later on I'll try to see her casually.

Love,
Eudora

Welty's next book would be One Time, One Place: Mississippi in the Depression, a Snapshot Album, *a collection of her 1930s photographs.*

April 21, 1971 • Jackson to Austin

Dear Frank,

The box is exquisite—beautiful in color and design—such a lovely present. And you know I love boxes anyway, even a cardboard soap box on a cracker tin—This one does rejoice my heart, and made my birthday a very happy one—it came exactly on the morning. Thank you ever so much.

It's been too long since I wrote. I had an unusable wrist and hand (R.) for a while—it went away after a shot of cortisone, finally, though I <u>refuse</u> to believe it was arthritis—and so much work had stacked up on me—Had presentation for the picture book (photos from you know when) underway (due fall or winter, I think)—a review to write (Mizener's biography of Ford Madox Ford—I <u>didn't</u> like M's treatment)[81]—Last week, as you probably already know, poor Mrs. Creekmore died, and as you may <u>not</u> know, the happy news—Elizabeth had her baby, a little girl, born yesterday, April 20. All seems well with both of them. I was glad for everybody's sake and for Mittie it was a blessing—couldn't have been better timed, after her trouble so recent and fresh.

It's fine you're planning on Europe—and I hope all's well and good here so you can leave without feeling anxious about your mother—It will be a bad disappointment if I don't get to see you—Must go to N. Y. [. . .] can't get back before June 7 [. . .] Maybe I can see you off in N. Y.? [. . .]

Many thanks again + best love,
Eudora

On her next trip to New York, Welty met another author she admired, Kenneth Millar, who wrote mystery novels under the name of Ross Macdonald. A year earlier, on May 3, 1970, Millar had written a fan letter to Welty, and the writers had begun corresponding. On May 15, 1971, Welty was delighted to discover that Kenneth Millar was staying at the Algonquin Hotel, as she was. She reported this meeting to Lyell, although she does not detail how emotionally charged the encounter was for both of them.

June 3, 1971 • Columbus, OH, to Jackson

Dear Frank,

Bon voyage! I hate not being there to say it. Have a marvelous trip, keep well, see all, hear all, + tell all, like The Pathé News rooster—I'll be waiting for the fine evening when you tell me your trip. And I hope your mother's feeling well and you're feeling secure about being gone—I know she wants you to go and to have the grand summer. As do I, but how I'll miss you—

I have so many things to report—How can I get it all in a letter quick enough to get there. I'll just give one-liners, and if time allows elaborate.

In NYC, I saw (of special interest to you)—

Reynolds, who came for a week to the Algonquin—

KAP, who came to the Institute—after the broken hip and cataract operations. Looking wonderful and with all her animation, though she leaned heavily on Red Warren to climb the stairs.

Mary Lavin! who'd been staying in the Algonquin a whole week the same time I was, + only found out the last night [. . .]

—And Ross Macdonald (Kenneth Miller)!—who came from California to accept a prize, at the same time I came from home and to the same hotel, and to the room next to mine! Amazing coincidence—but needless to say, Archer [*Macdonald's fictional detective*] discovered it at once. We had a fine time. I went to a party Alfred Knopf gave for him, and after that he took me to dinner. Lovely. [. . .]

About the little play—I'll have to tell you that—but it'll never, as it is, make Off-Broadway—It's been off-off, down in The Bowery[82]—[. . .]

Best love to you and best wishes on the trip. Postcard me when you can. Love to your mother, with whom I'll be in touch, and good luck—
Eudora

December 4, 1971 • Jackson to Austin

D.F.,

So good to get your communiqués and I see your mother must have still forgotten to give you the message I asked her to—I've had arthritis in my right hand since Sept so painful I couldn't do any writing or more than essential typing—hit me midway in revising Optimist's Daughter, which I did finish—Taking cortisone shots + aspirin but still frustrated—Especially when I'd like to write you a long letter—I did the Old Mags + some are good, aren't they? [. . .]

Mary Alice (now Mrs. White) is fine—back teaching after a weeklong honeymoon in Acapulco and Mex. City—Liz's baby is trying to stand up, making a lot of funny noises about it.

I would like to go to San Antonio in Feb, but will have to see. Will tell you about Duncan [*Aswell*][83]—Pretty well, I think.

Best love,
Eudora—

Newsclippings include New York Times *review of* One Time, One Place, *plus items apparently sent for Lyell to annotate, including photos of various celebrities and a child amongst Jesus Freaks.*

January 30, 1972 • Jackson to Austin

Dear Frank,

It looks as if we'll be seeing each other—and Mary Lou + Agi [*Agnes Simms*]—This next Saturday night in San Antonio![84] M.L. wrote me you were to come to the party from Agi, and I gathered she's been in touch with you. Just to put it all down from here on paper, I hope correctly + I hope the way it works out—I leave Jackson Friday the 4th on the Panama Ltd., connect in N.O. with the Sunset Ltd., spend the night in Houston (at the Downtowner) + leave on a Trailways bus next mid-morning which will bring me to San Antonio at about 3:15 Saturday. M.L. + Agi—unless they are assailed by a blizzard at the Pass driving from Santa Fe, + God forbid they are—will meet me + we'll go to the Merger. So let us be in touch when you arrive. I'm so looking forward to all.

I had such a nice letter from Jack Varner—also thanks to you, one from Donald Sutherland, P.S. by Gilberte—telling me of some therapeutic volcanic mud at an Italian health spot that helped Gilberte's arthritis—kind of them. My hand has had to sign the pages of the limited edition of Optimist these last few weeks—I took it slowly. Isn't it wonderful, the Institute [*of Arts and Letters*] is giving me the Gold Medal for Fiction this May. I am thrilled—Drive carefully—See you soon—

Much love,

E.

March 13, 1972 • New York to Austin

D.F,

Thanks for yours, and for the card Pamela [*Travers*] wrote, here enclosed. I hope she's feeling cheered these days. But what will you find to tell her about Friend Monkey [*book by Travers, panned by reviewers*] that will add any cheer?

I meant to write earlier—Felt washed up after sinus trouble for a couple of weeks + laryngitis—But came on up for an Institute meeting that was set for last week—Staying till Wednesday, + going down early to Washington to have lunch + spend the afternoon with KAP—I wrote her after the Gold Medal was announced as coming to me, to thank her for what I felt was the instigation or the support behind it, and asked if I might see her and she wrote me so warmly, even anxiously, to please come, time was rushing by—So I'm so looking forward. Called today to check on its being still good with her, + she said she was going to have catfish for us to eat—"I thought of having hominy grits too—but that seemed going a little too far!"—+ champagne—I'll write you about the visit + how she seemed—

Weather here awful—it's lightning + thunder + snow, all at the same time—Saw wonderful Rodin drawings at the Guggenheim, the Picasso + Matisse shows at the MMA—Had dinner with Eileen, whose husband is confined to his bed these days, phlebitis + other things—Saw Diarmuid for lunch, going out tonight with Walter Clemons—Saw Nash + Nora too—Albert + I are lunching tomorrow.

Hand bothers me in NY—perhaps the miserable weather—but I'll get a fresh shot after I get home (Thursday night). Will write better then.

Didn't we have a grand time in S.A.? A big treat, and you such a large part of it—I wish you hadn't had to miss the Edward Lear watercolors!

Much love,

Eudora

I feel sure your mother wrote you about Mrs. Robinson's death. John sailed from NYC on March 5—on the Leonardo—

Welty sent Lyell a letter of condolence after the March 31 death of his brother, Garland Lyell, who died when the car he was driving went into the Ross Barnett Reservoir. In the next letter, she thanks him for a birthday gift he had sent her shortly afterwards.

April 29, 1972 • Jackson to Austin

Dear Frank,

It was so very sweet of you to think of my birthday, in the middle of all your trouble, and I felt such a special pleasure in hearing from you and receiving Lady Bea and on April 13 itself Il Segno dell' Ariete of Ferrara—which I love and shall frame. [. . .]

It will be good that you'll be home now before too long. Your mother is, as well you know, brave + remarkable, but you can't imagine how much difference it always makes in her to have you about the house, and this time it is going to be a godsend. She called me last night (to say she was glad that what I'd sent you was a gift to St. Andrews in Garland's name) and sounded better, as she does each time from the time before. I'm planning to see her again real soon.

I've been having extra things to do that have got me behind in all I want to be doing—the latest of which was having a lady from Time here to interview me about my new book. She's Martha Duffy, whose reviews you probably know—young and very nice—I drove us down to Port Gibson the morning after she arrived, beautiful day—then to Grand Gulf + out a gravel road to a clearing on the bank of the Mississippi that looks like the very spot where we found that fisherman's camp so long ago—And what did we see but the Delta Queen, the steamboat—it happened at that very time to go by! Headed north up river. It was galvanizing—I've also had a book review to get written + copied, some necessary chores about the Arts + the Literary Festivals to do (pleasant too, but time consuming), Dr. Hughes about my eyes + new glasses, dentist, + legal problems (I'll have to complain at some length to you about the Internal Revenue Dep't!) ETC. Including serving a week on the Grand Jury!

Anyway, to start again at the beginning, I was of course delighted to have Beatrice Lillie in reach, and with the glorious photographs—not the cover, though—(those highlights in the dark lipstick had made it look to me, in the ads, like an open mouth with 2 lone white teeth in it—not the right choice for the cover, you agree).[85] My favorite among many good ones is, I believe, "Transatlantic Commuter grounded", the fur coat, ospreys (?) + space shoes, arms upflung, in seated position. Lovely young ones, of her, and young Noel + Gertrude [*Lawrence*]—and many as we saw and adored her in the 30's—I love having the book—[. . .] something of her own real story does somehow emerge—+ sad it is, too, + I'm glad she kept it private, though what she did tell would have been so much more interesting + worth reading if she'd simply told it herself—As it is, I wonder if we'll ever know what she really is like any better than we do already from her performance on stage—and that really is marvelous enough—It is allowed to come through, because of the photos—

KAP was in wonderful form when I saw her—She lives in a luxury, high-rise apartment about ½ hour's car drive from Washington, in the country really, near Silver Springs. She has 2 apts, together, (4 bedrooms, 2 baths, etc.) and a pleasant housekeeper-nurse-chauffeur comes daily, and a secretary comes regularly to type etc. (The apt., high up, lovely view, has restaurant, beauty parlor, and all that on ground floor—she has all her needs supplied right there.) She is very occupied in filing all sorts of stuff ready for the K.A.P. rooms in the U. of Maryland library ("9 rooms now, darling" (or is it 14? I forget)). Her health appears fairly stable, though of course she has had the broken hip, + cataract operations + takes medicine for her heart—she is frailer looking, but walks well enough, though always with the nurse alongside when she leaves the apt. Gay as could be—effervescent—We talked for 6 hours (mostly of course she did) + ate catfish which she'd fixed, along with other fine goodies, for lunch, + drank champagne—Then she came along, with nurse driving, to see me off in Penn Station in Washington. She says she is going to be the one to give me the Gold Medal at the ceremonial ("wearing a white Italian silk pants' suit, angel") which of course makes it still more wonderful. It's the 17th of May—the day of your last exam—How badly I wish you could be there. [. . .]

So many thanks again and much love and many thoughts—
Eudora

October 17, 1972 • Jackson to Austin

Dear Frank,

Writing this out in the car, as the painters are still in occupation. One reason to explain why I've been so bad about writing—please forgive. [. . .]—I have such a chaos of mail + papers, and those folders I've marked "Immediate" and "Keep" etc. have just about lost their meaning—mail backed up while I was away on top of the other, + being out of my room + away from my typewriter has me worried all the time about my getting so far behind.

Washington [*National Arts Institute*] was interesting in its way. Stayed at the Carlton + meetings + eating took place downstairs, so it was all sort of hermetically sealed. [. . .] Rosalind Russell, to answer your question, appeared to be a very nice woman—quiet and speaking up not too often (she was new, like me, we were learning). But intelligent when she offered a word. She looks startlingly like Bertha Ricketts Sumner in old age in the face and in benevolence of expression, even in the way she does her hair, [. . .] I can't tell you what she wore. I can tell you what Agnes de Mille wore to the dress-up occasion, when we were all bussed out to L'Enfant Theatre to see that awful TV Firebird by the French Ballet, preview, with Robert Merrill introducing the program. She wore a luscious, luminous short evening gown, full-skirted, filmy pink organza—really that thin bright silk from India—beautiful. [. . .] The last night, we were offered a chance to buy ($9.90) a ticket to Pippin + something also, but I called John + Catherine [*Prince*] instead and went out to their house for dinner—[. . .] So relaxing + refreshing after all that talk + money.

I went up to NY for a few days, mostly to see about sick friends—too sad to talk about. [*Diarmuid Russell had lung cancer; Henry Volkening died of cancer later that month.*] Walked around and saw some good art shows—Bonnard drawings, Whistler sketches (at the Met) a number of galleries on Madison. Saw Walter Clemons who brought me over to his house for a fine dinner. But came on back soon—didn't call Nash or any of them this time. [. . .]

You will be startled to hear I'm flying to Jacksonville, Fla this Friday. Some kind of "Southern Academy of Arts, Letters + Sciences" is being started up, [. . .] Dean Oliver of St. Andrews is involved and he is going to fly with me + pray the whole way. I'll try to report. Back Sat. Reynolds will be there too—we're asked to sit on a panel, a fruitless invention in my eyes. But we'll see.

Many thanks for all yours, to which this is an inadequate answer, but will write again soon + better, maybe.

Love,
Eudora

April 20, 1973 • Jackson to Austin

Dear Frank,

That scarf is extremely pretty, I think, and it fits in beautifully—it's really more violet than brown, with many subtle shades of pink, gold, amber, and yellow—and the paisley design is of course the latest as well as the loveliest.

I'm crazy about it. The shape, too, which I didn't have one like. Mary Alice also presented me with an Echo scarf, and hers is the loud one! Purple and green and what all—I like it too. You were grand to remember my birthday, with messages and present too—thank you ever so much.

[. . .] I've been at work getting ready for my company on May 2 [*The state of Mississippi was holding a Eudora Welty Day in Jackson*]. I was sorry you couldn't come but I of course thought it wasn't very likely that you could. We'll miss you. I believe about 40 people are coming from "away"—Bill Smith and Sonia, John and Catherine Prince, maybe Caroline (depending on arrival date of English lecturer she'd invited to this country), Reynolds, you knew Mary Lou and Agi and Mary Mian were coming, and KAP swore she was coming—she turned out to be in Columbia, teaching this semester! I nearly fainted, having last seen her leaning on the arm of her nurse—but although she declared she was going to introduce me at my reading, I have warned the Festival that this may be cancelled—(as you know) she's so generous and promises all, then collapses. Bill and Sonia are going to sort of look after her, come on same plane, etc. Ross Macdonald and wife are coming from Santa Barbara. Nona [*Balakian*] is coming—sorry Nash can't get away—and Joan and Olivia Kahn are—I think Walker Percy—and others. The finest news is this—Diarmuid is coming. He says he wants to, and he and Rosie are coming with the doctor's OK, and stay a week with me. They'll arrive the Sunday before EW day and of course I'll plan all around them—he's thin and tired easily, and I just want them to be comfortable. I am thrilled by such a wonderful gesture. They'd always planned to visit me this spring—when he was to retire—but now, of course, it had seemed out of the question—only it isn't!

I'm overwhelmed by the generosity and sweetness of all of them—coming so far, some of them, too—and poor Mary Lou and Agi, who're on their way to Europe, will have to fly straight back to Albuquerque to get on their charter plane to fly to NY and across—hideous expense—I tried though not hard, or hard enough, to talk them out of coming to Jackson when I found about the plane arrangements, plus the decline of the dollar in Europe. [. . .] I forgot to say I'm having all the out-of-town friends to my house on May 1, the eve. most arrive, for drinks and buffet which will certainly be the largest party I ever had—I'm getting in some help for the night, though, since of all times I want to be able to mingle with my guests.—My Norfolk cousin, Margaret Upshur Meacham, and her husband, Wm. S. Meacham are coming!

[. . .] I wonder who did the TLS one [*review of* One Time, One Place], it was the best. Kenneth Millar sent it to me. (His new books is dedicated to me—to come out next month. You must know how thrilled I was. I read the ms. last fall and have the book now—very good indeed.) Bethany

[*Swearingen*] just called—on way over for some books I'm giving for the AAUW book sale—must sweep the porch for her.

HAPPY EASTER. Many thanks and lots of love,

Eudora

Early October 1973 • Jackson to Austin

Dear Frank,

Thanks for your letter, and I was glad to know you got there all right [. . .] but <u>so</u> sorry about your back. Is it better? You <u>will</u> go to a doctor, won't you, if it persists in bothering you—a real doctor—and have it looked after? (Exercising can be the wrong thing sometimes, you know) Not to presume to advise you, but you are awfully stoic, and I hate to think of you sticking something out if it can be helped sooner. Let me hear how things go.

I know the death of Auden [*September 29, 1973*] saddened you—I learned of it in the most indirect way—the NYT Book Review called up to see if I'd take over a review Auden was to do for them. (I couldn't.) Got the Sunday <u>Times</u> today, + also read the obit. in Newsweek, also out last Sunday, which was remarkably quick—Eileen phoned me Sunday night, you remember she also knew him in the old days + he used to come out to Mt. Kisco—she talked of him a long time, and said she + Frank were driving in to N.Y. to the memorial service at St. John the Divine—or being driven ("That's a terrible neighborhood.")

I had a 2 week trip and will write more of it later. I saw Diarmuid, who is frail and valiant, spent 2 days with them—Talked to KAP twice on the phone, and would have gone out—she'd invited me, but then had a spell + was in bed—but her spirits rose while she talked, about half an hour each time. Take care, write a line when you can—

Much love,

Eudora

Mary Lou is going to spend next Tues. night with me on her way to see her children—wish you could be here!

November 6, 1973 • Jackson to Austin

[*Star sketched in top left corner next to Welty's message in all caps*]

MY NEWS: MARY ALICE HAD HER FIRST CHILD, A SON, ON OCT. 19, NAMED DONALD ALEXANDER WHITE JR, AND BEING CALLED ALEX. ALL DOING FINE.

Dear Frank,

Good to get your letter, and thank you too for the interesting one from James Stern. How much the same I feel about the losses so close together of the closest of friends—Elizabeth, and Dolly, and now before long—and I hope it won't be too long—Diarmuid.[86] It's int. to know Stephen Tennant is still going. I thought of him in Nebraska—almost wouldn't have batted an eye had he come dancing in in his auburn camelshair coat with his hair to match. Tell Jimmy that is really a good introduction he wrote for the Willa Cather on Writing, which Stephen presented me with in NY. [. . .]

In Chicago, where he is now on the faculty at the University, I ran into an old student of yours, Ham Hill, who was just brought out what is apparently a wildly successful book on Mark Twain. Do you remember him? He says he owes you everything. (Was it "everything?" I hedge a bit because I found him not all that likeable personally. But I have not seen his book yet. I rather shrink from what I'm afraid was a real "job" on Mark Twain, from his own description of his work.)

[. . .] I worked so hard both places that I came home exhausted and with a heavy cold—I'm still in bed (well, typing in my nightgown). Have to get up and go to NY Monday. The Museum of Modern Art is having a strike, as you may know—something internal, I'm not informed on the issues, but the strikers phoned me and said that unless I would withdraw my lecture and deliver it to them instead, in "another place", they would have to picket me. I don't at all care for being even mildly threatened, and intend to keep my date at the Museum of course. There's to be a little party afterward at a private house—I'll write you about it or tell you. Walter Clemons just phoned me to say he would like to take me to the Ballet and the party for Lincoln Kirstein afterwards on the Tuesday night I get to NY, so that will be a splendid evening—I'll report on that. [. . .]

Poor Tennessee [*Williams*]. I bet the joke he told is the same one he told as his response (in full) to the presentation of the Gold Medal for the drama at the Institute meeting. What a waste of himself and to everybody's loss.[87] It's hard on anybody even in good health to do that kind of program and then what comes afterwards (I just did it myself in Chicago)—people are merciless, without thinking or meaning to be. Sure, I've autographed many a paper napkin, and also "Moby Dick" and math books and match packets, nobody's particular!

Keep well, and come home soon for some good holiday meetings and cheer.

Much love,

E.

Thanks for the Observer review of Sleeping Beauty [*by Ross Macdonald*].

October 2, 1974 • Jackson to Austin

Dear Frank,

The enclosed is the purpose of this letter, and I'll write one of my own later. It's the first I've been able to see your mother and when I asked if she'd like to dictate a letter to you she was ready at ONCE—a good dictator, too. I only hope you can read my writing—[*Apparently Welty enclosed this letter from Clarena Lyell, but it is not at MDAH.*]

I thought she looked pretty well, her color good and her voice firm, but of course she is thin and she says she still hasn't too much of an appetite. The phone by her bed makes her feel much more in touch, I think, and I know she'll be glad when she hears your voice over it. [. . .]

I know you want this letter from your mother soon as possible so off to mail it. I think of you and hope you are not too unhappy or wearying yourself too much. Things are being done for Clarena there—the therapy + the getting up regularly—and that's the important thing—

Best love,

Eudora

December 9, 1974 • Jackson to Austin

Dear Frank,

I hope you haven't felt I've been living in oblivion of everybody and everything because I haven't written as I should and as I wanted to. I was glad to get your news. This is just a line to say more later. [. . .] When I got back (Nov. 25) my furnace, which had been giving me trouble (threatening to explode) on the day I left, gave it to me again. [. . .] what the cost will be I can't imagine—then more cost cleaning up the black dust everywhere. But how lucky I am to be not blown up. Tell Mrs. Friedel [*Lyell's landlady*] a valuable piece of information the plumbers gave me: a BOOM out of the gas furnace means fire.

[. . .] Do you think that Charlotte, Louise and I could get your mother over to the easiest house and entertain her somehow during Xmas? Somebody else (we can't) will have to do the fetching and carrying with the wheel chair etc., but I think she would like it, don't you? We can't let Xmas pass without her in it, in person.

I hope the internal convulsions at the University have not disrupted you too awfully, lately—what a mess for you to bear with.[88]

Some books came from you from England! I will save for Xmas—I put them wrapped up inside a drawer to preserve them from the flying soot and dust—I am so delighted that one is about grand Kenneth Clark and one is the words of Auden—you couldn't have chosen any that will give me more pleasure.

[. . .] I hope you will get a long vacation? I kept wishing you'd fly over for a weekend—you can always use my car, have a room here (I know your house is ready for you too) and even if I'm not in town you could make do in the kitchen. I'm so glad your mother is stronger now, and her spirits up and determined to get her home—I agree with Charlotte that she probably could swing it—she really is so MAGNIFICENT.

Best love,

Eudora

January 21, 1975 • Jackson to Austin

Dear Frank—

Are you all right? Your mother still hasn't heard anything from you. When I saw her yesterday, I told her I was going to write you, and it's mainly to say I hope you will write her or call her soon. I'm sure you don't need reminding, but I feel for her when she worries about you, on top of the rest. She is still coughing deep in her chest—I wish they could better help her get over that cold—She said tell you she was better but feeling tired + worn out with the coughing. They give her some sort of cough medicine, she says, and she thinks it's got a sedative in it that makes her sleep lots more than usual, but I gather the doctor hasn't been back to see her. Charlotte went to see her Sunday and we feel the same concern about her—she wouldn't tell you herself, she's so brave, but you must know she feels discouraged + worried when she doesn't hear from you. I told her that I believed a letter must have got lost in the mail—maybe one did—so anyway, do write a good one now—I hope you are fine—and am sure you're busy with the new semester. I hope all's going well.

I enclose a Buchwald, only one I've come across lately—

More next time—just had to write this after seeing her.

Love,

Eudora

May 11, 1975 • Jackson to Austin

Dear Frank,

You're probably going to be in Dallas the same night I am, May 17, but you'll be at the Opera and I'll be at a party of SMU [*Southern Methodist*

University] people. I get an honorary degree from them the 18th. It's true, I have been more pressed than I can say, but am all right, just tired. Haven't been able to get to my own work, which I suppose is what makes me feel the tiredness. Thanks for your messages. Also thank you for ordering me the Metropolitan reproduction of the Sandwich-glass flowerpot with its dish to sit in—you know how much I'll love having it [. . .]

My time goes like this: This Friday, 16th, to Tulane for hon. degree afternoon of 17th—fly to Dallas afterwards (Hilton Inn) for the night + ceremony next afternoon—fly to New Haven after that (close connections!) for honorary degree from Yale next day—down to N.Y. for a week, then home. (13th of June I'll have to be in Santa Barbara, where I'll be happy to see Ken Millar.) Having just got back from a 4-day Arts Council meeting in Seattle, I am wondering if I've really caught enough breath to start out again Friday. [. . .]

We also had the 50th reunion of the high school Class of '25 last night. I had charge of the program—George Stephenson gave a fine talk among other things. Nash couldn't make it, as I'd hoped—It was all rather fun—a nice party.

The last time I saw your mother she looked stronger and of better color and good spirits than ever. Her fortitude seems equal to anything at all. She has my whole admiration + love.

Liz + Mary Alice are both due to have their babies pretty soon. I hope I'm able to be on hand. It'll be good to be home again altogether after the 20th of June or thereabouts.

Must get to work—[. . .] Have a good trip home—

Love,

Eudora

Jackson arts columnist and theater director Frank Hains, a good friend of Welty's, was murdered in July. Lyell, who also knew Hains, may have been in town in July; there are no letters from Welty to Lyell from summer 1975, and her other letters to him do not mention the tragedy.

October 3, 1975 • New York to Austin

Dear Frank,

Glad to get word from you, and I hope the weather is cooler now and the new schedule is working out all right. I'm sitting in a shoe repair shop sort of like Haber's, having the strap of my handbag repaired—You know how sorry I was not to come to Austin, though the chances of seeing you were slim from the start. I saved the schedule we had, so you could see—and meant to write you from D.C. but never had so much we had to do—even a breakfast meeting beginning at 7:30 AM—I got to go to the Princes' for dinner the first night—fresh salmon!—and no chance even to phone them after that. N.Y. is lovely today—42° and bright and clear—after a soggy trip all the way up—[*Hurricane*] Eloise all the way. I was so tired I spent a lot of time in bed having food sent up and reading Middlemarch [. . .]

Best love,
Eudora

[*Enclosed postcard with a statue,* Dancer, *by Elie Nadelman*]

Dear Frank—

You'd have been amused by this Nadelman show at the Whitney—

Enclosed the Austin schedule I didn't get to try to see you in spite of. (Diagram that sentence, Prof.)

Love,
Eudora

Welty began working on a novel about a retired schoolteacher who is a victim of sexual assault and then begins to recover repressed childhood memories of witnessing her mother's infidelity, her father's murder of her mother, and her father's suicide. Welty never published this novel, The Shadow Club.

March 12, 1976 • Jackson to Austin

Dear Frank,

Two minds with but a single Buchwald—I'd cut out the wonderful Nixon poems to Mao to send to you. Many thanks though, and I hadn't seen the Lockheed ones. I hate to miss any single one of his. I'm returning Mao poems—and also the sad letter you sent about Anna and all the fine Riddick family and what has befallen them, which must be almost more than the younger Genie can bear. I hate it for Anna, and know you must hate it so very much, out of all the long years of closeness to her. What Lodwick said about the dance step brought me a sharp pang—seeing Anna so clearly as I do doing the Big Apple in my living room. [. . .]

I've been far behind with writing any letters at all (except for those declining those things people think up, terribly augmented by the Bicentennial, heaven knows why, unless they think I am aged 200, and sometimes I feel that way). I did attend the Feb. meeting in Washington but came straight home again and went back to work on a story I've been working hard at—still have not got it done, but hope to seize this weekend to do nothing else but clean up my first draft. [. . .]

I also had a visit with Miss Theora Hamblett wh. I can't even start here to tell you about, but I will.[89] Mercy!! and I'll also fill you in later on the Today show. Did the best I could in 7 minutes but the crux of the matter is they didn't give a damn about where they were and preferred skimming over it and getting out.[90] I didn't see the show, being at Council Meeting, and was glad—then to my embarrassment they got a cassette of it and showed it after day was done to the Council! I hope to see your mother very soon. Saw George in grocery store—looking so well, and had long chat.

Keep well—we are all OK here—and let me have word whenever you can, and I will do the same.

Best love,
Eudora.

April 21, 1976 • Jackson to Austin

Dear Frank,

Virginia Woolf and Her World arrived in the same mail with your postcard and it was lovely to receive both for my birthday—Thank you! I was particularly glad to set eyes on the John Lehmann book—I hated most of the recent What-the-Butler-Saw-in-Bloomsbury offerings, that is I had no wish to read them, and John Lehmann's approach will be the valuable one of a contemporary, and a literary mind, and an able observer and participant of what he tells about—I look forward enormously to beginning it—very soon.[91] I've already of course looked at the photographs in it—the unfamiliar ones so refreshing to the spirit, aren't they, and isn't the one of Virginia and Angelica Bell and the small bird beautiful? and the one of Virginia + Leonard sitting side by side + filled with those years + days in 1939 leaves you just without words. It was good to see them all young and fair—and the one of Rosamund + John + Lytton Strachey was like a scene from "Dusty Answer"—It's a marvelous book to have, and thank you so much once again—

I had a call from your mother for my birthday too—So very sweet of her to remember that—Messages and things from a number of old pals, I was cheered.

[ ] Am also working quite hard + hoping to get something done—When will you be home? Mary Mian sent me this notepaper—I thought it would amuse you too.

Best love,
Eudora

The stationery features "Fantasy Frolic," a wood engraving by Grandville portraying a frog-fish riding a turtle/snail, with pig/chicken marching solemnly behind.

June 23, 1976 • Santa Barbara to Jackson

[*Postcard from Moreton Bay Fig Tree in Santa Barbara, California. Welty was at the Writer's Conference in the company of Kenneth and Margaret Millar.*]

Dear Frank,

Perfect weather in this heavenly place[92]—It's just as fine being here as it was last year—nothing more to be said! Workshops in the morning, play in the afternoons and evenings. I go to Santa Fe on Friday (25th) and will be home on Monday. Let's meet soon + tell our trips—

Love,

E.

December 8, 1976 • Jackson to Austin

[*Postcard from the Treasures of Tutankhamun exhibit at the Met*]

D.F.

Thanks for yours—I heard about your mother's stroke when I got home from Washington, and have kept up with how she was. Just now I've talked to Tippy, who says she continues to do all right without any sign of recurrence, but is very thin and very weak. She (T.) said it would be OK to go in and see her and I certainly shall, promptly. I'm sure what she's counting the days for is your return. You didn't say when, but I wouldn't be surprised if it's not the same as ever, <u>just</u> before Christmas. Hope it's for a good long time.

We'll have to catch up on all news when you come—I <u>was</u> glad to get that of yours, + clippings. I know I'm worse than ever about writing. Am trying very hard to get work done through the thick and thin of interruptions—I thought of you at the King Tut show! The Council was let in after hours (normally there's a 3-hr wait in line). [. . .]

Love,

E

Welty's arthritis made writing and typing painful, and she wrote fewer letters during this period. She was concerned for Kenneth Millar, whose memory problems were beginning to seem serious. She did preserve a handful of letters from Lyell in this period, all of which confirm that Lyell treasured his long connection with his famous, busy friend.

March 4, 1977 • Austin to Jackson

Dear Eudora,

Many thanks for the good letter, so clairvoyant in analyzing all the main questions in my mind about current goings on at 1119 + departures therefrom on the spring traveling schedule! May is going to be quite a whirl, so you must calm + arm yourself for that after the return from Agnes Scott. The honorary degrees! All deservedly yours—many congrats—but won't you soon have to build an Annexe to store them in?? I'm assuming that the series of universities beginning with Washington U. indicate Doctor of Letters pick-up stations instead of lecture platforms—or do you go to Santa Barbara for another writer's conference? Harvard one day, S.B. the next?! That beats the New Orleans—Dallas—New Haven Hop. I wonder whether there's a Top-Mileage-Flown-for-Honorary-Degrees Degree? You should certainly have that too. Princeton is inexcusably laggard, but when invited there, as you're bound to be one day, shake them up a bit by asking whether they even considered rescinding the honoris causas they bestowed on Coretta King + Bobby Dylan. Yes, I know about Berry College if that's the Martha Berry charitable institution near Rome, Georgia. First heard of it when a fellow-graduate-student at Princeton went to teach there. Then one summer in the 30's Clarena + I drove to Mentone, Alabama, to bring Louis home from his summer camp, + we detoured to look at the nearby campus, which was then very beautifully laid out. I remember how handsome a dairy building looked—so much better than the building I was occupying + seeing every day in Raleigh during those years. The countryside all around is lovely + should look its best at that time of year.

Alarming news of KAP—I'm so sorry + do let me know of any significant ups or downs that follow. I've been pretty well—no colds, but plenty of nose drooling during the chilly weather + inevitable coughing in overheated, airless interiors out of which hot gas heat has removed all oxygen. [. . .]

K. Tynan's piece on R. Richardson was indeed excellent. Such an unusual personality revealed in the offstage Sir Ralph. Look at p 58 again. I can vouch for what Kenneth says about those productions establishing "the high-watermark of English acting in the 20th century" because I saw every one of them. Sweeping statement, since the century has 23 more years to run, + I'm glad to say I've seen as impressive performances in other years in New York, London, Paris, + elsewhere; but it's safe to say that no company could reasonably be expected to establish a higher watermark, + it's reassuring to note that Kenneth has been using the same critical yardstick I've been using ever since my wartime London days. I was lucky enough to see Uncle Vanya, Richard III + Arms + the Man again in June of 1945 in Hamburg at the unbombed Staatstheater where the whole old Vic Company came to entertain the troops (that was the British zone) during our Bomb Survey days in that city—+ those performances were free! Sybil Thorndike greeted me in the theatre lobby one morning when I went to get tickets, asking if I wasn't an American (there weren't many in that zone), I not recognizing her right away in her khaki uniform. Will never forget her in Peer Gynt as Aase—in the death scene, with Richardson riding the baseboard of the bed pretending it is a sled drawn by reindeers. At the marvelous Uncle Vanya in London I was so transported by the stormy night scenes especially Olivier's (as Dr. Ostrov) with Margaret Leighton (as the doddering Professor's wife) that I jumped when the curtain came down. I was sitting in the 3rd or 4th row, but the power of the acting—everybody's—had made me forget completely that I was in a theatre. For me a unique experience. What was so extraordinary was the versatility of the individual actors, combined with the imperishable excellence of the dramatic material in the repertory of both the 1944–45 + 1945–46 seasons—Olivier's shift from Hotspur to Shallow, for example. My friend Bob Whitfield took me to the opening nights of both parts—of Henry IV, at one of which I remember we sat behind Clementine Churchill + daughter Sarah. Sybil Thorndike was Quickly, Joyce Redman Doll Tearsheet . (Kenneth omits reference to ever-memorable Joyce + others equally versatile but less well known in America). [. . .]

In the Feb 14 NYer Andrew Porter produces a rave notice of San Antonio's Rienzi. I drove down with operatic pals for the Sunday matinee, + it was indeed interesting + very much worth seeing because it's so rarely performed, but it wasn't as good as he says it was. It lasted from 3 to 6:45. Uncut it lasts 6 hours. Wagner began to sound like Wagner in The Flying Dutchham which comes right after Rienzi. I hadn't done my homework except to read the plot + kept wondering, what does this derive from?? It was a real treat at the second interval to meet Freidelind Wagner, Richard's granddaughter and have her answer the question: early Italian opera [. . .] A wonderful surprise to see her and have a brief chat. She agreed with me that the ballet music (San Antonio substituted an elaborate procession + high school flag drill for dancing) could go straight into Swan Lake + not be thought of as Wagner's if the score weren't so familiar. Andrew also goes wild over San Antonio and wants it to exhume Die Feen + Das Liebesverbot, Wagner's first two operas, + other rarities he's never seen.

There's more to report and I have clippings for you, but I must stop now and continue in another envelope later—but soon. So glad to be thought of daily on your busy days (ditto, ca va sans dire,[93] at this end) + hope the creative-critical chores are speeding merrily along.

With lots of love,

Frank

[*Lyell encloses John Lehmann's typed essay "Publishing Under the Bombs—the Hogarth Press" annotated with these comments*]
So cheering to see John again. He has been at a Bloomburg powwow of some sort at the U of Calif at Santa Barbara + also lectured at UCLA + Santa Cruz—for 3 weeks. I met his plane + took him home for drinks + out to dinner after checking in at his hotel.

Excellent paper, to be part of yet another B'burg volume Thrown to the Woolfs, which he says is necessary to straighten out what Leonard says about him in the autobiography, i. e. [*illegible*]

There was sherry in a HRC room after the lecture for anyone who wanted to come, then a largish cocktail party given by a younger colleague to which I took John + Margaret Scarborough, + after that a very cozy supper à trois in Margaret Scarborough's kitchen. Next day I took him to the airport, so you see we had a thorough reunion. Hate to see him hobbling on a stick because of bad right-hip arthritis. [. . .] Was told that [. . .] he would get $450. Quite a contrast to Alex (Roots) Haley's $3500 fee—sic! sic! sic!—I said $3500, for an afternoon talk (about an hour) followed by 45 minutes answering written-out questions brought to the stage—of Hogg Auditorium, which was packed with hundreds listening to a loudspeaker on the lawns outside. He was here during the T.V version showing + I almost didn't go (saw none of TV + haven't seen book), but I'm so glad I did.[94] I was greatly taken with him—so sensible + unassuming + straightforward without any Civil Rights or Wrongs proved. All emphasis was on family as the preserving unit of human life—"ask your grandparents to tell you all they know about your family history + write it down. If you don't, it's gone forever." Haven't time to summarize fully—Marvelous for the students to hear, + none of his main points were properly summarized + most were ignored in the local papers + Daily Texan. Nothing said of his praise + thanks to God the Father for the gift of talent + energy + strength to endure the days of writing + research, + the need he felt to pray every day. Much about his own family + life in the small Tennessee town he comes from; really amusing anecdotes told without a trace of wisecrackery. I'll summarize when next we meet. I was overjoyed to hear him say things that half a class would denounce me or any other teacher for recommending to flaming Bicentennial youth. "The past—what's that?" Everything to Mr. Haley, if the present is going to be fit to live in.

The youth who told me about Clive Barnes' fee, told me about Haley's. I ran into him on campus the day after Haley's lecture, delighted to praise it after denouncing Barnes when he asked my opinion of him—but couldn't believe he said $3500—but he did!

March 14, 1977 • Austin to Jackson

D.E.—

In Washington I always wonder if I'll be able to guess the nationality of my taxi-driver before I get to the Baxters' from bus or train station. Never the same + usually unguessable for me. Some have looked pretty fearsome, + the current hostage-holding vogue prompts me to send you the enclosed modern terrorist roll-call to use on your NCA trips: look <u>hard</u> at every driver and tell him to assure you his name isn't listed.

The Slocums' photograph[95] was in the latest <u>English Speaking Union News</u>, sent to members 5 or 6 times a year. He looks nothing like my recollection of him, + both are now showing that, as Daddy used to put it, they've always lived off the fat of the land. (That button on Eileen's midriff looks pretty strained.) Mr. McCulloch was the speaker at the Austin branch's dinner meeting this year (at the Driskill in January just before I got back here). A brother of his is the man who bought London Bridge and transplanted it to Havasu, Arizona.

[. . .] More dust, alas, for the weekend. Hope it hasn't blown your way.

Best love,

Frank

[. . .]

April 27, 1977 • Jackson to Austin

Dear Frank,

So happy to get your letter—I certainly <u>would</u> be absolutely delighted to receive <u>Moments of Being</u>[96] for a birthday present—thank you so much, in advance! It is a fine + thoughtful idea you had, to do it—

Here is PLT's [*Pamela Travers*] letter back, which I enjoyed having a chance to look at—She must be in many ways more settled about things now—after all the trials and difficulties and false starts (Ireland), and I hope when Camillus's baby comes she will feel new pleasure—I expect they <u>do</u> need praying for (if she doesn't <u>tell</u> them about it!). How rotten a homecoming she must have had to the wrecked house. You want the letter back quickly so I'm sending without too much of a note myself—I'm submerged. More pressure than I almost can take, till May is over.

See other side for my Agnes Scott trip. It really was a pleasure to see the people I'd worked with 11 years ago there—and many figures from my past, John Lehmann appeared, sitting on the front row at my reading! Later we got to talk, over drinks at the president's house (Great changes at Agnes Scott!).

I was saddened to see him on his stick, but so pleased to be talking with him—of course we spoke of you. Also about Henry Green—[. . .]. Absolutely perfect weather—dogwood time—Decatur [*Georgia*] is heavenly—

More next time. I go to Cornell May 5 + 6, NYC 7–11, Berry College (which you tell me is attractive) 11 + 12, Council meeting, Washington, directly from there, home the Sunday it ends, the 15th. Then onward, but I don't look any farther than the 15th for now. When do you get back to Jackson? Let me know. I enjoyed your letters + seeing the enclosures so much, forgive the brief answer—But wanted you to know these matters—Va. Woolf, J Lehmann—

Much love,

Eudora

[. . .]

May 1, 1977 • San Antonio to Jackson

[*Picture on postcard is captioned River Dee & Suspension Bridge, Chester*]

D.E—

Thanks for the reply & forecast of coming events. Good luck at Cornell + everywhere else on the trip. Berry College may seem very rustic-homespun after all the highbrow places you've been. Better not get too elated over my impressions of long ago. I'll be hearing some of the operas in Dallas May 12–14 + may be able to come home from there as I did last year. In any case I'll be there shortly after the 15th + see you I hope before you have to go to St. Louis. I'm booked now to fly to NY on the 27th + to Luxembourg on the 31st. I now think of being a month in Europe. More of this when we meet. Don't mention this very recent decision because I may have to undecide.

Best love,

Frank.

June 28, 1977 • Nancy to Jackson

[*Postcard depicts detail from le Retable du Jugement Dernier L'archange Saint Michel*]

D.E.—

Can't remember whether you came to Beaune + Dijon on your French meanderings. The vistas + textures in the old parts of both towns are charming. This is part of Roger Van der Weyden's wonderful altarpiece in the Hotel-Dieu in Beaune—the finest painting I've seen, + I don't know why the card doesn't say Roger painted it. I'm now in Nancy + from my hotel room can see the deservedly renowned Place Stanislas, under the evening floodlights—a most elegant + beautiful sight. Will soon be turning in my car in Luxembourg + returning to N.Y. Will be around, then perhaps in W'ton for a bit before coming home. Hope everything was fun for you in Calif. and New Mexico. Want to hear All when next we meet.

Best love,
Frank.

When Lyell returned to Jackson in July, he had developed congestive heart failure and was hospitalized. Welty wrote Aswell that "when he felt like it," she visited him, and "he would talk lovingly of his trip."[97] *He died on July 19, 1977, at age sixty-five.*

Frank Lyell and Eudora Welty's friendship began in 1930, the year they had eagerly escaped their hometown to live in New York, its streets full of artists, intellectuals, and people who'd never heard of Jackson. In the ensuing decades, as Welty went from an unknown to a celebrity, she made many more friends, but always cherished her connection with Lyell.

A few weeks after his death, Welty wrote to Kenneth Millar of her grief and shock over losing "one of that inner circle of closest friends" from Jackson. Like Dolly Wells and Diarmuid Russell, who had died in 1973, Lyell had been part of her life for many decades. Losing friends "is not considered surprising" for someone in her late sixties, she mused to Millar. "But I am not going to learn to accept it for being not surprising, I'm going to hate it and protest it [. . .] up to my last breath,"[98] she wrote. Her loved ones' deaths, their permanent absence, struck Welty as an injustice, to be forever deplored and protested.

Welty's words call to mind the thoughts of one of her characters, Gloria Beecham, in *Losing Battles*: "There is only one way of depriving the ones you love—taking your living presence away from theirs; no one alive has ever deserved such punishment, although maybe the dead do; [. . .] no one alive can ever in honor forgive that wrong, which outshines shame, and is not to be forgiven until it has been righted."[99] Today, we are deprived of the "living presence" of Welty and of Lyell, but perhaps their absence can be "righted" through their correspondence. Within their letters, we can still glimpse the sensibilities they shared and took delight in performing for one another. We are left to enjoy this lively, decades-long conversation—playful, urbane, heartfelt—reflecting their deep love for art, for absurdity, and for the hometown where they never quite belonged.

NOTES

EDITORIAL NOTE

1. Mississippi Department of Archives and History has now digitized images of many of Welty's letters to Lyell but has not digitized clippings enclosed in these letters.

2. A few scholars have cited or quoted from the Welty–Lyell correspondence. Patti Carr Black, editor of Welty's *Early Escapades*, excerpts and quotes from two 1930s letters from Welty. Suzanne Marrs's essay "Eudora Welty's Enduring Images" cites two letters to Lyell, and her biography *Eudora Welty* quotes briefly from about forty of Welty's letters to Lyell, cites at length about a dozen more, and quotes from one letter Lyell wrote. Her essay "Welty, Race, and the Patterns of a Life" discusses the Welty–Lyell correspondence and quotes from two letters to Lyell. Stephen Fuller's *Eudora Welty and Surrealism* cites and briefly quotes from nineteen letters between Welty and Lyell. Pearl McHaney cites two letters to Lyell in her essay "The Observing Eye" and quotes briefly from eight Welty letters in *A Tyrannous Eye*. I cite three letters in my essay "Teaching the Art of Welty's Letters," and Jacob Agner cites five letters to Lyell in "Welty's Moonlighting Detective." Annette Trefzer cites three from Welty and one from Lyell in *Exposing Mississippi*.

3. I wish to thank Pearl McHaney and Lori Howard for their extensive editorial assistance and support in creating the Welty–Lyell "Correspondence Calendar."

DRAMATIS PERSONAE

1. Marrs, *Eudora Welty*, 214–15.

2. Hartston, "Beachcomber."

3. Wilkie, "Hodding Carter, Jr."

4. For a discussion of Welty's working relationship with Giroux, see Samway.

5. Marrs, *Eudora Welty*, 189.

6. A draft card has surfaced that suggests George Greenway was born in 1906, but the year of his death has not been identified.

7. Prenshaw, *Conversations*, 187–88.

8. For more on Frank Hains, see McMahand and Murphy.

9. Marrs, *Eudora Welty*, 50.

10. "Interview."

11. For the full Paris restaurant anecdote as Welty related it to one friend, see Cole, "Eudora on Stephan Tennant."

INTRODUCTION

1. Marrs's *Eudora Welty: A Biography* contains many quotations from Welty's correspondence to these friends. Michael Kreyling's *Author and Agent* quotes extensively from Welty's decades-long correspondence with her agent Diarmuid Russell, focusing especially on Russell's encouragement of Welty and his efforts to place her works in a competitive literary marketplace. Books devoted to Welty's correspondence include *What There Is to Say, We Have Said* (Welty's correspondence with William and Emmy Maxwell, edited by Suzanne Marrs), *Tell About Night Flowers: Welty's Gardening Letters, 1940–1949* (to Russell and John Robinson, edited by Julia Eichelberger), and *Meanwhile There Are Letters* (the Welty–Kenneth Millar correspondence, edited by Suzanne Marrs and Tom Nolan). As of 2025, letters between Welty and several other significant correspondents remain unpublished, including Mary Lou Aswell, Reynolds Price, Dolly Wells, Hubert Creekmore, and Welty's immediate family.

2. Stephen Fuller notes that the Welty–Lyell correspondence from this era "colorfully and comically reflects the zeitgeist of the thirties" (233). Fuller identifies surrealism throughout Welty's body of work; chapter 1 of his *Eudora Welty and Surrealism* discusses the many surrealist and avant-garde artists working during this era, some of whom Welty and Lyell encountered in galleries, in person, and by letter.

3. At least eighty-four of these local names also appeared in Jackson newspapers from the 1910s through the 1940s. *The Clarion-Ledger* (Jackson) articles quoted in this book were accessed via Newspapers.com. In a few instances, I discovered connections between the assumed name and the contents of the letter. Typically, though, the names seem to have no particular significance. After 1946, only two letters contain playfully assumed names.

4. Welty to John Robinson, July 13, 1944.

5. Marrs notes that the motto "Don't take it cereus, life's too mysterious" is a modification of a Rudy Valee song lyric (Marrs, *Eudora Welty*, 45). According to *The Clarion-Ledger*, a night-blooming cereus in Zula Cain's garden in 1933 attracted a number of guests who came to watch it open on July 31 ("Cereus Plant in Full Bloom," *Clarion-Ledger* [Jackson], July 31, 1933, 10).

6. *The Ponder Heart* originated as a short story by the same name, published in *The New Yorker* on December 5, 1953. The novella was reprinted in Welty, *Complete Novels*.

7. Marrs, *Eudora Welty*, 423–24.

8. June 23, 1976. To Hunter McKelva Cole, another friend of Welty's during these years, Welty would use a similar expression to ask for an account of his latest travels. "Tell me your trip," she would ask, upon his return (Cole, telephone interview).

9. Welty to Lyell, April 21, 1976.

10. Marrs and Nolan, *Meanwhile There Are Letters*, 348.

11. Welty to Lyell, October 30, 1960.

12. Welty to Lyell, June 15, 1967.

13. See chapter 5 of *A Tyrannous Eye* for McHaney's analysis of Welty's lifelong letter-writing practices.

14. Welty to Lyell, November 22, 1933.

15. Welty, *Stories, Essays, and Memoir*, 772, 760.

CHAPTER 1: 1931–1939

1. Prenshaw, *More Conversations*, 147.

2. Cole discusses the New York year and sample items from Lyell's scrapbook in his *China Grove* article "Frank Lyell: Eudora Welty's Bachelor of the Arts." I am grateful to Louis Lyell for furnishing me with a copy of this journal.

3. "Frank Lyell Sails for Europe," *Clarion Ledger* (Jackson), June 14, 1931, 14.

4. Welty, *One Writer's Beginnings*, repr. in *Stories, Essays and Memoir*, 936.

5. Marrs, *Eudora Welty*, 38.

6. Mary Wigman, a highly influential German Expressionist dancer, opened a branch of the Wigman School in New York in 1931, directed by German choreographer Hanya Holm. Eliza Butler was director of the women's residence hall at Columbia University, where Welty and other young women from Jackson had lived in 1930–1931.

7. *The Greeks Had a Word for Them* was the title of a 1932 movie based on Zoe Akins's 1930 play *The Greeks Had a Word for It*. Ina Claire starred as a gold digger. The movie was reissued as *Three Broadway Girls* after its pre-Code title and some of the scenes were deemed too suggestive.

8. "Mounting Misgivings" is the title of chapter 4 of Thomas Mann's *The Magic Mountain* (1924).

9. Steel record player needles lasted more than one playing but damaged a record after repeated playing. Fiber needles were softer but were quickly worn down.

10. The popular radio show *The Fire Chief*, hosted by Ed Wynn, was preempted by an address by Herbert Hoover, who had been president since 1929. Widely expected to lose his upcoming 1932 race against Franklin Delano Roosevelt, Hoover defended his administration's policies in a series of nine radio speeches, totaling more than ten hours, between August and November (Carcasson). "How Do You Do It" was a song and dance featured in the musical revue *Ballyhoo of 1932*.

11. Lady Diana Bridgeman Abdy, daughter of an English earl, was a poet, artist, wife of a baronet who was an art dealer, and glamorous enough to appear in Cecil Beaton's 1933 book of photographs *The Book of Beauty*. Her appearance is an example of Lyell and Welty's epistolary practice of assuming names of celebrities or of not-so-famous Jackson acquaintances.

12. In his letter dated September 26, 1932, Lyell, describing his new room's "dark paneling around fireplace," reported that his "pictures look marvelous—Thank God I brought them."

13. Welty and her brothers were beneficiaries of life insurance policies purchased by her late father. $42 in 1933 was equivalent to over $1000 in 2025.

14. Willia Wright Bennett, Evelyn O'Briant, and Leone Shotwell were friends of Welty's from Jackson. Leone Shotwell had attended Columbia in 1930–1931 along with Welty, Lyell, and other Jackson friends. *The Poor Little Rich Girl*, originally a Broadway play, was a 1917 film starring Mary Pickford.

15. The Sunday society page informed readers that the "popular young daughter of Mrs. C. W. Welty, Pinehurst Place, is the guest of the Barbizan-Plaza Hotel in New York City" ("Miss Eudora Welty in New York," *Clarion-Ledger* [Jackson], January 15, 1933).

16. The London flat of English composer and playwright Noel Coward was featured in the January 1933 *Harper's Bazaar*, with one caption stating the flat's interior was "far from the madding vortex" (41). The title of a 1925 drama Coward wrote and starred in, *The Vortex*, was presumably the source of the magazine's pun on *Far from the Madding Crowd*, the title of a Thomas Hardy novel.

17. John Martin was dance critic for *The New York Times* from 1927 to 1962. He was also a friend of Lehman Engel's (Engel, *This Bright Day*, 55).

18. Martha Graham, a pioneer of modern dance, had a long association with Lehman Engel. He composed music for seven ballets for her, including *Ekstasis*, which premiered in May 1933 (*Ekstasis Ballet*).

19. The Piccoli, an Italian puppet theater produced by Vittorio Podrecc with orchestra, singers, and marionettes, performed circus acts, classical opera scenes, a bullfight, and a marionette version of Josephine Baker (Carb, 71).

20. Welty and Lyell were lifelong fans of the ironic and zany Beatrice Lillie (1894–1989), a singer and comedienne who appeared in Broadway shows, movies, and radio programs.

21. Guy Lombardo and The Royal Canadians were broadcast on WJKS at 10 p.m. on February 4 (*Radio and Amusement Guide*, 23). "Blues in My Heart" was first recorded in 1931. "Between the Devil and the Deep Blue Sea" featured the refrain "You've got me in between/ The devil and the deep blue sea." Lombardo's orchestra was the first to record "Going Going Gone" in January 1933.

22. Painter Vanessa Bell (1879–1961) was the sister of Virginia Woolf.

23. The dean of Princeton University Chapel, Robert Wicks, preached there most Sundays. In January, one sermon was entitled "The Hypocrisy of Privileged People" ("Dean Wicks," 1). Norman Thomas, a 1905 Princeton graduate and Socialist candidate for president in 1932, spoke February 26, 1933, at the Princeton chapel service, criticizing the capitalist system ("Thomas," 1).

24. "Le sacre" refers to *Le Sacre du Printemps* (*Rite of Spring*) by Stravinsky.

25. In a 1986 interview with Patchy Wheatley, Welty discusses "skullduggery" by an advertising agency that the Columbia placement office had connected her with, where she worked without pay for several weeks (Prenshaw, *More Conversations*, 124). Lyell may be referring to this incident, which Welty said was in 1931, but Marrs suspects this date is not correct (*Eudora Welty*, 583 n28). This letter further suggests that Welty's experience occurred in 1933. It seems unlikely that an agency would have "duped" her twice.

26. The Mae West film was probably *She Done Him Wrong* (1933).

27. Tallulah Bankhead was making her American stage debut in the Broadway play *Forsaking All Others* (1933).

28. As director of the Columbia University women's residence hall, where Welty had lived in 1930–1931, Eliza Butler imposed strict rules for the residents' comportment. Butler's hauteur and her disdain for Southerners made her an object of energetic mockery by Welty and her friends.

29. Lyell earned an undergraduate English degree from the University of Virginia.

30. Welty used the same style of address Lyell used in his letter dated March 10, 1933, merging "d" and "f" just as he had merged "d" and "e."

31. Welty had been unable to find a job in the city.

32. Cecil Beaton (1904–1980) was a British photographer. In the 1920s and 30s, *Vogue* and *Vanity Fair* often published Beaton's images of unconventional, hedonistic, glamorous artists

and socialites known as "Bright Young Things," avidly followed by Lyell and Welty. A few years later, Beaton would be photographing Welty for an issue of *Harper's Bazaar.*

33. A *New Yorker* March 25, 1933, unsigned cartoon depicts a woman seated at a switchboard with spaghetti-like cords and a man leaning on the desk, inviting her to "go somewhere for a spaghetti dinner." Dorothy Parker's essay is "The Diary of a Lady During Days of Panic, Frenzy, and World Change" in the same issue (13–14).

34. Congress had passed the Twenty-First Amendment to repeal Prohibition in February 1933. In March, Roosevelt amended the Volsted Act, making it legal to produce and sell low-alcohol beer and wine. Outdoor beer gardens, therefore, could sell beer openly, rather than accepting back door deliveries and selling indoors, as most New York establishments were doing (Touba), including the one Lyell recommends in the previous letter. Welty would soon return to Mississippi, which would remain a dry state until 1966. There, bootleggers and their customers, including Welty, freely circumvented the law.

35. Sigmund Spaeth, whose brother was a Princeton English professor and author of *The Common Sense of Music*, was a radio personality appearing as "Tune Detective" on NBC radio programs. Having gained fame in the 1920s for his analysis of sources for "Yes, We Have No Bananas" (these included Handel's "Hallelujah Chorus," Cole Porter, "My Bonnie Lies Over the Ocean," etc.), he would soon propose that antecedents for the song "Going Going Gone" included the Oriental scale, "Water Boy," and "Willie the Weeper" (Rosen). His lecture at Princeton was "The Popular Song: An Index to American Life" ("Spaeth to Lecture," 1).

36. American poet Ezra Pound (1885–1972) lived for several years in Paris and first published *A Draft of XXX Cantos* there in 1930, which may be why Lyell refers to Pound as "M," for Monsieur. A United States edition of *A Draft* was published in 1933.

37. The musical *Gay Divorce*, with music by Cole Porter, preceded the 1934 film *The Gay Divorcee*. Welty's friend Malcolm, with whom Lyell seems to be acquainted, is unidentified.

38. Felicia White, the granddaughter of architect Stanford White, had studied at the University of Wisconsin with Welty. She was now back in New York.

39. Lear's limerick concludes "That unhappy Old Man in a boat" (*Limericks*, 32).

40. Stravinsky's *Sacre du Printemps* (*Rite of Spring*) was performed April 11. Critic Olin Downes wrote that the performance was "the most feral, the most brutal conception of the music that has been experienced here. [. . .] The orchestra was soon unchained and howling like a pack of wild beasts. [. . .] A better balanced interpretation, one that read into the music other things as well as brutality and violence, is to be preferred" (24).

41. Alia Nazimova performed the role of Madame Ranevsky.

42. The Scottsboro Boys were nine Black teenagers accused of raping two white women on an Alabama train in 1931. The Supreme Court ordered a retrial. At the 1933 trial of Haywood Patterson, Ruby Bates, who had been named one of the victims, was a surprise witness for the defense, stating she had not been raped. Welty enclosed a photo of Bates and Victoria Price, who was also named as a victim. The caption stated, "An interesting sidelight on the trial of Haywood Patterson was the comment of one of the jurors, who said that the 12 Morgan County men did not believe Ruby Bates (right) since she had admitted perjuring herself at previous trials." Patterson was reconvicted April 9. Protests in support of the Scottsboro Boys occurred in several cities. Stamps were sold to raise legal funds to appeal the teenagers' convictions; Welty pasted one of these stamps onto a May 25 letter to Lyell.

43. Wilma Segrest had been at Columbia with Welty (Marrs, *Eudora Welty*, 29). She seems to have been staying with Welty at the Barbizan. Bud, apparently a fellow resident, may have been an insect or someone's unauthorized pet.

44. *The Complete Novels of Jane Austen,* published by Modern Library Giants, 1933.

45. Nettie Norris had been at Columbia University with Welty (Marrs, *Eudora Welty*, 29). Their friend Noel, whom Lyell seems to know as well, is unidentified.

46. The passage Welty quotes is from James George Frazier's *The Golden Bough*, a Celtic tale of a beast who can only be killed when an egg, safeguarded inside a hind, is broken, destroying the beast's soul.

47. Mississippi was a dry state from 1907 until 1966. One of Welty's 1930s photographs, *Woman with Ice Pick*, depicts a Utica bootlegger on her porch, jokingly wielding an ice pick to defend herself from the photographer (Welty, *Photographs*, Image 12).

48. Barron Ricketts, a Jackson friend, later married Leone Shotwell, mentioned on the third of these four postcards.

49. "Too Too Divine," by E. Y. Harburg and Vernon Duke, appeared in the 1930 musical revue *The Garrick Gaieties*.

50. Ralph Hilton attended school with Welty and wrote for the *Jackson Daily News* before producing the *Jackson State Tribune*. He later worked for the Foreign Service. His last post was at a paper he edited and cofounded, the *Island Packet* in Hilton Head, SC. In 1981, *The New York Times* noted that some new manuscripts by Welty had surfaced, work that she had shown Hilton when she was a teenager. When Hilton told Welty he had these papers, she asked him to donate them to the Mississippi Department of Archives and History (McDowell, 68).

51. Prenshaw, *Conversations*, 204.

52. McHaney, *A Tyrannous Eye*, 32–33.

53. "Mr. Frank Lyell Arrives from Princeton," *Clarion-Ledger* (Jackson), July 5, 1933, 5. On July 22, "Misses Cook and Welty to Chicago" reported that Welty was spending a week attending the Fair with Jackson friends Martha and Bessie Cook (*Clarion-Ledger* [Jackson], July 22, 1933, 7).

54. Writer Beverly Nichols, one of London's "Bright Young Things," wrote *Crazy Pavements* (1927) about the activities of sophisticated and cynical English people like himself. He wrote columns in the 1930s about his attempts at gardening. His first book on this topic was *Down the Garden Path* (1932).

55. The bridge party was also reported in *The Clarion-Ledger* (Jackson) article "Dr. and Mrs. Price Honor Visitor from Washington, D. C." on July 25, 1933, 5.

56. Robert Daniel was a Sewanee student who became an English professor and poet; in the 1930s he contributed to Welty and Lyell's parody collection, never published, called *Lilies That Fester*.

57. Advertisement, *Clarion-Ledger* (Jackson), August 29, 1933, 5.

58. "Am. Life Since 1860" refers to a 1933 book of photographs assembled by Agnes Rogers, with text by Frederick Lewis Allen.

59. "Three Little Words" was first recorded in 1930. Guy Lombardo and the Royal Canadians' version of "Inka Dinka Do" was released in November 1933.

60. The Junior Auxiliary or Junior League was a young women's civic organization with chapters in many Southern cities. The Jackson chapter sponsored and edited an annual insert for *The Clarion-Ledger*. Welty's photography was in its beginning stages at this time. Gay Lee's society column "The Chatterbox" reported that Welty and Hubert Creekmore were "taking

snapshots" at the 1933 State Fair (*Clarion-Ledger* [Jackson], October 15, 1933, 8). Creekmore was two years older than Welty, and his family lived on the same street as the Welty family. In the 1930s he was one of Welty and Lyell's intellectual and artistic friends, part of a Jackson circle that also included Nash Burger and Lehman Engel; the group later called themselves the Night-Blooming Cereus Club. His sister, Mittie Creekmore, later married Welty's brother Walter.

61. *The Clarion-Ledger* (Jackson) ran a special Junior Auxiliary insert each December. In 1933, this contained a photograph including Welty and Lyell's friend Frances McWillie with the "Motor Corps and Milk Committee." Other photographs showed the "Operations and Dental Committee," "Advertising Committee," "Editorial Staff," "Welfare and Publicity Committee," "Provisional Members," as well as some Auxiliary members modeling current fashions and the queen and king of the Junior Auxiliary Ball in royal costume. Regrettably, the dog Welty says she and Creekmore photographed did not make it into print.

62. Paul Bowles (1910–1999) was a New Yorker who attended the University of Virginia, as did Lyell. He wrote poetry, music, and fiction, including *The Sheltering Sky* (1949).

63. Norma and Herschel Brickell, originally from Jackson, hosted gatherings that Lyell and Welty attended when they were students at Columbia. Herschel Brickell had edited the *Jackson Daily News* before writing for the *New York Evening Post*, then becoming an influential book reviewer and an editor at Henry Holt and Company. He would later edit the O. Henry Memorial Prize Stories collection as well as working for the US State Department (Arrington).

64. Conrad Salinger (1901–1962) was an orchestrator for Broadway and then for Hollywood musicals.

65. The 1933 film version of *Little Women*, directed by Frank Lloyd and starring Hepburn as Jo, had opened at the RCA theater November 16. *Cavalcade* was the film version of Noel Coward's 1931 play.

66. Princess Faucigny-Lucinge was another socialite often photographed by Cecil Beaton, as was Daisy Fellowes. Elsa Maxwell, gossip columnist, often hosted high-society events.

67. The account of Cecil lying on the tracks resembles a photo that of herself Welty staged, lying across the railroad tracks like a silent-movie damsel in mortal danger (Welty, *Early Escapades*, 150).

68. Welty's description of herself as "underfoot locally" is quoted in Porter's 1940 preface to *A Curtain of Green* (repr. in Welty, *Stories, Essays, and Memoir*, 966).

69. Welty's mother, Chestina, wrote a 1930 *Clarion-Ledger* article about the national Little Theatre movement and the local organization, which was limited to two hundred members "carefully selected from those lovers of the drama who are interested in it either from the production or the literary viewpoint" ("Little Theatre Players a Revival of Drama as Outgrowth of Church League," *Clarion-Ledger* [Jackson], October 5, 1930, 19).

70. Welty, *Occasions*, 151–52.

71. "And this was scarcely odd, because. . ." is a recurring line in Lewis Carroll's "The Walrus and the Carpenter" from *Through the Looking Glass* (1871).

72. Marshall Hurt owned an advertising firm in Jackson.

73. *Salammbô* is an 1862 historical novel by Gustave Flaubert, set in Carthage in 260s BCE. Welty probably saw the silent film released in 1925, directed by Pierre Maradon.

74. *The Vinegar Tree*, a 1930 play by Paul Osborn, was made into the 1933 movie *Should Ladies Behave*.

75. *The Woods Colt: A Novel of the Ozark Hills*, by Ross Thames Williamson, was a 1933 novel written entirely in dialect. *Twenty Years A-Growing* was Maurice O'Sullivan's 1933 memoir, published in English and in Irish.

76. Willia Wright Bennett's daughter was named Worth. Bitty Creekmore was a sister-in-law to Hubert Creekmore.

77. Emily White Stevens, Welty's high school classmate and roommate during their first year of college at MSCW, graduated from Millsaps, where she was president of the Kappa Delta sorority. By 1934 she had married John MacLachlan and earned a master's degree in sociology, and was teaching in North Carolina ("Interview").

78. *Ozma of Oz* is the title of one of the Oz novels by L. Frank Baum.

79. Welty is referring to the songs "Body and Soul," "Sweet and Lovely," "Sophisticated Lady," and "Blues in My Heart."

80. Edna Best and Herbert Marshall costarred in early talkies. Barbara Hutton, the "Poor Little Rich Girl" debutante, was unhappily married to Alexis Mdivani. Welty puns on the title of the 1930 song "Too Too Divine" (see n48).

81. "Theses" perhaps refers to Welty's undergraduate thesis in creative writing, for which she received a B. It has not been found among her papers.

82. A pageant with 2,500 schoolchildren was announced on April 29, 1934, in *The Clarion-Ledger* (Jackson). Welty was listed as one of the dance teachers and creators of Mother Goose costumes ("May Day Festival by Twenty-Five Hundred Children on Tuesday," 15).

83. Welty enclosed an "eraser card," a credit card–sized metal stencil with small openings, and a printed card that read "ADMIT ONE AND FRIENDS" to a Men's Bible Class at Istrione Theater on Sunday mornings.

84. Welty is referring to actors in the movie *The Barretts of Wimpole Street*, about poets Elizabeth Barrett (Norma Shearer) and Robert Browning (Fredric March). Katherine Cornell played Elizabeth Barrett in the stage version.

85. Adolphe Menjou costarred in the 1933 film *Morning Glory* with Katharine Hepburn, who won an Oscar for her performance.

86. Patsy Kelly appeared with Thelma Todd in several short comic films by Hal Roach. In 1930 she appeared with Jack Benny in the Broadway revue *Earl Carroll's Vanities*, which Welty and Lyell apparently saw while living in the city that year.

87. *The Decline and Fall of the Roman Empire* (1776–1788) by Edward Gibbon had been republished in 1932 by Modern Library Giants.

88. Works Welty mentioned were composed by Edvard Grieg (*Peer Gynt*) and Henri Ghys ("Amaryllis"). Clarena Lyell, a frequent soloist at Jackson church services, weddings, and recitals, sang in a quartet from Giuseppe Verdi's *Rigoletto*. An article in *The Clarion-Ledger* (Jackson), "Spring Festival Planned Monday," notes that the program was free, with "a section reserved for colored people" (April 1, 1934, 7).

89. Welty sometimes referred to two elderly Jackson women as "phantoms of the Jitney." They were great-aunts of the future writer Willie Morris and frequented Welty's neighborhood grocery store, the Jitney Jungle. Welty included a sketch of one "Phantom" in a letter to John Robinson on September 1, 1943.

90. Easter fell on April 1 in 1934. Pearl Spann was a mathematics teacher at Central High School and the sister of Lyell and Welty's friend Willie Spann.

91. In 1933, as a member of the second bass section, Lyell sang with the Princeton Glee Club in a production of *Parsifal* with the Philadelphia Orchestra, broadcast on successive nights on the radio ("Glee Club," 1).

92. Mittie Creekmore, Hubert's sister, later married Walter Welty. Mrs. Clifford Pullen, older than Welty and her friends, was a member of the Junior Auxiliary. Walter was now attending the University of Mississippi.

93. Millstein's was a dress shop in Jackson. The 1933 Junior Auxiliary edition of *The Clarion-Ledger* (Jackson), for which Welty and Creekmore took photographs, features several photos of Auxiliary members in Millstein's outfits.

94. The Welty family began growing camellias in the 1920s. Welty enjoyed sending blooms by express mail to friends in colder climates.

95. A Jackson contemporary, mentioned in Jackson newspapers during Welty's girlhood, was named Camille Penix.

96. Debussy's *Pelleas et Melisande* was broadcast April 7, 1934. George Burns and Gracie Allen were performing on Wednesday evening CBS broadcasts.

97. A member of the "Night-Blooming Cereus Club," Nash Burger became an editor for *The New York Times Book Review*. Bill Hamilton became a history professor at Duke University.

98. *At 33* is actress Eva Le Gallienne's 1934 memoir.

99. A dead bird figures prominently in Chekhov's 1895 play *The Seagull*.

100. George Greenway had dated Welty when he lived in Jackson and had visited her in New York during her year at Columbia (Marrs, *Eudora Welty*, 27).

101. The Carioca is a dance performed by Fred Astaire and Ginger Rogers in *Flying Down to Rio*.

102. There were two department stores in Jackson: the Emporium and Kennington's.

103. The Woman's Institute of Domestic Arts and Sciences, part of the International Correspondence School, had since 1916 been offering courses in dressmaking, millinery, and cooking.

104. Comedienne Beatrice Lillie (1894–1989) appeared in Broadway shows, movies, radio programs, and eventually on television. Lillie's estranged husband, Sir Robert Peel, had died April 6, 1934, so Lillie was newly single when Welty provided feathers to Lyell.

105. Elsie de Wolfe was an actress turned interior designer. She lived for almost forty years with theater producer Elisabeth Marbury, before and after marrying Sir Charles Mendl.

106. Fredric March played Death and Evelyn Venable costarred in *Death Takes a Holiday* (1934).

107. Alfred Tennyson's "The Charge of the Light Brigade" contains the line "Someone had blundered." ("Forward, the Light Brigade!" / Was there a man dismayed? / Not though the soldier knew / Someone had blundered. / Theirs not to make reply, / Theirs not to reason why, / Theirs but to do and die.")

108. Wealthy Manhattan model Mary Taylor was photographed by Cecil Beaton and other high-fashion photographers.

109. Presenting quantum physics to lay people, Eddington's 1929 book *The Nature of the Physical World* explained how matter could be both particle and wave and how it was theoretically possible for multiple things to occupy the same space simultaneously.

110. Sir Arthur Eddington was broadcast on NBC radio on Saturday, April 28, 1934, at 2 p.m. ("Eddington Sees Gains in Science," 26).

111. Welty had taken art lessons from Marie Hull and was friends with Hull's niece, Helen Lotterhos. For a discussion of Jackson artists, many of whom Welty knew, see Black's "At Home." Welty's and Creekmore's photographs were exhibited in the Municipal Art Gallery in July 1934 ("Miss Welty and Mr. Creekmore," *Clarion-Ledger* [Jackson], July 8, 1934); the following week, Marie Hull gave a gallery talk on these photos and the works of painter William Hollingsworth, which were also on exhibit ("Marie Hull to Make Gallery Talk This Evening," *Clarion-Ledger* [Jackson], July 13, 1934, 10). Helen McGehee (1892–1980), another member of the Mississippi Art Association, exhibited her paintings during the 1930s (Black, *Art*, 204). McGehee's awards, gallery talks, and another work with the Art Association are regularly mentioned in *The Clarion-Ledger*. In 1935, Welty wrote a review of the Art Association's exhibition, praising Hollingsworth's art and recalling a painting from an earlier exhibition by McGehee, "a factory scene . . . which was of fine interest too" ("City Critic Discusses Annual Exhibit of Mississippi Art Association Here," *Clarion-Ledger* [Jackson], November 5, 1935, 4). McGehee's daughter, Helen Gray McGehee, danced in Martha Graham's company and became an acclaimed teacher and choreographer.

112. Welty had seen Uday Shankar perform in New York. "Shan Kar's bro." may refer to a photograph of his brother Ravi, a dancer and sitarist who toured with the group in 1933–1934. In 1971 he and George Harrison performed together in *The Concert for Bangladesh*.

113. The photographs by Welty and by Hubert Creekmore were scheduled for an exhibit in July.

114. *The Clarion-Ledger* ran an article about the Hinds County Maternity Center and included an uncredited photograph of the house where the clinic operated, which could have come from Welty, as well as formal photographs of all the officers ("New Maternity Center Home Will Open Today," *Clarion-Ledger* [Jackson], May 25, 1934, 15, 18). Another article mentioned the clinic's insignia as that of a "Madonna and Child" ("Hinds County Maternity Center Scores Success in Annual Dinner Held at the Edwards House," *Clarion-Ledger* [Jackson], February 25, 1934, 8).

115. Russian dancer Vaslav Nijinsky choreographed the 1913 ballet danced to *Le Sacre du Printemps* and other controversial works. He was hospitalized for schizophrenia and did not dance after 1919. *Nijinsky* (1934) was by his wife, Romola.

116. *Eskimo*, also called *Mala the Magnificent*, was released in 1933; *It Happened One Night* in 1934.

117. The Fitzgerald contraction is an observation, made by physicists Hendrik Laurentz and George Francis Fitzgerald, that an object is shorter if at rest than if in motion. Presumably Welty, sending love to Lyell in her signoff, was including extra to account for shrinkage in transition.

118. William Hollingsworth (1910–1944) was a Jackson native who had just graduated from the Chicago Art Institute. A Mississippi painter, he later became highly acclaimed.

119. H. C. Speir (1895–1972) ran a record store on Farrish Street in Jackson; as a talent scout for numerous record companies, he also recorded blues artists including Robert Johnson. He used the metal disc recorder in his store for demo musical recordings, as well as the sort of novelty recording that Creekmore and Welty apparently made for Lyell.

120. Rarely playing the record and using a fibre needle would reduce damage to the record Welty and Creekmore sent, which apparently no longer exists.

121. *The Silver King's Daughter* is the title of a 1910 book by Laura Jean Libbey.

122. "Thurber of the day" refers to a 1934 cartoon in *The New Yorker* (Thurber, 31).

123. Frank Lyell's return to Jackson was reported in late June along with his brother's graduation from the University of Mississippi ("The Lyell Brothers at Home from 'Ole Miss' and Princeton," *Clarion-Ledger* [Jackson], June 27, 1934, 4).

124. When published in Welty's *Early Escapades*, these limericks were mistakenly identified as having been created for Lyell's journey to Princeton, but in this letter, Welty makes recommendations for the Fair, including a suggestion for Lyell's eight-year-old brother Louis. Lyell wrote to Welty from Chicago the following week, and on July 22, 1934, *The Clarion-Ledger* (Jackson) reported that Lyell, his parents, and Louis spent a week in Chicago ("Frank and Louis Lyell").

125. "Poet + Peasant" refers to the overture to the 1900 operetta of the same name, composed by Franz Von Suppé.

126. Sir Arthur Eddington's *The Nature of the Physical World* discussed the fact that atoms are primarily composed of empty space, which meant that solid objects could theoretically pass through a wall, or vice versa.

127. Japanese actor Sessue Hayakawa starred in silent films in the 1910s and 1920s.

128. Lee, "The Chatterbox," *Clarion-Ledger* (Jackson), July 29, 1934, 10.

129. Black, "Back," 34, and McHaney, *A Tyrannous Eye*, 57–59. Trefzer's *Exposing Mississippi* analyzes Welty's aspirations to become a professional photographer, noting that Abbott was only ten years older than Welty and was already becoming recognized for her photographs of New York City.

130. Welty had written at least one play while a student at MSCW, "The Gnat," a parody of *The Bat*. She seems to have taken up playwriting again in the mid-1930s. "The Waiting Room," apparently never produced, is dated 1935 in the Eudora Welty Collection at MDAH.

131. The Jack Benny football story was broadcast September 29, 1934, on *The General Tire Revue* ("General Tire Revue"). See Fuller-Seely for a history of Benny's radio career.

132. African American singer Mamie Smith (1891–1946) was appearing at the Alamo, a theater in a neighborhood of Black businesses on Farish Street (Marrs, *Eudora Welty*, 47).

133. Beatrice Lillie's "I'm a Camp Fire Girl," recorded in 1934, became a favorite of Welty's.

134. *Dodsworth* is a play based on Sinclair Lewis's 1929 novel of the same name.

135. Stein was touring the United States, beginning with a lecture the following evening at the Museum of Modern Art. *The New York Times* reported that the audience "listened intently for nearly an hour to the frequently puzzling involutions and repetitions of her diction and went away afterward to argue" ("Miss Stein Speaks," 25).

136. Etoile de Holland is the name of a red rose.

137. "Mrs. Slaughter and Miss Welty Arrive from New York and Washington," *Clarion-Ledger* (Jackson), November 7, 1934, 8.

138. Seta Alexander, another Jackson friend, later married Tom Sancton, writer and *New Republic* editor.

139. Luther Burbank (1849–1926) developed hundreds of hybrid plants.

140. Welty sent Lyell pun-laden postcards from New Orleans: "Banana awful stew—palm me for asking you, but orange you the man I saw in the Astor—Market down to a bad memory endive off—Minnie" (February 8, 1935).

141. Welty recalled years later that she had assisted Hubert Creekmore with producing a short-lived journal called *The Southern Review*, "getting ads and reading proof. When we had to quit, we dumped all the copies we had left, with a short bridge-side ceremony, into the Pearl River. Hubert said they should at least be rare" (Welty, *Occasions*, 196).

142. Karl Wolfe (1904–1985) was a Mississippi portrait painter and Jackson resident. In a 2023 tribute to Louis Lyell, son-in-law Luke Lampton reproduced the Wolfe sketch of Louis as well as two photographic portraits by Welty from this period, one of the Lyell family and one of Louis.

143. Gluck Sandor, New York choreographer, dancer, and visual artist, was married to dancer-choreographer Felicia Sorel, who allegedly signed Welty's message.

144. Charles Henri "Bubber" Ford (1913–2002), born in Brookhaven, Mississippi, was a surrealist poet and editor. In 1929 he began publishing *Blues: A Magazine of New Rhythms* in Columbus, Mississippi, featuring such modernist poets as William Carlos Williams, Ezra Pound, and Gertrude Stein. He then moved to Paris and lived with Djuna Barnes while she was writing *Nightwood*. He coauthored the 1933 novel *The Young and Evil*, about artists in Greenwich village. In 1934 he returned to New York with his partner, the Russian painter Pavel Tchelitchew (Chartier). Ford's sister Ruth was an actor and model photographed by Cecil Beaton, Man Ray, and Carl Van Vechten. Ruth Ford later adapted and starred in the dramatic version of Faulkner's *Requiem for a Nun* (Abadie). A party hosted by the Fords enabled Lyell to meet several notable artists, including fashion photographer George Hoyningen-Heune. For a detailed analysis of this letter, see Fuller, 24–25.

145. "Tigrett Announces 'Rebel' as Name for Streamliner," *Clarion-Ledger* (Jackson), April 2, 1935, 10.

146. Peter Lindamood (1914–1972) was an aspiring writer from Columbus, Mississippi, where Surrealist poet Charles Henri Ford (1908–2002) had also lived. By the 1930s Ford was living in New York City with his sister, the actress Ruth Ford, and Lyell had written Welty about attending a party they had hosted. Charles Henri Ford edited an art journal called *View*, and in 1940 Lindamood contributed an essay to a special issue on Marcel Duchamp ("I Cover the Cover").

147. Welty was a member of the Little Theatre of Jackson. Members were the primary audience; they also carried out all parts of the productions, including serving refreshments at intermission. Here Welty contemplates serving "trick food" from the Johnson Smith & Company, which relocated from Wisconsin to Michigan in 1935, and which sold novelties including whoopie cushions, joy buzzers, and fake food items.

148. Zula Cain was a Jackson woman whose invitation to watch her night-blooming cereus open had been published in 1933 ("Cereus," *Clarion-Ledger* [Jackson], July 31, 1933).

149. Bertha Ricketts Sumner (1890–1970) later published novels under the name of Cid Ricketts Sumner.

150. Welty had written the Jackson society columns for *The Commercial Appeal* (Memphis) regularly since August 1933. On August 29, 1933, *The Clarion-Ledger* (Jackson) ran an advertisement for *The Commercial Appeal* that listed Welty as the Society editor ("Advertisement," 5).

151. Winter lived on the same street as the Weltys, Pinehurst Street. *The Clarion-Ledger*'s 1932 Junior Auxiliary edition included an article on Mrs. Winter, listing the women's clubs that had published her work for their study programs. It noted, "It is very unusual for any poet, more especially for a southern poet, to be thus honored while living. We congratulate Mrs. Winter upon gaining such signal recognition, while we felicitate ourselves upon being able to claim her for Jackson" (Betty Bartee Tucker, "Capital City Is Proud of Its Poet," *Clarion-Ledger* [Jackson], December 4, 1932, 19). On March 26, 1933, a poem she wrote called "I Was Ever a Rover" had appeared in *The Clarion-Ledger*.

152. Emily White Stevens, Welty's high school classmate and roommate at MSCW, had married John MacLachlan and earned a master's in sociology from the University of North

Carolina. Both worked for the Rosenwald Foundation in addition to university teaching, and were friends with the editor of UNC Press, William T. Couch ("Interview," 42).

153. In the 1934 film *It Happened One Night*, Clark Gable and Claudette Colbert play bus passengers who meet on a ride from Florida to New York.

154. J. K. Huysmans's 1884 novel *À Rebours* (*Against the Grain*) was about an aesthete who retreats from his decadent life in Paris to read, collect art, concoct perfumes, and contemplate past love affairs. Huysman's 1894 *Là-Bas* features a character like Huysmans, a novelist, exploring the practice of Satanism in France.

155. "The Hottentot Potentate" was performed by Ethel Waters, the only Black cast member in *At Home Abroad* starring Beatrice Lillie, which Lyell reported having seen that September before moving to North Carolina.

156. "Phantoms of the Jitney" were eccentric women who shopped at Welty's grocery store.

157. Welty includes a photograph of this group of friends in *Photographs*, Image 236.

158. Probably the tenor Lauritz Melchior (1890–1973).

159. For discussions of Welty's development as a photographer and of photographers whose style may have influenced her, see McHaney's "Eudora Welty, Photographer" in *A Tyrannous Eye*, and Trefzer's *Exposing Mississippi*.

160. Unless otherwise noted, information on the publication history of Welty's works comes from the "Chronology" of Noel Polk's indispensable *Eudora Welty: A Bibliography of Her Work* (1994).

161. "The Doll" appeared in June 1936 in *Tanager*; "Magic" appeared in the September–October 1936 issue of *Manuscript*. In August 1936 *Manuscript* returned "Shape in Air."

162. Lyell taught at NC State in 1935–1936 but was not there in 1936–1937, according to the 1937 NC State yearbook *Agromeck*. *The Clarion-Ledger* reported Lyell was visiting Jackson from Princeton in June 1937 ("Visits Parents," *Clarion-Ledger* [Jackson], June 28, 1937, 2). Subsequent NC State yearbooks show Lyell on the faculty from 1937 to 1938 and then in 1941–1942.

163. Baker Wynne was an English professor who began teaching at NC State University the same year Lyell did.

164. Welty's photograph *Watching a Fire* documented a crowd gathering to watch a fire on a city street (*Photographs*, Image 77).

165. Welty is referencing the issue of *The New Yorker* published July 4, 1936.

166. Woolf's 1937 novel *The Years* had been scheduled for publication in fall 1936 ("Books").

167. The Weltys owned the lot next door, east of 1119 Pinehurst, and built a duplex there to generate rental income for the family. Edward Welty designed the house and for a time lived in one of the apartments with his wife, Elinor.

168. Dwight Fiske (1892–1959) performed in upscale New York nightclubs, delivering risqué comic monologues while accompanying himself on piano. Welty's Beatrice Lillie recordings probably include "I'm a Campfire Girl" and "Paree." Her Edith Sitwell record must have been a 1930 Decca recording of *Façade*, a sequence of Sitwell's poems she recited with musical accompaniment written by William Walton. Sitwell's biography of Queen Victoria, *Victoria of England*, was published in 1936.

169. Colonel Harry Hulen was the director of the state information bureau for the Works Progress Administration, where Welty and her friend Helen Lotterhos were working ("WPA Reductions Seen in State," *Clarion-Ledger* [Jackson], November 12, 1936, 10).

170. *Lilies that Fester*, described by Welty as a burlesque poetry anthology (Welty, *Occasions*, 207), was never published; Robert Daniel may have had the only complete copy, which Ann Waldron viewed and summarized for her biography of Welty (82). Photocopied pages from this work are at the Mississippi Department of Archives and History; they include a photograph of Welty for one of the spoof authors, Romola Knowles. On the archive's folder, Welty lists Lyell, Daniel, herself, and Hubert Creekmore as authors.

171. *Horsefeathers* is a 1932 Marx Brothers film. *A Day at the Races* appeared in 1937.

172. After a show at the Lugene, Inc. Opticians' gallery in 1936, Welty's photographs were exhibited in New York for the second time in March 1937 at The Camera House, owned by Samuel Robbins, a Lugene's employee who had started his own business (McHaney, "The Observing Eye," 13–14).

173. Welty took photographs of Mardi Gras revelers in New Orleans in this era, later published in "Literature and the Lens" and in *Photographs*.

174. Mona Williams, later Countess von Bismarck, was known to Welty through photographs in *Vanity Fair*; fashion designers had declared her the world's best-dressed woman.

175. Margaret Mitchell's bestseller *Gone with the Wind* was published in 1936.

176. "Years Progress for Jackson AAUW Discussed at Tea," *Clarion-Ledger* [Jackson], October 10, 1937, 10. Six of Welty's photographs were published in *Life* magazine, November 8, 1937.

177. "Frank H. Lyell Gets Doctorate," *Clarion-Ledger* (Jackson), May 14, 1938, 10; Lee, "The Chatterbox," *Clarion-Ledger* (Jackson), May 29, 1938, 24. The "accepted short story" was probably "Old Mr. Grenada," published in *The Southern Review*, revised and retitled "Old Mr. Marblehall" in the 1941 collection *A Curtain of Green*.

178. Modernist poet Edith Sitwell (1887–1964) was the subject of many photographs and portraits by artists drawn to her sharp features and her dramatic clothing, rings, and hats.

179. In his speech broadcast on September 27, 1938, Prime Minister Neville Chamberlain said,

> I am myself a man of peace to the depths of my soul. Armed conflict between nations is a nightmare to me; but if I were convinced that any nation had made up its mind to dominate the world by fear of its force, I should feel that it must be resisted. Under such a domination life for people who believe in liberty would not be worth living; but war is a fearful thing, and we must be very clear, before we embark on it, that it is really the great issues that are at stake, and that the call to risk everything in their defence, when all the consequences are weighed, is irresistible. (*In Search of Peace*, 175)

On September 30 Chamberlain announced a nonaggression pact with Germany, an agreement he believed would prevent another world war.

180. Annie Parker was the city librarian.

181. The 1938 Fair ran in Jackson from October 10 to 15, a few blocks from Welty's Belhaven neighborhood. On October 9 *The Clarion-Ledger* (Jackson) reported that a company called The Royal American would host "the world's largest midway" at the fair, with rides and performances including a "Follies Internationale" "with a cast of 100, including a singing, dancing chorus of 50."

182. Lee, "The Chatterbox," *Clarion-Ledger* (Jackson), September 25, 1938, 18.

183. The YWCA fund drive was reported as being October 4–6, 1938. Luncheons were held at the YWCA on October 4, 5, and 6 according to the October 6 society column of *The Clarion-Ledger* (Jackson).

184. Other reasons for Welty's lack of enthusiasm may be discerned from such *Clarion-Ledger* (Jackson) headlines as "Late September Finds Socialites Concentrating Time and Effort on Series of Stimulating Projects" (September 25, 1938, 16).

185. Shady Rest was a gambling establishment in an area of Rankin County sometimes called the Gold Coast, East Jackson, or "cross the river," an area near the Pearl River where bootleg liquor was readily available (Yancy, "Pearl River's"). A December 1938 news article included Shady Rest in a list of clubs that had abruptly closed, apparently tipped off that the district attorney was planning arrests ("Gold Coasters Again Fold Up Their Business," *Clarion-Ledger* [Jackson], December 11, 1938, 1).

186. "The Whistle," about impoverished tomato pickers who burned their furniture to stay warm, ran in *Prairie Schooner,* and "A Curtain of Green," about a widowed young gardener, ran in *The Southern Review* in fall 1938.

187. "The Lambeth Walk," named for a street in a working-class London neighborhood, was a song written by Noel Gay for the 1937 musical *Me and My Girl.* After it inspired a dance craze, numerous musicians released recordings in 1938. Dancers performed a strutting sequence that ended by pointing their thumbs over their shoulder in a "Cockney salute" while calling out "Oi!"

188. *The Clarion-Ledger* (Jackson) reported a high of 88 degrees on October 4, 84 on October 5, 88 on October 6 and 7, 86 on October 8, 1938.

189. Harriet Fletcher was in the same grade as Welty at Jackson Central High School. In 1928, *The Clarion-Ledger* (Jackson) reported that she was honored with a "debut party" before moving with her parents to Philadelphia, PA.

190. Ford Madox Ford (1873–1939) had first written Welty in November 1938, telling her that Katherine Anne Porter suggested he ask Welty to show him her stories. In January, Ford wrote Welty that he was impressed by her work (Marrs, *The Welty Collection*, 164–65). Lyell seems to have learned of this correspondence and used Ford's name as an alias when he sent Welty some records.

191. The card Welty enclosed bore the caption, "Congratulations! Sharing Your Joy at the Good News Today and Hoping Good Luck Keeps Coming Your Way!" It was a "talking card," featuring a strip of cellophane that apparently could make the sound of the word "Congratulations" when pulled through a slit on the card.

192. Soprano Jeannette MacDonald (1903–1965), who sang opera roles before becoming a movie star in the 1930s, was giving a recital tour. Her stop in Jackson was arranged by Armand Coullet (1899–1982), an Algerian musician who came to Jackson in 1928 to conduct a fourteen-piece orchestra for WJDX, the radio station sponsored by Christian Welty's firm, Lamar Life. Coullet later recalled that the same day he arrived, he submitted his resignation, because Jackson "was so primitive. They had streetcars being pulled down Capitol Street by mules." The radio station persuaded him to remain (Yancy, "Armand Coullet"). Welty worked as the station's newsletter editor from 1931 to 1934. In 1935, Coullet helped to organize the Jackson Music Association, which began its "All Star Series" in 1937. Coullet and his wife Magnolia Simpson Coullet, a Millsaps College professor, were members of Galloway United Methodist Church, as the Welty family was ("Arts Impresario Armand Coullet Dies at 84," *Clarion-Ledger* [Jackson], January 1, 1983, 1).

193. Charles Betts Galloway (1849–1909) was the founding pastor of the First Methodist Church, later known as Galloway Methodist Church, where Welty attended Sunday School.

"Master Charles Betts Galloway," presumably his grandson, played in a recital with Welty in 1921 ("Piano Recital Tomorrow," *Jackson Daily News*, June 9, 1921, 3).

194. Limerick author and artist Edward Lear (1812–1888), a favorite of the Welty siblings, wrote a recipe for Gosky patties in *Nonsense Cookery.* Readers were told to leave a pig out on their roof for three days and beat him each day, and if this didn't turn him into Gosky patties, nothing would. Welty shared this same quip in a September 1940 letter to Diarmuid Russell, discussing repeated attempts to get national publishers to publish a book of her stories (Eichelberger, *Tell About Night Flowers*, 7).

195. Charlie McCarthy, the character voiced by ventriloquist Edgar Bergen, was sawed in half in the 1939 movie *You Can't Cheat an Honest Man*, starring W. C. Fields.

196. In *The Welty Collection*, Marrs cites letters from publishers from 1936 through 1940 who rejected a collection of Welty's stories (158–67).

197. *Clarion-Ledger* (Jackson), November 26, 1939, 56.

198. "Fine Arts Club Holds Interesting Meet at Municipal Club House," *Clarion-Ledger* (Jackson), December 7, 1939, 8.

CHAPTER 2: 1940–1949

1. Vincent Rousseau, a college student from Charlotte, North Carolina, had met Welty in 1937 while sojourning in Mexico, where Welty went on a road trip with John, Will, and Anna Belle Robinson (Marrs, *Eudora Welty*, 56).

2. The much-acclaimed Southern fiction writer Katherine Anne Porter (1890–1980) had encouraged Welty in the 1930s after reading work she submitted to *The Southern Review*. Porter had recommended Welty's work to Ford Madox Ford.

3. Edith Mirrielees (1878–1962), a Bread Loaf Writers' Conference faculty member, was a Stanford creative writing professor and the author of *Story Writing* (1939).

4. Welty to Russell, December 5, 1940, quoted in Kreyling, *Author*, 54.

5. In addition to writing fiction, Welty donated some of her writing talents to the Jackson Little Theatre, which sponsored a workshop in playwriting; she was listed as an advisor in a *Clarion-Ledger* (Jackson) article published on September 11, 1940 ("Organization Meet Held by Workshop Group of Theatre," 4). The next month, she and Willie Spann were credited with a play called *Victory at Solferino*, apparently an adaptation of *A Memory of Solferino*, a book that inspired the formation of the Red Cross. The play was performed for a conference for the Mississippi Red Cross ("Red Cross Head to Speak Here," *Clarion-Ledger* [Jackson], October 15, 1940, 3).

6. Presumably Welty is referencing bootleggers, who may have raised their prices "up to the sky" as more military personnel came to the area for training.

7. Jose de Creeft (1884–1982) was a Spanish-born sculptor whom Welty met at Yaddo in 1941. His large sculpture of *Alice in Wonderland* characters was installed in Central Park in 1959.

8. Welty to Russell, September 30, 1941, in Eichelberger, *Tell About Night Flowers*, 35.

9. Lyell had received his initial draft notice in November 1940 ("Registrants Receiving Draft Questionnaire," *Clarion-Ledger* [Jackson], November 11, 1940, 5). Then he apparently obtained a deferral from the state's draft board. He enlisted in September 1942 ("World War II Army Enlistment Records").

10. In the Fu Manchu series by British novelist Sax Rohmer, characters attempt to stop the "Yellow Peril" that allegedly sought to destroy white Western societies.

11. Copies of *A Curtain of Green* were being sold by Kennington's department store and by Office Supply, where Mrs. W. C. Herbert managed book sales.

12. The party was sponsored by Russell & Volkening, the literary agency of Diarmuid Russell and Henry Volkening. John Slocum worked at this firm in its early years. Other friends at the party were Karnig Nalbandian, an etcher Welty met at Yaddo; Jackson friend Dolly Wells, who worked in New York; and Vicki Baum, author of *Grand Hotel* (1930). Doubleday, Doran was about to publish Baum's book *Marion Alive* (1942).

13. Henry Volkening's guests included Edward Aswell, who edited Thomas Wolfe, Richard Wright, and others at Harper & Brothers, and Mary Lou Aswell, fiction editor at *Harper's Bazaar*, where Welty's fiction would appear. Also present were *New York Times* book reviewer Peter Monro Jack, playwright Joseph Kesselring (*Arsenic and Old Lace*), "and their wives." Prolific author Kay Boyle (1902–1992) had published fourteen volumes (novels, short fiction, and poetry) by the time Welty met her in 1941.

14. Welty's interview with Robert Van Gelder, editor of *The New York Times Book Review*, was published in the *Review* on June 14, 1942 (repr. in Prenshaw, *Conversations*, 3–5).

15. Presumably Woodburn saw a resemblance to the author William Saroyan, whose play *The Time of Your Life* had received the an award he had refused, the 1940 Pulitzer Prize for Drama. In 1943 Saroyan wrote a bestseller novel and hit movie screenplay, *The Human Comedy*.

16. This typed poetry was attributed to "G. Garland Lyell" and dated November 25. Other letters indicate that Judge Lyell periodically wrote verse for special occasions. According to *The Clarion-Ledger* (Jackson), Lyell's mother, Clarena, hosted a party for Welty that day ("Mrs. Lyell Entertains Miss Welty," November 27, 1941, 12).

17. Men who had married before Pearl Harbor could defer being drafted, but that exemption ended in 1943. Lyell could have been eligible for deferment because he was teaching students who would need higher education to train for specialized military assignments. He may have also benefited from his father's influence with Mississippi officials who made these decisions. For draft-age men who were qualified and fortunate, noncombat military assignments could be found, including working in intelligence or conducting a military band, as Lehman Engel did.

18. Samuel Taylor Coleridge's *Biographia Literaria* (1817) discusses the poet's artistic and personal development as well as his spiritual philosophy and his views of poetry.

19. Eileen McGrath, whose sister was married to David Rockefeller, was a friend of Diarmuid and Rose Russell, who lived in Mt. Kisco. McGrath would later become a medical doctor.

20. The meeting at Miss Etta Mitchell's is noted in "M. S. C. W. Alumnae," *Clarion-Ledger* (Jackson), January 4, 1942, 14.

21. In "The Wide Net," a young woman named Hazel leaves a note for her husband, saying she has drowned herself. After a drunken evening out, her husband comes home and reads the note, drags the river for Hazel, and enjoys the day with his friends who are helping him. Hazel is actually safe at home. "The Wide Net" originally appeared in *Harper's Magazine*, May 1942; it was reprinted in Welty's *"The Wide Net" and Other Stories* and *Stories, Essays, and Memoir*.

22. Welty was a lifelong lover of mysteries. John Dickson Carr (1906–1977) wrote many "sealed-room" or "locked-room" mysteries featuring English detective Dr. Gideon Fell.

23. On May 26, 1942, Welty wrote Lyell, "The impossible has happened, or will happen today, God willing—I sign the contract for the 'Robber Bridegroom' alone—by itself—isn't that grand!

Maybe your harangue with Dr Elder caused the change of heart—Anyway, that's all fixed—for whatever comes now, that will be in print to my credit or blame—"

24. Fannie Thompson's connection with the Welty family is unclear. Aunt Mary was Mary Hammer, the aunt and guardian of Leone Shotwell, who went to study at Columbia in 1930 when Welty, Lyell, and other Jackson friends were also students there.

25. The story accepted by *The Atlantic* was "Livvie Is Back," later published in *The Wide Net and Other Stories* as "Livvie."

26. Edna Frederikson (1904–1998) was a writer who had been at Bread Loaf with Welty. Her novel *Three Parts Earth* was published in 1972.

27. The story about Rodney is "At the Landing."

28. In the back of the property at 1119 Pinehurst Street was a small building Welty's brothers called the "club house." Welty and her friends called it "the pent house, the house of passions pent" and gathered there for drinks in the 1930s because "Mrs. Welty didn't want illegal whiskey in the house," according to Suzanne Marrs.

29. The two-volume edition of Dorothy Wordsworth's journals was published by Macmillan in 1941.

30. A lifelong Jackson friend, Charlotte Capers, later published a humor column, "Miss Quote," in the *Jackson Daily News* (collected in *The Capers Papers*, with an introduction by Welty). From 1955 to 1969, Capers was the director of the Mississippi Department of Archives and History, to which Welty donated her manuscripts and correspondence.

31. Welty's abbreviations stand for Galatoire's, Antoine's, Pat O'Brien's, and the Monteleone Hotel.

32. Elizabeth Lawrence (1904–1985), author of *A Southern Garden* (1942), was from Raleigh, North Carolina, and became friends with Lyell while he was teaching there. The two met during one of Welty's North Carolina visits.

33. Lyell's military fortunes differed from those of John Robinson, whose draft card listed his occupation as sales. Lyell's occupation, teaching at a university that trained engineers, may have extended his deferment. Local draft boards, with whom Lyell's father may have had influence in Mississippi, had considerable autonomy to decide whether someone should begin serving. Amy J. Rutenberg noted that during the 1940s, "In the absence of central authority, board members had a tendency to bend regulations to their will or to ignore them entirely."

34. The dust jacket illustration showed a young woman in a forest walking in bare feet towards a log cabin (Polk, *Eudora Welty: A Bibliography*, 25).

35. Welty had bought an Ansley Dynaphone with some of her O. Henry Prize money.

36. This essay was "Ida M'Toy," *Accent* 2, no. 4 (1942): 214–22. It is reprinted in Welty, *The Eye of the Story*, 336–48.

37. *Li'l Abner*, a comic strip drawn by Al Capp featuring the misadventures of lovable country rube Abner Yokum, ran from 1934 to 1977.

38. This notice, consisting of two paragraphs in Benjamin De Casseres's column that ran November 19, 1942, in the Randolph Hearst publication *San Francisco Examiner*, has not been collected elsewhere.

> Do you love the crazy beauty? The crazy beauty—what is that? you ask. Well, you will find it in 'Alice in Wonderland,' in 'Snow White,' in 'Peter Pan,' in 'High Wind,' in 'Jamaica,' in 'Don Quixote,' and, in a way, in 'Superman' and 'Captain Flash.' It's the beauty of the

improbably, of fairyland, of the never-never world. And here it is today again in Eudora Welty's 'The Robber Bridegroom' (Doubleday, Doran).

It's all about Rosamond, down in the old Natchez country, who fell in love with a bandit. But the telling is everything, and Miss Welty has the authentic touch of magic in her pen. To me, it's the book of the year. Chuck Steinbeck and Hemingway and all the rest of the railriders of literature. Snuggle into 'The Robber Bridegroom' and kiss sourpuss reality goodby [*sic*] for three or four hours. In these black-browed days, 'The Robber Bridegroom' is, indeed, an event. ("March of Events," 16)

39. A *Clarion-Ledger* (Jackson) article on January 23, 1943, "National War Women's Saving Staff Member Says There Is Prestige In 'Doing Without,'" features a photo of officers in the local organization, including Welty, newsletter editor (5). Welty wrote Diarmuid Russell in February that her "publicity work" was "a little boring" (Eichelberger, *Tell About Night Flowers*, 78). For evidence, see an excerpt she wrote for a 1944 newsletter, reproduced in Welty's *Occasions*, 130–31.

40. Mack Sennett directed the Keystone Cops films and other slapstick comedies.

41. In 1942, men "deferred from service due to issues such as dependency" could become Volunteer Officer Candidates (VOC's). These men "were sent to OCS and in the event of their failure, were returned to citizenry rather than face a continuation of service in the enlisted ranks" (Wiegers, 132). Although the US had anticipated a shortage of officers early in the war, by 1943 it had more officers than it needed, with little opportunity for promotion of enlisted personnel, so the program was phased out (161–66).

42. Welty was visiting Diarmuid and Rose Russell and their children. Will Russell was Welty's godson.

43. "Some Notes on River Country" was published July 2, 1943, in *Harper's Bazaar* (repr. in Welty, *The Eye of the Story*, 286–99).

44. Faulkner was then in California writing screenplays for Warner Brothers. His letter praised Welty's *Robber Bridegroom* and also "The Gilded Six-Bits," by Zora Neale Hurston; some sentences suggest Faulkner was not sober when writing it (Welty, *On William Faulkner*, 20).

45. Japanese American soldiers in the US military were trained at Camp Shelby in a segregated regiment (Howard, 2). The US had incarcerated over 120,000 Japanese Americans in ten concentration camps, including two in Arkansas. Japanese American women incarcerated in Arkansas were bussed to Camp Shelby to attend dances with Japanese American members of this regiment, who in turn paid visits to the Arkansas camps (Howard, 124–49).

46. Lyell was looking for a path to noncombat military service in Army Air Force or Army Ground Forces. Given the glut of US officers that had developed by 1943, fewer slots were available in specialized training programs and fewer men were being accepted to Officer Candidate School (OCS).

47. Welty to Diarmuid Russell, August 6, 1943, in Eichelberger, *Tell About Night Flowers*, 90. Welty's worries eased a few weeks later when Robinson was posted to Algiers.

48. Welty mentioned seeing the OCS film to John Robinson in a June 23, 1943 letter.

49. Porter had still not finished her novel, then titled *Safe Harbor*. It was published in 1962 under the title *Ship of Fools*.

50. Doris Comby was a member of Delta Zeta at Millsaps in 1925 and often mentioned in society columns.

51. Pamela Travers (1899–1996) was the author of the Mary Poppins children's books and a client and friend of Diarmuid Russell, who had introduced her to Welty.

52. Mrs. Annie Parker, head of the Jackson Public Library, did not want Baha'i magazines to appear there. The Baha'i religion's humanist and universalist message may have been the source of the "Antichrist" designation; they were also unpopular with some whites because they opposed racial segregation. Martha Hamilton Cavelin was the sister of Bill Hamilton, who was a history professor at Duke University and a friend of Welty and Lyell. Martha Hamilton was a Julliard student when she met her husband, Borah Cavelin. He spoke at the Jackson Baha'i community center on December 24, 1943 ("Baha'i Community Member Speaks Here," *Clarion-Ledger* [Jackson], December 24, 1943, 8).

53. Martha Hamilton Cavelin's twin sons were born in Jackson on January 7, 1944.

54. Miriam J. Ezelle, another Jackson schoolmate, in 1928 wrote a letter to the editor of *The Clarion-Ledger* in support of prohibition, even if it meant crossing over and voting Republican ("Voice of the People," *Clarion-Ledger* [Jackson], August 31, 1928, 9). It is unclear whether this had anything to do with the "golden circle 4th degree" in Welty's signoff.

55. "A Pageant of Birds," *New Republic*, October 25, 1943. Repr. in Welty, *The Eye of the Story*, 315–20.

56. Tom Sancton, husband of Welty and Lyell's friend Seta Alexander Sancton, was managing editor of *The New Republic*.

57. Welty to John Robinson, December 3, 1943.

58. "The Great Image" is probably *The Land of the Great Image*, by Maurice Collis (Faber & Faber, 1943). Collis had lived in Burma and was critical of British colonial rule there. He was also a supporter of Irish nationalism and a friend of A. E., whose son was Welty's literary agent, Diarmuid Russell.

59. Emma Maud Slaughter, the faux addressee of Lyell's letter dated December 15, 1943, was cited in the 1928 *Clarion-Ledger* as an accompanist in a program by the Women's Club and a winner of a piano contest for high school players. Lee Gainey, Lyell's alias in this letter, was a high-school-aged tenor soloist in the 1920s.

60. Welty's essay on Jose de Creeft, published in the February 1944 *Magazine of Art*, is reprinted in Welty, *Occasions*, 89–94.

61. Lyell to Welty, March 3[?], 1944.

62. In a letter to Diarmuid Russell, Welty described A. Robins's performance, in which he pulled seemingly endless items—harmonicas, a drum, watermelons—out of his coat pockets, changing costumes throughout the act. "Everything multiplies. Really there is no end in the world, you feel, to his garments, treasures, and receptacles," Welty wrote Russell (June 8, 1942). Robins was also known for extracting from his clothing cardboard cut-outs of musicians that he then manipulated so they seemed to play while he hummed the sounds of their instruments. When Welty saw him in 1942, Robins was in a show called *Top Notchers*, and later appeared on television (Slide, 421–22).

63. *Life* had published a few of Welty's photographs in 1937. In "American Magazines in Wartime," published March 5, 1955, in *The New Republic*, Richard Rovere stated that during the war, fiction published in American magazines was "still unsubtly oriented to middle-class illusions and aspirations. [. . .] Some editors occasionally publish writers like William Faulkner, Kay Boyle, and Eudora Welty, but as a rule their courage fails them" (308–11). This must be what seemed "misleading" to Lyell, who asked Welty if any of the magazines mentioned had

published her work. The article named *The Reader's Digest, Saturday Evening Post, Ladies' Home Journal, McCall's,* and the *Woman's Home Companion.* None had published Welty's work by March 1944; her work had appeared in little magazines such as *The Southern Review* and *Prairie Schooner* and in larger magazines including *Atlantic Monthly, Harper's Magazine,* and *Harper's Bazaar.* By June 1944, *Ladies' Home Journal, Saturday Evening Post,* the *Woman's Home Companion,* and *Good Housekeeping* had passed on stories Welty's agent Diarmuid Russell had offered to them (Polk, 365–71).

64. "Mirrors for Reality," Welty's review of Woolf's *A Haunted House and Other Stories,* appeared in *The New York Times Book Review* on April 16, 1944; repr. in *A Writer's Eye,* 25–29.

65. *The Burning Court* is a 1937 locked-room mystery by John Dickson Carr.

66. Rosa "Dolly" Wells and Lyell graduated in the same high school class as covaledictorians. Both were the dedicatees for Welty's 1949 story cycle *The Golden Apples.*

67. Lyell to Welty, April 3, 1944.

68. Wealthy and fashionable, Lucius Beebe (1902–1966) wrote columns for the *New York Herald-Tribune* and, in 1938, published the photograph book *High Iron: A Book of Trains* with his partner, Charles Clegg.

69. Lyell to Welty, April 3, 1944; Welty to Robinson, June 2, 1944, June 19, 1944.

70. Marrs, *Eudora Welty,* 108–9.

71. Robert Van Gelder, Welty's boss at *The New York Times Book Review,* and his wife Dotty hosted the party for Welty. Other attendees were Dolly Wells; Alice and Nancy Farley; Diarmuid Russell and Henry Volkening; Margaret Cousins, fiction editor at *Good Housekeeping*; and Welty's Doubleday, Doran editor John Woodburn.

72. Mae West (1893–1980), whose 1930s films included the line "Come up and see me sometime," was returning to Broadway to star in a play she had written.

73. Welty to Robinson, October 18, 1944, in Eichelberger, *Tell About Night Flowers,* 142.

74. November 16, 1944, in Eichelberger, *Tell About Night Flowers,* 151.

75. Welty to John Robinson, November 20, 1944 and November 29, 1944.

76. Welty to John Robinson, December 25, 1944; January 4, 1945.

77. Jewell, "Art: Diverse Shows," 124.

78. Munsel would later sing in a 1955 recording of *Carousel* conducted by Lehman Engel.

79. Raines was famous as a star in war films and as a pinup girl. She divorced her first husband, a major in the Army Air Forces, in December 1945, and in 1947, married a fighter pilot.

80. The second group of names are other Jackson contemporaries of Lyell, seemingly not close friends, so Welty was likely teasing Lyell.

81. A recording of Richard Wagner's *Götterdämmerung,* a Christmas gift, had arrived damaged, so Lyell had another one shipped to Welty.

82. The Delta research visit inspired Welty to write what would become *Delta Wedding.*

83. The film noir movie *Laura* (1944), directed by Otto Preminger, starred Gene Tierney and Dana Andrews, with Judith Anderson and Clifton Webb in the cast.

84. Welty to John Robinson, February 14, 1945; Lyell to Welty, February 19, 1945; Welty to Robinson, February 20, 1945.

85. On February 19, 1945, *The Clarion-Ledger* (Jackson) reported that Welty had been a guest of Mrs. N. R. Fitzgerald in Sumner. The "nightlight story" became part of "A Little Triumph," a story Welty worked on throughout the spring, telling Robinson in a letter dated March 24,

1945, "it is astonishing how it grows" (Eichelberger, *Tell About Night Flowers*, 164). The story was reworked into the novel Welty didn't yet realize she was writing, *Delta Wedding*.

86. London socialite, arts patron, and friend of T. S. Eliot, Sybil Colefax, a high-end decorator, had orchestrated salons and dinner parties for artists, intellectuals, and other luminaries in London in the 1910s–1930s.

87. Maggie Teyte (1888–1976) was an English operatic soprano.

88. *The Circle* is a play by Somerset Maugham, produced that season at the Haymarket Theatre in London, with John Gielgud.

89. "My first Duchess" is Lyell's play on the Robert Browning poem title "My Last Duchess," which suggests that this production was the first performance of *The Duchess of Malfi* Lyell had seen. It was directed by George Rylands. John Gielgud, already a celebrated stage, film, and radio actor, played Ferdinand.

90. J. L. Roberts was principal of Central High School in Jackson when Lyell and Welty were students.

91. The English edition of *The Wide Net and Other Stories* was published in March 1945.

92. It is unclear what "Earl Beyard" meant to Lyell or Welty, but it may have been a variation of the name of knight called Pierre Terrail, Seigneur de Bayard. William Gilmore Simms's historical novel *The Life of Chevalier Bayard* presented this figure from the sixteenth century as a model of chivalric virtue. Many white Southerners believed in the holiness of the "Lost Cause" of the Confederacy and believed the Southern gentleman, who held benevolent control of his land and enslaved humans, was chivalrous and noble.

93. Donatallo's bronze sculpture *Judith and Holofernes* had been removed from the front of the Palazzo Vecchio for safekeeping during the war.

94. In his radio address delivered on V-E Day, May 8, 1945, Churchill asserted that "we, from this Island and from our united Empire, maintained the struggle single-handed for a whole year until we were joined" by Russia and the United States. "Finally almost the whole world was combined against the evil-doers, who are now prostrate before us. Our gratitude to our splendid Allies goes forth from all our hearts in this Island and throughout the British Empire." Churchill's speech concluded, "Advance, Britannia! Long live the cause of freedom! God save the King!"

95. An article by local writer Vary Thrower published April 29, 1945, in *The Clarion-Ledger* (Jackson) reviewed the show in glowing terms. "Have you seen his painted analysis of the music of Debussy? Who among us could paint portraits of music," she marveled, noting that Franklin "often incorporat[ed] his poetry within his paintings, poetry in which he has often excelled, having taken many prizes in this field" ("B. Franklin Has Show at Gallery"). An undated clipping from late spring 1945 noted that Franklin had won second prize for poetry published in the Jackson high school's literary anthology, edited by Nash Burger and judged by Welty. On the clipping next to Franklin's name, Welty scribbled a sentence that began "I had to, it was better than the [*illegible*]." *The Clarion-Ledger* also reported that Benjamin's mother, Mrs. Lester Franklin, was serving as the president of the Poetry Society when both she and her son received awards for their poetry in 1945 ("Mississippi Poets Inspired by Subject, 'Hands,'" *Clarion-Ledger* [Jackson], January 9, 1944).

96. This letter and several others are written on stationery printed with a stylized drawing of a piano player wearing a bow tie. This could be the same notepaper that Lyell had thanked Welty for earlier that year, a Christmas present that was "very chic—just my type."

97. Lyell's explicit, written request was required in order for civilians to purchase for service members items that were normally rationed.

98. Composer and writer Nicolas Nabokov was a cousin of novelist Vladimir Nabokov and a friend of Auden's.

99. In 1947 James Stern published *The Hidden Damage*, a slightly fictionalized account of his own experiences in 1945. The book presents numerous vignettes demonstrating ongoing psychic and physical damage caused by Nazism and the war.

100. Correspondence from July 9, 1945. Founded in 1918, the English-Speaking Union maintained a club in London that offered cultural events and celebrated the common interests and traditions of English-speaking nations. During World War II, the club provided hospitality to members of the American military. Lyell's letters suggest that, though he was an Anglophile, his contact with the club was not motivated by colonialist or xenophobic attitudes that are now associated with some English-Speaking Union members.

101. Welty was a fan of the radio quiz show *Information Please*, which featured celebrities' learned or humorous attempts to answer questions. It aired from 1938 to 1951.

102. Pearl McHaney's essay "Forays into the Surreal" analyzes the affinities between Welty's art and that of surrealist artist Joseph Cornell, who sent Welty a letter expressing his admiration for "The Winds" and for a photograph of Welty's published in *Vogue* in August 1944. Cornell's letter was decorated with a drawing of a chimney sweep stepping out of a chimney, presenting a letter to Welty. This letter is reproduced on page 29 of Fuller's *Eudora Welty and Surrealism*, which discusses the links between Cornell and Mississippi-born Charles Henri Ford (27–29). Welty replied to Cornell in a letter dated April 3, 1945.

103. Bessie Smith and Jane Power were names of students at Central High School in Lyell's and Welty's years there.

104. Lyell's photograph is published in *W. H. Auden: The Life of a Poet* by Charles Osborne (259) and in Paul Giles's *Atlantic Republic: The American Tradition in English Literature* (254).

105. Lyell was at the Führerbau or Führer's building, in Munich, where the leaders of Great Britain, Italy, and France signed the Munich Agreement with Germany in 1938. The building is on a square, the Königsplatz, next to a temple where Nazis killed in the Beer Hall Putsch were enshrined. Since the US military was now in control of the building, Lyell, in his uniform, had some authority to scold German passersby.

106. The phrase "infinite riches in a little room" is from Christopher Marlowe's *The Jew of Malta* (ca. 1589).

107. "Beachcomber" was the name used for the author of the humor column "By the Way" in the *Daily Express* (UK edition). The dispatches that Welty and Lyell enjoyed reading and sharing were by J. B. Morton, who wrote them from 1924 to 1975. The column had been written by John Bernard Arbuthnot from 1917 to 1919 and by Wyndham Lewis from 1919 to 1924.

108. Since Welty had not planned for this story, about a 1920s Delta family, to become a complete novel, she refers to it as "my novel (sic)." It was ultimately titled *Delta Wedding*.

109. On June 25, 1945, a B-52 bomber hit the Empire State building where Dolly Wells worked, destroying most of the 78th and 79th floors (Adams, 1). Fourteen people were killed.

110. Nash Burger had moved to New York City with his family to work for the *Times Book Review*.

111. Frank Faylen played Bim in *The Lost Weekend*, a 1945 film noir about an alcoholic writer. George Sanders played Jack Favell in the 1940 film *Rebecca*.

112. Clippings from three newspapers reported that the rain of the day was the first to fall in twenty-five, twenty-three, or nineteen days.

113. These letters span December 1945 to February 1946 and are available in Eichelberger, *Tell About Night Flowers*, 178, 182–85.

114. Presumably Lyell is referring to Grant Wood's 1930 painting, "American Gothic."

115. ASCAP is the American Society of Composers and Performers, with whom Garland Lyell Sr. was connected.

116. Marrs, *Eudora Welty*, 109.

117. Gilbert Adrian (1903–1959) was a Hollywood costume designer. In Lyell's letter, "Adrian" is written in large letters at a 45-degree angle.

118. Engel was musical director of *Call Me Mister*, which opened April 18, 1946.

119. Isaac Rosenfeld reviewed *Delta Wedding* for *The New Republic* on April 29, 1946. His negative review noted that he could not get past the first one hundred pages (633–34).

120. Christopher Isherwood's *Berlin Stories* includes one about a Berlin cabaret singer named Sally Bowles. Isherwood was a friend of W. H. Auden and collaborated with him on three plays and the nonfiction *Journey to a War*. This relationship may have called to Welty's mind Auden's handwritten review (no longer extant) as she wrote.

121. "The Whole World Knows" was originally published in *Harper's Bazaar* in March 1947. It was reprinted in Welty's *The Golden Apples* and *Stories, Essays, and Memoir*.

122. Welty to Russell, September 9, 1946.

123. Welty to Robinson, September 16, 1946, in Eichelberger, *Tell About Night Flowers*, 190.

124. "I couldn't have liked it more" is the refrain to a Noel Coward song Beatrice Lillie recorded, "I Went to a Marvelous Party." Welty and Lyell sometimes used this phrase in letters. Here she phonetically spells the last word, indicating Lillie's aristocratic pronunciation.

125. Andrés Segovia was a Spanish classical guitarist; Pierre Monteux was a French conductor. Cellist Gregor Piatigorsky, whose playing demonstrated that the cello could be a compelling solo instrument, was performing his "Variations on a Paganini Theme."

126. The play *Come on Up* toured the United States for nine months but never made it to Broadway. Mae West played an undercover FBI agent.

127. The story Welty was writing would become "Music from Spain."

128. The *Atlantic* eventually passed on Welty's "long 60 page" story, "Golden Apples," later titled "June Recital."

129. Bennett Cerf (1898–1971), a writer and humorist, was the cofounder of Random House.

130. Hubert Creekmore's latest book of poetry, *The Long Reprieve and Other Poems of New Caledonia*, was reviewed briefly in *The New Yorker* on February 8, 1947.

131. Welty's letter to Lyell on March 16, 1947, enclosed a clipping from the *San Francisco Chronicle* with a story and photo of nightclub owner Gypsy Buys. She and her husband had announced that a Black spiritual leader named Peace Peace It's Wonderful Brown would soon be purchasing their Los Altos mansion. Affluent neighbors, alarmed by the possibility, began bidding on the property.

132. Colin McPhee's *A House in Bali* (1947). Welty had been at Yaddo with McPhee in 1941.

133. "The Golden Apples," published in September 1947, would later be retitled "June Recital" in Welty's story cycle *The Golden Apples*. "June Recital" was also reprinted in *Stories, Essays, and Memoir*.

134. The letter from E. M. Forster is reprinted in Marrs, *Eudora* Welty, 156.

135. Presumably Lyell had read a draft of the story published as "Golden Apples" before reading it in *Harper's Bazaar*.

136. Seventeen *New Yorker* cartoonists posed for a group photograph by Irving Penn, which appeared along with a drawing by each cartoonist in the *Vogue* issue for September 15, 1947. Penn would later photograph Welty for the magazine.

137. Welty is paraphrasing lines from Keats's "To a Nightingale." Caroline Gordon was a novelist and critic, married to poet-essayist Allen Tate.

138. Welty had attended a summer camp in 1921 much like the one in "Moon Lake." An article on this camp identifies Willie Spann as one of the "councillors" ("Girls Reserves Home After 'Grand' Camp," *Jackson Daily News*, August 7, 1921, 6).

139. Chaplin starred in his 1947 film *Monsieur Verdoux*.

140. Available Jones and his cousin Stupefyin' Jones were recurring characters in *Li'l Abner*.

141. Caroline is probably Caroline Gordon.

142. Hodding Carter and Ben Wasson's Levee Press published "Music from Spain" as a seventy-two-page book in June 1948.

143. Welty to Russell, January 2, 1949.

144. Porter's article was "Gertrude Stein: A Self-Portrait," *Harper's Magazine*, December 1947.

145. Maxwell Anderson's 1946 play *Joan of Lorraine* was touring.

146. President Harry Truman had outraged many Southern Democrats by supporting federal measures to guarantee voting rights, enforce antilynching laws, and combat hiring discrimination in the United states. On February 7, 1948, *The Clarion-Ledger* (Jackson) reported that the legislature announced a mass meeting of "all loyal Mississippians" and another resolution offering a "free ticket out of Mississippi" or out of the United States, to all who believed they were being discriminated against because of their race ("Dislike the South? Solon Has Remedy / Merely Pick Up and Move Elsewhere," 1, 10). For more on 1940s Mississippi, see Marrs, "Welty, Race, and the Patterns of a Life."

147. *The Clarion-Ledger* ran a photo of Versie Rae Brown, of 1607 Pinehurst Place, costumed, for the Orpheus Ball in New Orleans, as Cleopatra; "her headpiece was an immense vulture made of sequins" ("Versie Rae Brown Reigns over Orpheus Pageant," *Clarion-Ledger* [Jackson], February 8, 1948, 31).

148. *Lions and Shadows* is Christopher Isherwood's autobiographical novel.

149. Probably Dorothy Simmons.

150. To Robinson, on March 19, 1948, she wrote of her hope that his writing would continue. "As long as a visit wouldn't interrupt what you came for but could help celebrate it," she wrote. "So glad we came—can look forward to another time. I think absence is no *light* thing—yours to me—ever" (Eichelberger, *Tell About Night Flowers*, 210–11). In her letters to him that spring, Welty devoted much time to his work in progress and to a story he had written the previous year that she was trying to help him place. Planning another trip a few weeks later, she wrote Robinson on March 30, 1948, "My love to you—the world like it is, and I love you and think of our lives in a real and prideful way. What will ever dim this?"

151. Woolf's posthumous collection *The Moment and Other Essays* was published by Harcourt in 1948, along with a reprint of her 1925 collection *The Common Reader*. Diana Trilling's essay review appeared in *The New York Times Book Review* on March 21, 1948 (68, 95, 96).

152. Having contracted malaria years earlier, Welty periodically suffered recurrences.

153. Jackson physician Levi McCarty was tried for the murder of two men he shot in a nightclub on December 30, 1947. He stated afterwards he had no memory of his action. He was convicted of manslaughter and in 1955, pardoned, reportedly leaving the state to resume medical practice elsewhere ("Physician Granted Complete Pardon," *Clarion-Ledger* [Jackson], December 21, 1955, 1). The portable electric chair Lyell mentions, constructed in 1940, was transported by truck to sites of execution. In 1951, for example, the chair was set up in front of the jury box in the Jones County courtroom, so that fifty witnesses could watch as an African American man, Willie McGee, was executed for the alleged rape of a white woman (Taylor).

154. Engel's composition *The Creation* premiered on June 20, 1948, in a broadcast of the CBS Symphony. Michael Redgrave was the narrator.

155. Welty, *Occasions*, 44.

156. Welty to Robinson, September 5, 1948.

157. Having published a comic memoir, *We Shook the Family Tree*, in 1946, Dolson published *The Husband Who Ran Away* in 1948.

158. *An Ideal Husband* is the 1947 British film adaptation of Oscar Wilde's 1895 play of the same name.

159. Lyell offered feedback on "The Hummingbirds," which was retitled "The Wanderers" when it appeared as the last story in *The Golden Apples*. It begins on the day Virgie Rainey's mother dies and ends after her funeral. "The Wanderers" was reprinted in Welty's *Stories, Essays, and Memoir*.

160. Hodding Carter and Ray Sprigle were the two panelists on "What Should We Do About Race Segregation?" broadcast on ABC Radio's *Town Meeting of the Air*, November 9, 1948.

161. In Creekmore's novel *The Welcome*, two men living in a small Mississippi town are in love but unable to be together. One character, Jim, is married to a woman, and the other, Don, is in a relationship somewhat similar to Welty and John Robinson's. Jim's marriage is not happy, but he values the respectability it brings him, and he convinces his wife to become pregnant in exchange for an expensive car, a Lincoln. Harriet Pollack discusses this novel and Welty's relationship with Robinson in chapter 3 of *Eudora Welty's Fiction and Photography*.

162. Welty wrote to *The New Yorker* in response to Wilson's remarks about Southern writers. On January 1, 1949, the magazine printed her letter in its "Department of Amplification" (repr. in Welty, *Occasions*, 225–28).

163. Creekmore's novel *The Welcome* received a mixed review from Warren E. Preece in the November 21, 1948, *New York Times* (BR42). John Woodburn reviewed it somewhat more favorably November 13, 1948, in *Saturday Review*.

164. Lyell enclosed *The Daily Texan*'s preview of Armstrong's appearance, "a four-hour dance," which noted that "tickets for the special white reserved section had been sold out at both selling points, but additional supplies were expected Wednesday morning" ("'Ol' Satchmo' Plays," 8).

165. Later that spring, Lyell enjoyed the troupe's performance in Austin. He wrote Welty that

> it was marvelous here too—never saw her or her group dance any better and everybody was properly bowled over. Liked Cave of the Heart as much as you did—a stage full of rattlesnakes couldn't have horrified or enthralled me more—And how remarkable in other ways Every Soul Is a Circus is—amazing how much such dancing communicates and how beautiful the stage pictures are at all times [. . .]—couldn't have liked it more

> and enjoyed so much the opportunity to tell them so according to your suggestion. [. . .] urged them to keep on touring the South and relieve us from the tired twirling of the pseudo Ballet Russe. For me they proved the third really satisfying evening I've spent in Hogg Auditorium. (April 8, 1949)

166. Stark Young wrote novels set in Mississippi and an essay for the collection *I'll Take My Stand*. He was also a playwright and a prolific drama critic. Lyell saw him occasionally at the home of Young's sister Julia Robertson, who lived in Austin.

167. Welty to Lyell, May 24, 1949, and August 5, 1949.

168. Lyell seems to have sent a Robert Benchley book, perhaps *Chips off the Old Benchley*, to her ship the day she left New York, but it did not arrive in time.

169. The year 1950 was an Anno Santo (Holy Year), a "Year of Jubilee" in which people who visited churches in Rome could receive pardons for past sins.

170. Aswell, fiction editor at *Harper's Bazaar*, had become a friend of Welty's and had recently married another writer, Fritz Peters. Genet was the pen name of Janet Flanner, author of *The New Yorker*'s "Letters from Paris."

171. Mary Mian was one of Diarmuid Russell's clients. Her husband, Aristide Mian, was a French sculptor. A photograph of their home in Meudon is found on page 3 of the *Eudora Welty Newsletter* 31, no. 2 (Summer 2005), illustrating an excerpt from Suzanne Marrs's biography.

172. Robinson's story "The Inspector," published June 1950 in *Harper's Magazine*, was dedicated to Welty.

CHAPTER 3: 1950–1959

1. Willie Morris, *North Toward Home*, 166.

2. Bales, *Conversations with Willie Morris*, 68.

3. *Short Stories*, a revised version of "The Reading and the Writing of Short Stories" that *The Atlantic* had published in February 1949 and March 1949, was published by Harcourt, Brace on January 1, 1950, as a sixty-four-page book "privately printed for the friends of the author and her publishers as a New Year's greeting" (Polk, *Eudora Welty: A Bibliography*, 74).

4. Lyell wrote twenty-four reviews for *The New York Times Book Review* between 1950 and 1962. His first, published January 15, 1950, was a brief, witheringly unfavorable review of Arthur Wormhoudt's *The Demon Lover: A Psychological Approach to Literature* ("Freud and the Writers," BR10).

5. This story has not been identified.

6. "Put Me in the Sky!" was later included in *The Bride of the Innisfallen* as "Circe."

7. Fiction writer Jean Stafford (1915–1979), who had been unhappily married to poet Robert Lowell, married Oliver Jensen in 1950. Jensen was a photographer for *Life* magazine, published by Henry Luce.

8. William Jay (Bill) Smith and Barbara Howe Smith, two of Welty's friends in Italy, were poets.

9. Art historian Bernard Berenson and his wife Mary Smith Costello hosted artists and intellectuals at "I Tatti," their country house and library. Berenson later willed the library to Harvard University.

10. Marrs, *Eudora Welty*, 189.

11. Hermione Gingold and Hermione Baddeley were performing in Noel Coward's *Fallen Angels. Venus Observed* was a blank verse drama by Christopher Fry.

12. Ruth Ford, actor and intellectual, was the sister of writer Charles Henri Ford. William Archibald's play *The Innocents*, based on James's *The Turn of the Screw*, was on Broadway.

13. On the verso of this letter, Welty copies out "the best item" from a recent Beachcomber column, with instructions on where to find his cat Humphrey's hat, boots, and food while he is away.

14. Welty to Lyell, February 28, 1951. Lee's *Clarion-Ledger* (Jackson) column "The Chatterbox" reported on February 18, "Looking attractive was Willia Wright Sessums as she boarded a plane for Mineral Wells, TX, while Dr. Wright and Ann Long and I waved goodbye to her."

15. Marrs, *What There Is to Say*, 26.

16. Gurdjieff was a mystic teacher who had died in 1949. For the spiritual awakening of his disciples, he developed exercises known as the Gurdjieff Movements ("Georgei Ivanovich Gurdjieff").

17. "Kin" originally appeared in *The New Yorker* on November 15, 1952. It was reprinted in Welty's *Bride of the Innisfallen* and *Stories, Essays, and Memoir.*

18. Marrs writes that by this time, Welty "had reached the breaking point in her relationship" with John Robinson (*Eudora Welty*, 217).

19. Carvel Collins, a Harvard professor, was doing research on Faulkner. Welty wrote Diarmuid Russell that Collins, who'd told Welty he'd met Russell at a party, "is down in these parts writing a book on Faulkner, and I saw him in Jackson and now he is here. Yesterday we took a trip down to the bit of road that follows the Mississippi down to the Gulf—Venice, La.—a wonderful country or world it is" (Welty to Russell, August 1951).

20. Jackson College for Negro Teachers, which later became Jackson State University, was celebrating its 75th anniversary. Welty was invited to participate by Ernestine Lipscomb, the college librarian, and Margaret Walker Alexander, the chair of the festival. The letter noted, "Langston Hughes, Sterling Brown, J. Suanders Redding, Arna Bontemps, Gwendolyn Brooks, Owen Dodson, Era Bell Thompson, and Elizabeth Vroman already have accepted invitations to participate, and we are expecting Williard Motley, William Gardner Smith and Frank Yerby.

We should very much like to have one evening devoted to the Negro as a theme in writing, particularly in the South, At this time we would like to have you, Hodding Carter, and William Faulkner as guest participants."

21. Robinson was seeking a job in order to relocate to Italy and be with Enzo Rochiggiani.

22. Alice was a Jackson friend.

23. Porter's essay, in the July 1952 issue of Mademoiselle, was entitled "Reflections on Willa Cather."

24. Lyell's review of Joanna Richardson's biography of Fanny Brawne, John Keats's fiancée, appeared November 9, 1952.

25. Engel was the conductor and musical director of a four-week series of Gilbert and Sullivan operettas (Zolotow, 9). Guests at the party Welty attended included Mississippi-born actor Wyatt Cooper, who would later marry artist, heiress, and designer Gloria Vanderbilt. No information has surfaced on the other guests Welty mentions, presumably all known to Lyell.

26. Illinois governor Adlai Stevenson, defeated in a 1952 landslide by General Dwight Eisenhower, was beloved by many writers and intellectuals. In her letter dated November 11, 1952, Welty enclosed a news clipping reporting votes for Eisenhower and Stevenson in Hinds

County, totaling 11,000 to 10,000. Welty and Lyell's precinct went 3–1 for Eisenhower. In "What Stevenson Started," an invited essay published in the *New Republic* on January 5, 1953, Welty praised Stevenson's "passionate intelligence [. . .] so alight with imagination" (repr. in Welty, *Occasions*, 229–31).

27. Jean-Louis Barrault and his wife Madeleine Renaud directed a French theater company that was performing in New York in November 1952.

28. In the letter, Louis Lyell had told Welty that in order to improve his German he needed to find a suitable young lady friend "with whom I can talk, talk, talk!"

29. Gilbert Harrison purchased *The New Republic* in 1953. Henry Wallace, Senator and from 1940 to 1944 FDR's vice president, became editor of *The New Republic* in 1946, then left to run for president as a Progressive Party candidate in 1948. During that campaign he refused to speak before segregated audiences, which made him even more unpopular with white Southerners.

30. On March 29, 1953, a poem entitled "Forever Young" appeared on page 26 of *The Clarion-Ledger* (Jackson). "This house that I inhabit / Will one day become derelict / Upon the land it clings to / With such tenacious thrills; / For termites of pain and care / Will, surely and inexorably, / Eat away its sills. / But when it does collapse / I, forever young, shall leave it / For a far more lovely one / Not made of hands."

31. Literary critic and University of Washington professor Robert Heilman wrote "The Southern Temper" in *Southern Renascence: Literature of the Modern South* (1953).

32. Welty's nine-year-old niece, Elizabeth, accompanied her aunt on her August trip to New York.

33. The Hungarian writer Eva Boros, a friend of Welty's, was married to photographer Bill Brandt.

34. William Roughead (1870–1952) was a Scottish solicitor who wrote nonfiction on trials and criminals, "true crime" books that Lyell and Welty greatly enjoyed, according to their friend Hunter McKelva Cole.

35. Elizabeth Spencer (1921–2019) was a Mississippi novelist who was a student at Belhaven College when she first met Welty.

36. Walter Pater's *The Renaissance* used the term "hard, gemlike flame" in characterizing intense "moments" of alertness and ecstasy. "How shall we pass most swiftly from point to point, and be present always at the focus where the greatest number of vital forces unite in their purest energy?" Pater wrote. "To burn always with this hard, gemlike flame, to maintain this ecstasy, is success in life."

37. This "authoritis" seems to have persisted through early 1954; Welty wrote to Aswell of being "low and weak in the health—nerves, I'm sure, the wretched nerves! Maybe after the book comes out and all is irrevocable I'll get over it" (Marrs, *Eudora Welty*, 229). Marrs speculates that Welty's somewhat low spirits in 1954 were partly due to her desire not to have to continue living at home (230–31).

38. William Maxwell to Eudora Welty, January 11, 1954, in Marrs, *What There Is to Say*, 58.

39. Louis Lyell took a photo of Frank Lyell, Mary Lou Aswell, and Welty before she sailed for England on June 26, 1954.

40. Welty had written, "Hamish Hamilton [*her London publisher*] is having party tonight and I believe Auden's to be there. Wish you were!" (Welty to Lyell, July 7, 1954).

41. "Going to Naples," originally published July 1954 in *Harper's Bazaar*, was revised and reprinted in *The Bride of the Innisfallen* and in *Stories, Essays, & Memoir*.

42. Shaun Wylie, Lyell's friend from his Princeton days, was teaching at Cambridge.

43. The Pamelas were Pamela Travers and Pamela Redmayne.

44. George Rylands (1902–1999) was a Cambridge professor who, like Forster, lived at Kings College. Rylands lectured in English literature and directed many plays, including the 1945 production of *The Duchess of Malfi* that Lyell described to Welty. Before becoming a Cambridge don, he worked for six months for Leonard and Virginia Woolf's Hogarth Press, which published two books of his poetry.

45. "The Confidential Clerk" is a comic verse play by T. S. Eliot, published in 1954.

46. "Place and Time: The Southern Writer's Inheritance" was published in *The Times Literary Supplement*, September 17, 1954 (repr. in Welty, *Occasions*, 161–69). A revised version was published in 1956 as "Place in Fiction."

47. Lehman Engel composed the music for a live telecast of *Macbeth,* with Maurice Evans as Macbeth and Judith Anderson as Lady Macbeth, on November 28, 1954.

48. Lyell's review of Mordecai Richler's *The Acrobats* appeared January 2, 1955. The Sulzberger family owned *The New York Times.*

49. "Life in the Barn Was Very Good," review of *Charlotte's Web*, by E. B. White. *New York Times Book Review*, October 19, 1952, 49; repr. in Welty, *The Eye of the Story*, 203–6.

50. These characters, some of them renamed, would eventually populate Welty's 1970 novel *Losing Battles*. Welty's essay was "How I Write," *Virginia Quarterly Review* 31 (1955): 240–51.

51. Capers's newspaper column, *Miss Quote*, was moving to the *State-Times*, a new afternoon newspaper. *Time* magazine reported that this new publication, in which many Jackson businesses had invested, was intended "as an answer to the monopoly of the Hederman family's Jackson Clarion-Ledger and Daily News" ("The Press"). The *State-Times* ran from 1954 to 1962.

52. *Paris* was likely the booklet of photographs by Jacques Donvez that Lyell had recommended Welty buy on her last trip abroad.

53. Lyell seems to have taken up residence at a new address, once again rooming in someone's home, as he had done in Princeton, Raleigh, and Washington.

54. The "reader" was probably a graduate student who assisted Lyell with grading, although she seems not to have been assigned to him full-time. As with earlier teaching schedules Lyell had described to Welty, Lyell taught every day of the week but Sunday. His was a very large department at a burgeoning university; he taught mostly general education courses and was never part of the graduate program, but his classes influenced some talented undergraduates, such as Willie Morris.

55. In the 1954 French film *The Sheep Has Five Legs*, Fernandel played five quintuplets, one of whom writes an advice column for lonely readers.

56. In the 1954 western *Johnny Guitar*, Crawford played a tough saloonkeeper. In *Female on the Beach* (1955), she played a widow who fends off a younger man's plot to marry and then murder her.

57. Playwrights Jerome Chodorov and Joseph Fields had entitled their play *The Prize in the Crackerjack Box* (Kreyling 179). Earlier that year, they had visited Jackson, a much larger town than her fictional Clay, Mississippi, and Welty wrote Russell, "They are looking for local color—don't know where that is" (February 1955, qtd. in Kreyling, 173).

58. Welty to Maxwell, December 21, 1955, in Marrs, *What There Is to Say*, 90.

59. David Wayne had starred in the 1954 Broadway production of *Teahouse of the August Moon.*

60. The 1955 film *The Big Knife* was based on Clifford Odets's 1949 play of the same name.

61. Lyell had written Welty that Stark Young, a longtime theater critic, had sent Brooks Atkinson's review to his sister Julia, who lived in Austin. Stark Young had written across the top of the clipping, "Very amiable. I'll ask Brooks what he really thought" (Lyell to Welty, February 23, 1956).

62. *Life* published nine photographs in its story "The Trials of Uncle Daniel" (111–16). A Faulkner essay, "Letter to the North," appeared in the same issue, in which he expressed his opposition both to segregation and to "forced integration." He argued that in the South, most whites and Blacks "prefer peace to equality," and that much racism and "communal race tension" existed outside the South. Faulkner warned the NAACP to "go slow now" lest the world begin to give white Southerners "automatic sympathy for the underdog simply because he is under." He added, "The rest of the United States knows next to nothing about the South" (51–52). A benign but simplistic interpretation of the region was then on display in the Broadway production of *Ponder Heart* and illustrated in the *Life* magazine photographs, portraying the characters as comically childlike country folk.

63. Ruth Gordon played Dolly Gallagher Levi in Thornton Wilder's *The Matchmaker*. Alfred Lunt and Lynn Fontanne starred in *The Great Sebastians: A Melodramatic Comedy*. Eugene O'Neill's *The Iceman Cometh* was in a production starring Jason Robards. Chekhov's *Uncle Vanya*, in translation by Stark Young, was playing off Broadway. Beckett's *Waiting for Godot* was having its US premiere, with Bert Lahr (Cowardly Lion of *Wizard of Oz*) playing Estragon.

64. At Vassar, Welty read her soon-to-be-published essay "Place in Fiction." William Rose published scholarship on British modernists and taught literature and writing classes at Vassar.

65. The envelope of her May 14 letter reads, "Got Lady DDC. Am exterminated." Welty seems to have passed on something from Lyell to S. J. Perelman. Three months later, Perelman published an essay, "Cuckoos Nesting," that may have been inspired by this material. In Perelman's essay, the narrator reads an account of Lady Diana Cooper avoiding middle-class, boorish picnic sites by setting up a feast in an unoccupied chateau. The narrator describes driving out to check on his house in Pennsylvania and discovering a similar invasion by wealthy trespassers who have set up a party there ("Cuckoos Nesting," 28–31).

66. Welty to Maxwell, July 1956, in Marrs, *What There Is to Say*, 96–97.

67. The recording of the 1956 musical *My Fair Lady*, adapted from George Bernard Shaw's *Pygmalion*, was a best-selling album that year.

68. Welty seems to have enclosed a letter from the Guggenheim Foundation inviting fellows to suggest applicants "for a prime vintage."

69. Alun Jones, a young Welsh scholar who had made friends with Welty when he was at the Cambridge summer institute with her, had been offered a position at the university, but this had not worked out. Welty had recommended him to Lyell after Lyell said he wished for more colleagues with cosmopolitan outlooks. An offer was made, but apparently it came to Jones while he was on a long spring break, and when he did not respond for several weeks, the department rescinded the offer. Disappointed and puzzled, Lyell wrote Welty that he did not wish to ask the chair of the hiring committee about what happened, for fear of giving offense. This incident further suggests that Lyell, now in his ninth year at the University of Texas, remained on the periphery of the English Department.

70. John Foster Dulles, secretary of state, underwent emergency surgery for a perforated colon on November 3, 1956, amidst international crisis, three days before the presidential

election. A revolution in Hungary (the Hungarian Uprising) had begun on October 23, 1956. Although the Eisenhower administration had voiced support for those resisting communism in other countries, the US did not intervene when Soviet forces invaded Hungary on November 1 and crushed the uprising on November 4. Meanwhile, in Egypt, President Nasser had announced his country's intention to purchase and control the French- and British-owned Suez Canal. In response, Israeli forces attacked bases in Egypt on October 29, and French and British forces followed suit on October 31. Back in the US, Eisenhower won reelection on November 6 in a landslide.

71. Katherine Anne Porter's article on writing *Noon Wine* (1937) is "'Noon Wine': The Sources."

72. Garnett's book *The Flowers of the Forest* included photographs of Lytton Strachey, Dora Carrington, and Vanessa Bell.

73. Welty was surely disappointed that Adlai Stevenson was trounced for the second time, earlier in November. She was also concerned for her Hungarian friend Eva Boros, who lived in England. Soviet troops crushed the Hungarian uprising and killed thousands of Hungarian citizens; many more fled the country. England's standing as a global power was also taking a beating after Great Britain and France attacked Egyptian bases to retain control of the Suez Canal. The US had not been informed, and Eisenhower condemned the action. Facing opposition at home and pressure from the UN, the British agreed to a ceasefire on November 6. Prime Minister Anthony Eden resigned two months later.

74. The Jackson Little Theatre produced *The Ponder Heart* in October 1956.

75. J. B. Ackerly's memoir *My Dog Tulip* included details of his dog's urination and defecation and accounts of Ackerly's attempts to satisfy his pet's sexual urges by arranging encounters with male dogs.

76. "A Sweet Devouring." *Mademoiselle*, December 1957. Repr. in Welty, *The Eye of the Story*, 279–85.

77. The title of a *New York Times* article probably caught Welty's attention: "Bayonets of Troops Bring School Order" (Fowle, 1).

78. *The Ordeal of Gilbert Penfield* is a 1957 novel by Evelyn Waugh.

79. Welty feared Lyell might have the Asian flu.

80. A few years later, Capers published a humorous account of this visit, in which Welty was treated like royalty and Capers cast in the role of devoted servant. Marrs summarizes Capers's description in *Eudora Welty*, 269.

81. Reynolds Price's book was published in 1963 as *The Names and Faces of Heroes.*

82. Actress Madge Evans (1909–1981) was married to the playwright Sidney Kingsley (1906–1995).

83. Welty's review of *The Most of S. J. Perelman* appeared October 12, 1958, in *The New York Times Book Review* ("All Is Grist for His Mill"); her review of Woolf's *Granite and Rainbow* was published on September 21, 1958. Both reviews were reprinted in Welty, *The Eye of the Story* (227–35 and 190–92). Mary Mian's 1958 novel was entitled *Young Men See Visions.*

84. Letter is undated, but October 18, 1958, was the date of the Schwarzkopf concert that Lyell mentions he just attended.

85. *The $64,000 Question* was a TV game show.

86. Welty read at the Library of Congress on November 3, 1958, then went to Bryn Mawr on a Lucy Donnell Fellowship.

87. Welty encloses a clipping about her reading at the Library of Congress, with photo by Frank Hains.

88. Marcella Comès (1905–2000), a portrait painter, had been a friend of Lyell's when he was stationed in Washington after the war; in 1946 she painted a portrait of Welty, which hangs in the Welty House. Welty's theater tickets were apparently for *The Visit*, *Touch of the Poet*, *The Pleasure of His Company*, *The World of Suzie Wong*, and *Goldilocks*. Engel would be conducting the premiere of his opera *The Soldier*, based on a story by Roald Dahl, as well as his composition "Malady of Love." *Time* magazine noted that in the same week, Engel also conducted *Goldilocks* and rehearsals for Bernstein's *Wonderful Town*, making him "one of the nation's busiest and most versatile men-about-music" ("Man About Music").

89. Mackie Jarrell was a colleague of Lyell's and ex-wife of poet Randall Jarrell.

90. Edward Aswell, former husband of Mary Lou Aswell, died in November 1958. Among the authors he edited were Thomas Wolfe and Richard Wright.

91. Edward Mulhare and Sally Ann Howes had replaced Rex Harrison and Julie Andrews in the *My Fair Lady* cast.

CHAPTER 4: 1959–1977

1. Welty to Lyell, August 30, 1963.

2. In 1973 when Alice Walker asked Welty if she knew any Black people well, Welty spoke of "a schoolteacher who helped me on weekends to nurse my mother through a long illness—she was beyond a nurse, she was a friend and still is, we keep in regular touch" (Prenshaw, *Conversations*, 137).

3. Marrs, *Eudora Welty*, 424.

4. Welty to Lyell, January 17, 1969.

5. To William Maxwell, Welty wrote, "Our yard man, who was old when Walter was a little boy, and who hasn't worked for us for years & years, paid us a call in his Chesterfield overcoat on that Sunday morning—had walked miles—'I just wanted to pay a call to say I hoped what I heard on the radio wasn't true'" (Marrs, *What There Is to Say*, 135).

6. Williams's *Cat on a Hot Tin Roof* treats subjects that some Jackson theatergoers likely did not believe should be discussed in public. In the play, a wealthy Southern planter has been treated at the Ochsner clinic (where Welty's late brother Walter was treated) and is told he is healthy, but his family is told he's terminally ill. Son Brick is an alcoholic who repressed his desire for his friend Skipper, who committed suicide shortly after expressing his attraction to Brick. Characters also discuss Brick and Maggie's now-sexless marriage. Welty's brief essay praised Williams for "his driving wish to show us something about ourselves. [. . .] The brutality of his characters [. . .] must be a cloak to hide the truth from themselves and one another." First printed in the Little Theatre program notes, then in *The Clarion-Ledger*, the 1959 essay also appears in Welty, *Occasions*, 106–7.

7. Ruth Ford played Temple Drake in *Requiem for A Nun*, a play based on Faulkner's novel that Ford and Faulkner adapted. Tynan wrote a Menckenesquely scornful review of the play in *The New Yorker* (Review, 82–87).

8. Welty to Lyell, July 15, 1959; September 19, 1959; September 20, 1959.

9. Una Merkel (1903–1986), who had played Edna Earle in the Broadway production of *The Ponder Heart*, was starring in the musical *Take Me Along*, an adaptation of Eugene O'Neill's *Ah, Wilderness.* Lehman Engel wrote vocal arrangements and was conductor and musical director.

10. Nancy Spain (1917–1964) wrote for *Daily Express* and other British publications, including *She* magazine, published by Spain's partner Joan Laurie. Spain was also a well-known radio personality and the author of detective novels.

11. Lyell reviewed Louise Cowan's *The Fugitive Group: A Literary History* in the February 14, 1960, edition of *The New York Times* ("Practical Purpose," BR5).

12. Osbert Lancaster, a cartoonist for the *Daily Express*, was also an architectural historian, stage designer, and illustrator.

13. The book Welty refers to is probably O'Connor's 1960 novel, *The Violent Bear It Away*.

14. Young had suffered a stroke in 1959 (Langdale).

15. Welty to Lyell, April 23, 1960.

16. Welty to Aswell, August 27, 1960 (Marrs, *Eudora Welty*, 281).

17. Samuel Richardson (1689–1761) was an eighteenth-century novelist.

18. Welty's "over-long" story was probably one she worked on for years but never published, called "The Last of the Figs" and, in other versions, "Nicotiana." It may reflect some of the difficulties Welty experienced with the household helpers and caregivers she relied on during her mother's illness. For more on this story, see Pollack, *Eudora Welty's Fiction and Photography*, 221–40.

19. *The Atlantic* did reject Welty's essay, as Welty had predicted, so Russell sent it to *Texas Quarterly*, which published it (*Texas Quarterly* 4 [1961]: 246–56). It is reprinted in Welty, *The Eye of the Story* as "Henry Green: Novelist of the Imagination," 14–29.

20. Lyell's father, Garland Lyell, was hospitalized for heart surgery.

21. Welty to Lyell, February 14, 1961.

22. The Disney interpretation of *Mary Poppins* would appear in 1964. "Little Mary" may have been the 1959 Off-Broadway hit musical *Little Mary Sunshine*. Ingmar Bergman's *Virgin Spring* was released in 1960, as was *Breathless* by Jean-Luc Godard.

23. Garland Lyell was in a nursing home when he passed away six weeks later, June 29, 1961. Hattibel Wilkinson Hallam, Clarena Lyell's sister-in-law, had been ill as well; she died the following year.

24. As the second Secretary-General of the United Nations, Hammarskjöld was traveling to the Congo to help negotiate a ceasefire there when his plane crashed, a circumstance that many have speculated was not an accident.

25. Marrs reports that during the New York portion of this trip, Welty and her Welsh friend Alun Jones "had long conversations about the southern resistance to integration—Eudora branded Jackson 'benighted'" (*Eudora Welty*, 286). At the same time, Welty was not eager to discuss the topic with most people, especially in front of strangers; this may partly explain why she was so discomfited when a Freedom Rider repeatedly told her story during meals at Yaddo.

26. Edward Welty suffered from clinical depression.

27. Welty's review of Eric Johannesson's *The World of Isak Dinesen* ran in *The New York Times Book Review* in December 1961.

28. Eddie Mae Polk was a longtime housekeeper for the Welty family. At Welty's funeral in 2001, she served as an honorary pallbearer, along with four other women who were Welty's caregivers in her final years. Two other longtime, important caregivers for Chestina Welty, Virgie and Carrie, are mentioned in Welty's letters to Lyell, but have not been further identified.

29. Maxwell to Welty, October 2, 1962, in Marrs, *What There Is to Say*, 155.

30. Ralph McGill, editor of *The Atlanta Constitution*, had faced hate mail and violence for his antisegregationist stance. He received death threats and bombs in his mailbox; crosses were burned on his lawn and shots fired into his house.

31. After the United States' unsuccessful attempt to overthrow Fidel Castro's government in Cuba that summer, US intelligence sighted Soviet nuclear missiles in Cuba. The US asserted that such weapons were an act of aggression against the US, and the Soviet Union stated that the US Navy was committing an "act of aggression" by preventing missiles from being delivered to Cuba. On October 28, 1962, the immediate threat of war was dispelled when Khrushchev announced that missiles would be removed from Cuba.

32. Welty notes that the Meridian bus station had different jukeboxes for white and Black passengers. In bus stations in the South, drinking fountains, seating areas, and restrooms were segregated, with some stations providing no facilities for Black passengers. To challenge this practice, the Freedom Riders had crossed the color line in bus stations where their bus stopped, and were often met with violence and/or arrests. Discrimination in public accommodations was eventually prohibited by the 1964 Civil Rights Act.

33. Marrs, *Eudora Welty*, 295.

34. Welty to Aswell, March 9, 1963, in Marrs, *Eudora Welty*, 297.

35. Welty lectured at the University of Texas on May 13, 1963 ("Eudora Welty to Talk Monday"). She read "Why I Live at the P.O." and "Words into Fiction" (Brewer).

36. Warfield, 151–52.

37. For a discussion of the kerfuffle over canceled interview plans, see Marrs, *Eudora Welty*, 304–5.

38. Marrs, *Eudora Welty*, 306.

39. Welty, *Stories, Essays, and Memoir*, 78.

40. In "Paree," part of the musical *At Home Abroad* that Lyell saw in 1936, Lillie performs as a French chanteuse who loves Paris so much that she "could kiss Montparnasse, kiss your Right Bank, your Left Bank [. . .]."

41. Welty and her like-minded friends, even from their more protected vantage points, knew that their attendance at interracial gatherings might be surveilled. They suspected that a law enforcement officer recorded the license plates of white visitors to Tougaloo, a Black college near Jackson where Welty sometimes attended events (Marrs, *Eudora Welty*, 273).

42. Welty had met English journalist Nancy Spain during her travels. Lyell may have gotten a copy of *The Nancy Spain Colour Cookery Book*, published in 1963 in London, during his summer abroad.

43. Howard Zinn, "Mississippi 'Chronology,' 1963–1964."

44. Welty to Aswell, April 1964, in Marrs, *Eudora Welty*, 309.

45. Civil rights organizers had announced their plans for Freedom Summer, a voter registration campaign aided by hundreds of young volunteers who would spend the summer in Mississippi. The state's governor and other lawmakers responded with new measures against picketing or leafleting and gave the police broader authority to intervene in these efforts (Zinn).

46. Mississippi-born Willie Morris was the editor of *Harper's Magazine*. Morris had been Frank Lyell's student at the University of Texas while editing the student newspaper, which administrators criticized for arguing that the university should admit nonwhite students.

47. *Harper's Magazine* ultimately passed on Welty's "Must the Novelist Crusade?" It was accepted by *The Atlantic Monthly* and published in October 1965. "Must the Novelist Crusade?" was reprinted in Welty, *Stories, Essays, and Memoir*, 803–14.

48. Welty, *Stories, Essays, and Memoir*, 809, 811, 813.

49. Kreyling, 203.

50. Welty's niece Elizabeth was a University of Mississippi student.

51. In New Orleans in 1951, Welty and Faulkner scholar Carvel Collins took a car ride together, an experience that inspired her story "No Place for You, My Love."

52. The United States was expanding its military presence in Vietnam, sending ground troops to augment the bombing it had been carrying out. The Johnson administration continued its attempts to defeat the North Vietnamese amid increasing opposition and protests in the US.

53. *Stories, Essays, and Memoir*, 806.

54. Welty to William Maxwell, December 2, 1965, in Marrs, *What There Is to Say*, 184.

55. Monroe Wheeler was director of exhibitions and publications at the Museum of Modern Art.

56. Painter Loren MacIver (1909–1988) had an exhibition in 1966 at the Pierre Matisse Gallery in New York, "Paintings, Pastels, and Drawings."

57. To Katherine Anne Porter, Welty described her appearance in Alabama alongside her friend Caroline Gordon (Tate), who took the train with Welty back to the Northeast. "The first thing Caroline said to me as we gained our roomettes was: 'I hate every word you've ever written and I can't *stand* you!' And I thankfully replied, 'The Same!'" (Marrs, *Eudora Welty*, 326).

58. Creekmore and Welty had many other mutual friends, including the poets William Jay Smith and Barbara Howes, with whom Welty traveled during her 1949–1950 sojourn in Europe. Both poets wrote verse in honor of Creekmore.

59. Marrs, *Eudora Welty*, 327.

60. For a detailed description of the Houston banquet reading, see Welty's letter to William Maxwell (Marrs, *What There Is to Say*, 208).

61. Welty to Lyell, February 18, 1967. This letter is filed at MDAH with an enclosure, an undated letter from Seta Sancton Alexander.

62. Marrs, *Eudora Welty*, 331.

63. Marrs, *Eudora Welty*, 333.

64. North Vietnam was attacking cities, towns, and military bases in South Vietnam during the Tet Lunar New Year, a campaign known as the Tet Offensive. With over 485,000 US soldiers now stationed in Vietnam, American opposition to the war had intensified in recent months.

65. Maxwell wrote Welty that her story "The Optimist's Daughter" had been intended to run the week of Mardi Gras, when some of the story takes place, but there was not room for it until March (Marrs, *What There Is to Say*, 252). The story appeared in *The New Yorker* on March 15, 1969. Revised and published as novella, it was reprinted in Welty, *Complete Novels*.

66. Elizabeth Welty worked at Mississippi Department of Archives and History, with Charlotte Capers as director.

67. Richard Nixon won the 1968 presidential election, to Welty's dismay.

68. Marrs, *Eudora Welty*, 329–30.

69. Apollo XI's lunar module had landed July 20, 1969. Neil Armstrong's first steps on the moon's surface were broadcast worldwide July 21, 2:56 a.m. for BBC viewers.

70. A total eclipse was visible along much of the East Coast of the US on March 7, 1970. A partial eclipse was visible over most of North America, except areas shrouded in clouds, as Jackson was.

71. Aycock is a character in *Losing Battles*. In the novel, Jack Renfro has been serving time in Parchman Penitentiary for his part in a fight in Curly Stovall's store.

72. *Losing Battles* was to be published April 13, 1970, Welty's sixty-first birthday. Lyell had received an advance copy.

73. This group of friends, "The Basic Eight," included Welty, Lyell, Charlotte Capers, Bill and Ann Morrison, Jimmie Wooldridge, and Major White. The eighth member had been the late Hubert Creekmore (Marrs, *Eudora Welty*, 214–15).

74. The book of essays Welty mentions is *The Collected Essays and Occasional Writings of Katherine Anne Porter*, Delacorte, 1970. Welty enclosed the *New York Times* review she described, with the headline "Katherine Anne Porter Is 79 and Sovereign."

75. Welty may have sent Lyell *A Certain World: A Commonplace Book* (Viking, 1970). Auden's anthology of passages by other writers, with his brief commentaries on each, was "a sort of autobiography," Auden wrote (vii). Welty missed seeing "Sonnet XXI" of Auden's 1938 "Sonnets from China," dedicated to E. M. Forster. It begins "Though Italy and King's are far away, / And Truth a subject only bombs discuss, / Our ears unfriendly, still you speak to us / Insisting that the inner life can pay." For more on Forster's influence on Auden, see Stuart Christie's "Disorientations: Canon Without Context in Auden's 'Sonnets from China.'"

76. *A Season of Dreams* was first produced at the New Stage Theater in May 1968. ETV broadcast this play on November 19, 1970.

77. Reynolds Price, *Permanent Errors*, Atheneum, 1970.

78. Maeve Brennan (1917–1993) was an Irish-born fiction writer whose works appeared in *The New Yorker*.

79. Jack Storey's play *Home* had come to Broadway, with Ralph Richardson and John Gielgud in the cast.

80. Apollo 14 had reentered the Earth's atmosphere and splashed down successfully in the Pacific Ocean on February 9, 1971. On the same day, a 6.6 magnitude earthquake struck Los Angeles.

81. Welty's review of *The Saddest Story: A Biography of Ford Madox Ford* was originally published in *The New York Times Book Review*, May 2, 1971; repr. in Welty, *The Eye of the Story*, 241–50.

82. The "little play" Welty mentions is "Bye-Bye, Brevoort." For more on its performance history, see Gordon.

83. Mary Lou Aswell's adult son Duncan had had a nervous breakdown the previous year. For months his family was unable to locate him, but he later recovered and reconnected with his mother (Marrs, *Eudora Welty*, 355, 361–64).

84. The McNay Art Institute in San Antonio had mounted an exhibition of Sims's art entitled "Man and Magic."

85. The book Welty mentions is *Every Other Inch a Lady* by Beatrice Lillie (Doubleday, 1972). The photograph Welty describes appears in the insert before page 289. The title page credits Lillie as author, "Aided and Abetted by John Philip/Written With James Brough."

86. Diarmuid Russell was dying from cancer. When Elizabeth Bowen died earlier in 1973, Welty had not been aware that she was ill. Welty's friend Dolly Wells died alone at her home in Jackson, a few days after Welty had been there for a drink (Marrs, *Eudora Welty*, 391).

87. Tennessee Williams had spoken at the University of Texas on November 1, 1973 ("Tennessee Williams," 45). In 1969, he was awarded the Gold Medal for Drama by the American Academy of Arts and Letters. After Lillian Hellman presented the award, Williams did not acknowledge her praise, but announced he was "essentially a humorist" and would tell the audience "something that makes you laugh." He recounted a phone conversation between Maureen Stapleton and another woman, who reported to Stapleton that a woman they knew who was a lesbian was marrying a gay man. Stapleton asked the caller to invite Williams to the wedding, since he would say the couple were "just plain folks" ("American Academy"). This was the entirety of his speech—as Welty put it, "his response in full."

88. The University of Texas's president Stephen H. Spurr had been fired by the chancellor. No cause was given, but a *New York Times* article suggested Spurr had not shown adequate favoritism to a law school applicant recommended by a board member (Reinhold, 75).

89. Theora Hamblett (1875–1977) was a painter from Oxford, Mississippi.

90. Welty was interviewed by Jim Hartz for the Today Show's bicentennial special on the state of Mississippi. A year later, she told an interviewer,

> I was so disappointed in their idea of coverage. It was just that they had such a chance to find out things for the rest of the country about Mississippi. I told Mr. Hartz and some of the others that in one or two sentences I, for instance, could give them a picture of the great amount of work in the arts that's been going on here—writing—painting—music—and they said, "Well, we don't have time to go into anything. We've got to get to Arkansas." I really was so cross, because everybody here was trying and ready to help them with things: show them the backgrounds and give information. (Prenshaw, *Conversations*, 184)

91. John Lehmann's *Virginia Woolf and Her World* was published by Harcourt Brace Jovanovich in 1975.

92. This was Welty's second trip to the Santa Barbara Writers Conference, where she spent much of her time with Kenneth Millar and his wife Margaret. Her next publication, *The Eye of the Story*, was dedicated to him.

93. The phrase "ça va sans dire" is French for "that goes without saying."

94. Alex Haley's 1976 novel *Roots: The Saga of an American Family* describes generations of his family that he traced back to Africa where his ancestor was kidnapped and enslaved. *Roots* was made into a miniseries that aired for eight nights in January 1977.

95. John Slocum was originally the junior member of the Russell & Volkening literary agency. He later served as an aide to Mayor Fiorella LaGuardia and became a diplomat, philanthropist, and prominent Republican donor.

96. *Moments of Being* is a collection of autobiographical essays by Virginia Woolf, found by her nephew/biographer in 1972 and published in 1976.

97. Welty to Aswell, July 19, 1977. Marrs, E*udora Welty*, 428.

98. Welty to Millar, August 7, 1977. Marrs and Nolan, *Meanwhile There Are Letters*, 348.

99. Welty, *Complete Novels*, 803.

BIBLIOGRAPHY

Abadie, Ann J., and Lisa Speer. "Ruth Ford." In *Mississippi Encyclopedia*. Last updated April 30, 2018. http://mississippiencyclopedia.org/entries/ruth-ford/.

Adams, Frank. "B-25 Crashes in Fog." *New York Times*, July 29, 1945.

Agner, Jacob. "Welty's Moonlighting Detective." In Pollack, *New Essays on Eudora Welty, Class, and Race*.

Allard, Mike. "World War II Prisoner of War Camps." In *Mississippi Encyclopedia*. Last updated February 6, 2024. http://mississippiencyclopedia.org/entries/world-war-ii-prisoner-of-war-camps/.

"American Academy of Arts and Letters Ceremonial Awards." May 21, 1969. WNYC: New York Public Radio Archive Collections. https://www.wnyc.org/story/the-american-academy-of-arts-and-letters-ceremonial-awards/.

Arrington, Melvin S., Jr. "Herschel Brickell." In *Mississippi Encyclopedia*. Last updated April 13, 2018. https://mississippiencyclopedia.org/entries/herschel-brickell/.

Atkinson, Brooks. "Theater: Comedy of Rural Manners: Music Box Welcomes 'The Ponder Heart.'" *New York Times*, February 17, 1956.

Auden, W. H. *A Certain World: A Commonplace Book*. Viking, 1970.

Bales, Jack, ed. *Conversations with Willie Morris*. University Press of Mississippi, 2000.

Barilleaux, Rene Paul, ed. *Passionate Observer: Eudora Welty Among Artists of the Thirties*. Mississippi Museum of Art, 2002.

Beaton, Cecil. *The Book of Beauty*. Duckworth, 1930.

Black, Patti Carr. *Art in Mississippi, 1720–1980*. University Press of Mississippi, 1998.

Black, Patti Carr. "At Home in Jackson." In Barilleaux, *Passionate Observer*.

Black, Patti Carr. "Comic Energy: Eudora Welty's Young Art." In *Early Escapades*, by Eudora Welty. University Press of Mississippi, 2005.

"Books to Be Published During the Autumn Months." *New York Times*, September 20, 1936.

Bowen, Elizabeth. "Book Shelf." Review of *Delta Wedding*, by Eudora Welty. *Tatler and Bystander*, August 6, 1947.

Brewer, Anita. "Act of Vision Writer Need!" *Austin-American Statesman*, May 14, 1963.

Capers, Charlotte. *The Capers Papers*. With foreword by Eudora Welty. University Press of Mississippi, 1982.

Carb, David. "Seen on the Stage." *Vogue*, February 15, 1933.

Carcasson, Martin. "Herbert Hoover and the Presidential Campaign of 1932: The Failure of Apologia." *Presidential Studies Quarterly* 28, no. 2 (spring 1998): 349–65. Gale Academic OneFile.

Chamberlain, Neville. *In Search of Peace: Speeches, 1937–1938*. National Book Association, 1939.

Chartier, Courtney. "Charles Henri Ford." In *Mississippi Encyclopedia*. Last updated February 19, 2024. https://mississippiencyclopedia.org/entries/charles-henri-ford/.

Christie, Stuart. "Disorientations: Canon Without Context in Auden's 'Sonnets from China.'" *PMLA* 120, no. 5 (2005): 1576–87. https://www.jstor.org/stable/25486269.

Churchill, Winston. *Winston S. Churchill: His Complete Speeches, 1897–1963*. Vol. 7. Chelsea House Publishers, 1974.

Cole, Hunter McKelva. "Eudora on Stephen Tennant: A Personal Conversation." *Eudora Welty Newsletter* 29, no. 2 (2005): 10–12.

Cole, Hunter McKelva. "Frank Lyell: Eudora Welty's Bachelor of the Arts," *China Grove* no. 4 (2016): 52–75. Rpt in *Eudora Welty Review* 14 (2022): 5–20.

Cole, Hunter McKelva. Telephone interview by the author. October 29, 2021.

Collis, Maurice. *The Land of the Great Image*. Faber & Faber, 1943.

Creekmore, Hubert. *The Fingers of Night*. Appleton-Century, 1946.

Creekmore, Hubert. *The Long Reprieve and Other Poems of New Caledonia*. New Directions Press, 1946.

Creekmore, Hubert. *The Welcome*. Appleton-Century, 1948.

Crews, Elizabeth. "'The Still-Existing Parts of Life,' Part I: The Early Correspondence of Eudora Welty and Mary Louise Aswell." *Eudora Welty Review* 11 (2019): 33–46. https://www.jstor.org/stable/48590839.

"Dean Wicks to Give Sermon in Chapel Services Tomorrow." *Daily Princetonian*, January 21, 1933.

De Casseres, Benjamin. "March of Events." *San Francisco Examiner*, November 19, 1942.

Dolson, Hildegarde. *The Husband Who Ran Away*. Random House, 1948.

Dolson, Hildegarde. *We Shook the Family Tree*. Random House, 1946.

Donvez, Jacques. *Paris*. Panoramas, 1951.

Downes, Olin. "Stowkowski Brings Color and Contrast to a Program of Rimsky-Korsakoff, Stravinsky and Sibelius." *New York Times*, April 12, 1933.

Eddington, Arthur. *The Nature of the Physical World*. Macmillan, 1929.

"Eddington Sees Gains in Science." *New York Times*, April 29, 1934.

Eichelberger, Julia. "Correspondence Calendar, 1931–1977: Letters Between Welty and Frank Lyell." *Eudora Welty Review* 13 (2021): 7–165.

Eichelberger, Julia. "Teaching the Art of Welty's Letters." In *Teaching the Works of Eudora Welty: Twenty-First-Century Approaches*, edited by Mae Miller Claxton and Julia Eichelberger. University Press of Mississippi, 2018.

Eichelberger, Julia, ed. *Tell About Night Flowers: Eudora Welty's Gardening Letters, 1940–1949*. University Press of Mississippi, 2013.

"Ekstasis." *Martha Graham at the Library of Congress: Articles and Essays*. https://www.loc.gov/collections/martha-graham/articles-and-essays/

Engel, Lehman. *This Bright Day: An Autobiography*. Macmillan, 1974.

Eudora Welty House Accession Register: Books. Eudora Welty House, August 12, 2011.

"Eudora Welty's House: A Conversation with Charlotte Capers, 1987." *Eudora Welty Review* 16 (2024): 43–81. https://dx.doi.org/10.1353/ewr.2024.a932404.

Faulkner, William. "Letter to the North." *Life*, March 5, 1956.

Foff, Arthur. *Glorious in Another Day*. Lippincott, 1947.

Fowle, Farnsworth. "Bayonets of Troops Bring School Order." *New York Times*, September 26, 1957.

Fuller, Stephen. *Eudora Welty and Surrealism*. University Press of Mississippi, 2012.

Fuller-Seeley, Kathryn H. *Jack Benny and the Golden Age of American Radio Comedy*. University of California Press, 2017. https://doi.org/10.1525/9780520967946.

"General Tire Revue, September 28, 1934." *Jack Benny Single Episodes 1934–1935*. Old Time Radio Researchers Group. The Internet Archive, December 30, 2019. https://archive.org/details/OTRR_Jack_Benny_Singles_1934-1935.

"Georgei Ivanovitch Gurdjieff." In *Religious Leaders of America*. Gale, 1999. *Gale In Context: Biography*. Accessed May 23, 2024. link.gale.com/apps/doc/K1627500473/BIC?u=cofc_main&sid=bookmark-BIC&xid=6c7153fc.

Giles, Paul. *Atlantic Republic: The American Tradition in English Literature*. Oxford University Press, 2006.

"Glee Club to Hold Rehearsal Tonight." *Daily Princetonian*, March 28, 1933.

Gordon, Leslie H., "Eudora Welty's Theatrical Sketches of 1948: Summer Diversion or Lost Potential? *Bye-Bye Brevoort* and Other Sketches." Master's thesis, Georgia State University, 2010.

Hartston, William. "Beachcomber: The World's Oldest Newspaper Columnist Is 100 Years Old Today." *Daily Express* (UK edition), August 2, 2017. https://www.express.co.uk/news/history/836022/beachcomber-column-turns-100-years-old.

Heilman, Robert. "The Southern Temper." In *Southern Renascence: Literature of the Modern South*, edited by Louis D. Rubin. Johns Hopkins Press, 1953.

Howard, John. *Concentration Camps on the Home Front: Japanese Americans in the House of Jim Crow*. University of Chicago Press, 2008.

"Interview with Emily White Stevens Maclachlan Ring." University of Florida Campus (General) Oral History Collection. November 3, 1977. https://ufdc.ufl.edu/UF00005945/00001.

Jewell, Edward Alden. "Art: Diverse Shows." *New York Times*, January 14, 1945.

Kreyling, Michael. *Author and Agent*. Farrar, Straus and Giroux, 1991.

Lampton, Luke. "Louis J. Lyell, 1925–2023: A Tribute to a Gentle Giant of Mississippi." *Hinds County Gazette*, April 7, 2023.

Langdale, Jay. "Stark Young." In *Mississippi Encyclopedia*. Last updated October 11, 2019. https://mississippiencyclopedia.org/entries/stark-young/.

Lear, Edward. *A Book of Limericks*. Little, Brown, 1888.

Lehman, John. *Virginia Woolf and Her World*, Harcourt Brace Jovanovich, 1975.

Lillie, Beatrice. *Every Other Inch a Lady*. Doubleday, 1972.

Lindamood, Peter. "I Cover the Cover." *View* 5, no. 1 (March 1945): 3. Repr. in *Tout Fait* 1, no. 2 (May 2000). https://www.toutfait.com/issues/issue_2/Interviews/pop_cover.html.

Lyell, Frank. "An Expatriate's Search for Truth." Review of *The Acrobats*, by Mordecai Richler. *New York Times Book Review*, January 2, 1955.

Lyell, Frank. "Freud and the Writers." Review of *The Demon Lover*, by Arthur Wormhoudt. *New York Times Book Review*. January 15, 1950.

Lyell, Frank. "Keats' One Enduring Passion." Review of *Fanny Brawne: A Biography*, by Joanna Richardson. *New York Times Book Review*. November 9, 1952.

Lyell, Frank. Letters to Eudora Welty. Eudora Welty Collection, Mississippi Department of Archives and History.

Lyell, Frank. *The Novels of John Galt*. Princeton University Press, 1942.

Lyell, Frank. "The Practical Purpose Was to Woo the Muse Toward Nashville." Review of *The Fugitive Group: A Literary History*, by Louise Cowan. *New York Times Book Review*. February 14, 1960.

"Man About Music." *Time*, December 8, 1959. https://time.com/archive/6802153/music-man-about-music/.

Marrs, Suzanne. *Eudora Welty: A Biography*. Harcourt, 2005.

Marrs, Suzanne. "Eudora Welty's Enduring Images: Photography and Fiction." In Barilleaux, *Passionate Observer*.

Marrs, Suzanne. *The Welty Collection: A Guide to the Eudora Welty Manuscripts and Documents at the Mississippi Department of Archives and History*. University Press of Mississippi, 1988.

Marrs, Suzanne. "Welty, Race, and the Patterns of a Life." In *Eudora Welty, Whiteness, and Race*, edited by Harriet Pollack. University of Georgia Press, 2013.

Marrs, Suzanne, ed. *What There Is to Say We Have Said: The Correspondence of Eudora Welty and William Maxwell*. Houghton Mifflin Harcourt, 2011.

Marrs, Suzanne, and Tom Nolan, eds. *Meanwhile There Are Letters: The Correspondence of Eudora Welty and Ross Macdonald*. Arcade, 2015.

McDowell, Edwin. "Publishing: Lost Papers of Eudora Welty Found." *New York Times*, June 19, 1981.

McHaney, Pearl. *Eudora Welty: The Contemporary Reviews*. Cambridge University Press, 2005.

McHaney, Pearl. "Forays into the Surreal: Eudora Welty's 'The Winds' and 'A Sketching Trip' and Joseph Cornell." *Miranda*, July 2012. https://doi.org/10.4000/miranda.4501.

McHaney, Pearl. "The Observing Eye." In *Eudora Welty as Photographer*, edited by McHaney. University Press of Mississippi, 2009.

McHaney, Pearl. *A Tyrannous Eye: Eudora Welty's Nonfiction and Photographs*. University Press of Mississippi, 2014.

McMahand, Donnie, and Kevin Murphy. "'Remember Right': Disenfranchised Grief and the Commemoration of Queer Bodies in Welty's Fiction and Life." *Eudora Welty Review* 6 (2014): 69–82. http://www.jstor.org/stable/24742697.

"Miss Stein Speaks to Bewildered 500." *New York Times*, November 2, 1934.

Morris, Willie. *North Toward Home*. Houghton Mifflin, 1967.

North Carolina State University. *Agromeck* (yearbook). Special Collections Research Center, NC State University Libraries.

"'Ol' Satchmo' Plays in Austin Tonight." *Daily Texan*. February 23, 1949.

Osborne, Charles. *W. H. Auden: The Life of a Poet*. Harcourt Brace Jovanovich, 1979.

Parker, Dorothy. "The Diary of a Lady During Days of Panic, Frenzy, and World Change." *New Yorker*, March 25, 1933.

Pater, Walter. *The Renaissance: Studies in Art and Poetry*. 1893. Project Gutenberg, 2009. https://www.gutenberg.org/files/2398/2398-h/2398-h.htm.

Perelman, S. J. "Cuckoos Nesting," *New Yorker*, August 25, 1956.

Polk, Noel. *Eudora Welty: A Bibliography of Her Work*. University Press of Mississippi, 1994.

Pollack, Harriet. *Eudora Welty's Fiction and Photography: The Body of the Other Woman.* University of Georgia Press, 2016.

Pollack, Harriet, ed. *New Essays on Eudora Welty, Class, and Race.* University Press of Mississippi, 2020.

Porter, Katherine Anne. *The Collected Essays and Occasional Writings of Katherine Anne Porter.* Delacorte, 1970.

Porter, Katherine Anne. "'Noon Wine': The Sources." *Yale Review* 46 (1956): 22–39.

Preece, Warren. "Dixie, C-Rations, City Rooms." Review of *The Welcome*, by Hubert Creekmore." *New York Times*, November 21, 1948.

Prenshaw, Peggy, ed. *Conversations with Eudora Welty.* University Press of Mississippi, 1984.

Prenshaw, Peggy, ed. *More Conversations with Eudora Welty.* University Press of Mississippi, 1996.

Prescott, Orville. "Books of the Times." Review of *Delta Wedding*, by Eudora Welty. *New York Times*, April 17, 1946.

"The Press: New Daily in Mississippi." *Time*, March 7, 1955.

Price, Reynolds. *The Names and Faces of Heroes.* Atheneum, 1963.

Price, Reynolds. *Permanent Errors.* Atheneum, 1970.

Radio and Amusement Guide: The National Weekly of Programs and Personalities, January 29–February 4, 1933.

Reinhold, Robert. "Abrupt Ouster of Austin Campus President Revives Turmoil at the University of Texas." *New York Times*, November 3, 1974.

Robinson, John. "The Inspector." *Harper's Magazine*, June 1950.

Rogers, Agnes, compiler, and Fredrick Lewis Allen. *The American Procession: American Life Since 1860 in Photographs.* Harper & Brothers, 1933.

Rosen, Gary A., "The Tune Detective." In *Unfair to Genius: The Strange and Litigious Career of Ira B. Arnstein.* Oxford University Press, 2012. Oxford Academic, 2015. https://doi.org/10.1093/acprof:osobl/9780199733484.003.0006.

Rosenfeld, Isaac. "Double Standard." Review of *Delta Wedding*, by Eudora Welty. *New Republic*, April 29, 1946.

Rovere, Richard. "American Magazines in Wartime," *New Republic*, March 6, 1944.

Rutenberg, Amy J. *Rough Draft: Cold War Military Manpower Policy and the Origins of Vietnam-Era Draft Resistance.* Cornell, 2019. EBSCO.

Samway, Patrick. "Tracing a Literary and Epistolary Relationship: Eudora Welty and Her Editor, Robert Giroux." *Eudora Welty Review* 8 (2016): 69–108. http://www.jstor.org/stable/24742206.

Slide, Anthony. "A. Robins." *Encyclopedia of Vaudeville.* University Press of Mississippi, 2012.

"Spaeth to Lecture in McCosh Tonight." *Daily Princetonian*, March 28, 1933.

Spain, Nancy. *Nancy Spain Colour Cookery Book.* World Distributors, 1963.

Stern, James. *The Hidden Damage.* Harcourt, Brace, 1947.

"T. S. Eliot Reviews Influence of Bible." *Daily Princetonian*, March 24, 1933.

Taylor, Kieran. "Willie McGee." In *Mississippi Encyclopedia.* Last updated April 14, 2018. https://mississippiencyclopedia.org/entries/willie-mcgee/.

Tennant, Stephen. "The Room Beyond." Foreword to *Willa Cather on Writing*, by Willa Cather. Knopf, 1949.

"Tennessee Williams Speaking on UT Campus Tonight at 8." *Austin-American Statesman*, November 1, 1973.

"Thomas Discusses Need for New Code of Living." *Daily Princetonian*, February 27, 1933.

Thurber, James. Cartoon. *New Yorker*, May 5, 1934.

Touba, Mariam. "Now on View: 'Padlocked': New York City's Prohibition Years." New York Historical Society and Library. March 6, 2019. https://www.nyhistory.org/blogs/now-on-view-padlocked-new-yorks-prohibition-years.

Trefzer, Annette. *Exposing Mississippi: Eudora Welty's Photographic Reflections*. University Press of Mississippi, 2021.

"The Trials of Uncle Daniel," *Life*, March 5, 1956.

Trilling, Diana. "Virginia Woolf's Special Realm." *New York Times Book Review*, March 21, 1948.

Tynan, Kenneth. Review of *Requiem for A Nun*, stage adaptation by William Faulkner and Ruth Ford. *New Yorker*, February 7, 1959.

United States Commission on Civil Rights. *Justice in Jackson, Mississippi: Hearings Held in Jackson, Miss., February 16–20, 1965: Vol. 2* (Police in America Series). Arno Press, 1971.

Warfield, Adrienne Akins. "Insiders, Outsiders, and Class Anxiety: Eudora Welty and Bob Dylan on the Medgar Evers Murder." In Pollack, *New Essays on Eudora Welty, Class, and Race*.

Welty, Eudora. *The Bride of the Innisfallen and Other Stories*. Harcourt, Brace, 1955.

Welty, Eudora. *Bye-Bye Brevoort*. New Stage Theatre, 1980.

Welty, Eudora. *Complete Novels*. Library of America, 1998.

Welty, Eudora. *A Curtain of Green and Other Stories*. Doubleday, Doran, 1941.

Welty, Eudora. *Delta Wedding*. Harcourt, Brace, 1946.

Welty, Eudora. *Early Escapades*. Edited by Patti Carr Black. University Press of Mississippi, 2005.

Welty, Eudora. *The Eye of the Story: Selected Essays and Reviews*. Random House, 1978.

Welty, Eudora. "The Golden Apples." *Harper's Bazaar*, September 1947.

Welty, Eudora. *The Golden Apples*. Harcourt, Brace, 1949.

Welty, Eudora. "The Hummingbirds." *Harper's Bazaar*, March 1949.

Welty, Eudora. Letters to Diarmuid Russell. Eudora Welty Collection, Mississippi Department of Archives and History.

Welty, Eudora. Letters to Frank Lyell. Eudora Welty Collection, Mississippi Department of Archives and History.

Welty, Eudora. Letters to John Robinson. Eudora Welty Collection, Mississippi Department of Archives and History.

Welty, Eudora. *Lilies That Fester*. 1937. Coauthored with Frank Lyell, Robert Daniel, and Hubert Creekmore. Photocopied pages; n.d. 7 pieces. Eudora Welty Collection, Mississippi Department of Archives and History. Series 40, Box 365, folders 3–4.

Welty, Eudora. "Literature and the Lens." *Vogue*, August 1, 1944.

Welty, Eudora. *Losing Battles*. Random House, 1970.

Welty, Eudora. *Music From Spain*. Levee Press, 1948.

Welty, Eudora. *Occasions: Selected Writings*. Edited by Pearl McHaney. University Press of Mississippi 2009.

Welty, Eudora. *On William Faulkner*. University Press of Mississippi, 2003.

Welty, Eudora. *One Time, One Place: Mississippi in the Depression, A Snapshot Album*. Random House, 1971.

Welty, Eudora. "The Optimist's Daughter." *New Yorker*, March 15, 1969.

Welty, Eudora. *The Optimist's Daughter*. Random House, 1972.

Welty, Eudora. *Photographs*. 1989. University Press of Mississippi, 2019.

Welty, Eudora. *The Ponder Heart*. Harcourt, Brace, 1954.
Welty, Eudora. *The Robber Bridegroom*. Doubleday, Doran, 1942.
Welty, Eudora. *The Shoe Bird*. Harcourt, Brace, 1964.
Welty, Eudora. *Short Stories*. Harcourt, Brace, 1950.
Welty, Eudora. *Stories, Essays, and Memoir*. Edited by Richard Ford and Michael Kreyling. Library of America, 1998.
Welty, Eudora. "The Waiting Room." 1935. Eudora Welty Collection. Mississippi Department of Archives and History.
Welty, Eudora. *The Wide Net and Other Stories*. Harcourt, Brace, 1943.
Welty, Eudora. *A Writer's Eye: Collected Book Reviews*. Edited by Pearl Amelia McHaney. University Press of Mississippi, 1994.
"What Should We Do About Race Segregation?" *Bulletin of America's Town Meeting of the Air* (ABC Radio's Town Meeting of the Air. Town Hall, Inc.), November 9, 1948.
Wiegers, Trevor C. *The Leadership Gap in Extremis: Challenges of Officer Procurement in World War II*. Master's thesis. US Army Command and General Staff College, 2019. https://apps.dtic.mil/sti/pdfs/AD1111720.pdf.
Wilkie, Curtis. "Hodding Carter, Jr." In *Mississippi Encyclopedia*. Last updated May 1, 2018. http://mississippiencyclopedia.org/entries/hodding-carter-jr/.
Woodburn, John. Review of *The Welcome*, by Hubert Creekmore. *Saturday Review*, November 13, 1948.
World War II Army Enlistment Records. Electronic Army Serial Number Merged File, ca. 1938–1946. United States National Archives and Records Administration, 2002. Archives.gov. Accessed March 1, 2021.
Yancy, Jesse. "Armand Coullet: The Rise of a Mississippi Impresario." *Magnolia Tribune*, July 6, 2023.
Yancy, Jesse. "The Pearl River's Gold Coast." *Magnolia Tribune*, May 4, 2023.
Zinn, Howard. "Mississippi 'Chronology,' 1963–1964." Howard Zinn Papers. Freedom Summer Digital Collection. Wisconsin Historical Society. https://content.wisconsinhistory.org/digital/collection/p15932coll2/id/11425.
Zolotow, Sam. "Chartock Singers to Bow in 'Mikado.'" *New York Times*, October 20, 1952.

INDEX

ABOUT THE EDITOR

Photo by Cassandra Foster

Julia Eichelberger, Marybelle Higgins Howe Professor of Southern Literature at the College of Charleston, edited *Tell About Night Flowers: Eudora Welty's Gardening Letters, 1940–1949* and coedited *Teaching the Works of Eudora Welty: Twenty-First-Century Approaches*. She is past president of the Eudora Welty Society and a recipient of their Phoenix Award for her scholarship on Welty. A graduate of Davidson College and the University of North Carolina at Chapel Hill, she has taught at the College of Charleston since 1992. In addition to her literary criticism on Welty and other writers, her scholarship and public history explores Charleston and the College's historic neighborhood. In 2024 she received a South Carolina Humanities Governor's Award.